41: *Afro-American Poets Since 1955*, edited by Trudier Harris and Thadious M. Davis (1985)

42: *American Writers for Children Before 1900*, edited by Glenn E. Estes (1985)

43: *American Newspaper Journalists, 1690-1872*, edited by Perry J. Ashley (1986)

44: *American Screenwriters*, Second Series, edited by Randall Clark, Robert E. Morsberger, and Stephen O. Lesser (1986)

45: *American Poets, 1880-1945*, First Series, edited by Peter Quartermain (1986)

46: *American Literary Publishing Houses, 1900-1980: Trade and Paperback*, edited by Peter Dzwonkoski (1986)

47: *American Historians, 1866-1912*, edited by Clyde N. Wilson (1986)

48: *American Poets, 1880-1945*, Second Series, edited by Peter Quartermain (1986)

49: *American Literary Publishing Houses, 1638-1899*, 2 parts, edited by Peter Dzwonkoski (1986)

50: *Afro-American Writers Before the Harlem Renaissance*, edited by Trudier Harris (1986)

51: *Afro-American Writers from the Harlem Renaissance to 1940*, edited by Trudier Harris (1987)

52: *American Writers for Children Since 1960: Fiction*, edited by Glenn E. Estes (1986)

53: *Canadian Writers Since 1960*, First Series, edited by W. H. New (1986)

54: *American Poets, 1880-1945*, Third Series, 2 parts, edited by Peter Quartermain (1987)

55: *Victorian Prose Writers Before 1867*, edited by William B. Thesing (1987)

56: *German Fiction Writers, 1914-1945*, edited by James Hardin (1987)

57: *Victorian Prose Writers After 1867*, edited by William B. Thesing (1987)

58: *Jacobean and Caroline Dramatists*, edited by Fredson Bowers (1987)

59: *American Literary Critics and Scholars, 1800-1850*, dited by John W. Rathbun and Monica M. Grecu (1987)

60: *Canadian Writers Since 1960*, Second Series, edited by W. H. New (1987)

61: *American Writers for Children Since 1960: Poets, Illustrators, and Nonfiction Authors*, edited by Glenn E. Estes (1987)

62: *Elizabethan Dramatists*, edited by Fredson Bowers (1987)

63: *Modern American Critics, 1920-1955*, edited by Gregory S. Jay (1988)

64: *American Literary Critics and Scholars, 1850-1880*, edited by John W. Rathbun and Monica M. Grecu (1988)

65: *French Novelists, 1900-1930*, edited by Catharine Savage Brosman (1988)

66: *German Fiction Writers, 1885-1913*, 2 parts, edited by James Hardin (1988)

67: *Modern American Critics Since 1955*, edited by Gregory S. Jay (1988)

68: *Canadian Writers, 1920-1959*, First Series, edited by W. H. New (1988)

69: *Contemporary German Fiction Writers*, First Series, edited by Wolfgang D. Elfe and James Hardin (1988)

70: *British Mystery Writers, 1860-1919*, edited by Bernard Benstock and Thomas F. Staley (1988)

71: *American Literary Critics and Scholars, 1880-1900*, edited by John W. Rathbun and Monica M. Grecu (1988)

72: *French Novelists, 1930-1960*, edited by Catharine Savage Brosman (1988)

73: *American Magazine Journalists, 1741-1850*, edited by Sam G. Riley (1988)

74: *American Short-Story Writers Before 1880*, edited by Bobby Ellen Kimbel, with the assistance of William E. Grant (1988)

75: *Contemporary German Fiction Writers*, Second Series, edited by Wolfgang D. Elfe and James Hardin (1988)

76: *Afro-American Writers, 1940-1955*, edited by Trudier Harris (1988)

77: *British Mystery Writers, 1920-1939*, edited by Bernard Benstock and Thomas F. Staley (1988)

78: *American Short-Story Writers, 1880-1910*, edited by Bobby Ellen Kimbel, with the assistance of William E. Grant (1988)

79: *American Magazine Journalists, 1850-1900*, edited by Sam G. Riley (1988)

(Continued on back endsheets)

Dictionary of Literary Biography®
Yearbook: 1991

Dictionary of Literary Biography®
Yearbook: 1991

**Edited by
James W. Hipp**

A Bruccoli Clark Layman Book
Gale Research Inc.
Detroit, London

Printed in the United States of America

Published simultaneously in the United Kingdom
by Gale Research International Limited
(An affiliated company of Gale Research Inc.)

The paper used in this publication meets the minimum requirements
of American National Standard for Information Sciences—Permanence
Paper for Printed Library Materials, ANSI Z39.48-1984. ∞™

Library of Congress Catalog Card Number 82-645187
ISSN 0731-7867
ISBN 0-8103-7601-6

Contents

Plan of the Series

The advisory board, the editors, and the publisher of the *Dictionary of Literary Biography* are joined in endorsing Mark Twain's declaration. The literature of a nation provides an inexhaustible resource of permanent worth. We intend to make literature and its creators better understood and more accessible to students and the reading public, while satisfying the standards of teachers and scholars.

To meet these requirements, *literary biography* has been construed in terms of the author's achievement. The most important thing about a writer is his writing. Accordingly, the entries in *DLB* are career biographies, tracing the development of the author's canon and the evolution of his reputation.

The purpose of *DLB* is not only to provide reliable information in a convenient format but also to place the figures in the larger perspective of literary history and to offer appraisals of their accomplishments by qualified scholars.

The publication plan for *DLB* resulted from two years of preparation. The project was proposed to Bruccoli Clark by Frederick C. Ruffner, president of the Gale Research Company, in November 1975. After specimen entries were prepared and typeset, an advisory board was formed to refine the entry format and develop the series rationale. In meetings held during 1976, the publisher, series editors, and advisory board approved the scheme for a comprehensive biographical dictionary of persons who contributed to North American literature. Editorial work on the first volume began in January 1977, and it was published in 1978. In order to make *DLB* more than a reference tool and to compile volumes

that individually have claim to status as literary history, it was decided to organize volumes by topic, period, or genre. Each of these freestanding volumes provides a biographical-bibliographical guide and overview for a particular area of literature. We are convinced that this organization—as opposed to a single alphabet method—constitutes a valuable innovation in the presentation of reference material. The volume plan necessarily requires many decisions for the placement and treatment of authors who might properly be included in two or three volumes. In some instances a major figure will be included in separate volumes, but with different entries emphasizing the aspect of his career appropriate to each volume. Ernest Hemingway, for example, is represented in *American Writers in Paris, 1920-1939* by an entry focusing on his expatriate apprenticeship; he is also in *American Novelists, 1910-1945* with an entry surveying his entire career. Each volume includes a cumulative index of the subject authors and articles. Comprehensive indexes to the entire series are planned.

With volume ten in 1982 it was decided to enlarge the scope of *DLB*. By the end of 1986 twenty-one volumes treating British literature had been published, and volumes for Commonwealth and Modern European literature were in progress. The series has been further augmented by the *DLB Yearbooks* (since 1981) which update published entries and add new entries to keep the *DLB* current with contemporary activity. There have also been *DLB Documentary Series* volumes which provide biographical and critical source materials for figures whose work is judged to have particular interest for students. One of these companion volumes is entirely devoted to Tennessee Williams.

We define literature as the *intellectual commerce of a nation:* not merely as belles lettres but as that ample and complex process by which ideas are generated, shaped, and transmitted. *DLB* entries are not limited to "creative writers" but extend to other figures who in their time and in their way influenced the mind of a people. Thus the series encompasses historians, journalists, publishers, and screenwriters. By this means readers of *DLB* may be aided to perceive literature not as cult scripture in the keeping of intellectual high priests but firmly positioned at the center of a nation's life.

DLB includes the major writers appropriate to each volume and those standing in the ranks immediately behind them. Scholarly and critical counsel has been sought in deciding which minor figures to include and how full their entries should be. Wherever possible, useful references are made to figures who do not warrant separate entries.

Each *DLB* volume has a volume editor responsible for planning the volume, selecting the figures for inclusion, and assigning the entries. Volume editors are also responsible for preparing, where appropriate, appendices surveying the major periodicals and literary and intellectual movements for their volumes, as well as lists of further readings. Work on the series as a whole is coordinated at the Bruccoli Clark Layman editorial center in Columbia, South Carolina, where the editorial staff is responsible for accuracy of the published volumes.

One feature that distinguishes *DLB* is the illustration policy—its concern with the iconography of literature. Just as an author is influenced by his surroundings, so is the reader's understanding of the author enhanced by a knowledge of his environment. Therefore *DLB* volumes include not only drawings, paintings, and photographs of authors, often depicting them at various stages in their careers, but also illustrations of their families and places where they lived. Title pages are regularly reproduced in facsimile along with dust jackets for modern authors. The dust jackets are a special feature of *DLB* because they often document better than anything else the way in which an author's work was perceived in its own time. Specimens of the writers' manuscripts are included when feasible.

Samuel Johnson rightly decreed that "The chief glory of every people arises from its authors." The purpose of the *Dictionary of Literary Biography* is to compile literary history in the surest way available to us—by accurate and comprehensive treatment of the lives and work of those who contributed to it.

The *DLB* Advisory Board

Foreword

The *Dictionary of Literary Biography Yearbook* is guided by the same principles that have provided the basic rationale for the entire *DLB* series: 1) the literature of a nation represents an inexhaustible resource of permanent worth; 2) the surest way to trace the outlines of literary history is by a comprehensive treatment of the lives and works of those who contributed to it; and 3) the greatest service the series can provide is to make literary achievement better understood and more accessible to students and the literate public, while serving the needs of scholars. In keeping with those principles, the *Yearbook* has been planned to augment *DLB* by reflecting the vitality of contemporary literature and summarizing current literary activity. The librarian, scholar, or student attempting to stay informed of literary developments is faced with an endless task. The purpose of *DLB Yearbook* is to serve these readers while at the same time enlarging the scope of *DLB*.

The *Yearbook* is divided into two sections: articles about the past year's literary events or topics; and obituaries and tributes. The updates and new author entries previously included as supplements to published *DLB* volumes have been omitted. (These essays will appear in future *DLB* volumes.) Included in the articles section are an overview of the Nabokov archive at New York Pub-

lic Library, a facsimile reprint of one of Dashiell Hammett's last magazine publications, interviews with James Ellroy, David Rabe, and literary agent George Greenfield, and extended discussions of the year's work in fiction, poetry, drama, and literary biography. The *Yearbook* continues two surveys begun in 1987, an overview of new literary journals, and an in-depth examination of the practice of book reviewing in America. In addition, the *Yearbook* features an article on the recipient of the 1991 Nobel Prize in Literature, Nadine Gordimer, including Gordimer's Nobel lectures.

The death of a literary figure prompts an assessment of his achievements and reputation. The obituaries section marks the passing of Fredson Bowers, Theodor Seuss Geisel, Graham Greene, Fletcher Markle, Véra Nabokov, Isaac Bashevis Singer, and Alden Whitman, who died in 1990.

Each *Yearbook* includes a list of literary prizes and awards, a necrology, and a checklist of books about literary history and biography published during the year.

From the outset, the *DLB* series has undertaken to compile literary history as it is revealed in the lives and works of authors. The *Yearbook* supports that commitment, providing a useful and necessary current record.

Acknowledgments

This book was produced by Bruccoli Clark Layman, Inc. Karen L. Rood is senior editor for the *Dictionary of Literary Biography* series. James W. Hipp was the in-house editor.

Projects manager is Charles D. Brower. Photography editors are Edward Scott and Timothy C. Lundy. Layout and graphics supervisor is Penney L. Haughton. Copyediting supervisor is Bill Adams. Typesetting supervisor is Kathleen M. Flanagan. Systems manager is George F. Dodge. The production staff includes Rowena Betts, Teresa Chaney, Patricia Coate, Janet Connor, Gail Crouch, Henry Cuningham, Margaret McGinty Cureton, Bonita Dingle, Mary Scott Dye, Denise Edwards, Sarah A. Estes, Robert Fowler, Avril E. Gregory, Ellen McCracken, Kathy Lawler Merlette, John Myrick, Pamela D. Norton, Jean W. Ross, Thomasina Singleton, Maxine K. Smalls, Jennifer C. J. Turley, and Betsy L. Weinberg.

Walter W. Ross and Dennis Lynch did library research. They were assisted by the following librarians at the Thomas Cooper Library of the University of South Carolina: Jens Holley and the interlibrary-loan staff; reference librarians Gwen Baxter, Daniel Boice, Faye Chadwell, Jo Cottingham, Cathy Eckman, Rhonda Felder, Gary Geer, Jackie Kinder, Laurie Preston, Jean Rhyne, Carol Tobin, Virginia Weathers, and Connie Widney; circulation-department head Thomas Marcil; and acquisitions-searching supervisor David Haggard.

The editor wishes to thank Karl Kirchwey of the Poetry Center of the 92nd Street Y, New York, New York, for his help in obtaining several of the tributes to Isaac Bashevis Singer.

Dictionary of Literary Biography®
Yearbook: 1991

Dictionary of Literary Biography

The 1991 Nobel Prize in Literature
Nadine Gordimer
(20 November 1923 -)

Stephen Clingman
University of Massachusetts, Amherst

BOOKS: *Face to Face* (Johannesburg, S.A.: Silver
    Leaf, 1949);

The Soft Voice of the Serpent (New York: Simon &
    Schuster, 1952; London: Gollancz, 1953);

The Lying Days (London: Gollancz, 1953; New
    York: Simon & Schuster, 1953);

Six Feet of the Country (London: Gollancz, 1956;
    New York: Simon & Schuster, 1956);

A World of Strangers (London: Gollancz, 1958;
    New York: Simon & Schuster, 1958);

Friday's Footprint (London: Gollancz, 1960; New
    York: Viking, 1960);

Occasion for Loving (London: Gollancz, 1963; New
    York: Viking, 1963);

Not For Publication (London: Gollancz, 1965; New
    York: Viking, 1965);

The Late Bourgeois World (London: Gollancz, 1966;
    New York: Viking, 1966);

A Guest of Honour (New York: Viking, 1970; Lon-
    don: Cape, 1971);

Livingstone's Companions (New York: Viking, 1971;
    London: Cape, 1972);

The Black Interpreters—Notes on African Writing (Jo-
    hannesburg, S.A.: Spro-Cas/Ravan, 1973);

On the Mines, with David Goldblatt (Cape Town,
    S.A.: Struik, 1973);

The Conservationist (London: Cape, 1974; New
    York: Viking, 1975);

Selected Stories (London: Cape, 1975; New York: Vi-
    king, 1976);

Some Monday for Sure (London: Heinemann,
    1976);

*Nadine Gordimer (photograph copyright © The
Nobel Foundation)*

Burger's Daughter (London: Cape, 1979; New
    York: Viking, 1979);

A Soldier's Embrace (London: Cape, 1980; New York: Viking, 1980);

What Happened to the Burger's Daughter, or How South African Censorship Works, with John Dugard and others (Johannesburg, S.A.: Taurus, 1980);

July's People (London: Cape, 1981; New York: Viking, 1981; Johannesburg, S.A.: Ravan, 1981);

Something Out There (London: Cape, 1984; New York: Viking, 1984; Johannesburg, S.A.: Ravan/Taurus, 1984);

Lifetimes: Under Apartheid, with David Goldblatt (London: Cape, 1986; New York: Knopf, 1986);

A Sport of Nature (London: Cape, 1987; New York: Knopf, 1987; Cape Town, S.A.: David Philip, 1987);

The Essential Gesture: Writing, Politics and Places, edited, with an introduction, by Stephen Clingman (London: Cape, 1988; New York: Knopf, 1988; Cape Town, S.A.: Taurus/David Philip, 1988);

My Son's Story (London: Bloomsbury, 1990; New York: Farrar, Straus & Giroux, 1990; Cape Town, S.A.: David Philip, 1990);

Crimes of Conscience (London and Portsmouth, N.H.: Heinemann, 1991);

Jump and Other Stories (London: Bloomsbury, 1991; New York: Farrar, Straus & Giroux, 1991; Cape Town, S.A.: David Philip, 1991);

OTHER: *South African Writing Today*, edited by Gordimer with Lionel Abrahams (Harmondsworth, U.K.: Penguin, 1967).

Nadine Gordimer's writing life has held in balance two distinct yet inseparable commitments. The first, ever since her earliest short stories, has been to the craft of her writing; this has been unassailable, inalienable all along. The second, because of the pressures of living in South Africa—at first under a general regime of racial segregation, then for the last forty years under the formalized oppression and depredations of apartheid—has been a gathering commitment, over the years, to the *responsibilities* of writing in her time and place. Beyond the superficial categorizations of being an "anti-apartheid" writer, it is the balance and productive tension between these two commitments that has provided the signature of Gordimer's fiction, the specific kind of vision that has allowed her to render the complex so-

cial, political, and psychological realities of South Africa in equally complex artistic exploration and form.

Nadine Gordimer was born on 20 November 1923 in Springs, a small gold-mining town on Johannesburg's East Rand. Her father, a Lithuanian Jewish immigrant to South Africa, was initially a watch-seller and repairman; later he had a more established watch and jewelry store in town. Gordimer's mother was also of Jewish extraction, but came to South Africa from England. In answer to questions regarding her Jewish background, Gordimer has said that it hardly played any part in her life. Her mother, who seems to have been dominant in the family in this respect, had little connection with Jewish culture, and felt more at home with the Scots Presbyterian women of the town. For her early schooling, Gordimer went to the Convent of Our Lady of Mercy in Springs; this was not due to any religious preference, but simply because one could get a better education there; it was fairly common practice to attend such schools at the time. Still, we could say that from early on, crossing cultural and ethnic boundaries was built into Gordimer's life.

Not in one respect, however. The color line, in South Africa, was a hard and fast one when Gordimer was growing up, and no one in her family would have dreamed of crossing it. In her fiction and in essays and interviews, Gordimer has indicated how alienated she was from the world of blacks in South Africa—their language completely foreign, unspoken, and therefore unheard except as continuous, undifferentiated background, their culture unexplored, their very being, for whites in Gordimer's situation, placed almost in the realm of nature, to be exploited as such, or ignored, but never engaged with. There were express limitations to such engagement. Gordimer remembers as a young child hearing the sound of drumming from the mining compounds, and asking what it was; the reply would come that it was just noise. It was some time before Gordimer made the symbolic shift in her mind, to understand that what seemed alien in that setting—African culture—was quite at home, and what seemed "natural"—the culture of white superiority—was in fact quite alienated.

Gordimer has described herself as being a "bolter" during her early years at school—a child of irrepressible energy who would skip school to go exploring the allure of the veld around her ("A Bolter and the Invincible Summer"). It is an attraction and an attachment she has never lost, the South African landscape being a vividly observed presence in her fiction. In these years she also studied ballet and wanted to be a dancer. There were other capacities, and they added to the repertoire of a future writer—an ear for voice and an acute skill for mimicry. Yet the life of unbounded physical expression did not last long. For obscure reasons (Gordimer has only been gradually forthcoming on this point) when Gordimer was ten or eleven, her mother seems to have invented the idea that Gordimer had a heart ailment, and, as a consequence, she was withdrawn from school and taught at home by a tutor. At that point the energy expended in other ways became invested in something else: reading. Gordimer has mentioned how during her adolescence her literary appetite was voracious and completely unformed; she would go to the library and devour everything from Samuel Pepys's *Diary* to Robert Burton's *Anatomy of Melancholy*. She is convinced that good writing comes from wide reading, so this too may have been a turning point.

During these years she did indeed turn to writing. At first—at the ages of thirteen and fourteen—she wrote fables which were published in the children's section of the *Sunday Express* in Johannesburg. Then, at the age of fifteen, her first full-fledged short story, "Come Again Tomorrow," was published, and it marked the beginning of Gordimer's self-awareness as a writer. Yet this did not come easily. In a late-colonial world in which young white girls seemed destined for typing courses, secretarial work, and then marriage, Gordimer knew that was not what she wanted, but she did not know what else was possible. She has described this period of her life as one of "sybaritic meagreness," lazing around, writing some stories, until finally going off at the age of twenty-two to the University of the Witwatersrand for her one year of higher education. At this time she came into contact with the poet, translator, and editor Uys Krige, and with his encouragement and that of others her existence was transformed. Her stories began to be published by the *New Yorker*, and an international career began.

Gordimer's early short stories followed wherever her ranging interest led her. With a precise eye for detail, whether environmental or psychological, she would pick out the inner workings of human motivation, exploring moments of despair, betrayal, transcendence. Yet, under the influence of writers such as Katherine Mansfield

Dust jacket for the American edition of Gordimer's 1965 collection of stories (courtesy of Elizabeth Wessels)

and Eudora Welty, a further awareness was growing: that one could be a *local* writer, and that this *locality* could be a worthy subject. It involved a question of literary identity, captured exactly by Helen Shaw, the central character of Gordimer's first novel, *The Lying Days* (1953):

> I had never read a book in which I myself was recognizable; in which there was a "girl" like Anna who did the housework and cooking and called the mother and father Missus and Baas.

Although Gordimer has never written to any kind of program, there came this gathering sense of identity in her work, that she would explore what she found in the South African world around her. And so even her early short stories came to have characteristic settings and terrains: small-town cafés, police raids for illicit African beer-brewing, the agonized relations between white mistresses and black servants, all observed with the penetrating and unremittingly ironic eye which has become Gordimer's other signature.

The point is a crucial one. When asked why she writes, time and again Gordimer's answer has been the same: "To make sense of life." She quotes Goethe: "Thrust your hand deep into life, and whatever you bring up in it, that is you, that is your subject." It is not as if Gordimer in some sense "found" her political topic or even perspective, and then wrote according to that principle of selection. On the contrary, it was making sense of life, thrusting her hand in, that brought up her topics and perspectives. On this she has been nothing less than emphatic:

> So it was that I didn't wake up to Africans and the shameful enormity of the colour bar through a youthful spell in the Communist Party, as did some of my contemporaries with whom I share the rejection of white supremacy, but through the apparently esoteric speleology of doubt, led by Kafka rather than Marx. And the "problems" of my country did not set me writing; on the contrary, it was learning to write that sent me falling, falling through the surface of "the South African way of life" ("A Bolter and the Invincible Summer").

This fundamental artistic integrity has meant two things: first, that Gordimer has been unafraid to explore in all of its labyrinthine psychological intricacy the social and political world around her; second, that what she finds there is never predictable in either political or artistic terms.

It is a question of great subtlety which few writers in the world have either had to, or had the capacity to confront in this way. Gordimer has no doubt that one of the effects of her writing is to lay bare the destructive and immoral nature of apartheid. As she puts it, "If you write honestly about life in South Africa, apartheid damns itself." Yet this is not the intention—if one can speak so placidly of complex processes that by and large operate at deeper levels than any notion of conscious choice would indicate—that underlies her work when she sets out to write. As she has said, Gordimer sets out to write what is *there* and what she is drawn to, and any political implications follow afterward. Her courage, for which she is duly celebrated, is as much artistic as political.

Gordimer's notion of "honesty" and of apartheid revealing itself in her fiction indicates a basic trust in the realism and truth-telling capacities of fiction to which not everyone in this postmodern era would subscribe. In that sense her literary roots are in the nineteenth century,

for instance in the like-minded commitments of Ivan Turgenev, to whom she pays homage, who saw his own artistic duty in writing of life as it "happened to be." At the same time, and emerging directly out of the social realities of her situation, Gordimer has an acute and thoroughly contemporary awareness of her own position in society, and of the fact that it by no means gives any neutral or objective vantage point from which her world is to be surveyed. She does not underestimate the power of the writer; on the contrary, she believes firmly that writers are endowed with extraordinary powers of perspicacity. Nor will she observe any formulaic limits: when the Black Consciousness movement of the 1970s began to put forward the idea that white authors should not write about blacks because they did not know them and it was a form of aesthetic exploitation, Gordimer insisted that whites and blacks in South Africa did know one another in all kinds of peculiar ways, and that writers have a capacity of the imagination that allows them to enter into the lives of others, whether across racial or gender lines. And yet, for all that, she has an extraordinary self-awareness, which makes her turn the sharp eye of her observation on no one more clearly than herself and the specific kind of world from which she comes.

For many readers, that eye, and Gordimer's ability to render what she sees into words, are most persuasively and compellingly evident in her short stories. And there is no doubt of her capacities in this medium; in her skills of pace, poise, insight, reversal, revelation, *epiphany*, there are few writers in the world to equal her. Obviously, not all of Gordimer's stories are socially or politically minded. Along the way, she has consistently found time to explore the things that might come to any "ordinary" life—love, betrayal, aging, death, even more recently a fictionalized musing on the origins and implications of her father's life ("My Father Leaves Home"). As time has gone on, Gordimer's writing has become tauter, more adventurous, poetic. In the workshop of her short stories she hones her writing to its finest precision—a precision then evident in the deeper substance of her very best novels.

Gordimer's short stories do give an astonishing inner picture of South African life. Her early story, "Is There Nowhere Else We Can Meet?," explores in highly charged form the symbolic terrain of the white psyche—its inner narratives of threat, desire, and repression. A story such as "Which New Era Would That Be?" dissects with ruthless psychological accuracy the hypocrisies and pretensions of a self-serving kind of white liberalism; but "The Smell of Death and Flowers," written at about the same time, movingly shows the moment of conversion of a young white woman to political commitment. Gordimer has given visions of an Africa beyond and untrammeled by histories of political degradation ("No Place Like"). She has shown the inner innocence and then the institutionalized corruption of cross-racial love affairs ("Town and Country Lovers"). She has, in the voices of black characters, drawn out the temptations and traumas of personal and political betrayal ("A City of the Dead, A City of the Living") and suggested realms of infinite loss ("The Ultimate Safari"). She has, in symbolic and poetic form, represented the emerging and irrepressible promise of a coming liberation, allegorized as a narrative of threat, desire, and inevitability ("A Lion on the Freeway").

To this repertoire Gordimer has, in her novels, added two dimensions: those of historical placement and historic *responsibility*. Time and again her novels appear to pose and then address the following question: given the situation in South Africa, what obligations fall to the (usually white) individual, and how is he or she to live? Gordimer's fundamental commitment to the realism of truth-telling means that the answers she finds have undergone significant changes over the years. And her novels help clarify the fact that, from early on, Gordimer's biographical life has been inseparable from her writing life, for it is in her writing that she has addressed (and in some respects resolved, in the developing form that a life has) the most significant questions that her society has posed for her as it too has transformed historically.

This is apparent in the chronological sweep of her novels. Thus *The Lying Days* (1953) and *A World of Strangers* (1958), besides their energized encounter with a local social and cultural identity, explore in successive forms the possibilities of liberalism in South Africa—measured specifically as the potential for interracial commitment transcending the color bar. Yet, in the midst of South Africa's political traumas of the early 1960s, in *Occasion for Loving* (1963) such potential seems all but unavailable, and *The Late Bourgeois World* (1966), published in the middle of that decade, delves into a realm of much more demanding commitment. *A Guest of Honour* (1970) is not set in South Africa at all, but in a fictional African country. Yet here Gordimer explores two further kinds of affiliation: of finding an identity as a white African, and of the apparent necessity of socialism in Africa. By the early 1970s Gordimer was describing herself not as a liberal but a "white radical," understanding in her own lifetime the need for a thorough transformation in South Africa. Her novel of 1974, *The Conservationist*, is undoubtedly one of her masterpieces, combining an intensified descriptive naturalism with an underlying symbolic vision which comes to prophesy an eventual transfer of power in South Africa and the resumption of black history.

Gordimer's later novels extend further the parabola of Gordimer's changing and developing vision. *Burger's Daughter* (1979), utilizing the experimental narrative skills fashioned in *The Conservationist*, turns to the white revolutionary heritage to explore the question of historic obligation in the aftermath of the Soweto Revolt; it too is widely recognized as a masterpiece of political fiction, not only for its affirmations but for its extraordinary self-interrogations. In what—drawing on Antonio Gramsci—Gordimer has described as the "interregnum" of South Africa in the early 1980s, a period when "the old is dying and the new cannot be born," *July's People* (1981) turns its eye to an apocalyptic moment of revolutionary change; but its inner project is to decode the "morbid symptoms" (again Gramsci's formulation) of the present. In a much misunderstood novel, *A Sport of Nature* (1987), Gordimer was able to envision a post-apartheid South Africa; but here, just as important as this vision, is the novel's interrogation of the nature of power in bringing it about, and the kind of power it will introduce. This inner dialogue is continued in Gordimer's most recent novel, *My Son's Story* (1990), the first novel in which her central characters are not white but "coloured" (mixed race). And here Gordimer appears to have approached her original point of departure, for the ultimate tension in the novel (and there are many) appears to be between the claims of politics and the claims of fiction. The one is the "offspring" of the other, but how is it to assert its own vision, its independence?

In all of her fiction Gordimer has, like the buried black body which rises to the surface in *The Conservationist*, resurrected much that normally lies buried in South Africa: what shapes life, what shapes individuality, even what shapes the unconscious. As if that were not enough, in a substantial output of nonfictional writing, she has turned her attention to the situation in which she writes. Essays on politics, on censorship, biographi-

40.

to smoke. Yet the craving was just another appetite,

~~something~~ some petty recurrence, ~~satisfied~~ assuaged a

thousand thousand times and easily ~~assuag~~ again, with

something bought across a ~~shop~~ corner shop counter. Around

~~outlin~~ an horizon

him in the dark, ~~shapes~~ darker ~~than~~ the dark, ~~were~~ the strange

~~shapes his life had taken~~ forms the old, real, ~~great~~ needs

of his life, his father's life and his father's father's

life ~~sought~~ had so strangely ~~come to claim their realization~~

were now so ~~abstractly~~ realized. He had sat at school

gases

farting the ~~gas~~ of an empty stomach, he had seen ~~the~~ everyday

fathers, uncles, brothers, come home without work from

days-long queues, ~~he had had his~~ bare feet shod in shoes

worn to the shape of a white child's feet. He had sniffed

glue to see a rosy future. He had taken a ~~simplex~~ diploma

by correspondence to better himself. He had ~~spoken~~ spoken

~~nobodyx~~ nobody's name under interrogation. He had left a

girl and baby without hope of being able to show himself

to them again. You could not eat the ~~four~~ AKM assault

rifles that Charles had brought in ~~in a~~ golf-bags. ~~You~~

dig a road or   make   turn a lathe with

could not ~~grow anything, make anything~~ with the ~~seven~~ grey

limpet mines, ~~with detonators and it~~. ~~You~~ could not ~~clothe~~

~~your~~ feet and body with the ~~three~~ offensive and ~~three~~

the AKM bayonets

defensive handgrenades ~~with out~~, ~~compete with a white~~ for

skills

~~job applicant a white man's job~~ with AKM, you could not

assault rifles

use the AKM ~~bayonets~~ to compete with ~~white applicants for~~

the AKM bayonets

~~a job~~ the white man's education, or ~~use them~~ as wire-cutters

to get you out of solitary confinement in maximum security,

, and the boxes of hundreds of rounds of ammunition

would not make even a squatter's shack for the girl and child.

He had watched, too young to understand, the tin and board that had been the shack he was born in, carted away by government demolishers, his

---

Two pages, with revisions, from Gordimer's typescript for Something Out There *(Pierpont Morgan Library, MA 4710; by permission of Nadine Gordimer)*

34

Pablo Neruda

her maiden name on the fly-leaf and read ~~Garcia Lorca~~ to

him. Afterwards they fell asleep, and then woke to make love

safely ~~xxfxtyxxafx~~

once' more before losing each other in the rush hour traffic

back to town.

They were secure in that cottage—for as long as they

would need security. Sometimes he would find the opportunity

to remark: We are not children. I know, she would agree.

has loved

He could be ~~satisfied~~ she accepted that ~~even if~~ this ~~was to~~

One late afternoon they were lying timelessly, although there had only less

~~be her last love, it~~ could ~~only~~ have its span. They were

about 15 minutes left   *one late afternoon*

~~lying timelessly~~ (it was the ~~only~~ way to deal with ~~times~~

absolutely

an association restricting to the hours between ~~2~~ 3 and 6)

after love-making

~~inxthexafternoonxxonexdayx~~ one late afternoon, ~~although they~~

~~had only about fifteen minutes left~~, naked, quiet, her

comforting

hand languidly ~~for comfort~~ ~~holding~~ his lolling penis, when

~~behind them~~

they heard a scratching ~~sound~~ at the ox-eye window above

the bedhead. He sat up. Jumped up, standing on the bed.

She rolled over onto her face. There was the sound of

something, feet, a body, landing on earth, scuffling, slap

spray

of branches. ~~A strandxafxthex~~ branch of the old bougainvillea

that climbed the roof, snapped back against the window.

The window was empty.

freed

He gently ~~turned~~ her face ~~away~~ from the pillow.

—It's all right.—

She lay there looking at him. —She's hired someone

to follow you.—

—Don't be silly.—

I know it,

—Did you see ~~who it was~~? A white man?—

He began to get dressed.

—Don't go out, my darling. For God's sake. Wait for

him to go away.—

cal pieces, even some remarkable travel pieces (on the Congo, Egypt, Botswana) have flowed consistently over the years. An essay such as "Living in the Interregnum," deriving from the same apocalyptic moment as *July's People*, is the definitive nonfictional examination of the period, again not least for Gordimer's unremittingly clear self-inspection in the midst of it. "The Essential Gesture" is a heightened, searching investigation of Gordimer's two commitments—to her fiction and its responsibilities. In all of this—and in her many interviews—Gordimer has shown herself a highly intelligent and insistently independent thinker. She has, for instance, consistently refused the mantle of feminism, saying that in South Africa white men and white women have more in common than white women and black women, and that these issues have to be resolved first. She reads as widely as ever, and her writing and commentary show the absorption of a searching range of world literature as well as an interest, at various times, in some of the major figures in literary criticism and theory.

As a writer and an individual Gordimer has been fully involved in South African literary and political life. From the 1950s on she formed friendships and associations with black writers which have endured to this day, even through the difficult years of the Black Consciousness movement. She has, over the years, put a tremendous amount of energy into workshops, mainly for young black writers. She is a founding and executive member of the Congress of South African Writers, the major aim of which is to democratize and make available more generally a culture of writing and reading in South Africa. Even before the unbanning of the African National Congress in February 1990 it was clear she was close to it as an organization, and she has since become a member. Yet as soon as she puts pen to paper she reserves the right to question, to doubt—with the same doubt that led her to write in the first place. "Nothing I say," Gordimer has said, "will be as true as my fiction" ("Living in the Interregnum"). It is this questioning and doubting capacity that will be her surest guide—as it has been all along—into the world of a postapartheid literature and culture.

It is easy now to forget what Gordimer has been through as a writer in South Africa (though she would not exaggerate its significance, given what others have suffered): the banning of some of her books, the barely grudging acceptance by a literary establishment. Yet inroads have been

Dust jacket for the American edition of Gordimer's 1987 novel, presenting her vision of a postapartheid South Africa (courtesy of Elizabeth Wessels)

made there too: she has won the CNA Prize four times, and among her nonracial circle of writers she is regarded with deepest affection. In the outside world her rewards have been many, as even an inexhaustive list would indicate: the W. H. Smith Commonwealth Literary Award (1961), the James Tait Black Memorial Prize (1972), the Booker Prize (1974), the Grand Aigle d'Or (1975), the Nelly Sachs Prize (1986), the Malaparte Prize (1987). Gordimer has held the Scottish Arts Council Neil M. Gunn Fellowship (1981), she is a Fellow of the Royal Society of Literature, an Honorary Member of the American Academy of Arts and Sciences, and of the American Academy and Institute of Arts and Letters; she has been decorated *Commandeur de l'Ordre des Arts et des Lettres* (France). Honorary degrees have flowed like water. And most recently has come the Nobel Prize.

Other forms of writing have begun to and will emerge in South Africa; Gordimer's own writing has changed and will transform further. The era of apartheid appears to be ending, and we hope is never to return. But there is no doubt that the writer who—in so many senses of the phrase—*saw through* South Africa during the years of apartheid, and who managed simultaneously during that period to keep both her artistic and political faith, was, preeminently, Nadine Gordimer. Beyond her intentions or expectations she has been witness to, and chronicler of, the inner life of apartheid. Out of evil times she has made great writing and shown that when literature is true to itself it does have a function beyond anything that might be predicted. In these ways, keeping alive the dialogue between her fiction and politics, she has served not only her country and its culture but the world and the world of literature.

References:

Nancy Topping Bazin and Marylin Dallman Seymour, eds., *Conversations with Nadine Gordimer* (Jackson and London: University Press of Mississippi, 1990);

Stephen Clingman, *The Novels of Nadine Gordimer: History from the Inside* (London and Cambridge, Mass.: Allen & Unwin, 1986; Johannesburg: Ravan; 1986; second edition, Amherst: University of Massachusetts Press, 1992);

John Cooke, *The Novels of Nadine Gordimer: Private Lives / Public Landscapes* (Baton Rouge and London: Louisiana State University Press, 1985);

Judie Newman, *Nadine Gordimer* (London and New York: Routledge, 1988);

Michael Wade, *Nadine Gordimer* (London: Evans, 1978).

NOBEL BANQUET SPEECH
Nadine Gordimer

Your Majesties, Your Royal Highnesses, Your Excellencies, Fellow Laureates, Ladies and Gentlemen:

When the six-year-old daughter of a friend of mine overheard her father telling someone that I had been awarded the Nobel Prize, she asked whether I had ever received it before. He re-plied that the Prize was something you could get only once. Whereupon the small girl thought a moment: "Oh" she said, "so it's like chicken-pox."

Well, Flaubert said that "honours dishonour" the writer, and Jean-Paul Sartre declined this particular honour, but whether as malediction or malady one cannot say. I certainly find being the recipient at this celebratory dinner more pleasurable and rewarding than chicken-pox, having now in my life experienced both.

But the small girl was not entirely wrong. Writing is indeed, some kind of affliction in its demands as the most solitary and introspective of occupations. We writers do not have the encouragement and mateyness I imagine, and even observe, among people whose work is a group activity. We are not orchestrated; poets sing unaccompanied, and prose writers have no cue on which to come in, each with an individual instrument of expression to make the harmony or dissonance complete. We must live fully in order to secrete the substance of our work, but we have to work alone. From this paradoxical inner solitude our writing is what Roland Barthes called "the essential gesture" towards the people among whom we live, and to the world; it is the hand held out with the best we have to give.

When I began to write as a very young person in a rigidly racist and inhibited colonial society, I felt, as many others did, that I existed marginally on the edge of the world of ideas, of imagination and beauty. These, taking shape in poetry and fiction, drama, painting and sculpture, were exclusive to that distant realm known as "overseas." It was the dream of my contemporaries, white and black, to venture there as the only way to enter the world as artists. I took the realization that the colour bar—I use that old, concrete image of racism, was like the gate of the law in Kafka's parable, which was closed to the supplicant throughout his life because he didn't understand that only he could open it. It took this to make us realize that what we had to do to find the world was to enter our own world fully, first. We had to enter through the tragedy of our own particular place.

If the Nobel awards have a special meaning, it is that they carry this concept further. In their global eclecticism they recognize that no single society, no country or continent can presume to create a truly human culture for the world. To be among Laureates past and present is at least to belong to some sort of one world.

NOBEL LECTURE 1991
Nadine Gordimer

WRITING AND BEING

In the beginning was the Word.

The Word was with God, signified God's Word, the word that was Creation. But over the centuries of human culture the word has taken on other meanings, secular as well as religious. To have the word has come to be synonymous with ultimate authority, with prestige, with awesome, sometimes dangerous persuasion, to have Prime Time, a TV talk show, to have the gift of the gab as well as that of speaking in tongues. The word flies through space, it is bounced from satellites, now nearer than it has ever been to the heaven from which it was believed to have come. But its most significant transformation occurred for me and my kind long ago, when it was first scratched on a stone tablet or traced on papyrus, when it materialized from sound to spectacle, from being heard to being read as a series of signs, and then a script; and travelled through time from parchment to Gutenberg. For this is the genesis story of the writer. It is the story that wrote her or him into being.

It was, strangely, a double process, creating at the same time both the writer and the very purpose of the writer as a mutation in the agency of human culture. It was both ontogenesis as the origin and development of an individual being, and the adaptation, in the nature of that individual, specifically to the exploration of ontogenesis, the origin and development of the individual being. For we writers are evolved for that task. Like the prisoner incarcerated with the jaguar in Borges' story[1], "The God's Script," who was trying to read, in a ray of light which fell only once a day, the meaning of being from the markings on the creature's pelt, we spend our lives attempting to interpret through the word the readings we take in the societies, the world of which we are part. It is in this sense, this inextricable, ineffable participation, that writing is always and at once an exploration of self and of the world; of individual and collective being.

Being here.

Humans, the only self-regarding animals, blessed or cursed with this torturing higher faculty, have always wanted to know why. And this is not just the great ontological question of why

Dust jacket for Gordimer's 1988 collection of essays on censorship, apartheid, writers and writing, and Africa

we are here at all, for which religions and philosophies have tried to answer conclusively for various peoples at various times, and science tentatively attempts dazzling bits of explanation we are perhaps going to die out in our millennia, like dinosaurs, without having developed the necessary comprehension to understand as a whole. Since humans became self-regarding they have sought, as well, explanations for the common phenomena of procreation, death, the cycle of seasons, the earth, sea, wind and stars, sun and moon, plenty and disaster. With myth, the writer's ancestors, the oral storytellers, began to feel out and formulate these mysteries, using the elements of daily life—observable reality—and the faculty of the imagination—the power of projection into the hidden—to make stories.

Roland Barthes[2] asks, "What is characteristic of myth?" And answers: "To transform a meaning into form." Myths are stories that mediate in this way between the known and unknown. Claude Lévi-Strauss[3] wittily demythologizes myth as a genre between a fairy tale and a detective story. Being here; we don't know who-dun-it. But something satisfying, if not the answer, can be invented. Myth was the mystery plus the fantasy—gods, anthropomorphized animals and birds, chimera, phantasmagorical creatures—that posits out of the imagination some sort of explanation for the mystery. Humans and their fellow creatures were the materiality of the story, but, as Nikos Kazantzakis[4] once wrote, "Art is the representation not of the body but of the forces which created the body."

There are many proven explanations for natural phenomena now; and there are new questions of being arising out of some of the answers. For this reason, the genre of myth has never been entirely abandoned, although we are inclined to think of it as archaic. If it dwindled to the children's bedtime tale in some societies, in parts of the world protected by forests or deserts from international megaculture it has continued, alive, to offer art as a system of mediation between the individual and being. And it has made a whirling comeback out of Space, an Icarus in the avatar of Batman and his kind, who never fall into the ocean of failure to deal with the gravity forces of life. These new myths, however, do not seek so much to enlighten and provide some sort of answers as to distract, to provide a fantasy escape route for people who no longer want to face even the hazard of answers to the terrors of their existence. (Perhaps it is the positive knowledge that humans now possess the means to destroy their whole planet, the fear that they have in this way themselves become the gods, dreadfully charged with their own continued existence, that has made comicbook and moviemyth escapist.) The forces of being remain. They are what the writer, as distinct from the contemporary popular mythmaker, still engages today, as myth in its ancient form attempted to do.

How writers have approached this engagement and continue to experiment with it has been and is, perhaps more than ever, the study of literary scholars. The writer in relation to the nature of perceivable reality and what is beyond—imperceivable reality—is the basis for all these studies, no matter what resulting concepts are labelled, and no matter in what categorized microfiles writers are stowed away for the annals of literary historiography. Reality is constructed out of many elements and entities, seen and unseen, expressed, and left unexpressed for breathing space in the mind. Yet from what is regarded

as old-hat psychological analysis to modernism and post-modernism, structuralism and post-structuralism, all literary studies are aimed at the same end: to pin down to a consistency (and what is consistency if not the principle hidden within the riddle?); to make definitive through methodology the writer's grasp at the forces of being. But life is aleatory in itself; being is constantly pulled and shaped this way and that by circumstances and different levels of consciousness. There is no pure state of being, and it follows that there is now pure text, "real" text, totally incorporating the aleatory. It surely cannot be reached by any critical methodology, however interesting the attempt. To deconstruct a text is in a way a contradiction, since to deconstruct it is to make another construction out of the pieces, as Roland Barthes[5] does so fascinatingly, and admits to, in his linguistic and semantical dissection of Balzac's story, "Sarrasine." So the literary scholars end up being some kind of storyteller, too.

Perhaps there is no other way of reaching some understanding of being than through art? Writers themselves don't analyze what they do; to analyze would be to look down while crossing a canyon on a tightrope. To say this is not to mystify the process of writing but to make an image out of the intense inner concentration the writer must have to cross the chasms of the aleatory and make them the word's own, as an explorer plants a flag. Yeats' inner "lonely impulse of delight" in the pilot's solitary flight, and his "terrible beauty" born of mass uprising, both opposed and conjoined; E. M. Forster's modest "only connect"; Joyce's chosen, wily "silence, cunning and exile"; more contemporary, Gabriel García Márquez's labyrinth in which power over others, in the person of Simon Bolivar, is led to the thrall of the only unassailable power, death—these are some examples of the writer's endlessly varied ways of approaching the state of being through the word. Any writer of any worth at all hopes to play only a pocket-torch of light—and rarely, through genius, a sudden flambeau—into the bloody yet beautiful labyrinth of human experience, of being.

Anthony Burgess[6] once gave a summary definition of literature as "the aesthetic exploration of the word." I would say that writing only begins there, for the exploration of much beyond, which nevertheless only aesthetic means can express.

How does the writer become one, having been given the word? I do not know if my own be-

Dust jacket for the American edition of Gordimer's 1991 collection of short stories

ginnings have any particular interest. No doubt they have much in common with those of others, have been described too often before as a result of this yearly assembly before which a writer stands. For myself, I have said that nothing factual that I write or say will be as truthful as my fiction. The life, the opinions, are not the work, for it is in the tension between standing apart and being involved that the imagination transforms both. Let me give some minimal account of myself. I am what I suppose would be called a natural writer. I did not make any decision to become one. I did not, at the beginning, expect to earn a living by being read. I wrote as a child out of the joy of apprehending life through my senses—the look and scent and feel of things; and soon out of the emotions that puzzled me or raged within me and which took form, found some enlightenment, solace and delight, shaped in the written word. There is a little Kafka[7] parable that goes like this: "I have three dogs: Hold-him, Seize-him, and Nevermore. Hold-him and Seize-him

are ordinary little Schipperkes and nobody would notice them if they were alone. But there is Nevermore, too. Nevermore is a mongrel Great Dane and has an appearance that centuries of the most careful breeding could never have produced. Nevermore is a gypsy." In the small South African gold-mining town where I was growing up I was Nevermore the mongrel (although I could scarcely have been described as a Great Dane . . .) in whom the accepted characteristics of the townspeople could not be traced. I was the Gypsy, tinkering with words second-hand, mending my own efforts at writing by learning from what I read. For my school was the local library. Proust, Chekhov and Dostoevsky, to name only a few to whom I owe my existence as a writer, were my professors. In that period of my life, yes, I was evidence of the theory that books are made out of other books . . . But I did not remain so for long, nor do I believe any potential writer could.

With adolescence comes the first reaching out to otherness through the drive of sexuality. For most children, from then on the faculty of the imagination, manifest in play, is lost in the focus on day dreams of desire and love, but for those who are going to be artists of one kind or another the first life-crisis after that of birth does something else in addition: the imagination gains range and extends by the subjective flex of new and turbulent emotions. There are new perceptions. The writer begins to be able to enter into other lives. The process of standing apart and being involved has come.

Unknowingly, I had been addressing myself on the subject of being, whether, as in my first stories, there was a child's contemplation of death and murder in the necessity to finish off, with a death blow, a dove mauled by a cat, or whether there was wondering dismay and early consciousness of racism that came of my walk to school, when on the way I passed storekeepers, themselves East European immigrants kept lowest in the ranks of the Anglo-Colonial social scale for whites in the mining town, roughly abusing those whom colonial society ranked lowest of all, discounted as less than human—the black miners who were the stores' customers. Only many years later was I to realize that if I had been a child in that category—black—I might not have become a writer at all, since the library that made this possible for me was not open to any black child. For my formal schooling was sketchy, at best.

To address oneself to others begins a writer's next stage of development. To publish: to publish to anyone who would read what I wrote. That was my natural, innocent assumption of what publication meant, and it has not changed, that is what it means to me today, in spite of my awareness that most people refuse to believe that a writer does not have a particular audience in mind; and my other awareness: of the temptations, conscious and unconscious, which lure the writer into keeping a corner of the eye on who will take offense, who will approve what is on the page—a temptation that like Eurydice's straying glance, will lead the writer back into the Shades of a destroyed talent.

The alternative is not the malediction of the ivory tower, another destroyer of creativity. Borges once said he wrote for his friends and to pass the time. I think this was an irritated flippant response to the crass question—often an accusation —"For whom do you write?," just as Sartre's admonition that there are times when a writer should cease to write, and act upon being only in another way, was given in the frustration of an unresolved conflict between distress at injustice in the world and the knowledge that what he knew how to do best was write. Both Borges and Sartre, from their totally different extremes of denying literature a social purpose, were certainly perfectly aware that it has its implicit and unalterable social role in exploring the state of being, from which all other roles, personal among friends, public at the protest demonstration, derive. Borges was not writing for his friends, for he published and we all have received the bounty of his work. Sartre did not stop writing, although he stood at the barricades in 1968.

The question of for whom do we write nevertheless plagues the writer, a tin can attached to the tail of every work published. Principally it jangles the inference of tendentiousness as praise or denigration. In this context, Camus[8] dealt with the question best. He said that he liked individuals who take sides more than literatures that do. "One either serves the whole of man or one does not serve him at all. And if man needs bread and justice, and if what has to be done must be done to serve this need, he also needs pure beauty, which is the bread of his heart." So Camus called for "Courage in one's life and talent in one's work." And Márquez[9] redefined tendenz fiction thus: "The best way a writer can serve a revolution is to write as well as he can."

I believe that these two statements might be the credo for all of us who write. They do not resolve the conflicts that have come, and will continue to come, to contemporary writers. But they state plainly an honest possibility of doing so, they turn the face of the writer squarely to her and his existence, the reason to be, as a writer, and the reason to be, as a responsible human, acting, like any other, within a social context.

Being here: in a particular time and place. That is the existential position with particular implications for literature. Czeslaw Milosz[10] once wrote the cry: "What is poetry which does not serve nations or people?" and Brecht[11] wrote of a time when "to speak of trees is almost a crime." Many of us have had such despairing thoughts while living and writing through such times, in such places, and Sartre's solution makes no sense in a world where writers were—and still are— censored and forbidden to write, where, far from abandoning the word, lives were and are at risk in smuggling it, on scraps of paper, out of prisons. The state of being whose ontogenesis we explore has overwhelmingly included such experiences. Our approaches, in Nikos Kazantzakis's[12] words, have to "make the decision which harmonizes with the fearsome rhythm of our time."

Some of us have seen our books lie for years unread in our own countries, banned, and we have gone on writing. Many writers have been imprisoned. Looking at Africa alone— Soyinka, Ngugi wa Thiong'o, Jack Mapanje, in their countries, and in my own country, South Africa, Jeremy Cronin, Mongane Wally Serote, Breyten Breytenbach, Dennis Brutus, Jaki Seroke: all these went to prison for the courage shown in their lives, and have continued to take the right, as poets, to speak of trees. Many of the greats, from Thomas Mann to Chinua Achebe, cast out by political conflict and oppression in different countries, have endured the trauma of exile, from which some never recover as writers, and some do not survive at all. I think of the South Africans, Can Themba, Alex la Guma, Nat Nakasa, Todd Matshikiza. And some writers, over half a century from Joseph Roth to Milan Kundera, have had to publish new works first in the word that is not their own, a foreign language.

Then in 1988 the fearsome rhythm of our time quickened in an unprecedented frenzy to which the writer was summoned to submit the word. In the broad span of modern times since the Enlightenment writers have suffered opprobrium, bannings and even exile for other than po-

litical reasons. Flaubert dragged into court for in-
decency, over *Madame Bovary*, Strindberg ar-
raigned for blasphemy, over *Married*, Lawrence's
Lady Chatterley's Lover banned—there have been
many examples of so-called offense against hypocritical bourgeois mores, just as there have been
of treason against political dictatorships. But in a
period when it would be unheard of for countries such as France, Sweden and Britain to bring
such charges against freedom of expression,
there has risen a force that takes its appalling authority from something far more widespread
than social mores, and far more powerful than
the power of any single political regime. The
edict of a world religion has sentenced a writer
to death.

For more than three years, now, wherever
he is hidden, wherever he might go, Salman
Rushdie has existed under the Muslim pronounce-
ment upon him of the *fatwa*. There is no asylum
for him anywhere. Every morning when this
writer sits down to write, he does not know if he
will live through the day; he does not know
whether the page will ever be filled. Salman
Rushdie happens to be a brilliant writer, and the
novel for which he is being pilloried, *The Satanic
Verses*, is an innovative exploration of one of the
most intense experiences of being in our era, the
individual personality in transition between two
cultures brought together in a post-colonial
world. All is reexamined through the refraction
of the imagination; the meaning of sexual and fil-
ial love, the rituals of social acceptance, the meaning of a formative religious faith for individuals removed from its subjectivity by circumstance
opposing different systems of belief, religious
and secular, in a different context of living. His
novel is a true mythology. But although he has
done for the postcolonial consciousness in Europe what Günter Grass did for the post-Nazi
one with *The Tin Drum* and *Dog Years*, perhaps
even has tried to approach what Beckett did for
our existential anguish in *Waiting For Godot*, the
level of his achievement should not matter. Even
if he were a mediocre writer, his situation is the terrible concern of every fellow writer for, apart
from his personal plight, what implications, what
new threat against the carrier of the word does it
bring? It should be the concern of individuals
and above all, of governments and human rights
organizations all over the world. With dictatorships apparently vanquished, this murderous new
dictate invoking the power of international terror-
ism in the name of a great and respected religion

Nadine Gordimer (photograph © 1991 by Horst Tappe)

should and can be dealt with only by democratic
governments and the United Nations, as an offense against humanity.

To return from the horrific singular threat
to those that have been general for writers of this
century now in its final, summing-up decade. In
repressive regimes anywhere—whether in what
was the Soviet bloc, Latin America, Africa,
China—most imprisoned writers have been shut
away for their activities as citizens striving for liberation against the oppression of the general society to which they belong. Others have been condemned by repressive regimes for serving society
by writing as well as they can; for this aesthetic venture of ours becomes subversive when the shame-
ful secrets of our times are explored deeply, with
the artist's rebellious integrity to the state of
being manifest in life around her or him; then
the writer's themes and characters inevitably are
formed by the pressures and distortions of that society as the life of the fisherman is determined
by the power of the sea.

There is a paradox. In retaining this integrity, the writer sometimes must risk both the
state's indictment of treason, and the liberation
forces' complaint of lack of blind commitment.
As a human being, no writer can stoop to the lie

of Manichean "balance." The devil always has lead in his shoes, when placed on his side of the scale. Yet, to paraphrase coarsely Márquez's dictum given by him both as a writer and a fighter for justice, the writer must take the right to explore, warts and all, both the enemy and the beloved comrade in arms, since only a try for the truth makes sense of being, only a try for the truth edges towards justice just ahead of Yeats's beast slouching to be born. In literature, from life,

> we page through each other's faces
> we read each looking eye
> . . . It has taken lives to be able to do so.

These are the words of the South African poet and fighter for justice and peace in our country, Mongane Serote[13].

The writer is of service to humankind only insofar as the writer uses the word even against his or her own loyalties, trusts the state of being, as it is revealed, to hold somewhere in its complexity filaments of the cord of truth, able to be bound together, here and there, in art: trusts the state of being to yield somewhere fragmentary phrases of truth, which is the final word of words, never changed by our stumbling efforts to spell it out and write it down, never changed by lies, by semantic sophistry, by the dirtying of the word for the purposes of racism, sexism, prejudice, domination, the glorification of destruction, the curses and the praise-songs.

NOTES

1. "The God's Script" from *Labyrinths & Other Writings* by Jorge Luis Borges. Translator unknown. Edited by Donald H. Yates & James E. Kirby. Penguin Modern Classics, page 71.

2. *Mythologies* by Roland Barthes. Translated by Annette Lavers. Hill & Wang, page 131.

3. *Histoire de Lynx* by Claude Lévi-Strauss. ". . je les situais à mi-chemin entre le conte de fées et le roman policier". Plon, page 13.

4. *Report to Greco* by Nikos Kazantzakis. Faber & Faber, page 150.

5. *S/Z* by Roland Barthes. Translated by Richard Miller. Jonathan Cape.

6. London *Observer* review. 19/4/81. Anthony Burgess.

7. The Third Octavo Notebook from *Wedding Preparations in the Country* by Franz Kafka. Definitive Edition. Secker & Warburg.

8. *Carnets 1942-5* by Albert Camus.

9. Gabriel García Márquez. In an interview; my notes do not give the journal or date.

10. "Dedication" from *Selected Poems* by Czeslaw Milosz. The Ecco Press.

11. "To Posterity" from *Selected Poems* by Bertolt Brecht. Translated by H. R. Hays. Grove Press, page 173.

12. *Report to Greco* by Nikos Kazantzakis. Faber & Faber.

13. *A Tough Tale* by Mongane Wally Serote. Kliptown Books.

The Year in the Novel

David R. Slavitt
University of Pennsylvania

What we have here—not even the president has had the effrontery to deny it—is an intellectual recession. I cannot think of a year in which more bad books have received more serious attention. These aren't just lapses but a pattern, and one need not be paranoid to look for explanations. What people do is, mostly, what they want to do and intend to have done. And if the non-book has been promoted to a new eminence, there must be some significant intention, however malign.

What we're talking about are the big books of the season—Norman Mailer's *Harlot's Ghost* (Random House), Harold Brodkey's *Runaway Soul* (Farrar, Straus, and Giroux), and, in a slightly different and more traditional vein, Alexandra Ripley's *Scarlett* (Warner). I find myself in the bizarre position of having not only to admit but having to boast that I haven't read them. Anyone dopey enough to slog all the way through these novels isn't smart enough to write intelligently about them. I've dipped and skimmed, browsed and sniffed and held my not so delicate nose (in my needier years, I committed some bestsellers myself in order to keep my children's rapacious bursars at bay). It was ridiculous, not just a matter of three random disasters but a conspiracy of discontented, misanthropic, dyspeptic crazies in New York who are trying to get back at literature itself for having betrayed them. These are English majors, most of them, who know nothing about literature or business and who find themselves working for much less than they would be making in any other industry (if, indeed, they were employable in any other industry). And they hate it, hate the books, and hate the readers, and want to get even, which they contrive to do by forcing down the gullets of a retching public these scabrous libroid monstrosities.

These volumes are printed in large numbers, shipped, reviewed, sold, displayed on shelves and coffee tables, but never (one supposes, or one hopes) actually read. My guess is the breakthrough title was Umberto Eco's *The Name of the Rose* (1983), which proved, almost ten years ago, that one could sell vast quantities of a volume nobody would read—because nobody could. This was a text about 10 percent in Latin, and most readers in this Jacobin society have only the loosest grip on English. But the concept was enticing—the display book, the unreadable book, the book as a pure piece of merchandising rather than literature. Indeed, the worse a book is as literature, the better and purer it is as an act of merchandising.

This perversity is not new but seems to have reached a new intensity this year. And Mailer and Brodkey are the appropriate heroes of this antiliteracy ecstasy. Mailer for years has been doing a kind of Mexican hat dance on the broad brim of his talent, as if to invite us to share the joke he has learned to be amused by—that it is absurd to be gifted in a time when nobody notices gifts, and quality counts for nothing or can't be distinguished from arrant fakery and trumpery. He will then, sometimes ruefully and sometimes with ebullience, devote his talent to foolishness and fatuousness, thus reclaiming the initiative from his operating editor, Jason Epstein, and making the game his own.

Brodkey, meanwhile, seems to be an invention of the *New Yorker* on the one hand and Gordon Lish on the other, and has been running an amazing scam, claiming to have been working on this book for twenty-seven years! (Wonderful! Excellent! Superb! One more year, and he'd have doubled Flaubert's stint on *Madame Bovary* [1854]!) Just think what it would mean for the literary world if all authors took this long to spin out their sentences. There'd be so much less on the table. John Updike, Joyce Carol Oates, and their like just don't get it—that people don't like to read, find it a good deal of work to get through one book, let alone a slew of them, and rather resent it when they are put in the dreadful position of turning pages as fast as they possibly can and nevertheless falling perceptibly behind.

The *New York Times Book Review* has figured this out and proclaims the message in a not so subtle way almost every Sunday with a bottom-half-of-

Richard Moore, author of The Investigator *(photograph by Virginia Cazort)*

the-first-page essay, which is *not* a book review and which therefore doesn't even put us at risk of having to read yet another damned, thick, fat, square book. The subjects of these essays are often revealing: "Books I've Never Finished" or "Writer's Block." If there were more writer's block, think how much less time we'd have to spend reading those books, after all.

Brodkey is probably the champion blocked writer. Past sixty now, he has made a career— and a living!—with this book in progress, which is of course the best place for a book to be, for once it is down on paper, the editors' dreams for any literary work begin to come undone. It isn't a piece of high art that will sell a jillion copies and then move to the backlist and do well in university survey courses forever, but merely another title, a commodity like any other that one must pitch to the sales force, send out to unappreciative reviewers, and then try to sell to a fickle and anyway dense public. The dream book is the "supreme fiction" of Wallace Stevens's title. It is not embarrassed by any advance orders from

which to figure a first print run, and there isn't an advertising and publicity budget that seems not only undreamlike but actually constrained. Unwritten books are the ones the industry lives on, by, and for.

But after twenty-seven years of throat clearing, even a Brodkey must turn in something to someone, because there are only so many excuses, postures, and dodges with which to put off editors who have authorized checks and are responsible to corporate executives. The CEOs, who may be pleased to list these oneiric assets but object after a time to the paying of so much interest, aren't Millkens or Keatings after all— which is not exactly a compliment: they're no more scrupulous but lack the nerve, the sheer brashness of those pirates.

So I'm all for Brodkey for taking publishers to the cleaners for as much as possible and as long as possible. It's only that eventually even he had to hand in a manuscript. And they get (and we get in turn) this ... first novel actually, a vastly pretentious and even more vastly boring, tiresome, all but incoherent hodgepodge that gets respectful treatment in the *New York Times Book Review*, and prominent space in the *New York Review of Books* and the *Times Literary Supplement*. In the *New York Review*, Brodkey is on page three with a David Levine caricature—the other caricatures in the issue are Jacques Derrida, Nadine Gordimer and Adrienne Rich, and Alexander Hamilton. That's fairly grand treatment for what seems essentially a prank, a demonstration that taste is dead and intelligence has turned upon itself, that, with a sufficiently intimidating headwaiter, one can serve up whale slunk, pass it off as milk-fed veal, and get away with it.

Indeed, the outrageous unreadability of the book is probably a part of its success—the notion being that art isn't merely entertaining but ought to uplift, ought to be serious, difficult, and, not to put too fine a point on it, boring. If it feels bad enough, it must be—like church, medicine, or aerobic exercise—good for you. Thus, in a review in the *TLS* that turns out to be finally unfavorable, Gabriel Jospovici feels obliged to register his credentials by making comparisons, or invocations, or allusions to "the greatest modernist novels, from *À la Recherche* to Georges Perec's *La Vie, mode d'emploi* and Yavok Shabtai's *Past Continuous*" which, he says, "have found a means of sailing between the Scylla of plot and the Charybdis of total plotlessness."

Is it necessary to trot out all that just to say that in these 835 pages, there isn't any basic narrative? What we have here is the collected outtakes from Brodkey's short stories and has to do one way or another with the same Brodkey-like figure, a poor orphaned boy who goes to Harvard, discovers women, but then finds out that there's also literature to screw around with. To suggest that this is an almost incoherent, mostly maundering, often even ungrammatical book ought not be so intimidating that a reviewer feels the need to gird himself up, get defensive, and allude to Perec and Shabtai to let us know that he was, in the first grade, in the bluebird group of fast readers and is still pretty good at it.

The only other interesting thing to remark about *The Runaway Soul* is its runaway price—it is the second novel in the history of American publishing to come out with a list price of thirty dollars. The first, only a few weeks earlier, was, naturally enough, Norman Mailer's *Harlot's Ghost*. This was noted on the business news pages of the *Times*, which is where the project ought properly to be discussed. Mailer's book and Brodkey's have a lot in common, actually, for Mailer's novel is also big, dopey, but grandly ambitious, and clearly IMPORTANT. It is so big that it doesn't even end but only indicates that this is "To Be Continued," which is more of a threat, I think, than a promise. It's so big that nobody at Random House had either the nerve or the energy to edit any of it. There is a dangling modifier in the first sentence that would not pass muster in the bonehead composition course of any cow college, and, for the rest of the long way, we get paragraphs that start out with first person pronouns and wander distractedly through syntactical thickets to end up astonishingly in the second person.

We might expect of a large novel about the CIA a certain degree of political savvy, some historical background, a sense of what has been going on in the world. If Gore Vidal had written such a book, a good part of the fun of it would have been in his impish suggestions about which country did what and to whom and for what reason. Indeed, if John le Carré had written such a book, we'd have at the very least a mordant entertainment about the psychological tribulations of spying and the philosophical stresses of the bad faith that spies not only encounter, but are required to enact themselves. These are ambitions that Mailer doesn't condescend to acknowledge, let alone fulfill. What he gives us is a father-son story, an Oedipal farrago onto which he grafts

his own peculiar (one might also say loony) metapsychology of the yin and yang of things that he labels *alpha* and *omega*.

It isn't all dreadful. There are pages, even whole scenes here and there, in which Mailer's tendentious silliness disappears because he has latched onto some piece of action too good to let go, and where his craftsmanly experience takes him onto firm narrative ground in spite of the arrant dumbness of the book's grand strategy. I found these passages not only not redemptive but actually distressing, for I took them as evidence of what our novelist could have been doing had he any shred left of the modesty and humor that keep most writers from making fools of themselves.

The trouble is that Mailer is smart enough to have understood that his real relation with his audience has nothing to do with his writing. He can produce a good book such as *Executioner's Song* (1979), or a windy and insane one such as *Ancient Evenings* (1983), and it makes no difference at all. He gets the same media attention either way, achieves the same impressive sales, and thus for his next book can command the same hefty advances. At the time of this writing—early December—some 185,000 copies of *Harlot's Ghost* had been shipped, and the newspapers were reporting that Random House, although indifferent to the content of the novel, had been much concerned about its cover. The core beliefs of publishing are diametrically opposite to those most of us hold. Lightning always strikes in the same place, they assume, and one should always judge a book by its cover. Therefore, the rather handsome, dark gray dust jacket with "CIA" as an overall design and the author's name and the title in striking embossed white letters has been judged by the merchandisers as too somber. Another jacket in raspberry has been whipped up for the Christmas season in the hope of greater sales.

There is no room for any gloss on this, and surely no need for one. But I am reminded of the observation of an old teacher of mine who lives in Washington, D.C., and finds it depressing to see, each year, another generation of bright young men and women, all of them filled with some degree of idealism and the wish to do good, arrive from colleges and graduate schools. They are socialized, however, by the bureaucratic system and learn—in the State Department, the Justice Department, or wherever else—not to take any initiative, never to incur risks, never to follow their instincts but always to implement the policies of higher-ups until their naive but precious idealism has been finally extinguished and it is too late for them to dream about doing anything that may have consequences for good in the world.

Well, it happens in publishing too, evidently. The love of literature that drew these young men and women to be English majors has to be killed before they can be trusted to run even modest amounts of capital. Hard lessons must be learned about quality counting for nothing. They must be made to realize that this is a business, a series of feats of merchandising, a kind of fraud practiced upon a public that deserves nothing better because it demands nothing better.

This leads us, at last, to *Scarlett*, the other big book of the fall season. Or big nonbook, one might better say, an expensive rehash of the lower-middle-brow nonsense of Margaret Mitchell's *Gone With the Wind* (1936). That was—let us not kid ourselves—a more or less stupid exercise, a feminist tract *avant la lettre* with a predictably romantic setting in the South of the Civil War and the Reconstruction period. The film was rather better than the book, mostly because Clark Gable and Vivian Leigh and Leslie Howard imposed their personalities on it and gave it a schlocky sheen—so that this sequel, once the Mitchell heirs could be brought round, was an attractive, or at least economically viable, proposition.

The book is not readable, is even duller and more mawkish than Mitchell's, and seems to be rather prudish. (The estate, in a high-minded way, wanted to protect the "property" from vulgarization and insisted that there be no explicit sexuality in the sequel, as if there had been no changes at all in public taste and standards since the 1930s. These restrictions only guaranteed a different and more serious kind of vulgarity.) But to talk about the text of the novel is entirely to miss the point. The publishers knew quite well that literary quality was irrelevant, and that the writing and editing were merely preliminary chores annoyingly prerequisite to the real business of selling books and subsidiary rights. I am reliably informed that the editor, a bright young woman, sent down by Warner for the first look at Ripley's manuscript, had a good dinner and a night's rest, and then, in the morning, was left alone for some hours with the manuscript and a pot of coffee. When she got up to stretch and take a turn around the garden, she was asked what she thought, and her reaction, after the

first couple of hundred typescript pages was: "It's very Southern."

It turned out that she had never actually read *Gone With the Wind*. She had not seen the film either. She had no clear idea, then, what she was looking at. But never mind. The book sold a record number of copies in its first month in the stores, and producer Robert Halmi in partnership with CBS put up eight million dollars for the film rights—an all-time record, even making allowances for inflation. Not only was *Scarlett* the number one title on the best-seller list, it even dragged Margaret Mitchell's old book back onto the hardcover list (at $21.95) and onto the paperback list too (at $5.99). It is therefore difficult to try to maintain that these cynics in publishing are wrong. All one can do is gnash one's teeth and mutter how they are all villains, churls, fools, knaves, rogues, swine, dogs, vermin.

And what if they knew writers and readers were doing this? They would delight, exulting and enjoying every moment of what they would take as an acknowledgment of their triumph—because, as I have suggested, they detest their own old and foolish notions about quality. They understand that publishing is a business, that in the marketplace of ideas, ideas are the last things that readers can bear. On a best-seller list toward the close of the year, *Scarlett* was followed by a Stephen King horror story, a Tom Clancy high-tech novel, a Ken Follett suspense story, a Dick Francis horse story, a couple of novels by Sidney Sheldon and Barbara Taylor Bradford, and then an Anne McCaffrey science-fiction work in the "Dragonriders of Pern" series. What claptrap! What a monumental disgrace! It is a triumph of kitsch over art, of the demos over the aristos. If we do not see this as an indictment of the folly of free, universal, compulsory education, it is at the least a mordant demonstration of entropy in the sphere of culture. The minions of these publishing houses learn to delight in their ability to manipulate such offenses against good taste to produce, from time to time, impressive results on the real books—which are those the accountants keep. There has to be a perverse delight these editors take in what they're doing, a kind of blithe nihilism or a literary schadenfreude.

Real publishing, what little there is left, is mostly by inadvertence—good books young editors sneak through on small budgets—or is elsewhere, out in the sticks where the little presses seem not to have been informed of the death of civilization and are reading manuscripts, printing

*Dust jacket for Rush's novel about love, Africa,
and anthropology*

the story of one Archibald Bromley, an odd duck who lives with his brother and sister in a large house in some Boston suburb and has convinced himself that his siblings are involved in an incestuous affair. Archibald's oddity, if not actual craziness, doesn't necessarily affect the likeliness of the truth or falsity of his suspicion, and, while he is not a particularly sympathetic character, Moore writes about him with such crafted and precise sentences (he's a poet, after all) that Archibald comes across with a vividness that makes it impossible for the reader not to respond to him. Archibald's eccentricity informs the rest of the world and accounts for it better than sanity might be able to do. "His very peculiarities, he believed, put some things in a newer, clearer light, just as a photographer's filter, held up to some familiar scene, brings out aspects of the scene that were unnoticed before." A brisk, intelligent, ghastly comedy, it seems to me a bit like Alfred Hitchcock in the moviemaker's lighter mode (*The Trouble with Harry* [1955], for instance), or William Gerhardie's odd, wonderful, and sadly underappreciated novels of the 1920s and 1930s, such as *Futility* (1922) and *Doom* (1928). My information is that this elegant book was written in the late 1970s, has been shopped around since then, was rejected "thirty or forty times" by the trade houses, and that Moore's agent finally gave up on it, leaving the author to plod onward, writing cover letters and shipping out the manuscript until Story Line took it.

There are worse publishing stories, of course, insane tales from the crypt about indifference and ill luck that good writers tell one another for consolation. The worst I've heard this year is about a book out of my purview (American novels are enough, are more than any one person can handle). Still, rules are made only to be broken, and the appearance this year of Ingeborg Bachmann's *Malina* (Holmes and Meier) is instructive, to say the least. Bachmann was an influential and eminent Austrian writer, a member of the "Group 47," and, in 1964, a winner of the Georg Büchner prize in poetry. This first and last novel of hers—she died in a fire in her apartment in Rome in 1973—was published in 1971 and has been translated into ten languages including, finally, English. None of the high-toned prestigious trade houses was interested, and it was left to a small press to bring her book out in New York and London. On the first page of Philip Boehm's translator's note is a paragraph announcing that, "shortly before this book

the best books they can find, and are, if anything, surprised that so many works of such high quality are coming out to the silos and bayous and log cabins where they are stashing their hordes of good writing. Twenty years ago there was a kind of coherence to the lit biz, and Knopf and Random House and Farrar Straus and Viking were doing a reasonable enough job so that one could ask why there was such a need for small presses. Today, the question is reversed, and one looks to Dalkey Archive, the University of Chicago, Louisiana State University Press, Story Line Press, Coffeehouse Press, and such operations, and one wonders what it is that Knopf, and Random House and Farrar Straus and Viking suppose themselves to be doing. Or, given what they are doing, we might better ask, who needs them anyway?

To get down to cases, I thought Richard Moore's *The Investigator* (Story Line Press) was an absolutely brilliant piece of work, nervous, jangly, shrewd, and altogether engrossing. It is went to press, Max Holmes, the co-founder of Holmes & Meier, suffered a fatal heart attack." The cream of this grim jest is that A) the novel is extraordinarily fine, a brooding, soaring, and extremely serious elaboration of a conventional love story to include all of Vienna and, finally, all modern experience, and B) a film version directed by Werner Schroeter and starring Isabelle Huppert has appeared in Europe, has won the 1991 Bavarian Film Prize and makes *Malina*, despite its quality, a viable commercial "property." Which proves that the odds against these longshots hitting the target are no worse when the attack is from the small bore guns of the little presses.

Such disasters are not at all unusual. I remember hearing some years ago—eight? maybe ten?— at a writers' conference at Bennington College an extraordinary reading by Richard Elman of a wonderful piece of writing from his novel, *Tar Beach* (the title refers to the place on the roof of a Brooklyn synagogue where, in 1947, a bunch of Jews are sunbathing). Elman is an elegant, experienced, and quite funny writer, and this was his nineteenth book. With some confidence I looked forward to having a copy of the text in my hand—and here it is, in 1991, a dog's age later, from Sun and Moon Press. The book is a medley of the lively and enlivening rhythms of Yiddish, Hebrew, Brooklynese, and an imaginary African language the protagonist dreams up, having decided that the Zionists might have passed up an attractive offer when the British offered them Uganda as a homeland instead of Israel.

Sandra Scofield's novel, *Beyond Deserving* (Permanent Press), garrulous and hip, is a book one might have expected any trade editor to leap at for its obvious commercial potential. Scofield writes about the women of the Fisher family and how they manage their roughneck menfolk in what is virtually a *roman à thèse* in support of the notions of machismo that Robert Bly has been promoting with his bizarrely successful *Iron John*. It wouldn't have taken much calculation to figure out that somewhere between the Bly book and Camille Paglia's *Sexual Personae*, which also has enjoyed a phenomenal run, there should have been an audience of some size and enthusiasm for this impish, poised, funny performance. And Scofield's credentials were impeccable—she'd had an NEA fellowship, and her first novel, *Gringa* (1989), had been nominated for the Sue Kaufman Prize for First Fiction of the American Academy and Institute of Arts and Letters. Indeed,

the only thing I can see that might have put off some editors is the fact that *Beyond Deserving* is clearly well written, intelligent, poised—and warning bells go off to announce that this is quality stuff. Such bells are death knells of manuscripts in the offices of editors looking for books that can sell in large numbers to mass audiences that prefer something else. Even with the prestige that comes of having been a National Book Award finalist, the sales of *Beyond Deserving* were modest. The first printing was a minuscule twenty-two hundred copies, there was a second printing of four thousand copies, and, by the end of the year, a third printing had been ordered of three thousand more. At this level, a large trade house, with its expensive overhead (real estate costs as much as editorial salaries) would just about break even.

A Cure for Dreams by Kaye Gibbons (Algonquin) ought to have been another safe bet, for Gibbons had actually won the American Academy and Institute of Arts and Letters' Sue Kaufman Prize with *Ellen Foster* (1987), had an NEA fellowship in fiction, and, with *A Virtuous Woman* (1989), had further established herself with what one would suppose to be a loyal following as a sort of woman's novelist—if only because her characters are mostly female and their concerns are largely those of ordinary family life. Gibbons's prose is brisk and clean, and her eyes and ears are sharp for whatever is funny or sad in the lives of women who are trying to work out their own identities in a distinctively regional and male-dominated world. In a similar vein, Kay Sloan's first novel, *Worry Beads* (L.S.U. Press), is a finely worked study of family life in the South. It is about two brothers, and the hopeless love of one of them for the other's wife and what this does to them all on the gulf coast of Mississippi over a forty-year span. An impressive debut!

Another finalist in fiction for the National Book Award was Stephen Dixon's *Frog* (British American Publications), a huge sprawl of a book in which, for some 769 pages, Howard Tetch, a writer, chronicles real and imaginary events, alternative universes, recollections of things that happened, or only ought to have happened. The title, here, comes from the name of the narrator's pet turtle, and the book leaps about and croaks, basks, and does everything a frog can do except turn into a prince—which would be a kind of betrayal. This is a big burly book, expansive and ambitious, the kind of thing we had perhaps been led to expect from the Brodkey novel,

Dust jacket for Busch's novel about a lawyer-client relationship that is influenced by memories of Vietnam and childhood abuse

a slightly oafish but enormously powerful book about how at least some of us live now.

There were some books that the major trade houses brought out that were of obvious quality. These houses have salesmen going out each season, and they need to construct a list one way or another. Unlike producers of plays, they can't make a full-time career of saying no. From time to time, then, good books get through the chicanes and actually appear—but whether they fare better or worse bearing these better-known imprints is difficult to tell. I was surprised but not astonished when I called, at the beginning of December, for copies of *Mating* (Knopf), Norman Rush's novel that won the National Book Award, to find that it was out of stock. This was the day after a full page ad had run in the *New York Times Book Review*. The same thing happened with *Mariette in Ecstasy* (HarperCollins), Ron Hansen's book about a novice nun who embarrasses the order and, indeed, the whole church when she develops the stigmata. John Leonard

had done an enthusiastic piece on the CBS "Sunday Morning" show, and I called the publisher the next day and was told that this too was out of stock. This happened in December, when a large proportion of the book business is transacted and when a sane publisher might expect to exploit the listings of some of his books in the various lists of editors' recommendations? Go, know what they're thinking. Or *if* they're thinking. A little flurry of interest, and they're helpless, utterly perplexed by what they were unable to predict because they were blinded by their own cynicism.

Both of those were engaging, interesting books. I enjoyed Hansen's delicate and careful writing, found myself caring a lot about these quite plausible nuns, and mean no faint praise when I suggest that the book is less limited in its appeal than one might expect. Rush's *Mating* was much less modest, indeed was rather showy and bristling with low-frequency words from American and British slang, French, Latin, Setswana, and the argots of anthropology and rock music. An ambitious piece about a love affair in Africa, it dazzled for a while, then tried my patience. But I was, at that point, reading a lot of books in a relatively short time to get this piece done, and my patience was perhaps not at its best. I shall go back to this and give Rush's nameless anthropologist narrator and her peculiar lover, Nelson Denoon, another shot. Maybe there is something in their utopian settlement in the backcountry of Botswana that will speak better to me in a less harried, more receptive moment.

U&I, a short and brilliant book by Nicholson Baker (Random House) carried on its dust jacket the blazon "A True Story," which got it put, more often than not, with biography, or literary criticism, or memoirs, or in other inappropriate places; or no place in stores that don't sell a lot of literary criticism and memoirs. That a novel can be, in various senses, "true" or that Baker, an extremely playful fellow, might be entertaining himself with a little game just didn't get through to the gatekeepers of the culture (editors, salesmen, book buyers, and, finally, clerks). I had to flick my dog whip menacingly across my thigh to get someone to find me a copy in a large store where the computer said there was one in stock. It's an account of a younger writer, the "I," and his romance with John Updike, the "U" of the title. The love-smitten younger writer wants a token from his beloved, and in this case he succeeds when he can persuade himself that Updike has quoted—and been influenced by—

him, rather than the other way around. It is a crazy, extremely intellectual, extremely engaging performance, the kind of thing that Harold Bloom or Stanley Fish would be doing if they had a sense of humor, for the issues are theirs, really: how does one author influence another and how do we distinguish between the author on the page and the imperfect copy of his work that is in our own heads? These serious lit-crit questions are the occasion for a sprightly and engaging book, a book so good that I felt I had discovered a new friend and betook myself to a series of bookstores until I'd managed to get hold of his earlier works, *Room Temperature* (1990) and *The Mezzanine* (1988), both of which I admired—and both of which made me laugh aloud.

Baker's success is the kind of thing that is supposed to happen to talent and persistence and still can happen—often enough to keep us all off balance, to give the rest of us hope, to make us suppose that our unsuccess must be in some measure our own fault. There are literary careers, Updike's for instance, that suggest that the world of letters is still functioning in a reasonable way. And there are others who write well and who have managed to attract a large enough and faithful enough audience so that the publishers can make a profit on their books without actually having to do anything. Anne Tyler's *Saint Maybe* (Knopf), Gail Godwin's *Father Melancholy's Daughter* (Morrow), John Barth's *The Last Voyage of Somebody the Sailor* (Little Brown), Don De Lillo's *Mao II* (Viking), Amy Tan's *The Kitchen God's Wife* (Putnam's), Stanley Elkin's *The Macguffin* (Linden/ Simon and Schuster), and Alice Adams's *Caroline's Daughters* (Knopf) were all accomplished and impressive if not particularly innovative works of reliable, established performers.

Isaac Bashevis Singer was as established as any performer can get, and his farewell appearance was *Scum* (Farrar, Straus, and Giroux), another anguished consideration of sex and faith. If this book isn't up to the level of *Enemies, A Love Story* (1972), that is no reason not to like it. Singer's death makes much of this business of ranking and discrimination seem silly anyway. His protagonist Max Barabander is a familiar bumbler with a bad case of priapism—which is a peculiarly modern complaint, and modernity is the real monster in Singer's work.

On a cheerier note, Frederick Busch is a by now familiar name, and his career is one of persistent excellence. *Closing Arguments* (Ticknor and Fields) is his seventeenth book, and evidently he

does well enough for his publishers to stick with him while they are making only modest sums and hoping for that big breakthrough book. This one ought to be it—a passionate novel about love and pain, sex and pain, love and war, torture and justice. By turns erotic, frightening, and abruptly moving, it is an enormously intelligent book that combines the heritage of Vietnam with the scars of child abuse and transforms their sordidness into art. What else could one ask for? A movie? That is how Anthony Burgess emerged from the modest obscurity of being a merely excellent novelist to the eminence of celebrity and stardom. The trouble is that one can't imagine a movie version of *Closing Arguments* that would be any more vivid. The way in which Busch intertwines his lawyer-protagonist's affair with his client and the lawyer's memories of interrogation as a prisoner of war and then folds in their earlier recollections of being abused as small children is breathtaking, unsentimental, powerful, moving, and above all, literary. It would almost certainly vulgarize it to move it all from the page to the screen. As far as I'm concerned, *Closing Arguments* was one of the very best books of 1991.

The movies don't work anymore anyway, unless they are huge monster hits. One would have supposed that the John Frankenheimer film of Michael Mewshaw's *The Year of the Gun* (1984) would have paved the way for some heavy play for Mewshaw's *True Crime* (Poseidon), a crackerjack yarn about a crime writer who returns from Rome to his Maryland home and gets involved in the investigation of his father's murder. It's a slightly slick story, but it has all the virtues of good crime writing and many of those things one looks for in non-genre fiction—an evocation of place, a texture of lived lives, a plausibly rumpled sense of reality. I was up into the wee hours with this book that I couldn't put down, and I have no idea why it wasn't a huge success. It surely had more appealing characters then we encounter in Pete Dexter's *Brotherly Love* (Random House), which enjoyed considerable success and received a lot of critical attention. Some of this respectful treatment was no doubt the result of Dexter's having won the National Book Award for *Paris Trout* (1988), which was, I thought, a piece of fake Faulkner, and in any event a relatively nasty book. This new one, about gangsters and violence in Philadelphia unions, is rather less nasty, and has a plausible patina of local color, but I am nonetheless mystified by the seriousness with which Dexter's work is taken. This may be

Dust jacket for Evanier's comic novel about communism and the Ethel and Julius Rosenberg case

my own failure; some perfectly sensible friends of mine maintain that Dexter is worth reading.

Another Philadelphia writer, much funnier and more to my taste, is Mike Malone, whose *Foolscap* (Little, Brown) is a vastly entertaining, academic novel about the conflicts in an English department of Cavendish University. Malone has taught at the University of Pennsylvania, where his wife, Maureen Quilligan, is a member of the department and of the standing faculty. I teach there too and looked for smart (or at least unkind) observations about some of my colleagues, but what I found was a large, hearty, complicated, and quite satisfying entertainment.

Madison Smartt Bell is a young, showy writer, always Smartt and often Brilliantt, and in his latest novel, *Doctor Sleep* (Harcourt Brace Jovanovich), he is at the top of his form, writing about an insomniac hypnotherapist in London whose distorted perceptions of the world seem more and more to be a correct and inevitable description of external reality. An even younger

writer, with whose short stories I was quite taken in *Emperor of Air* (1988), has a first novel now, *Blue River* (Houghton Mifflin), about a doctor, a decent respectable fellow, whose brother turns up one day—a gambler and a drifter and not respectable at all. Ethan Canin, a student still at Harvard Medical School, has apparently been imagining otherness, and this is a quite impressive performance. *All-Bright Court* (Houghton Mifflin) is Connie Porter's first novel, a vivid account of grim existence in a slum in Buffalo, New York, not altogether unlike the one in which Porter grew up, a melting-pot community of blacks, Arabs, Spaniards, Poles, and Italians. Convincing and lively, the perhaps disproportionate success of Porter's book—a Book of the Month Club selection—may have been to some degree predictable (they could call her "another Toni Morrison," "another Alice Walker"), but her writing is good enough so that one can't quibble and, indeed, is glad to have found her.

What's left? Another handful of interesting volumes I can't fit into any organized piece but wouldn't want to omit. *Dead Certainties* (Knopf), by Simon Schama, is fiction—as he says, a series of "historical novellas"—by the extremely literate historian whose *Citizens* (1989) had a deservedly grand success a couple of years back. *The Weight of Winter* (Viking), by Cathie Pelletier, is the final volume of a trilogy about life in Mattagash, Maine. (The first two were *The Funeral Makers*, published in 1986, and *Once Upon a Time on the Banks*, from 1989.) I haven't read the first two and have only flipped through this last installment, but it looks just fine, and I approve of the undertaking which, if it is anywhere near as good as Ivan Doig's trilogy, completed last year, about Montana, could be a grand thing. I look forward to a little leisure and the chance to make a serious foray. *Los Gusanos* (HarperCollins) by John Sayles, the moviemaker who this year brought us *City of Hope*, is an interesting, gritty, complicated, and persuasive representation of four decades of the lives of Cuban émigrés and exiles in Miami. *Red Love* (Scribners) by David Evanier is a quite funny book about communism and Ethel and Julius Rosenberg—which seems an obvious idea only because someone has now thought of it. The utter collapse of communism allows us to look back at the rape of language of those old apparatchik types, and the most appropriate reaction now is to giggle. The idea of a comedy about two characters who are electrocuted is admittedly sassy, but then I admire sass. *The Late*

Night Muse (HarperCollins), by Bette Pesetsky, a strange, rather self-conscious but finally successful book, is about a young woman dying of some neurological ailment whose swan song we are offered. An ambitious project, Pesetsky brings it off quite creditably.

So, despite the disarray of publishing and bookselling, there were good books. A friend of mine once observed that while publishing is a relatively trivial undertaking, measured in terms of its share of the gross national product, writing is important, serious, and worth paying attention to. That still seems to be going on. One way or another, at least some good books find their way sooner or later into the hands of the right readers. It does take a degree of luck for this to happen. One of the books I admired most this year was David Markson's *Wittgenstein's Mistress*, which I'd picked up by mistake actually—I'd been looking for Ray Monk's book, *Ludwig Wittgenstein*. Anyway I read a few lines, then a few pages, of the Markson, then bought it and brought it home. It had been published in 1988, and the paperback, from Dalkey Archive Press in Elmwood Park, Illinois, came out in 1990. How it got into a bookstore relaxed enough not to ship it back right away, and how it then got into my hands, was pure luck, but, as Napoleon is reported to have said, luck will do.

The Year in the Short Story

George Garrett
University of Virginia

At the end of 1990, a banner year for the short story, the word was out that the publication of books of short fiction had now peaked and would seriously decline in 1991. Final numbers are not in yet, but that guesswork looks to be wrong. Eighteen percent of the "Notable Books of the Year" selected by the editors of the *New York Times Book Review* for the "Christmas Books 1991" issue (1 December 1991) were collections of stories as compared to 19 percent in 1990; but that one-point difference is modified by the fact that the editors chose more books as "Notable" in 1991 (122) than in 1990 (94). In both years two of the ten books listed as "Editors' Choice: The Best Books of 1991" are collections of short stories; for 1991, V. S. Pritchett's *Complete Collected Stories* (Random House) and *Two Lives* (Viking) by William Trevor. All meaningless numbers games aside, it appears that 1991 was another fine year for the publication of short stories in America. The big reviewing institutions, newspapers and popular magazines, could not keep up, but *Publishers Weekly* managed to publish brief notices of a multitude of story collections including those brought out by major publishers, university presses, small presses of all kinds, both in hard-cover and in original paperback editions. Once in the marketplace many of these books received uneven attention in the review media. As for the health of the short story in general, there was the good news and the bad news. Exemplary of the latter were the remarks of Eudora Welty quoted in the *Richmond Times Dispatch* (23 June): "I feel so much for writers today. There are not many magazines that publish short stories anymore. I suppose no book of short stories ever sells." Somewhat more optimistic views found space in Deirdre Carmody's "Short Stories Thrive Out of Mainstream" (*New York Times*, 23 April). There, after acknowledging the surprising resurgence of the contemporary short story, she turned to experts for confirmation. "If there is any cultural significance in what the literary community is doing," said Daniel Menaker of the *New Yorker*, "it resides in the short story." Shannon Ravenel, editorial director of Algonquin Books, seemed to agree, though she made the literary community sound a bit like some kind of exclusive club: "There is a very real community of American short story writers. Everybody knows who everybody is, although there is no real way to make much of a splash."

Roughly fifteen thousand short stories are submitted annually to the *New Yorker*. *Atlantic*, which publishes from twelve to fifteen stories a year, chooses them from among approximately twelve thousand submissions. From the editors' point of view there is plenty of activity among story writers. Just before summer the *New York Times Book Review* took note of this with a special feature—"Keeping It Short: A Season of Stories" (26 May). And by the end of 1991 there was already attention being paid to the collection of stories due to come along in early 1992. Among those spring 1992 books of stories already in circulation in bound galleys before year's end, some of the outstanding collections by old and new hands were Hilary Masters's *Success* (St. Martin's Press); *Cowboys Are My Weakness* (Norton) by Pam Houston; *Let the Dead Bury Their Dead* (Harcourt Brace Jovanovich) by Randall Kenan; and Pinckney Benedict's second collection, *The Wrecking Yard* (Doubleday/Talese). Benedict's book was being massively promoted before year's end. It remains to be seen if this extraordinary effort will pay off beyond capturing review space. Never shy when it comes to promotion, Random House is hustling three new story writers on their list, by means of an advance sampler of their stories— Leo Berenstain, *The Wind Monkey*; Jacqueline Carey, *Good Gossip*; and Susan Thames, *As Much As I Know*. Another forthcoming book that looks likely to gain significant attention is Robert Olen Butler's *A Good Scent From a Strange Mountain* (Holt). Butler, who has published several highly regarded novels and who, thanks to the U.S. Army, is fluent in the Vietnamese language, writes from the inside about Vietnamese characters. The fifteen stories in the volume have already earned interest and awards as they have been appearing in the quarterlies.

Any other signs and portents? Not long before year's end the *New Yorker* published a story utterly atypical of anything they have published for years. Not clever or cute or chic, not, except for some moments, marked by the elegant style of its sentences, and riddled with four-letter words which have seldom appeared in the slick pages of that magazine and, also, a story with loose ends and rough edges in construction, not at all perfectly wrapped and packaged, "The Pugilist At Rest," by Thom Jones (2 December), is a Marine Corps and Vietnam story, full of bitter energy, though familiar enough for those who have read the other books and stories or seen the films about Vietnam. Whatever the reason for the re-

Dust jacket for Abbott's fifth collection, which includes a novella about two old college friends who rob convenience stores for recreation

markable publication of this story in the national gallery of the *New Yorker*, it must signal that the times are a-changing there too.

In any given year any critic will have special favorites. Though these may not be "better" than many other books of the year, these are books the critic would like to recommend and to share with others. I found many first-rate collections during the year, some by authors of great reputation and importance. Here is a list, in alphabetical order so as not to be hierarchical, of my special favorites among story collections published during 1991.

Lee K. Abbott's *Living After Midnight* (Putnam's), his fifth collection in what is a brilliant career, is his finest work so far. Five stories, four of them told adroitly in first person, and a novella, "Living After Midnight," show Abbott at the peak of considerable powers, able to make his habits and obsessions work for him as he deals with complex characters in a variety of places. The novella about a pair of old college chums who drift into a life of dope and the robbery of convenience stores, more for fun than profit, is Abbott's most powerfully ambitious work to date.

Charles Baxter continues to grow as a creator of short fiction, encouraged by Norton, publisher for many outstanding collections in recent years. Baxter's *A Relative Stranger* (Norton), dealing with characters in a Michigan town, has an unusual twist to the final story, "Saul and Patsy Are Pregnant," establishing the collection as more tightly linked than the reader might have suspected. As in the Oz books of L. Frank Baum, all the characters reappear in a new context, and the town turns out to have a name: Five Oaks, Michigan.

Ann Beattie brought out her fifth collection, *What Was Mine* (Random House), twelve stories, of various kinds and characters, set in suburbia. Widely reviewed, *What Was Mine* received mixed notices. Favorable reviewers found the stories more developed than her earlier work, more dependent upon dimensional characterization and, thus, more compassionate as well. Less enthusiastic notices focused on the persistence of narrative habits and, as some reviewers saw it, the limited content of her fables. Typical was Patricia Storace's "Seeing Double" (*New York Review of Books*, 15 August), where she argues that the apparent implications of Beattie's works come more from technical sleight of hand than anything else: "Beattie achieves the illusion of alienation and unknowability between character and character by limiting severely what the reader can know about them."

Another writer of distinction and achievement in poetry (twelve volumes) and the novel (six), and many uncollected essays and reviews, Fred Chappell also faced mixed reviews with his second book of stories—*More Shapes Than One* (St. Martin's Press). Though he did not fare so well at the hands of *Publishers Weekly*, Chappell received extraordinary praise from *Kirkus Reviews*, which called the stories "marvelous" and described them as being "as circular as Borges, as richly symbolic as Kafka, and as zany as Woody Allen." The thirteen stories gathered in *More Shapes Than One* are boldly various and richly imaginative in language, form, and content, demonstrating next to no limitations on Chappell's abilities. In a laudatory review in the *Washington Post Book World* (6 October), editor Michael Dirda wrote: "Here are low-keyed tales of ghosts and strange beings, historical imaginings (about the bi-

ologist [Carolus] Linnaeus, the explorer-scientist [Pierre Louis Moreau de] Maupertuis, the mathematician [Ludwig] Feuerbach), a comic gem about a symbolist poem blocking a small country road." Just for the record, Jacques Offenbach and Hart Crane also visit Chappell's inimitable world.

Arriving on the scene with eight strong endorsements from some very prominent short-story writers, its author likewise having earned personal recognition and several awards, *The Way That Water Enters Stone* (Norton), by John Dufresne, brings together thirteen stories, divided in setting between North and South. Dufresne is a virtuoso of the vernacular, master of many voices, and a collaborator with all his eccentric characters. He writes of "ordinary" people who are as odd in reality as anyone you can imagine. The stories are not at all minimal and not in the least predictable. Novelist and screenwriter William Harrison is precise in the metaphor of his book-jacket endorsement: "John Dufresne is like a musician with a mysterious new instrument, one with unique tone, perfect pitch, and haunting power."

In *The Golden Boys* (Norton), Joseph Epstein, essayist and editor of the *American Scholar*, produced his first collection of short fiction, nine stories, two previously published in the *Hudson Review* and the others from *Commentary*, all primarily set in Chicago and involving a variety of characters, yet joined by certain recurring patterns and concerns. Above all, these quite wonderful stories share the realized sense of a place with its nuances and shadows as well as its relentless energy and aggressive power of continual change. These are stories of weight and density with enough differences from the trends of literary fashion to have the shine of originality. Although a mobster and a literary biographer appear as protagonists, the majority are businessmen. Language binds the stories—all are accessible and characterized by clarity and decorum.

Another first collection from a mature writer is by Philip Gould. After thirty-one years as an information officer in the Foreign Service, serving in nine foreign cities on four continents, Gould retired in 1986. His first novel, *Kitty Collins* (Algonquin), was published that year, and now Algonquin has brought out *The Eighth Continent: Tales of the Foreign Service*, a gathering of three long stories built around the same characters, Charlie McKay and Caroline Draper McKay, and moving chronologically forward from the mid 1950s through the Cold War. Writing with authority and smooth clarity about the times and places—Central Europe, India, a voyage to the Seychelles—Gould has a documentary authority at the heart of these compelling tales.

Winner of the *Los Angeles Times* fiction award for 1991, Alan Gurganus's *White People* (Knopf) consists of two novellas and ten stories culled from his short fiction of the past twenty years. In the wake of the success of his first novel, *Oldest Living Confederate Widow Tells All* (1989), Gurganus's *White People* was widely reviewed. The stories range from pure fable in "It Had Wings" (an angel falls out of the sky and into an old lady's backyard), to a real letter by Walt Whitman, joined with the imaginary letter of the ghost of a Union soldier to his mother, "Reassurance," to personal recollections, as in the case of "Nativity, Caucasian." The spine of the collection is in three autobiographical stories— "Minor Heroism: Something About My Father," "Breathing Room: Something About My Brother," and "A Hog Loves Its Life: Something About My Grandfather." *Publishers Weekly* was accurate in characterizing *White People* as "a virtuoso collection, to be savored and reread."

Another important collection, this one southern also in its settings and background, was Alyson Hagy's second volume—*Hardware River* (Poseidon). Arriving with the highest kinds of book-jacket praise from some of the best new writers in the country—Charles Baxter, Carolyn Chute, Susan Dodd, Madison Smartt Bell— *Hardware River* has seven stories, all but one, "Ballad and Sadness," which takes place mainly in Scotland, set in the Shenandoah Valley and the mountains and hollows of southwest Virginia. Violence and sex, some of it, as in "Kettle of Hawks," frankly deviant, are present, yet richly clothed by a lyrical style. The stories are various but characterized by a controlled craft and a rare compassion. Hagy's voice is at once traditional and original and adds up to something distinctly her own.

David Wong Louie's *Pangs of Love* (Knopf) won the Art Seidenbaum Award, given by the *Los Angeles Times* for the best first book of fiction in 1991. Here are eleven stories dealing with the lives and cultural conflicts of Asian Americans. A graduate of the Iowa Writers Workshop, Louie came up through the literary magazines, these stories appearing in *Agni Review, Colorado State Review, Iowa Review, Kansas Quarterly, Midamerican Review*, and in a special "Discovery" issue of *Plough-*

shares. One story, "Displacement," was chosen for *The Best American Short Stories 1989*. Writing about *Pangs of Love* in the *Los Angeles Times Book Review* (16 June), Richard Eder wrote: "He is elegant, a touch spooky, and has as fine a hair-trigger control of alienation and absurdity as any of the best of his generation."

For several years now some of the best fiction, novels as well as stories, about the American West, the "new" West of our times, has been coming from Kent Nelson, a writer who grew up in Colorado. Nelson's stories have earned honors and awards and attracted the favorable attention of prominent writers such as Tim O'Brien and Larry McMurtry. *The Middle of Nowhere* (Gibbs Smith) gathers thirteen of his stories of the past decade. The settings are various, from Tucson and Mexico to a vacation cabin in the Adirondacks, and the characters and situations are varied as well. Nelson is at his finest in stories such as "Discoveries," about a fishing day on the Elk River where landscape works its own messages and magic on the people: "He wished the road did not end at the trailhead. He wanted to keep driving right on through the aspen glades and past the beaver dams and up into the dark timber. He would gun the engine up the rocky scree and roll past the high lakes to the top of Zirkel Peak, where he could see out across the mountains to Wyoming. His doubts would seem inconsequential. . . ."

After two well-received novels—*Edisto* and *A Woman Named Drown*, Padgett Powell brought out *Typical* (Farrar, Straus and Giroux), twenty-three stories, some full length and longer ("The Modern Italian"), others ("Wait" and "Florida," for example) no more than a brisk page or two. What these tales, set all over the place and involving all kinds of people, have in common is the particular charged language, an electric colloquial, which has characterized all of Powell's fiction. Powell's fiction takes all kinds of chances; and when that daring pays off, the effect is devastating. Josephine Humphreys wrote (in her book-jacket blurb): "The stories are new, true, honest, funny—and brilliant, brilliant." In a *New York Times* review (16 August), Michiko Kakutani praised the "fireworks of language, language that runs, jumps and sometimes performs acrobatics in the air." But, like several other leading reviewers, she had reservations—"Unfortunately, Mr. Powell does not always employ his marvelous language to any recognizable end."

The Foreseeable Future (Atheneum) is the twenty-second book in the career of Reynolds Price, which began in 1962 with the highly praised *A Long and Happy Life*. This volume is devoted to three long stories, "The Fare to the Moon," "The Foreseeable Future," and "Back Before Day." "The Fare to the Moon" concerns one day in the life of Kayes Paschal, the day he must report for his preinduction physical in World War II. "The Foreseeable Future" takes place between Sunday, 6 May 1945, and Friday, 11 May 1945. Its central figure is Whit Wade, a badly wounded veteran of the D-Day landing. "Back Before Day" features Dean Walker, football coach and Vietnam veteran. In each of these stories of good country people from North Carolina peace gradually replaces war and the memories of war, family love works to overcome troubles and temptations, and dreams and visions enlarge consciousness and light the way forward into the foreseeable future.

David R. Slavitt is one of the most productive and versatile writers alive, even allowing for the inimitable Joyce Carol Oates. Slavitt has written eleven books of poems, five books of translations (Ovid, Virgil, Seneca, Albius Tibullus), fifteen novels under his own name (not counting those written under several pseudonyms), three works of nonfiction, and several plays and screenplays. But he has not until now published a book of stories. Now with the fourteen stories of *Short Stories Are Not Real Life* (Louisiana State University), Slavitt takes his place among the best story writers of the times. He has a voice so fully developed and at ease—colloquial, witty, direct, relaxed, self-reflexive, and quietly different from any other—that his work seems as original as any published for a long time. It is not difficult or demanding except insofar as life, the "real life" that short stories are ostensibly not, is difficult and demanding. Quickly moving and accessible, these stories stand up to rereading, indeed ask for it. They are thoughtful, wearing their wisdom lightly. Herbert Gold says it well and accurately in his (rare) blurb: "Here is a comfortable talemaker who sheds light on fathers and sons, on the conflict of generations, on the confusions of marriage, on the reuse of time passing, speaking easily with the natural eloquence of a raconteur in whose presence one wants to listen." In his explorations of the subtle interactions of facts and fiction, Slavitt has done pioneering work in exploiting the autobiographical in fiction, the facts of his "real life," transformed, giving his stories

the overwhelming authority of verisimilitude. With this book he has pointed toward new directions for story writers.

Any literary season that witnesses the publication of a collection of stories by Elizabeth Spencer is not without excitement. This year *On the Gulf* (University of Mississippi), a volume in the "Author and Artist Series" (for the book offers artwork by artist and naturalist Walter Anderson), gathered six Spencer stories, one of them previously uncollected, set on the Mississippi Gulf Coast. In a lively "Introduction" to the book Spencer tells what the Gulf Coast means to her. To do so she has to tell something about the inland towns of her native state which was one of the chief sources of her story-telling art:

> In such towns people lived on stories of each other's sayings and doings, repeating and checking for the facts, speculating and measuring and fitting together the present to the past, the known to the suspected, weaving numberless patterns. It was a complex and at times beautiful society; much fine literature has been created to do it justice; but the smell of salt air did not reach it, and none can deny that it was confined and confining.

The gulf, as these six stories testify, served to expand and to liberate Spencer's already active story-telling imagination.

Melanie Rae Thon's first novel, *Meteors in August* (1990), received praise and aroused interest in the future of this young writer who grew up in Montana, went to school at the University of Michigan (where she won a Hopwood Award for her fiction), and now lives in Cambridge, Massachusetts. *Girls in the Grass* (Random House) is her first collection of short stories, eleven of them, various in subject and set in and against a diversity of American landscapes—suburban Arizona, rural Idaho, and downtown Boston. If there is a dominant theme, it is the sudden awakenings of adolescence to the reality of the adult world. Sometimes it is the clash of uncomprehending generations, as in one of her best stories, "Small Crimes," in which an aging and self-destructive poet, real enough to be almost recognizable, uses the occasion of a manuscript conference to try to seduce a young woman. Melanie Rae Thon's voice, which has been praised by writers such as Andre Dubus, Shirley Hazzard, and Daniel Halpern, is appropriately a delicate balance between the plain and the purely lyrical.

One of the most widely reviewed story collections was Marianne Wiggins's *Bet They'll Miss Us When We're Gone* (HarperCollins). The initial reason for attention was the fact that Wiggins, as the wife of Salman Rushdie, had, until they separated, shared his life on the run. "We were on the Lam in Wales, running through the Black Mountains like unarmed smugglers from the righteous with their guns," begins the autobiographical story—"Croeso I Gymrui." But whatever the source of press attention, this book, her sixth book of fiction and her first since the successful novel *John Dollar*, stands on its own. With thirteen stories of extraordinary variety and virtuosity, *Bet They'll Miss Us When We're Gone* ranks among the most innovative collections published in 1991. Three of the stories are directly autobiographical. The others, distinctly different from each other in style and tone, in length and form, are set in a variety of places—the United States (especially Tidewater Virginia), Amsterdam, Zaragoza, London, Wales. Something of her energy is revealed in her theory of inspiration, declared in "Zelf-Portret": "Stories come like storms, they come like weather or natural disasters." This is modified in the same story by a kind of confession on behalf of all writers—"The list of possibilities is endless and the writer always lies."

The year was marked by books of stories by old masters, living and dead. Joining together previously and separately published novellas, "The Theft" and "The Bellarosa Connection," with the long title story (itself separately dedicated "To My Children and Grandchildren"), Nobel Laureate Saul Bellow brought out *Something To Remember Me By* (Penguin), which was first published in a mass-market paperbook edition. In a lively "Foreword," Bellow makes some points about his recent interest in shorter forms: "There is a modern taste for brevity and condensation. Kafka, Beckett, and Borges wrote short. People of course do write long, and write successfully, but to write short is felt by a growing public to be a very good thing—perhaps the best." "Something To Remember Me By" turns out to be a classic Bellow story, made out of the specifics of love and death, the wonderful absurd world of his adolescence ("a high-minded Jewish school boy") in Chicago ("These are the plain facts, they have to be uttered. This, remember, is the New World, and here one of its mysterious cities."), and the grit of bitter wisdom at the end—"I myself know the power of nonpathos, in these low, devious days."

David R. Slavitt, author of Short Stories Are Not Real Life, *a collection exploring and exploiting the interactions between fact and fiction (photograph by Bernard Gotfryd)*

Other books by masters include R. W. B. Lewis's editorial selection—*The Selected Short Stories of Edith Wharton* (Scribners), twenty-one representative stories of various kinds, including the famous "Roman Fever," published from the 1890s to the 1930s. Another Scribners book, *Zelda Fitzgerald: The Collected Writings*, edited by Matthew J. Bruccoli, includes eleven stories by her, one which was originally published under F. Scott Fitzgerald's name. *Louisa May Alcott: Selected Fiction* (Little, Brown), edited by Daniel Shealy, is an uneven gathering, but certainly worth preserving. *The Ancient Memory and Other Stories* (University of Nebraska) follows the earlier volume, *The End of the Dream*, and completes the publication of the late John G. Neihardt's short fiction. The nine stories in the book, originally published from 1905 to 1908, are concerned with the frontier. There is a foreword by the author's daughter, Hilda Neihardt Petri. Two other posthumous collections are E. F. Benson's *Desirable Residences* (Oxford), edited by Jack Adrian and containing twenty-six stories from 1896 to 1932; and *A How-*

ard Nemerov Reader, which, with novel excerpts, poems, essays, etc., collects some short stories. Writing in *Washington Post Book World* (21 April), Michael Dirda particularly praised "the half-dozen enigmatic, fantastic short stories that introduce professional dreamers, mysterious sky-writers, stylized water ballets at the end of the world." Finally, Ecco Press, always alert to trends, weighed in with the first volume of *The Complete Short Fiction of Joseph Conrad*, edited by Samuel Hynes.

Out of the French tradition come two books, *Early Writings of Gustave Flaubert* (University of Nebraska), the first English translation, by Robert Berry Griffin, of Flaubert's juvenilia, including eleven essays and stories; and *Hesitant Fire: Selected Prose of Max Jacob* (University of Nebraska). It is good to have in English (translated by Moishe Black and Maria Green) some of the prose work of the great French surrealist poet, founder, among other things, of the Babowinist movement, who was killed in World War II.

Prominent writers, all of them literary stars and a few acknowledged masters, published collections in 1991. Kobo Abe, celebrated ever since the appearance of his *The Women in the Dunes* (1960), is represented by *Beyond the Curve* (Kodansha America), twelve stories first published between 1949 and 1961. There are forty-six stories of all kinds in *Isaac Asimov: The Complete Stories, Vol. 1* (Doubleday). Asimov authored more than four hundred books before his death on 6 April 1992. At his prolific rate of production, it will be many more volumes before Doubleday finishes *The Complete Stories*.

Another Doubleday star is Margaret Atwood, whose third collection of stories, *Wilderness Tips*, is her twenty-third book. There are ten stories, mostly urban in setting though various in subject, linked together (in the publisher's words) by shared themes "of loss and discovery, of how we connect with others and with the sometimes hidden parts of ourselves...." Novelist James Wilcox, writing in the *New York Times Book Review* (24 November), praised the collection, though he reported, accurately, that the language is sometimes mannered and sometimes flat. He added: "Well constructed as these stories are, some may seem to belabor their themes with built-in explanations."

Following her 1988 novel, *Eva Luna*, Isabel Allende brought out *The Stories of Eva Luna* (Macmillan). Taking its model and epigraph from *A Thousand and One Nights*, Allende creates her own

situation. In bed with Eva Luna, her lover, Rolf Carle, tells her: "Tell me a story you have never told anyone before. Make it up for me." What follows are twenty-three stories in the Latin American "magic realism" manner, told with high energy.

Despite being J. G. Ballard's twenty-first book and his first story collection in a decade, *War Fever* (Farrar, Straus and Giroux) did not receive the attention it should have; though, since the huge success of his autobiographical novel, *Empire of the Sun* (1984), the writer, himself, has been the subject of a great deal of literary journalism. It may be that this gathering of fourteen typical (which is to say uniformly surprising and non-traditional) Ballard narratives has been eclipsed by his second autobiographical novel, also published during 1991—*The Kindness of Women* (Farrar, Straus, and Giroux).

Correspondent Philip Caputo offers a book not easy to classify with *Means of Escape* (HarperCollins). In a note, "An Explanation ...," Caputo explains that the book is mainly an autobiographical work, but not exactly: "There is too much fact in this book to properly call it a novel, too much fiction to call it reportage." Searching for a way to find "the emotional-truth," Caputo hit upon the device of inter-chapters which he calls "sketches." "The sketches entitled 'Disasters of War,' for example," he writes, "are fictional recreations of actual incidents." There are nine of these pieces, reminiscent of the interchapters of Ernest Hemingway's *In Our Time* (1925) and tightly linked in place, subject, theme to the longer "factual" pieces.

Michael Chabon earned serious critical attention for his first novel, *The Mysteries of Pittsburgh* (1988). His first collection of stories is *A Model World* (Morrow). The volume contains eleven stories in two parts—"A Model World," six stories thematically related; and "The Lost World," a sequence about a central character, young Nathan Shapiro, whose world is breaking apart under the weight of his parents' divorce.

Poet Edward Field has edited a collection of thirteen stories, together with seventy pages of memoirs about the author, of the late Alfred Chester—*The Head of a Sad Angel* (Black Sparrow). These stories, from 1953 to 1966, deal with characters on the rough edges of life in respectable society. As if in explanation of his narrative goals, Chester wrote: "God preserve us from the invasion of good fairies. Where are the screaming queens, the gigolos, the outrageous Harlem faggots?"

One of the most widely praised collections of the year, a book which was one of the finalists for the *Los Angeles Times* fiction award, was *Woman Hollering Creek* (Random House), by the outstanding Chicana writer Sandra Cisneros. Twenty-two stories, mostly set in and around San Antonio and all involving Mexicans and Mexican Americans, *Woman Hollering Creek* follows the author's successful first collection—*The House on Mango Street* (Random House). Since Cisneros is a poet as well, the language surprises with a fine excess. She has more purposes than aesthetic, however. In an essay-review (*The World & I*, September), Kaye Northcott quotes Cisneros naming her goal as "taking all these Mexican myths and reinventing them in a way that's not restrictive to women but empowering." In this book she tells the imaginary history of the "real" mistress of Emiliano Zapata ("Eyes of Zapata"), of the custom of posting petitions to saints ("Little Miracles, Kept Promises"), of an artist who falls in love with an exterminator ("Bien Pretty"), and so forth, with a bilingual voice she has made her own.

Seventeen years after *The Murphy Stories* (1974), Mark Costello reappears with six new stories about his singular protagonist—*Middle Murphy* (University of Illinois). Of these stories of the middle-aged and middle-western Murphy, now a husband and a father, only the longest one, "The Soybean Capital of the World," is told in third person. In the others Murphy speaks for himself. Reviewing the collection for the *Washington Post* (9 December), Elizabeth Ferber wrote: "Despite its inconsistencies and occasional lack of coherence, Costello's near novel redeems itself in the strong and evocative writing in most of the stories."

Admired teacher and author of thrillers, James Crumley did not earn much critical admiration for *Muddy Fork & Other Things* (Clark City), a collection of nonfiction and fiction set mostly in south Texas. Of the eight stories, gathered under the rubric "Fictional Truths," the author disarmingly writes: "My problem with the short story seems to be that I neither understand it nor think in that form."

More successful in catching and holding the public eye was Rick DeMarinis, whose *The Voice of America* (Norton) started as a (rare) featured book in *Publishers Weekly* (29 March) and was well-received and widely reviewed. DeMarinis, who has published six novels and two earlier collec-

tions of stories, brings together fifteen stories, two previously published in *Harper's*, the others in literary magazines. DeMarinis is a stylist and a very funny writer, though his general subjects, as described by his publisher, might not quite sound that way: "The characters in these stories try to keep the ravages of depression, boredom, illness, middle age, and a faltering economy at bay with the usual postmodern palliatives: booze, travel, adultery, Prozac, television." But the publisher also points to his "special energy and wizardry," his "compassion and affection for outré Americans," among other virtues.

Author of three novels and of a highly praised earlier collection of stories, *New Yorker* writer John Rolfe Gardiner did not fare so well with reviewers of *The Incubator Ballroom* (Knopf), a collection of four stories and a novella. His characters, who have been aptly described as "agrarian misfits" (by Wanda Urbanska in the *Washington Post Book World*, 19 May), are well realized, and his settings (usually northern Virginia) are efficiently evoked. His troubles with this collection may have resulted from the title piece. Set, in part, in and around Roanoke, it is far off the mark in its rendering of the place and the kinds of people there.

Brought out shortly before Nadine Gordimer was awarded the Nobel Prize for Literature, *Jump* (Farrar, Straus and Giroux) is her eighth collection of stories. There are sixteen stories, diverse in their settings (England, South Africa, Mozambique) and united in their concern for the great political and social issues of our times. Nadine Gordimer is anything but politically incorrect, but her demonstrable love of good, accessible writing and her compassion for her characters tend constantly to modify, if not to overturn, any sociopolitical agenda. Certainly her fiction gives late-twentieth-century liberalism a good name.

Another writer of international distinction and strong political views, one who like Gordimer seldom allows his political notions to ruin a good story or distort a characterization, Graham Greene published *The Last Word* (Viking). Although the stories date from 1923 ("The New House") to 1989 ("An Old Man's Memory"), only four have ever appeared in any book, and none of them was published in *Collected Stories* (1970). One story, "A Branch of the Service," is published for the first time anywhere. This tale, replete with Greene's particular edges of irony, tells of a kind of spy, an inspector for the "International Guide to Good Restaurants." The final story of the collection, "An Appointment with the General," is vintage Greene. A French woman journalist, who knows no Spanish, is assigned to interview a Latin American revolutionary general and carries on a strange, and strongly moving, conversation with the general through an interpreter.

There are ten stories in *Every Hunter Wants To Know: A Leningrad Life* (Norton), by recent immigrant (1986) Mikhail Iossel. Iossel, who attended the University of New Hampshire and was a Wallace Stegner Fellow at Stanford, has written autobiographical stories of the Brezhnev years, from his own childhood until, in the final story, "Insomnia," he recounts his complicated, almost crippling experiences as a Soviet émigré. These are thoughtful, honest, original stories with a point of view we have not seen before.

Another shifting point of view is found in Ursula K. Le Guin's *Searoad* (HarperCollins), what her publisher calls her "first completely mainstream book of fiction." These are linked stories set in the small coastal town of Klatsand and dealing with characters of several generations. The longest story in the collection, "Hernes," tells of the lives of four generations of Klatsand women. "Mainstream" or not, Le Guin's world is still a home for the fabulous. Reviewing the book for the *Washington Post Book World* (8 December), Francis Taliaferro writes: "The real-life mothers and daughters of Klatsand are the sisters of rain and foam, or of Demeter and Persephone, crying in their kitchens the elemental sorrows of the world."

Another Nobel Prize winner (1988), Egypt's Naguib Mahfouz, had published his first collection of short stories in English—*The Time and the Place* (Doubleday), selected and translated by Denys Johnson-Davies. These twenty stories were culled from fourteen volumes of stories published in Arabic from 1962 to 1988. Though the stories are various in subject matter and narrative mode, all but one are set in Cairo. Chronologically the stories follow, roughly, a line of growth from childhood to maturity. There is a calm absurdity and savagery, so matter of fact as to seem surreal in many of these stories, as, for example, in "At the Bus Stop," where an innocent man observes a series of strangely horrible events—a thief being beaten, a terrible car accident, a man and a woman making love in the street—under the impression that it all must be the making of a film. Only at the very end, when the people at the bus stop are shot down by a policeman for no known reason, does the story prove itself to be "real."

From Australia comes a posthumous collection, *The Rose Farmer* (Norton), by Olga Masters. Of the seventeen stories, eight were in finished drafts and forms before the author died in 1986.

Heat (Dutton/Abrahams) is the latest addition to the growing oeuvre of Joyce Carol Oates, twenty-five stories, various except in their exploration of violence. Three of these stories have received O. Henry Awards, and in 1990 Oates received the coveted Rea Award for the Short Story. Of this collection *Publishers Weekly* (5 July) wrote: "Each story, fluent, ironic, and deeply intelligent, encompasses its own compact fictional cosmos, holding sway over the reader's imagination."

One of the monumental collections of our time is V. S. Pritchett's *Complete Collected Stories* (Random House), twelve hundred pages containing eighty stories written over more than fifty years. Pritchett published first in the early 1920s. One of the most thorough and interesting responses to this massive volume was the review, "Child of the Century" (*New York Review of Books* (13 June), by William Trevor, himself one of the most highly regarded story writers of the age. Trevor was not shy about picking his favorite story among them all, "When My Girl Comes Home," and concluded that "Pritchett is at his best when his cast is large and the story twenty or thirty pages long."

Though he has published some twenty-five books of fiction since he first appeared on the scene (with the blessing of a blurb by Edith Sitwell) in 1956, James Purdy has also, in the words of reviewer Richard McCann, "been so highly praised and so steadily ignored that he has become that most difficult of literary phenomena: the important but neglected writer" ("Lives of Quiet Desperation," *Washington Post Book World*, 12 January 1992). Purdy selected from three previous collections for *63: Dream Palace: Selected Stories 1956-1987* (Black Sparrow). What these stories have in common is the author's overwhelming nihilism and the depiction of (in McCann's words) "a meticulously gothic and hallucinatory America." Purdy's pessimism overwhelms his pitiable and/or merciless characters. Describing the fates of people in the world of James Purdy, McCann writes: "As for those who neither maim nor are maimed—they exploit or are exploited."

Every bit as serious and sometimes every bit as pessimistic, but never a nihilist, William Trevor has not been ignored by readers. His *Two Lives* (Viking) consists of two novellas, both set in the summer of 1987 and both with a remarkable woman at the center of the story. Mary Louise Quarry is the memorable protagonist of "Reading Turgenev," and Emily Delahunty, whose first-person account forms "My House in Umbria," is a writer of successful romance novels. These are sad stories, very subtly connected to each other, and the characters are complex and splendidly realized.

Paul West is a prolific and greatly gifted writer who is often found among the year's best makers of fiction. Here he is represented by the oddly original *Portable People* (Paris Review), one hundred brief biographical sketches of historical figures—athletes, writers, aviators, and everybody else from Samuel Pepys to the Shah of Iran, from Helen Keller to Chris Evert.

Then there are those writers who are not quite beginners nor yet well known enough to be called stars—for example, David Ely, whose second collection, *Always Home* (Fine), concerns itself with "the treachery of the familiar." *The Tomcat's Wife* (HarperCollins) is a second collection, by Carol Bly, and perhaps received the attention it did because of her former husband's (poet and guru Robert Bly) huge success with the cult book *Iron John* (Addison-Wesley). Her slender collection of eight stories about Minnesotans received considerable review attention. In the *New York Times Book Review* (31 March), Louis B. Jones made her work sound somewhat less than perky and cheerful: "Her stories describe loveless marriages, lifelong rancor, quiet happiness over the death of husbands, wife beating, the murder of the smartest girl in town, the suicide of the only clever woman in town, arson by respectable citizens." Another second collection is by a writer whose star is in the ascendant, Peter Cameron, who has been called by *Booklist* "one of the best writers about middle-class youth since Salinger." His first collection, *One Way or Another* (1986), earned favorable notice by people such as David Leavitt and Lorrie Moore. His new collection, *Far-Flung* (HarperCollins), has twelve stories, most of them first-person narratives, and is divided into three sections, the last being three linked stories concerned with a single Indiana family. Two of the book's stories, "Slowly" and "The Winter Bazaar," first appeared in the *New Yorker*.

J. California Cooper, an African-American writer from Texas, brought out her fourth collection of stories, *The Matter Is Life* (Doubleday), eight stories characterized by what her publisher describes as "a knowing wit that can always discern the tear within a chuckle." She often writes in dialect and in a lively vernacular idiom—"Everybody talkin bout how Time is such a great, forever, long thing, makes me wonder why the little piece of life we get is such a short one" ("No Lie"). A new and posthumous book by Maria Thomas (she was on the plane with Congressman Mickey Leland which crashed in the mountains of Ethiopia), *American Visas* (Soho), has a novella, "The Jiru Road," and six short stories about East Africa and the clash of cultures, western and African, and the impact, at once limited yet magical, of one or the other. Thomas spent almost twenty years living in Africa, and these stories are precisely set in Ethiopia, Kenya, Tanzania, and Nigeria. She had published a novel and an earlier collection of stories—*Come to Africa* (1987) and *Save Your Marriage* (1987).

Joan Chace made her mark with two well-received novels—*The Evening Wolves* (1989) and *During the Reign of the Queen of Persia* (1983), works which won her a string of awards and honors: the *PEN* Ernest Hemingway Award, the Janet Heidinger Kafka Prize, a Whiting Award, a Guggenheim Fellowship. *Bonneville Blue* (Farrar, Straus and Giroux) is her first collection of short stories, composed of eleven stories, various in setting, situation, matter, and manner, alike mainly in their unsentimental compassion for the troubled characters. There is also an oddly original twitch in the author's style, a kind of poetry of non sequiturs and irrepressible imagination as in this woman's description of a departure in "The Harrier":

> We left town by the iron bridge that had been inadvertently laid in backward by feckless engineers after the flood of '32, splashed through salt pools from the runoff, stagnant atop frozen snow, salt that would by spring soak down into the roots and wells, the earth saturated to the salinity of human blood, so that finally it might rise and scream.

Foreign short fiction came from all over in 1991. From Ireland came Maeve Binchy's *The Lilac Bus* (Delacorte), eight interrelated stories about people who travel to Dublin on the bus to work and go home to the country on weekends. The stories are evenly divided between country and city. Victoria White's *Raving Autumn* (Dufour) is also Irish, the title story telling of an Irish servant during the days of the 1919 rebellion. *The World of Kate Roberts: Selected Short Stories 1925-1981* (Temple University) has some thirty-five stories focusing on modern Wales, many concerned with intractable poverty. The late Kate Roberts wrote in Welsh; these stories were translated by Joseph P. Clancy. First published in Australia in 1979, Thea Astley's *Hunting the Wild Pineapple* (Putnam's) was described in a *Washington Post* review (1 February) by James Polk as "fiercely funny, bizarre and precisely observed tales of smalltown shenanigans in Northern Australia." Highly honored in her own country, Astley says, "I'm very interested in oddballs." She proves it in this excellent collection.

Among Canadian collections to be published in the United States are those by two women, both of them identified by their publishers as being peers of the highly successful Alice Munro—Janice Kulyk Keefer and Sandra Birdsell. Keefer's *Traveling Ladies* (Morrow) has a dozen stories, various except for their unifying emphasis on real or metaphorical traveling. Sandra Birdsell subtitles her collection of twenty-three related stories in *Agassiz* (Milkweed) as "A Novel in Stories." Its stories concern three generations of the Lafreniere family in the fictional Manitoba town of Agassiz. Alice Munro praises Sandra Birdsell's work for its "sense of the story's being alive—all hot, rude, contrary, funny, unbearable." A somewhat different view of things, a worldview more appropriate to his own experience (born and raised in Trinidad in 1955, immigrated to Canada in 1973), haunts the beautifully written work of Neil Bissoondath. *On the Eve of Uncertain Tomorrows* (Potter) has ten stories of a variety of situations and characters, alike in their sense of exile and loss. Bissoondath has his own very distinct voice and is accurately described by his publisher as "a master of comic detail, a sly conjurer of the unexpected, and a compassionate chronicler of people's hopes, fears, dreams, and needs."

Latin American writers continue to gain the attention of North American publishers and readers. Antonia Skarmeta's *Watch Where the Wolf Is Going* (Readers International) translated that Chilean writer into English for the first time. *Cape Horn and Other Stories From the End of the World* (Latin American Literary Review Press), by another Chilean, Francisco Coloane, tells of survival in the hostile environment of Patagonia and

Tierra del Fuego. From neighboring Argentina, with a preface by Susan Sontag, comes *Urban Voodoo* (Lumen), by Edgardo Cozarinsky. After years of exile, in Argentina and in Spain, Eduardo Galeano has returned to Montevideo, Uruguay. Having finished his three-volume history of the Americas, he offers his latest work, *The Book of Embraces* (Norton). As in his other work, this one is a sequence of very brief vignettes—anecdotes, dreams, pieces of autobiography, *pensées*, variations on stated themes—the longest two and a half pages, the briefest no more than a sentence or two ("The Night/2": "Woman strip me of my clothes and my doubts. Undress me, undoubt me."). Of his special importance Alan Cheuse writes (in the *Chicago Tribune*): "Galeano's work offers all of the engaging power of a historical novel and the compelling force of fact."

Asia remains a place of great interest and is of special interest to Americans of Asiatic background. R. A. Sasaki, a third-generation San Franciscan, wrote stories of the conflict of cultures in *The Loom* (Graywolf). In "Another Writer's Beginnings" she portrays a narrator, like herself a Japanese American, who longs above all things to be a Mouseketeer. There are nine stories here, dealing with three generations of Japanese Americans in San Francisco. From Japan, itself, we have *Self Portraits* (Kodansha American), eighteen autobiographical stories by Osama Dazai, who committed suicide in 1948. These stories are laced with self-pity and assert a misogyny not easily acceptable in today's culture: "I assume even the most pathetic female life story to be a pack of arbitrary lies and am no longer capable of shedding a single tear in response."

From China there were several collections. *As Long As Nothing Happens, Nothing Will* (Grove Weidenfeld) is made up of five stories by the celebrated Zhang Jie. Reviews were mixed as reviewers argued that the stories were uneven in quality. Praise was accorded to *Getting Used to Dying* (HarperCollins), by Zhang Xianliang ,and to the translation by Martha Avery. This collection was first published in Beijing in April 1989 and then withdrawn. The protagonist in all these stories is nameless yet seems autobiographical. *Black Walls* (University of Washington) is the first translation into English of work by Liu Xinwu, the former editor of *People's Literature*. Also from the University of Washington came *Silent Operas*, six stories of the late Ming Dynasty by its great author Li Yu.

From the Indian subcontinent came the *Crows of Deliverance* (Readers International) by

Nirmal Verma, stories about Indians in a variety of settings. Russell Lucas, a former bank manager from Bombay, who grew up and lived there before moving to London, generated considerable critical interest with his first book, *Evenings at Mongini's* (Summit). With the exception of the story "Keep Smiling," the stories all take place in Bombay in the 1940s. Writing in the daily *New York Times*, Michiko Kakutani (1 February) particularly praised Lucas for his handling of character: "He not only allows us to see the absurdity of their situations, but he also enables us to commiserate with their flight and understand their self-delusions." Reviewing the book for the *Washington Post Book World* (20 January), story writer Janette Turner Hospital praised Lucas's evocation of the city of Bombay: "It is a polyglot megalopolis of fabulous wealth and appalling poverty, of violence and vibrancy, of wholesale dealers in flesh, ecstasy, dreams and nightmares."

Out of the Arabian Peninsula came *Dubai Tales* (Dufour), twenty-one old-fashioned, strongly plotted tales of people in Dubai, by Muhammad al Murr. A. B. Yehoshua's *The Continuing Silence of a Poet* (Viking Penguin), listed among the recommended "Books for Vacation Reading" by the editors of the *New York Times Book Review*, represents the collected stories of a master Israeli storyteller. Yehoshua writes both realistic stories (set in Israel in the 1960s and 1970s) and parables. His chief protagonists are teachers, students, and professionals.

There seem to have been fewer European collections of stories this year. Among the more interesting were: from Italy, Goffredo Parise's *ABECEDARY* (Marlboro Press), a series of anecdotes arranged in alphabetical order (from "Amore" to "Famiglia") generally illustrating an aristocratic point of view. There is a certain similarity, in a very different form, found in Henryk Sienkiewicz's *Charcoal Sketches* (Dufour Edition), a century-old account of Polish life in three novellas. One of the most interesting books of 1991, of any kind, was Russian writer Nina Berberova's *The Tattered Cloak* (Knopf), six long stories (she calls them "novels") concerned with the aristocratic Russian émigré population in Paris, exiles in the years following the 1917 revolution. Berberova's writings were originally published in Europe from the late 1930s into the 1950s. Since 1950 Berberova, now eighty-nine years old, has lived in the United States. This is her first American publication, and it was widely reviewed and praised.

Small presses and university presses continue to publish a lot of short fiction. These are more and more noted and reviewed (though unevenly) in the media. Distribution, of course, remains an enormous, perhaps insolvable problem; but, in any case, fighting the odds, these publishers have continued to bring out all kinds and sorts of short fiction, by both new and known writers. Robert H. Abel, for example, whose *Ghost Traps* (University of Georgia) received the Flannery O'Connor Award for Short Fiction, is the author of four previously published books, including a collection of stories. Here he has twelve stories (three about fishing and fishermen), characterized by a wide variety of subject and setting. Also from the University of Georgia Press was Ted Poston's *The Dark Side of Hopkinsville*, a sequence of autobiographical stories, set in Hopkinsville, Kentucky, by this African-American journalist (1906-1974). Tom McNally's *Low Flying Aircraft* (University of Georgia) was also a Flannery O'Connor Award winner. Here the characters are connected with each other and the emphasis is on the search for meaning from experience. As a woman in "The Anonymity of Flight" says: "We spend our lives looking for signs—for thin, brief moments of direction." More explicitly unified is *The Doll House* (University of Nebraska) by Puerto Rican writer Rosario Ferré, fourteen stories all about the oppression of a patriarchial society. This is the first volume of the new series Latin American Women Writers.

The University of Missouri Press, now directed by Beverly Jarrett, who for years was editor for Louisiana State University Press, moved strongly into the short-fiction scene with an impressive group of collections. Earliest in creation (five stories written in the eighteenth century) is Denis Diderot's *This Is Not A Story*. Veteran story writer and novelist Gladys Swan joined ten diverse stories, out of literary magazines, to make her latest—*Do You Believe in Cabeza de Vaca?* The basic theme is the power of history and the past upon present lives. A new voice is found in Susan Hubbard's *Walking on Ice*, winner of the AWP Award for Short Fiction. A former student of both Raymond Carver and Tobias Wolff, she is represented by nine stories about "ordinary people," written in the minimalist mode. The stories of Sandy Hull's *Labor For Love* are linked together in their concern with the lives of independent women. The University of Missouri-Kansas City Press published a significant posthumous collection—Daniel Curley's *The Curandero*. Several of the stories are set in Mexico.

Louisiana State University Press continues to set the pace and the standards for first-rate fiction. In addition to David Slavitt's distinguished and original first collection, *Short Stories Are Not Real Life* (discussed above), Louisiana State University came forward with other outstanding short fiction. Janette Turner Hospital, an Australian by birth whose four novels and earlier collection of stories, *Dislocations* (Louisiana State University, 1988) have won major literary prizes in Britain, Canada, and Australia, brought out fifteen stories in *Isobars*. Different from each other in matter and manner, set variously in Manhattan and Sydney, Ontario, and Queensland, the stories are subtly bonded by a pattern of concern. *Isobars* received considerable review attention.

Not as widely noted and known as it ought to be is *A Kind of Redemption* (Louisiana State University), by Stephen Hathaway. Mainly concerned with aspects of the war in Vietnam (the last three of the eleven stories are set twenty years after the war), many of the stories concern the same character, Timothy Grote, who was kicked out of the Peace Corps to find himself, soon after, pulling a tour of duty in Nam. At the end, in "Grote Discovers Himself Trapped in Time," we find the middle-aged protagonist sipping a Budweiser, listening to classical music on KFRZ, and thinking some deep, historical thoughts:

> More recently, when Roman legions marauded in Britain, who was favored or not favored, murdered or not murdered, raped or not raped that Grote might sip his beer in smug satisfaction over the results of a baseball game? Who did the Danes, William the Conqueror, or Oliver Cromwell spare that Grote might live?

Including books published in 1991, the Illinois Short Fiction Series of the University of Illinois Press has published fifty-nine volumes. This year, in addition to the significant Mark Costello volume (mentioned above), the press published *Private Fame*, by Richard Burgin, his second book in the series, these eleven stories being mainly about seriously "disturbed" characters; and Stephen Schwartz's *Lives of the Fathers*, ten stories alike in their exploration of family bonds, especially those between fathers and sons.

The support of specific prizes and awards has served to encourage the publication of fiction by various university presses. *The Ant Generator* (University of Iowa), by Elizabeth Harris, eleven realistic short stories, won the 1991 John Simmons Short Fiction Award. One of the high-status annual prizes offered through a university press is Pittsburgh's Drue Heinz Literature Prize. Winner of the 1991 award was *Have You Seen Me?*, by Elizabeth Graver. Selected by writer Richard Ford from more than 275 competing manuscripts, the work consists of ten various stories. In a sense, the powers and limits of imagination serve as a central thematic thread; for Graver's characters are, themselves, fantasists and storytellers.

Other good university press volumes include Ruth Zenova's *Mute Phone Calls* (Rutgers University), autobiographical stories of life in a police state (the Soviet Union); *Stories From Mesa Country* (Ohio University), a first collection by Jane Candia Coleman, fourteen stories, six of them set in the old West ("Tumbleweed" is told from the point of view of Wyatt Earp's wife, Mattie); Carolyn Osborn's third collection, *Warriors and Maidens* (Texas Christian University), twelve stories of Texas and the Mexican border; and Gerald Vizenor's *Landfill Meditation: Crossblood Stories* (University Press of New England), fourteen stories by a Native American who has been called, by N. Scott Momaday, "the supreme ironist among American Indian writers of the twentieth century." Another university press which has planned and scheduled an impressive new program for fiction, both novels and stories, is the Southern Methodist University Press, here represented with *Red Wolf, Red Wolf* by W. P. Kinsella. Kinsella, who wrote *Shoeless Joe* which was made into the film *Field of Dreams* (1988), has included thirteen stories in this volume, alike in a wacky use of real and literary characters in odd situations. Billy the Kid stars in "Billy in Trinidad," for example, and the title story deals with a character out of the fiction of Flannery O'Connor, Enoch Emery, who pays a house call on his author and originator.

Even though some small presses, most notably North Point Press, have stepped out of the picture, many others continue to bring out books of short fiction. In addition to maintaining an important backlist (Constance Urdang, Marianne Luban, Jonis Agee, W. P. Kinsella, Carol Emschwiller), Coffee House Press in Minneapolis, Minnesota, keeps publishing good new books. Nancy Lord's *Survival* contains fifteen stories about Alaska and Alaskans of all ages, in the towns and in the wilderness. Nancy Lord, herself, is a commercial fisher in Alaska. Galileo in

Sparks, Maryland, brought out *Puzzling Through the News* by Pat Rushin, a new writer described by Stephen Dixon as "an original, energetic, tough, comical, gifted writer"; and also published *Inventions in a Grieving House* by Patricia Grossman, stories about childhood and adolescence highly praised by writer James McConkey.

Lewis Nordan's *The Music of the Swamp* (Algonquin) has ten interrelated stories (Sugar Mecklin is narrator of nine of them) of a boy growing up in the Mississippi Delta country. Barry Gifford, whose *Wild at Heart* was turned into a cult movie, put together four stories described in *Library Journal* as "a combination of wild fantasy and straightforward fact," in *New Mysteries of Paris* (Clark City). Real people appear too—painter August Macke in "The Tunisian Notebook" and King Farouk in "The Yellow Palace"—to liven up things. Predictably wilder than that was Gilbert Sorrentino's latest, *Under the Shadow* (Dalkey Archive), fifty-nine very short and very much off-the-wall stories. Another old-timer with a reputation for experimental fiction and for his particular interest in voice is Fielding Dawson. His latest, *The Trick* (Black Sparrow), has twenty of his inimitable stories and is enhanced by photographs and collages by the author. Author of four novels and five previous story collections, winner of many prizes and awards, Gordon Weaver published his latest, a novella and six stories, with Tri-Quarterly Books—*Men Who Would Be Good*. Contemporary and wide-ranging in setting (from middle America to the middle of Vietnam), these are stories of "men pushed to the limits of their lives." The collection appeared to mixed early reviews. It was recommended by *Library Journal* (1 April), and *Booklist* (15 March) praised the "masterfully written stories." But *Publishers Weekly* was intensely critical of the central characters and their feelings: "These selfish men are incapable of examining their own flaws, and instead blame everyone around them for their predicaments. Worse yet, the reader is constantly repelled by their outrageous racist and sexist sentiments." Perhaps more politically correct are the various stories, ranging from domestic strife to an account of the decimation of the Taskachulo Indians of Texas, in Lisa Sandlin's *The Famous Thing About Death* (Cinco Puntos). The eighteen stories of all kinds, though the tendency is toward fable and contemporary allegory, in *Distant Journeys* (Bilingual Press), by Rafael Catillo, are sometimes solemn enough to be PC, more often they are touched by a saving irony, as in "The

Goy from Aztlan," about a Chicano author who has written a successful holocaust novel under a pseudonym.

"People who read my stories are always surprised to find out that I have blue eyes and blond hair," said Susan Straight of her collection *Aquaboogie* (Milkweed), exclusively concerned with an all-black community. "You must really want to be doing something else but you won't let yourself admit it," asserts one character to another, one of many people desperately trying to impose order on chaos in Mary Scott's *Nudists May Be Encountered* (Serpent's Tail). "You almost thump your foot as you read them," writes author Carolyn Chute of the seventeen stories of Anne Brashler's *Getting Jesus in the Mood* (Cane Hill). "You almost dance."

Other small-press books with essentially mainstream matter and manners were *John Logan: The Collected Fiction* (BOA Editions), eighteen autobiographical stories; Anzia Yezierska's *How I Found America* (Persea Books), essentially autobiographical tales of Jewish immigrants on New York's Lower East Side, taken from two previously published collections and with seven new stories; *Breeding Leah* (Signature), seven stories set in Utah desert country, many with a specific Mormon context, by John Bennion; Charles Nicholson's *The Skinner's Tale* (Stackpole), a series of stories, with much hunting detail, about a black deer-skinner named Jericho Walker; and Merrill Joan Gerber's novella and stories, *Chattering Man* (Longstreet).

Not surprisingly, small-press publishers also brought out a good deal of genre fiction. Mercury House published Carol Emschwilller's latest collection, *The Start of the End of It All*, twenty feminist science fiction stories. David Streitfeld of the *Washington Post Book World* called *The Brains of Rats* (Scream Press), by Michael Blumlein, "one of the best science fiction/horror collections to appear in the last few years" (April 28). *Grimscribe* (Carroll and Graf), by Thomas Ligotti, has twelve separate thrillers in the gothic manner, joined together by a single narrator's voice, a voice "always speaking of terrible secrets." As might be inferred from the title, Richard Sutphen's *Sexpunks and Savage Sagas* (Spine-Tingling) is a collection of occult stories of sex, violence, and revenge. Joanne Greenberg's well-received *With the Snow Queen* (Arcade) has fourteen futuristic stories, mostly set in Colorado. *The Petrus Borel Stories* (Sun and Moon) gathers seven fragmentary tales of pain and sadism by

Tom Ahern. Set in Florida, the Bay Area, and New York, Ruthann Robson's *Cecile* (Firebrand) has nineteen first-person stories about a lesbian couple trying to bring up a young son. Chris Mazza's *Is It Sexual Harassment Yet?* (Fiction Collective Two) was described by Bill Christophersen in the *New York Times Book Review* as "a collection in which absurdist sitcoms alternate with offbeat psychodramas and tales of trauma." Jane Byrne called them "creepy" stories in the *Wall Street Journal* (29 November) and focused on Mazza's characters: "They are repressed, always a hairbreath from psychosis and operate in a world where frayed nerves and people's mistreatment of one another have finally won out, and there is no question of redemption."

More and more publishers are willing to do collections of stories as first books. A good many of these are collections in which the stories are, in one way and another, clearly linked, creating a fiction that could as well be called a novel. R. M. Kinder's *Sweet Angel Band* (Helicon Nine), for example, has connections among its stories. Most deal with a life of uniformly grinding rural poverty in Bootheel County, Missouri. Several follow a single character, Cora Leban, who has moved away yet never fully escaped her place and past. Another collection in which place—Berkeley in the late 1940s and during the 1960s—is important is *Now You See It* (Little, Brown), by Cornelia Nixon. These stories also deal with the same family—philosophy professor Edward Hooper, his German-born wife, Ella, who becomes a photographer, and their four children. Widely reviewed, the book was singled out for praise by the *New York Times* reviewer Michiko Kakutani (29 March) and here defined by the critic as joining together "Alice Munro's sympathetic understanding of character with Ann Beattie's radar-sharp eye for the dislocations of contemporary culture." The settings are various and so are the characters in *No Peace at Versailles* (New Rivers), by Nina Barragan, but the basic subject matter, women working to find themselves, unifies the collection. Gay characters in their thirties dominate the stories (with one, "Saying the Truth," about AIDS) of Philip Gambone's *The Language We Use Up Here* (Dutton); while the novellas and stories of *Naked to the Waist* (Houghton Mifflin), by Alice Elliott Dark, deal with "straight love" stories involving characters *Publishers Weekly* compared to those of television's *thirty-something*. More obviously linked are the fifteen stories of Julia Alvarez's *How the Garcia Girls Lost Their Accents* (Al-

gonquin), closely interwoven tales of the adolescence and young adulthood in New York of four young women, sisters—Carla, Sandra, Yolanda, and Sofia—who, like their creator, come from the Dominican Republic. All of Paul Gervais's stories in *Extraordinary People* (HarperCollins) deal with the same family—the Beelers of North Tewksbury, Massachusetts.

Although most of the twelve stories in Eileen Pollack's extravagantly praised (by Dan Wakefield, James Alan McPherson, David Leavitt, Lynne Sharon Schwartz) *The Rabbi in the Attic* (Delphinium) are about young women coming to maturity, and some are set in the Catskills, the stories are various in manner and matter, linked only in the singularity of the author's voice and concerns. The stories of Deborah Rebollar Pintonelli's *Ego Monkey* (Another Chicago Press) are experimental, as one might expect from John Hawkes's book-jacket praise for her as "an extremely promising young writer." Variety, the deliberate and effective use of many voices in sixteen stories, especially in "Something About Ireland," is the hallmark of Rick Rofihe's *Father Must* (Farrar, Straus and Giroux). Another among the handful of genuinely experimental books by newcomers is *A Modern Way to Die* (Fromm), by Peter Workman, a careful and original mix of fantasy and reportage, as in the title story in which death becomes a spectator sport. Another example of the mixing of genres is found in Australian Michael Wilding's *Her Most Bizarre Sexual Experience* (Norton), twelve stories, mostly involving artists and intellectuals in Australia, and showing strong elements of science fiction in such stories as "The West Midlands Underground," "See You Later," and "The Man of Slow Feeling." Trying to pinpoint precisely the "new-wave" qualities of Wilding's work, his publisher writes: "*Her Most Bizarre Sexual Experience* is hip, but not flippant; up-to-the-minute, but not instantly obsolescent."

Other outstanding first collections of stories published during the year were: *Under the Light* (Knopf), by Sam Michel, fifteen highly praised (by James Dickey, Barry Hannah, John Graves), stories about the life and times of a memorable man of the new West—Harry Drake; *The Art of Cartography* (Knopf), by J. S. Marcus, twelve diverse stories, set all over the world and involving distinctly different characters, though several deal with the same character—a woman named Sheila. These are people "on the edge," whose attitude is announced in the second paragraph of the collection—"Physically, economically, politically, nobody wants to be in the middle, and everybody wants to be on the edge."

Rosana Robinson, having already received respectful attention for a first novel and a biography of painter Georgia O'Keefe, brought out a collection of stories which have appeared in the best places—the *Atlantic*, the *New Yorker*, *Wigwag*. The fourteen stories of *A Glimpse of Scarlet* (Burlingame/HarperCollins) are various in their settings and circumstances, but generally united by their concern for (in the words of the publisher) "the hidden realities beneath the serene and gleaming surface of old-guard WASP family life." This book was widely reviewed. So was Gretel Ehrlich's *Drinking Dry Clouds: Stories From Wyoming* (Capra). Author of an earlier collection of essays and a novel, recipient of a Guggenheim Fellowship and a Whiting Award (1988), Ehrlich divides her collection in two parts—"During the War," with four stories written from a third-person point of view, and "After the War," consisting of ten stories told in first-person by a variety of characters. All the stories are set in Wyoming in the 1940s.

Another book of stories singled out for honor is *Imagine a Great White Light* (Pushcart), by Sheila Schwartz. This collection of nine stories, various in its characters and themes, was chosen as the Ninth Annual Editors' Book Award for "overlooked manuscripts of enduring literary value." Marly Swick, who was awarded, by judge Jayne Anne Phillips, the Iowa Short Fiction Award for *A Hole in the Language* (University of Iowa), also of nine full-length stories, is, like Ehrlich, a writer whose work has earned her a James Michener Award and a National Endowment for the Arts Fellowship. Besides the usual literary magazines, her stories have appeared in *Playgirl*, *Redbook*, and *McCall's*.

Two first collections which were treated much more as work by accomplished masters than debuts of promise were: *The Clay that Breathes* (Milkweed), by Catherine Browder, and Pauline Melville's *Shape-Shifter* (Pantheon). *Shape-Shifter*, which arrived in the United States with Britain's distinguished Guardian Prize and International PEN's Macmillan Silver Pen Award to its credit, together with strong endorsements from Fay Weldon and (from his hiding place) Salman Rushdie, contains twelve stories involving both poor Londoners and Caribs, particularly from Guyana, of which Melville, now living in London, is a native. A different kind of cultural interplay, the interaction of Americans and Asians, is

found in *The Clay that Breathes*. The title novella (there are also six short stories) is about an American apprentice, Eve Sandler, who goes to Kyoto to work under a Japanese master potter. The stories are set in both Japan and America. The review attention given to this small-press book is testimony to the growing importance of fiction coming from small presses. Graywolf brought out *Through and Through: Toledo Stories*, by Joseph Geha. Born in Zahleh, Lebanon, Joseph Geha came with his family to Toledo, Ohio, in 1946. His eight stories treat three generations of Arab Americans (from the 1930s to the present).

Among other first collections which made a mark in 1991, *In the Air* (Johns Hopkins), by Robert Nichols (husband of master storyteller Grace Paley), offers a baker's dozen of stories with a matter-of-fact element of the fabulous and powerful political implications. "Moral outrage," with a touch of surrealism, is the order of the day. Two younger writers, David Means and Louis Berney, both having recently studied in creative writing programs, demonstrate a high level of craft and competence and the kind of originality in language and point of view that lead reviewers and blurb-writers to use words like "dazzling." Since 1989 stories from Berney's *The Road to Bobby Joe* (Harcourt Brace Jovanovich) have appeared all over the lot, from the *New Yorker* to *Crescent Review*. Needless to say, the stories are various. They also usually involve some surprising and extraordinary development in a very ordinary situation. Diversity is also the chief characteristic of Means's well-received collection, *A Quick Kiss of Redemption* (Morrow). Although the stories are distinctly different, the characters would often be at home in the world of Robert Nichols, as, for example, here where the first-person narrator of "Seed" reflects on the ironies of American life and language: "You pick up the family and move West because, well, sometimes you just have to do what you have to do. Sitting in New York that night, I thought about the way this country was founded on such convoluted, in-turning, snake-eating-its-tale phrases. No guts, glory, pride, oppression, stagecoach dreaming drive: just routine, run-of-the-mill phrase turning."

Anthologies are gallery exhibitions of the work of literary stars, some old and established and others new and ascending to prominence. Probably the two most important anthologies of the year were: *Prize Stories 1991: The O. Henry Awards* (Doubleday), edited by William Abrahams; and *Best American Short Stories 1991*

Dust jacket for Trevor's volume of two short novels, which was shortlisted for the 1991 Booker Prize in England

(Houghton Mifflin), edited by Alice Adams. This is Abrahams's twenty-fifth anniversary as editor of *Prize Stories* and the seventy-first in the series. Most of Abrahams's "Introduction" is taken up with the list of the 307 authors whose work he has selected over the years of his editorship—a very distinguished and impressive list. For the 1991 issue first prize was awarded to solid citizen John Updike for his story "A Sandstone Farmhouse," from the *New Yorker* which has only three stories out of the twenty on this year's list. The other stories come from a variety of places—slick magazines like *Glamour* and *Playboy*; two from the *Atlantic*, and the rest from various literary magazines—and are widely diverse in their ways and means of storytelling. Some of the writers are very well known—Alice Adams, Charles Baxter, Ursula K. LeGuin, Joyce Carol Oates, Ronald Sukenick. Others, for example Marly Swick, Helen Norris, Sharon Sheehe Stark, Martha Lacy Hall, are well along their way. There is some overlap in authors in Alice Adams's choices for *Best American Short Stories 1991* (Updike, Oates, Baxter, et al.), and six of her twenty stories came from the *New Yorker*, but the range in both writ-

ers and publications is wide and representative of the present eclectic scene. As good as any story in the book is the account by Rick Bass, in "Contributors' Notes," of how "Madame A.," fiction editor for "a famous men's publication"—"one of those magazines that runs fiction between pictures of breasts and groins, pubic hair and hineys"—first accepted, then later rejected his story "The Legend of Pig-Eye," which ended up in this anthology. Another annual gathering of prizewinners, its fifteenth, is *The Pushcart Prize* (Simon and Schuster), edited by Bill Henderson. Henderson's product is a bit of a hustle, but, all things considered, a worthwhile one, and has twenty-four stories, in the company of poems and essays. He, too, in the past has included many writers from the roster of established stars. This time his collection is more various (and, inevitably, uneven) and has first-rate work by excellent writers such Padgett Powell, Lydia Davis, Molly Best Tinsley, Kent Nelson, Robin Hemley, and Sarah Glasscock.

Another anthology with the aura of a prize collection about it—in part because its editor, Shannon Ravenel, was formerly the editor of *Best*

American Short Stories—is *New Stories From the South: The Year's Best 1991* (Algonquin). Here familiar names are firmly in place—Peter Taylor, Lee Smith, Bobbie Ann Mason, Larry Brown, Jill McCorkle, Rick Bass, Reynolds Price. But so are some others less familiar and likely to be better known: Robert Olen Butler, Barbara Hudson, Hilding Johnson, Susan Starr Richards. Shannon Ravenel's prefaces have become an annual treat as she seeks to define the ever-changing elements of the "southern" in form and content. This time she is busy defending herself from a piece by Marc K. Stengel, "Why Is Nobody Writing about the South We Know?," first published in "The Nashville Scene" and later reprinted all across the South. Neither the criticism of Stengel nor the defense of Ravenel says much about the variety of forms and voices to be found in the contemporary southern short story. What needs to be said about that is in Fred Chappell's "Introduction: The Contemporary Southern Short Story and the Long Dark Shadow of Its Origins," in *Contemporary Southern Short Fiction* (Texas Review), a gathering, wholly written for this book of thirteen stories, some by better known writers (Richard Bausch, Kelly Cherry, Ellen Douglas, Percival Everett, Ellen Gilchrist, David Madden, Allen Weir, Heather Ross Miller), others by writers who soon will be better known—Cathryn Hankla, Clay Reynolds, Anita Thompson, Tom Whalen. Chappell's critical essay makes complex and exciting points, not least of which is that there are more threads in the southern tradition than others, including Ravenel, seem to be fully aware of: "If much of such writing imitates the porch whittler's drawl, as Mark Twain's and Calder Willingham's did, or the beauty shop's twitter as Eudora Welty and Lee Smith have done, much of it is also spoken in the white-faced feverish stammer of the fearful and disordered personality, of the spirit trying to break free."

Another and somewhat more conventional southern anthology is *Growing Up in the South* (Mentor/Penguin), edited by Suzanne W. Jones and including a rainbow coalition of twenty-five southern writers, from Katherine Anne Porter to Mary Hood, from William Faulkner to Fred Chappell. The stories are concerned with childhood, adolescence, young adulthood—growing up. *Something in Common* (Louisiana State University), edited by Ann Brewster Dobie, has nineteen stories, all by contemporary writers from Louisiana. The book has work by a variety of writers, including major figures in short fiction such as Walker Percy, Shirley Ann Grau, Andre Dubus, and Ernest Gaines, and equally gifted writers from that special area with its unique American history. Writing in the "Introduction," editor and critic Lewis P. Simpson makes a good deal of the changing history of Louisiana and the changes in the second half of this century which are demonstrated in the work of these writers:

> If the writers we associate with Louisiana today tell us, as Ann Dobie says, who Louisianians are at this moment in history, the writers present, I have meant to say, a different sense of life in Louisiana from the one dominantly conveyed by the Louisiana literary sensibility down to the 1950s.

The South was not alone, by any means, in the production of anthologies of short fiction. *The Best of the West 4* (Norton), edited by James and Denise Thomas, offered up fifteen recent stories of the old and new West. *Tales from the American Frontier* (Pantheon), edited by Richard Erddes, contains tales of figures such as Billy the Kid, Paul Bunyan, and Jim Bowie. Other anthologies were put together around similar subjects, themes, and purposes. For example: *Revenge: Short Stories by Women Writers* (Faber), edited by Kate Saunders, features twenty women writers, including, among the better-known contemporaries, Ellen Gilchrist, Muriel Spark, Alice Walker; *Dreams in a Minor Key* (Crossing), edited by Susanna J. Sturgis, is also devoted to women writers (fifteen), but deals with examples of "magic realism"; Diane Wolkstein meanwhile edited "creative renditions" in *The First Love Stories: From Isis and Osiris to Tristan and Iseult* (HarperCollins). Jeffrey Archer and Simon Bainbridge edited ten "political" stories (from Jack London and Mark Twain to Kingsley Amis's "I Spy Strangers") in *Fools, Knaves and Heroes* (Norton).

The year saw many "gay" anthologies, among the better known being: *Indivisible: New Short Fiction by Gay and Lesbian West Coast Writers* (Plume), edited by Robert Drake and Terry Wolverton; *Lesbian Love Stories: Volume 2* (Crossing), edited by Irene Zahava, some thirty stories of uneven quality, though some (see Merrill Mushroom's "How to Engage in Courting Rituals 1950s Butch-Style in the Bar") have been singled out by reviewers for special praise. Probably the most significant anthology of this kind to appear in 1991 was *The Faber Book of Gay Short Fiction* (Faber), edited by Edmund White and made up of thirty-two old and new writers, British and American, including Alan Gurganus, E. M. Forster, Henry James, Ronald Firbank, Christopher Isherwood, Alfred Chester, Tennessee Williams, and James Baldwin.

Doubleday published *Memory of Kin*, edited by Mary Helen Washington, nineteen stories (Toni Cade Bambara, Ernest Gaines, Alice Walker, etc.) and twelve poems about family by black writers. Advertising itself as "the first comprehensive, multicultural anthology of twentieth-century American fiction ever published," *Imagining America: Stories from the Promised Land* (Persea), edited by Wesley Brown and Amy Ling, has thirty-six stories, by not only people of color but also Jews (Bernard Malamud, Grace Paley, Lynne Sharon Schwartz), Irish (Mary Gordon), Italian (Jo Pagano), and even a white male (Richard Bausch). Some other ethnic anthologies were more limited in scope. *The Boundaries of Twilight* (New Rivers), edited by C. J. Hribal, contains stories and poems by Americans of Czechoslovakian descent. Short stories, poetry, and essays, some as recent as a story by Tony Ardizzone ("Nonna"), make up the contents of *From the Margin: Writings in Italian Americana* (Purdue); while *The Big AIIIEEEEE* (Meridian) brings together stories by Asian American writers. *Publishers Weekly* called the angry introduction "incendiary" and noted that a significant number of these Japanese- and Chinese-American writers are women. Native Americans are the writers in Craig Lesley's anthology *Talking Leaves* (Dell) and likewise in *The Lightning Within* (University of Nebraska), edited by Alan R. Velie.

Foreign cultures also furnished anthologies for this year's marketplace. *Green Cane and Juicy Flotsam* (Rutgers University), edited by Carmen C. Esteves and Elizabeth Paravisini Gerbert, contains twenty-seven stories by Caribbean women including Jamaica Kincaid and Jean Rhys. From Britain came *Best English Short Stories III* (Norton), edited by Giles Gordon and David Hughes, twenty-five stories that *Publishers Weekly* called "well rounded narratives," and including the work of major figures such as Nadine Gordimer, Alice Munro, Julian Barnes, and William Trevor. *The Penguin Book of British Comic Stories* (Viking), edited by Patricia Craig, has forty-two stories by three generations of British authors, from Rudyard Kipling to V. S. Naipaul, from Evelyn Waugh to Julian Barnes. Exclusively Irish is *The Field Day Anthology of Irish Writing* (Field Day), three volumes edited by Seamus Deane and others. Volume three deals with the modern period. *Soviet Women Writing* (Abbeville) has fifteen writ-

Dust jacket for Marcus's collection of twelve stories set in geographically diverse locations

ers and stories. Some of them—for example, Tatyana Tolstaya, Galina Kornilova, and Victoriya Tokareva—are already known here; most are not. *Stories by Iranian Women Since the Revolution* (University of Texas) contains thirteen stories translated by Soraya Paknazar Sullivan and includes contemporary Iranian writers such as Goli Taraghi, Simin Daneshvar, Lyly Riahi, and Mihan Bahrami. *Stories From Iran* (Image) has a chronological arrangement (1929-1991) of thirty Iranian stories. *Fool of Life* (Image) collects some fifty stories, with illustrations, from the whole history of Persia. From Japan came several anthologies of short fiction. *Tales of Tears and Laughter* (University of Hawaii) has thirteen exemplary stories from Medieval Japan. *Unmapped Territories: New Women's Fiction from Japan* (Women in Translation) has seven stories concerning conflicts of women with male sexuality and with assigned roles in Japanese society. *Monkey Brain Sushi* (Kodansha American), edited by Alfred Birnbaum, collects eleven works of short fiction by a new generation of Japanese writers that, in the words of the editor,

"Has emerged to capture the electric, eclectic spirit of contemporary life in Japan's mega-cities." Another gathering of the latest Japanese writers is *New Japanese Voices* (Atlantic Monthly), a selection including twelve young Japanese writers, edited by Helen Mitsios and sporting an introduction by Jay McInerney. McInerney, sensing a collegiality among the young and the restless everywhere, concludes: "Hollywood, Madison Avenue, and rock and roll have generated a global reservoir of images, icons, and modern myths."

Two new anthologies of the works of women writers from India were produced by the Feminist Press of the City University of New York—*Women Writing in India* and *Truth Tales: Contemporary Stories by Women Writers of India*. These two books were given a full-scale review by Anita Desai in the *New York Review of Books* (16 January 1992). The leading Latin American anthology was *A Hammock Beneath the Mangoes* (Dutton), edited by Thomas Colchie and containing work, among its twenty-six authors from eight countries, by new writers as well as Olympians such as Gabriel García Márquez, Jorges Luis Borges, Isabel Allende, Carlos Fuentes, Julio Cortazar, and Manuel Puig.

Genre fiction of various kinds resulted in some anthologies. Edward D. Hoch edited *The Year's Best Mystery and Suspense Stories* (Walker), with thirteen writers, including five Edgar nominees. Selected by editor Eleanor Sullivan from some eight thousand published stories were the fifty stories of *Fifty Years of the Best from Ellery Queen* (Carroll and Graf). Carroll and Graf also published *Dark Crimes: Great Noir Fiction from the 50s to the 90s*, edited by Ed Gorman; and *Scarlet Letters*, edited by Eleanor Sullivan, some sixteen stories about adultery from the pages of the mystery magazine *Ellery Queen*.

Forms of horror fiction seemed more popular than ever. *The New Gothic* (Random House), edited by Bradford Morrow and Patrick McGrath, has twenty-one stories by contemporary writers as wildly different as Martin Amis and Robert Coover. It is worth the price of admission for the sake of Paul West's "Banquo and the Black Banana." For a gripping title, consider *I Shudder at Your Touch: 22 Tales of Sex and Horror* (NAL/Dutton), edited by Michele Slung. Here, along with six stories published for the first time, are stories from as early as 1900 and as recently as 1990. *Masques IV: All-New Works of Horror and the Supernatural* (McClay), edited by J. N. Williamson, has twenty-four stories, all but one

of which were written exclusively for this volume. Editor Larry Dark chose twenty-eight contemporary ghost stories, from writers such as Donald Barthelme, Muriel Spark, I. B. Singer, Nadine Gordimer, for *The Literary Ghost* (Atlantic Monthly). Meanwhile Oxford published *Victorian Ghost Stories*, representing masters of the genre such as J. S. LeFanu, Henry James, Charlotte Riddell, Mary Elizabeth Braddon, and Elizabeth Gaskell. Carroll and Graf is the source of two horror anthologies—*Best New Horror 2*, twenty-eight new thrillers edited by Stephen Jones and Ramsey Campbell; and, edited by Robert Silverberg and Martin H. Greenberg, *The Horror Hall of Fame*, eighteen stories from a period of 138 years chosen by a poll at the World Fantasy Convention and including writers from Edgar Allan Poe to Robert Bloch and Harlan Ellison. *A Whisper of Blood* (Morrow), as its title suggests, is composed of vampire tales, eighteen of them edited by Ellen Datlow.

All sorts of organizing principles are evoked to justify (or unify) anthologies. *One Step in the Clouds* (Sierra Club), for example, has some thirty-one stories concerning mountaineering. *Vital Signs* (Graywolf), edited by Dorothy Sennett and Ann Czarniecki, is an international collection of contemporary stories on aging. *From the Center of the Earth* (Clover Park) is entirely concerned with stories and autobiographical accounts coming out of the Peace Corps experiences. *You Haven't To Deserve: A Gift to the Homeless* (Longstreet), edited by Jane Hill, is one of several 1991 anthologies of fiction dedicated to the homeless. Exactly how this fiction is supposed to offer aid and comfort to homeless people is left to the reader's imagination. Jane Hill also edited *Street Songs 2: New Voices in Fiction* (Longstreet). More conventional (and successful in terms of review notice and sales) were books such as the highly praised *Writers on World War II* (Knopf), edited by Mordecai Richler; and Jack Newcombe's *A New Christmas Treasury* (Viking), with eighty-nine stories, essays, and poems from Charles Dickens and Thomas Hardy to George Plimpton and Peter Matthiessen. *Los Angeles Stories: Great Writers on the City* (Chronicle), edited by John Miller, has twenty-five pieces—stories, excerpts from novels, poems, and a shard of the screenplay for *Sunset Boulevard*, from F. Scott Fitzgerald ("Crazy Sunday") to Charles Bukowski and Kate Brauerman. Odd and oddly beautiful, both as a book and because of the handsome color photographs by Jane Gottlieb, is *Car Tales: Classic Stories About Dream Ma-*

chines (Viking). With five offbeat stories by writers from Arthur Conan Doyle ("How It Happened") to F. Scott Fitzgerald ("The Family Bus") and an "Introduction" by Mario Andretti, it is a unique little book.

Two anthologies originated with radio programs. *The Sound of Writing* (Doubleday), edited by Alan Cheuse and Caroline Marshall, is a compilation of thirty-eight original stories selected from the National Public Radio (and PEN syndicated fiction project) program "The Sound of Writing." Here, in the brief format of the story for broadcast, new writers are side by side with established masters. Another anthology derived from a National Public Radio program, "Weekend Edition," is *The Wedding Cake in the Middle of the Road: 23 Variations on a Theme* (Norton), edited by Susan Stamberg and George Garrett. All these stories were written for the radio show or for the anthology and include prominent writers (Mary Lee Settle, Ann Beattie, Joy Williams) and newcomers such as Beverly Goodrum, Brian Klam, and Hannah Wilson.

Finally, there were those anthologies from a particular press or magazine. The University of Iowa Press celebrated an anniversary with *The Iowa Award: The Best Stories from Twenty Years*, edited by Frank Conroy. Because some years saw double winners there are twenty-five stories in the book. There are significant "discoveries" here, writers such as Susan Dodd, Philip F. O'Connor, and Barry Targan were Iowa Award winners. *Disorderly Conduct: The VLS Fiction Reader* (Serpent's Tail) has twenty-five writers and stories from the *Village Voice*, people such as Kathy Acker and Blanche McCrary Boyd, Harry Matthews and Russell Banks. *The Best of the Missouri Review* (Missouri), edited by Speer Morgan and others, contains twenty-five stories from 1978 to the present and offers an interesting, eclectic mix, from Paul Bowles and Naguib Mahfouz to Amy Hempel and the late Raymond Carver. In his position as senior editor at the *Atlantic Monthly*, C. Michael Curtis has the duty of rejecting close to twelve thousand short stories a year in order to publish the twelve to fifteen stories the magazine publishes annually. Therefore his second collection, culled from the pages of that magazine—*American Stories II: Fiction From The Atlantic Monthly* (Chronicle)—can be taken as representing his eclectic view of the best of the best. Here, William Faulkner ("Gold Is Not Always") to Amy Tan ("Two Kinds"), are twenty stories from, roughly, three generations of American

writers; and it would be eminently worthwhile if only for the appearance of Edmund Wilson's "The Man Who Shot Snapping Turtles" and Richard Bausch's "The Man Who Knew Belle Starr."

In his lively "Introduction" Curtis (who ought to know, if anybody does) seeks to make a distinction between *stories* and *story-telling*. It sounds a little mystical and mysterious, but why not? "Story-telling is a sort of controlled catharsis," he writes, "a review of historical evidence, a rehearsal of imagined tomorrows. Story-telling allows us to look for connections between injuries of the past and uncertainties of the future.... Story-telling is our way of reminding ourselves who we are or want to be or might have been." Got it . . . ?

There are three special cases among the many collections by prominent writers during 1991. Two are based on performances. Wallace Shawn's *The Fever* (Farrar, Straus and Giroux) is a first-person narrative monologue of long-story or novella length, based on a performance piece created and acted by Shawn. The narrator gets sick with a fever in a Third World country and, as the jacket tells us, "is visited by cherished memories of a privileged past." It is not without irony or humor, but its overwhelming impact is of politically correct sincerity: "Without the money, your face would become the face of a rat, your hands would be paws—sharp, nimble, ready to scratch, ready to tear.

"Sure, sometimes you think about the suffering of the poor. . . ."

Eric Bogosian, also an actor and performer, has published two previous books, *Drinking in America* and *Talk Radio*. The latter had separate lives as a book, play, TV movie, and, finally, as a film. *Sex, Drugs, Rock & Roll* (HarperCollins) has seventeen first-person performance monologues, each with a central character-narrator—an English rock star, a bottle collector, a phone sex hostess, a wheeling-dealing executive, a good old boy, etc.—involved in a narrative situation. That is, each monologue (he calls them "solos") is a short-short story. "I've spent most of my life stuck between idealism and hedonism, between selfishness and selflessness, between love and sex, between chaos and clarity," he states in his "Introduction," indicating the conflicts out of which his fiction is formed.

Broken Vessels (Godine), by the highly honored story writer Andre Dubus, is a book of twenty-two personal essays, autobiographical and various yet sequential, building steadily toward the central narrative events, the terrible accident in which Dubus lost his leg, its aftereffects, and, in the final title piece, the earned self-reconciliation: "So my crippling is a daily and living sculpture of certain truths: we receive and we lose, and we must try to achieve gratitude; and with that gratitude to embrace with whole hearts whatever of life remains after the losses." Call it what you will, essay or story, Dubus cannot write without writing narrative; and in a real sense this, his ninth book, may be one of the finest collections of stories of the year.

The Year in Poetry

R. S. Gwynn
Lamar University

Every year seems to bring at least one major magazine article that addresses the current state of American poetry and, in calling attention to some of its shortcomings, precipitates a flurry of controversy. In 1983 Donald Hall's "Poetry and Ambition," first printed in the *Kenyon Review* and reprinted as the title essay in his 1988 collection, blasted the predictable sameness of much contemporary poetry, labeling the typical product of a writing workshop the "McPoem," with the result that "every year, Ronald McDonald takes the Pulitzer." Greg Kuzma's "The Catastrophe of Creative Writing," a 1987 review in *Poetry* ostensibly of a book of poems by Martha Collins, detailed the metastasis of creative-writing programs throughout the country by speculating that "[W]ithin five years there will be a creative writing program available for anyone in America within safe driving distance of his home," a prediction seemingly borne out by the latest edition of *The AWP Official Guide to Writing Programs*, the Sears catalogue of the Associated Writing Programs.

In 1988 Joseph Epstein's essay "Who Killed Poetry?" appeared in *Commentary* and was reprinted the next spring in *AWP Chronicle*. Epstein lamented that poetry no longer is part of the nation's intellectual life, having become "a sadly peripheral art form" practiced and for the most part appreciated only by those he labels "poetry professionals," a generation of poet-teachers who inhabit the cloistered halls of university English departments. Responses to Epstein's article, most of them angry, filled the next two issues of the magazine.

In 1991 the role of Jeremiah was undertaken, in the May issue of the *Atlantic*, by poet and critic Dana Gioia, who asked "Can Poetry Matter?" Gioia warns of a species in danger of extinction, the vanishing general audience for poetry that existed in this country only a few decades ago; in doing so, he finds it paradoxical that poets "as individual artists . . . are almost invisible" in a time when, judging by the sheer numbers of publications, readings, and professional sinecures, the art and its practitioners would seem to be in the middle of an American quattrocento. Gioia does not slight the complexity of the cultural antecedents of a "boom [that] has been a distressingly confined phenomenon," but his chief culprits are the wildly proliferating spawn of creative-writing programs, which have stratified into "a large professional class for the production and reception of new poetry, comprising legions of teachers, graduate students, editors, publishers, and administrators." The result of this increasingly inbred "poetry subculture" is that "the energy of American poetry, which was once directed outward, is now increasingly focused inward. Reputations are made and rewards distributed within the poetry subculture. . . . [A] 'famous' poet now means someone famous only to other poets. But there are enough poets to make that local fame relatively meaningful. Not long ago, 'only poets read poetry' was meant as damning criticism. Now it is a proven marketing strategy." Gioia is not alone in these fears and is by no means the first to voice them. As early as 1957 Hugh Kenner remarked, "I cannot help thinking that a civilization is in very perilous condition when all its writers have been driven into the universities." After all, when we refer to a question as "academic" aren't we in fact dismissing it as unimportant?

Gioia offers a few suggestions by which "poets and poetry teachers [might] take more responsibility for bringing their art to the public," among them, reading from other authors at their own readings and perhaps allowing performance of other art forms to be integrated with their own; greater candor by poets in reviewing and rigor in editing, especially in the production of anthologies which "should not be used as pork barrels for the creative-writing trade"; and an increased attention to the public performance of poetry, both in the classroom and over college and public-supported radio, a medium hitherto largely neglected. These are indeed modest proposals, more of a wish list than anything, but they and the article's other remarks, even though Gioia for the most part refrained from naming names, occasioned several hundred letters to the *Atlantic* and other essays and symposia published both here and in Great Britain. Typical of the negative respondents was poet Peter Sears, who, pointing out Gioia's politically incorrect sins of using "American" to refer only to poetry written in the United States and of daring to suggest that Adrienne Rich ("a major poet by any standard," said Gioia) occasionally writes "often overbearing polemics," denounced his thesis as "romantic, patriarchal, Eurocentric, and elitist." On the other hand, Michael Heffernan, poet and director of a creative-writing program, saw Gioia's evidence of "hundreds of thousands of Americans attend[ing] poetry readings" as revealing the strengths, rather than the weaknesses, of contemporary American poetry. Writing in *PSA News*, the quarterly publication of the Poetry Society of America, critic Robert McPhillips, in an essay that the PSA was careful to note "represents its author's opinions, not the collective position of the membership," suggested that the intense response to the article was proof "that there is a wide audience for poetry, albeit one that has largely been disenchanted with much contemporary verse" and went on to argue that such fundamental techniques of pedagogy as memorization, imitation, and basic instruction in metrical technique have been slighted by creative-writing classes, which all too often, to cite one case from the author's own experience, consist of student-poets "getting in

touch with nature and their inner feelings by writing poems on pieces of bark."

Even the editors of the *Atlantic* were surprised by the breadth of the response, observing several months later that they had received many newspaper articles from around the country commenting on Gioia's article, for the most part favorably. Typical of these sentiments (and one I have heard expressed countless times) is that of Jack Kestner in the Bristol, Virginia, *Herald-Courier*: "For years, I'd been wondering what had happened to the verse I enjoyed as a child and youth." Kestner decries the lack of rhymed verse in today's magazines, naming the *Atlantic* as one of the chief offenders. It is again paradoxical that so few poets today use rhyme when the reading public so consistently mourns its absence. If American poetry existed in a true market economy, wouldn't such consistent demand for verse of this sort eventually force its suppliers to provide it? Since traditional versification is one of the few elements of poetry that can be taught with any degree of precision, it is a mystery that so few graduates of the creative-writing programs employ it in their own work. On the other hand, one could be cynical and counter that when a member of the public says that he or she wants poetry that rhymes the real desire is for the undemanding banalities of the Muse of Hallmark.

With that in mind, one has to have mixed feelings about Joseph Brodsky's appointment as poet laureate, succeeding Mark Strand. The first foreign-born appointee and the only Nobel Prize laureate so named, he too wishes to make poetry more widely available to Americans. According to an Associated Press story, Brodsky argues that poetry should be sold in drugstores and supermarkets ("People who buy the *National Enquirer* would buy poetry.") and placed in motel rooms: "Anthologies of American poetry should be sitting there . . . next to the Bible. The Bible won't mind this. It doesn't mind being next to the telephone book." Witty remarks, but I, for one, would feel better about Brodsky's appointment if he showed any facility for writing in his adopted tongue. It was easy to make a case for his importance as long as he was being translated by the likes of Anthony Hecht or Richard Wilbur, but his efforts in English, where the problems are compounded by his attempts at rhythm and rhyme, remain something of an embarrassment. Here is a stanza from "A Song," one of the poet's favorites, which appeared in the *New Yorker*:

I wish you were here, dear.
I wish you were here.
I wish we were in my car,
and you'd shift the gear.
We'd find ourselves elsewhere,
on an unknown shore.
Or else we'd repair
to where we've been before.

Shouldn't someone along the way have pointed out that in idiomatic English one shifts gears in the plural, that "unknown shore" is trite, that "repair / to where" is a rhyme-forced archaism? Reading Brodsky's Russian poetry in translation sometimes I do get the sense of a god in ruins, like Rainer Maria Rilke's broken statue of Apollo, but Brodsky's English originals more often than not summon up only a pitying shake of the head and turn of the page.

In this year of the collapse of the Soviet Union it is appropriate that two of Brodsky's former fellow citizens appeared in American editions. Yevgeny Yevtushenko's *The Collected Poems 1952-1990* (Henry Holt) is a hefty tome of over six hundred pages, with English versions by many hands. Yevtushenko, of course, differs from Brodsky in that he managed, for forty years, to hold on to an international reputation as something of a dissident while at the same time exercising enough prudence to stay out of serious trouble with the authorities. I doubt if he can be compared to any American poet of this century, but I would suggest certain parallels between his protests (though mild enough now they were daring in their time) and those of Langston Hughes. As soon as black rage exploded in the late 1960s many younger black writers turned on Hughes for what they saw as pusillanimity; such, I suspect, will be the fate of Yevtushenko's reputation as more barriers fall in his own country.

F. D. Reeve's edition of Bella Akhmadulina's *The Garden: New and Selected Poetry and Prose* (Henry Holt) also bears brief mention, since most readers are not likely to be able to name any Russian women poets after Anna Akhmatova. Reeve's translations contain hints of the rhymes and rather more of the meters of the originals, if I may judge solely from the look of the words in the facing Russian texts. It would be interesting to learn whether this sort of strict formalism is typical of contemporary Russian poetry, of which one still hears rumors of huge audiences filling soccer stadiums to hear readings by major figures such as Yevtushenko, to whom, incidentally, Akhmadulina was once married. Reeve makes

Dust jacket for the fourth annual edition of the anthology intended "to glean the best work being done today"

some points in his introduction for her as a chronicler of social injustice, but she seems more often a poet whose apostrophes are intimate:

Remember how in Manege Square
you tossed money in the snow
and tried to get the coins to say
does she love me, yes or no?

In lyrics such as this she, like Brodsky, seems to be drawing on a lyrical tradition that in America has almost completely been co-opted by writers of popular songs. How strange it is that millions of listeners (and a few of them must be poets and editors) go around humming Mariah Carey's latest hit, but a poem attempting to use some of the same techniques would be rejected by virtually every mainstream literary magazine in the country (unless, of course, it was written by Brodsky).

The attempt to satisfy the call for rhyme and meter without falling prey to poetic reaction and sentimentality remains the program of the New Formalists, an eclectic group of younger poets whose work is gathered together, in poems and essays, in a special issue of *Verse* (Spring 1991), edited by Robert McPhillips, who argues that this generation of formalist poets, unlike their elders (Wilbur, Hecht, and others), is more likely to draw subjects as "freely from popular American as from high-brow culture, as well as with more ease from their own quotidian lives. Their urns are more openly accessible than they are self-consciously well-wrought." One poem from the issue that elegantly mixes the levels of the brows is "At Home with Eros & Psyche," by Charles Martin:

1

Not much of a reader or writer
Himself, but always hot for a good fable,
    Eros has heaped the tabloids that he bought
    her
On Psyche's coffee table;
    The *HOUSEWIFE* who is *TAKEN UP IN RAP-*
    TURE
Rubs elbows with the ALIENS that CAPTURE
BIGFOOT'S PREGNANT DAUGHTER!

Now why, exactly, is a delicious verbal cartoon like this encountered in a small circulation university quarterly instead of in the pages of the *New Yorker*? Surely there is a large potential audience for sophisticated verse, yet other than the now defunct *Light Year* anthologies from Robert Wallace's Bits Press there have been no publishing outlets for this sort of thing for many years. Perhaps sensing a potential demand, a poet named Al Kracht recently ran a magazine advertisement for a company called Limerick Lane Poetryworks (5 Birch Lane, Chappaqua, NY 10514), which offers verses on order for all occasions:

To answer your need, provide word and deed,
There's our workshop on Limerick Lane,
Selling verse rated best, tailored to your request,
FAXed to you when time is a strain.

In an age when freshmen can purchase research papers on virtually any academic subject out of the back pages of *Rolling Stone*, I wonder how long it will be before some hard-pressed M.F.A. candidate places an order in with Kracht for a creative thesis-to-go.

Who *are* the members of the audience for contemporary poetry? For whom does the poet imagine he or she is writing? This question was addressed in a symposium organized by Fred Chappell in the Spring 1991 issue of *Mānoa*, a literary journal published at the University of Hawaii, which solicited responses from twenty American poets. Chappell raises questions that must at one time or another have crossed the mind of anyone who writes poetry:

[S]hould the poet attempt, willingly or unwillingly, to imagine what the poet's insubstantial reader must be like? What gender? What ethnicity? What age? To which economic class this reader belongs? To what community or region? How intelligent should the poet expect the reader to be?

If the responses have anything in common, it is simply that they reflect the increasing fragmentation—the "Balkanization," as one critic put it—of contemporary poetry, or what Robert Creeley calls "the plurality of poetries—a fact significantly changed since I began, and usefully."

Relatively few of the respondents seem to imagine the ideal reader as a college-educated man or woman who shares certain cultural assumptions and values with the poet and who includes contemporary poetry among the choices that reading for pleasure presents—the so-called common reader that Gioia and others deduce must have existed in the not-so-distant past if poets such as Robinson Jeffers, Edna St. Vincent Millay, Robert Frost, and Edwin Arlington Robinson were to be published by major houses expecting some degree of financial return on their investment. Today, the reader who was once called "common" more often than not seems an oppressive representative of white, middle-class, patriarchal values. Thus, Joseph Bruchac, in replying to Chappell's questions that "my own answer to all of them is a simple one—*no*," nevertheless establishes his frame of reference almost totally in the context of native American culture and literature. Brenda Hillman, listening to a friend claim that she writes for "the woman in the Shop-Rite," has reservations about the anonymous woman:

I have a terrible feeling she won't like me. She's the other group in seventh grade, the normal group. I am the group of one: weird, ugly, no friends. Secretly, I talk to lizards, believe God reuses souls to save time.

Nell Altizer, getting up on one of 1973's tallest soapboxes, speaks of trying to reach "the reader . . . who has no time for my poems, so pledged is she to reading the work of her more intimate sisters" instead of "the reader I try not to write to, my old college professor," the poet's bête noire of established (read *male*) literary culture. David Baker and Philip Levine seem admirably candid. "Let's get real," says Baker. "First of all, I write poems *for* people who read poems." Levine, remembering his early career, summons up "three readers: myself, my identical twin brother and something or someone else whose identity remained a mystery to me . . . , that being or soul that I thought we all partook of." T. R. Hummer, who is rarely at a loss for words on any subject, rambles on for eight pages before addressing a Marxian (Groucho, not Karl) audience that contains "even *me*, however reluctant I may be to join a club that would have me as a member." The ever-equivocating Robert Pinsky imagines "an actual reader very much like me, yet not me. But that begs the question—what do I mean by 'like me'?" All in all, the *Mānoa* symposium (followed in the Fall issue by a similar one on book reviewing) makes one look forward to reading more of these meetings of the minds in the future.

One could argue endlessly about all of the fine points raised both by Gioia and by the poets in Chappell's symposium, but it is undeniable that most Americans outside of the universities are exposed to very little contemporary poetry. With only a few exceptions, poetry does not appear in our popular magazines or newspapers, and the poems that do appear in mass-circulation periodicals, if I may judge by what I have seen lately in the *New Republic* and the *New Yorker*, are not likely to hold much appeal for even the most loyal subscribers. Other than an occasional sop from the Public Broadcasting Service such as Bill Moyers's *The Power of the Word* (which gave many the impression that being a poet today has largely to do with having an affinity for tom-toms and believing that wolves live under one's bed) or a short poem recited in the wee hours on National Public Radio, poetry has not captured the interest of the electronic media. Most chain bookstores do not stock any contemporary poetry beyond that written by celebrities or Rod McKuen (who, his vogue long past, is even in short supply these days), and the average man or woman wandering down the mall's corridors would be hard pressed to come up with the name of a *single* living contemporary American poet.

Thus, at least at first glance, we should be gladdened by anthologies such as *The Best American Poetry* series from Collier, the two latest editions edited by Jorie Graham and Mark Strand, respectively. Collections such as these do much of the legwork for us, collecting poems from some thirty-five magazines ranging from the well known (the *New Yorker*, the *Atlantic*) to the obscure (*Hambone*, *O.blek*, *Temblor*). Series editor David Lehman speaks of an attempt "to glean the best work being done today, irrespective of the biases of this man's region and that woman's literary allegiances"; and the editor of the 1990 edition, Jorie Graham, describes her choices as reflecting "the American moment: still in the story we've told ourselves of ourselves, . . . crackling on the surface in that dizzy irreverent self-knowledge that passes today for freedom." Strand, a recent poet laureate, observes,

> The way poetry has of setting our internal houses in order, of formalizing emotion difficult to articulate, is one of the reasons we still depend on it in moments of crisis and during those times when it is important that we know in so many words what we are going through.

High aims, indeed. But what are the results?

When the first edition of *The Best American Poetry* (edited by John Ashbery) appeared in 1988, Fred Chappell published a review titled "Poetry Is So Bad, Book's Pages Must Writhe in Agony," and his list of descriptive adjectives included "banal, empty, cute, exhibitionistic, silly, clumsy, sniveling, arch, smug, prissy, lunatic, sycophantic, snobbish, gossipy, vicious, surly, whorish, and self-gratulatory." Most of Graham's edition is too bland to inspire epithets like these, though "self-indulgent" would certainly head any list I might wish to assemble. To put the problem as simply as possible, the poems in *The Best American Poetry 1990* aren't *about* very much. Amy Clampitt and Thom Gunn provide coherent elegiac pieces, Richard Wilbur has a fine descriptive poem about a wall in "Mr. Bryant's // Homiletic woods" near his home in Cummington, Massachusetts, and a few other poets such as Rodney Jones and Yusef Komunyakaa manage to focus on a specific event or character; but so many of these poems seem such empty exercises in word spinning that one begins to wonder what ever happened to *subject matter* as a necessary part of poems. As much as we try to envision a common reader, it is well nigh impossible to conceive of a being who might derive much delight or instruction from opening passages such as these four:

> The ant stood up on two legs looks like a chesspiece
>   maybe a bishop.
>
> Toppled
> down backward six feet through stifled heat
> onto dry grass. The sacrificial
> smell of grilling beef.
> Telephone cables jammed with chit-chatting starlings
>   make self-consciousness the sky.
>
> Attention was commanded through a simple, unadorned, unexplained,
>   often decentered presence,
> up to now, a margin of empty space like water, its surface
>   contracting, then melting
> along buried pipelines, where gulls gather in euphoric buoyancy.
>
> A yak is a prehistoric cabbage: of that, at least, we
>   may be sure.

If this represents the best of the year, what, in Graham's estimation, could the *worst* be like?

Strand's 1991 edition seems a little better, on the whole, than Graham's, starting off strongly with the second poem in the book, Ai's "Evidence: From a Reporter's Notebook," a monologue filled with the journalist-persona's bitter ambivalence about an alleged incident of racial and sexual violence reminiscent of the Tawana Brawley affair:

> It could have happened. That is the bridge
> that links the world of Kafka to us still,
> the black pearl in pig's mouth
> that won't be blasted out no matter what we do,
> that finds us both on Oprah
> or on Donahue, facing the packed pews
> of the damned and the saved,
> to send out innocence,
> our guilt, across the crowded airwaves
> to be filtered through
> the ultimate democracy of TV. . . .

Among many others collected here in almost three hundred pages of verse and an additional section of authors' comments about their work are poems by James Merrill, David Trinidad (from "Reruns," a tart cycle of haiku drawn from vintage television shows: "Samantha looked at / the dirty dishes. 'Just this / once,' she thought, and twitched."), Katha Pollitt, and James

McManus, whose "Smash and Scatteration" is a wild and woolly sequence of thirteen fifteen-line poems that weaves together bits of vintage rock trivia, snatches of televised violence from China and the third world, and the speaker's affair with Linda, a performance artist with a unique specialty: "Linda stands on a table in green suede high / heels about two feet apart and pees into a teacup." All too often, though, the anthology's pages teem with the bland or the simply unbelievable, as witness these representative lines from Kenneth Koch's "A Time Zone," an autobiographical narrative about the poetry and art scene in New York in the early 1950s:

> I am of New York not a native
> I'm from Cincinnati which is to this place nominative like a remote dative
> In 1948 from college I come here and finally settle
> The city is hot and bright and noisy like a giant boiling kettle
> My first connection to it aside from touristy is sexual
> A girl met here or there at first nothing serious or contextual
> That is earlier now I'm here to live on street subway and bus
> I find people exciting unrecognizable and of unknown-to-me social class
> Finally they start to come into focus

A few lines of this—it goes on for eleven pages—should be enough to cure anyone of nostalgia for rhyme. Koch (who can, believe it or not, write traditional metrics skillfully—a book-length narrative poem of his some years ago was composed in ottava rima) has here, in what seems a misguided attempt to imitate Guillaume Apollinaire, adopted instead the manner of William McGonagall, whose interminable doggerel earned him the reputation of being the world's most wretched poet. Koch pushes one's tolerance for campy performances to the limit, but at least he is entertainingly bad; more typically we get a blandness such as Louise Glück's in the opening stanza of "Celestial Music":

> I have a friend who still believes in heaven.
> Not a stupid person, yet with all she knows, she
>   literally talks to god,
> she thinks someone listens in heaven.
> On earth, she's usually competent.
> Brave, too, able to face unpleasantness.

There probably aren't enough good poems in *The Best American Poetry 1991* to make it worth

Still autographing balls for boys,
Mother of mercy, what's the answer?

Is there a heaven with rainbow flags,
Silver trophies hung on walls,
A horseshoe grandstand, mobs of fans,
Webbed gloves and official balls?

Mother of mercy, if you're there,
Pray to the high celestial czar
For all of these, the early dead,
Who've gone where no ovations are.

As novelist W. P. Kinsella points out about this "most literary of sports": "Baseball is poetry. Baseball is ballet. Baseball is chess. Baseball is mystery. Most of all mystery." As the title of a poem by Jack Ridl states, adjusting to the game's place in a changing society provides "Good Training for Poetry": "Now, one week each spring / I watch my daughter / take her cuts, slap her hand / into the pocket of her mitt." About all I miss seeing here is a sample of Kenneth Koch's *Ko, or a Season on Earth*, a wacky mock-epic about a Japanese baseball player that stands as the sport's *Orlando Furioso* (which has nothing to do, incidentally, with the anger of the great slugger of the Giants and Cardinals).

Two anthologies of poems about music will appeal to many readers. *Mixed Voices: Contemporary Poems about Music* (Milkweed), edited by Emilie Buchwald and Ruth Boston, uses Wallace Stevens's "Mozart, 1935" for a preparatory piece:

Poet, be seated at the piano.
Play the present, its hoo-hoo-hoo.
Its shoo-shoo-shoo, its ric-a-nic,
Its envious cachinnation.

Of the two anthologies, *Mixed Voices* ranges more widely, from poems on Johann Sebastian Bach's *Goldberg Variations* (1741) and Wolfgang Amadeus Mozart to others on Charlie Parker and The Platters. Grace Bauer poses one universal question of the generation of the 1960s, remembering how, years later, "we still wondered what the Kingsmen / really sang in *Louie, Louie*." Oddly, the volume contains no poems on opera, a subject that has attracted many contemporary poets.

The Jazz Poetry Anthology (Indiana University Press), edited by Sascha Feinstein and Yusef Komunyakaa, contains 250 pages of poetry, probably more than anyone would ever desire on the subject. Poems by Stevens, Carl Sandburg, and William Carlos Williams come as something of a

surprise; on the other hand, I looked in vain for anything by Weldon Kees, a poet who was also a jazz composer, or poems by E. E. Cummings or Vachel Lindsay, probably the first American poet (antedating even Langston Hughes) whose rhythms show the influence of jazz, or an individual favorite of mine, Richard Hugo's "My Buddy." The anthology contains a helpful appendix listing the individual artists, from Cannonball Adderly to Lester Young, dealt with in the poems. It does seem to be stretching the book's limits a bit to include two poems about Janis Joplin (by Marilyn Hacker and Alice Fulton) and absolutely nothing about any other rock musician. Which jazz artists have inspired the most homage? It looks like a three-way dead heat among John Coltrane, Thelonious Monk, and Charlie Parker. Coltrane's memory will probably survive Sonia Sanchez's dissonances:

EECCCCHHHHHHH
SCREEEEEEEEEEEEEEEEEEEEEEEEEEEEEE
    EEEEEECHHHHHHHHHH
BRING IN THE WITE/LIBERALS ON THE
    SOLO
SOUND OF YO/FIGHT IS MY FIGHT
            SAXOPHONE.
        TORTURE
THEM FIRST AS THEY HAVE
        TORTURED US WITH
PROMISES/
    PROMISES. IN WITE/AMURICA.

Perhaps more fitting as a tribute are these lines from Michael S. Harper's "Dear John, Dear Coltrane":

You plod up into the electric city—
your song now crystal and
the blues. You pick up the horn
with some will and blow
into the freezing night:
a love supreme, a love supreme. . . .

Three other anthologies bear brief mention. *Blood to Remember: American Poets on the Holocaust* (Texas Tech University Press) was edited by Charles Fishman, himself the author of a book on the subject, *The Death Mazurka* (1987). With over four hundred pages of unrelieved grimness, the collection is not likely to attract casual readers of poetry, but its amplitude is proof of the event's impact on artists' sensibilities. I particularly admire the closing of Enid Shomer's "Women Bathing at Bergen-Belsen," which de-

picts the camp a scant twelve hours after its liberation:

> Though nudity was
> a death sentence here, they have undressed,
> oblivious to the soldiers and the cameras.
> The corpses push through the limed earth like up-
>   ended
> headstones. The bathers scrub their feet, bending
> in beautiful curves, mapping the contours
> of the body, that kingdom to which they've re-
>   turned.

*American Indian Poetry: An Anthology of Songs
and Chants* (Fawcett Columbine), edited by
George W. Cronyn, is a reissue of a collection
first published in 1918. Those who think that interest in things Native American begins with
Kevin Costner would do well to peruse this volume, which, as Kenneth Lincoln's new introduction points out, came out of the post-World War I
sense of cultural exhaustion that produced Ezra
Pound's *Hugh Selwyn Mauberly* (1920) and stimulated poets worldwide—T. S. Eliot and William
Butler Yeats are only two—to reinvigorate old mythologies. I did not know that *Poetry* ran two issues devoted to what was then called "aboriginal"
poetry in 1917 and 1920; the first of these was apparently Cronyn's chief stimulus to assemble the
anthology, which, according to Lincoln, occupied
"the position of lead text in Jorge Luis Borge's
classes on the American canon."

*The Space Between: Poets from Notre Dame,
1950-1990* (University of Notre Dame), edited by
James Walton, was produced for that university's
sesquicentennial. I was tempted at first to dismiss
it as a mere public relations ploy, but a quick
look at the table of contents reveals several distinguished poets—John Frederick Nims, Samuel
Hazo, John Logan, Michael Ryan—who have
been either students or faculty members there;
two of the latter group, Ernest Sandeen and
Sonia Gernes, published individual collections
with the same press in recent years and were reviewed in these pages. Still, I can't imagine that
many readers or even libraries will rush their orders in for an anthology of such limited appeal.

Relatively few large collected editions appeared in 1991; of the year's crop, *If I Had
Wheels or Love: Collected Poems of Vassar Miller*
(Southern Methodist University) must rank as a
must for serious libraries. Over the years Miller
has garnered praise from other poets as diverse
as George Garrett (who provides an introduction
to the present volume), James Wright, Donald

*Dust jacket for a selection of poems by a poet who committed sui-
cide in 1978 at the age of twenty-nine*

Hall, Henry Taylor, Denise Levertov, and Richard Wilbur, yet, after early books from Wesleyan
University Press and appearances in key anthologies of the 1950s such as *New Poets of England and
America* (1957), she seems to have been pigeon-
holed in a way that has discouraged any important reevaluation of her accomplishments.

Miller's formal conservatism is exemplified
by the title itself, part of the collection's final
line: "If I had wheels or love, I would be gone."
The meter is strict iambic; the line part of the re-
frain of a villanelle. Miller early developed a compact repertoire of traditional verse forms—
sonnet, couplet, quatrain, blank verse—which she
has frequently utilized, and, since the mid 1960s,
she has also written a considerable amount of
free verse. In this respect she invites comparison
with another woman of her generation,
Gwendolyn Brooks. Here, in the much admired
"Autumnal Spring Song," Miller demonstrates
her skills with the formal lyric:

When every branch is whole
The bitter sword of spring
Will scar the forest's soul
And mine remembering
   That the trees bloom on forever,
   But with the same leaves never.

The two alternative wishes in Miller's title should also be noted. The first is the desire to have "wheels." Miller has cerebral palsy, and her own perception of her physical condition is essential, as subtext, to understanding her fully. From the book's first poem, which mentions "My crooked step wrenched straight," through lines such as "I even carry my own rock / hard in my mouth, / grinding it out bit by bit," we are made aware of how perilously close she has always felt to one like the "Spastic Child," with "His mind, bright bird, forever trapped in silence." When she deals directly with her handicap, it is with the restraint and tact of the aptly titled "Subterfuge":

I remember my father, slight,
staggering in with his Underwood,
bearing it in his arms like an awkward bouquet

for his spastic child who sits down
on the floor, one knee on the frame
of the typewriter, and holding her left wrist

with her right hand, in that precision known
to the crippled, pecks at the keys
with a sparrow's preoccupation.

The other wish in the book's title is for love, and there is a powerful erotic element in Miller's poetry. Perhaps because we find ourselves embarrassed to imagine the sexual lives of the physically handicapped, it becomes too easy to write off Miller's yearnings as mystical, turning her into a sort of regional Christina Rossetti. When asked about the way certain poets fuse sensual imagery and religious passion, Miller replied, "whoever wrote the Song of Solomon was writing a straight love poem. It was the Church Fathers who gave it the allegorical interpretation." The predominance of sexual imagery, often autoerotic ("lust's one-finger exercise"), in poems with no discernible religious context indicates to me that a desire for physical fulfillment precedes the spiritual in Miller's list of priorities. When, again in the book's title poem, she speaks of being "Kissed on my breast or belly where I'd play" or of "Fonding your flanks, my dear, made clouds from clay" she is much closer to the spirit of Walt Whitman than to that of Saint John of the Cross.

Now nearing her seventies, she strikes me as one of the most representative, and most often overlooked, poets of her generation.

Four other retrospective editions by American women poets, two of them deceased, appeared in 1991. The centenary edition of Edna St. Vincent Millay's *Selected Poems* (HarperCollins), edited by Colin Falck, will doubtless cause some reassessment of her place in the modernist canon, which was already in jeopardy when she died in 1950. Falck's introduction does not make hyperbolic claims for Millay's work and contains some straight talk about the reasons for the fluctuations of her literary reputation:

Millay is no longer a part of any trend or tendency that is seen as having helped to make American poetry what it is today . . . , and her distinctive achievement, like that of any poet whose work relies on lyrical directness or firmness of tone, is almost entirely incapable of being discussed within the reflexive and involuted terms of present-day critical debate.

Yet, as Richard Wilbur observes, "I know that Millay is a good poet because there are so many of her lines in my memory," a claim many will substantiate when they come across "What lips my lips have kissed, and where, and why, / I have forgotten . . ." or "My candle burns at both ends; / It will not last the night" or "Love is not all: it is not meat nor drink / Nor slumber nor a roof against the rain." Allen Tate once noted that she "stood athwart two ages," and her blend of late-Romantic lyrical techniques with Roaring Twenties subject matter (she is the F. Scott Fitzgerald of American poetry—read "Recuerdo") helps to explain the phenomenal appeal that put upwards of a quarter million of her books in print. For the most part, she will still seem too much the affected "poetess," prisoner of a bygone perception of what a woman poet was expected to be; at times, however, when she tones down her lyrical mannerisms, she can sound strikingly contemporary, as in these lines from the last section of "Sonnets from an Ungrafted Tree," a sequence describing a wife's reaction to her husband's final illness:

Gazing upon him now, severe and dead,
  It seemed a curious thing that she had lain
Beside him many a night in that cold bed,
  And that had been which would not be again.

Kay Boyle, born in 1902, was part of the Parisian literary scene of the 1920s; she was married for a time to Robert McAlmon and traveled in the same circles as Samuel Beckett, James Joyce, the Fitzgeralds, and Ernest Hemingway. Really now, what living American poet could wish for more than a jacket photograph by Man Ray? The *Collected Poems of Kay Boyle* (Copper Canyon) sports one. Remarkably, after a versatile career as novelist, journalist, and poet that started in 1917, she is still active; the most recent poem here, completed with the help of her son, Ian Franckenstein, is dated November 1990. Obviously a poet who, in 1925, could title a poem "In Defense of Homosexuality" ("I speak of it as a thing with a future") has long been on the cutting edge of things. Like her mentor, Marianne Moore, Boyle favors the outrageous opening assertion; "A Poem About the Jews" begins, "I have had enough of them, more than enough; / Enough of the pages alloted to them, the margins / Crowded with faces." Some of the best work in this slim (172 pages) collection of her total poetic output dates from the late 1960s, when Boyle, teaching at San Francisco State University, apparently found that the expatriate disaffections of an earlier era had come home to roost among her own students.

Louise McNeill (born in 1911) is a true anomaly, a regional poet whose traditional lyrics and ballads about rural West Virginia (she has been that state's poet laureate since 1979) will invite comparison with Jesse Stuart's work. *Hill Daughter: New & Selected Poems* (University of Pittsburgh) contains work from her first book, published by Harcourt Brace in 1939 when regional work such as hers could find populist champions such as Archibald MacLeish and Stephen Vincent Benét. McNeill's verse provides yet another reminder of how mistaken the notion is that "people's poetry" is supposed to sound like the plainspoken non-measures of William Carlos Williams. Here, in a passage about a 1907 disaster in Monongah that killed 361 coal miners, McNeill chooses quatrains of dactylic tetrameter for her form:

Say that these men were from far-distant countries:
"Hunkies" and "Tallies," and Russian and Pole,
Welshman and Irish—then some from the mountains—
And all of them diggers, who dug in the coal.

See how they come to the portals that morning,

Lamps on their foreheads and lunch pails that shine;
See how they stand for a hesitant moment;
Watch how they vanish down into the mine.

Maggie Anderson's introduction, while perhaps too inclusive in its definition of populism (Muriel Rukeyser and Thomas Wolfe, to mention only two, seem ill fitted to this discussion), does discuss some of the reasons by which, until recently, the "populist literature of the 1930s [was] relegated to historical eccentricity, and . . . effectively erased from the literary canon."

May Swenson (1911-1989) was a prolific and endlessly inventive poet who still seems, despite having won the Bollingen Prize and many other awards, to get something of a slight whenever a list of major contemporary figures is compiled. *The Love Poems of May Swenson* (Houghton Mifflin) reveals her intimate side, an aspect of her poetry I would not automatically have thought of amid so many poems that succeed on the strength of sheer verbal and formal *fun*. This brief (eighty-five pages) collection makes a good claim for her as a brilliant, if somewhat limited, erotic lyricist. There is, perhaps, an overabundance of apostrophes, personifications, and overpretty nature imagery, though at their best these poems seem almost the verbal equivalent of Georgia O'Keeffe's "gynomorphic" flowers. Here is a bee, not so innocently at work:

He scrubs
himself
in her creamy
folds;
a bullet, soft, imposes
her spiral and, spinning, burrows
to her dewy
shadows.

Swenson's personal orientation was homoerotic, but she wrote poems that do not necessarily exclude readers of other persuasions. Marriage, after all, is marriage:

Asleep you flip
over roll
everything under
you and off
me. I'm always grabbing
for my share of the sheets.

It may be something of a left-handed compliment, but I suspect that this collection will hold a large measure of appeal for readers who do not ordinarily read contemporary poetry.

As I write this, reviews of E. E. Cummings's *Complete Poems 1904-1962* (Norton) are beginning to appear. Lacking a review copy, I can make only secondhand comments borrowed from Brad Leithauser's review in the *New Yorker* (3 February 1992). Leithauser notes that Cummings's current "appeal for anthologists and composers of college syllabi looks precarious" and that, unlike most of the other major modernists, he failed "to win a substantial following among today's younger writers," finding his most consistent devotees among adolescents who perhaps identify with a poet who "steadfastly remained mr. lower case." This is a huge volume containing approximately a thousand poems, and, as one might expect, more than enough bad apples to taint at least, if not spoil, the barrel. Still, Cummings's inventiveness had its moments (I still take delight in the columnar poem describing the fall of a lonely leaf or the cubist attempt at capturing a grasshopper's leap), and he was an excellent, if eccentric, sonneteer and lyricist. I can still remember hearing, in an inspired defense of his talents, John Ciardi pausing in the middle of a recitation to marvel at "up so floating many bells down." Leithauser observes that the primary targets of Cummings's satirical sting—in particular the machine age and the all-trampling progress of modern "manunkind"—were identical to those of the generation that came of age shortly after his death in 1962, but he ironically speculates that Cummings might not have responded in wholehearted manner to the Aquarian Age:

> Is it unfair to suppose that this antimaterialist, pacifist, protoenvironmentalist would have been profoundly discomfited by the triumph of so much of what he stood for? Wouldn't his constant cranky desire to be seen as a hard-pressed loner have insured his recoiling from the hippie's brotherly embrace?

So many editions of new and selected poems by poets with established reputations arrived that it is impossible to do justice to more than a handful of them. Twenty years ago I purchased an anthology called *The Major Young Poets* (1971), edited by Al Lee, and among the eight poets included (all male, all under thirty-five at the time) were Mark Strand, C. K. Williams, Marvin Bell, and Charles Simic, all of whom have established reputations that have seemed to support the editor's claims. Among the others in the anthology, James Tate and David Young issued selected editions in 1991, both from the same publisher. Tate's *Selected Poems* (Wesleyan University Press) gathers two decades of work, from his 1967 Yale Series of Younger Poets winner *The Lost Pilot* (the title poem of which, an elegy to the poet's father, remains one of his strongest, though least typical, poems) through *Reckoner* of 1986; for some reason no poems appear from *Distance from Loved Ones* (1990), which was reviewed in these pages last year. At that time I observed, "Tate's brand of surrealism has always seemed to me a peculiarly homegrown variant; if he resembles any past writers, it is not Breton or Eluard but Americans such as James Thurber and Robert Benchley." Here is an indicative sample, "Teaching the Ape to Write Poems":

> They didn't have much trouble
> teaching the ape to write poems:
> first they strapped him into the chair
> then tied the pencil around his hand
> (the paper had already been nailed down).
> Then Dr. Bluespire leaned over his shoulder
> and whispered into his ear:
> "You look like a god sitting there.
> Why don't you try writing something?"

Tate and Russell Edson are the only two poets who come to mind currently working this vein of skewed satire; when Tate avoids Edson's extremes and does not allow the dogs in his narratives to grow too shaggy he can be very entertaining. True, it is entertainment without a great deal of substance—somewhat like a performance by a hip comic like the Steve Martin of years past—but in the face of so much mock solemnity from Tate's contemporaries, this "kook's tour" is breezy and diverting. It is practically impossible to resist an opening like that of "The Chaste Stranger": "All the sexually active people in Westport / look so clean and certain, I wonder / if they're dead." Too often, though, the rest of the poems don't live up to their initial promise, and the reader is left with associations as random as the one of a child "lumbering through the lumberyard / like a titmouse with goosebumps." Imagery like this, so much in vogue in the graduate schools of the early 1970s (Tate is a University of Iowa M.F.A.) has almost vanished from the contemporary scene.

David Young (writing then as David P. Young) struck me at the time of *The Major Young Poets* as being the weakest of the eight, given to gooey passages such as "She's my summer /

peaches, corn, long moondawn dusks / watermelons chilling in a tub / of ice and water," and, unlike the other poets in the anthology, overly fond of writing fragmentary poems, in the manner of Stevens, in numbered sections. The title poem of *The Planet on the Desk: Selected and New Poems 1960-1990* (Wesleyan University Press) will bring the modernist master to mind, even if the voice does not:

> The planet on the desk, illuminated globe
> we ordered for Bo's birthday,
> sits in its Lucite crescent, a medicine ball
> of Rand McNally plastic. A brown cord
> runs from the South Pole toward a socket.

One of the anthology poems that I did like (not, alas, included in the new collection) was a satirical piece in five deadpan sections called "The Death of the Novel." Here is the fourth:

> And now the glade
> where Stan was sprawled
> grew still. A bird
> twittered, insects drowsed.
>
> And then
> a shrill scream came
> from the middle distance,
> came again, and Stan's
> heart jumped. The noon
> express! Would Anne, or Kim,
> be on that train?

Today, Young remains a highly literary poet; among the new pieces is a "Stevens Ghazal," and there are other poems for or about James Wright, Vladimir Nabokov, Osip Mandelstam, and Jean Follain. One of the best concerns the thoughts of the century's most significant *poète maudit*, Chairman Mao Tse-tung:

> I would have done it
> with poems! Instead
> I have come to be
> a red book, a pumped-up myth,
> from Long March to Big Swim
> surfacing, always surfacing. . . .

Despite his ability to come up with good ideas for poems, Young employs a flat, uninspired idiom; on occasion, though, he can rise above sea level, as in these parodic lines that anyone who has ever wrestled with "easy assembly" instructions will recognize: "Put tip of pot through loop. Pull tight. / Call this position B. File flash

and sand. / Use adze to strike off wobbly-pump / of Handley-Page or Spad. Dry roller stocks, / make notch in carrick bits with extra pick / and fit in spindle bush."

Robert Sward is another Iowa product. "Iowa Writers' Workshop—1958," from *Incarnations: New & Selected Poems 1957-1991* (Coffee House), will doubtless strike a familiar chord with anyone who has spent an evening slogging through a worksheet full of bad poems-in-progress:

> "The poet has here been impressed
> by the relationship
> between blue birds and black. In the octet
> we note the crow. And its iambic death."
> "On page three, *The Poet upon His Wife*
> (by his wife), we note the symbols
> for the poet: the bird
> in flight, the collapsing crow, the blue bird . . .
> Note too the resemblance between sonnets."

Fittingly, the poem is dedicated to Paul Engle. Some poets (Edward Field comes to mind) have the magical ability to succeed on the sheer appeal of personality, and Sward is one of them. His foreword to the collection, here describing his teenage stint as corresponding secretary for a Chicago street gang, sets the tone for much of the poetry that is to follow: "My job was to write postcards to inform my brother thugs—who carried switchblade knives and stole cars for fun and profit—as to when, where and why we were meeting. Rhyming couplets seemed the appropriate form. . . ." Later, Sward informs us that he has lately worked as a Jewish "Rent-a-Santa Claus." One of the best poems in the book describes one of the poet's personal "incarnations," when he was hit by a car in 1966 and suffered from spells of amnesia intermittently for years thereafter:

> "Making love, it's always as if it were happening
> For the first time," I said after ten years of marriage.
> "When a woman chooses an amnesiac as her husband,
> she has to expect things like that," she laughed.

Carolyn Kizer describes Sward's poems as the kind you want to read over the phone to friends you have called up—high praise in my book.

Robert Morgan's thoughtful bucolics were on display in last year's *Sigodlin* (the title refers to Appalachian slang for buildings that are slightly out of square) and even more extensively in

Green River: New and Selected Poems (Wesleyan University Press). Over the years Morgan has become more expansive in his forms and in his subjects. The early poems collected here often seem to speak in the voice of a southern-accented Charles Simic; their gnomic quality is best exhibited in "White Pines":

> Standing beneath huge pilings.
> Up there where the sea broke, browsed along the
> sand
> millions of years ago.
> A faint surf breaks far overhead.

As he develops confidence in his own poetic voice, Morgan leaves this sort of elliptical conceit for deeper explorations of the possibilities his subjects afford. Anyone who has worked around cut cedar will recall the "Faint musk of old arrows, canoe ribs. / Wood still giving / its breath, radioactive—releasing / a subtle verb for years / to fill whatever room or closet it lies in." Similarly Morgan's poetry has become more richly peopled over the years; he does not sentimentalize his mountain kith and kin, and their stories are often bluntly tragic. "Mountain Bride" tells of a new husband unwittingly awaking a nest of rattlesnakes when he lights a fire on his wedding night. In the morning he rises from bed and is fatally bitten:

> he died yelling her to stay
> on the big four-poster.
> Her uncle coming up the hollow
> with a gift bearham two days later
>
> found her shivering there
> marooned above a pool
> of hungry snakes,
> and the body beginning to swell.

Diane Ackerman, who is barely in her forties, probably does not yet merit a 250-page volume of poetry, but the best-selling nonfiction book *A Natural History of the Senses* and her reporting on the animal kingdom have made her a hot literary property of late, and one should not be greatly surprised that *Jaguar of Sweet Laughter: New and Selected Poems* (Random House) has the look and heft of a major production backed by the full force of a large publishing house (as I write this, it has just been nominated for the National Book Critics Circle Award). Ackerman's poems don't always measure up to the promise of her titles—"A. R. Ammons amid the Fungi,"

"How like a Virus Entering a Cell"—but she mixes together such a smorgasbord of subjects, from Patrick Ewing to Antarctica, that the reader rarely feels that she is merely repeating herself. About half the time, though, these subjects seem somewhat undercooked—good ideas for poems that might have been allowed to simmer awhile longer. Most readers will recognize the details in "Letter to Wallace Stevens" and will doubtless feel that Ackerman hasn't found a way to approach a subject she knows solely from her reading:

> The new biography makes me a fortuneteller
> in reverse. I watch you weaken
> in your garden robust with peonies
> where you ushered in the world
> and escaped your wife (whose face, on the liberty
> dime,
> sat in your pants pocket all day).

When her language rises to the same level as her inventiveness, however, she can be quite formidable. "Life Sentence" is a dizzy catalogue of primal natural forces linked by anaphora: "aside from the winter/spring / polemic quibbling over a dry seedpod till it / sounds like a hooded mamba or a harpist." Here is the conceit's denouement:

> aside from that vague psoriasis
> of the spirit that threatens my bone-house
> with foreclosure, the brainpantry teeming,
> and the will as bloodthirsty as a tick; I mean
> aside from all these obvious concessions,
> I keep asking myself: what does gravity demand?

I have the feeling that Ackerman, somewhere far back in her academic career, must have cut her poetic teeth on the English Metaphysicals.

The Light the Dead See: The Selected Poems of Frank Stanford (University of Arkansas Press) collects the best of a remarkable body of work (including an epic poem of over five hundred pages) completed by the poet before his suicide in 1978 at age twenty-nine. Editor Leon Stokesbury's introduction tells us of a childhood along the Mississippi River, where Stanford, the adopted son of an engineer, was often the only white child in the levee camps his father ran. After his father's death, these early years, largely spent among rural blacks and their folklore and superstitions, loomed larger, eventually providing him the basis of his poetry. As he educated himself through wide reading in European literature and desultory attendance at the University of Arkansas, Stanford developed a homegrown brand of surrealism that sounds like no one else; if he resembles anyone it is the "magical realists" of South America, with a healthy dose of Arthur Rimbaud thrown in for good measure. Here is a stanza from "The Snake Doctors":

> I carved wild hog out of a cypress knee
> I made it the handle
> I made four tushes out of the hambone
> I used the blade I brought out of the fire
> And sealed the pig with
> It was the blade I put the burning horse to sleep
>   with
> I called the knife the Holy Ghost

Stanford's chief originality lies in long, cryptic narratives such as this one, which merges realistic regional details with a revenge plot straight out of Norse legend. As Stokesbury notes, Stanford "possessed an unusual ability to assimilate what he read into his style," and he read a great deal. In another vein, he is quite effective as a strictly regional lyricist. Here, in "Allegory of Death and Night," he describes the nightly ritual of a rural couple:

> When he's dead to the world
> She reaches into the pocket
> Of his trousers for a white pouch.
> She rolls a cigarette with one hand.
> She smokes in the dark. Clouds
> Go by, turning under the soil.
> She turns a flashlight on
> The man's body, looking for seed
> Ticks that have been there since dawn.

All of Stanford's nine books were published by small presses and are thus almost impossible to find; this compact edition provides a useful service in keeping his work available.

So many other new and selected editions crossed my desk in 1991 that I can only give short notice of some of the more significant ones. Peter Meinke's *Liquid Paper: New and Selected Poems* (University of Pittsburgh Press) doesn't quite live up to a jacket note stating that the poet "was a master of traditional poetic forms long before the current interest in 'the new formalism' "; I am hard pressed to find much to support this claim, though Meinke does occasionally use very relaxed versions of traditional forms such as quatrains and sonnets. I like him best as a chronicler of aging, a poet who can open a love poem with "Today is our sixteenth anniversary / the suet anniversay, everything / turning to fat." He is the

Dust jacket for Levine's collection of poems about labor

only poet I have ever read who has the candor to say, apropos the poetry-in-the-schools program, "Come off it, Rousseau. / The eyes roll inward, the brain coughs / like a motor at ten below // and doesn't start: they're not bad kids. / Too dumb for poetry, and smart enough to know / they don't need it: no one needs it. . . ." Like Meinke a writer of prose as well as poetry, James B. Hall has had a distinguished academic career. *Bereavements: Selected and Collected Poems* (Story Line Press) gathers poems written since the author's single published collection. I particularly enjoy "Our Masters, Revisited," a dream vision in which the poet engages in dialogue with the spirits of Theodore Dreiser, Wallace Stevens, and William Faulkner, and the title poem, which eloquently laments moments and companions past: "In the rim of smoke / Above their poker / Table or beyond a fairway / Marker, when I miss them / So, for one moment, / Silently, I show myself." From the same publisher comes Vern Rutsala's *Selected Poems* (Story Line Press), which also contains some good lines on the progress of time. In

"Drinking Late," the collection's most ambitious poem, the poet meditates among the sobering detritus of a New Year's Eve party: "We become our own shadows. / We live by proxy. Yes, yes / and some nights I am scarcely here. / Some nights I must think hard to find / myself. Some force thinks me away. / Some vagueness erases me and I'm / carried into mists, into clouds without shape / or voice."

Other selected volumes include Allen Grossman's *The Ether Dome: New and Selected Poems 1979-1991* (New Directions), a collection recommended by both Harold Bloom and Richard Howard that will doubtless hold appeal for those who miss high modernist effusions like "his voice is carried up by the thermals / At the sea's edge, or down among the dark / Anfractuous trees, and the textile moss" or "The poet is dead, and from his stare released / The stars weary of dance divest themselves / Of countenance." Ruth Whitman's *Laughing Gas: Poems New & Selected 1963-1990* (Wayne State University Press) collects poems dating from the last year before World War II, when the young poet was a student at Bread Loaf Institute, to a large section of new work written in the last decade. Among the new poems, I admire "The Drowned Mountain," a fourteen-part poem about the poet's first husband. The eleventh section describes a hospital room where she finds herself with the dying man and his "second wife and new mistress": "The nurse comes in to adjust the plastic bottles. / She looks at the three of us and says: // *You have many friends.* // *No*, your wife says, *wives*." Joseph Langland's *Selected Poems* (University of Massachusetts Press) contains some unpitying descriptions of farm life, all with titles beginning with "Sacrifice." These lines describe the killing of a sow so wild she eats her own pigs: "And since the old sow had fed / On the offspring she conceived, we strung her up / And slit her throat and stripped her down and ate / That succulent rib with which we kept alive." One of Langland's earlier collections was a selection of the National Poetry Series in 1980. Also received were *Night Perimeter: New and Selected Poems 1958-1990* (Greenfield Review Press), by Gogisigi (Carroll Arnett), a Cherokee poet from Oklahoma; *What Madness Brought Me Here: New and Selected Poems, 1968-1988* (Wesleyan University Press), by Colleen J. McElroy, a poet who draws on her experience as a speech therapist; *Clock of Clay: New and Selected Poems* (Louisiana State University Press), by Robert Hazel, a retired professor living in Florida; and *Sudden Dreams: New & Selected Poems* (Coffee House Press), by George Evans, whose previous work was published in England.

The winners of the year's major awards did not stir up the sort of controversy that arose in 1990 when a book of prose poems by Charles Simic was awarded the Pulitzer Prize, prompting a stern lecture (in the *New Criterion*) to the judges from Louis Simpson on the difference between prose and verse, the mode stipulated by the Pulitzer rules. This year's winner was Mona Van Duyn for *Near Changes* (Knopf), a choice that has followed the pattern set during the last few years of apparently awarding the prize for lifetime achievement (appropriately, Van Duyn turned seventy in 1991) rather than for the strength of the individual collection (Is there anyone out there seriously willing to defend Simic's *The World Doesn't End* (1989) as an important book? I doubt it). Reviewing *Near Changes* (1990) in these pages last year, I noted that Van Duyn had won every major prize except the Pulitzer, though I did not make any predictions that the present volume would rectify the omission. Van Duyn's best work, it still seems to me, is to be found in her 1982 collection, *Letters from a Father, and Other Poems*, the title poem of which is a remarkable sequence of dramatic monologues describing how an aged couple experiences a spiritual renewal through their fascination with observing a bird-feeder, a gift from their child. *Near Changes* is a more personally autumnal collection, with many poems addressed to the poet's husband of many years, Jarvis Thurston, and an equal number of elegiac pieces, including one for critic David Kalstone, the subject of similar poems in recent collections by James Merrill and Anthony Hecht. Van Duyn's forte lies in her genius at finding the usable contemporary detail in newspaper stories or even on the supermarket shelves (in this respect she resembles Karl Shapiro and the late Howard Nemerov, her sometime colleague at Washington University in Saint Louis); her main faults, lack of compression and occasional sentimentality, often seem to go hand in hand with slack meters and awkward rhymes. These stanzas, which come perilously close to doggerel, are from "Condemned Site," a villanelle:

No one answers the ring of phone, the knocks from
   dusk to dawn
of Sorrow's cost-accountant, the would-be re-
   arranger

of Love's old boardinghouse. The shades of five
    rooms are drawn

on the Heart's unlicensed embalming. Soon, fenced
    from the lawn,
only the watching world, privacy's dog-in-the-
    manger,
can say Peter, Tom, David, Jim and Howard are
    gone,

and even the world, turning, will glimpse them
    alive in a spawn
of unchanging images they tore from Time, the
    changer.

A rigorously pruned selected volume of Van
Duyn's work, long overdue, might have proven a
more appropriate recipient of American poetry's
most prestigious award.

    After an absence of almost a decade a po-
etry prize was reinstated this year by the National
Book Awards. The winner was Philip Levine,
also a recipient in 1980, for *What Work Is*
(Knopf). Levine embodies most of the strengths
and weaknesses of contemporary American poetry. On the one hand, he can make poetry out
of the slag heaps and greasy waters of the modern industrial landscape, and he has shown a
whole generation of poets what to do with such traditionally "unpoetic" subject matter as minimum-
wage employment or chance encounters with the
scarred and scared. Here is a description of one
of the dreary yet dangerous industrial jobs to
which the book's title alludes:

>   I would descend
> step by slow step into the dim world
> of the pickling tank and there prepare
> the new solutions from the great carboys
> of acids lowered to me on ropes—all from a recipe
> I shared with nobody and learned from Frank
>   O'Mera
> before he went off to the bars on Vernor Highway
> to drink himself to death. A gallon of hydrochloric
> steaming from the wide glass mouth, a dash
> of pale nitric to bubble up, sulphuric to calm,
> metals for sweeteners, cleansers for salts,
> until I knew the burning stew was done.

When Levine lists the "friends who helped me
with these poems and encouraged me to complete them" it comes as no surprise that Larry
Levis, Garrett Hongo, Edward Hirsh, and C. K.
Williams are among them—all younger poets
who betray his influence. Still, I think that some
of the least appealing qualities of American po-

etry today—uninspired idiom, a literalism that
does not transcend the surface of the subject, pro-
saic rhythms and syntax, and general neglect of
the full rhetorical possibilities of language—can
be traced to Levine and, through him, back to William Carlos Williams; this is not to lay the blame
at Levine's feet but merely to point out that
many young poets, in imitating Williams's or
Levine's mature styles, *begin* with a manner that
their elders arrived at only after years of apprenticeship. To refresh my memory I went back to
Levine's work in *New Poets of England and America, Second Selection* (1962). Here is what he
sounded like thirty years ago:

> At last the tiger leaps, and when it hits
> A putrid surf breaks in the drunkard's soul.
> The tiger, done, returns to his patrol.
> The world takes up its trades; the man his wits,
> And, bottom up, he mumbles from the deep,
> "Life was a dream, Oh, may this death be sleep."

No reader in his right mind would, I think, prefer this, but it should at least indicate that Levine
is no untutored "natural." As with Williams,
Levine's "American Grain" aesthetic forces a deliberately anti-intellectual stance, and at times the
poet sounds as pugnacious as actor Robert Conrad: "All this month I've / gone in search of the
right cross, the punch / which had I mastered it
forty years ago / might have saved me from the
worst." But, these demurrals notwithstanding, he
remains one of the most readable of contemporary poets, and he has an abundance of good stories to tell. Knopf also issued Levine's *New Selected Poems* this year, an updated version of the
selected edition that appeared in 1984.

    The winner of the National Book Critics Cir-
cle Award for poetry was Amy Gerstler's *Bitter
Angel* (North Point Press), published in 1990 and
reviewed here last year. Since this prize is determined by ballot of the entire membership of the
NBCC someone must have lobbied extensively
for Gerstler; her book did not come from a
major press, and her periodical publications, with
the exception of poems in *Paris Review*, have
mostly been in small magazines. But both Tom
Clark, perhaps the most influential West Coast
critic, and Jorie Graham ("subtle yet energetic negotiations between the voltages of experimenta-
tion and the undertow of classical balance"—a
heady mix of metaphors there) have been her
champions. *Bitter Angel* has some interesting moments, combining some rather traditional love poetry with prose poems on a variety of subjects.

One section of "The Sexuality of Objects" is addressed to an absent (dead?) lover, who once said, "'Take good care of my piano and hammer, they'll outlast us both.'"

> Well, every item you ever had has outlasted you, from the essential to the useless, regardless of its intentions, including me. The photo album full of small squares of treated paper outlived you, enabling me to kiss your picture, but the acid from my lips is slowly causing the sensitive paper to disintegrate, probably from embarrassment. So I kiss the less delicate handle of your golf club (the putter), and the Oldsmobile's steering wheel, where you gripped it. I kiss the kitchen table where your elbows rested at breakfast, right by the ashtray, and it tastes like Lemon Pledge. I must love what you touched, scouring it for tidbits of you left there.

This is not exactly what I would call *distinguished* writing, but it's hard to dislike it. Granted, Gerstler has wit. I would never have thought of subjecting Nancy Drew to a sexual assault, but I'm glad that *someone* has:

> The stranger's face descending toward hers and his unpleasant breath are the last items to register clearly on the amateur detective's mind as his stout, chapped hands find her sweater clasp. Nancy's miffed when she comes to, lying alone in the road. The culprit's vanished. She notices immediately her purse is gone, and with it, her car keys. Her intuition clicking like a geiger counter, she has a revelation she may have lost more than her compact and billfold to this ruffian, as, with leaden feet, she begins the long walk home.

But it's still difficult to accept this as the best book of the year.

It is even harder to account for the rationale that led to naming Susan Wood's *Canto Santo* (Louisiana State University Press) the Lamont Poetry Selection for 1991, a prize annually awarded to support publication of an American poet's second book. Wood's uniformly one-dimensional poems draw on Texas locales remembered from her childhood ("On Sunday drives / we'd pass the signs for Bug Tussle / and Jot 'Em Down but never see the towns"), relatives like the alcoholic baseball-bum uncle of "Four Roses," who made "The Fort Worth Cats . . . all the sport / there is" for the six-year-old poet, and so many elegiac subjects that the poet at times sounds like a new apostle of the Graveyard School. Wood can sometimes shape an apt simile, as when residents of a declining small town are described as looking "like people on the news, the ones / shoved into police cars just after pictures / of the child's back tattooed by cigarettes," but even here the syntax is flatly expository, and the book's series of garrulous autobiographical narratives (virtually every poem in the book exceeds a page in length) often indulges in bald sentimentalizing and falls victim to what I take to be unintentional humor. Thus one poem describes a lover's young son learning that "It's hard to be a just god, ruling / a universe of hamsters" when he finds "one gerbil dead, / the other eating it": "It's a wonder we don't all fail / growing up. He's inconsolable, sobs / he never wants another thing." In another unguarded passage the poet learns of a close friend's death while eating Chinese food, sparking a moment of bathos worthy of *The Stuffed Owl*: "What I felt / was the shock of a current suddenly shot / through my body, so that the chopsticks flew / from my hands." With sexual harrassment becoming a serious campus issue, one finds it hard to imagine a male poet daring to write lines such as Wood's about a teenage student: "I, for instance, / his teacher, would like, right now, to touch / the fine down on his bare thigh just beneath / his khaki shorts. . . ." This year's judges for the Lamont were Marvin Bell, Robert Morgan, and Lucille Clifton.

The Poets' Prize, established during the period when the National Book Awards gave no poetry award, is annually awarded by a jury of peers, a group of poets who themselves donate the prize money. This year's cowinners were John Haines, for *New Poems: 1980-88* (Story Line Press), and Mark Jarman, for *The Black Riviera* (Wesleyan University Press). A poet primarily associated with the Alaskan wilderness, where he was a homesteader for twenty-five years, Haines is a poet of few flourishes who succeeds through the sheer integrity of his vision. His separation from a once-loved place and the lost treasure of friendships that thrived there constitute the theme of "Rain Country," the book's longest poem and a Pushcart Prize winner. The recent success of *Northern Exposure*, a television series that makes inventive use of Alaskan locales, may influence readers to look into Haines's attempts to get at both the physical and spiritual landscapes he inhabits. Jarman, the poet most often cited when discussions of contemporary narrative poetry surface, recently contributed the thirty-page "Iris," a poem-in-progress, to the *Hudson Review*. The story of a single mother escaping both her abu-

Dust jacket for Middleton's collection of poems influenced by the "mythos of the Old South" and the Agrarians

sive ex-husband and the drug-related murder of her relatives, "Iris" promises to be a classic when it is published as a complete book-length poem. The narratives in *The Black Riviera* are shorter, for the most part, anecdotal vignettes that attract other associations, as if by the centripetal force of the incidents themselves. The title poem relates the ritual of adolescent encounters with a shadowy drug dealer. "The Shrine and the Burning Wheel," the most original piece in the book, makes a symbol of transcendence out of "a gang of boys, / Local boys probably, / Burning the front wheel of a ten-speed" outside a convenience store, an image that magically connects Edna St. Vincent Millay, Janis Joplin, and an unnamed poet Jarman describes who "rested her head / On the heel of her left hand, / Full hair falling to the propped elbow, / And, as the prologue ran on, / Shook a little dandruff from her hair."

　　Competitions provide a means of publication for both unknown and established poets. Among the former, the Yale Series of Younger Poets, open to poets under forty, is perhaps the most prestigious. In 1991 James Dickey suc-

ceeded James Merrill as judge, and his choice was *Bears Dancing in the Northern Air* (Yale University Press) by Christiane Jacox Kyle, a poet and translator who teaches at Eastern Washington University. After several years of puzzling and generally disappointing selections by Merrill, one hoped that Dickey would restore some of the former glory of the series; he explains that he chose Kyle's collection "because of her clear, clean, and highly personal mysticism, the quiet and balance of her imagination, and her ability to articulate both sourced and sourceless joy." Well and good, but when I encounter, in the book's opening poem, such phrases as "the silence between them is a thin scream / splitting open the round terrible silence / of the rising moon" or "the redolent splendor of dust in the spheres" I hear, instead of the thrumming of the oversoul, the approving murmur of the advanced poetry workshop. The book does contain two poems that rise above the ordinary. "Fire Stolen from Heaven" describes the deaf Ludwig van Beethoven conducting the Ninth Symphony (1824): "all stare / in horror as the deaf man, the magician / keeps on lashing the air, his eyes / fixed on a measure all light denies." Another fine poem is "Dialogue in Jordan, Montana," an extended marital colloquy that describes a life made up almost solely of hard winters. The husband speaks:

> Look, my hands know what it is
> to split frozen ground, to drive
> those cedar posts, begging for calluses,
> to winter deep in cold and survive
> again and again, to burden my bones with this. . . .

Kyle's collection contains several sonnets and poems in terza rima, a poetic form rarely encountered these days.

Kathleen Peirce's *Mercy* (University of Pittsburgh Press) is the winner of the Associated Writing Programs Award Series in Poetry, selected this year by Ellen Bryant Voight. At first *Mercy* seems distanced from the reader, with an opening section filled with zoological poems that bring Marianne Moore to mind, as in the case of the continuation of the title "Out of Disappearance Comes":

> the means to disappoint. But the lungfish
> go and go in African Water and who would miss
>   them,
> swimming from under the photographer's boat?
> With their hardy spines, with decorative and useful
> gills, with muscular fins,
> they live to leave us alone.

There is a similarly detached quality throughout the book though Peirce does move into the familiar ground of family history in its second half. Still, the collection gathers strength as it goes along, culminating in the impressive "Parts," a meditation on varieties of amputation and how "the body can be / subtracted into grace":

> I can tell you this now,
> that girl on her honeymoon,
>   I think about her one leg
> clasping at her new husband's waist,
>   how she was especially
> kind to the man with the pincher
>   hand, putting money in it.

The Nicholas Roerich Prize is annually awarded for a first book published by Story Line Press. In 1991 there were two winners, David Mason and Lee McCarthy. Mason's *The Buried Houses* is the more impressive of the two. When it first appeared several years ago in *Crosscurrents* I greatly admired "Blackened Peaches," a longish narrative spoken by a farm woman who remembers her youth at the beginning of the century, the unrequited love an elderly doctor has for her, and the end of a long marriage. On the night of her husband's death she is visited by the doctor's ghost:

> I turned and saw a man beside the door,
> knew him by the wire rims of his glasses,
> his smile peaceful though he was covered with rain.
> I heard his voice with so much gentleness:
> "Sally, all of our illnesses will end."
> When he said my name it was like the sound
> grew inside me till the tears had to fall.
> I could almost feel his hand on my hair.
> By the time I dried my eyes he was gone.

Equally good is "The Nightingales of Andritsena," a monologue spoken by an American woman serving as a translator and guide in Greece. An infatuation with a young man in the tour group makes her aware of her own aging and estrangement from the world of sensual pleasure: "Because of who I am, who I've always been, / I know the nightingales won't let me sleep. / I do not think that I have ever been young. / I do not think I have let myself be young." This is a beautifully sustained collection, and Mason is adept at drawing characters who can make their emotions both believable and recognizable.

Lee McCarthy's *Desire's Door*, the cowinner of the Roerich award, lies much more squarely in the confessional tradition; most of McCarthy's poems display the kind of flip toughness of the born survivor, like a character straight out of a Jim Thompson novel. She is definitely unafraid of being unfashionable, writing a poem made up of tart responses to an individual who asks, "Must you smoke?":

> The truest reply is, "You know I came out here to get
> away from assholes. Neither of us has been success-
>   ful,
> have we?" backed up with a dead-level look. I pull
>   my
> dead-ringer sunglasses down to my lips.

Similarly outspoken is a prose poem on Emily Dickinson, "In the Flesh":

> I am tired of males swearing undying love for
> Emily Dickinson, praising her with a tongue usu-
> ally reserved for Saturday night. I protest it each
> time. *Her poems suffer the confines of her life,* I say.

Think what she could have been, given Venice, Paris, a baby, emeralds in her ears.

This is a collection that succeeds largely on the strength of McCarthy's tart tongue; *Desire's Door* contains several poems about the poet's relationship with her son that poignantly tally the emotional balance sheet of single parenthood.

An important new first-book award comes from the University of Arkansas Press, with the initial competition judged by poet Reed Whittemore. Eric Nelson's *The Interpretation of Waking Life* (University of Arkansas Press) collects work by a poet who has appeared in *Poetry*, *Shenandoah*, and *Western Humanities Review*. I generally find Nelson's poetry too reliant on abstract diction; a poem titled "The Target" contains "innocent," "fatally," "Mercy," "Sovereignty," "sacred," "knowledge," and "grief" in eighteen lines, and as a result the poem fails to come to life. He is best with small triumphs of the quotidian—a house's elderly previous owner who inadvertently dropped sewing needles in the carpet so that "With our shoes off / we step like guests"; a collection of free first volumes of reference books the poet's mother, "a sucker for grocery store / promotions of encyclopedias for children," accumulated; the lessons, learned from Little League, of "How the mediocre, like myself, might / shine in the team's larger light." The title poem relates a truly spooky incident; the poet is wakened in the middle of the night to find a naked, disoriented woman standing in his infant son's doorway. He grabs her and pushes her roughly out the door, later feeling guilty about "the young / drunk girl who wandered lost into our house / expecting something or someone else." When he looks out in the morning, he steps "back / from a drift of deep, unpredicted snow."

The Juniper Prize, awarded by the University of Massachusetts Press, went to Dennis Finnell for *Red Cottage* (University of Massachusetts Press). When an ore boat on Lake Michigan is described as "floating on nothing / but water, and all of the words for water" and when the poet, meditating on his first name, observes, "we may as well be named / for milk, fingers, an orange sliced in half," the uneasy fear surfaces that the reader is in for another session of Semiotics 101. Donald Revell, blurbing the book, says, "If you were to ask me where the American language lives, I would, without hesitation, answer 'in *Red Cottage*'"; it also lives in Finnell's "The Peaceable Kingdom," where the poet seconds the motion by apparently alluding ("I don't know / how to liberate you from your Gaza / of marriage") to Revell's own 1988 collection, *The Gaza of Winter* ("A marriage is a Gaza. Ours is blind at a mill . . ."). Intertextuality, anyone?

The Iowa Poetry Prize, which has been awarded since 1987, was renamed the Edwin Ford Piper Poetry Award in 1991. Winners were Philip Dacey and Lynda Hull. Dacey's *Night Shift at the Crucifix Factory* (University of Iowa Press) is another strong collection from a poet many readers will know best as the coeditor (with David Jauss) of *Strong Measures*, an anthology of contemporary poems in traditional forms that has been widely used in creative-writing classes. This is Dacey's fifth collection and, to my mind, his best—inventive and deeply moving at times. Even if the subsequent poem doesn't quite equal it, "Upon His Mailing a Child Support Check to L.L. Bean and a Check for Sleeping Bags to his Ex-Wife" has to rank as the juiciest title of the year. Poems worth noting include a fine dramatic monologue, "Thomas Eakins: The Secret Whitman Sitting," in which the painter remembers doing a nude study of the dying poet, and "Ars Poetica: A Reply to an Actor Who Complained that Poetry Is Aethereal and Doesn't Have Sweat in It, the Way the Acting Art Does" (possibly the year's worst title), composed in the sweatiest of meters, the Anglo-Saxon alliterative line:

I propose this:

                    poetry's impure

Splendidly soiled

                    with the solid world:

Our armpits are not

                    deodorized by artifice;

Rather, form selves

                    to fan the fumes. . . .

"Coke" begins with the poet's memory of a time when "Coca-Cola was America / and my dad drove its truck." The meditation grows progressively more hyperbolic as the child-persona thanks God for his favorite drink:

And sometimes I even thought of his
son on the cross, getting vinegar
but wanting Coke. I knew that if I
had been there, I would have handed a Coke
up to him, who would have figured out
how to take it, even though his hands
were nailed down good, because he was God.
And I would have said when he took it,
"That's from America, Jesus."

Whatever reservations one might have about Dacey's work, it would be impossible for even the most demanding reader to fault him for lack of originality.

Lynda Hull's *Star Ledger* (University of Iowa Press) conflates memories of a Newark childhood ("Traffic stalls to bricks shattering, / the windows, inside her, bitch I love you, city breaking / down and pawnshops disgorge their contraband of saxophones // and wedding rings. Give me a wig, give me / a pistol.") with movie fantasies that begin with the book's first poem and continue through allusions to Myrna Loy, Jean Harlow, Lauren Bacall, and other figures of romance. "Utsori" is an intriguing meditation on an unfamiliar word:

> The Japanese call this *utsori*,
>
> a way of finding beauty at the point
> it is altered, so it is not the beauty
>
> of the rose, but its evanescence
> which tenders the greater joy.

Four of the five winners of the National Poetry Series arrived for review and merit mention. John Balaban's *Words for My Daughter* (Copper Canyon Press) was selected by W. S. Merwin. Many will remember Balaban as one of the best poets to have written about Vietnam (where he did alternative service as a conscientious objector) and as a former winner of the Lamont. The title poem recalls an incredibly motley assortment of the poet's childhood friends, most of whom escaped childhood with no shortage of scars:

> So, these were my playmates. I love them still
> for their justice and valor and desperate loves
> twisted into shapes of hammer and shard.
> I want you to know about their pain
> and about the pain they could loose on others.
> If you're reading this, I hope you will think,
> Well, my Dad had it rough as a kid, so what?
> If you're reading this, you can read the news
> and you know that children suffer worse.

A deeply felt compassion has always been the hallmark of Balaban's poetry, and it is in evidence here. This generally likable collection includes several poems about the poet's experiences hitchhiking through the western states.

Billy Collins's *Questions About Angels* (William Morrow) was selected by Edward Hirsch. The book opens with "American Sonnet," a meditation on a peculiarly native mode of self-expression:

> We do not speak like Petrarch or wear a hat like Spenser
> and it is not fourteen lines
> like furrows in a small, carefully plowed field
> but the picture postcard, a poem on vacation,
> that forces us to sing our songs in little rooms
> or pour our sentiments into measuring cups.

Collins is an example of that increasingly endangered bird, the poet with a sense of humor. He writes of "The History Teacher" who, to protect his students' innocence, tells them that "The Spanish Inquisition was nothing more / than an outbreak of questions such as / 'How far is it from here to Madrid?' / 'What do you call the matador's hat?'" At times, Collins sounds a bit too much like Kenneth Koch ("Where has the summer of 1572 gone? Brocade and sonnet / marathons were the rage. We used to dress up in the flags / of rival baronies and conquer one another in cold rooms of stone."), but one could pick few better mentors for this sort of thing. This is Collins's fourth collection, and it is a pleasure to make his acquaintance belatedly.

The three other winners bear brief mention. Laura Mullen's *The Surface* (University of Illinois Press), selected by C. K. Williams, is a first book. Mullen has a variety of prose poems and poems with long lines which link her to Williams. The most interesting sustained piece is "The Holmes Poems," a sequence of seven sonnetlike poems which integrates "found" elements from the Sherlock Holmes stories in the sections' speculations on the sleuth's own obsessions. Thylias Moss's *Rainboy Remnants in Rock Bottom Ghetto Sky* (Persea), selected by Charles Simic, follows quickly on the heels of Moss's two recent books, *Pyramid of Bone* (1989) and *At Redbones* (1990). Moss's mix of black folk themes (one poem is about asafetida, a home remedy for colds and flu) with surrealistic techniques makes her a rather obscure and difficult poet, though "Interpretation of a Poem by Frost," which reimagines "Stopping by Woods on a Snowy Evening" from the perspective of a young black girl, admits a few more rays of light than most of Moss's other poems. The fifth winner of the series, Roger Fanning's *The Island Itself* (Viking), chosen by Michael Ryan, was not received for review.

Nineteen ninety-one was not a vintage year for collections by the senior generation of American poets. Two useful posthumous editions did appear, by Kenneth Rexroth (1905-1982) and Thomas McGrath (1916-1990). Rexroth's *Flower Wreath Hill: Later Poems* (New Directions) is a reprint of two collections originally published in the 1970s. Rexroth, paterfamilias of the extended tribe of San Francisco poets, turned increasingly to the East for his subjects in his later years, living in Kyoto during the last decade of his life and translating from both Chinese and Japanese. He did not, however, totally abandon his aesthetic heritage, which even a cursory glance will reveal is deeply rooted in the rank soil of Dr. William Carlos Williams's Rutherford, New Jersey:

> Chestnut flowers are falling
> In the empty street that smells
> Of hospitals and cooking.
> The radio is breaking
> Somebody's heart somewhere
> In a dirty bedroom. Nobody
> Is listening. For ten miles
> In either direction
> There are no spots on the dice.
> The houses are all empty.

I was momentarily taken aback by Eliot Weinberger's jacket note (". . . Rexroth, the great celebrant of heterosexual love . . . devoted the last years of his life to becoming a woman poet.") until I realized that he was referring to one of the poet's late sequences, "The Love Poems of Marichiko." Here Rexroth pulls off a Borgesian stunt, inventing a woman poet as his persona and then presenting the resulting poems as "translations" of her work—the kind of conceit one would gladly salute if the poems rose above the ordinary. Too often, though, they sound no more original than the stock responses of bus-station erotica:

> I scream as you bite
> My nipples, and orgasm
> Drains my body, as if I
> Had been cut in two.

An interesting test of Rexroth's success or failure at gender reversal would be to present these poems, under the name of "Marichiko," to a class in feminist literary criticism and wait to see if anyone deduces that they were written by a man.

Thomas McGrath's *Death Song* (Copper Canyon Press) collects the last work of one of our most resolutely leftist poets, one whose life and subsequent career were permanently marked by being blacklisted during the McCarthy era. Though coming from the other side of the political spectrum, McGrath appropriates the invective

tones of Pound's "Usura" canto in railing against the Nicaraguan Contras and their accommodations with "The U. S. of A. and Everywhere":

> The spirit of capitalism and exploitation—a vile
> spirit
> That poisons their wells with the dead bodies of peasants,
> That sours the sweat of workers and fills their
> shoes with stones
> That stuffs their beds with barbwire: mortgages:
> debts—
>
> Plagues of lawyers follow this foul creation as flies
> Beelzebub. . . .

As McGrath himself notes, his poems are "Totally out of date / According to the bourgeois seasons." McGrath's brand of populist radicalism links him to the wandering bards of the Great Depression such as Woody Guthrie and Pete Seeger, or the folksinger in the James Dickey poem who is crucified against the side of a boxcar. McGrath reveals this kinship in "Legends, Heroes, Myth-Figures and Other American Liars," an uncharacteristic bit of balladeering:

> Westward, always westerly,
> Toward all desires,
> Toward mountain and ocean
> And the great Western liars:
>
> Mike Fink, Joe Stink—
> Who gave the lie luster—
> Helped by Windy Bill
> And G.A. Custer.
>
> So the nation became
>
> What legend made of it:
>
> Half exaggeration
>
> Half pure bullshit.

McGrath has occasional moments of charm, but for the most part his cheerlessness—he can't even listen to Garrison Keillor without mentioning "starving masses near Lake Wobegon"—quickly becomes tiresome. Readers who are having a hard enough time keeping their financial heads above water in the current recession may have trouble empathizing with McGrath's "Last Will and Testament," in which he begs his son's pardon for having "made some money, / Once, / And saved it / For what they call / Your 'future,'" adding that this "agreement with / the enemy" was done "without / Robbing a bank." This shame at having done business with the robber barons and the bureaucrats notwithstanding, the book's cover proudly notes that McGrath "was named to two Bush Foundation Fellowships, a Guggenheim Fellowship, a National Endowment for the Arts Senior Fellowship, and a Shelley Memorial Award."

Another older contemporary poet whose poetry has become inseparable from her political agenda is Adrienne Rich. Twenty-five years ago, she was handing out "Leaflets" with this entreaty:

> I want to hand you this
> leaflet streaming with rain or tears
> but the words coming clear
> something you might find crushed into your hand
> after passing a barricade
> and stuff in your raincoat pocket.
> I want this to reach you
> who told me once that poetry is nothing sacred....

Now, in *An Atlas of the Difficult World* (Norton), though almost everything else in Rich's personal orientation has changed (it hardly seems possible that in *Leaflets* this poet could have begun a poem with "When your sperm enters me, it is altered"), the urgency of her message remains the same, though its scope has become global:

> I know you are reading this poem as you pace beside the stove
> warming milk, a crying child on your shoulder, a book in your hand
> because life is short and you too are thirsty.
> I know you are reading this poem which is not in your language
> guessing at some words while others keep you reading
> and I want to know which words they are.

No matter how impatient one may grow listening to Rich's familiar litanies of victimization, it should be apparent from almost any sample of her work that she still possesses one of the finest ears and deftest lyrical techniques of any poet on the scene.

In a perceptive review in the *New York Review of Books* Helen Vendler identifies Rich as a moral allegorist in the manner of William Langland or John Bunyan. Her view of good and evil in our "difficult world" seems typical of much contemporary political activism, which strives to reduce bewildering moral complexities to a single set of axioms—ecological or gender-based political programs, for example—and the resulting ethical scheme can become disturbingly oversimplistic. As Vendler observes, "The good in Rich are the weak, the social underdogs—women, blacks, lesbians, the poor, prisoners, Jews, mothers of the disappeared.... But because ... she never places herself among the reprobates (even in imagination) and never tarnishes the victims with evil qualities of their own, we may feel she imperfectly understands social phenomena." What Vendler is taking excessive pains to avoid saying, it seems to me, is that Rich has, in essence, become a propagandist who limits herself to preaching to the converted. Of course, this reduction gives her poetic vision the strength that can come only from the assurance of her own rectitude (in this respect she resembles the religious poets of earlier centuries), but its constricted range of subjects—a woman writer beaten and then run over by her husband, schoolchildren being fed by "Black Panthers spooning cereal," migrant laborers, among them pregnant women, being dusted with malathion while they pick strawberries—seems drawn solely from the front pages of underground newspapers. Even with contemporary boundaries of taste being what they are, I don't know how to respond to Rich's account ("I don't want to know how he tracked them") of a murder on the Appalachian Trail, in which two women, according to Rich's note, were attacked "because they were lesbians":

> I don't want to know
> but this is not a bad dream of mine   these are the materials
> and so are the smell of wild mint and coursing water remembered
> and the sweet salt darkred tissue I lay my face upon, my tongue within.

As I write this, Jeffrey Dahmer has just been sentenced in Milwaukee, Wisconsin, for a horrifying series of sexual murders of young men, most of whom were black homosexuals. I wonder what the response would be if a contemporary gay male poet eulogized Dahmer's victims in such explicitly erotic terms as these.

Several other books by poets over sixty deserve brief mention. Possibly the most widely discussed was John Ashbery's long poem of over two hundred pages, *Flow Chart* (Knopf), which was not received for review—for which favor I offer no small thanks to the publisher. Discussing it in the *New York Review of Books*, John Bayley observes that "Ashbery's bland undisturbing clarity has learned how to flow toward, between, and over meaning without rupturing the surface," words meant, I suppose, as praise. Nobel Prize-winner Czelaw Milosz published *Provinces: Poems 1987-1991* (Ecco), translated by the author and his Berkeley colleague Robert Hass. Milosz may have his champions and indeed may be a considerable poet in his native tongue, but for the most part he seems here to be dedicated to giving new dimensions to the meaning of *sententious*:

—When I die, I will see the lining of the world.
The other side, beyond bird, mountain, sunset.
The true meaning, ready to be decoded.
What never added up will add up,
What was incomprehensible will be comprehended.

Two books by David Ignatow arrived. *Despite the Plainness of the Day: Love Poems* (Mill Hunk Press) reprints erotic work from four decades. It's hard to resist lines such as "We are like two freight cars, / headed for each other cautiously / on the one track and about to couple / and take on freight for the nearest port." *Shadowing the Ground* (Wesleyan University Press) is a touching valediction from a poet nearing his eighties who notes that life is "difficult to give up" and delays his departure as long as possible: "I am watching, / unable to leave, for something / is happening, and so I stand / in a shower of rain / or under a hot sun, worn out / with looking." The unsentimental quality of many of these short, untitled poems recalls the epigrams Walter Savage Landor wrote when he was almost the same age as Ignatow. Even older is Brewster Ghiselin (born in 1903), whose *Flame* (University of Utah Press) collects work from the last twenty years. In an introduction (written in 1971) Allen Tate praises this Western poet's "wide and magnificent sweep of vision," which is most evident in a seven-part poem titled "Elemental."

Several other new books allow us to keep up with the doings of veterans of several countercultures. Gary Snyder's *Riprap and Cold Mountain Poems* (North Point Press) reprints two of the poet's early collections with a new afterword by the author that details his youthful wanderings through lumber camps, the merchant marine, and Japan. *Rebel Lions*, by Michael McClure (New Directions), provides a continuation of that poet's bad habits, namely an overuse of capital letters and poem after poem centered on the page, the kind of thing one might have applauded, in the years before the word processor, for the poet's typ-

ing skills. Following his expulsion from the University of Bucharest in 1966, Andrei Codrescu began his American career as a late joiner of the New York poets associated with the late Ted Berrigan and the St. Mark's Poetry Project; it comes as something of a surprise to find that he is only forty-five. Now he is a professor of English at Louisiana State University: "Nel mezzo del camino I found myself / in the middle class / looking at two diverging options: / ideology and addiction." *Belligerence* (Coffee House Press) is his first book of poetry since 1986 but has precious little to say about the upheavals that have changed his native Romania in those years. Another poet who emerged from the same New York milieu is Clark Coolidge, whose random scatterings of words anticipated by almost twenty years the work of the contemporary L = A = N = G = U = A = G = E poets. *Sound as Thought: Poems 1982-1984* (Sun and Moon Press) is, for the most part, grammatically more coherent than Coolidge's earlier work though scarcely more accessible. *Nice to See You: Homage to Ted Berrigan* (Coffee House Press) should also be mentioned in this regard: an affectionate miscellany of poems, memoirs, interviews, and journal entries by and about Berrigan, who died in 1983 and was the guiding spirit of the New York poets of the 1960s. Poet Anne Waldman, a longtime friend and colleague of Berrigan, has edited a surprisingly touching collection of reminiscences that captures something of the wildness of the era in words and photographs. Of roughly the same vintage (though from the opposite coast) is Diane Wakoski, who checks in with *Medea: The Sorceress* (Black Sparrow Press), almost two hundred pages of poems and letters. Wakoski's endless fascination with herself rivals that of any other American poet: "By the way, another aspect of feminism which didn't appeal to me was the idea that it was odious to be seen as a sexual object. I think I spent most of my California youth and adolescence trying to figure out HOW to be perceived as a sexual object." She is contemporary poetry's equivalent of the heroine of the popular comic strip *Cathy*.

Trying to make some generalizations about the scores of individual collections that arrive each year is a futile task, and about all one can do is plunge into the stack and try to find single poems that are memorable and the occasional whole collection that coheres. One that does both is Dana Gioia's *The Gods of Winter* (Graywolf). Since Gioia called another pantheon of gods into

Dust jacket for Hudgins's third collection of poems about history, religion, and the South

question in his *Atlantic* article, he has, I suspect, placed himself permanently outside the circle of power controlled by the AWP establishment and will pay the price of its indifference—*The Gods of Winter* has been only sparingly reviewed. But debate over Gioia's prose should not be allowed to obscure his talents as a poet; this is as good a book as one is likely to encounter—varied, formally complex, ambitious in its two longer poems, and unusually free from the sort of adolescent self-indulgence that characterizes much contemporary American poetry. In this second collection Gioia is writing for *adults*, not the captive college-reading crowd, and it is clear that he respects his audience's intelligence. Here, in "The Next Poem," he presents a modest aesthetic program:

> The music that of common speech
> but slanted so that each detail
> sounds unexpected as a sharp
> inserted in a simple scale.

No jumble box of imagery
dumped glumly in the reader's lap
or elegantly packaged junk
the unsuspecting must unwrap.

But words that could direct a friend
precisely to an unknown place,
those few unshakeable details
that no confusion can erase.

Despite having produced a considerable amount of work in open forms, Gioia is often listed among the New Formalists, and in such rhymed, metrical poems as "The Next Poem" he manages to avoid the sort of artificiality that too often seems the bane of the generation of formalists known disparagingly in the 1960s as "Academics." Yet, appealing as these witty turns are, I prefer the voice that speaks in the loosely metered lines of "Planting a Sequoia," one of several poems in the collection contrasting evanescence (in this case a son who died in infancy) and permanence:

> We plant you in the corner of the grove, bathed in
>   western light,
> A slender shoot against the sunset.
>
> And when our family is no more, all of his unborn
>   brothers dead,
> Every niece and nephew scattered, the house torn
>   down,
> His mother's beauty ashes in the air,
> I want you to stand among strangers, all young and
>   ephemeral to you,
> Silently keeping the secret of your birth.

The most impressive single poem in the volume is "Counting the Children," a narrative of slightly over 150 lines. The persona, a Chinese-American accountant named Choi, has come to the home of an eccentric female intestate to take inventory. In one of the dead woman's rooms he finds an astonishing collection:

> I walked into a room of wooden shelves
> Stretching from floor to ceiling, wall to wall,
> With smaller shelves arranged along the center.
>
> A crowd of faces looked up silently.
> Shoulder to shoulder, standing all in rows,
> Hundreds of dolls were lining every wall.
>
> Not a collection anyone would want—
> Just ordinary dolls salvaged from the trash
> With dozens of each kind all set together.

Some battered, others missing arms and legs,
Shelf after shelf of the same dusty stare
As if despair could be assuaged by order.

He speculates about the whereabouts of "the children who promised them love . . . / The small, caressing hands, the lips which whispered / Secrets in the dark," and later, in his own home, a nightmare wakes him to thoughts of his own daughter:

How delicate this vessel in our care,
This gentle soul we summoned to the world,
A life we treasured but could not protect.

Gioia took considerable risks in releasing this book hard on the heels of his critique of the contemporary scene, but he has indeed produced poetry that "can matter" to the intelligent common reader. *The Gods of Winter* was a selection of the British Poetry Book Society, an extremely rare honor for a book by an American poet.

Andrew Hudgins continues to develop in interesting directions. His first book, *Saints and Strangers* (1985), contains a nice mix of lyrics, narratives, and dramatic monologues, the best of which was the title poem, a sequence of reminiscences spoken by the daughter of an itinerant fundamentalist preacher. *After the Lost War* (1989) is even more unusual, a complete book of monologues in the voice of Sidney Lanier, the Southern soldier-poet who died of tuberculosis at thirty-nine. *The Never-Ending: New Poems* (Houghton Mifflin), his third collection, is for the most part lyrical and autobiographical. "The Unpromised Land" recalls a summer spent working in George Wallace's capital:

Once, standing where Jeff Davis took his oath,
I saw the crippled governor wheeled into
the Capitol. He shrank into his chair,
so flaccid with paralysis he looked
like melting flesh, white as a maggot. He's fatter
  now.
He courts black votes, and life is calmer than
when Muslims shot whites on this street, and calmer
than when the Klan blew up Judge Johnson's house
or Martin Luther King's. My history could be
  worse.

History, particularly that of the South, and religion are two of Hudgins's favorite subjects; there are several poems on the person and body of Christ, both imagined and, as in this case, recalled from works of art:

One blood-drop trickles toward his wrist. Somehow
the grieving women missed it when they bathed,
today, the empty corpse. Most Christs return.
But this one's flesh. He isn't coming back.

The most impressive poem in the collection is "Heat Lightning in a Time of Drought," a funny yet poignant lyrical ramble—on love, loss, and the dog days—that should become an impressive performance piece:

And then one day the doorbell rang.
A salesman said, *Watch this!* He stripped my bed
and vacuumed it. The nozzle sucked up two
full, measured cups of light gray flakes. He said,
That's human skin. I stood, refusing the purchase,
stood staring at her flesh and mine commingled
inside the measuring cup, stood there and thought,
*She's been gone two years, she's married, and all this time
her flesh has been in bed with me.*

The offbeat tonal mix here recalls similar poems by other Southern poets of roughly the same age as Hudgins—Leon Stokesbury, Rodney Jones, T. R. Hummer come to mind—and it is interesting to speculate about the influences that may lie behind seriocomic monologues such as these.

David Middleton's *The Burning Fields* (Louisiana State University Press) is, like Hudgins's book, consciously Southern in its orientation; the title poem describes the annual ritual of burning off sugarcane fields after the harvest:

Cupped matches struck by the older men
Kindled in undergrowth a steady flame
And the empyrean crossed cremated ground.
Like gods in the choking sweetness of the air,
They watched the holocaust their need compelled. . . .

Middleton is barely in his forties, but his rigid meters, host of classical references, and the total seriousness with which he approaches the mythos of the Old South mark him as something of a throwback to an earlier generation; indeed, his assumption, in "The Planters," of the mantle of the Agrarians recalls Donald Davidson, that most unfashionable of the Fugitives:

Then, just at harvest time, those people came,
Obtusest slaves to Luciferic dreams,
Deniers both of history and guilt
Who seized on present evil to postpone
Awareness of their own millennial sins.
We called them Satan's angels, the crude recruits
Of Sherman and his kind. . . .

David Baker is a native of Maine but may well qualify for honorary Southern citizenship; *Sweet Home, Saturday Night* (University of Arkansas Press) takes its title from the song "Sweet Home Alabama" by the quintessential Southern rock band Lynyrd Skynyrd and also contains an ironic meditation on the Southern anthem "Dixie," about which Ohioan Dan Emmett was reputed to have said, "I wish I had never writ that God-damn song." The title poem perhaps shows the influence of T. R. Hummer, Baker's sometime colleague at the *Kenyon Review* and one of the book's dedicatees. Several years ago Hummer published in the *Georgia Review* a long, ambitious poem called "Bluegrass Wasteland," a remarkable conflation of erotic and autobiographical passages unified with a contrapuntal musical structure. Baker's poem, over twenty pages long, might best be described as "Prufrock at the Com-On-Inn," a postmodernist celebration of the joys of pure honky tonk and

> this rhetorically sexual
> concoction of ruckus and rhythm, of rock-and-roll
> and country / swing, so given over
>
> to it all, so like those two
> lovers spooning in their dark corner
> where they've been lip-locked and buckle-to-buckle
>
> since the last set's last
> slow song, four legs pressed into two,
> so convinced of love and beauty, so lost....

Aside from the amp-busting energy level this recreation of a memorable evening on the dance floor generates (one can almost work up a sweat reading it), Baker deserves credit for his clever manipulation of poetic distance ("I am, and am not, that guitar player, and these are and are not / my friends and partners and paying customers. / I am sitting here watching myself / sitting at a beer-slopped table watching myself...") and for the way he is able to make this poem more than just an empty exercise in the mimetic mode. "Sweet Home, Saturday Night" may be the closest any poet in memory has come to re-creating the spirit of a Dionysian dithyrambic.

The celebrations in Linda Pastan's *Heroes in Disguise* (Norton) are somewhat quieter than those in Baker's book; in "Autumn" the poet expresses a wish "to mention / summer ending / without meaning the death / of somebody loved // or even the death / of the trees." Another poem de-

scribes the experience of finding "A New Poet," comparing it to

> finding a new wildflower
> out in the woods. You don't see
>
> its name in the flower books, and
> nobody you tell believes
> in its odd color or the way
>
> its leaves grow in splayed rows
> down the whole length of the page. In fact
> the very page smells of spilled
>
> red wine and the mustiness of the sea
> on a foggy day—the odor of truth
> and of lying.

The book contains a section of autobiographical poems, "Only Child"; here are Pastan's lines on the death of her mother and the birth of a grandson:

> The new child will not
> fill precisely the space
> that death has emptied,
> though the space around the baby
> expands already to fit it in.
>
> The wheel of generations turns
> with such excruciating logic,
> a kind of rack to stretch us on.

In a year when all too often it seems that poets are trying to outdo the guests on daytime talk shows with horror stories from their childhoods, Pastan's healthy version of her own family romance is positively tonic.

Linda Gregg's *The Sacraments of Desire* (Graywolf) contains poems set in Greece, Mexico, and other foreign locales, but the poet is so solipsistic ("We live alone in our self") that landscape is subordinated to reports on her physical and emotional state of the moment: "It is summer and I am in the middle / of my life. Alone and happy." Or "I am not feeling strong yet, but I am taking / good care of myself. The weather is perfect." Or "I am alone writing as quickly as I can, / dulled by being awake at four in the morning." The sacraments of the book's title are primarily those relating to Aphrodite, invoked only as a capitalized pronoun in several of the Greek poems: "I will bring Her my story of loss / like a broken toy and see it mended / miraculously in Her hands." Gregg rarely ventures far from her absorption in her own interior romance; in one poem, "The War," she spins a provocative allegory describing a group of border guards torturing a scorpion whose stinger one of them has cut off, but this leads her only to the limp conclusion that "Maybe morality does change, / I was thinking, but suffering does not." Nor are her speculations on the consolations of art any less tentative:

> Perhaps poetry replaces something
> in me that others receive more naturally.
> Perhaps my happiness proves a weakness in
> my life.
> Even my failures in poetry please me.
> Time is very different here. It is very good
> to be away from public ambition.

The dust jacket of this book contains one of the year's most curious blurbs, from Joseph Brodsky: "The blinding intensity of Ms. Gregg's lines stains the reader's psyche the way lightning or heartbreak do." It do, indeed.

Albert Goldbarth, Jorie Graham, and Larry Levis all seem to be vying for the title of "Ramblin' Man" (or "Woman") of American Poetry. Goldbarth has long been our champion of comic garrulity, and the pleasure one takes in *Heaven and Earth: A Cosmology* (University of Georgia Press) will largely depend on one's patience and the size of the dose. "The Children of Elmer" is a fairly typical example of Goldbarth's "flypaper" approach to a subject. He begins by speculating on the fate of a missing twelve-year-old, who is "happy or thinks she's happy" in a Mexican whorehouse, while her distraught mother and classmates appear on television begging for her return. This leads the poet into memories of the ritual of "milk break" in his own sixth-grade days and the evolution of bottles into "half-quart / cartons with a coat of wax a kid could thickly / scrape up under his nails" to, in the present, "these joyless things" with the faces of missing children printed on them. In the midst of all this there is a cameo by "Elsie the Cow" and her husband, "stolid Elmer"—hence the poem's title. Goldbarth's shtick would probably play better at *Live at the Improv* than on the cold page, but his book has been named one of the finalists for the National Book Critics Circle Award.

Graham and Levis used to write poems; Graham, in particular, now seems to be devoting herself exclusively to the writing of Poetry, which is a different matter altogether. *Region of Unlikeness* (Ecco) takes its title from the same quote from Augustine's *Confessions* that provided Robert Lowell with the title of his first collection, *Land of Un-*

Dust jacket for Pastan's collection of poems focusing on, among other things, her family

likeness (1944). The similarities don't end there, for Graham seems at times to be writing her own version of Lowell's *History*:

> The last time I saw it was 1968.
> Paris, France. The time of the *disturbances*.
> We had claims. Schools shut down.
> A million *workers* and *students* on strike.
>
> Marches, sit-ins, helicopters, gas.
> They stopped you at gunpoint asking for papers.

The book's jacket notes speak of how "Graham explores how we join our need for a linear version of time—a 'story'—with our desire for a defining world view, or metaphor." Unfortunately, Graham's "defining ... metaphor" is expressed in the title of the book's opening poem, "Fission," which interrupts a description of a matinee showing of *Lolita* with the news of President John F. Kennedy's assassination. Unfortunately, as the houselights go up a promising situation trails off into abstract chatter:

where the long thin arm of day came in from the
    top
to touch my head,
    reaching down along my staring face—
where they flared up around my body unable to

merge into each other
    over my likeness,
slamming down one side of me, unquenchable—
    here static

    there flaming—
sifting grays into other grays—
    mixing the split second into the long haul. . . .

This pseudosentence goes on for about thirty more lines, ending in a dash; "Six Participles in Search of a Verb" might have been a more appropriate title. In other poems Graham often seems to be making much over precious little; "The Phase After History," a poem seemingly written for an audience solely composed of the Duke University English department, describes the poet's efforts to free two small birds trapped in her house. How we get from that simple situation to this rhetorical summit is beyond me:

High-pitched the sound it makes with its throat,
    low and too tender the sound it makes with its

    body—against the walls now,
down.
    Which America is it in?
Which America are we in here?
    Is there an America comprised wholly
of its waiting and my waiting and all forms of the
    thing

oven the green's—
    a large uncut fabric floating above the soil—
a place of *attention*?
    The voice says wait. Taking a lot of words.

No kidding.

    Levis is not much more concise. *The Widening Spell of the Leaves* (University of Pittsburgh Press) opens with a four-and-one-half-page autobiographical poem, "Self Portrait with Radio," which the poet begins in the far branches of the family tree ("I'm the Levis of the Levis of the Levis, / Descendant of slaves, yes, but also / Of the owners of slaves. . . .") and, after a couple of pages, is born, develops picky habits at table, and speculates in an admiring fashion on his parents, who have

    joined hands to listen
    In disbelief & pity

To what I now know
Were the McCarthy hearings
Barking over a radio. . . .
How noble they both looked
In that moment that composes
Entirely my first
Memory of the world. . . .

This really stretches credulity, I'm afraid. The title poem, running to almost six pages, literally runs into a dead end when the speaker finds himself lost on the Carpathian frontier, the road playing out into "a complete stillness of yellow leaves filling / A wide field." From this point we leap to a memory from childhood, when a Japanese neighbor and his family were shipped off "To a place called Manzanar, a detention camp." Since Levis was born in 1946, he must be using a persona here, but he provides no clue to the identity save in his dedication to his brother. After yet another topical reference that mentions how the poet "made love once / To a woman in broad daylight in an empty classroom" on "a bright May morning, the day after Kent State" I begin to suspect that Levis is primarily concerned with establishing to his readers that he has been politically correct since his days in his mother's womb, or even earlier.

    After these three poets it is a relief to turn to two poets, Gibbons Ruark and Sydney Lea, who have mastered the respective virtues of compression and narrative coherence. Ruark, to my mind, is one of the most underrated poets writing today. Many of the poems (sonnets for the most part) in *Rescue the Perishing* (Louisiana State University Press) reflect the poet's travels in Ireland in a time of civil strife. I particularly like this description of two ancient warriors, serene amid the unending native "troubles":

Backs to the window of the bar in Donnybrook,
Two bent but elegant soldiers remember
The Somme, living through it, how the river looked
Recalling the Liffey, the chilling number
Of wild Irish boys among the casualties.
The younger one lost an arm for his trouble;
The older, ninety-eight, first of the British
Officers to cross the Hindenburg. . . .

Ruark is a skillful elegist; "Larkin" eloquently sums up the dead poet's appeal:

Surefooting through the rain of rice and horn blare
Flattering some lovely daughter's wedding ride,
His tune is brassy, muted, grave, and just—

Jelly Roll's "Dead Man Blues" as the slow hearse glides.

Sydney Lea's *The Blainville Testament* (Story Line Press) collects the poet's narrative poems. One of these, "The Feud," appeared previously in the poet's 1982 collection, *The Floating Candles*, and should become a classic contemporary narrative. Set in rural New England, the poem describes the steady escalation of retaliatory acts after a bunch of lowlife neighbors, coming in from hunting, scatters deer guts along the road in front of the narrator's house. The poem builds steadily to a truly terrifying climax, when the narrator returns home to find his house on fire:

> *My* kid, meanwhile cried
> from behind a big storm window, "Daddy? Daddy?"
> It sounded like a question. I gave up
> and tried to call back up to him. I couldn't. . . .
>
> He threw a model boat, a book, a drumstick.
> He couldn't make a crack. I flung the ax.
> It missed by half a mile. I threw again
> and broke a hole, and scared the boy back in.
>
> That was the last I saw him. Like a woman
> sighing, the old house huffed once and fell.

The conclusion is painfully bitter:

> No man can find revenge for a thing like this.
> They say revenge is something for the Lord.
> And let Him have it. Him, such as He is.

Nothing else in the book quite matches the brilliantly sustained action Lea builds here, but the other poems do draw quite effectively on the poet's familiarity with regional locales and characters.

A little levity is worth cherishing, and four collections of (mostly) light verse arrived this year. Tom Disch's *Dark Verses & Light* (Johns Hopkins University Press) is a mixed bag, comprising a longish Christmas poem, a "Masque in Five Tableaux," a parodic "biography" and selection of poems by a hopelessly untalented 1960s underground filmmaker, one "Joycelin Shrager," and a variety of Disch's shorter pieces of verse. Here is part of his apostrophe "To Fame": "Let me appear / On *Time*, my dear, and make John Simon praise / What he has utterly misunderstood." *New Yorker* cartoonist Jack Prelutsky offers *There'll Be a Slight Delay and Other Poems for Grown-ups* (William Morrow), which includes a sonnet sequence on fa-

miliar vexations. Here is the close of one, about "a timid wimp" who becomes a terror behind the wheel:

> He glowers at pedestrians with scorn,
> Accelerates through every yellow light.
> He weaves through traffic, leaning on the horn,
> Then flips a bird, and passes on the right.
> Inherently, he seems to understand
> The power of vehicular command.

Richard Moore's *No More Bottom* (Orchises) specializes in more radical types of surgery, often with an extra twist of the knife. Here is "Parting Wish":

> May she find solace with her lovers—
> writhe with them underneath the covers;
> then may age bring, to ease her slumbers,
> carrots, bananas, and cucumbers.

And "The Seventeenth Century":

> Men led in that unhealthy age
> short lives of feverish endeavor.
> Poor old Moliere dropped dead on stage.
> Now Johnny Carson talks forever.

From the same publisher comes Bruce Bennett's *Taking Off* (Orchises), parodic poems of a decidedly literary bent. Here is "Upstate," which I admired when it appeared in a chapbook called *The Garden & Other Abridged Versions*:

> "If Winter comes, can Spring be far behind?"
> Where I live, yes; long months, so grim and glum
> The snow lies blanker than a poet's mind
> Who'd say a thing so pitiful and dumb.

I also admire "New Book, Old Poet," a snippet of literary criticism I can verify as dead on target:

> The packaging is better than ever.
> It blares: I'm here, and here to stay.
> But underneath the trim and tinsel,
> the same tired words, with less to say.

From two poets of the Southwest have appeared books with strong regional emphases. Editor of the *New Mexico Humanities Review*, Jerry Bradley takes the title of *Simple Versions of Disaster* (University of North Texas Press) from the afterimages of catastrophe, loss, and failure that show up in all-too-familiar roadside environments. "Singles Bar at the Ramada" ends with a wry observation: "And they stare at each other through their campari-and-beer breath / as if all waiting would be forgiven by a kiss / yet fearful still to know that two out of three / marriages end in divorce, but the other ends in death." "Motel on the San Augustine Plains" opens by noting how "hawks sit on posts / and perch like large women / wearing necklaces of fencewire / and surveying a sea of dust." Bradley has a good eye for incongruous details. Walter McDonald's *The Digs in Escondido Canyon* (Texas Tech University Press) is the poet's twelfth collection since the mid 1970s. The title poem refers to archaeological excavations along the Brazos River, where a campfire's "pale flames waver like ghosts / of tribes drawn to this stream ten thousand years / before railroad trestles and beef." It is disturbing that McDonald's range of subjects has not grown perceptibly over the years; nevertheless, within his limits of experience—the West Texas "hardscrabble" country and an air force tour as a pilot in Vietnam have provided him with many poems—he is an enviable craftsman of lyrics and short narratives.

Space remains for only short mention of other books that were published in 1991 which will hold some interest for readers. Many of these came from established poets. Norman Dubie's *Radio Sky* (Norton) completes a trilogy of lyrical volumes which also includes *The Springhouse* (1986) and *Groom Falconer* (1989). Dubie's surrealistic pastiches of historical and biographical incidents never quite seem to jibe with his personal poems. "Radio Sky" is of the latter type, a memory of lovemaking in front of a snow-filled television screen tuned to "the original light of Creation." In other poems, though, Dubie is in full flight, as in one that describes how "Samuel Taylor Coleridge tossed / Raw chunks of a disquieting muse / to three ragged mermaids." Stephen Dunn's *Landscape at the End of the Century* (Norton) concludes with a thirteen-page poem called "Loves," which takes the year's top prize for smug self-congratulation: "When students fall in love with me / I want to tell them / I'm the dream that won't last; / there are more pleasures in the text." This interminable catalogue ("In spite of their lack of humor / I love Thoreau and Jesus, Marx, / Malcolm X.") ought to be set to music by Tom T. Hall. Gary Gildner's *Clackamas* (Carnegie Mellon University Press) takes its title from a Michigan river of the poet's childhood. The book contains several strong poems written during a year the poet spent as a Fulbright Lecturer at the University of Warsaw, including a longish narrative about a trip to Auschwitz and two

Dust jacket for the third collection of lyrical poems in the trilogy that also includes The Springhouse *(1986) and* Groom Falconer *(1989)*

shorter ones recounting his funny experiences as coach of the Warsaw baseball (!) team: "thirty-five guys who throw—excuse me—like girls. / They are trying to catch up on something / they don't even know they've missed. . . ." Reginald Gibbons's *Maybe It Was So* (University of Chicago Press) has as its centerpiece "From a Paper Boat," winner of the John Masefield Memorial Award from the Poetry Society of America. The poem is a long, fragmented dramatic monologue spoken by an unidentified survivor of the destruction of his city and family. At times ("At one end of the huge square soldiers shouted / Through trumpets and raised a huge flag. / At the other, defiant students in their faded caps / Stood thick as the grain before the harvest.") the poem seems to allude to events in wartime Japan and contemporary China, but nothing here is ever quite specified. Even though the poem has a simple surface, I keep hearing echoes of "The Waste Land" in its apocalyptic tones.

Three books by women poets who have been on the scene for a good while arrived for review. *Days Going/Days Coming Back* by Eleanor Ross Taylor (University of Utah Press) contains several poems set in Virginia, which must have endeared the collection to series editor Dave Smith. I particularly enjoyed "Casting About," a long meditation on fishing that alludes to Dame Juliana Berners, the legendary English nun whose treatise on angling preceded Walton's *The Compleat Angler* (1653) by almost two centuries. Lucille Clifton's *Quilting: Poems 1987-1990* (BOA Editions) collects recent work by a leading black woman poet. "to my last period" is a witty apostrophe: "you / never arrived / splendid in your red dress / without trouble for me. . . ." Clifton's avoidance of punctuation and capital letters tends to make reading her a bit more of a chore than one really wants, though. Pinky Gordon Lane, poet laureate of Louisiana, offers *Girl at the Window* (Louisiana State University Press), a collection that gathers work from three decades. Lane, another black female academic who has been publishing for years, is only belatedly receiving the recognition she deserves.

Poets usually singled out in discussions of minority writers continued to be prominent in 1991, among them two Native American women poets. Linda Hogan's *Red Clay* (Greenfield Review Press) collects poems and stories drawing on subjects from the poet's native Oklahoma. *The Light on the Tent Wall: A Bridging*, by Mary TallMountain (American Indian Studies Center), gathers work by a Native Alaskan who was featured on Bill Moyers's *Power of the Word* series. Brenda Marie Osbey's *Desperate Circumstance, Dangerous Woman* (Story Line Press) is a narrative sequence set in the New Orleans district called the Trémé, settled in the early 1800s by free blacks. The book contains a glossary explaining ethnic words and customs relating to the practice of Hoodoo. Victor Hernandez Cruz's *Red Beans* (Coffee House Press) is a long collection of poetry and prose by the leading Puerto Rican poet. One of the concluding prose poems is a verse-essay on the five hundredth anniversary of Columbus's voyage of discovery, an event that has stimulated no mean amount of controversy and reevaluation of late.

Many important collections by women appeared in 1991. Pamela Alexander's *Commonwealth of Wings: An Ornithological Biography* (Wesleyan University Press), a poetic account of John James Audubon's life, covers some of the same ground as Robert Penn Warren's earlier poems on the subject. Cathy Hankla's *Afterimages* (Louisi-

ana State University Press) comes highly recommended by William Stafford and Fred Chappell and contains two solid meditative poems on the Apollo space flights. C. D. Wright's *String Light* (University of Georgia Press) contains surrealistic poems (a sort of homegrown version of South American magic realism) set in the poet's native Ozarks. Ann Lauterbach's *Clamor* (Viking Penguin) seems aptly named, randomly assembled lines ("In the full heroic flush, we // Am I A? Each line is a quibble // How can I keep an even keel. . . .") for the delectation of deconstructionists and Ashberians. *The Deed*, by Carole Simmons Oles (Louisiana State University Press), contains a touching personal narrative with an absolutely dreadful title, "Visiting My Formerly Runaway Daughter and Her Husband at the Orchard in Vermont." Jo McDougall's second collection, *Towns Facing Railroads* (University of Arkansas Press), consists for the most part of short poems describing lives of not-so-quiet desperation in America's whistle-stops. Susan Hahn's oddly titled *Harriet Rubin's Mother's Wooden Hand* (University of Chicago Press) contains one poem, "Tricholtillomania," (the title refers to obsessive hair pulling) that I recalled seeing in *Shenandoah*. If the contents of Hahn's poems could consistently rise to the level of her titles ("Lana Turner in the Butcher Shop" is one) she would be a force to reckon with.

Other books from poets whose names will spark some glimmers of recognition include A. Poulin's *Cave Dwellers* (Graywolf) a longish selection of mostly lyrical poems, including one section described as "A Bestiary of Angels." Ronald Wallace's *The Makings of Happiness* (University of Pittsburgh Press) contains some good descriptions of labor on the poet's Wisconsin farm. Frederick Feirstein's *City Life* (Story Line Press) has more than half its pages devoted to "The Psychiatrist at the Cocktail Party," a dramatic poem drawing on the poet's own experiences as a New York psychoanalyst. Gerard Malanga's *Three Diamonds* (Black Sparrow Press) is almost beyond belief: a collection of erotic photographs of women in various stages of undress which are accompanied by poems by the author, a sometime associate of the late Andy Warhol. I would be interested to see what its honoree thinks of "Photographing Jorie Graham," which may indeed herald a new genre, the "mash note" poem. Matthew Graham's *1946* (Galileo) contains poems set some years before the poet's birth in 1954, including one based on an uncle's eyewitness account of the Bikini hydrogen bomb tests. R. T. Smith's *The Cardinal Heart* (Livingston University Press) collects work by one of the ablest observers of the landscape of the South. Dan Masterson's *World Without End* (University of Arkansas Press) focuses mainly on the outdoors, particularly the wildlife and human predators near the poet's cabin in the Adirondacks. P. H. Liotta's *Rules of Engagement* (Cleveland State University Press) includes an assortment of poems about flying (including one spoken by a U-2!) in which Liotta draws on his experiences as a military pilot. Thomas Carper's *Fiddle Lane* (Johns Hopkins University Press) is somewhat unusual in the number of fairly regular sonnets it contains. Linda Bierds's *Heart and Perimeter* (Henry Holt) includes poems on historical subjects, including one on Tom Thumb, the celebrated dwarf made famous by P. T. Barnum.

I would be remiss if I did not close this essay without two recommendations for further reading and two fond farewells. Jacques Barzun's *An Essay on French Verse* (New Directions) is a book I would recommend to anyone who is interested either in prosody or in translating poetry. Barzun, who remains one of the most delightfully readable of academic critics, manages to answer a host of questions I have had about the difference between French and English meters. Along the way he provides a brief history of French poetry which is also a spirited defense. Jonathan Holden has become the chief defender of the faith as far as his own generation's poetic efforts are concerned, and *The Fate of American Poetry* (University of Georgia Press) provides a clear overview of the doings of the poets of the center while also looking at their two main groups of challengers, the New Formalists on the one side and the L= A= N= G= U= A= G= E poets on the other. Holden is the most useful critic currently writing about American poetry.

Two deaths diminished the ranks of American poets in 1991. Judson Jerome died on 5 August, after having written the poetry column in *Writer's Digest* for over thirty years. Because he wrote for a popular magazine, Jerome was aware that his criticism was not taken seriously by the academic establishment, yet I doubt if any other individual gave more devoted service to the art than Jerome. For many poets in the hinterlands he was the only contact with the mainstream of poetry, and his solid practical advice benefited thousands of beginners. In the last months of his life he published three books—*Nude* (Applezaba), a novel; *Jonah and Job* (John Daniel), a pair of biblical poems with a prose commentary; and *The Youthful Look: A Memoir 1947-1952* (University of Arkansas Press), a continuation of his earlier autobiographical book, *Flight from Innocence* (1990). The other death was that of Howard Nemerov, late poet laureate of the United States. *The Collected Poems of Howard Nemerov* (University of Chicago Press), which won both the Pulitzer Prize and the National Book Award in 1978, should be on everyone's bookshelf. *A Howard Nemerov Reader*, a retrospective volume of poetry and prose, including samples of Nemerov's fiction, was issued in 1991 by the University of Missouri Press.

And as long as farewells are the order of the day, I will take my own. Having produced this column annually since 1987, I turn it over to other hands in hopes that, having lectured everybody else on how to write poetry for five years, I can still remember how to write it myself.

The Year in Drama

Howard Kissel
New York Daily News

Since the 1960s some of the most interesting theater in New York has not been listed in the daily *New York Times* directory. Thirty years ago that meant the Off-Off-Broadway experimental pieces that were performed at times and in places known only to cognoscenti. Such pieces are still presented, but they have become standardized. Once daring, they are now entirely predictable.

The most involving theater these days is announced in the *Times*, though not in its daily directory of plays. I refer to the memorial services that take place with increasing frequency in the New York theater. One reason for this frequency is, of course, AIDS, which has taken a heavy toll. But old age, other illnesses, and the odd circumstances of life have also had their impact.

The growing "literature" of these memorial services is interesting because it includes many of the qualities that used to characterize theater but are now seldom in evidence—wit, literacy, an eagerness to explore and celebrate human character, a sense of the complexity and beauty of life. Even the burgeoning crop of plays that focuses on AIDS seldom attains the simple, moving eloquence of friends paying tribute to people they loved.

By contrast, the year's theatrical offerings are marked by a predilection for the esoteric, the perverse. There are, of course, notable exceptions, but it seemed oddly appropriate that the year 1991 began with a war and a Stephen Sondheim musical. The war ends with surprising swiftness and success. The musical, *Assassins*, which also had a very brief run, ends with a surreal scene in the Texas Book Depository on 22 November 1963. The ghosts of America's presidential assassins urge a distraught young man to join their ranks and enter history by shooting John F. Kennedy.

Unlike most of his earlier musicals, which incorporate discursiveness into skillful narratives, *Assassins* is a kind of variety show. Each of the assassins is given the moment in the spotlight earned by his or her act of daring. Sondheim and his collaborator John Weidman gave equal time even to such unsuccessful assassins as Squeaky Fromme and Sara Jane Moore, both of whom failed in their attempts to murder Gerald Ford. (Their dialogue, in which the acidhead and the suburban matron seem remarkably similar, was the comic high point of the evening.)

The show begins with a carnival pitchman urging the audience to shoot a president, or, as the sign on the booth behind him declares, "Shoot the Prez and Win a Prize." The lyrics throughout seemed deliberately restrained, as if an abundance of overt wit might be untoward, but the overall theme of the show—that assassins share with their victims a yearning to be Somebody, a hunger for Success fostered by the American Dream—seemed quite unoriginal for so perverse a project.

The score makes extensive use of period materials, parodying Stephen Foster, incorporating a Sousa march into the musical structures. The most interesting number is a barbershop quartet in which the assassins of Lincoln, Garfield, McKinley and a would-be assassin of Ford sing, "It takes a lot of men to make a gun / And all you have to do is move your little finger," to eerily beautiful harmonies. Sondheim has invariably tried to rile and disturb his audience, but here the desired result seemed too easily obtainable.

Of the new plays, the most interesting, both as literature and as theater, was Brian Friel's *Dancing at Lughnasa*, which was imported from London in October. As the narrator of the play explains in an opening monologue, Lugh (pronounced Loo) was the Celtic God of the Harvest, and his feast day, the first of August, was called La Lughnasa (pronounced Loo'na-sa, the same rhythm as lunacy). The narrator, looking back to the summer of 1936, when the action takes place, explains Celtic myth in relation to his family's acquisition of its first radio.

At the time, the narrator, Michael, is a boy. He lives with his mother and her four sisters in Ballybeg, county Donegal, Ireland. His aunts are all spinsters, his mother unmarried, and virtually the only action of the play is the brief visit of his father, a charmer to whom even the starchiest of the sisters is drawn. (One other significant event is the brief disappearance of one of the sisters, Rose, who would now be called "retarded" but who they call "simple.")

There are two other characters in the play: their brother, Father Jack, a missionary who has just returned from many years in Africa; and, of course, the radio. Because it arrived in early August one of the sisters wanted to name the radio after Lugh, but another sister, the schoolmarm, thought this improper. Instead, they named the radio Marconi. Just as the shrines of "Our Lady" that dot the landscape of rural France are thought to mark (and conceal) altars once sacred to primitive goddesses, so the name of the modern inventor cannot mask the essentially primal nature of the instrument reposed in a corner of their cottage kitchen.

Marconi is the sisters' link to Dublin. It is also their link to their own primitive nature. Halfway through the first act the radio begins making bleating sounds to a rhythm so marked, so profound that for a second it sounds as if it might be the sort of thing their brother heard in Africa. Then the melody begins and is recognizable as Irish folk music. It is one of the many parallels Friel draws throughout the play between the Dark Continent and the sunny Irish countryside.

At first the women, engaged in their homely tasks, listen to the melody. Then Maggie, the earthiest of them, begins to dance. It is not a harmless folk dance. It is a dance of savage frenzy, punctuated by an occasional sensual moan. The fact that Maggie wears boots might make the dance comic, but in fact it accentuates the brutality of her movements. In short order even the most straitlaced of her sisters joins her, and one has a keen sense of their kinship with pagan harvesters millennia before.

In the second act something similar happens. Marconi is broadcasting the haunting dance music of the 1930s, a lovely arrangement of Cole Porter's "Anything Goes." Michael's father, who happens to be visiting, dances elegantly with several of the sisters. This time their movements follow the dictates of convention, but the sensuality lying just beneath the surface is apparent.

The play is essentially static. Without being verbose, it has a discursive quality. We learn that Father Jack, who has ostensibly returned from Uganda because he contracted malaria, has in

Program cover for the Plymouth Theatre production of Brian Friel's play about memory and ritual

fact been sent back because his order was disturbed that he had, in effect, gone native. As he describes native customs, analogies are made between rural Africa and the world depicted on the stage. Similarly the audience finds itself, like attentive students, drawing similar analogies between the primitive dance of the first act and that of the second. Lest the parallel go unnoticed, Michael's father actually sings Porter's words.

What disrupts the generally soothing flow of life in Ballybeg is something that happens offstage. A knitting factory opens in the nearby town, depriving the two sisters who do handknitting (one of whom is Rose) of their income. They go off. So does Michael's father, never making good on his promise to marry Michael's mother—or to give his son a bicycle. Michael's mother goes to work in the factory. Father Jack dies. Years later Michael discovers his father had another family in another little town. All this is related in a monologue.

The idyll has ended. The once joyful house becomes bleak, and Michael is left with the memory of the summer Marconi took up residence and of the dancing he inspired: "Dancing with eyes half closed because to open them would break the spell," Michael says in the haunting closing monologue, "Dancing as if language had surrendered to movement—as if this ritual, this wordless ceremony, was now the only way to speak, to whisper private and sacred things, to be in touch with some otherness. . . . Dancing as if language no longer existed because words were no longer necessary."

Friel, whose plays have appeared on Broadway since *Philadelphia, Here I Come* in 1966, has become increasingly Chekhovian over the years, particularly in his 1989 study of a decaying rural gentry in *Aristocrats*. In *Dancing at Lughnasa* he achieves a style all his own, a sense of loss and futility reminiscent of Chekhov, but a poetry based on the unmistakable rhythms and pulses of primitive Ireland.

Both the Pulitzer Prize and the Tony Award for Best Play of the 1990-1991 season went to Neil Simon's *Lost in Yonkers*, which might be considered as belonging to the genre of wartime plays set in bunkers or trenches of the Great War, except that it takes place in 1942 in a Spartan but comfortable apartment in Yonkers, a suburb of New York City. The tension is palpable. In some of Simon's plays there is an air of specious hysteria that stems from his own fear that the laughs might stop. Here, that is unnecessary. The laughs all grow out of the situation.

A widower who owes a large amount of money gets a job as a traveling salesman and has to leave his two young sons with his mother, a glacial woman who has never shown affection to anyone. At first the play, which abounds in grotesque characters, seems Dickensian in its understanding of childhood as a time of terror and immense strangeness. Then Simon's real concerns become clearer. In many of his plays he has milked Jewish characters and situations for comic effect. In the last few years he has begun to take Jewish values more seriously, which he does to great effect in *Lost in Yonkers*.

The play focuses on an elderly German-Jewish woman, the matriarch of a family that includes a retarded, pathetically affectionate daughter, a gangster son, a daughter whose breathing goes haywire whenever she visits the dowager, and the son whose spirit the mother has broken, who nervously leaves his own sons in her care. At

Danny Gerard and Irene Worth in a scene from the Richard Rodgers Theatre production of Neil Simon's Lost in Yonkers *(photograph by Martha Swope)*

first the mother seems more German than Jewish. She came of age in Berlin before World War I, and her iron will and her punctiliousness make her seem more a kinsman of Otto von Bismarck and Karl von Clausewitz than a daughter of Zion. And yet, late in the second act, when she speaks—almost contemptuously—in her own defense, it is clear that what has motivated her has been an obsession with survival. Moreover, although she does not luxuriate in self-sacrifice in the way that has inspired countless Jewish-mother jokes, the audience sees, to its great surprise, that she is profoundly capable of it.

Survival and self-sacrifice have traditionally been Jewish concerns. By addressing them without the usual Jewish stereotypes or cozy humor, Simon has written an unusually tough play. The production was distinguished by powerful performances from Irene Worth as the matriarch and Mercedes Ruehl as the pathetic daughter, who is liberated by her opportunity to "mother" the two boys.

Undoubtedly the most literate play of the year was *A Room of One's Own*, based entirely on the essay by Virginia Woolf, judiciously pruned by Patrick Garland. Eileen Atkins played Woolf lecturing young women on what they need to be independent and creative. Atkins never seemed merely to be lecturing the audience—or the young women. Everything she uttered grew out of a passionate concern, which made the evening emotionally powerful, not simply an opportunity to savor a pungent, sharply reasoned text.

An unusual play is based on Thomas Keneally's novel *The Playmaker* (1987). Using Keneally as an inspiration, Timberlake Wertenbaker, an American playwright who lives in London, wrote *Our Country's Good*, about an actual episode in Australian history. The governor of the English prison colony orders one of his lieutenants to direct some of the prisoners in a production of George Farquhar's comedy *The Recruiting Officer* (1829), the first piece of Western theater presented "down under."

In a curious way *Our Country's Good* is about the recovery of innocence. When the prisoners first appear they are justifiably embittered, antisocial creatures, their reflexes as keen and mistrustful as animals'. The play presents their gradual, sometimes comic, sometimes deeply moving transformation into nervous, deeply vulnerable human beings, reclaiming the dignity and modesty their years of criminal activity and the inequities of the judicial system have stripped from them.

As the prison governor tells the lieutenant who must direct the play, he wants to see if putting on the play can redeem the prisoners' humanity. The lieutenant is dubious about how much humanity remains in a woman with whom the governor is particularly concerned. "I'm afraid there may not be much there," he suggests. "How do we know what humanity lies hidden under the rags and filth of a mangled life?" the governor asks him.

In this description it might be imagined that Wertenbaker depicts a kind of eighteenth-century group therapy. What keeps the play from either sentimentality or solemnity is its sharp, often brutal humor. In a particularly thrilling moment one of the prisoners, a woman the governor has described as "lower than a slave, full of loathing, foul-mouthed, desperate," has undergone unfair trial. Despite her own refusal to cooperate, the governor saves her from hanging.

She does not thank him directly, but she fulfills his belief that she is redeemable when, in response to his remark that he hopes she will be good in the play, she says, with unexpected fervor, "Your Excellency, I will endeavor to speak Mr. Farquhar's lines with the elegance and clarity

their own worth commands." The play is a testament to the transforming power of art, but couched in an eloquence so earthy, so hardheaded it can persuade the least sentimental of its truth.

Our Country's Good was one of two plays to reach New York under a new plan designed to encourage the production of nonmusicals on Broadway. (At one point last year there were only eleven lit theaters on Broadway, offering four British musicals, five American musicals, and two American plays.) The distinction between Broadway, Off Broadway, and Off-Off-Broadway is an economic one, defining union contracts. Only on Broadway can writers and actors make a living from the theater.

The Broadway Alliance, as the scheme is called, is a tightly structured plan in which all the unions make concessions so that a play can be presented for a weekly cost of $70,000. The normal cost for a straight play is $125,000. Under the Alliance, when the box office takes in $100,000—with a ticket price of $24 as opposed to $45—the producers make a $30,000 profit (compared to the $25,000 loss they would bear under normal circumstances).

The second play presented under the Alliance was Steve Tesich's *The Speed of Darkness*. Tesich's play appears to be about Vietnam, about environmentalism, and about the American family. Ultimately it is about all of these things and none of them, achieving its greatest successes in its free flights of imagination.

Its plot concerns the reunion of two Vietnam veterans, one a prosperous contractor in a small South Dakota town, the other a homeless drifter. The play seems to be moving steadily toward the revelation of some My Lai-like affair, but instead it swerves into the description of an act of environmental sacrilege.

The play's constantly shifting focus makes it seem like a ride on a puddle jumper, which lurches up and down but then affords splendid vistas. These vistas occur in the speeches of the drifter. None of them, happily, is the harangue or lecture that a less imaginative, less whimsical playwright than Tesich might have written.

At one point, for example, the drifter explains why the homeless prefer to take shelter under a statue of Giuseppe Verdi rather than some untitled piece of modern sculpture. He leaps from this explanation to a conjecture about what the universe might be like if God had been a modernist and left his work untitled ("I don't

Program cover for the Nederlander Theatre production of Timberlake Wertenbaker's play based on Thomas Keneally's novel The Playmaker *(1987)*

want to be pinned down"). Len Cariou, as the prosperous vet, and Stephen Lang, as the drifter, made the play, for all its awkwardness, seem one of great eloquence.

Caryl Churchill's *Mad Forest* was conceived in collaboration with students of the Central School of Speech and Drama in London. Churchill; the director, Mark Wing-Davey; and a group of students went to Bucharest six months after the overthrow of Nicolae Ceauşescu and interviewed people from all walks of life about their experiences during the three days of the coup.

These recollections form the second act of the play, which draws its title from the name of the plain where Bucharest now stands. In ancient times it consisted of many small muddy streams and had to be crossed by foot. It was impenetrable to foreigners who did not know the paths, and horsemen, irritated at having to skirt it, named it "Mad Forest."

The first act of the play consists of vividly etched sketches of life under the Ceauşescus. The most memorable of the vignettes shows a young girl returning home with a treasure—four fresh eggs. Shortly afterward, an argument ensues. Her father flings one of the eggs to the floor. Without reproaching him, she fetches a plate and a piece of cardboard. She puts the shell on the plate, then skillfully scoops up the precious egg with the cardboard and places it on the plate, discarding the shell in the cardboard.

These vignettes in the lives of two families, some bitterly comic, all palpably full of the tension of life under a totalitarian regime, culminate in a wedding scene accompanied by the rich, haunting music of the Romanian church, which is then supplanted by one of the banal marches honoring the Ceauşescus.

From this evocation of a dark and oppressive world the play moves immediately into a bright scene where the participants in the rebellion sit on stools and simply recount their experiences during the overthrow of the dictators. These are the monologues transcribed by the students during their stay in Romania, artfully assembled and shaped by Churchill. The emotional effect of these simple narratives, delivered by the actors in wonderfully authentic Romanian accents, is shattering.

The third act shows that not much has changed. Power has not shifted significantly. Lives are brighter, filled with a new sense of promise, but there is an underlying sense of disquiet and even uncertainty about what actually happened during the three tumultuous days of revolution. The play ends with the characters' peasant roots emerging. A wedding party turns into a fracas. The spirit of the plain that preceded Bucharest still predominates.

Mule Bone is a work of historical reconstruction. The play, written in the early 1930s, was a collaboration between Langston Hughes and Zora Neale Hurston based on an unpublished story by Hurston. The two had a falling-out before it was finished, but Hurston did further work on it. Until the Lincoln Center Theater's production in February, it had never been produced.

The needs of scholarly reconstruction and those of the theater did not always mesh in this production. George Bass, professor of English at Brown University and a former secretary of Hughes, prepared the text. He added a prologue, in which Hurston describes her return to rural Florida. It was intended to put the backwoods humor of the play into context, but, in production, it seemed unnecessary. (The text Bass prepared was presented in its entirety, partly out of respect to the scholar, who died shortly before production began.)

Mule Bone is a simple story. Two men fight over the same woman. One hits the other over the head with a mule bone. This act of assault leads to a hilarious trial in the second act. The trial is characterized by a kind of folk humor that both Hughes and Hurston cherished but that, during the intervening decades, has become associated with negative stereotyping. The production was directed and acted with so much affection for the material that only the most humorless liberal could not laugh when a minister prosecuting the assailant, combining Anglo-Saxon jurisprudence and biblical exegesis, declares, "An y'all know dat de further back you gits on uh mule de more dangerous it gits an' if de jaw-bone slewed three thousand people, by de time you gits back to his hocks, it's pizin enough tuh kill a thousand."

The cast also had historic elements, featuring actors from all the prominent New York African-American theater companies of the last few decades. In a small part there was even the venerable Robert Earl Jones, a protégé of Hughes and the father of James Earl Jones.

From the Mississippi Delta, by Dr. Endesha Ida Mae Holland, also had the feel of folk theater though it tells the remarkable odyssey of the playwright in the last thirty years. Dr. Holland is the daughter of a woman who served as both midwife and brothel keeper in a small Mississippi town. Much of the first act tells about her mother. The second act is about herself. She had followed the less humanitarian of her mother's callings. When civil rights workers came to the delta, they encouraged the young woman to look beyond her tiny world. After intense political activisim, she went to Minnesota, where she eventually received a doctorate in American studies.

The description of her mother lingers over vignettes of regional color and eccentric personalities. The second act is less interesting because we learn little about Dr. Holland's education, more about how she spent time with the prostitutes of St. Paul, who later came to cheer at her commencement.

The play is written in the fashionable theatrical style of the present day, dividing Dr. Holland's voice among three actresses, who narrate sometimes in the first person, sometimes in the

Program cover for the Walter Kerr Theatre production of Paul Rudnick's comedy about a television actor who is tutored in Shakespearian acting by the ghost of John Barrymore

third. This kind of storytelling enhances the overall feeling of a communal experience. It also intensifies the piece's theatricality. But sometimes the audience wishes that instead of three voices, invariably in a state of feverish excitement, there could be one voice making the tale more personal than theatrical.

Jon Robin Baitz, the young playwright who made an auspicious debut three years ago with *The Film Society*, wrote about a Holocaust survivor in a play called *The Substance of Fire*. The protagonist has founded a New York publishing house to barricade himself against the cruelty of the world. He has erected walls of books around himself, which, he discovers, provide only rudimentary protection against time and economic necessity. More unhappily, the books have also served as barriers to understanding his three children. As one of them reproachfully declares, "People's lives are ruined by books, and they're all you relate to, Dad."

In the second act he converses with a psychiatric social worker the children send. It turns out they had met at a party many years before and have an unexpected kinship. Both have been gravely wounded, he by the civilization of the Old World, in which he continues to put so much trust, she by a husband who embodied all the charm of the New.

Their conversation is so beautifully delineated it might be an extremely satisfying one act. The first act, a series of confrontations with the publisher's malcontent children, seems, by contrast, tacked on as a way of providing background that could have been given without spelling everything out quite so literally. *The Substance of Fire*, whatever its weaknesses, is an unusually civilized piece of writing, especially so in view of the fact that its author is not yet thirty.

A thriving genre in the New York theater is camp, generally send-ups of old movies. Twenty years ago such plays had a vaguely subversive quality in their attacks on popular culture. Now they are as predictable as the culture they set out to parody. A notable exception was Charles Busch's *Red Scare on Sunset*, a play set in the McCarthy period. It ends with a Hollywood actress, who has come to Washington to "name names," all dolled up for the occasion, standing gallantly before a silhouette of the Capitol and reading from her list of names, one of which is her husband's. Normally this should horrify the audience, but it is a tribute to Busch's skills as both writer and actor (he plays the actress) that the scene is hilarious.

It is no mean feat to take a subject as ugly as McCarthyism and put it in the context of camp, but when Busch has a Communist cell masquerading as a method acting school (hideous grunts are heard in the background as the students work on a scene from *Life With Father*) and has the Commies trying, in the context of the play, to subvert the Freed Unit (the M-G-M division that, in the context of the play, created splashy musicals such as *Singin' in the Rain* to reconcile exploited Americans to the circumstances of their economic enslavement), it puts the Red Scare into a fresh and oddly amusing perspective.

Paul Rudnick's *I Hate Hamlet* had an amusing premise. A Los Angeles television actor has been cast as Hamlet in a Central Park production. By chance he rents the Greenwich Village apartment where John Barrymore once lived, and the ghost of Barrymore tutors him in the role. This promising idea was never developed.

It was simply a pretext for admittedly funny one-liners about the state of the theater. (His agent, for example, outraged that he is even considering performing Shakespeare in New York, explains, "Think reputation. Word on the street. When folks—let's call 'em Hollywood—when they hear that you're doing the greatest play in the English-speaking world, they're gonna know you're washed up.")

Two Alan Ayckbourn plays, *Absent Friends*, an unsettling comedy about an abortive reunion, and *Taking Steps*, a remarkable farce written for a theater-in-the-round, were imported by Off-Broadway groups. Instead of the door slamming that is generally at the heart of farce, and which would be awkward in a theater-in-the-round, Ayckbourn has his characters pantomime going up and down staircases on the perimeter of the stage. Each character has his own distinctive way of climbing stairs, so that their frequent sorties up and down take on the quality of a grand comic ballet.

Four plays with AIDS as a theme, spoken or not, were produced this year. The most successful was Terrence McNally's *Lips Together, Teeth Apart*. The play is set at a house on Fire Island. A young man who died of AIDS left the house to his sister, a Sunday painter. She and her dumpy husband, his pretentious sister, and the sister's sexually roving husband are spending a weekend there. The houses on either side are occupied by gay men who are unseen (though the dumpy husband gives a stunned account of a frenzied sexual encounter he sees in the bushes). In the foreground of the set is a swimming pool all four of the houseguests avoid, imagining it is full of deadly germs. McNally's image is potent: Surrounded by reminders of mortality, his two couples pursue lives of absurd and relentless triviality.

It is a daring play that sometimes goes too far. One of its assertions is that none of its characters—the audience, as well—is committed to life. One of the men says, "I don't believe in enough to be a father." The Sunday painter watches a young man swim far out to sea. Before he dives in, their eyes meet. Though she senses his suicidal mission, she makes no attempt to stop him. "My eyes didn't say, 'Stay, life is worth living.' They said, 'Go, Godspeed, God bless . . . I know where you're going. I've wanted to go there too.'" In the context of a comedy filled with contrivances and miscalculations, such nihilism seemed far too overstated.

In *Raft of the Medusa* Joe Pintauro depicts a therapy group in which all the participants have AIDS. The particular session presented in the play occurs just after one of the members has died. (His painful final moments begin the play, and members of the group carry him off in his hospital bed like a funeral cortege.) The man who died was, in the 1970s, a rabbinical student unable to reconcile his homosexuality with the demands of his chosen profession. The psychiatrist who guides the group had encouraged him not to deny the demands of his sexuality. Now, of course, the doctor feels remorseful. The relationship of these two men, embodying central conflicts of sexuality and society, might have made an absorbing play. Pintauro, however, has tried to represent a dozen different dilemmas, a variety of classes, and the result seems largely rhetorical.

There was also an unexpected amount of rhetoric in A. R. Gurney's *The Old Boy*. The play marked a departure for Gurney, the consummate chronicler of WASP life. It concerns an aspiring politician's return to his New England prep school to be honored himself and to honor a school friend who has died. He discovers his friend died of AIDS, which triggers a series of painful memories.

When they were school chums in the 1960s, the friend confessed his homosexual inclinations. Horrified, the aspiring politician tricked him into marrying a girl he himself was discarding. The result is that all their lives have been blighted. Understanding that he has been responsible, the politico uses his chapel speech the following morning to decry society's attitudes toward gays.

The speech has a grace one would expect of Gurney, but the play that precedes it seemed overly schematized and histrionic. Gurney has always understood that there is something deeply theatrical, even Chekhovian, about WASPs unconsciously saying simple things that conceal a wealth of emotions. He was unable to portray overstatement convincingly.

Scott McPherson's *Marvin's Room* is not technically about AIDS. But it has two terminally ill characters, and nowadays that is enough to give it an importance its writing would not merit in less agitated times. In the first scene, for example, a doctor appears who does not know how to apply a tourniquet, a high-school-level joke. Also reduced to a sophomoric joke is another character, who has three collapsed vertebrae. To quiet the pain she has an electronic anesthetizer con-nected to her brain. Unfortunately if she uses it in the kitchen it operates the automatic garage door.

This juxtaposition of humor and seriousness was taken as a sign of McPherson's sophistication, but it seemed more a symptom of the press's eagerness to discover profundity in increasingly meaningless theater. What interest the play offers comes from a subplot in which an immature woman has to cope with her rebellious son.

The desperation with which playwrights are attempting to transfer the dislocations of the 1990s—social and particularly sexual—to the stage was apparent in many plays that opened this year. Timothy Mason's *Babylon Gardens* is a portrait of a Yuppie couple who are drawn to their social inferiors. He "adopts" a homeless woman who, he eventually realizes, is suckering him, a fact which does not diminish his commitment to her. His wife has a penchant for drawing slum children, one of whom, late in the play, victimizes her. She accepts it cheerfully, even gratefully.

Keith Curran's *Walking the Dead* takes place at the wake for a lesbian who has become a man through surgery. As friends talk about her life, the play flashes back to Veronica's announcement that she wants to change sex. She meets with surprisingly little resistance from her female lover, an artist who melts plastic dildos in a toaster oven. The only opposition comes from her strident, bigoted mother. Nevertheless Veronica becomes Ronald, complete with beard and Hitler-like mustache. Veronica's mother is remarrying and begs Ronald to wear a dress to the ceremony. Ronald, who never wore dresses even when he was Veronica, acquiesces, shaving and wearing a flashy chartreuse number. On the way home from the wedding Ronald is attacked by ruffians who want to rape him and are outraged to discover he has male genitals. Had Marston or Webster tackled this material, the result might at least have offered some explosive poetry. Curran achieved only adolescent *epatisme*.

Sexual identity was also explored—at least theoretically—in Constance Congdon's *Casanova*. Congdon treats a potentially fascinating subject, the life of the eighteenth-century seducer, in an entirely clichéd way. She alludes to several of Giovanni Giacomo Casanova's actual contemporaries—Lorenzo Da Ponte, the librettist of Wolfgang Amadeus Mozart's *Don Giovanni* (1787), himself a tireless seducer, and the Chevalier D'Eon, a secret agent for Louis XV. Louis

Program cover for the Playwrights Horizons production of Scott McPherson's play about terminal illness

XVI sent Pierre-Augustin Caron Beaumarchais (who had not yet written that troublesome play) to London to persuade D'Eon, a transvestite with a passion for grandly feminine costumes, to end some intrigues instigated by Louis XV. As a reward D'Eon received a generous settlement that included money for a feminine wardrobe.

These historic figures might have served as studies of how modern sexual anxieties took root in prerevolutionary France, but Congdon was content merely to portray Casanova as a charmless, pompous ravisher of innocence. Even the most shameless male chauvinist would be hard put to defend Casanova from the many charges a contemporary feminist could place against him. But why spend two hours and forty minutes watching seduction after seduction in which the women are as stereotyped as Casanova himself? He may not deserve better, but *we* do.

Arthur Kopit's *Road to Nirvana* is about a Hollywood producer who, to secure the rights to the life of a Madonna-like rock star, must eat a bowl of nuns' feces and sacrifice one of his testicles.

The pleasantest light in which it could be seen was as a parody of David Mamet's *Speed-the-Plow*. But it was neither funny nor skillful enough to succeed as satire; overall, it seemed merely exploitative.

In Jane Anderson's *The Baby Dance*, a pair of Los Angeles yuppies pays a pair of crackers living in a trailer in Louisiana to bring to term the baby the latter cannot afford to keep. The contrast between their two worlds is drawn out relentlessly and tiresomely, though there are occasional moments of insight. At one point the yuppie woman remonstrates with the cracker husband about his racist remarks. "Lemme ask you something," he retorts. "If you're into civil rights, then how come you advertised for a white baby? How come you're paying so much for a white baby when you could of gotten a black baby for free?"

The playwright cannot sustain such honesty. Halfway through the second act the characters discover the baby may be retarded (the preparation for this surprise is presumably that the mother drank coffee and smoked during her pregnancy, much against the wishes of the health-conscious yuppies). Neither couple wants to keep the baby. It is put up for adoption. The yuppies will presumably be able to buy another one, and the crackers, comforting one another on the hospital bed, will doubtless soon be back "in production."

David Hirson's *La Bete* was a rarity, a comedy in verse. The play is set in seventeenth-century France, where an acting troupe in the patronage of Prince Conti is asked to add a new member, whom the leader considers a buffoon. The leader, whose name is Elomire (a sophomoric anagram for Molière), despises Valere. Valere is supposed to be a bewitchingly amusing fellow. Hirson gives him a twenty-minute monologue early in the first act that is an old-fashioned virtuoso piece for an actor. The role was originally to be played by Ron Silver, who left the cast shortly before the Broadway opening. He was replaced by an amiable if undistinguished actor named Tom McGowan. Even the more accomplished Silver, however, probably could not have enhanced a play whose major interest seemed the demonstration of how facile Hirson was with verse.

Admittedly some of Hirson's verse is very skillful. One of Valere's speeches makes a good example. It begins with extreme assurance, then makes a joke of the author's eagerness to be clever:

"Diction, like aesthetics, is more free:
It's where we show our creativity
By choosing metaphors and ways of speech—
I'd say 'the shell-crushed strand'; you'd say 'the
    beach'.
Semantics is like . . . (hang on . . . let me see . . .
I've *used* aesthetics and morality . . .)
Semantics is like . . . SWIMMING! . . . (no, that's
    bad!
O, DAMMIT! DAMMIT! DAMN! I thought I had
A brilliant speech developing! DOMMAGE!)
Well . . . back to our exciting persiflage . . .[.]"

Eventually the rhyming becomes exhausting because it is so self-involved and so unmistakably self-satisfied. Toward the end Elomire observes, "When the honest word is stripped of sense / Its *form* assumes unnatural consequence," Hirson's self-conscious self-criticism. Whatever virtues the script had were buried under a foppish production.

If *La Bete* was the most fascinating of the failures of 1991 the most disappointing was *States of Shock*, a Sam Shepard play that seemed like a piece of 1960s nostalgia. The action takes place around two tables in a "family restaurant." At one sit two WASPs, from whom all life seems to have been drained. The other is occupied by two crazed Vietnam War veterans, one in a wheelchair, trying to determine exactly what happened when one veteran's son was killed in battle.

The only interesting image in the play is the need for an "enemy." What Shepard intends is an ironic comment on the end of the cold war, on America's psychological dependence on a Communist foe. But there is another "enemy," the one Shepard and his fellow 1960s playwrights needed—the stolid WASPs, the smug bourgeois audience he here lampoons. Not even in darkest Connecticut are there WASPs as benighted as the ones Shepard portrays. The adolescent play suggests Shepard is as much sealed in another time frame as the "enemy" he so glibly attacks.

In the minds of many New York theatergoers the high point of the year was the visit to the Brooklyn Academy of Music by the Royal Swedish Theater, which presented three classic plays directed by Ingmar Bergman.

The production of Eugene O'Neill's *Long Day's Journey Into Night* (1957) was a much more lighthearted view of the play than is customary. The most radical of the productions was Henrik Ibsen's *A Doll's House* (1879), in which Bergman tinkered with the last act. At the point where Nora goes to change into her street clothes,

Bergman brought down the curtain. When it rises, the scene is Nora and Torvald's bedroom. Torvald is asleep when she enters. Because he is naked he must remain defensively under the covers while Nora lectures him. (This has less to do with Torvald's modesty, I suspect, than various strictures of the Royal Swedish Theater.) Whatever the alteration's shortcomings, it made the all too familiar play fresh again.

The most satisfying of the three productions was August Strindberg's *Miss Julie* (1888), starring Lena Olin and Peter Stormare. It was a surprisingly theatrical production. Theatricality, of course, is a dangerous word in New York, especially in relation to *Miss Julie*. Strindberg portrays a woman who is a sexual aggressor, who relentlessly sheds everything about her identity that serves as a barrier to sleeping with her servant Jean. By the end of the play she is left with no class, no religion, no sense of herself, seemingly no course but suicide.

In the wisdom of New York theater the only way to present such a story is through dreary, humorless naturalism, avoiding anything that smacks of *theater*. By contrast, Bergman brought the play to harrowing life by accentuating its theatricality. Toward the end, for example, at the mention of sunrise, the stage lights come up suddenly, unsubtly, to their brightest, heightening the sense that all until then happened in the half-light of Midsummer Eve. Now mythic time is over. The harsh light of day has returned.

Such moments work only when the actors project a heightened sense of reality. Stormare, who was Bergman's Hamlet four years ago, gave Jean sardonic humor. The conventional approach to Jean is that he is a hunk in lackey's clothing. By contrast, Stormare made him comically servile. Even when he dragged Miss Julie into the bedroom it seemed an act of inebriated recklessness rather than assertive masculinity. Throughout the play, in fact, he seemed more reluctant to shed his class than Miss Julie hers, perhaps because his craven position gave him more security than her "liberation" gave her.

As Julie, Olin made an extraordinary transition from a boldly superior figure to one of Edvard Munch-like anxiety, ultimately to someone mindless and poignant. Even the normally awkward peasant dance, a sort of satyr element Strindberg seems to have thrown into the play in a moment of pretension, worked in Bergman's production. He had one of the drunken peasants try to bathe in the water barrel in Miss Julie's kitchen. Everytime thereafter that someone drew water (even to brew coffee) there was the sense that the communal life had been soiled. Such details made this an unusually illuminating *Miss Julie*.

The noted director and acting teacher Rob-ert Lewis declared that the Bergman productions were "the only theater we had in New York last year. The rest was show business." As this survey indicates, there was not even much in the way of show business.

The Year in Literary Biography

William Foltz
University of Hawaii

This year marks the end of one and the beginning of two massive (and often unwieldy) biographies. Michael Holroyd's *Bernard Shaw: The Lure of Fantasy, 1918-1951* (Random House) almost ends his trilogy (1988-); notes and bibliography will be published separately. But two other lives have begun: the first of three volumes of John Worthen, David Ellis, and Mark Kinkead-Weekes's joint biography of D. H. Lawrence, an assemblage of too many facts, and another first volume (of two, fortunately) on Johann Wolfgang von Goethe, by Nicholas Boyle. Then we have the large blockbuster *Dickens* (HarperCollins), a book which in more civilized times would be published in two volumes. The paperback version promises to be as fat and ugly as the post-esparto grass horrors of Charles Dickens's century now decaying on college shelves.

However one defines a "good read"—surely one of biography's crucial aims—the book should lie easy on the lap, and the text should please, not offend the eye: fine printing has, of course, become expensive, but the print of too many of this year's indexes becomes a gray blur, and not just to the vision of a presbyope. The indexes, themselves, are another matter. Biography is about people. The force of this truism is often lost on the maker of indexes who not only neglects to compile a full list of those mentioned in the text, but even puts them on the wrong page; it would seem that the computer-assisted index does not solve this problem. And the reader of biography who is often curious will not appreciate sloppy, inconsistent, or nonexistent documenta-tion. But there is much for which we should be grateful: amazing industry. Many biographers have visited enough archives and libraries that their frequent-flier bonuses, taken together, would push them beyond *Voyager 2*.

Most of the subjects reviewed below are British or American. Two German writers are included, Johann Wolfgang von Goethe and Franz Kafka, for their biographers present not only a life, but an age and sensibility. That big names are done again is not surprising, but it is refreshing to see the scope of interest expand: James Baldwin's essays, Goethe's fiscal policy, Henry Fielding's pamphlets, Samuel Butler's (1835-1902) paintings, and Anthony Burgess's music are topics which aid in explicating purely literary endeavors. The same problems recur: sympathy that becomes uncritical and dispassion that becomes dull. Then there is the biographical inference: that John Keats (or D. H. Lawrence) ate porridge is a given, but trivial; that Keats drank wine (or Lawrence beer) needs no archive's bill of fare. But generally this has been a good year.

To understand Henry Fielding is not to understand England in the first half of the eighteenth century: he, like Goethe, should not be seen as a representative figure. But since both were so involved in the public life of their times, those times must be presented. Donald Thomas's *Henry Fielding: A Life* (St. Martin's Press), like Boyle's life of Goethe, gives us the writer and his age—but considerably more concisely. Though Martin and Ruthe Battestin's *Henry Fielding* (1990) is more officially scholarly, this biography reads better. Thomas is well qualified for a biography of Fielding; not only has he burrowed in the Public Record Office and located new letters, but his earlier *A Long Time Burning: The History of Literary Censorship in England* (1969) and biographies of James Cardigan, Algernon Charles Swinburne, Robert Browning, and—in this case most usefully—Marquis de Sade all recognized an ingrained sense of evil in man's nature. It also helps to be a witty poet. Now, the social setting can become confusing in a time of political patronage, but Thomas shows the lines of power and the push of the propertied classes, especially Sir Robert Walpole, Arthur Lyttelton, and John of Lancaster, Duke of Bedford. Political controversy was complex; and London was a brutal city. The violence of the mob and Fielding's responses to it, both as an overworked magistrate and indignant pamphleteer, are remarkable: the first for savagery, the second for tempered compassion. We see initially an educated fortune hunter, then the successful, scurrilous, and dissipated playwright who attacked the abuse of lotteries, the pedantry of Richard Bentley, and the promiscuity and self-righteousness of those who would frequent a brothel one night and burn it the next. With family lawsuits, arrest for debt, marriage, the death of his daughter, and remarriage to what Walpole and Fielding himself called a "whore," the pregnant maid of his late wife, Fielding was no Allworthy.

But he was a fine novelist and extraordinary playwright. Thomas revives the plays, and his introductions to the novels, though necessarily succinct, are splendid and cogent. The novels are distinguished by a self-conscious intellectual power, a power Samuel Richardson and his followers could never equal. Thomas makes the unfashionable claim that the intelligence and tradition which most distinguish Fielding's novels were soon to be defeated by the romances of "female writers and readers and their evangelical bodyguards." *Tom Jones* (1749) is the culmination of a tradition. William Makepeace Thackeray, a hundred years after Fielding's death in 1754, sensed and deplored the triumph of feminine sensibilities. The Victorian age began early.

And above the Victorians there looms Charles Dickens. The Dickens scholar or fan (since this is a Book-of-the-Month Club selection) can choose to subscribe to the *Dickensian*, now in its eighty-sixth year, purchase a reproduction of the Gad's Hill desk at forty-four hundred dollars or buy Peter Ackroyd's twelve-hundred-page biog-

Dust jacket for the first American edition of the biography that, according to Anthony Burgess, "supersedes all other Dickens biographies"

raphy. Opt for the book: Ackroyd has read all the scholarship, and the desk is only similar to the one in Robert William Buss's famous 1870 painting, *Dickens's Dreams*. But start first with a re-reading of the novels: Ackroyd refuses to indulge the quasi-lettered with tedious plot summaries.

What sort of biography is *Dickens*? Ackroyd's answer is found in one of seven two- to three-page breaks that interrupt the narrative; in some Dickens speaks to Ackroyd, in one Thomas Chatterton, George Eliot, and Oscar Wilde chat with Dickens, and in the last Ackroyd dreams of Dickens, but in the sixth he defines his biography's aim: to "interanimate" the orthodox split between life and works in a new way.

What exactly is Ackroyd's interanimation and how does it work so well? It is the linking of isolated episodes into cumulative significance: "the biographer must behave like an archeologist and go field walking over the life of his subject, looking for those faint traces and furrows which indicate the presence of a time long gone"; this is a method that is most successful dealing with the childhood of Dickens and with early-Victorian London. This is partly accomplished by re-creating the streets of vanished London (the book could use maps); with statistics, for example, how many had typhus in 1847 (25 percent); through extensive and superb citation of both published and unpublished letters; recollections of foreign travelers; and the author's experience as he weeps, reliving the anguish of Dickens the child. But more important is the astonishing ability to organize biographical details. In Ackroyd's analysis of the early novels we are persuaded that Dickens's visual memory of the blacking warehouse informs *Oliver Twist* (1837-1839), *Nicholas Nickleby* (1838-1839), *The Old Curiosity Shop* (1840-1841), and then later *The Mystery of Edwin Drood* (1870); the Marshalsea in *Little Dorrit* (1855-1857), *David Copperfield* (1849-1850), and earlier *The Pickwick Papers* (1836-1837); Oliver Twist is traced in the deaths of Nell, Florence Dombey, Rosa Maylie, and Mary Hogarth. In Dickens's later novel *A Tale of Two Cities* (1859), Ackroyd examines, as have other critics, the literary antetypes of Thomas Carlyle and Edward Bulwer-Lytton, but he adds otherwise disparate childhood memories of prisoners to Dickens's relations with Ellen Ternan, and Dickens's earlier research for *Barnaby Rudge* (1841) to the play he was then producing with Wilkie Collins, *The Frozen Deep*. Ackroyd is right: Dickens had planned this novel all his life.

But such a method can go wrong and not only with the isolated excessively analytical comment. For example Dickens's speculation that were he born in America he would have "died, poor, unnoticed, and a 'black sheep'" does not make America one vast blacking factory. Ackroyd's analysis of *Dombey and Son* (1846-1848) begins masterfully: childhood chapel attendance, Lord Grey's fishiness, the Paris morgue, railroads, traveling in the Alps, editing the *Daily News*, meeting a rich monomaniac in Lausanne, Babbage's machine, and assisted emigration, all these Ackroyd finds in the dense texture of the novel. But among the twenty pages of critical explanation, the novelist—the biographer himself—emerges: as Paul Dombey dies, Dickens's text is interrupted rather than illuminated by Ackroyd's fanciful re-creation. The page, 520, has *Dickens* in italics, *Ackroyd* in regular type. This desire to shape a life into a novel also ends the biography: Dickens, whose last walk in June 1870 had been

"beautifully anticipated" thirty-four years earlier in *The Pickwick Papers*, a novel whose imagery of light subdues the dark of his last novel, sinks to the floor of Gad's Hill citing *Hard Times* (1854). It is, perhaps, too good to be true.

Ackroyd is better with Dickens's "struggle and work and anxiety lit by the glare of intense flame." And Dickens's hard times begin with his childhood and youth to which the biographer devotes nine chapters, arguing—as is surely correct—that these years formed the adult man and novelist. The remaining twenty-six chapters proceed generally two years at a time: this means that the fifteen or twenty pages devoted to literary analysis may be split between two chapters, and some of the later, longer chapters can focus only on life, that is, marital misery. On the topics of Dickens's marriage and Ellen Ternan, Ackroyd insists that, given the evidence of Dickens's character and fictional fantasies, the affair was not consummated. For Dickens safe sex was fraternal and infantile, a "concatenation of infatuation, obsession, and disavowal," and this was true, Ackroyd argues, of his relation with his sisters-in-law, Mary (dead at seventeen) and Georgina Hogarth, his sister Fanny (dead at thirty-seven), and Ellen Ternan who was with him when he died. Perhaps. Much more likely is Ackroyd's speculation that the public readings kept Dickens alive rather than killing him as his first biographer, John Forster, insisted.

Though Ackroyd has read extensively, he often gives the impression in his text that his is the first biography of Dickens: Edgar Johnson's *Charles Dickens: His Tragedy and Triumph* (1952) is alluded to only once. Other biographies can serve as a corrective: surely Dickens was pulling Ralph Waldo Emerson's leg when he said a son who was particularly chaste would not be in good health, rather than defining the moral order of the world as sympathy combined with discipline, pity with control, as Ackroyd portentously insists. He is much more convincing in his initial excellent chapter on America: it was there that Dickens discovered his Englishness.

When Ackroyd avoids sounding like Thomas Carlyle—writing sham-Dickens such as solemn sentence fragments; the purple such as "we are left with the image of the young boy writhing in agony on the rat-infested floor"; the digressive such as migraines suggest "latent anxiety" about the world; and the frankly inhuman such as Dickens was lucky that Mary Hogarth died when he was twenty-five, for if later, the death would not have shaped his imagination—and sticks to the life and works, then this biography succeeds.

Ackroyd demonstrates time and time again that it was power that drove Dickens, the power to create a fictional world and his own life: "when he recreates the world, he recreates his own self," and Ackroyd traces the causal relationship between life and works: Dickens is a novelist writing himself from the romantic vocabulary of *Oliver Twist*, the theatrical of *Nicholas Nickleby*, to the social of *Little Dorrit*, to the ethical of *Martin Chuzzlewit*. So perhaps Dickens died living his fictional world.

No doubt some buyers will actually believe that academic footnotes merely perpetuate a nineteenth-century illusion that literary scholarship can be empirical. For them Ackroyd has written "little essays"—and they are splendidly succinct—for each chapter. But the reader who may wish to pursue a topic is too often frustrated. It is clear that exact page references to specific journals and books are often not needed: indexes do the work; and Ackroyd always provides the location of various manuscripts he has consulted and documents the "more arcane references" to Dickens's published works. But it would be helpful to know exactly where one could find Karl Marx's comment to Friedrich Engels on Dickens's "social truths," where Aleksandr Blok reported that he felt more horror in Dickens than in Edgar Allan Poe. It is essential to provide at least a chapter number to the novels: because Ackroyd's style is so allusive, unless the title of a novel appears on the page, the index is silent. Orphans are reorphaned: David Copperfield, Little Dorrit, and Nell occur as characters in the text, but not in the index. Ackroyd's austerely titled *Dickens* then is the richest biography we are likely to have for the next seventy years, rich not only in detail but in argument, and equally rich with its re-creation of nineteenth-century London.

The other major nineteenth-century biography of this year is that of "the most original poet of the nineteenth century." Avoiding the hagiographical which has made him a priest not a poet and the historical which makes him a paradigmatic Victorian, Robert Martin (the biographer of Alfred, Lord Tennyson and Edward FitzGerald) succeeds with *Gerard Manley Hopkins: A Very Private Life* (Putnam's) in presenting the life of a suffering man. Whether readers will accept all his conclusions is another matter. Martin draws upon recently available material, especially the facsimile edition of the now unexpurgated note-

books and early poems, and previously neglected material such as the diaries of Hopkins's acquaintance Samuel Brooke, the working notes of Humphrey House, the Bridges Deposit in the Bodleian Library, and the scattered muniments of the Dolben family. Nor is he reticent in using the poems to illustrate the poet's life: to ignore parallels would be, as he rightly insists, "pig-headed."

What then is our new picture of this complex poet? A man—not just a poet or a Jesuit or a teacher—stubborn, possessed of an "overworked moral consciousness," who never took the easy way out of his church, out of his family, or out of common poetic practice, but also a man with close friends and close ties to his surroundings. And it is with friendship and setting that Martin most often succeeds. It is not just his ability to distinguish between the Oxford of Hopkins the undergraduate and the changed city upon his return twelve years later, but his accuracy in presenting the dark valleys near St. Beuno's, the florid plasterwork of St. Stephen's Green, and the cold granite of Hopkins's tomb that forces one who has seen these places to realize what was not noticed.

Hopkins, who briefly met many famous figures (Dante Gabriel Rossetti, William Holman Hunt, Jenny Lind, William Butler Yeats), and to whose aunt John Henry Newman's brother proposed, and whose uncles lived from Peking to Kahuku, was more lucky in his friendships than in his vocations. And of these his friendship with Robert Bridges looks better and better: not only was his tolerance and patience often tried, but Bridges has become a major source for information concerning the relationship between Hopkins and Digby Dolben. But not an entirely open source: Bridges seems to have suppressed what Martin emphasizes in his life of Hopkins—the homoerotic impulse. This impulse, suppressed by Hopkins, led to his priestly vocation and his poetry. This will remain controversial. But Martin argues well: since Hopkins's intellect, personality, and spiritual cast of mind were formed before his conversion, Martin spends many pages on the poet's Oxford years, and to examine these years is to examine Bridges's strange, beautiful, and young cousin who amazed Henry James and attracted Hopkins, only to drown before his twentieth year. Dolben was a tractarian, a Mariolater, a ritualist, and a poet: all this and his dangerous beauty attracted the twenty-one-year-old future Jesuit. Hopkins's poetry at Oxford records an anguished and unrequited love. True, Martin says, we have to change the gender of the addressee in some poems, and true, we should like more detailed evidence (most convincing is Bridges's note "these two sonnets must *never* be printed"), but the extent to which his disappointed passion influenced his poetry even into the "terrible sonnets" of the Dublin years is another matter. The topic of the poet's homoeroticism can no longer be politely ignored after the publication of the full text of the notebooks and this important biography.

After Hopkins embraced Rome rather than Dolben, the biography traces Hopkins's bewildering series of moves; his order simply did not know what to do with him. And this was not, Martin makes clear in the two thorough chapters devoted to the Dublin years, the fault of his order. The extent of Hopkins's happiness or misery, faith or despair, academic success or failure in Dublin is a question that has vexed scholars for fifty years: on it hinges the meaning of his last poems. Martin argues that Hopkins's perhaps too scrupulous consistency isolated him from others. This led to an increased self-inflicted isolation and almost madness. For us this is fortunate— as it was for George Orwell, who recited Hopkins's work to keep off the cold of the Spanish front; we have some of the most moving and oddly beautiful poems in English. For him, tragic; he died estranged and a stranger. Whereas Hopkins's life is dull and tedious, his poetry is not. Martin's integration of life and works is succinctly seen in poems such as "Harry Ploughman" (among the other fifty considered): here events and documents over a twelve-year period (three specific paintings, an Irish laborer, dialect study, sexual admiration, letters, journal entries) unite in a dense and persuasive reading. But as thorough as Martin's explication and narratives are, both are marked, even from the title, by wit and sympathy. The thoroughness and variety of Martin's narrative and explications—we learn of William Gladstone's politics, William Butterfield's architecture, God's private communications—do not prevent but encourage humor and humanity. Of all biographies reviewed here, *Gerard Manley Hopkins: A Very Private Life*, is the most graceful and rewarding.

There is some need for a new biography of Samuel Butler (1835-1902); like Hopkins his training was clerical and his thought at variance with orthodoxy. Peter Raby's work will help supplement Philip Henderson's *Samuel Butler: The Incarnate Bachelor* (1953). Raby's *Samuel Butler: A Biography* (University of Iowa Press) has made use of much

material published in the last thirty years, especially Bassington's book on Butler in New Zealand and the continuing volumes of the published letters. The photographs of four of Butler's paintings are good additions. All in all, this biography is aimed at the general reader: Raby's literary criticism is often judicious, and the extensive plot summaries, ten pages on *Erewhon* (1872), for example, will jog the memory; but his defense of some of Butler's opinions is too often untenable.

As with Orwell, one must separate the author's life from his quasi-autobiographical writings. Can Butler's family be as horrible as that of Ernest Pontifex in *The Way of All Flesh* (1903)? The answer is a qualified yes: his father was a typical Victorian, but often with a vengeance. The elder Butler claimed that *Erewhon* killed his mother, though Samuel knew it was stomach cancer. Raby's early chapters, which rehearse, as other biographers have done, Butler's childhood, school days, and student life at Cambridge, restore what the novelist excluded: Shrewsbury, according to other old boys, was not that bad; St. John's (a brief ten pages), not full of bloated aristocrats. One realizes that Butler left St. John's as an ordained clergyman theologically ignorant—or innocent—of the last twenty years of biblical scholarship: this topic could use expansion.

Perhaps the best treatment of the life are the sections on New Zealand; here autopsy, examination of memoirs of (to most of us) obscure settlers in New Zealand, and interviews are put to good use. And it was in New Zealand that Butler read Charles Darwin and formed that series of puzzling friendships with young men. Raby is sane here: he refuses to play pop psychologist with either the leechlike Charles Paine Pauli whom Butler met in New Zealand or the "professional invalid" and future biographer Henry Festing Jones, whom he met upon his return to London. Raby argues that friendship did exist, not only with these two men, but with Miss Savage, the Aunt Alethea of *The Way of All Flesh*. In fact, Butler's sex life was probably no different than that of some of our great-grandfathers: many kept mistresses, but most were also married.

There has been considerable work on Butler's quarrel with Darwin since Basil Willey's book of thirty years ago, and Darwin was a family acquaintance and later surrogate, that is, hated, father figure. Raby does a useful job untangling Butler's thoughts and arguments, for But-

Dust jacket for the first American edition of Holroyd's biography of Shaw from the time he wrote Heartbreak House *(1919) until his death*

ler had a mind deeply suspicious and isolated from current thought. After one hundred years it is difficult to put straight the morass of innuendo and insult caused by sloppy book reviews in *Nature* and *The Popular Science Review*, but Raby succeeds. In fact, we have almost a defense of Butler's position in those pre-DNA and RNA days. Not that Butler was all that isolated: he had, as Raby makes clear, a wide circle of friends rather than followers, for example, Yeats's father, Robert Bridges, Algernon Charles Swinburne (whose name does not appear in the index), and the actor Sir Johnston Forbes-Robertson. And having overthrown, as he thought, Darwin, Butler went on to Homer: the outrage when he insisted that Homer was a she and the odyssey a circumnavigation of Sicily may be compared to Harold Bloom's recent assertions about the author(ess) of the Old Testament. Alas, no amount of citation from Robert Graves can back up either Butler's argument about Homer or his later *Shakespeare's Sonnets Reconsidered* (1899), though

Raby tries. Butler was not, as George Bernard Shaw would have us believe, the greatest English writer since 1850. Raby says he is "unclassifiable," but this serviceable biography will assist in classifying him.

Among Butler's fans was Shaw, and the third and concluding volume of Michael Holroyd's extraordinary biography, *Bernard Shaw, The Lure of Fantasy, 1918-1951* (Random House), brings to an end one of the best, if not the longest, English literary biographies of recent years— say a generation or more. To condense over forty years of lecturing, pamphleteering, play writing, filming, and travel is a considerable accomplishment. And Shaw lived a long time; so did William Wordsworth. And that is the problem: Edward Gibbon's best work was done after the age of forty, but can we say the same of Shaw? This may account for the third volume being not quite as witty as it is condensed (it would have been longer except the ten thousand references are to be published later).

One thing the book will do is encourage the reader to go back to (assuming he has read them in the first place) the later plays: *Too True to be Good* (1932), *The Six of Calais* (1934), *The Simpleton of the Unexpected Isles* (1935), *The Millionairess* (1936), and *In Good King Charles's Golden Days* (1939). Or perhaps not. Part of the reason for this book's length is the extensive recapitulation of plots: this suggests either the reader's unfamiliarity or Shaw's, not obscurity, but datedness. In duscussing *Back to Methuselah* (1922), Holroyd masterfully links Samuel Butler's anti-Darwinism to Shaw's (from the playwright's 1887 review of Butler's *Luck or Cunning?*), quickly deals with the play's reception by New Yorkers, Londoners, and V. I. Lenin (who called Shaw "a good man fallen among the Fabians"), selects a superb photo of Edith Evans as the Serpent, but has to spend ten pages retelling the plot. Granted, *Back to Methuselah* is long, but Holroyd does the same for *Heartbreak House* (1920), *Saint Joan* (1923), *Too True to be Good* (ten pages), and most of the other later plays. This would seem to suggest that one of the biographer's aims is to resuscitate the literary reputation of an aging Edwardian about whom there were already fifty works by 1930.

Since this is a biography of Shaw, we get not only the standard life and works, but the opinions. The index lists seventy topics, excluding what he said about people. The opinions are rarely dull, but often as offensively wrong as they are witty. After two volumes a biographer must become close to his subject. Holroyd at times comes too close. The end of *Heartbreak House* is the beginning of another Great War, not a prophecy of "nuclear holocaust." Often Holroyd sees his subject's faults: after an extensive examination of the 1928 *The Intelligent Woman's Guide to Capitalism and Socialism*, he admits Shaw is late by fifty years, that *Back to Methuselah* needs a preface to Shaw's preface, and *The Apple Cart* (1929) can be revived. But just as often Holroyd tries to get him off the hook. This is particularly true of his 1931 trip to Russia. Shaw is in good company— we recall Lincoln Stevens and the brothers Reuther—(he is also accompanied by Lady Astor). If it was true, as Holroyd says, that Shaw's "theatricalizing of reality has become a habit of mind," this fantasizing also obscures moral realities: to liquidate does not mean, as Shaw defined it, to cause unemployment by technology. Perhaps it is this moral blindness which infects the last plays of Shaw.

The reader will encounter people and references to people from the first volumes, such as William Archer, the Webbs (Sydney and Beatrice), the burial of Thomas Hardy, the ghostly letters of Ellen Terry, and will also meet new faces. Of them, some are still famous (Lady Astor, Mrs. Patrick Campbell, Winston Churchill, Edward Elgar, Frank Harris, T. E. Lawrence, Gene Tunney, Joseph Stalin ["Like Undershaft, Stalin is UNASHAMED"]); and others still obscure (the critic St. John Ervine; the actor Sir Barry Jackson; the filmmaker Gabriel Pascal; the Viennese playwright whom the Germanless Shaw translated, Seigfried Trebitsch). In addition, there are the women: his wife Charlotte and Molly Tompkins, an ex-Zeigfeld dancer but chaste-with-Shaw admirer; Dame Laurentia McLachlan, the prioress of Stanbrook Abbey and Shaw's splendidly sane secretary, Blanch Patch. Charlotte Shaw, shyer than Dorothy Wordsworth, in addition to suggesting subjects for his plays, simply and amazingly kept Shaw going; it is in his almost confessional letters to her that we see Shaw most clearly, though not always most pleasantly.

Holroyd suggests that we see Shaw's last quarter century as a rewriting of the first seventy years: two editions of his collected works in the 1930s, new plays with the old themes, and old plays in the new forms (films). In general, he "followed a mode of phrase-making more commonly used by those in power (final solutions, acceptable losses)." This perceptive remark would explain his attraction to Stalin, Benito Mussolini,

and initially to the early Keynesian Oswald Mosely, but when Holroyd adds that this phrase making is "sometimes echoed by academics prepared to sacrifice populations for libraries," some readers will be mystified: it sounds vaguely Shavian but lacks the punch. Holroyd is better with Shaw's travels during his last twenty years to Italy, Switzerland, Palestine, South Africa, Greece, Hong Kong, New Zealand, where the Sage, often like Carlyle, sought to cure by epigram: one Chinese diplomat boasted Shaw had insulted his country more than Japan. Holroyd's treatment of Shaw's arrival in Hollywood and subsequent ability to edit his plays and interrupt shooting is very thorough; it was in films that Shaw found the final lure of fantasy.

Far north of Hollywood, in Canada, is the Laurentian, a mountain range: massive, usually cold, and difficult of access. So is John Worthen's (and Mark Kinkead-Weekes's and David Ellis's) *D. H. Lawrence, The Early Years, 1885-1912* (Cambridge). It is massive in its details: Paul Morel's last name, we are told, is, among other things, a surname common in France, the bitter (morello) cherry, and an edible, dusky mushroom. Perhaps this will come as news to the stay-at-home with anaesthetized taste buds, but to add—and this by page 8—"a sense of darkness is conveyed by them all" is too, too serious: the dark gods have invaded biography. How did this happen?

It begins with the publisher's hype. Title page: Cambridge now has a blurb to the right of its armorial bearings, then: *The Cambridge Biography of D. H. Lawrence*. It continues in the Authors' Preface: a new type of biography, that is, three separate authors for the projected three volumes, each responsible for a different volume but all working in tandem. Why? Because "no synoptic view" could achieve a picture of a Lawrence "evolving with a steady emotional logic." Natural piety no longer binds the man to the boy. And with three on the committee, this is not biography, but Sabellianism.

Having said this, there is no doubt that this series will lay the foundation for any future consideration of Lawrence as a writer. It will become indispensable. The "facts" are all here. The authors' skepticism about oral interviews and the re-collected letters of Jessie Chambers (Lawrence's first love and mentor) are sound; the seventy pages of notes are models of bibliography (see pages 573-574 on "Paul Morel" manuscript fragments). We may need five hundred words on two postcards from Glashütte re-creating a morn-

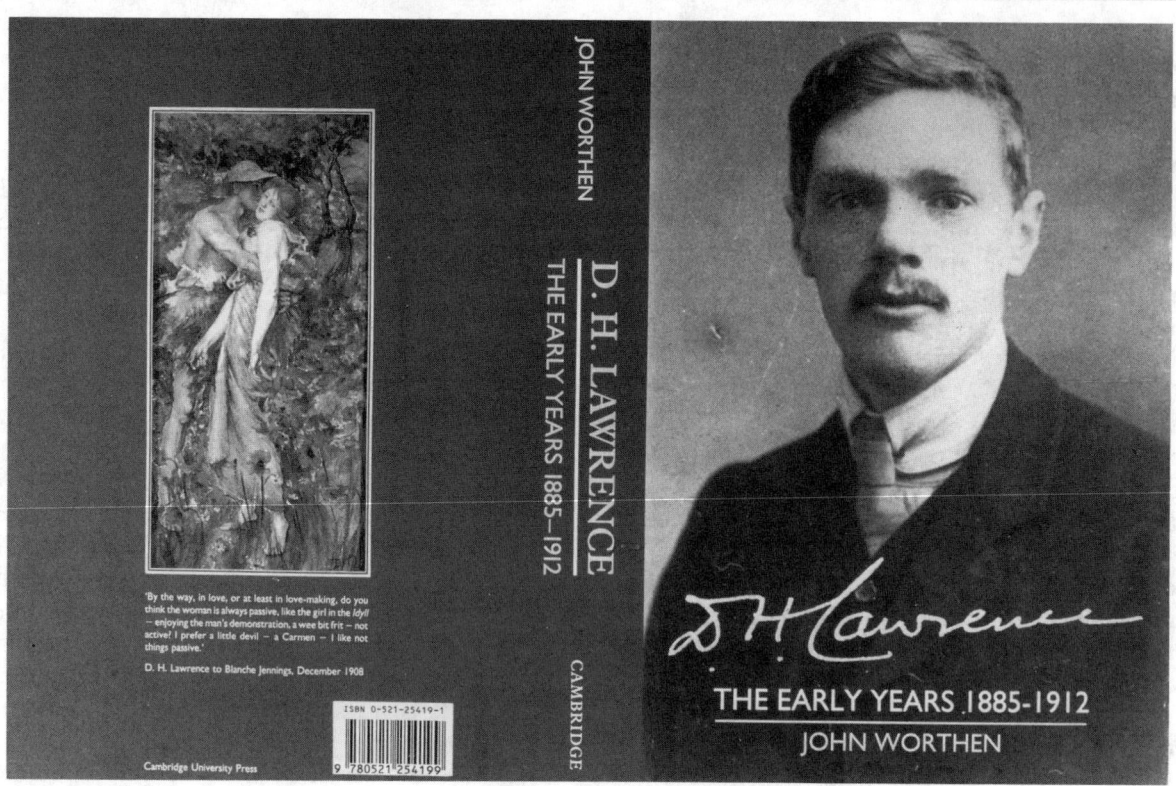

Dust jacket for Worthen's biography of Lawrence during the part of his life he fictionalized in Sons and Lovers *(1913)*

ing walk (from the Röhrlmoos Alm one can only reach the east side of the Schiffbach) and meal at a café with Freida and so on, but do enough of these details find their way into *Mr. Noon* (1984)? At least the Via Dolorosa has an end in sight. This prodigality of detail can produce satiety with major works. Worthen "frequently" cites *Sons and Lovers* (1913) because, along with his cobiographers, he acknowledges Lawrence to be a writer, but cites it "only sparingly" to illustrate events in the Lawrence household. My count is 461 references to the novel; of these 93 are biographically "significant," some because they correspond to real life, others because they alter real life. Consequently, this biography which tells us so much is difficult to access for that same reason. Even more than Ackroyd's *Dickens*, it is meant—though I do not think that this was the intent—to be consulted by readers rather than read, or read only by specialists (which is much the same thing). The thorough end matter, then, becomes invaluable: appendixes locate date, title, manuscript, and printed text of the prose and poetry; the index, interpretations and a quick overview of the life.

And among the major events receiving full treatment is the affair with Freida. Worthen pre-

sents the origin of this affair as though Lawrence had found a muse with whom he could sleep: he saw in her the "sleeping beauty whom he could release from imprisonment." That this beauty had slept with three others since her marriage Worthen dispassionately acknowledges: Otto Gross, her sister's friend's husband; Ernst Frick, the ex-lover of that friend; and William Dowson, one of the earliest motorcar owners in Nottingham and the godfather of her third child. This is the thirty-three-year-old muse who made Lawrence the kind of writer he became. And off they went: "What better subject for a biographer than the passionate elopement of the hero with the heroine?" Worthen ironically asks, but misses the comic possibilities: the lieutenant who interrupts pastoral content when they wander into a forbidden military zone, Lawrence's letter confessing to Freida's husband, and his poor French at teatime with her father, Baron von Richthofen.

The authors state that the same voice for three volumes "might be more than flesh and blood could bear." And even though one text in Lawrence's grim and well-documented childhood must have been "By these, my son, be admonished: of making many books there is no end; and much study is a weariness of the flesh," still this first volume has become essential, but tedious.

Among those novelists Lawrence would most dislike for their prose, their manners, and perhaps their gender, might be Gertrude Atherton. But Mary Leider's *California's Daughter: Gertrude Atherton and Her Times* (Stanford University Press) is well worth reading. If not a gem, this is certainly a semiprecious stone of a biography; Leider has clarified the popular literary taste of Britain, of the United States, and especially of California from the 1890s to just before World War II. And we may not like what we see. But that is not the fault of Leider who has spent ten years visiting twenty-two libraries, reading all the fifty novels, all the essays, and all the columns in the *San Francisco Examiner*. The fourteen illustrations flesh out Atherton; the most extraordinary is that of a mural painted in 1913 for the St. Francis Hotel, which depicts Gertrude Atherton as "California Welcoming the World."

But who was Gertrude Atherton? It seems she was an Edith Wharton gone bad; it is sobering to read that in 1923 *Black Oxen* outsold Sinclair Lewis's *Babbitt* (1922), but tied Emily Post's *Etiquette* (1922), and almost frightening to learn she was the most popular American novelist in Europe in the same decade. Yet her novels, especially those set in California, were controversial—at that time. The family into which she married insisted that ladies, especially Athertons, did not write; her husband's death in 1897, when she was thirty, fortunately freed her from them. She left for New York and, eventually, Europe. She returned to California permanently when she was sixty. Publishers in Britain and the United States were wary of "The New Woman" novels: 1895 was the year of Thomas Hardy's *Jude the Obscure* and Atherton's *Patience Sparhawk*. Even though Sir Walter Besant compared it to *Jane Eyre* (1847), others were outraged: physical sensations portrayed "with a frankness that is nothing short of indecent" (*Edinburgh Review*), a novel that belongs "in a refrigerator rather than a bookcase" (*Critic*). The *New York Times* simply howled "Balderdash."

The initial reaction to these carefully documented reviews probably is to think the novel cannot be all that bad and might be interesting. But Leider has the critical distance to judge and condemn Atherton's novels as baggy sensationalism: Patience is no Sue Bridehead. Leider provides quick and useful plot summaries for the major works (Patience, unhappily married, writes for

the papers, is accused of poisoning her husband with morphine, and condemned to electrocution at Sing Sing), links this summary to widely reported trials in England and America and Atherton's research (she went to Sing Sing and sat in the chair). *Black Oxen* (1923) was a novel about glandular rejuvenation. From it she received thirty-one thousand dollars the first year, a denunciation, again, from the *New York Times*, and her caricature on the front cover of the catalogue of Boni and Liveright: she stands between Theodore Dreiser and George Moore, above Edgar Lee Masters, but underneath Warner Fabian. The book then became a movie starring Corinne Griffith as the new and improved Countess Zattiany.

Leider also keeps her critical distance from Atherton's life. Other writers, for example, Gertrude Stein and Ambrose Bierce, were her acquaintances rather than her friends; if she was hard-working, she was also an intolerably pushy snob; if she met the famous, her judgments were as shallow as her characters: Big Bill Heywood, the leader of the Wobblies, merely "most interesting and likeable." Was Gertrude Atherton important and does she deserve this careful biography? The answer is a muted maybe followed by a forceful yes.

If we might recall Gertrude Atherton from Hollywood, we surely remember the next author from television. And what we probably did not know is that the four volumes, published between 1966 and 1975, that made up that series were not called *The Raj Quartet* until Heinemann, in a fit of publicity, gave these novels the title in 1976. For this fact, if not for much else, we are indebted to Hilary Spurling's *Paul Scott: A Life of the Author of The Raj Quartet* (Norton). This biography has all the literary merit of his novels. It is at times titillating: like a character in *The Bender* (1963) "Paul looked well and knew it in a pair of black bathing trunks." This teaser leads, three pages later, to a revelation of bisexuality! The reader's prurience is flattered. The trunks appear in the midst of a discussion of his apprenticeship as an accountant: not quite office dress. Then the ill-documented: Scott meets and falls suddenly in love with his future wife (this twelve days after making a pass at a drunken fellow soldier, an event not commented upon). What does his wife write "long after?" "Paul Scott didn't court nor woo me. He was there." But how long after? The notes refuse to say—and it makes a difference; instead we are referred to a mass of papers at the University of Tulsa, where Scott taught and taught well. This is uncritical; so is the acceptance of nearly everything an interviewee says; the improbable equation of novelistic events back into the life; weird pronouncements, for example, Victoria, like most respectable women until 1950, knew nothing about buggery; intolerable phrases ("The lonely little poet with his head in the clouds"); and an index printed on the head of a pin. Surely Scott, a professional (it took him twenty-five years to break into the market), an entertaining and, at times, a serious novelist, deserves better treatment. So does his internal torment. Wait for the sequel.

The Indian subcontinent that Michael Shelden, the biographer of Orwell's classmate Cyril Connolly and the author of a study of *Horizon*, presents in *Orwell: The Authorized Biography* (HarperCollins) is not Paul Scott's. Shelden has beat many of the problems a biographer is confronted with in Orwell, who kept a closed mouth over his life: we know of his first affair, with Eleanor Jaques, only by the chance preservation of some letters. Even his letters are highly elusive (a mention of a meeting with his maternal grandmother in Burma is merely tagged on to a letter); he was just as likely to call himself a poultry farmer as a novelist. Shelden realizes this about a third of the way through his at times otiose biography: Orwell's works "occupy a border zone between fact and fiction, which makes them more interesting as literature, but makes his biography harder to write." Apparently, it has been this paucity of primary texts that encouraged earlier biographers to find the life in the work. But Shelden, by using interviews with seventy survivors (pupils, friends, family), documents in the India Office Library, unpublished letters, publishers' accounts, marginalia, and common sense, has added to our understanding of the writer and his works. Now, not everything is all that important, for example, a romantic attachment with a schoolboy at his first school, St. Cyprian's, but most is. His work then does more than supplement Bernard Crick's life of ten years ago: it almost replaces it. The real St. Cyprian's is not the school of "Such, Such Were the Joys." His days in Burma were not *Burmese Days* (1934): Orwell was not unpopular (though he read a lot), was not bullied by his superiors, was not exiled to bad posts, did not suffer from a vague illness but dengue fever. Ditto *Down and Out in Paris and London* (1933): he was not that out; *The Road to Wigan Pier* (1937) is not a real road map. And *Homage*

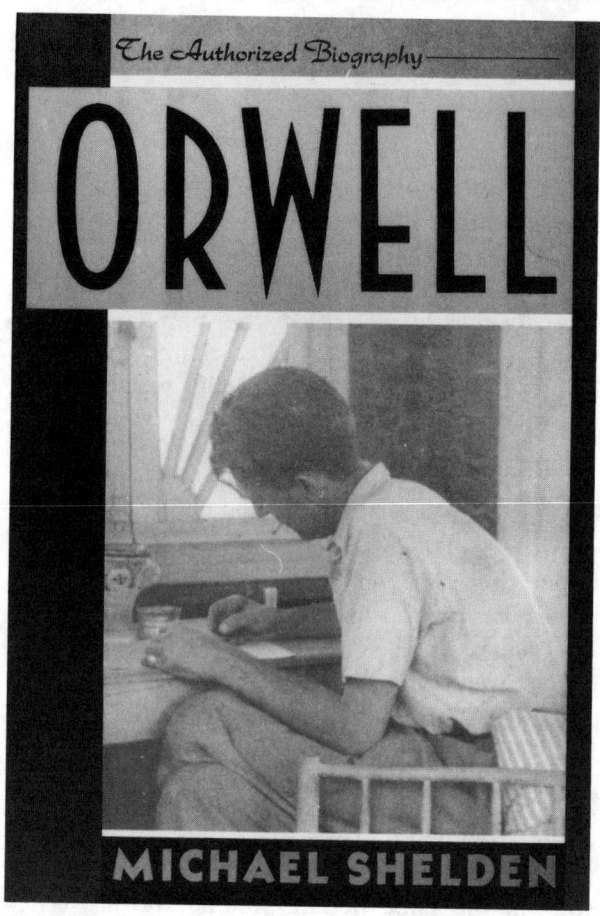

Dust jacket for Shelden's biography of the writer V. S. Pritchett has called "the conscience of his generation"

to Catalonia (1938) underplays his courage and his wife's infidelity with his CO, a sleazy and ubiquitous fake Belgian (and Shelden has interviewed everyone on this).

The clear explanations of Orwell's problems with censorious publishers, libel laws, compensation, and American rights fill in the trials of an overworked professional writer (130 articles in the year after his first wife's sudden death). The chapters on the BBC at war document egregious government folly. The last one hundred pages focus on his best-known works: *Animal Farm* (1945) and *Nineteen Eighty-Four* (1949). The former was rejected by three publishers, including T. S. Eliot at Faber and Faber, before its success (590,000 copies in the United States in four years; Britain bought 25,000 in five). Shelden's analysis of the latter is acute: *Nineteen Eighty-Four* is a prophecy of the future, a condemnation of the present, but also a summary of Orwell's past: the vanished past of a child marvelling at a glass paperweight, the bullying at St. Cyprian's, police interrogation in Burma, censorship at the BBC, and perhaps the sexual frankness of his second wife of sixty-six days, who learned of his death while she was in a Soho nightclub.

Like Orwell, the young Carl Sandburg wandered if not over an empire, at least a continent, and unlike Orwell, he often celebrated his country. Their ends did differ. And a poet who publishes over twenty volumes of verse, and wins a Pulitzer Prize, and who earlier wrote a four-volume biography of Abraham Lincoln for which he won another Pulitzer, and who dies in his ninth decade to national mourning, will have a life with seven hundred text pages, ninety-nine pages of clear and accurate notes, and a three-hundred-item Select Bibliography. And that is what Penelope Niven has given us in her comprehensive *Carl Sandburg: A Biography* (Scribners). But do we still read his poetry? After all, a standard text such as the huge *Norton Anthology of Modern Verse* has only six poems including the inevitable "Chicago/Hog Butcher for the World." Has America changed, have our standards for poetry altered that much? In answering these questions, Niven's life is an elegiac chronicle of what has vanished from our land and our sensibilities. Chicago closed its stockyards thirty years ago; its poet was shut out from academic criticism even before World War II. In 1916 Ezra Pound pushed in London to find a fellowship for Sandburg at the University of Pennsylvania: Sandburg was a "lumberjack who has taught himself all that he knows. He is on the way to simplicity," but Edgar Lee Masters "has gone off into gas." Yet a year later Conrad Aiken would damn Sandburg in *Poetry Journal* both for his socialist morals and for a "rather rudimentary sense of balance and echo." It is no wonder, as Niven explains, that Sandburg held aloof from literary feuds, preferring the performance circuit to the cloister. Nine years ago Malcolm Cowley observed that Sandburg "turned the Midwestern voice into a sort of music"; apparently, Little Gidding must modify the flat *a*'s of St. Louis. Sandburg, then, is too centrist a poet and his biographer's balanced and valiant attempts to revive him are almost doomed in the current climate of critical opinion. But Niven almost succeeds.

The amount of work in this biography is prodigious. Starting in 1976 Niven spent every summer, often on her knees and once sifting through the ashes of a wood-burning stove, in her successful attempt to locate and file six decades of letters, unpublished manuscripts, first drafts, and private journals; she organized the Carl Sandburg Oral History Project ten years ago, and finally charted each month of his life. The facts, then, are in. Future scholars will remain indebted for her meticulous sense and documentation of the past. To read Sandburg's life is to relive the first fifty years of his century: the Spanish-American War, in which he served; socialist agitation with the mayor of Milwaukee; the "Red Scare," which he reported. Not the least of her achievements is clarifying an often confused publication history and the occasional vagaries of Sandburg's memory, for example, the poet's 1956 recollection of how Lenin's *Letter to American Workers* (1934) got to the United States is massively documented. We see the interior of Sandburg as it bounces off his letters to his wife, Paula, the sister of Edward Steichen. Her assistance was unfailing, her devotion inspiring, and the marriage almost too happy. Perhaps his letters recount too often his public activities rather than any extensive inner turmoil; if so, once again, Sandburg is too much of a centrist for contemporary taste. We hear in this excellent biography the public voice of a self-proclaimed bard, but rarely, even in the 150 poems Niven glances at, a private whisper.

To turn to Henry Miller, and other allied voices below, is to move from public celebration of America to public exposure of *ego* and *id*, terms that entered common usage in English a generation after Sandburg's birth. And despite Mary Dearborn's earlier success with *Pocahantas's Daughters: Gender and Ethnicity in American Culture* (1986), her thorough documentation, seven research assistants, an insistence to tell Miller's life "as a story of the twentieth-century male identity," Robert Ferguson's *Henry Miller: A Life* (Norton), despite its faulty documentation, is better than Dearborn's *The Happiest Man Alive* (Simon and Schuster). Since this is the centennial year, perhaps Dearborn began her notes on time. Ferguson refuses to type Miller as a sinister bully oppressing women or an unholy apostle of irresponsible sex. Ironically, it is Dearborn who reports Miller's "When I move I have only to pack a few condoms and I'm off."

One, if not the major, problem with writing a life of Miller is the copiousness of material, eighteen volumes of letters and novels after his move to Europe in 1930. Further, and Ferguson is good on this, Miller read indiscriminately: Marcel Proust, the ominous Mme Blavatsky, the Norwegian novelist Knut Hamsun. And his own novels are a real problem as both biographers freely admit: Miller changes venues, events, and names around and rarely consistently. Worse, even his friends changed their own names. The problem of what or whom to include surfaces especially just before Miller sails to Europe. When June, Miller's second, ex-taxi dancer of a wife meets Mara (or Jean in Dearborn's account), Ferguson, unlike Dearborn, begins in context with a discussion of fashionable lesbianism in the Village, continues with the Sullivan Ordinance of 1907 on women smoking in public, then adds a later outside view (that of Cyril Connolly), before the narrative proper of Miller and June and Mara (Jean). In his despair and incomprehension Miller tucks the marriage certificate (and the divorce papers: Dearborn) in a doll's arm against the headboard (on a pillow: Ferguson). Were his remarks on old love letters merely annotations (Ferguson) or clownishness and self-effacment (Dearborn)? Conaston, a coconspirator in Dearborn, examines Mara's (Jean's) genitals for normalcy. Not so in Ferguson. Did Conaston telegram June after Miller's (fake) suicide attempt (Ferguson) or rush to tell her (Dearborn)? Both biographers say the returning June ignored the suicide note and went out for a meal with Mara (Jean). Did Miller chase June with a stick, knife her door, then brush her hair and pare her nails (as the notes to *The Tropic of Capricorn* [1939] suggest: Dearborn)? Ferguson corrects the Latin of a Virgilian tag; Dearborn says the gold digger (or is she a "prick tease"?) wrote it correctly on the toilet's back. Mara (Jean) and June leave for Europe, but was their farewell note read by a surprised Miller by the light of a match before he raged and howled (Dearborn), or did he expect it from all the conversation and preparations for packing he silently observed over the last few weeks (Ferguson)? And what is Ferguson's source for the unquoted-by-Dearborn farewell note?

Which account makes more sense of Miller as a writer? I think Ferguson's for he argues that Conaston's failure to help the couple had literary consequences: Miller saw the failure of psychoanalysis. And there are further inferences: that the suicide attempt allowed Miller to write a good note, and that Miller decided to defeat women through his books; consequently the impossibility of the triangle allowed him to write. It is also interesting, though hardly redeeming, to learn that Miller's account in *Playboy* (for which a friend posed) was an exaggeration: he did not urinate on Mara (Jean) and then sleep in the bath-

tub, but dragged her from the bed and urinated in the bathtub.

The pre-1930 erotic contretemps are confusing, and even the film *Henry and June* (1991) can't assist our full understanding of Anaïs Nin and the novelist in Paris, but it was in Paris that Miller achieved his fame: recognition in the United States only came when censorship ended in 1960. These two biographies differ here: from who met whom where and wearing what to questions of the quality of the ménage, yet it is Ferguson who makes the more convincing analysis of Nin, the sexual and literary participant in Miller's heady prose and exuberant life. But the reader must keep in mind that Miller's works break down the barrier between fiction and life; Ferguson reminds us of this, but can he, as a biographer, keep them separate? That Knut Hamsun, the subject of Ferguson's earlier biography, figures large in this work is not unexpected, Miller read him attentively. But the adjective *Strindbergian* figures too large. As Miller approached fame in his own country he approached his own death. On his death both biographers are excellent: Dearborn on his fame finds him unclassifiable, but Ferguson's dispassionate summation puts him in the tradition of Arthur Rimbaud and Bob Dylan. Will we ever know the truth? Miller would say "shit no!"

Once during his time on the West Coast Kenneth Rexroth defended Allen Ginsberg's *Howl* (1956) from prosecution for words similar to Miller's. On the date set for trial the accused was in Paul Bowles's Tangier, a city that made San Francisco look like a quieter suburb of Topeka. Michelle Green's *The Dream at the End of the World: Paul Bowles and the Literary Renegades in Tangier* (HarperCollins) is a biography of a place and sensibility as well as of various writers. When Rexroth complained that the Beat movement was turning into "pot and pussy," Tangier included pederasts and drugs, and the drugs appear all the more potent in their italicized and transliterated gutturals.

Readers may remember Paul Bowles from the wretched prose of Robert Ruark when the journalist, along with *Time* and *Life*, lamented the fall of Tangier when it lost its status as an international free port after Morocco asserted its rights in 1958, an event mentioned rather briefly halfway through this book. Bowles was not obscure then, nor was his fellow Tangerine Barbara Hutton. Bowles wrote *The Sheltering Sky* in 1950, and the novel was praised by the *Times Literary Sup-*

plement (London), *Time*, and by an earlier visitor, Tennessee Williams, in the *New York Times*. Nine years later, in *Advertisements for Myself* (1959), Mailer claimed Bowles "opened the world of Hip . . . the call of the orgy, the end of civilization"— in fact, one mysteriously uncaptioned photo shows Bowles petting a sheep. But there is more; and not just parlor games—though this is part— like Daisy Chain, where players reconstruct the doxographical tradition of illicit amours in this tolerant city: here Green's position as a senior writer at *People* comes into play. An amazing number of writers arrived for R and R and then, more importantly, left. Truman Capote decamped after a few months in 1949, two years after Bowles settled in Tangier. Jack Kerouac cut his visit short after providing the title for William Burroughs's novel, but Allen Ginsberg stayed on a few more months in 1957 to edit the re-named *Naked Lunch* (1959) into a two-hundred-page workable draft. Burroughs left soon after. But many returned in the 1960s to a Tangier invaded by beatniks and then left for good. In 1991 Bowles said Tangier was like a gong that still resonates after forty years, and among the writers in this book it is Burroughs we still read and hear the most: a knifed lover, with an unrequited passion for Ginsberg, who experiments with the pharmacopoeia, and engages in literary surrealism.

It was Paul Bowles and his wife Jane, his Moorish lovers, and her Moorish lovers (especially the veiled and bizarre Cherifa) who held together this drugged miasma of socialites, writers, and ex-diplomats, but the hold was tenuous as is this biography's narrative line: too many people simply come and go. To what extent Green could achieve accuracy in her account is difficult to judge: even assuming the reminiscences, thirty years later, of a fifteen-year-old catamite turned artist are truthful; if the contemporary letters of Burroughs and Ginsberg reflect actual events, these events are clouded by passion and chemicals. If we are to believe the book jacket, Tangier was "the last great paradise of our century." It is to Green's credit that she records another reality.

The temptation in this next biography is to turn immediately to the seven chapters, a good fourth of the book, on the 1950s and early 1960s of another port, San Francisco. And, for literary purposes, these are the best chapters of Linda Hamalian's *A Life of Kenneth Rexroth* (Norton). In them, she carefully traces Rexroth's unexpected but deserved promotion to what a newspaper called (in a phrase he would despise), the "elder

statesman" of the Beats and also evaluates his consistent confusion of his private life with his public voice. This voice of "vituperation and spleen wiped out" his critical acumen; vituperative because his third physically and emotionally abused wife fell in love with his fellow poet Robert Creeley, splenetic because he extended his hatred to Creeley's friends, most notably Kerouac, whom he attacked in a series of savagely irresponsible reviews. Further reviews angered the academics whom Rexroth damned for "grinding out little Donnes and Hopkinses" in their "seven types of ambiguity factories": little wonder deans harassed him over tenure. Incapable, then, of the dispassionate in action or language, his candor has still kept him out of most college anthologies.

But his passionate deeds and words encouraged a renaissance of poets General and Mrs. Eisenhower would never read but the literate eagerly awaited: Ginsberg, whom he defended in court, Lawrence Ferlinghetti, Gary Snyder, and Denise Levertov. Frank Sinatra's companion is reputed to have decided that Rexroth sounded like "John Donne in the fourth dimension." But Rexroth seems to have put these words in Shirley MacLaine's lovely mouth.

But to read only this section would be unfortunate because Hamalian is excellent on the poet's first forty-five years, years that show that San Francisco was a state of mind before it became the City of Beats. Hamalian presents Rexroth's orphaned childhood; analyzes his marriage to the radical and unstable Andrée Schafer, whose romanticized presence informs much of his later poetry. The marriage was unconventional: overcome by sacramental glory he fainted during the high nuptial mass; so did she, but later, during his reading of *The Duchess of Malfi* (1623). Hamalian documents the fading of the Chicago renaissance (Al Capone was Rexroth's neighbor) and thoroughly discusses the poet's political and literary pacifism before and during the war. His founding of a John Reed club in San Francisco ("putative writers and unputative Communists" was his phrase), serving as cosecretary of the League for the Struggle of Negro Rights, led to his first national political recognition in the Federal Writers Project in the 1930s, at least ten years before he achieved national literary recognition in a review by William Carlos Williams. Protesting against the roundup of Japanese civilians, he also had to fight for conscientous objector status. And all the while he wrote poetry of various merit, had affairs (some brief, some serious, all confused), married again (to Marie Kass), met the famous (the index is a list of illuminati, but not, alas, of individual poems), and created enemies. One foe accused him of cofounding a "New Cult of Sex [Henry Miller] and Anarchy [Rexroth]." And anarchy, lowercased and sympathetically documented, is the best description for Rexroth's life since the age of twelve: an anarchy of people (caught copulating on his library floor before his nuptials with his fourth wife) and of places (he once was a botanical guide in the Sierra Nevada), but an anarchy which, once mythologized and subverted, created Rexroth's controlled, elegiac tone.

Hamalian, who began her study of Rexroth as a romantic admirer, reached the mild conclusion readers may share: she "ended up disappointed by some of the truths." But she is able by a judicious use of interviews, FBI files, a moderate attention to his "autobiographical novel" and its unpublished sequel to demonstrate how this not-quite-accepted poet and often unacceptable man resolved the turmoil of his life in his verse.

Tom Clark is the best choice for another fine biography, this of one of Rexroth's friends, for he brings to *Charles Olsen: The Allegory of a Poet's Life* (Norton) as acute an ear as a poet himself, literary acumen, and earlier practice as a biographer (Damon Runyon). His scholarship is as thorough and as current as possible: the Olsen Archives at the University of Connecticut for his notebooks, Robert Creeley's encouragement and nine volumes of letters, family recollections, Butterick's recent (1989) assemblage of poems not in the collected edition, and even Senator Alan Cranston (Olsen's boss during World War II).

This biography examines both the public career of Charles Olsen and his inner turmoil of hypochondria and requited loves; often they overlap, but Clark can keep both in focus. Many readers of Olsen may not know that his poetic career did not begin until 1944 when the poet was thirty-four. We have a smooth narrative of Olsen's earlier literary, erotic, and political endeavors provided by the lover of Herman Melville (and a Harvard faculty wife) who located 124 books from the novelist's dispersed library and whose notes F. O. Matthiessen used for *American Renaissance* (1941). It was this love that, twelve years later, became the stimulating and compact essay in poetic historiography *Call Me Ishmael* (1958). We view his work in Washington during the war in the Office of War Information where

Dust jacket for the British edition of Amis's episodic portraits of himself and others

he and his common-law wife, Constance Wilcock, entertained colleagues Archibald MacLeish, Robert Sherwood, Owen Lattimore, Bernard De Voto, and Malcolm Cowley. It is a mark of Clark's thoroughness that he not only located the *New York Times* announcement of Olsen's resignation over censorship, but also read the surrounding stories. Overriding all was the early friendship with Edmund Dahlberg, paternal adviser and pander. But Dahlberg was replaced by a maternal Constance whose financial assistance (she worked as a typist) allowed Olsen to write. Dahlberg was also replaced by the incarcerated Ezra Pound, whose contacts—and here Olsen's friendship was not disinterested—found him a publisher for the Melville study. Clark's recreation of Olsen's meeting with St. Elizabeth's most famous inmate provides an emphasis at odds with Olsen's later 1975 account.

His general argument, that the poet's sexual behavior was a mixture of the desire to conquer, the desire to flee, and a (usually unsatisfied) desire for love does not seem to apply to Constance. This may be because Clark has much more information on Olson's next liaison, Frances Boldereff, even though he interviewed her thirty-five years after the affair's inception. Clark's attitude to the initial subterfuges of this pair is marked more by bemused sympathy than by a tolerant approbation. Boldereff provided much else for Olsen: the inspiration and background for the *Maximus* (1953-1975) poems. Unfortunately her readings were indiscriminately eclectic. This makes Clark's achievement all the more remarkable for he untangles the private myths of Olsen. This poet who already took Melville as a fifth gospeler was now exposed to Egyptian, Sumerian, and Mayan mythology, an obscure Austrian art historian, Saint Anthony of Padua (the patron of fishermen and, by extension, Gloucester, Massachusetts), and to the glories ("mio chorego!") of a new lover. All this came together in a typo ("nest" for "next") or, in Clark's happy phrase, "a lucky accident instigated by Eros and the Muse." This is another major merit of his biography: Clark has assembled much of the earlier literary criticism, selected the germane, and presented it in succinct form. But as much as Boldereff offered the charming and witty Olsen, it was not enough to overcome the obdurate coldness of his intellect. Olsen's works are morally preferable to his life. Ultimately and inevitably, the women in his life were a source.

But Olsen did more, as Clark's analysis of Black Mountain College makes clear. Olsen, despite his political work during the war, was not a college administrator. The history of this experimental college, placed in what Olsen saw as a mythic setting, has been done before, but Clark neatly ties its failure into Olsen's private and public maladministration. A person whose talk is "circular not linear" (as one student put it thirty years later) cannot fend from his campus both FBI agents and creditors. Nor should he—and Clark's distaste is clear—become a father while corresponding with a muse and living with a wife. By 1957 both the college and his marriage had failed, but his new, typewriter-based poetry (Projective verse) continued with the help of Robert Creeley. The argument that Olsen started postmodernism is the publisher's wishful thinking. By the late 1950s and 1960s he had made the eternal return to the scene of his nativity, Gloucester. It was a time of psychic misery (most

of it self-caused), of the public acceptance of his verse, and of financial sponging.

In a work devoted to a poet whose craft was often founded on the appearance of the printed page, it is surprising to find the occasional typo and an index whose print, the size of that used in the compact Oxford English Dictionary, misses material in quotations (Pindar, Washington Irving). The *Maximus* poems bulk large. So did Charles Olsen at six feet, seven inches: we could use a picture of him, the women in his life, the Black Mountains, and Gloucester. But despite these few faults, this interpretation will become a text essential for a sympathetic understanding of this poet's life, soul, and verse.

The United States figure briefly, but tellingly, in the next two works. The first, the breezy and hasty *Memoirs* of Sir Kingsley Amis, who received his knighthood in 1991, is not an autobiography, but instead, as he claims, an *allobiography*, that is, his impression of others. And rather than attempting to record his own "intimate, domestic, and sexual experiences" which would "hurt" people, he puts in those of others. In this case, twenty-eight others, some of whom may be still his friends or "chums." No doubt, Great Britain and America have their quotas of drunken, adulterous, pretentious, and silly men and women; but Amis seems to have met the most famous. There are some he admires, but more he dislikes: Enoch Powell because the editor of Thucydides pedantically shows that he knows Latin, Freddie [A. J.] Ayer because the philosopher was not just a "cocksman" but a successful if egoistical one, Anthony Burgess because the novelist not only loves but is infatuated with language. This list could proceed for another fifteen people. And if one enjoys—and most readers will—witty dirt, these sketches are ideal. Amis has a good eye for the physical: the repellent hairy nose of his grandmother, the gold and scarlet cuffs of Margaret Thatcher. Better is his dramatic sense of where to place the telling anecdote: Francis Bacon offers soft gay porn surrounded by Cardiff's dry mud; Leo Rosten's parsimony with drinks over the telephone. But after reading more than three in a row, the *Memoirs* pale: calloused humanity asserts itself. In addition, and often more successfully, Sir Kingsley writes about places: Oxford, Cambridge, the United States (Princeton and Vanderbilt). His specific topics, "Jazz," "Czechs," "The Army" (surely all literate people suffer the same), and "Booze can be skipped."

But the author is capable of appreciation. The reprint of his 1982 sketch of Philip Larkin nicely balances that poet's "jovial acerbity" and isolation with his humor and wit. Larkin's dislike of the English curriculum at Oxford, a type of commodity, is only matched by Amis's—or rather John Wain's—extraordinary parody of Lord David Cecil. But even Lord David, Amis admits, encouraged his students to find pleasure rather than polemic in literature. The visits to the United States in 1958 and 1967 are worth rereading both for their humor (his tattooed Uncle Virg gets Walter Lippmann to explain Shanghai Shek) and outrage (a Vanderbilt professor with an attractive Southern lilt says he "can't find it in his heart to give a nigra or a Jew an A"). Like *Lucky Jim* (1954), his best-known novel, Amis's *Memoirs* are best remembered and read in bits.

The second part of Anthony Burgess's *Confessions, You've Had Your Time* (Grove Weidenfeld) lacks the willful dysphonia of Amis's *Memoirs* and presents instead the career and travels of a professional writer, a professing Catholic, and a happily remarried widower—not that Burgess is a flavicomous saint (to use one of his words). This volume continues his first and covers 1960 to 1981, the years of the then notorious *A Clockwork Orange* (1962), novel and movie, and the movie *Jesus of Nazareth* (1977). But it would be a mistake to focus only on these two works and ignore his comments and those of purblind reviewers about the other thirty-plus novels, ten film scripts, his music, and his odyssey.

Like his novels, this is a well-organized work: it begins with his arrival and that of his touching and suicidally ill first wife; then a mysterious engendering in 1962 (one-fourth of the way through); self-exile to Malta; his marriage to the mother of a four-year-old son and the child's baptism in the rains of Provence (where typically Burgess worries whether Andrea takes a Greek accusative); another self-exile from Malta, an island as petty as its bureaucrats; eventual resettlement and the interruption of well-wishers in Monaco; and finally a return (paid for) to Malaya. In between: lectures, including one with quotations from a nonexistent Elizabethan dramatist, at City College, Chapel Hill, Duke, Princeton; bad food in three continents; run-ins with a Bedford Dormobile; celibacy at Niagara Falls; and a mugging at Avignon. And there are the novels and screenplays and translations and musicals and incessant reviewing. Burgess's activity makes Gissing's Grub Street an indolent lane. Fortu-

nately, the lot of this humane man of letters has improved, and he has retained his humor. He aims in his novels to entertain himself—he does the same in his memoirs—and us too. The humor is not simply the anecdote: the Neapolitan who, having dyed his penis purple, intended to kill his bride if she expressed surprise. It is also in the trials of his craft: on a Baltic liner he discovers how to integrate Russian loanwords into *A Clockwork Orange* while spelling out "toilet" in Cyrillic; the incredulity of early reviewers; later Stanley Kubrick's wordless purdah after the release of the film (with the American ending and not the British one) leaving Burgess to defend himself from theologically illiterate reviewers, an Indian who waved a tomahawk, and a Jesuit who offered riches. And again: General Motors withdrew sponsorship of *Jesus of Nazareth*, objecting to—though Detroit would not know the heresy—Nestorianism, Italian radio wanted to edit the Lord's Prayer, and Tunisian Arabs extras participated in the Second Coming. More serious is Burgess's argument that St. John is a better novelist than the synoptics: hence, after the movie's spectacular Rising of Lazarus, the Resurrection is anticlimactic. What most readers will fail to appreciate is Burgess's comments on his musical activities; we have not heard his lyrics. But what we all must acknowledge is the unflagging professionalism of a writer committed to educating and changing his country and his readers.

Among those who tried to effect change in America was James Baldwin. And James Campbell's *Talking at the Gates: A Life of James Baldwin* (Viking) takes its title from a work Baldwin planned, talked about, and brooded over for six years but never finished. In some ways this is an incomplete work also, though to accept the author's characterization of this biography as only a host of sketches and perceptions would be a mistake; the disclaimer is too modest. Campbell's treatment of Baldwin's life upon his return to the United States after nine years in Europe forms one-half of his biography; this means that Baldwin's best works, *Go Tell It on the Mountain* (1953), *Notes of a Native Son* (1955), and *Giovanni's Room* (1956), are comparatively neglected. Campbell's emphasis instead is on the essays, interviews, and public pronouncements when the novelist "parted company with his own privacy." In Paris and before 1953, Baldwin had no public life; by 1963 he had become an interviewee for *Mademoiselle*.

By page 50, Baldwin is in Paris and the reader remains puzzled: how could a black preacher's son born in Harlem—and illegitimate too—get to Paris? Did he follow the transatlantic path of Richard Wright with whom his later feud still remains unclear? Was he driven from his country by racism, or did he need breathing room and a cheap place to live? That Campbell can provide no sure answer is in part due to Baldwin's continual capacity for self-dramatization: he considered the interview as an art form. Further, biographical inferences from novels, Campbell demonstrates, can only provide "something of atmosphere and feeling, but not much specific detail." There are, however, the journals of others that Campbell did rely on to fill in the gaps. The general outline of his initial literary career is clear: early reviews (the first was on Maksim Gorky) in *Commentary* and *New Leader*, off to Paris and lower than genteel poverty, final acceptance of *Go Tell It on the Mountain* in 1952, and the often-anthologized "Stranger in the Village" published in *Harper's* a year later. The record of his emotional life is less clear. Lucien Happersberger, whose chalet was outside the stranger's village, is defined, but his successor, Arnold, remains only a name.

And so does Brown (of *Brown v. Board of Education*) in 1954. Campbell's narrative and discussion of Baldwin's eventual involvement in the civil rights movement are perhaps the best parts of this biography (probably because Campbell was born in Glasgow). In 1956, having seen on the Boulevard St-Germain newspaper reports about integration in Charlotte, North Carolina, Baldwin took on the drunken William Faulkner in the *Partisan Review*; traveled, for the first time, to the South to be "there"; and wrote. Yet his value to the movement was, as Campbell argues, mainly symbolic: "an intellectual with a fearsome articulacy" and "a worldwide readership." Should anyone need further examples of the FBI's witless paranoia, the censored cullings from the bureau's 1,302-page report are a feast of the inaccurate and illiterate; the bureau's ultimate boss, Attorney General Robert Kennedy, comes off more of a politician than a martyr during his meeting with Baldwin (insofar as Campbell can reconstruct the confused accounts).

As the level of political rhetoric rose, Baldwin's confidence and style sank: the earlier "compact and jewelled prose . . . turns to paste" in *Another Country* (1962). His essays, which get full treatment, became best-sellers, but his play was panned. This odd response was typical of Baldwin's success and failure as a writer; he felt him-

self isolated from the *Négritude* of emerging Africa, the white hipdom of the late 1950s, the poetic diction of others. So he quarreled with Langston Hughes, Norman Mailer, and Richard Wright. Campbell's analysis of Baldwin's literary failure and social success during his last twenty years is prescient, sad, and convincing. But in some ways *Talking at the Gates* does not convince: no page numbers to works cited in the notes, an incomplete index. When Baldwin's funeral is held at something called the Cathedral of St. John the Devine [sic], neither of these imaginative writers is well served.

Ronald Hayman's *The Death and Life of Sylvia Plath* (Birch Lane Press Book) is another sad book, and in many ways is the most painstaking and painful biography of 1991. Perhaps better is Hayman's phrase, a biographical study. What Sylvia Plath's death meant and means can only be answered when one decides what died. A woman, a wife, a poetess, a spurned druggie, a madwoman, or an archetype? Other biographers have tried to answer this question, but only under two severe restraints: first, her husband, Ted Hughes, severely limited access to her published works, and his sister, Olwyn Hughes, insisted on prepublication censorship. All these problems and more (disappeared poems, journals, and a novel, even a nonexistent suicide note) have bedeviled the earlier attempts of A. Alvarez in the first chapter of his *The Savage God* in 1971 and of Ann Stevenson's *Bitter Fame* of 1989. Hayman's thesis is, to put it cruelly, that nothing became her life and works better than the leaving of them. But here is the problem: Hayman in his last chapter argues from the works that it was "the triple convergence of the deep-seated death drive" along with, "the demoralizing circumstances in which she was living, and the effects of drugs" that caused her death. Now, to avoid even the appearance of the Hughes's censorship, Hayman never quotes directly from her works. But is the title of a poem the same as the text? And, even with quick paraphrases of this most confessional poet, the answer must be a considered no. Can Hayman bridge the week in which the "dead Sylvia Plath was still a fiction in the poetry" and the next in which she was dead? Not, I think, by the titles alone.

This is not to say that Hayman has ignored the suicide motifs in *The Bell Jar* (1963) and the poems her husband selected for posthumous publication in *Ariel* (1965), but we have to have the texts at hand to understand even the biogra-

Dust jacket for Boyle's biography of Goethe through his second trip to Italy, in 1790

pher's general remarks. Nor has he failed to present a fair picture of her family, her years at Smith, her first meeting with Hughes at Cambridge, the dislike of the English, her marriage, her husband's initial adultery in Boston, and his last with Assia Wevill who, having born him a daughter, gassed herself and the daughter two years later. At what is Hayman best? At doing what no one could stop him from writing about: the misery of a woman living in a small, cold ill-furnished apartment with frozen sewage pipes, in vile London weather, tending two young children, apart from her husband, writing extraordinary poems.

If Hayman's life focuses on death, what is Neeli Cherkovsky's *Hank: The Life of Charles Bukowski* (Random House) about? Hank, or Charles, a late recognized serious rival to the Beats, or a drunk, a poseur, and a cult figure? After reading it, a bad picaresque novel, the questions are not answered. Bukowski may be a worthy successor to Henry Miller, but this biography serves him ill. Perhaps we should see this as an "appreciation," that most genteel of Edwardian forms, but the subject matter forbids it. Cherkovsky himself enters halfway through the book, at its end in a "Personal Memoir," and in a

dozen entries in the index—but where is Madonna, who figures briefly in the filming of *Barfly* (1987)? What we have much too often is "My Life As Told To."

In his introduction Cherkovsky claims Bukowski often cannot remember his early "unverifiable years." This, however, has not deterred the biographer: his uncritical use of interviews with family and friends does result in some sort of narrative. This narrative includes the serious adolescent who concludes "adults, and children, too, were not very nice" and "the entire structure of society was populated by smooth-talking phonies" (see under "worldview of"—one of 103 entries), the morning salutations of the just married: " 'Good morning, Mrs. Bukowski.' 'Good morning, dear husband,' she replied." After this sort of flabby prose, the excerpts from Bukowski's oeuvre refresh.

Yet there are believable sections: the 1930s' cure for acne resembles Saint Sebastian's martyrdom. And this sense of ugliness drove the young Bukowski to novels which stripped the face from society such as Upton Sinclair's *The Jungle* (1906) and Sinclair Lewis's *Main Street* (1920) and later Fydor Dostoyevski's *Notes from the Underground* (1864) and led the writer to hate the conventional and pretty (two adjectives that cannot be predicated of his verse or prose). The literate reader will also appreciate the sections on the chaos, enthusiasm, and occasional skill of small publishers' work such as Jon Webb's *The Outsider* in 1961, Douglas Blazek's mimeographed *Ole* (1965), John Martin's finely printed Black Sparrow Press edition (1966), and eventually the Penguin Modern Poets series in 1969. Bukowski's wandering decades of the 1940s and 1950s are rehearsed: the sleazy rented rooms of New Orleans, Saint Louis, Fort Worth, and constant, we are told, drinking, brawls, and mayhem. But always Bukowski returned to Los Angeles. Cherkovsky is good on the pre-World War II Los Angeles which underlies many of Bukowski's short stories and poems, especially "Crucifix in a Deathhand." And his fight with the U.S. Post Office becomes an interrupted mock-epic (though much of this is the poet's doings—and words). What is frankly not credible is an invitation to join a Philly gang ("Because you've got guts, man"), that the last words he heard his mother say were "You were right Henry. Your father is a horrible man," that he received his first acceptance of a short story hours after being mocked by a cigar-chewing lout his boss called a "writer," that his first wife (who published his first poem) would insist on marriage before a fifteen-hour sexual marathon, or that his second was his "shelter against the raging storm." But Cherkovsky's" interpretations are worth consideration: Bukowski expresses "the profane sacredness of the commonplace" and that much of his present appeal to young writers is his "anarchic sensibility and a consciousness divorced from the usual literature of rebellion." But for how long? Is Bukowski a poet whose reputation arrived after the efflorescence of the Beats, or a figure whose cultus blossomed after a 1967 article in the New Orleans *Billboard*, in a city in which he wrote over ten poems daily, or perhaps after his first reading on Sunset Boulevard in the spring of 1969? We know his San Francisco reading three years later was famous for dope, drink, and vomit. What about the fifty thousand copies of his poems in Germany? In the United States his fame reached its apogee with the television documentary of 1973 which the National Endowment for the Arts wanted to broadcast nationwide (but could not, given the language). Bukowski, from the laureate of Los Angeles, perhaps has become its agent. Or Hollywood's with the filming of *Barfly* and *Love is a Dog from Hell* (1987). The latter ends with what

Cherkovsky would have us believe is a redemptive act of necrophilia. What *Hank* is and who Hank is remains unclear—perhaps a poseur manqué?

If Los Angeles is strange, so is New York. And we might ask, do we need another life of Norman Kingsley Mailer? Do we not know enough—or too much—already? Apparently not, Carl Rollyson argues in *The Lives of Norman Mailer* (Paragon House). And his biography does give us data we didn't know, for example, the novelist's middle name (from Charles Kingsley, the Victorian author of the manly *Hereward the Wake* [1865]). Rollyson's goal is to explain what sort of man could say, having bailed out a wife abuser from jail, "God, I wish I had the courage to stab a woman like that. That was a real gutsy act." And Rollyson's answer is: "A man who was not himself, a man who saw society as conspiring to take away his true self." That is it. But in 1992 on television, the sixty-nine-year-old Mailer said to David Frost that he had made some mistakes. His biographer disagrees. Can anyone be this objective?

We are told the biographer draws on new material; but too often these are lightweight interviews with heavies: Irving Howe, part of an afternoon with William Styron, a phone call to Max Lerner, discussion with Henry Levin, who, though he did not know about the Harvard Mailer, could still provide information about the "milieu." The bibliography is impressive: almost two hundred items. Rollyson has made equally impressive use of much important secondary material in *Harper's*, the *New Republic*, *Commonweal*, the *New York Times*; his encapsulation of reviews is balanced and succinct. This spade work, even in an age of printouts, is admirable. But *Time, Life, People, Parade*? Surely this is tertiary. Further, the documentation is incomplete: where is Joyce Carol Oates's review of the witty *A Prisoner of Sex* (1971) Rollyson cites on page 237? Not in the notes, not in the bibliography. The index is faulty: people show up before they should and sometimes not at all, as in the case of a quick, topical and sleazy reference to a current candidate for the presidency. In addition he draws heavily on earlier book-length studies, such as Philip Bufithis's 1978 *Norman Mailer*, Peter Manso's 1985 *Mailer: His Life and Times* and the 1969 *Running Against the Machine*, and Hilary Mills's 1982 *Mailer: A Biography*. Rollyson is better with information available after 1985, but neither *Ancient Evenings* (1983) nor Mailer's life since 1985 is particularly interesting, or rather, not as bizarrely interesting. Rollyson never interviewed Mailer.

The treatment of Mailer's childhood is perfunctory, that of his Harvard years padded, and surely the seven months Mailer saw something approaching combat deserve more than eight paragraphs. Yet for one reason *The Lives* is often splendid entertainment: it is a book not simply rich in anecdote but obsessed with the minipsycho-drama. All the stories are worth recalling or, for a few events of the last six years, reading. There is the onstage literary brouhaha over *The Prisoner of Sex* when Mailer—to the dismay of Susan Sontag—used the word *lady* of Jill Johnson who was one of a trio of roiling lesbians trying to prove something. Then during the evening party before the formal announcement of his campaign for mayor of New York Norman Podhoretz is berated for not bringing the "power structure" to this group of three hundred intellectuals and disenfranchised. An eight-foot table of food and drinks flies through the air, as well as drunken accusations of anomalous sexual preferences. This seems grotesque and sad and pathetic. Except he stabbed his wife. Then the next day alleged he did it "to relieve her of cancer." Now this was, and remains, a notorious event. What has Rollyson added to the earlier accounts of Peter Manso and Hilary Mills? Nothing, but (and this is important) a certain narrative verve.

Rollyson's main argument is that Mailer changed during his writing of *The Deer Park* (1955). He began "to enjoy his status as outcast" after his publisher, Rinehart, found a veiled reference to fellatio objectionable. So Mailer writes of controversy in controversial language while leading a controversial series of lives. Nu? The biographer is often better with plot summaries and interpretation than with the lives. *An American Dream* (1965) gets full treatment: all the plot, immense citations from the text, examples of what *Esquire* censored, judicious comparisons between Rojak and Lieutenant Hearn of *The Naked and the Dead* (1948), and lit. crit. that we generally do not find in Honors theses: "Shago is right. Rojak has been a 'bugger' and has wanted it up his ass but instead has given it that way to Ruta [*Esquire* excised that passage] and the other Germans who have tried to invade his [fox]hole." But this is Mailer. The Jack Henry Abbot scandal—and Abbot did for Mailer what Willie Horton did for Governor Dukakis—is handled well, involving a quick summary of the facts, Mailer's mishandling of the subsequent press conference, and even the

rare judgement on the biographer's part: "If Abbot played Mailer like a violin, it was because Mailer had taught him how to use the instrument." What this biography most lacks is a serious investigation of the connection between the willed violence of Mailer's life and the violence of his works, a violence that began with "The White Negro" twenty-five years ago.

The next two biographies move beyond a person to include an age. And as Nicholas Boyle in *Goethe: The Poet and His Age* (volume one, "The Poetry of Desire, 1749-1790") defines the second half of the eighteenth century, Frederick Karl's work on Kafka investigates the first half of ours. Boyle's is the first of a two-volume life, and precedes his "The Age of Renunciation, 1790-1832": we can anticipate a six-pound biography, the first major one since the 1930s. And six pounds, when we consider the collected works (including twelve thousand letters) come to 138 volumes, seems about right. The problem is making these volumes of works and eighty years of life manageable. If Boyle succeeds, as he has done with the first forty years of Goethe's life, a period leading up to the French Revolution, we will have one of the most comprehensive biographies not just of Johann Wolfgang von Goethe, but of any writer and his age. Boyle's claim to be only a synthesizer is excessively modest: the specialist will find the poet in his context; the nonspecialist will find the poet and his context. The timing is perfect for both these biographies if we are to understand the reunification of the Germanies and what appears to be the emergence of a new European culture.

In Boyle's work literal translations are always provided; the top of each page has a running title; the bottom is clean of dense footnotes; the general bibliography and index of Goethe's works comprehensive; thirty-seven illustrations flesh out the writer, his family and his landscapes; and the ninety pages of notes are mercifully clear.

After two introductory chapters on late-eighteenth-century Germany and Frankfurt, Boyle breaks the narrative into three five-year spans, reserving two final chapters for Italy and Goethe's reaction, from 1786 to 1790. Boyle's rhythm is to alternate life (reading, friends, travels) with works: the proportion is about one to two throughout this volume except for a needed extensive chronology of the Italian visits. The method works well. Twenty pages on the early 1770s, his meeting with Johann Gottfried von

Herder, the "affair" with Friederike Biron (who was never to marry—reflecting, as do most of his relationships with women, "little credit" on Goethe), and his detachment from Christian belief move into a forty-page analysis of immediate succeeding works followed by a general statement about the next nine years (to 1779). While admitting that Goethe has become the supreme master of the peculiar form of autobiographical literature, Boyle insists that Goethe's works are neither "encoded memoirs" nor "decoratively independent" of his life.

We have here a life in detail, but not dull detail: as he investigated the (vestigial) intermaxillary bone of the human jaw, we also learn that he hid the skull of an elephant in a trunk to avoid frightening his landlady, this while attending a conference on fiscal reform. Boyle analyzes both the poet's financial platform and contribution to anatomy. There is also the panorama that recreates the age: Frankfurt, Leipzig, and especially the chapter devoted to the demographics, political organization, and cultural life of Weimar. And it is this panoramic view of the age, the setting of Naples and Herculaneum, the succinct treatment of the French Revolution, the literary climate of the German-speaking regions of Europe, that makes this massive study an introduction to the origins of the twentieth century. But Goethe's age was not the Age of Goethe, as Boyle rightfully insists, but rather the age he stood above, removed and, at times, coldly Olympian.

Boyle's Goethe surmounted his times; Frederick Karl's Kafka is in the thick of them for eight hundred pages in *Franz Kafka: Representative Man* (Ticknor and Fields). Karl, a biographer of Joseph Conrad and just recently William Faulkner, does for Kafka what Walter Pater did to the Mona Lisa, he makes him the embodiment of the old fancy, the symbol of the modern idea, a man who fought against what he assimilated: "all destruction, all violence and brutality." These three qualities are the touchstones of "High Modernism"; Karl's goal is to demonstrate their prevalence in Kafka's art, his life, and his city. This is no easy task. Karl argues that the late era and fall of the Kaiserreich ushered in a European nationalism, virulent in its anti-Semitism, and intolerant of almost all the twenty-seven forms of modernism which filtered, from Paris or Vienna, into Kafka's Prague. The biography becomes extraordinarily dense in those pages and chapters, perhaps a good third of the book, which seek to re-

create Kafka's intellectual climate and his response to it. And for this we will remain heavily indebted. Karl's presentation of Prague may not read too well, but it is convincing (but surely its German minority was more than the 5 percent figure Karl cites; Leipzig published Kafka, but some of his fellow citizens read him). Karl's history of the Kafka family is thorough, from *shtetl* to fashionable haberdashery, from orthodoxy to secular Judaism. But is this the family of the modern Everyman? Karl argues it is because the more disassociated, the more alienated one is forced to be, or chooses to be, in a deconstructed society, the more one is modern. If Pater's Mona Lisa "in to which the soul with all its maladies has passed" is the archetype of the late nineteenth century, then Kafka is that of a modern godless world which has no soul, but only a mind, or perhaps, given Karl's critical stance, a subconscious. Not that the novelist was physically healthy: in 1917 tuberculosis kept him writing and out of marriage; but to see his attacks of hemorrhaging as "vicarious suffering" for soldiers at the front metamorphosizes Kafka from an Emersonian representative man into an independent symbol. Karl's life tends to become an allegory.

But when it comes to the reconstruction of the outward events of Kafka's life, this will become the standard English biography. In addition to his analysis of the cultural setting, Karl has found new letters to Kafka's parents and assimilated a great deal of German scholarship. The interior of Kafka's life, despite the revealing diaries, probably can never be clear; his affectional existence is as opaque as the causality implied by the prose of *The Castle* (1941). Nevertheless, Karl does untangle the dynamics between Kafka and his fiancée, Felice Bauer: Kafka chose art rather than heavy furniture. And not the least of this biography's excellence is the stimulating Freudian interpretation of literary texts, though at times one may wish Sigmund Freud had followed Homer's account and left Jocasta's son securely ruling Thebes. No doubt Kafka's texts call for tortuous psychoanalytic interpretations, and Karl's are never dull, but does Kafka's time call for the same treatment? Are Slovenian nationalists oedipodes who have ambushed Francis Joseph II?

These last two biographies can serve to illustrate the problems inherent in the genre of biography. Should the subject be examined from the inside or the outside? Karl, despite his chapters on intellectual history, works from inside out; Boyle from the times to the author. This accounts for their essentially different assessments of our century: to write of an age is to assume order exists; to treat of the psyche is to welcome the near form-

less. The more successful biographer finds in the author's works that mediation which links the causal and the inchoate.

BOOK REVIEWING IN AMERICA: V

George Garrett
University of Virginia

I.

The whole book business, including the Washington Post's *esteemed section, is horrendous and rife with personal dealings and all kinds of stuff.*
—*Bob Haring of the* Tulsa World, *quoted in the* Washington Post

Publishing, as anyone who's in it can tell you, has always been a business that pretends to feed on fact but prefers to feed on rumor.
—*David Streitfeld, "Life at Random,"* New York Magazine

On the occasion of this fifth year of following the ups and downs, the ins and outs of book reviewing in America, one is hard-pressed to discover facts and to come up with any conclusions that could be called positive unless it is simply this—that the topic remains a problem, still worthy of some serious consideration and, if only by logical implication, still a problem in need of some kind of solution. The problem proved the occasion for a public challenge by National Public Radio critic Alan Cheuse, a challenge which elicited concerned responses from twelve people—writers (Bob Shacochis, Madison Smartt Bell, Jay Parini, Josephine Humphreys, Herbert Gold, Carolyn See), all of whom are at least part-time book reviewers; four editors (George Core of the *Sewanee Review*, Robert S. Fogarty of the *Antioch Review*, Carol Houck Smith of Norton, Jack Shoemaker of Pantheon); a bookseller, Carla Cohen; and a literary agent, Timothy Schaffner. All these responses were published as a "Symposium:

Alan Cheuse, fiction reviewer and critic for National Public Radio (photograph by Carol Bullard)

The Situation of Reviewing," in *Mānoa: A Pacific Journal of International Writing* (Fall 1991). Points of view and angles of attack were, of course, different, sometimes contradictory. But the subject received a good and lively airing. There were good moments—for example, Carol Houck Smith's nononsense declaration of the desperate importance of one particular review in the case of literary fiction: "Though there are other papers whose reviews we publishers await eagerly, the *New York Times Book Review* still weighs in heavily, and I don't think I feel this way simply because I am situated in the East. When a book is poorly reviewed or overlooked by the *Times*, there's a difference in its sales trajectory. In addition to the tenor of the review (what follows is true for all newspapers), placement and visuals (jacket photo, author photo) are important." There were bad moments: for instance, Jay Parini mending (or whitewashing) political fences by pausing to praise "such excellent post-structuralist critics as Terry Eagleton, Edward Said, Katherine Stimpson, Elaine Showalter, Frank Lentricchia and Donald Pease, just to name a few of my personal favorites." There are precious few answers advanced in the "Symposium," but the questioning seems worthwhile.

Before facing the gloomy details and dealing with discouraging works (and facts), it may be wise to point to some things that have not changed for the worse. True, the *Kenyon Review* has opted for an updated role as an example of trendiness and unblushing political correctness (and can the *Georgia Review* and the *Southern Review* be far behind?), but the principal quarterlies, especially the *Sewanee*, the *Hudson*, the *Virginia Quarterly*, and, of course, the *American Scholar*, continue to publish many book reviews and critical pieces, occupying undiminished space in each issue, offering a responsible mix of recently published and older books.

Of course, on the downside there were seemingly inevitable developments like the taking over of *Grand Street* by Jean Stein, an event celebrated by an article, "Stein's Way" by Guy Trebay, in *Vanity Fair* (July). "Jean Stein's *Grand Street* has all the loopy charm of a world's fair," wrote Trebay. "*Paris Review* move over. *Granta* watch your ass." To which George Plimpton of the *Paris Review* replied with a shrug: "Jean couldn't edit her way out of a paper bag." (Also quoted is William Faulkner's long-ago estimate of her in a letter to his editor, Saxe Commins: "She is charming, delightful, completely transparent, completely trustful. I will not hurt her at any price.")

Meanwhile other periodicals kept their book pages alive or, in some cases, expanded them. Among the former was the *New Criterion*, especially in the regular reviews and essays of Bruce Bawer (see his "Literary Life in the 1990s," September 1991). The conservative monthly *Chronicles* hired former *National Review* literary editor

Chilton Williamson, Jr. to be their full-time senior editor for books. Williamson considerably expanded the space devoted to book reviewing, including both essay reviews and "Brief Mentions," and is also building up a crew of regular reviewers, among them Gregory McNamee, M. E. Bradford, and Richard S. Wheeler. Together with editor Thomas Fleming, Williamson and others on the staff brought out excellent special issues on "Southern Writing" (March), "Penny Dreadfuls"— science fiction, westerns and adventure fiction (August), and "Western Writing" (November). Similarly the *World & I*, the opulent monthly magazine produced by the *Washington Times*, continued to offer in its "Book World" section more than one hundred pages of book reviews, often dealing with books not treated so seriously or extensively elsewhere. For example, there is Lucy Mazareski's essay-review, "Waging War on Silence," of *If I Had Wheels of Love: Collected Poems of Vassar Miller*, in the June issue, surely the most thoroughgoing review of a new book of poems published during the year.

Other poetry reviews of any length and value dealt with well-known and well-established poets and tended to be disguised, in the places they were to be found, as profiles or "personality pieces." Typical of this form, in which a book appears (if at all) mostly as the occasion and justification for a personal profile, is Dinitia Smith's "Poem Alone: The Cryptic John Ashbery, America's Foremost Poet, Goes the Distance" (*New York*, 20 May). Another sort of celebration, a labor of love put together over some years by Vince Clemente, is "Remembering John Hall Wheelock," in the *North Atlantic Review* (Summer), which includes contributions by Richard Wilbur, Richard Eberhart, Paul Engle, James Dickey, David Slavitt, and others. The usually dormant American poetry scene was witness to one of the minor crises of the literary year. The trouble, a strong candidate for the Tempest-in-a-Teapot Award, began with a lengthy article in the May issue of the *Atlantic*—"Can Poetry Matter?," by Dana Gioia—which itself was a response to a 1988 piece, "Who Killed Poetry?," by Joseph Epstein, published in *Commentary*. There had been a firestorm of reaction to Epstein's essay, in places like the *AWP Chronicle*, reactions here described by Gioia as "extravagantly acrimonious"; but the public noise had mostly died down until Gioia's article came along, cheerfully blaming the poets, their mind-set and habits, as much as the system and the times for the decline of any real au-

Dana Gioia, poet and author of "Can Poetry Matter?," a controversial essay about the disappearance of a general audience for poetry (photograph by Michael Spano)

dience for poetry except among poets themselves. A lot of toes were intentionally and firmly stepped upon before Gioia wrapped up his show-and-tell with six general, if practical, suggestions of ways and means to turn things around for the better. More people evidently read articles about poetry in the *Atlantic* than actually contend with the thing in itself. And, as the *Atlantic* editors must surely have hoped, the Gioia article generated a wealth of letters to them and more public responses elsewhere. More or less typical of the latter is Robert McPhillips's "Poetry Still Matters," published in the Poetry Society of America's *PSA News* (Fall), which, while acknowledging much truth in the Gioia article, nevertheless pauses to praise the contributions of disinterested poetry lovers such as critic Helen Vendler and sees signs and clues "that a genuine audience for poetry exists outside the subculture of poetry." More pertinent is the essay by poet Louis Simpson in the *New Criterion* (September), "On the Neglect of Poetry in the United States." Simpson dismisses the practical suggestions of Dana Gioia, together with some ideas of approximately equal weight advanced by Donald Hall, with a simpler and more

direct suggestion. "The way to overcome the present neglect of poetry is to write great poems."

Another brief and fiery crisis among the poets was a battlefield of letters in *Poets and Writers* (March/April and July/August issues) over the fact that Maxine Kumin, acting as 1991 judge, had awarded the Virginia Poetry Prize to her close friend Carole Oles. These sometimes angry arguments seeking to define the outlines of conflict of interest became somewhat moot when, as an act of budget writing, the Commonwealth of Virginia ceased and desisted from offering its cornucopia of literary prizes and awards. . . .

INTERMISSION

Before returning to the general subject of book reviewing in America, here is an interview, done for *DLB*, on the subject of the criticism and reviewing of poetry. The interview was conducted by Brendan Galvin, whose twelfth book of poetry, *Saints in Their Ox-Hide Boat* (Louisiana State University), has recently been published. He questions Neal Bowers, poet and editor, who teaches at Iowa State University. Bowers is editor of *Poet & Critic* and is author of two books of poems, *The Golf Ball Diver* (1983) and *Night Vision* (1992), as well as two critical books.

DLB: Ours has been called an age of criticism as opposed to an age of poetry. Do you feel this is true, and if so has it been beneficial to poets?

BOWERS: Well, let me begin with the last part first. No, I don't think the gathering dominance of criticism has been beneficial to poets. Criticism is inevitably analytical, while poetry is essentially intuitive (good poetry is, anyway). So, to whatever extent criticism becomes confused with poetry, poetry suffers. Of course, there's always been an uneasy relationship between poetry and criticism, dating back to Aristotle's *Poetics*, which illustrates perfectly how simple description can become prescription (or even proscription). That's the trouble with criticism, generally—it's always shouldering in and telling artists how to do their jobs.

The twentieth century has confused poetry and criticism to a greater extent than any previous age, largely because of the self-involved nature of modern and postmodern art. The analytical properties of criticism perfectly suit the modern and contemporary inclination to make the materials of each artistic field—poetry, painting, music, etc.—the subject of the work itself. The result is an art that is all head and almost no heart. That's probably why art in our time generally appeals to no one but other artists.

The epitome of this problem is the so-called L = A = N = G = U = A = G = E poetry, which has adopted the worst aspects of deconstruction theory as its guiding aesthetic. The result, according to the "movement's" poets, is a poetry created by each individual reader. If that sounds like a nifty transmigration of artistic souls, it's actually something significantly less. It's the abandonment of a personal aesthetic in favor of a theory, and that amounts to the death of poetry at the expense of criticism. You can see this same process at work in the New Formalism, which in itself is an exciting development. Unfortunately, some of the movement's principal writers (Timothy Steele primary among them) have helped precipitate an inane debate over the value of form; and, in the end, poets have spent more time arguing the theory and politics of form than in testing form's potential in honest-to-God poems.

DLB: What are the duties of a conscientious poetry reviewer? What pitfalls does he have to avoid? For instance do you ever have to prevent yourself from imposing your own obsessions on a book under review?

BOWERS: I can honestly say that I've never imposed my own views on anyone who's reviewed for *Poet & Critic.* There've been times that I've wanted to, but I've resisted the urge. Even so, an editor may influence the process in more subtle ways—simply by sending a certain book to a certain reviewer, for example. And I think that's permissible, as long as the reviewer is left free to say what she feels is true about the work under consideration. Who can blame the editor if he is able to guess in advance what that truth is likely to be?

The one inviolable rule of reviewing for all parties concerned is honesty. A false positive review doesn't help anyone, and probably even the beneficiary of such intended kindness usually knows he's undeserving. Similarly, a calculated negative review, one written just for the hell of it, is likely to do harm all around. All I ever tell reviewers is to say what they really feel. And even in those instances when I'm guessing about the

Neal Bowers, editor of Poet & Critic *(photograph by Douglas E. Smith)*

outcome and am wrong, I don't interfere or try to modify the results.

DLB: As editor of *Poet & Critic,* as well as being a scholar and poet, you must see pretty much the entire spectrum of contemporary poems. What do you admire in what you see? Are there things you feel we could live with less of ?

BOWERS: The shortest answer is to say we could definitely live with less. That's the cry of every beleaguered editor on the planet. There's simply too much stuff being written, most of it god-awful, and a hell of a lot of it ends up in my mailbox and on my desk.

I'd say that about 25 percent of the manuscripts I receive are essentially incompetent. That is, they aren't worth the time it takes to read them because they're Robert Service imitations or Gibran paraphrases. About 50 percent are competent, probably written by people getting or holding M.F.A.'s, but there's nothing in them. They're hollow at the heart, void of feeling, vision, understanding. And the final 25 percent are the ones I spend most of my time with, because I end up accepting less than 1 percent of them.

I'm all the time telling writers who are angry at being rejected that an editor is nothing more than one person with an opinion. No editor is a final authority on anything other than his own tastes and perceptions, and even those are subject to change. Every time I take a poem, I take something that I simply cannot send back. The poem won't let me. It would haunt me forever if I let it get away.

To say what I most admire in poems is relatively easy, although it's of absolutely no use to any poet wanting to psych me out. I want—make that *need*—poems that convey a sureness about themselves. The voice has to make me feel, from the very first word, that I can give myself over to the poem, that it will take me somewhere I'll be glad to go. Think of it as a plane ride. Would you climb into the cockpit with someone who was thumbing the manual in search of the starter?

DLB: Are there poets whom you feel criticism has given reputations they don't deserve?

BOWERS: This is my opportunity to be nasty, right? I mean, I could make up a long, long list. Maybe it's best if I focus on a representative poet, like Marvin Bell, whose dominant solipsism is one of the ailments of our age. Bell represents better than anyone else the attenuations of confessionalism—that progressive decline from "I myself am hell" (to quote Milton via Lowell) to "I myself am." Bell is the only poet I know who can turn any subject into an occasion for reflection on himself. Denise Levertov once said, and I don't think she would mind my paraphrasing her here, that Marvin Bell begins each poem by asking the same question, "Self, what do I think of this?"

If you conclude from this example that I abhor phoniness and self-involvement, I won't argue with you. It's curious how poetic reputations are made, often of pretty shoddy stuff. Meanwhile, the deserving poets who go unnoticed by the self-elected powers that be are legion.

DLB: As a poet, what do you feel your attitude toward reviews of your own work ought to be?

BOWERS: I wish I could say I have the courage not to read any reviews of my work. Unfortunately, I'm always perversely interested in what anyone has to say, good or bad. No use pretending that a bad review doesn't hurt, and I've been known to fire off a letter of complaint when I've felt badly treated, but this sometimes precipitates an even more infuriating exchange as the reviewer and I become more entrenched in our separate opinions. Right now, I'm studying a benign dismissal of reviews, regardless of their flavor. I keep telling myself that the good ones are probably as specious as the bad ones, so none of them matters. The only essential thing is the work itself.

DLB: Do you approach a first book differently than you would a book by a poet in midcareer? How so?

BOWERS: Definitely. I think first books are almost always pretty much the same, because they're usually highly autobiographical. Mine certainly was. They should be good, of course, but they may be permitted some errors and excesses that subsequent books may not. A poet in midcareer is in a very different situation. We may forgive him, or even praise him, for the noble failure; but there's no reason to excuse arrested development.

DLB: In general, what's your feeling about how poetry is reviewed in this country now?

BOWERS: In recent years, many people have said poetry reviews are without value because they're so uniformly positive. I tend to agree with that assessment, because I rarely see a really tough review. Nothing of the sort that Randall Jarrell produced for the *Southern Review* over thirty years ago can be found today. I mean, when was the last time you read a review you could honestly describe as witty, urbane, or acerbic? Hell, it's even hard to find a review we could honestly describe as incisive. In most cases, it's hard to tell the language in a review from that found in jacket blurbs: "X's telling vision is of such a compelling nature that it enables us again to call our world our own." Yeah, right.

I don't mean to suggest that reviews should be nasty, but it's definitely telling when almost no reviews are. Kind of makes the value of the stock go down. And, anyway, if a reviewer is charged with telling the truth, as I said earlier, she should occasionally find herself writing about things that don't move her to paroxysms of adulation.

I would be remiss here if I failed to mention Robert Peters's testy "Black and Blue Review" that appears regularly in the *Small Press Review*. Having been the victim of one of his columns, I can tell you that he's no chronic celebrator. Unfortunately, as his column's title suggests, he may be as wedded to negativism as most of his counterparts are to positivism. Surely, there's some reasonable middle ground on the landscape of honesty.

DLB: Who are your models as critics and reviewers?

BOWERS: I've probably already tipped my answer to this one by mentioning Jarrell as a reviewer, so let me pick on someone I don't like—Helen Vendler. Her taste is almost infallibly bad, and she seems to be more engaged in her own fantasy of "making" reputations than in doing the job right.

In the realm of critics, I still admire anyone who can execute a good explication of text. Call me a dinosaur if you like, but I think criticism should function in the service of art rather than displace it. Among contemporaries, I'm a great admirer of Jonathan Holden, whose critical essays always set me to thinking in ways that I wouldn't otherwise. Dana Gioia, too, is a stimulating critical essayist, although I don't always agree with him point by point.

To be completely honest, though, I must admit that I read as little criticism as I can get by with. Most of it bores me, especially the nihilistic drift of the state-of-the-art stuff. In some ways, I've cut back on my exposure to criticism because I think it's bad for me as a poet. Probably, it's already marked my poems in ways I'd prefer it hadn't; but I'm struggling in this over-intellectualizing age of ours to hold firm to my own aesthetic rather than to conform to a critical theory.

II.

Meanwhile 1991 saw the space allotted for book reviewing beginning to shrink and to dwindle in many places which had earlier seemed positive in support of contemporary literature—not merely the news magazines, which have clearly concluded that the making of books is less a matter of interest, of *news*, than it used to be a few short years ago, but also other places presented

less in the way of book reviewing than in previous years. Losses were greatest in the women's magazines—*Vogue, Harper's Bazaar, Elle, Mirabella*, etc. *Elle*, which a couple of years ago was devoting good pages to reviews of quality books, proved to be particularly disappointing over the year; although, in fairness it must be pointed out that one of the better pieces on the subject of new first novels—"Going Home, Cheating, And Chewing the Fat: Untrue Confessions in New Novels," by Margaret Rausch—appeared in the June issue. *Mirabella* remains serious enough to have taken on, out of the literary magazine arena, Sven Birkerts as a regular reviewer. His choices of books on which to bestow his attention and ours have thus far been solid and interesting if unexceptional, a little safe at the outset. But more troubling than the critic's conservative literary stance have been occasional hints of a mind-set more purely journalistic than critical. In an otherwise worthy review of new novels by Elizabeth Spencer and Frederick Busch, Birkerts feels compelled to "place" them in a larger literary setting. "Frederick Busch and Elizabeth Spencer are both storytellers who have been suffering the curse—peculiar to America—of being very good but very unread. They win prizes, accolades from fellow writers, and are stubbornly prolific (Busch has published sixteen books of fiction, Spencer twelve), but neither has struck the magnesium flare of celebrity." Never mind the "peculiar to America" aside; it is unsupported and most likely insupportable. More to the point is that "magnesium flare of celebrity," here assumed to be as necessary as it might be (to some) desirable. Fascination with celebrity (and, to a lesser extent, with good fame) is real enough and offers blame enough all around—to the assumed audience as well as the creators and purveyors of celebrity and, finally, to the celebrities themselves, who, if they do not fully possess the power to bestow this quality upon themselves, nevertheless do have the freedom, not often exercised, to deny and ignore it.

Even though book reviewing in and of itself has become strictly limited, the literary journalists have discovered how to call attention to a book, newly published or, more often, (when magazines have a longer and longer lead-time and when books in the marketplace have a shorter and shorter shelf life, roughly three to four weeks these days), before the book has been published. The way to earn space, and with that space to capture some readers' interest, is to center the piece around the bright "magnesium flare of celebrity."

The easiest and most acceptable way for the literary journalist to make hay is to write about writers and their works which separately or together are, in a relative sense of the word, established, already recognized for one reason or another. Thus you have a piece such as Robert Love's "Bret Easton Ellis: Psycho Analysis" in the April issue of *Rolling Stone*, which combines a brief history of the coming and going of *Psycho* with an interview with its author. From Ellis we can learn some surprising (and doubtful) things: "I did so much research for this book. I read criminology textbooks. I read every pulp and true-life crime book I could get my hands on." Or we can flip the pages of *Vanity Fair*, already a model for celebrity journalism, perhaps with a particularly literary bent like the October issue with its review of *The Journals of John Cheever* (Knopf)—"Leave It to Cheever"—where James Wolcott can provide an upbeat if ironic ending to the sad Cheever story: "The mess of Cheever's life is a mud slide. Yet it's provided such posthumous fame that his fiction has finally been elevated to the big league." Posthumous fame is better than no fame at all. Sometimes death can be a good career move. In the same issue one finds Toby Thompson's "Mailer's Alpha and Omega," a lengthy piece welcoming Mailer's blockbuster novel *Harlot's Ghost* (Random House) to the world and recapitulating the not altogether untheatrical facts and legends of Mailer's life. (See also another almost simultaneous piece about Mailer, one among many, "Norman Mailer: A Legend in his Own Mind," by Helle Bering-Jensen, the *Washington Times*, 6 October.) In the June *Vanity Fair* is Anthony Haden-Guest's "Kosinski's Masque," with new photographs of the late writer, which at once serves as a memorial for Kosinski and offers some clues to the logic of his suicide. (For another version of the trials and tribulations of the late Jerzy Kosinski see "The Haunted Bird," by John Taylor, in *New York*, 15 July.) In the December issue of *Vanity Fair* British poet and editor Craig Crane ("Famous Seamus") takes the occasion of the publication of Seamus Heaney's new book, *Seeing Things* (Farrar, Straus and Giroux), to use the undeniable fact of Heaney's fame in the small world of poets and readers of poetry, and the anecdotes and memoirs that serve at once to isolate and to surround him like a performer's spotlight, to talk a little in an appreciative way (no point in wasting space and print on a seri-

ous critical questioning) about Heaney's work. Of course the writing inevitably suffers a little from the context of glitz and chic and soft-shoe irony (Crane refers to Heaney's study as "the nest where his golden eggs are produced"); nonetheless the article adds up to about as extensive and thorough a review as the book will receive. Again, however, celebrity is the fuel that runs the engine: "At the time (Christmas 1975) Lowell's poetry could command a review on the front page of the arts section in a national Sunday newspaper—a thing inconceivable now, even for Seamus Heaney—and he was easily the most charismatic and influential living poet." It is hard to imagine how a *dead* poet could be charismatic except through his words and works, but the point is there made that Robert Lowell in a sense created the celebrity of Seamus Heaney by a book review which was a kind of laying on of hands.

Crane's piece points toward another direction. If one celebrity is good news and reason enough for a piece of literary journalism, think how two celebrities increase the impact. This certainly occurred to some editors and journalists in 1991 with mixed results. An example whose pretensions are limited is "Rank and Style: Tom Wolfe talks to *M Inc.*'s Clay Felker About the Hidden Meaning in Men's Clothes." (Somewhere in the big sophisticated middle of things, a place where celebrity is not explained or justified, merely assumed, is another conversation, "Mailer and Vidal: The Big Schmooze," *Esquire* [May].) It is a dramatization of the peace process among the rich and famous. Where these two at least seemed to disagree strongly in days gone by, they now agree in almost everything. The only moment of brief disagreement is over the quality and value of Truman Capote's literary work. But that potential argument is quickly dissipated by Mailer's assertion (and Vidal's acceptance) that Capote's death has made the issue moot: "Mailer: Why should we argue about it? He's behind us. No one cares. Vidal: No one cares." Another odd pairing, in this case of the living and the dead (perhaps in the hope that some of the light of a famous ghost will shine on an ambitious young writer), was achieved by the *New York Review of Books*, assigning Jay McInerney to review *The Short Stories of F. Scott Fitzgerald* (Scribners)—"Fitzgerald Revisited," (15 August). More strictly literary in intent is James Wolcott's "The Sunshine Boys" (*Vanity Fair*, June), a linked book review of Don DeLillo's *Mao II* (Viking) and *My Romance* (Norton) by Gordon Lish, whom Wolcott casually refers to (as if everyone in the world already knew this and agreed without qualification) as "the very model of a bullshit artist." DeLillo makes out a bit better, though he, too, must suffer, if only from the lighthearted excesses of hip criticism. Without an overt wink Wolcott can write: "A Lone Ranger, DeLillo fires his perceptions like a beltload of silver bullets."

This kind of critical writing is suddenly much the fashion among magazine reviewers. Witness this metaphorical description, by Barbara Jones, of the writing of Ethan Canin in *Blue River* ("*Blue River*: Wading Into Troubled Waters," *Elle*, October): "*Blue River* is a knot of unhappiness tied so tight that even Ethan Canin can't tease a neat bow out of it." Another characteristic aspect of the writing of celebrity journalism even of the literary variety is the little prose snapshot of person or place even if a published photograph renders such detail at best redundant. Here is the gifted David Streitfeld performing that required figure early on in "Vonnegut, Existentially Speaking: The Writer and Failed Suicide Still Tempting the Fates" (*Washington Post*, 29 August): "He'll be 70 next year. He's smoked unfiltered Pall Malls since the Depression but nevertheless looks good, all crinkly hair and golden tan. The Tobacco Institute ought to sign him up as a spokesman. It's true he sometimes has a tendency to cough, especially when laughing, but today he's not doing much of either." Similarly, evoking first of all the details of place, here is Jacqueline Trescott's lead paragraph of her article "The Daughter of the Mother Poets: Novelist Paule Marshall, Exploring the World of Black Immigrants" (*Washington Post*, October 8): "On a rainy day in this city of Confederate monuments [Richmond], Paule Marshall is sitting at a polished oak table in her apartment. There's a clear vase of waxy anthericum behind her. A Haitian iron sculpture hanging on the exposed-brick wall takes note of her connections to the Caribbean." The habits and tropes of the writing remain much the same, almost interchangeable now, except in the rare case of somebody with a very special energy and style, not always, not even often, devoted to pieces about authors. When Henry Allen is put on the case there is a difference: "There is no solitude like the solitude of an angry woman. An angry woman is Camille Paglia, lost scholar and found celebrity." (*Washington Post*, 15 April).

But the range of this kind of reportage reviewing is limited, and the differences in matter and manner are slight. The biggest difference lies in the subject. Occasionally, instead of the constant reiteration of the power and glory and hierarchy of the Establishment, a contemporary critic-journalist may opt for the discovery of new talent or the celebration of talent which seems to have been ignored or, anyway, has avoided the statues of celebrity. A superior example of the latter is Dinitia Smith's "Just So: The Odyssey of a Quintessentially American Novelist" (*New York*, 19 August), a profile of writer Ward Just and a review of his new novel, *The Translator* (Houghton Mifflin). Of course, unless the writer is absolutely brand new on the scene, it is necessary to establish the need for attention and public discovery. Thus, having pointed to the exceptional critical reputation of Just's work, Smith seeks to surprise everyone (except other living novelists) with his relative obscurity: "Despite the praise, Just's fourteen books have rarely sold more than 20,000 copies each, and until recently, some of the best didn't even get a paperback sale." More toward the "discovery" side, though, in truth, all of these writers are relatively well known, even if not to most busy journalists. Good examples from the year are: John Anderson's "Pete Dexter's Fighting Words" (*M Inc.*, September); Will Dana's "The Raymond Chandler of the Bayou" (*M Inc.*, May), a profile appreciation of James Lee Burke, cousin of writer Andre Dubus and author of, among other things, four Dave Robicheaux novels; "Dangerous Dan DeLillo" (*New York Times Magazine*, 19 May: "His books are not friendly, but their architecture brings an odd pleasure no matter how unsettling the world they illumine."), by Vince Passaro; and James Wolcott's "Jungle Boogie" (*Vanity Fair*, January), a piece on Charles Portis and his most recent book, *Gringos* (Simon and Schuster). True to the form and fashion, Wolcott writes: "*Gringos* isn't a bust, just a book bumpily in bed with itself. What makes Portis's novels knockabout treats is that they're good company, even when they stray." The June issue of (the now defunct) *Fame* had a similar "discovery" piece by David Streitfeld—"Maxwell the Smart"— all about writer William Maxwell, who at the *New Yorker* served as the editor of J. D. Salinger, John Cheever, Harold Brodkey, and many others, well known and not.

The same issue of *Fame* demonstrates the other end of the spectrum of contemporary literary journalism—the unlikely candidate for attention—"Write Trash," by Dana Kennedy, all about "the glittering life of Judith Krantz." Krantz has been, Kennedy asserts, as influential in a literary way as she was commercially success-ful: "She set the tone for all the shopping-and-screwing novels that came later."

Promotion and publicity, emphasis on the personal and subjective, and, yes, shopping-and-screwing are now as firmly, deeply rooted in the publishing business as in the writing trade. It fol-lows. If the "facts" of a life (real and imaginary) are more important than any text, then all texts, having reached a level of modest competence, are equally important or unimportant, and, in ei-ther case, mostly irrelevant except insofar as they may be inflated by hype, inflected by celebrityhood. We have come very close to arriv-ing at the once-satirical point where all publicity of any kind, true or false, good or evil, is desir-able. Dealing with this problem directly is Meg Cox's article "When It Comes to Novel Hyping, The Wellspring Seems Bottomless" (*Wall Street Jour-nal*, 12 August). The piece concerns the promo-tional plans of Random House for a new novel, *Topless* by D. Keith Mano, plans beginning with "a book party tonight in a topless bar, complete with performances by eight bare-breasted danc-ers." Alberto Vitale, chairman of Random House, Inc., is quoted as follows, walking a fine line: "It's a bit unusual, but unusual things cause un-usual sales. The reputation of a publishing house is based on the book it publishes, not the parties it throws." To which Meg Cox later responds by noting: "But then, despite its exalted reputation, Random House divisions have published some pretty racy material of late, including *American Psy-cho*, a novel about a kinky sex killer that was re-jected elsewhere for reasons of taste. Another Ran-dom House division had a book party in Las Vegas last year during the booksellers' conven-tion at a topless ice-skating show called 'Nudes On Ice.' "

The next step, already taken, is to move away from texts and their creators and to focus on the party givers. No surprise that this year saw publishers, themselves, becoming public fig-ures, celebrity images created by the literary press.

Joni Evans and Richard Snyder, the story of whose marriage and divorce had enlivened the news of 1990, were back in the limelight. She was in the news chiefly because she left her position as publisher at Random House (maybe by free choice and maybe not) to form, still within that cor-poration, her own imprint—Turtle Bay Books. With a half-page photo of Evans and the four young women who comprise her staff and a lengthy, full-scale story, the *New York Times* "Busi-ness" section covered the ground and the gossip ("Random House's Glitzy New Imprint," by N. R. Kleinfield, 17 March), bestowing a publicity bless-ing on Evans and her new enterprise. It was not, however, without some condescending, if friendly, needling, as, for example, when Evans is quoted as opening the weekly editorial meeting at Turtle Bay: "What we normally talk about at these meetings is our hair. But today nothing about hair." The inimitable Evans seems even more at home on the pages of *W* ("A House of Her Own: Joni Evans is Creating Her Own Im-print with Turtle Bay Books," by Lorna Koski, 16-23 September), where she is quoted on interna-tional affairs ("You can't be a Stalinist any more. Ever since CNN, you can't look like those disgust-ing hard-liners.") as well as literary matters—"I love Norman Mailer more than any other writer, even when he's not writing well." (We must con-tinue to remind ourselves, that these public fig-ures, authors and publishers alike, participate in the creative process of image building.)

June 1991 appeared to be payback time as Richard Snyder occupied even more of the *New York Times* business pages (even larger photo-graph, even longer story) with "Profits—Dick Snyder's Ugly Word: Publishing's Legend Whips Simon and Schuster into the 21st Century. But is Literature Getting Lost?," by Roger Cohen. This piece which, while judicious, was highly positive in its evaluation of Snyder as corporate leader, was somewhat undercut by Adam Begley's "A Taste of His Own Medicine" (*Spy*, June). Begley's article rejoiced in the fact that Snyder now has a boss as tough as he is reputed to be; Begley's tone and point of view are swiftly established in the article's first two sentences: "Petty, ferocious behavior is nothing new to longtime Simon and Schuster boss Dick Snyder. But this time he's on the receiving end, and *his* boss, Paramount Com-munication's Marty Davis, is the bully." Another June piece which tended to personalize (maybe to heroize) corporate character in terms of celeb-rity was Roger Cohen's "Ruffled Feathers in Ran-dom Eaves" (*New York Times*, 17 June), which con-cerned the first eight months of leadership at Random House by British newspaperman Harold Evans, who replaced Joni Evans as publisher.

Once publishers found themselves as poten-tial celebrities and journalists noted how they could personalize complicated events and situa-tions, there seemed to be no end of it. Among the principal examples of this trend: Roger

Cohen's "In Unforgiving Haste, A Shift Atop Bantam" (*New York Times*, 25 June), about the appointment of Jack Hoeft, "a former Pepsico marketing executive as the second new chief of Bantam Doubleday Dell in just nine months"; David Streitfeld's "Life At Random: Reading Between the Lines at America's Hottest Publishing House" (*New York*, 5 August), an article effectively covering all the above news from publishers now, but settling in as a positive profile of Knopf's Sonny Mehta; "Editor to the Stars: HarperCollins's Craig Nelson" (*M Inc.*, June), by Richard B. Woodward, praising his subject whose goal is to make publishing as lively and profitable as other forms of mass media show business (Craig Nelson: "Publishing is in pathetic shape in relation to every other media industry."); and, finally, a scintillating puff piece about one of the best and the brightest, most publicized young editors in the history of American publishing—Gary Fisketjon ("Blond Ambition," by Lucy Kaylin, *GQ*, April), ostensibly celebrating Fisketjon's triumphant return to Knopf after a time at Atlantic Monthly Press.

At times, when the tone is less enthusiastically celebratory, these new publishing celebrities snap back. Case in point in 1991 was Jacob Weisberg's "Rough Trade: The Sad Decline of American Publishing" (*New Republic*, 17 June), which blew the whistle on the unspoken fact that most working editors are too busy making deals to do much, if any, editing, and that therefore the cultivated image of publishers does not conform to reality. Where publishers argued that they had to publish a certain amount of commercial trash to support the publication of literature, Weisberg seriously doubted this: "Except at a few independent-minded houses, of which Farrar Straus is the most prominent example, the situation is now reversed: the literature is an afterthought to the schlock, a garnishing of literary prestige to soothe the conscience and placate the ghosts." What stung publishers most (and many out of their stables of writers) was Weisberg's singling out of a couple of examples, Jason Epstein of Random House and Alice Mayhew of Simon and Schuster, to personalize and prove his case. The reaction was a little media firestorm as reporters and feature writers cranked out copy, and so many writers rose to the defense of Alice Mayhew that Jacob Weisberg concluded, "Alice Mayhew is organizing a chain-writing campaign." Indeed *Washington Post* writer Howard Kurtz found Weisberg's story, while fundamentally accurate and maybe even overdue, "less interesting than the chorus of denunciations it triggered from big-name authors who rallied to the defense of Simon & Schuster's Alice Mayhew and other editors Weisberg had criticized." Kurtz wrote: "Watch out, Jake: You'll never publish in this town again."

Some of Weisberg's observations about the contemporary publishing scene were echoed in an angry column in the 4 November *Washington Post* by critic Jonathan Yardley. Yardley attacked and ridiculed a recent issue of *Entertainment Weekly* which had elected to name the 101 most powerful people in the world of American entertainment. Ten names from publishing were cited in the issue, described thus by Yardley: "Four publishers, two editors, one journalist—and three hack novelists (Stephen King, Tom Clancy, Danielle Steel)." Yardley went on to pass judgment on the works and ways of these "powerful" people: "These are people who got where they are not by breaking new ground but by paving the old ground more slickly than anyone else."

At the core of the new personalized literary journalism is the straightforward interview, not disguised as a book review or a news story or anything else except itself. Somehow in the whole confusing context the interview has arrived at a certain kind of respectability, becoming almost a new genre. At one end, partly because of the success and repute of the *Paris Review* interviews, university presses regularly publish collections of interviews, the most extensive being the University Press of Mississippi's *Literary Conversations Series*, thirty-four volumes (so far) of collected interviews of "notable modern writers," living or dead. On the other hand there is *Publishers Weekly*, which has regularly, week by week, published interviews with writers of all kinds, many of them unquestionably "literary." A few among the many interviewed by *PW* in 1991 include Carolyn See, Diane Ackerman, Thomas Disch, Larry Brown, Mary McGarry Morris, Rick DeMarinis, Sandra Cisneros, and Barry Gifford. *PW* has also from time to time featured brief personal statements by prominent literary writers (see "Speaking of Books," *Publishers Weekly*, 8 August, for statements by "top authors"—Maeve Binchy, Harold Brodkey, Pete Dexter, Ethan Canin, Paule Marshall, Jane Smiley) and longer pieces by very well-known literary figures, for example John Irving (24 January) and Margaret Atwood (8 August). Even more limited and specialized literary publications have begun to publish interviews with some regularity. For example

Dust jacket for Baker's exploration of his obsession with the writing, life, and person of John Updike

AWP Chronicle, the newsletter for the Associated Writing Programs, published several author interviews in 1991, two of which, with Robert Coover (February) and poet and novelist John Williams (December), are outstanding. *Poets & Writers* has also begun to publish interviews with literary stars as a matter of course. Typical are interviews with John Irving (May/June) and Amy Tan (September/October) and Hubert Selby (March/April). Selby, author of the cult novel *Last Exit To Brooklyn* (1964), raises a few eyebrows with remarks like "I want to write the most politically correct book I can think of."

Public figures, even in such an essentially solitary enterprise as the creating of books, seem to have waived or forfeited, not always unwillingly, most of their rights to privacy. And so it is not surprising that in such a climate there should be fables reflecting that reality. Oddly exemplary is *U and I: A True Story* (Random House) by Nicholson Baker, a highly regarded young novelist. Described by the publisher as "an entirely new genre of creative exploration—an examination of how a life's worth of reading colors and affects the mind," *U and I* documents the author's apparent obsession with John Updike, his life, his works, his influence. Nabokovian brilliance and a certain insouciant self-reflexiveness make this tour de force somehow work even though there are some moments in which the author's urge for intimacy seems excessive. "I myself have never successfully masturbated to Updike's writing, though I have to certain scenes in Iris Murdoch; but someone I know says she achieved a number of quality orgasms from *Couples* when she first read it at age thirteen." Joke, to be sure, and all the funnier for the thought of possible readers of Nicholson's work turning to the huge, dense, complex fiction of Iris Murdoch, looking for excitement. Joke and satire, but nevertheless such writing reflects another sign of the disappearance of private life in a celebrity culture. A final example among many of the same distressing deterioration of late-twentieth-century literary sensibility.

Surely not since the Watergate tapes has a set of tape recordings attracted as much media interest and debate as followed after the disclosure that poet Anne Sexton and her psychiatrist had cooperated in making more than three hundred audiotapes, most of them recording her psychiatric sessions from 1956-1964. These were made available by the doctor to biographer Diane Wood for her biography *Anne Sexton* (Houghton Mifflin). The first revelation merited a page-one story—"Poet Told All: Therapist Provides the Record," by Alessandra Stanley (*New York Times*, 15 July). Another *Times* story (26 August), "Publicity Obsession Pays Off For Suicide-Book Publisher," by Roger Cohen, sums up the scene in its opening paragraph: "The stunning success of *Final Exit*, a how-to book for suicides, is just the latest exploit for Steven Schragis and his successful Carol Publishing Group, an innovative publisher whose obsession with marketing and publicity may point the way to the industry's future." Here the position of the publisher is that, in today's publishing marketplace, quality, indeed content itself, is of less importance than the capacity of a given book to generate publicity. Old-fashioned notions such as word-of-mouth advertising are no longer applicable. Even advertising is of less importance than direct publicity for the author and/or the book. It follows that the more apparently controversial the book, the more likely it is that publicity will follow. It seems to follow, also, that any kind of publicity is good publicity.

Not everything recorded and reported about the literary and publishing scene of 1991 proved to be a matter of constant personnel changes or the good and bad habits of personalities. Not everything was frivolous. A certain amount of business was accomplished and dutifully given attention by the literary press, which includes *Publishers Weekly* (surely the most complete coverage of the industry), the major national and regional newspapers, and other more specialized publications which, from time to time, sometimes regularly, deal in some detail with industry news. For example the expanded newsletter, *Authors Guild Bulletin*, edited by Hugh Rawson, has a regular and thorough feature aimed at authors—"Along Publishers Row." It was here (Spring-Summer) that correct and surprising numbers were culled and collated from a variety of sources proving that during the 1980s the sales of adult hardcover books increased at an annual average of 12 percent, or roughly twice the growth of mass market paperback sales. Here also (Winter) the full extent of foreign ownership of American publishing companies was highlighted: "In book publishing, Germans, English, Australians, and Scots own or run Doubleday, Macmillan, Penguin, and HarperCollins. An Iranian, Nader Dareshori, heads Houghton Mifflin. The Japanese electronic giant Matsushita picked up the Putnam Berkley Group when it bought MCA in November for $6.13 billion (considered something of a bargain). The trade magazine of the U.S. book business, *Publishers Weekly*, is owned by Britain's Reed International." Foreign ownership did not inhibit *Publishers Weekly* from firm political and social action in *this* country. On September 27, in a very rare, if not unique, gesture, *PW* took over its own front cover (usually reserved for publishers' advertisements) to address a letter to the president of the United States urging him to read a book about our public schools—*Savage Inequalities* (Crown), by Jonathan Kozol—and to take a strong stand against "the inequitable distribution of public funds."

Even though its main thrust remains political, the *Voice Literary Supplement*, being a New York publication, sometimes publishes pieces concerning the industry. In February *VLS* offered one of the better articles on the growing success and importance of independent bookstores—"Independents' Day: Good Stores Come in Small Packages," by Geoffrey Stokes. Other publications with at least irregular, but often intensive coverage of publishing include *AWP Chronicle, Poets*

& Writers, and *Poetry Plot* (published monthly by the Academy of American Poets); and for two issues the *PEN American Center Newsletter* (Summer and Autumn) devoted space to an ongoing symposium on the publishing scene.

Sales of books, to be sure, are what the business is all about. For most of the year publishers and booksellers faced the economy with apprehension. (See "Booksellers Fret Over How Fall Stacks Up," by Meg Cox, *Wall Street Journal*, 31 May.) Even in the absence of final statistics, it seems that the Christmas season of 1991 was a strong one in the book stores. Other retailers of various kinds faced real problems, but it appears that consumers bought a lot of books in the last months of the year. (See Esther Fein, "Booksellers Surprised by Strong Sales," *New York Times*, 23 December.)

The big story of the publishing year, covered by everyone, was the happy ending of a season of troubles for Harcourt Brace Jovanovich. All year long, still debt-ridden and struggling after fighting off a hostile takeover attempt in 1988 by the late Robert Maxwell, HBJ hovered right on the edge of bankruptcy. Then, at the last minute, in late November, this major publisher was acquired for $1.5 billion in cash by General Cinema Corporation, a move considered by qualified observers to be highly beneficial to both parties. (For a thorough analysis of the details, together with an interview with Richard E. Smith, General Cinema's chairman, see Geraldine Fabrikant, "General Cinema's Big Bet On Harcourt Brace's Revival," *New York Times*, 6 January.)

The almighty dollar earns a lot of critical interest, and no single literary work earned more dollars more quickly than Alexandra Ripley's *Scarlett* (Warner). From a rash of news and feature stories certain basic facts emerged. If critics and book reviewers hated it (and they certainly seemed unable to resist such a large and slow-moving target), a lot of readers at home and abroad seemed ready to trust their own judgment. *Scarlett* sold 500,000 copies in the United States in the first week of publication. It was officially published on 25 September in forty countries and in twenty languages. It has remained the number one best-seller here since then, selling a total (in America) of 1.2 million copies in six weeks, and was anticipated to sell 3 million copies by year's end. It also dragged Margaret Mitchell's original back on the best-seller list with it. Two excellent pieces (before and after as it were) on the *Scarlett* phenomenon are: (a) "The Global Launch of Scarlett," by Peggy Langstaff, *Publishers Weekly*, 30 August; and (b) "Success of 'Scarlett' Is an Epic in Itself," by Meg Cox, *Wall Street Journal*, 14 November. Oh yes, and the TV rights to the novel sold for a record $10 million. Through all this, writer Ripley bore herself with grace and courage, though she took the opportunity afforded by a podium at the Southeastern Booksellers Association (Atlanta, September 22) to speak for writers in general to the publishing industry: "There are many thousands of people in the world outside of midtown Manhattan who are hungry for good books to read. And they are being put on starvation diets by American publishers." (see "Alexandra Ripley Attacks Publishing Industry," *Publishers Weekly*, 4 October.)

All the excitement about *Scarlett* was primed by an initial promotion budget of $600,000, or roughly three times the usual budget for an anticipated best-seller. Well? Random House spent between $200,000 and $250,000 for a single evening party at the Rainbow Room in honor of a few of its authors at the American Booksellers Association in New York in June. And Viking Penguin announced a promotion budget of $750,000 for a forthcoming Stephen King book. Earlier in the year, during the brief war of Desert Storm, some publishers, perhaps motivated by patriotism as well as the bottom line, cut back on promotional ventures and expenses. (See Edwin McDowell, "War Cuts Publicity For Many Books," *New York Times*, 18 February.)

One measure of the state of the publishing industry, and a sure source of publicity, is the size of advances publishers are offering. The big ones—$5 million for General Norman Schwarzkopf (Bantam) and $4 million to Magic Johnson (Random House)—inevitably cause a stir. Random House was in the thick of things, reportedly offering Pamela Harriman $1.8 million for her memoirs and Marlon Brando something like $5 million for his autobiography. Those two were reported rumors, but it was official that Random House advanced $600,000 for a book about a Xerox sales team—"The Force," by David Dorsey—and came up with $375,000 for a first book by *Washington Post* reporter Nathan McCall about growing up black in America. Knopf paid $450,000 for a first novel, *The God of Illusions*, by Donna Tartt; and the indefatigable crew at Doubleday paid a $700,000 advance for a first and not yet written, though based on an article in *Granta* (37), book of nonfiction, "Shot in the

Heart: The Story of an American Family in Murder," by Mikal Gilmore. Mikal is the brother of Gary Gilmore, the convicted and executed murderer who featured in Norman Mailer's *The Executioner's Song*. The average upper limit for advances on first books of any kind is reported to be about $15,000.

The story of one first book occupied much space in newspapers and magazines and, as well, the time and energy of some of the leading literary reporters in the country. It was a thriller, "Just Killing Time," written by Derek Goodwin under the pseudonym of Derek Van Arman. This 787-page manuscript gained attention first because Simon and Schuster paid a huge advance, $920,000, for it. Soon thereafter it became apparent that part of the attraction of "Just Killing Time" was that the manuscript had strong endorsements from John le Carré and Joseph Wambaugh. When these two writers announced that they had never seen or heard of the manuscript and certainly not endorsed it, the story was everywhere. Simon and Schuster backed out of the deal. Other publishers took a look at the manuscript, some with reported interest. One of these was not Joni Evans, who was quoted in the *Washington Post* (26 April): "It's been tainted too much for me. There are too many smoking guns out there." Soon enough this example of fraud was food for personal journalism. Kim Masters and David Streitfeld produced an extensive profile in "The Bizarre Case of Derek Goodwin" (*Washington Post*, 18 April). A little later (23 April), in the same newspaper, Paula Span managed to locate the event in a larger general context ("All this means is that publishing has lost whatever insulation it once had from the demands and tensions of American capitalism.") in "What's Up With the Book Biz?: Behind the Gossip and Tales of Deceit, a High-Stakes World." On the whole it is a good piece, reflecting well the split between readers and purveyors: "How could a no-name novelist touch off a bidding war that brings close to a million bucks when would-be buyers hadn't ascertained whether those intriguing blurbs from noted authors were for real? What the hell is going on?"

There were other interesting examples of fraud, chicanery, and general hanky-panky in the literary year gone by. A very popular and politically correct book, sitting firmly at number six on the *Publishers Weekly* best-seller list and with a reported six hundred thousand copies in print, was *The Education of Little Tree* (New Mexico), by Forrest Carter. This autobiographical account of growing up as a native American was first published by Delacorte in 1976 and reprinted by the University of New Mexico Press in 1986. To make a long story shorter: the whistle was blown on Carter by his kinsman, Professor Dan T. Carter of Emory University. Turns out the late Forrest Carter was really one Asa Carter, who was (as Professor Carter was widely quoted) "a Ku Klux Klan terrorist, right-wing radio announcer, home-grown American fascist and anti-semitic, rabble-rousing demagogue." Carter's publisher blinked, declared *The Education of Little Tree* to be fiction, and went right on turning out books and coining profits. Another odd, if oddly appropriate, form of fraud for our celebrity-ridden culture surfaced in Larry McMurtry's introduction to *Texfake: An Account of the Theft and Forgery of Early Texas Printed Documents* (Taylor). Here McMurtry tells how, following the great success of *Lonesome Dove* on television, several impostors, at least four, have been professing to be Larry McMurtry. "Their aims were mainly sexual," he writes, "though one may have been in it for the money." McMurtry adds that at least one victim was not at all happy to hear the truth. Hearing that a young woman in Houston was just about to marry a McMurtry impostor, McMurtry writes that "When I reached her mother and informed her that her daughter's fiance was definitely not myself, the news was neither welcomed nor, so far as I could tell, accepted." The perennial problem of plagiarism offered examples like that of a Stanford Business School professor who was charged with lifting words and pages from work by Gregg Easterbrook for his book *Managing on the Edge*. And there was a great deal of give and take over plagiarism charges against Stephen B. Oates and his 1977 biography of Abraham Lincoln. More direct pilferage, possibly felonious, occurred when the *New Yorker* lost a chunk of its archives while moving from one location to another. Alessandra Stanley made the most of it in a *New York Times* piece, "How The New Yorker Lost 72 Boxes of Archives" (20 June). She quotes *New Yorker* editor Robert Gottlieb as trying not to make too much of the loss from his own perspective and in his own inimitable syntax: "Of course it is distressing. But compared to 100,000 dead Iraqis, where are you going to concentrate your anguish?" Felonies and misdemeanors may have been few and far between in the literary world, but litigation of all kinds, like grace in kinder, gentler times, was everywhere abounding.

Cases were many. A few examples will have to suffice. Among the more serious cases or cases with potentially serious consequences was one in which Kinko's was found to have been infringing copyrights. This was in connection with the reproduction of material for professors and their courses, a widespread practice of all copying services, including institutional ones, at hundreds of American colleges and universities. Prior to the lawsuit (which lost Kinko's five hundred thousand dollars), it had been widely agreed in academic circles that this kind of copying, for educational use, constituted "fair use." Not any more. Fair use has been a somewhat flexible concept, allowing for limited quotation from an author's copyrighted work, mainly for scholarly purposes, provided that the source is acknowledged and identified. Definition of fair use also depended on the nature of the source; thus, two or three hundred sustained words might be permissible fair use as a quotation from a work of expository prose, yet not be acceptable for poetry. The practice of professorial "course packs," homemade anthologies containing whole chapters, stories, and excerpts from book-length works of fiction, groups of poems, etc., published without permission of the copyright holder, was deemed to be above and beyond the intention of fair use.

Nobody is yet quite sure what will follow from the decision of the U.S. Supreme Court in the case of *Masson v. The New Yorker*. The only certainty is that the Court returned the case to be decided in a trial by jury. This is a complex case in which the plaintiff, Jeffrey Masson, argues that, among other things, he had been libelously misquoted by Janet Malcolm in a profile she wrote for the *New Yorker*. The defense against this was First Amendment rights and the necessity of the plaintiff to prove "actual malice." The court left it to a jury to decide, but asserted in opinion that quotes may be altered provided there is no "material change in the meaning." Where this leaves things remains to be seen. Certainly it complicates matters. If quotations may be inaccurate or altered, provided the inaccuracy or alteration does not change the "meaning," it would appear that the burden of proof rests on the party who has been misquoted to establish that content as well as form has been changed. As in any number of other complicated recent legal decisions, this one will lead to an explosion of litigation or to a climate that will force those who have been injured by inaccurate quotations simply to accept the consequences. It is not a strong incentive to careful and judicious quotation.

On the more cheerful and frivolous side of legal things, there is the news which greeted readers of "News of the Week" in *Publishers Weekly* (22 February)—"Knopf Editor Lish Sues *Harper's* Over Letter." Seems that *Harper's*, possibly for satirical purposes, published a slightly edited and abridged version of a letter Lish had sent to students in his celebrated private creative-writing course. (See "A Kind of Magnificence," *Harper's*, December 1990.) Lish brought suit. *PW* writes: "The lawsuit charges *Harper's* with copyright infringement, unfair competition, defamation and publishing the letter with the intent to inflict distress." The president of *Harper's* is quoted as allowing: "It's a frivolous lawsuit, although not a frivolous issue." None of it seems to have been especially frivolous to Lish, who advises his students: "Listen to me—whatever your life is, there can be an excellence in it, a garden of achievement that no jealous god can drive you out of and whose walkways, however narrow, can keep you safe and steady on your course for all the rest of your given days." Stay tuned, fans. This could turn out to be more fun than watching reruns of *Divorce Court*.

Lish's problems seem pale, if not frivolous, compared with those of Salman Rushdie, now well into his third year of hiding out under guard from anyone who might seek to carry out the death sentence passed against him by the late and influential Ayatollah Khomeini. Just before the turn of the year, on Christmas Eve 1990, he publicly embraced the Muslim faith. And according to *Newsweek* ("Rushdie Embraces the Faith: Trying to make peace after two years in hiding," 7 January 1991), there were other concessions to his enemies: "He promised not to publish *The Satanic Verses* in paperback or allow further translations in the foreseeable future." His recantation and promises brought him nothing much beyond a lot more publicity, at least some of which was strongly negative. (For an example of the latter stance see Raymond Sokolov, "Posturing in Vain for the Ayatollahs," *Wall Street Journal*, 9 January: "In the weeks before Christmas, Mr. Rushdie's light had begun to fade. His own martyrdom to Arab ire no longer was news. His sufferings in a state-funded environment looked cozy compared with the domestic situations of Western hostages held as human shields in Iraq.") The living spiritual leader of Iran, Ayatollah Ali Khomeini, simply renewed the sentence or fatwa; and it was

back to square one. After that one might have expected to encounter fewer media stories about Rushdie and his flight while he continued to lay low, protected by British policemen, and news of the real world, of wars and of the breaking of nations and empires, held the world's attention. Certainly 1991 revealed less about the thoughts, words, and deeds of Rushdie than the previous year. But even though he was forced to be (mostly) out of sight, he and his determined supporters struggled manfully not to allow him to be out of mind.

In March, James Fenton of the *New York Review of Books* (28 March) brought out "Keeping Up with Salman Rushdie," a piece whose occasion was ostensibly a late review of Rushdie's children's book, *Haroun and the Sea of Stories* (Granta), but whose center was a lengthy memoir of and interview with Rushdie ("Friend, You have achieved a fame beyond Byron's."). Another, perhaps more useful and significant article, dealing mainly with "the Islamic legal and historical implications of the Rushdie affair" and firmly based on a chronology of the events, is "Behind the Rushdie Affair," by Bernard Lewis (*American Scholar*, Spring). Lewis is one of the few writers on the subject who does not allow himself to become entangled in aesthetic arguments: "Good books enjoy no immunities from the law, bad books are subject to no penalties from the law, merely because they are good or bad. To condemn the one or privilege the other on the basis of literary merit would give to literary critics the right to determine not only the publication or suppression of a book but the life or death of its author, and that might seem excessive even by present-day norms of literary criticism." In April Rushdie was found in the papers by indirection; for his estranged wife, the writer Marianne Wiggins, was touring the United States to publicize her newly published collection of stories, *Bet They'll Miss Us When We're Gone* (HarperCollins). Under "Headliners" in the *New York Times* (7 April), she was quoted as explaining their separation and forthcoming divorce on the basis of "ideological differences": "I am incredibly sad about him, not because our marriage is over, but sad as a writer because all the attention he has gathered in the past two years has been about Salman Rushdie. The great fallacy he committed was to think he was the issue." Two days later Caryn James, in "Marianne Wiggins and Life on the Run" (*New York Times*, 9 April), quoted another criticism of Rushdie—"The very fact that he would go on television and announce a personal conversion shows how far his personality has been broken down."

In the May issue of *PMLA* (Publications of the Modern Language Association), Betty Jean Craige claimed Rushdie as exemplary for the people some would define as "politically correct" and whom Ms. Craige prefers to call *cultural holists* ("Literature in a Global Society"). From that point of view she praised him for things and views he might have preferred to leave unasserted: "In the eyes of religious Muslims, Rushdie was certainly guilty of blasphemy. But his achievement went beyond blasphemy, for he had treated Islamic tradition with disrespect in front of a world audience." A great blow for cultural holism. ("To cultural holists, even the Bible and the Koran are socially constructed texts, neither sacred nor profane.") One can hope that assassins do not find inspiration in or take comfort from the pages of *PMLA*, but by June newspapers reported that a "hit squad" was planning to kill Rushdie. Writing from London on 18 June ("Rushdie Under New Death Threat," *Washington Post*, 19 June), Glenn Frankel wrote: "Rushdie has been warned that the new threat against him remains acute and has been forced to return to a regimen of deep secrecy and constant shifts to various safe houses that he had tried to move away from last year, the sources said." The same story earned Rushdie a picture and a paragraph in the "People" section of *Time* (1 July). By mid July the whole situation was considerably more serious when Rushdie's Italian translator, Ettore Capriolo, was stabbed and wounded and his Japanese translator, Hitoshi Igarashi, was stabbed to death. Nevertheless Rushdie managed to make surprise appearances from time to time while he and his supporters urged the West to do more in his behalf. In September *Publishers Weekly* (27 September) announced that he had won and accepted, in person, a prize: "On September 15, flanked by bodyguards, he made a brief appearance at a Writers Guild awards ceremony at London's Dorchester Hotel, where he was presented with a prize for his *Haroun and the Sea of Stories*."

However, nothing all year equaled the gesture which earned him a page-one story in the *New York Times* ("Rushdie, Defying Death Threats, Suddenly Appears in New York," 12 December) and interviews and laudatory editorials in the nation's leading newspapers. Flown to the United States courtesy of the Royal Air Force and brought safely, by a score of New York City police-

Dinesh D'Souza, author of Illiberal Education: The Politics of Race and Sex on Campus *(photograph by Susan Muniak)*

men, to New York and to an assembly at Columbia University's Graduate School of Journalism, Rushdie participated in a salute to the First Amendment and Justice William J. Brennan, Jr. There he allowed that "I felt I needed to talk to Americans as well as British people." And he told his audience, "free speech is the whole thing, the whole ball game." It was a message agreeably received by the American media.

There was certainly more drama in Rushdie's story (even though the protagonist has lost little so far except, by choice, some of his liberty to move about as much as he pleases), but for sustained thunder and lightning nothing else on the intellectual scene could equal the dedication of space and a wealth of words, coming from the battles about an old Marxist term, rejuvenated in American colleges and universities (especially in English departments) even as, throughout the rest of the world, Marxist institutions are crumbling and the ideology and words are fading out of the noise of public discourse. In a sense another Indian (by birth; he is now an American citizen) was responsible for helping to focus attention on the subject. Dinesh D'Souza wrote and published a book, *Illiberal Education: The Politics of Race and Sex on Campus* (Free Press), which was, inevitably, widely reviewed and discussed together with the larger general topic of *political correctness* (hereinafter abbreviated as PC) and its place in the American literary and intellectual establishment. The range of publications—newspapers, magazines of all kinds, indeed all the media including commercial television—attracted by the subject was (and remains) astonishing. Yet in a society where everything imaginable, from fast foods and soft drinks and cartoon strips to classical music and classical literature, has been politicized and freighted with symbolic meaning and import, perhaps even our surprise is disingenuous. Nothing could be more disingenuous than the repeated, if belated, denials in the face of overwhelming empirical and anecdotal evidence otherwise, by prominent exponents of PC that any such thing exists outside the paranoid minds of reactionary critics.

D'Souza's *Illiberal Education* is a popular book, built in part on the success of earlier books about the politicization of American education and the bare-knuckle battles, beginning in the 1960s and continuing to the present moment, about the curriculum, the canon, and who shall control the power (and funds) of administrations and faculty. Allan Bloom's *The Closing of the American Mind* (1987) and Roger Kimball's *Tenured Radicals* (1990), among others, prepared the public and the way for D'Souza. His book was replete with lively anecdotes of PC in action, accounts of events at PC places (Berkeley, Stanford, Howard, Michigan, Duke, Harvard) and interviews with prominent PC people, many of whom are depicted as speaking with forked tongues. The book is adversarial and challenging.

People lined up, pro and con, to respond to the challenge. Reprints of the book reviews, articles, features, and letters generated by the book and the topic would easily fill a fat volume. Here it seems worthwhile merely to mention some of the more striking examples and some odd surprises. One of the best and certainly among the most judicious reviews of *Illiberal Education* came from the distinguished Yale professor emeritus C. Vann Woodward in, of all places, the *New York Review of Books* ("Freedom and the Universities," 18 July). Woodward does not spend much time praising or blaming D'Souza, but he argues strenuously that there is a very real problem here and now: "The most critical issue raised by the current academic upheaval is the denial of freedom

of thought, speech, and teaching—academic freedom." Is it serious? Consider what Woodward describes as the problems being avoided by most administrators: "University presidents and administrators have generally distinguished themselves for their acquiescence, timidity, and silence rather than for courageous resistance in the face of campus anarchy, violence, and barbarism." *Anarchy, violence, and barbarism . . .* can't get much worse than that. Even so a lot of PC people were outraged by a summarizing piece in *New York* magazine by John Taylor— "Are you politically correct?" (21 January). Because *New York* works at being sophisticated and chic ("hip" in the familiar sense of the term), the piece is smart-alecky enough to annoy those, academics among them, who would like to think of themselves as at once PC and hip. "Right thinking people attack capitalism and privilege, sexual power games, and even the notion of the nuclear family." Another mild surprise, from the other side, was to see the *New Yorker* devote its "Books" section to a lengthy, heavy-handed attack on D'Souza (personally) and his book: "It is not pleasant to see a man who did so much to poison the wells now turning up dressed as the water commissioner, and it will be apparent to most people who read *Illiberal Education* that the book's promise of balance is a false one" (Louis Menand, "Illiberalisms," 20 May).

Other stances were interesting enough if more or less predictable. For example, *National Review* (18 March) and *Chronicles* (September) weighed in more or less for D'Souza and definitely against PC. Not surprisingly *Mother Jones* ("Return Fire: We Take Aim at the Patriotically Correct," September/October) and the *Village Voice* ("Wanted For Intellectual Fraud: BeRube and Goldstein take on the PC Bashers," 18 June) fought back with all the weapons at hand. *Harper's*, it would seem, could have offered a balanced judgment, but in its special December "Campus Issue" it elected to follow Louis Menand ("What are Universities For?") and Rosa Ehrenreich, a recent Harvard graduate who didn't notice any PC chickens in her school ("What Campus Radicals?"). Another surprise, at least to this reader and reviewer, was the *Chronicle of Higher Education*, which was relentlessly and regularly an organ for PC opinion and positions. As if to prove me wrong—or perhaps because others have recognized and responded to the constant tub-thumping for PC, the *Chronicle* commenced 1992 with an even-handed approach. Page one offered an article on Clark University's Christina Hoff Sommers ("Philosophy Professor Portrays Her Feminist Colleagues as Out of Touch and 'Relentlessly Hostile to the Family,'" 15 January); and the "Opinion" piece, almost invariably a PC manifesto, is given over to John M. Ellis of the National Association of Scholars ("The Origins of PC"). But lest we should be overwhelmed with gratitude for once being allowed to debate the issue, there are well-placed pieces of purely advocacy journalism throughout. For example, Karen J. Winkler's "Literary Scholars Mount a Counteroffensive Against a Bad Press, Conservative Critics," wherein we learn that the mutual leaders of PC and the MLA believe their problems are the simple result of misperception, disinformation, unfair criticism, and bad public relations, clearly falls into this classification. As Berkeley's Stephen J. Greenblatt is quoted as saying (with remarkably disingenuous aplomb): "We in the profession have been inept in explaining to the public what we are doing." Another article, "'Squelching' the Opposition," matter of factly tells how feminist pressure on the venerable *Atlantic* apparently prevailed to prevent publication of a critical article by Christina Hoff Sommers, which had been commissioned and written in early 1990. And the last word in this issue, in "Point of View," is given over to PC leader Catharine R. Stimpson, whose seemingly back-pedaling piece, "It Is Time to Rethink Affirmative Action," is less than meets the eye, at least as far as any thinking or rethinking about affirmative action is concerned. Does it have anything to do with books and book reviewing? To be sure; for she slyly turns the discussion into a manifesto for the new, improved canon (and thus new books and textbooks by the thousands): "Thus, rethinking affirmative action means accepting the new scholarship about women and gender, race and ethnicity, domination and freedom, class and sexuality." *Same old bunch of bananas.* . . .

People—columnists, feature writers, op-ed performers and the like—were generally in character and as good as their positions allowed them to be. Surprising to some, though not to many who have followed his columns over the years, was Nat Hentoff's strong and persistently anti-PC stance. Hentoff has a passion for free speech and takes his cases one at a time. One of his better pieces, among a goodly number, was "Stars and Bars at Harvard" (*Washington Post*, 13 July), about one Brigit Kerrigan, who hung a Confederate flag from her window in Kirkland House and

withstood great pressure from all levels of the university to make her remove it, including a letter from faculty members and housemasters, who accused her of trying to "undermine all that is admirable about this House." Hentoff's reaction to that is instructive: "Apparently freedom of expression is not considered a quality to be admired 'in this House.' And did these self-satisfied faculty members ever wonder whether Thomas Jefferson or James Madison would have signed their letter? But then, neither of them went to Harvard."

Some of the best pieces written on the PC phenomenon were the works of *Wall Street Journal* editorial writer Dorothy Rabinowitz. Perhaps her finest piece, certainly a devastating one, came from her coverage of a conference, "The PC Frame-Up," at the University of Michigan ("On the Ramparts with PC's Defenders," 12 December). Her ending is brilliant. Leaving conference for campus, she sees students all around her happily stuffing junk food: "Years and years of nutritional indoctrination and education have, it seems, left no mark on these young. It is a not altogether discouraging thought as I contemplate the possibility that their political education could, with luck, suffer the same fate."

Writing about PC, Roger Kimball pointed out: "The cardinal rule is never treat literature as literature when you can make it serve some other agenda" ("Cleanth Brooks and the New Criticism," *New Criterion*, October). In one of the best critical attacks on PC, in terms of a particular book with a not-so-hidden agenda, Bruce Bawer separated the skin and bones of *The Columbia History of the American Novel* (Columbia University Press) in "Columbia's assault on the American novel" (*New Criterion*, December). Having done a chapter-by-chapter critique of this distorted PC history, Bawer calls them to account on their claims that they favor pluralism and diversity: "But *The Columbia History of the American Novel* reminds us dramatically that pluralism is not a tenet of Marxism and that what we call academic freedom and individual rights are, in the eyes of academic Marxists, not cherished concepts but abominations."

Perhaps it is only fair to allow a dedicated defender of PC, poet William Greenway, to explain the value of that kind of mind-set to a writer who fears the worst will follow if we do not learn our PC lesson (see "Politically Correct Language," *Poets & Writers*, January/February): "The New Awareness has done something good already. It's made us think harder about the words

Bruce Bawer, book reviewer and essayist for the New Criterion *(photograph by Ted Bawer)*

we use, to examine them carefully before we use them, to look for other shades of meaning, political meaning, in them. We will use them with more caution knowing that in the best-case scenario, we may be called to account for them, and that, in the worst case, we won't be around to have the opportunity to defend ourselves, even if we could."

Who will *call us to account*—the PC Patrol? the ghost of Marx? And who is going to *kill us* ("we won't be around") because we have used the unacceptable word or expression?

To be sure there were larger, wider, deeper political involvements in the PC issue. One of the principal ones was the speech of President Bush at the University of Michigan on 4 May in which he attacked PC as a dangerous threat to free speech, and thus to free thinking, teaching, and learning as well. This raised the volume and intensity on both sides of the PC issue. A second open political conflict concerned the failed nomination of Carol Iannone to the National Endowment for the Humanities. Iannone was ostensibly found wanting in the matter of credentials. She had her

Ph.D., some years of teaching experience, and a checklist of publications. However, the latter were mostly essays and book reviews, not in primarily scholarly publications, but in popular periodicals, especially *Commentary*. Her antagonists asserted that it was not the conservative content of her writings that concerned them, but rather the absence of demonstrably academic and scholarly contributions. Others, including Iannone, saw her defeat differently, purely and simply in PC terms. "My credentials were scarcely an issue with most of the senators and aides I visited," she wrote ("The Debate—on Me—that Missed the Mark," *Washington Post*, 25 July). "Instead I was questioned, with an admittedly unavoidable superficiality, about my literary and intellectual standards, about my views of feminism, minority writing, multiculturalism and even mental illness." The kind of thing that seems most to have worried Iannone's detractors is represented in her article "Literature by Quota" (*Commentary*, March 1991), in which she questioned the "tribalism" of bestowing awards on black writers Alice Walker, Gloria Naylor, and Toni Morrison, quoting black writer Charles Johnson to support her argument—"I find it very difficult to swallow the idea that one individual, black or white, can speak for the experience of 30 million people." A piece published near the end of the year— "Meet the Press: Cultural Criticism for the 1990s," by Marianna Torgovnick of Duke (*ADE [Association of Departments of English] Bulletin*, Winter)—runs head on into the Iannone problem. Arguing that academics ought to cultivate journalists and even write some journalism themselves, if only to ease the heat of this whole PC thing (in spite of the fact that "journalists tend not to care about distinctions between movements like deconstruction, feminism, and Marxism—so important and clear to most people inside the profession"), Torgovnick has to deal with the fact that Iannone was criticized precisely for writing for "popular" magazines such as *Commentary*. Her disposal of the problem, in a footnote, is typically disingenuous. "I admire public intellectuals and agree with the goal of making academic work accessible to the public," Torgovnick writes. "But in this case, Cheney's [Lynn Cheney, director of the National Endowment for the Humanities and the nominator of Iannone] use of the term 'distinguished public intellectual' was bogus; there was nothing in Iannone's record in her career to suggest distinction, and her nomination was rejected."

At year's end, leaders and members of the Modern Language Association at their meeting in San Francisco, by and large, maintained ranks and held firm to the obvious fiction that there is no such thing as PC. Michael Abramowitz ("Literature Professors Look Inward and Find Scant Evidence of 'PC': But Right-Wing Misinformation, Media Hype are Problems, Many Agree," *Washington Post*, 3 January 1992) quotes Houston Baker, the new president, as dismissing the idea as "someone else's invention." And outgoing president Catharine R. Stimpson, whose 1990 presidential address, "On Differences," was dedicated "to our colleagues who have met AIDS with exemplary rage, gallantry, and courage" and predicted that "the PC phenomenon, now hyped up, will eventually dry up" (*PMLA*, May 1991), sounded sweetly evenhanded, even moderate, in her remarks to Abramowitz ("I am about as left-wing as Barbara Bush"); but the reporter wasn't buying the whole nine yards: "Not everyone here was buying the kind of moderate image that Stimpson and others sought to present." Among those who were willing to be quoted and named in disagreement were Anna Balakian of N.Y.U. ("If you are not politically correct, you're not going to get great appointments") and Gerald Graff of Chicago, whose incisive description of the way things are offers not a lot of hope for the future: "The left has its own sessions in which they preach to the converted, and the other side has its own sessions. This contributes to the rising paranoia on both sides." Early in 1992 Dell published a trade paperback, edited by journalist and critic (and MacArthur Fellow) Paul Berman—*Debating P.C.: The Controversy Over Political Correctness On College Campuses*—which manages to bring together many of the major texts by the important players on both sides. In six related parts—"Debating Political Correctness," "Politics and the Canon," "Free Speech and Speech Codes," "Texas Shoot-Out," "The Public Schools," and "Diverse Views"—the book presents a representative outline of the principal arguments about PC made during 1990 and 1991. It seems unlikely, given the nature of the subject, that many, if any minds will be changed. But here at least are the words in print, frozen in fact if not in understanding and clarity, for all to read and to judge.

Some good things and good news deserve at least a brief mention. In Portland and Seattle Randy Byrd has created a publishing company called Dime Novels which sells little pocket-sized, twenty-thousand-word books in supermarkets for $1.99. He produces a book in each of twelve popular genres each month. It is Byrd's hope and expectation to go nationwide in 1992. On 28 May the *Wall Street Journal* published an article on a potentially important and probably unique library—the Brautigan Library of Burlington, Vermont, created by Todd Lockwood. In "A Fictional Library Becomes a Real Place With Unreal Fiction," Lawrence Ingrassia told the story of the only known library exclusively for unpublished books: "Nowhere else but here can you find 'Sure Beats Watching Trains; the tale of a 'burned-out shoe salesman . . . overtaken by an alien personna.' Or 'Theories of Father,' 'a video-image-script-novel narrated by a house fly, with help from Ed Sullivan.' Or 'Rory Stories, Vol. 1,' the 'humorous adventures of a talking Shetland sheepdog named Rory O'More.' " Surely there is hope for a world which has the Brautigan Library in it.

It is more difficult than usual to come up with an obvious choice for the Golden Hatchet Award (most negative review) for 1991. A year that saw the publication of such outstanding challenges to book reviewers as Bret Easton Ellis's *American Psycho* (Vintage), Alexandra Ripley's dauntingly successful *Scarlett* (Warner), and Norman Mailer's *Harlot's Ghost* (Random) had whetstones whirling, blade edges scattering sparks. Given the unavoidable choice, this reviewer of reviewers singles out Jonathan Yardley's review of Ellis as an outstanding hatchet job—"*American Psycho*: Essence of Trash" (*Washington Post*, 27 February). Yardley's finish is almost enough to win by a nose: "Of course Ellis has every right to write it, and Vintage every right to publish it. But the rest of us have every right not to read it; as one who did so out of duty, and who feels thoroughly soiled by the experience, I can only urge—no, pray—that everyone else refuse to do so by choice." It is a finalist for the sake of the final subjunctive construction alone.

Both early and late, *Scarlett* took a savage beating from reviewers, a condition rendered somewhat less painful to both author and publisher by the enormous sales of the book. It seems altogether possible that many reviewers, understanding that one strong reason for the writing of the sequel was to reestablish copyright on the materials and the characters of *Gone With the Wind* just as they were passing out of copyright protection and into public domain, felt justified in writing strongly negative reviews. If so, however, very few reviewers bothered to mention this practical incentive for a sequel in their reviews.

An early attack, well before publication date, was Diane White's "Scarlett suffers, and so do readers" (*Boston Globe*, 14 August). "Look Away Dixieland" (*New York Review of Books*, 19 December), by Patricia Storace, poetry editor for the *Paris Review* and a native of Mobile, Alabama, was a more complete mutilation, taking time and space to dispose of the original and its creator as well as the sequel. She finds Margaret Mitchell irredeemably racist: "Mitchell's failure to imagine black people as fully human is a devastating artistic failure, although it mirrors her culture's failure to do so; and that failure falsifies her view of the relationships she describes while it overtly distorts her book's picture of the past." Ripley and the sequel are keelhauled too: "Ripley's book is nothing more than a promotion for a novel she didn't write; Scarlett, Rhett and other characters recycled from Mitchell's novel show up in the sequel like guests on TV talk shows, flogging their forthcoming movies, or in this case, their appearance in Ripley's novel." After a barrage of lesser jabs and punches—the book is "excruciatingly dull" and written on a "fourth-grade reading level," a reference to "the tiny gnat of Ms. Ripley's imagination"—Storace too calls her a racist: "Far more important than anything else Alexandra Ripley has written is the contract she signed with the Mitchell estate not to include miscegenation in her sequel."

Another strong contender for hatchet honors is the celebrated John Simon, whose front-page review of *Harlot's Ghost* for the *New York Times Book Review* (29 September) is a masterpiece of suspense as he goes on and on, without any apparent judgmental fits or tics, describing in detail the almost indescribable plot, before in the last couple of paragraphs building to a guillotine ending—"What he lacks is his editor." Simon noticed something that at least some other reviewers noticed and reacted to—the fact that this vast work began, in its first sentence, with a bold grammatical mistake, a classic example of a dangling modifier: "On a late-winter evening in 1983," Mailer's opening sentence reads, "While driving

through fog along the Maine coast, recollections of old campfires began to drift into the March mist, and I thought of the Abenaki Indians of the Algonquin tribe who dwelt near Bangor a thousand years ago." Never daunted, Mailer, in full mask, costume, and character (*Trick or Treat!*), fired back a letter longer than most book reviews, defending himself and his art and attacking everyone else in sight, especially John Simon, who in turn counterpunched. Even the editor, Becky Sinkler, felt it necessary to publish a brief (and very rare) reply. By accident or design, the whole thing had the feeling of what was known and called, in simpler times, a publicity stunt.

If the sport is Mailer bashing, another strong and lively contender would have to be Lee Lescaze's *Wall Street Journal* (1 October) review—"spies strut their stuff." Responding to Mailer's three-word ending—"to be continued"—Lescaze writes: "This wasn't a blue-book exam. No proctor required Mr. Mailer to put down his pen as time ran out, yet, there is no conclusion, no climax and dozens of loose ends. Talk about risk taking. Tell it to Scheherazade."

After much consideration, prayer, and fasting, I award the 1991 Golden Hatchet Award to Suzanne Fields for her *Washington Times* (20 May) review of *The Beauty Myth* (Morrow), by Naomi Wolf. There is nothing false or phony about it, and it is rich with a variety of rhetorical tap dancing on the grave of a bad book, as, for example, in this neat example of perfectly controlled and insulting sarcasm:

Only the author who was once anorexic and bulimic and has lived to tell the tale, and a few contemporary feminists of her acquaintance are clever enough to notice how evil men are. Only they have transcended "the myth of beauty." The rest of us are dolts and drudges, sellouts to vanity and frivolity, shackled by a beauty backlash that triples our burdens after careers and domestic chores. Miss Wolf has written this book to save us from ourselves.

One golden hatchet coming up. . . .

Dashiell Hammett: An Appeal in *TAC*

Richard Layman

The previously unrecorded magazine publication by Dashiell Hammett reproduced on the following page is among the earliest of a curious set of political statements between 1938 and 1948 that is virtually the last published work attributed to him. Stylistically atypical of his better-known work, these pieces are of a type: they all espouse a liberal, usually Communist, cause or protest some injustice to the Communist party. It is unlikely that these statements are personal expressions of Hammett's beliefs, though they certainly reflect his sentiments. It is far more plausible that they were prepared by a political committee that sought a celebrity endorsement, which he provided.

TAC introduces Hammett as the president of the Motion Picture Artists Committee of Hollywood, an organization that was identified in typical fashion by the "California Committee on Un-American Activities, Report 1948" as a Communist front whose personnel "clearly indicates its character." Hammett was elected president in 1938, with Sylvia Sydney as his vice-president. His tenure presumably ended when he left Hollywood more or less for good in July 1939 after he was released for the last time from his writing contract at M-G-M. Beginning in 1937, Hammett was very active in leftist political causes. He had signed petitions in the *Daily Worker* favoring the lifting of the American embargo on Spain during the Spanish civil war; he added his signature to a public petition in support of the Moscow Trials; he spoke at Communist-sponsored anti-Nazi rallies in New York in the winter of 1938; he headed an organization called the Professionals Conference against Nazi Persecutions and a group called Equality Publishers, which launched *Equality*, a pro-Communist monthly that lasted for some eighteen months.

The Theatre Arts Committee, which published *TAC* in Manhattan from July 1938 to August 1940, was a leftist, if not Communist, organization. Such distinctions are clouded in the flighty atmosphere of the entertainment world and meaningfully refer to the administration and not necessarily to membership or supporters. The Theatre Arts Committee was formed in 1938 to serve the interests of political and social activists in the movies, theater, music, and radio. It was the successor to the Theatre Committee to Aid Spanish Democracy, and, according to the "California Committee on Un-American Activities, Report 1948," it was affiliated with the American League for Peace and Democracy, Medical Bureau, and the North American Committee to Aid Spanish Democracy, both of which had demonstrable ties to the Communist Party USA. TAC sponsored cultural events such as public lectures, cabarets, jazz concerts, and theater evenings, always featuring a celebrity to rally support for such causes as the Spanish Children's Milk Fund, and continued funding for the Federal Arts Project. The Christmas Refugee Aid Fund raised money by charging supporters twenty-five cents to light one of a thousand candles on each of four Christmas trees in different parts of Manhattan. Two of the five organizations identified as recipients of funds raised by the Christmas Refugee Aid Fund were listed in the House Committee on Un-American Activities's *Guide To Subversive Organizations and Publications* (3 March 1951).

Reasonable as the opposition to fascism and particularly to Nazism expressed in "Christmas for Refugees" may seem today, antifascism was a decidedly liberal attitude in 1939. The Roper Public Opinion Research Center conducted a poll in April 1937 asking the question: "If you HAD to choose between Fascism and Communism, which would you choose?" Sixty-one percent of the respondents chose fascism. Benito Mussolini was widely admired through the end of the decade, and, in the isolationist spirit of the time when anti-Semitism was a common attitude, Adolf Hitler was generally considered to be a distant threat at worst. He was the declared enemy of Communists, who perceived his potential military threat to the Soviet Union (a situation hardly affected by the Nazi-Soviet Pact of August 1939). As a result, much of the vocal anti-Fascist and anti-Nazi

A Christmas for Refugees

An appeal by Dashiell Hammett

HUMANITY must not be crucified on a swastika!

This year, as never before, we must prove to the world that "peace on earth, good will toward men" is not a mere beautiful figure of speech. We must prove that a Christmas tree really can be a symbol of Christianity, of human kindness and of love for our fellows. We must prove that there is a Christmas spirit. . . .

This year, as never before, we must prove to the world that Christmas does not come but once a year; we must prove that the Christmas spirit knows no calendar.

There is a Christmas tree in Times Square. There are trees in Union Square, in Columbus Circle and in Stuyvesant Square. Have you seen them?

Each tree asks a question of the world and each tree supplies the answer. "So yours is a merry Christmas," the trees say. "But what are you doing for the others—for those Nazi-stricken Jews and Catholics and Protestants in Germany, those Chinese peasants torn by Japanese bullets, those women and children starving to death in Fascist-besieged Spain? Christmas belongs to them, too. Can your Christmas really bring you joy when theirs brings death?"

And those trees in Times Square and Columbus Circle and Union Square and Stuyvesant Square give the answer.

Unless it is gaily lighted, a Christmas tree signifies nothing; it is just a tree. But the Christmas Refugee Aid trees which now occupy four of Manhattan's busiest corners will not be gaily lighted except by the hearts they reach. Each candle, each star, represents a con-

Photograph by Paul Strand

tribution to the Theatre Arts Committee campaign for refugee aid. And only when that contribution has been received is that candle or star lighted.

The question . . . "Will you help?"

The answer . . . "I have helped."

The Theatre Arts Committee, sponsoring the Christmas Refugee Aid campaign, is not stopping with these trees. Cans for contributions have been placed in all department stores, in railroad terminals, in theatres. Wherever people gather, there they will be reminded that Christmas is not the property of America and that the people of America cannot conscientiously speak of peace on earth, of good will toward men, so long as Fascism endures.

On Monday, December 19th, the nation listened to the dedication ceremonies of the Christmas Refugee Aid trees. Dorothy Thompson, Raymond Massey, Walter Huston and Eddie Cantor took part in the proceedings, which were broadcast by the Columbia Broadcasting System on a coast-to-coast hook-up from Times Square, where Miss Thompson lighted the first candle, the lowermost, on the tree.

Raymond Massey lighted by remote control the tree in Union Square, which stands near the statue of Abraham Lincoln. Mr. Huston, who is the Peter Stuyvesant of the current stage, similarly lighted the tree in Stuyvesant Square and Mr. Cantor, the tree in Columbus Circle.

On Christmas Eve, under the Times Square tree, a rabbi, a priest and a minister delivered their sermons and the German Choral Society sang Christmas carols. These services, too, were broadcast by CBS. Too much cannot be said for this demonstration of spiritual affinity. America, dedicated to religious

liberty, to racial equality, has learned that Christmas belongs to no *one* creed. Christmas belongs to all men, and Christmas this year represents civilization.

The moneys raised by Christmas Refugee Aid will be distributed among the American Committee for Christian German Refugees, the American Friends of the Chinese People, the American Jewish Joint Distribution Committee, the North American Committee to Aid Spanish Democracy and the Committee for Catholic Refugees from Germany.

Jew, Catholic, Protestant, Spaniard or Chinese . . . Fascist death knows no difference!

When disaster strikes a community—a plague, a flood, a fire—our cause of action is clearly defined. We help the victims and, concurrently if possible, we attempt to minimize or rid ourselves of that disaster. And once the danger is safely past, we try to prevent its recurrence.

Borders and oceans to the contrary, the world today is a single community struck by the plague of Fascism. Today we are devoting our efforts to save from the horror its immediate victims. Will we, tomorrow, destroy the plague?

These are the Christmas holidays, the days of "peace on earth," of human kindness and love for our fellows. These are the days when hearts expand. . . . Do you believe it?

These are the days when hearts break with tragedy!

Where Fascism lives there is no merry Christmas, there is no happy New Year . . . there is only the shadow of a swastika, death for some and the threat of death for others.

Humanity will never be crucified on a swastika!

[5]

Feature editorial from TAC, the politically radical arts magazine published in New York City from July 1938 to August 1940. This previously unrecorded fund-raising appeal is among Hammett's last magazine publications.

sentiment in America in the late 1930s originated with the Communist party. Thus Hammett's humanitarian plea has political overtones entirely consistent with his apparent membership in the CPUSA, dating from about 1937.

An Interview with George Greenfield, Literary Agent

George Greenfield is a major figure in Anglo-American publishing who has amalgamated literature with business. Born in 1917, he earned a double first at Cambridge under F. R. Leavis, and intended to become a schoolmaster. After serving in The Buffs at El Alamein, ending the war as a major, he commenced publisher with the firm of T. Werner Laurie. In 1953 Mr. Greenfield joined the John Farquharson literary agency, from which he retired as managing director. George Greenfield has written three novels: *Desert Episode* (Macmillan Centenary Award, 1945), *This World is Wide Enough* (1948), and *At Bay* (1955). In 1989 he published *Scribblers for Bread: Aspects of the English Novel Since 1945*.

George Greenfield was interviewed in his London office in October 1991.

DLB: You were a publisher before you commenced as an agent.

GREENFIELD: Yes, I left the army in 1946. At the beginning of '47 I became a publisher with T. Werner Laurie. I started at the top because I was a friend of the family. I stayed as a publisher for five or six years and then became an agent.

DLB: In the agenting world you retired as managing director of Farquharson.

GREENFIELD: I retired September 1986 after thirty-five or thirty-six years as an agent. So I did see the changes as they occurred.

DLB: There are those who describe agents as middlemen, as take-the-commission-and-run

men. Would you, please, define the proper role of a good agent?

GREENFIELD: I'm of the impression it's changed to a large degree over the last twenty years. But basically the agent is the author's representative. The agent, of course, is dealing all of the time on the author's behalf, but he (including she; I'll say he for this discussion) has always to bear in mind it is his author's interest he is representing. It is very easy for the powerful publisher to say, "Well, give me this book cheap and I'll make it up to you in other ways." Some of that goes on. The publisher says, "I'll buy this book cheaply, but in the future you'll get preferential treatment from me." Well, the agent has to say, "Forget it. I'm not selling this book cheap." One must restrain the feeling that the past was great and the present is lousy; but I think that up to about 1965—in the United Kingdom and to a large degree in New York—there was a certain integrity about agencies and agents that I don't notice today, not across the board. Although I'm five years retired, I have kept in fairly close touch with the trade.

Take the Paul Reynolds agency in New York, which was the first, founded in 1893. It is now absorbed with the John Hawkins agency, but it still exists and in almost a hundred years has only had three chiefs. It had Paul R. Reynolds, Sr., who founded the firm, Paul R. Reynolds, Jr., and John Hawkins, who married one of Paul Jr.'s daughters. So you have a certain continuity there that doesn't necessarily exist with other agencies. There are probably only four or five leading New York agencies that were actually in existence before 1939. Russell and Volkening, Harold Matson, Harold Ober. Ober broke away from Reynolds and took F. Scott Fitzgerald with him.

George Greenfield (photograph by Jonathan Rich)

There were a lot of rather old-fashioned, proper Bostonian types who entered the literary agency world. In London the Curtis Brown agency started in 1905. Farquharson himself started in 1919; and Heath at about that time; and Pinker was of course Arnold Bennett's agent and Conrad's agent and Stephen Crane's. His son turned out to be a crook and went to jail, and that ended the agency. But my general feeling is that there was more of a loyalty and respect for authors from those tough old boys. Alfred Knopf once remarked that Paul Reynolds would sell his grandmother, but being an honest man would deliver her by the due date. Paul was a toughie, but he played it straight down the middle. And there was little of the fancy wheeling and dealing that happens these days.

Talking on the general side of the agencies, one interesting difference is that lawyers in the United Kingdom are only allowed to charge fees. I believe that there's some legislation pending that may alter the situation, but at present lawyers in England are not allowed to charge any form of commission. Therefore, in effect, they can't become literary agents. There are several well-known law firms in the United Kingdom that specialize in copyright matters or libel or plagiarism, but they have to charge a blanket fee for their services.

DLB: In the States now more and more there are lawyers who are not agents but dealmakers. . . .

GREENFIELD: And lawyers who *are* agents. Back in the early 1960s, there was only one such I can recall—Paul Gitlin, who had a few best-selling clients like Harold Robbins and for a long while Irving Wallace. Lawyers have always swarmed round the Hollywood honeypots, but my hunch is that for many years they thought the publishing business was too small beer. That changed twenty-some years ago when there was a big and much publicized lawsuit. Allen Drury, the well-known journalist and author of that blockbusting book *Advise and Consent* [1959], sued his publisher for rejecting a later novel on the grounds that it was substandard. There was a massive advance involved, and the number of naughts that were bounced to and fro across the court had the effect of fresh blood in shark-infested waters. The lawyers homed in.

Their pitch to big authors—they're not basically interested in the new or small ones—is this: Not only can we produce you a copper-bottomed watertight contract but our tax department can sort out your taxes to the best advantage and our litigation department can handle your divorce and so on and so forth. In other words, you will get a comprehensive service from us that literary agents can't match.

DLB: This new breed of lawyer-agents, do they function differently than the old straight agents?

GREENFIELD: Indeed, they do. Let's face it, they will get top dollar for big clients as often as—probably more often than—the straightforward agent. But they're really operating from outside the trade, not from within. It would never cross their minds that squeezing a publishing house dry could have long-term ill effects on the publishing trade. They tend to deal only with the major houses—and they love doing a huge three-book deal—world rights—for the client in question. Which means that if the client fires them after the first book, they will still get their commission on the next two.

And, by handing over world rights, they save themselves the trouble and expense of setting up subagencies in London, Paris, Amsterdam, Barcelona, and so forth. But that makes a mockery of the promise to give global support.

Publishers on the whole cannot match good literary agents in selling serial and translation and anthology rights in a book, not only at home but throughout the world.

Every author starts off as a nobody. He/she needs careful nursing and a good slice of luck to have a chance of hitting the big time. If the lawyers are only interested in the ones who've arrived, who's going to look after the beginners? (If you hear an edge to my tone, it could be because I nursed and encouraged Barbara Taylor Bradford for over ten years and set up her first—actually, her second—novel, *A Woman of Substance* [1979]. After she had been right up there on the best-seller lists in New York and in London, Morton Janklow, the lawyer, stepped in and took over her future novels on the promise of universal service.)

Agenting is not just selling a book and then sitting back. The agent has to follow through. He has to keep in touch with the publisher, make sure the publicity's there, that the jacket's not left to chance.

DLB: What else does an agent do besides read the contract and haggle over the terms?

GREENFIELD: Well, an agent is two things . . . three things. First, the agent should find markets.

DLB: That is, place the manuscript with the right publisher.

GREENFIELD: Exactly. And also, of course, have the services to be able to exploit film rights, television rights, translation rights—which are increasingly important.

DLB: Subrights: the tail wags the dog.

GREENFIELD: Right. He finds the market. Not every author springs like Athene fully armed out of somebody's head. They must start somewhere, and the real agent has to pick potentially good new authors, and find markets for them. The new authors can't do that themselves, because the agent has the clout. If Joe Blow sends his novel in to HarperCollins or Bantam, it may get read by somebody, it may not. They could turn around and send it straight back. But if a leading agent says, "Listen, I've picked this and I think it's good. You really must read it," then

that agent's going to be listened to as long as he doesn't keep crying wolf.

DLB: You've used the word *pick*: the agent *picking* an author. How do you go about picking?

GREENFIELD: We used to get between five hundred and a thousand scripts in a year.

DLB: Over the transom?

GREENFIELD: Well, a minority were our clients repeating, but probably 85-90 percent would be unsolicited. We read, or looked very closely at, every single one.

DLB: How many outside readers did that require?

GREENFIELD: Didn't have any readers at all.

DLB: You did it in-house?

GREENFIELD: In-house. But there are various techniques. You read the first ten pages. If the author starts badly—usually a new novelist doesn't know where to begin, rambles along, starts with the little boy growing up, then the real story gets going with the little boy by now twenty-five years of age—you read the first fifteen or twenty pages. Sometimes it's so awful that you don't need to go any further . . . for instance, if the author can't spell, can't even write a proper sentence, or writes totally conventional crap. Then you read ten or twenty pages in the middle and ten or twenty pages at the end and you really can have an idea of whether this is worth pursuing or not. At Farquharson, we never in our lives sent out a rejection slip. I used to tell young colleagues joining us that if I ever saw anybody using a rejection slip he or she would be fired that week. You had to write a personal letter. It was a fairly standard letter; but it was "Dear Mr. Blow: Your novel which you sent us for consideration . . . times are tough, only the best get through. . . ." We didn't tell lies and say it was highly commendable if it was rubbish; but we phrased it, "I'm afraid it's not what we are looking for, but don't take me as a judge. I've been found wrong often before. So if you do offer it somewhere else I'd like to wish you the best of luck. Thank you for showing it to us." You'd be surprised the number of good authors who came as friends of dud authors. Because the dud authors would say, "I got this letter. . . ." As I said it was more or less a standard letter, but it never went out without a real signature. Once you said, yes, my goodness, this one's got talent, then I would have the author in for a chat.

Now I come to the part about agents doing some preliminary editing, and my feeling there is that you must be very, very careful. Spencer Curtis Brown once said to me, "He who pays the piper must call the tune." The piper is the publisher, and it is dangerous for the agent to say, "The opening is marvelous and the end is marvelous but I think you should totally regroup the middle." That may be just what a publisher doesn't want. So I think an agent's criticism has to be on fairly broad terms. You can say, "I thought the opening really rather dragged up until page 33, and then it suddenly took off and it was fine then, but I do honestly suggest you look at the first thirty-odd pages and see where they need cutting." But if the author says, "No way. This is what I wanted," well then, I guess depending on the author and the relationship, you let it go. If the publisher then came out and said, "I think the first thirty pages should be cut," your stock might go up in your client's view.

DLB: Are you willing to cite a book or an author in which your advice was accepted and proved efficacious?

GREENFIELD: Well, there were a number, not necessarily authors who would mean anything to an American market. Oh, well, yes, yes . . . the "great" Sidney Sheldon. Now Sidney, when he finished a novel, wherever he happened to be, would summon his agent, his American hardback publisher, and his American paperback publisher; and you all merged on the spot and had to read the novel, feeling Sidney prowling around—not in the room, but in the background somewhere. I remember on one occasion he was living outside Rome with his wife in a castella. He met me at the airport, drove me out, we had a pleasant lunch, wine. He said, "Right, George, it's two o'clock." The publishers had been to the Jerusalem Bookfair; they were on their way back and were to arrive the next day—Howard Kaminsky, then of Warner Books, and Hillel Black of William Morrow. I read from two until six, and there was a feeling in the air. I thought, "If this is a stinkeroo, do I have to walk back to the airport twenty miles? What's going to hap-

pen?" As it turned out I liked it—it was a good yarn. But he'd been quizzing me a lot during the writing because the villain is an Englishman of some aristocratic rank.

DLB: Do you recall the title of this novel?

GREENFIELD: Bloodline [1977]. The villain was this high-ranking Englishman, a member of Parliament, who is impotent, and because he is impotent he has to wreak vengeance on this lovely girl who's inherited this enormous chemical firm. And I said, "You haven't got it quite right; he wouldn't be a member of *that* club, he'd be a member of *this* one, I think. No, he wouldn't lunch *there* because it's about ten miles from the House of Commons; he'd lunch at Lockets which is just down the road," and a few other things like this. And "He wouldn't say, 'Oh, how frightfully, frightfully,' all the time." So Sidney accepted that, yes.

Then the following morning before I left, Jorja, his wife, took me for a walk around the grounds and said, "Did you *really* like the book?" I said, "Honestly, Jorja, I *did*. It was jolly good. A very good read." She said, "I'm so glad. Did you recognize any of the characters?" I said, "No." She said, "Sir Lancelot (or whatever the villain was named)—Sidney based him on you." That's a fact. There's a case of an author I helped.

What's important is that the relationship doesn't remain a business one; it usually becomes a friendly one, a personal relationship. And it has to be based on trust on both sides; the author has implicitly to trust the agent. And more and more these days. One thing I'd like to discuss is what's going to happen in the future, which is another can of worms. But to make the point, the first thing the agent has to do is to select: both select titles to take on and try to match them with the right publisher. Some books no publisher is going to take, but if you've got a bit of a choice you want to go where the publisher is stable. An author could well stay with a publishing house twenty-five or thirty years. The agent has to know his author, his personality, and put him with an editor he'll get on with and a publishing house that will understand him and one hopes stick with him. There was a prewar saying that went right on until the 1960s: "It takes seven books to make an author." Today it's one book very often, and if that author's not made it, that could be good-bye.

Then, of course, there is the ability to know what the market will stand. When John le Carré came to me as a client and stayed nearly twenty years until I retired. . . .

DLB: What was the first book you handled for him?

GREENFIELD: It was called *The Naive and Sentimental Lover* [1971], and it was the first straight novel he had done. And when he came to me, at the time it was largely because he had married my ex-secretary, I have to say—there was no damned merit about it—I wasn't going to say he must go with Collins or he must go with this one or that one, so we had a little beauty contest in a most laid-back, informal way. I had picked a short list of publishers based on prestige, editorial status, and publicity and sales, which he approved. We then met these people over a meal or drinks, and he decided to go with Hodder and Stoughton. On the Monday when I was about to go to the Hodder office to discuss terms for the novel, David Cornwell—that's le Carré's real name—called me and said, "George, it's entirely in your hands, whatever terms you agree, you don't have to call me back and ask my approval, you have it now. I leave it entirely to you. But I just want to say one thing: Would you please leave him with a slight smile on his face? I know you want to do the best job you can, but don't nail him to the wall because I hope this is for good now." At that stage this was his sixth novel and it would be with his third different publisher.

DLB: He started with Gollancz.

GREENFIELD: Gollancz, then he moved to Heinemann briefly. And he said, "Look, I'd like to stay with these people but I don't want them to start with a kind of incipient grudge, the feeling they've been pushed too hard, so leave him with a slight smile on his face." And that's the best advice I think I've ever as an agent got from an author of mine. This was an author everybody wanted, and it would have been so easy to squeeze Hodder's dry. This is old-fashioned now. I'm talking about 1970. Nowadays it's the idea of "sock-em," because they're such fools, they're going to pay double what the book's worth anyway, so let's take 'em to the cleaners. . . . £650,000 advance for Michael Holroyd's three-decker biography of Bernard Shaw. What will it have earned—£200,000? Less than £200,000? Chatto and Windus and those houses have

thrown away, maybe, £400,000. It's money straight down the drain; it's gone out of the business; it's going straight into the author's pocket. That's great—for him—but it'll never come back into the business, that money, unless the author goes out and buys £400,000 worth of books.

DLB: Now, we've talked about picking the property, picking the author, finding the right publisher, putting them together, and giving the author as much help as he'll stand. Do you have any role during the publishing process? Hand-holding?

GREENFIELD: Indeed. Yes, hand-holding and keeping the publisher on his toes, which is important because as we all know there's a gap between delivery and acceptance, a contract being signed and a book being published, usually something like nine months. And if it's a big publishing house they may be putting through four hundred, five hundred titles a year, thirty or forty a month. . . .

DLB: Two every working day.

GREENFIELD: Yes, it's very easy for that book to get lost unless it's one of their big bestsellers. Then, of course, it won't get lost, but I'm talking now about the. . . .

DLB: What they call in American a middle book.

GREENFIELD: Yes, except the midlist has virtually gone, alas.

DLB: Everybody's shooting craps for the blockbuster.

GREENFIELD: Yes. But back in the old days I think it was very important that you kept in touch with the publisher and kept in touch with the author. What I often used to say, certainly to first novelists, was, "Try to get as much of your next novel done as you can before this one comes out, because once it comes out you're a marked man (or a marked woman). You're going to get reviews. Some will love it; some will hate it. You'll feel totally confused. You may have to do so much publicity. . . . If you just sit back now it's going to be much more difficult to get going, because quite often I've seen authors' careers to some degree blighted in that they had a

Dust jacket for Greenfield's Macmillan Centenary Award-winning 1945 novel based on his World War II experiences

natural, spontaneous story-telling ability, and then they would take the critics too much to heart. They would get confused, and then they realized the difficulty of writing a novel. Wasn't it Monsieur Jourdain in [Moliere's] *Le Bourgeois Gentilhomme* [1671] who discovered he spoke prose without realizing it? In the same way some of these people could *write* prose without realizing it. But once they start thinking about tension and conflict and developing character and this, that, and the other. . . .

DLB: What's called the second-novel jinx.

GREENFIELD: Right. So my advice has always been—go away somewhere. You've got a little bit of money now; sit down and get on with the new book. I don't mean you've got to have it finished in nine months, when the first one

should come out, but if you're halfway there that's a good start.

Lunching is an important and yet delicate tool for an agent. A few drinks in a congenial atmosphere will help to loosen a shy author's tongue, and you get to know your clients so much better in that way. On the other hand, the agent must be very careful to match the venue to the client. You know that old Hollywood story about the film agent whose arrogant actor-client cut him dead at a party? The agent said, "There goes that sonofabitch who takes 90 percent of my income!" Well, authors feel the same—in reverse. If you take them to the Connaught Grill, they think you must be stinking rich at their expense; if you take them to MacDonald's they think you're either a cheapskate or must be doing badly, which makes you a lousy agent.

And lunching can have positive results. Away from the telephone, no interruptions, you can often kick around ideas that would never have surfaced in a formal atmosphere. I remember one lunch with Noel Barber. He was aged seventy and no longer the great traveling journalist he once had been. He had a solid but medium track record for nonfiction books, usually set in exotic places. Toward the end of a bibulous lunch, I suggested he should try his hand at novels. It was just a case, I said airily, of putting Boy Meets Girl in front of those exotic backgrounds: Singapore, Shanghai, the South Pacific Islands. He went home after lunch and wrote a thousand words that afternoon. For the next eight years until his death, Noel Barber produced a string of best-selling novels, starting with *Tanamera* [1981].

John le Carré left his first agent and his first publisher for reasons connected with lunch—or the lack of it. He left his previous agency because of their meanness. He was then mainly living abroad, but he always sent them a case of champagne for Christmas. On the few occasions he visited London, they would ask him to call at four o'clock in the afternoon, too late for lunch and too early for dinner. They would give him a cup of tea. They were making a fortune out of him in commission and hadn't the wit to make a gesture in return.

Now I'll tell you why he left his first publisher, Victor Gollancz. Gollancz did a pretty good job in selling *The Spy Who Came In from the Cold* [1963]. Victor was a nasty old hypocrite, in my view, espousing lost causes in public and screwing authors in private. He lunched most days at the Savoy Grill while crying over the starving Africans or whatever. This young author, le Carré, had just published *The Spy Who Came In from the Cold*, and it was going to be the biggest thing ever. Le Carré had taught at Eton and served in the Foreign Office, and he didn't really know the ways of the business world. Up till then, he had had no money. But he was a very generous man, and he said, "I must give Victor a celebration lunch—after all he's done for me." So he wanted to choose a smart and expensive place. He hit on the Savoy Grill. Now, if Victor had been wise, he would have said, "Oh, don't let's go to the Savoy Grill, if you don't mind. Let's go somewhere else." But oh no, he was going to show up his author, who had never been to the Grill before. When they arrived, the headwaiter came up and said, "Oh, Mr. Gollancz, your usual table, sir?" And then the wine waiter came rushing up and said, "Here, Mr. Gollancz, your usual drink, sir. Enjoy your lunch, Mr. Gollancz, sir." And so it totally deflated the poor author, who moved to Heinemann with his next novel. Authors need watching carefully, don't they?

Coming back to our previous discussion, let's not forget that once the book's been sold, all sorts of other things are happening. The foreign department is trying to sell it, so the news is coming through there on the foreign side; and there may be a film possibility that's being pursued, so there's a lot to keep in touch with.

DLB: Then the book comes out. What role does the good agent, the attentive agent, have at that point?

GREENFIELD: Usually as a soother. Not a soothsayer but a soother. Long ago, a British prime minister said the popular press had power without responsibility—like a harlot. In a way, that goes for agents, too. Somewhere along the line, even with the most perfect publisher and the most perfect author, there's going to be a row. "Why did they advertise so-and-so in the Sunday *Times* and not me? What a lousy jacket that is. Why didn't they put that I won the hundred-yard dash in school in my biographical note?" When an author gets irritated with his publisher—and sooner or later they all do—the conscientious agent has to make a big decision: Is it a genuine, irretrievable grievance or a momentary spurt of anger?

For example, at literary parties authors always tell each other lies. Or—shall we say?—they tend to exaggerate. The following day, a client would call me and say, "Hey, X gets twice the advance I do, and his publishers sell nearly twenty thousand copies of him in hard covers. Why don't you shift me from my lousy publishers to X's?" Very often, I was able to reply, "Forget it. I happen to know that X gets a *smaller* advance than you do—and he's lucky to move more than five thousand copies per book in hard covers."

But it's so easy for an agent to reply, when his author comes up with a real or imagined complaint, "Joe, you've got a great point there. I'll think of some way to break the contract and then we can shift you to a publisher who'll appreciate you." Or he can say, "Well, Joe, come and have a drink and we'll talk it over. You have a point—but let's look at it from all sides. Tell you what, let's both sleep on it overnight and then you call me tomorrow morning and we can set up that drink." Quite often, Joe Blow would have cooled off by the next day. Of course, if the complaint was a solid one and the agent knew he could easily place him elsewhere, firm action should be taken. But, overall, the agent should consider himself a marriage broker, not a divorce lawyer.

DLB: All authors feel that publishers fail to promote their books properly. All authors feel that there aren't enough review copies sent out, that there aren't enough ads; and publishers always say, "A good book makes its own way. You can't make a book by advertising." Every publisher I know says that advertising exists only to gratify the author; it doesn't translate into book sales. That's what publishers say. Authors believe in advertising. What do you, as an agent, try to do about reconciling these two irreconcilable positions? Do you—if you feel the author is indeed being treated shabbily—get on the phone and raise hell with the publisher?

GREENFIELD: Yes. I would take a midway stance here. Word of mouth sells books, and advertising alone won't do it—you can't flog a dead horse. In short, a book that's not going to sell—I've seen publishers take substantial funds and splash ads in the underground and posters on hoardings—but if the public doesn't want that book you can't sell it. But on the other hand, with a word-of-mouth recommendation people will actually start buying the book in shops. Unless there are displays and unless there is enough advertising the reading public—which is a minority thing I suppose, 10 percent of the population are readers in the United States or the United

Kingdom—is not aware of it. And it's fairly cheap advertising to let them know the book's available. In this country there's the *Times Literary Supplement*, the *London Review of Books*, the *Bookseller*, and *Publishing News*. I don't think you have to take a page in the Sunday *Times* for twenty-five thousand pounds or whatever, but there should be a certain amount of advertising. A lot of publishers and a lot of bookshops will cooperate over advertising to some degree, especially if it's an author who means something to the public. If the publisher will take an ad in the local paper they'll go half-cost, perhaps tie it in with an author signing. So, yes, I don't think publishers really ever just publish a book and walk away. There would be a row very certainly between the agent and the top man responsible, and the agent would get tough with him. This is why the agent is the *author's* agent.

DLB: You said earlier that you wanted to get around to talking about the future of agenting and publishing, what the next twenty years are going to look like.

GREENFIELD: Up to perhaps the mid 1970s, there was real stability in the publishing world. Many houses on both sides of the Atlantic were family-owned, and, although they may have been patriarchal, the senior staff tended to stay put. On this side, for example, David Farrer spent his working career as a top editor with Secker and Warburg; Roger Machell did the same with Hamish Hamilton. Roland Gant, Harold Harris, Alan Maclean, Lord Hardinge of Penshurst—these people were fixed stars in their own little firmaments. And, in the States, Ned Bradford at Little, Brown; Marshall Best and then Alan Williams at Viking; Bob Gottlieb at Knopf; John Dodds at Putnam's; Albert Erskine at Random House—I could name a dozen more—were constantly there to select and encourage writing talent.

But, since the conglomerates took over, with even the biggest publishing houses being bought and sold, editors are shifted, they get fired, they move to another house—there's just no continuity. The only fixed star is the agent. Authors on the whole leave publishers or are dropped by publishers more frequently than they leave their agents. If the agent is doing a reasonably good job and he's a reasonably nice guy or gal, it's like having a divorce. An author leaving an agent is happening more than it used to, but not as much

as changing publishers. And so I have a feeling that we really need to go back to the eighteenth century where publishers were printers and sellers of books—not bookshop owners but selling books to bookshops. And the editing side would become allied with the agency, particularly with big novels.

I recall authors saying to me, "X got fired, or X has moved to somewhere else, and I read it first in the paper, and my publisher hadn't even the wit to say, 'I'm awfully sorry but X is leaving us.'" Or X himself—well, in the awful trauma of being fired, X wasn't going to write to every single author he met there.

DLB: You said that you foresee the editorial process becoming closely aligned to the agency side rather than the publishing side. How is this going to work?

GREENFIELD: In practice, a lot of good editors have been fired and are loose at the moment.

DLB: Yes. And they become employees of the author.

GREENFIELD: Exactly. On a free-lance basis. Initially, this will only work with pretty successful authors who are not totally wedded to an editor at their existing publishing house. You say, "Look, Y has been fired by publisher Z. I have a lot of time for Y; I reckon he's an imaginative and constructive editor. Your novels are right up his street. Why don't we have him in for a drink?" If they meet and get on well together, the agent then negotiates a lump-sum editorial fee with Y, based on time spent.

When the author has completed his revisions and is happy with the final typescript, the agent says to the publisher, "Look, here is an absolute finished work down to the last comma and full stop. All you have to do is pop it straight into production. You don't even have to read it." So you save the publisher's overhead, and if there isn't a contract existing already you make sure that your author picks up the cost of the editorial fee on top of his advance. Anyway, that money is tax deductible, the money paid to the editor. So an author on a 40 percent tax level isn't going to lose all that much money, and he's got in effect control of the editing: one editor is not going to be editing his book among ten others.

DLB: Is this a crystal ball? Is this a prediction of things to come?

GREENFIELD: This is a prediction.

DLB: The next step then would be to deliver to the publisher not setting copy but the text on disk.

GREENFIELD: Yes, because strangely a lot of very successful novelists write with felt-tip pens: John le Carré uses a felt-tip pen; Jeffrey Archer, to mention a couple of big names, uses a felt-tip pen; quite a few do. They don't type. But somebody's got to change the handwriting into typing, so if you've got a word processor it's a professional service, all part of the deal. So really the publisher becomes a producer and a purveyor of books.

DLB: The publisher may or may not want to look at the galleys, the proofs. Theoretically the publisher—under the Greenfield plan—could publish the book without seeing it before the bound copies came from the binder?

GREENFIELD: Well, one hopes that there would be enough curiosity to see what they've got, but yes.

DLB: The publisher then becomes just that.

GREENFIELD: The publisher then becomes a publisher.

DLB: And the editorial relationship is more intimately bound to the author under this system because the editor is in effect an employee of the author.

GREENFIELD: Oh indeed, yes. In fact, he is, because it's the author who's paying the editorial fee. Because wars are too important to be left to the generals, and books are too important to be left to publishers, really. If you cut their function down to what they ought to be best at— actually getting the book into the shops—maybe you don't even need that, the way book distribution is going. You just need a free-lancer who goes around wining and dining the top buyers at the chains, but then, of course, that defeats the object because you're not getting out into the countryside. But in this country the independents, small independents, look like they're disappear-

ing, particularly as the net book agreement is under threat. You do have a lot of small towns that usually have at least one good bookshop, don't you, in the States?

DLB: They're called "Mom-and-Pops" because usually it's a husband and wife running it, and they used to make a living until five or six years ago, and now the Walden and Dalton chains at the shopping malls are driving the "Mom-and-Pops" out of business. Americans shop at these unspeakable malls, and the "Mom-and-Pops" rarely can afford mall rent.

GREENFIELD: Yes, on the periphery of London these great big shopping centers are setting up with several-hundred-acre sites.

DLB: Malls of any size will have a Walden or a Dalton or both.

GREENFIELD: But then they mainly carry pulp fiction, don't they? Do they have a wide selection of books?

DLB: Best-sellers and remainders. Not a wide selection there.

GREENFIELD: So if, for example, you wanted to get Willa Cather . . . I should think she is mostly out of print now.

DLB: They'll order it for you, but they don't stock her—except possibly for *My Antonia* [1918].

GREENFIELD: But then you could do that anywhere, I suppose, even at the "Mom-and-Pops." That's very sad, but that's the way it's going. Well, it wouldn't work right across the board, clearly, because with a new novelist who may end up selling a thousand copies in this country if he's lucky, there's not the margin for editorial fees. However, in the States, I can see this happening with established authors.

DLB: And you've seen the reports in *Publishers Weekly* about publishers submitting manuscripts to the chain-store buyers saying, "Shall we publish this?" That is to say, "Will you guarantee an order if we publish it?" There are those who feel that this is very dangerous.

GREENFIELD: Well, it used to happen here in the days before there were in-house paperback firms. You sent a typescript to the hardcover publisher, who would rush around to Pan or Corgi, saying, "Would you take this?" Sometimes weeks went by. Once I was having a drink with a paperback publisher, and he said, "That was an interesting novel of so-and-so's that I just read." He knew it was one of my authors. I said, "How the hell did you get hold of it? Did the author send the manuscript in?" And he said, "No, no, no, Heinemann or Collins, or whatever it was." So I thought about it and I said, "This is fraud. They don't have the right to show it to anybody. Submission of a script is supposed to be privileged. What they have sent to you is confidential." And he said, "Oh no, you don't understand, that century ended back in 1900." So who knows? But I have a feeling something of the kind is going to happen more and more with big authors.

DLB: Conceivably with a big enough author, with a hot enough property, the author could hire the publisher, pay the publisher a commission to distribute the book.

GREENFIELD: That is the Hill Plan. Tim Hill is an American publisher who ran *American Heritage* for Little, Brown. He put together this idea—which I wrote about in *Scribblers for Bread* [1989] at some length—in which an author and his agent would have a package of their book done through Hill with a free-lance editor, free-lance designer, and so forth. Under the Hill Plan everything is done rather like the modern free-lance movie producers and directors who merely use the Hollywood system for distribution; an ad hoc team is put together for the movie. So here you put together an ad hoc team for the book. But it requires a very established author; and the Hill Plan has never taken off because of the mad advances that are being paid.

Under the Hill Plan up to the point of actually printing the book you had previously gone to let's say Simon and Schuster or whomever and said, "Look, will you take a hundred thousand copies?" And you've shown them a sample jacket design and so forth and they know the author's name and you even show them the text. And they say yes, and all they then do is act as distributor in effect for the book. And then you've got a guaranteed price from them; the publisher knows what he's going to get from the distributor, from the chains, and he has a cut in the mid-

GEORGE GREENFIELD

SCRIBBLERS FOR BREAD

Aspects of the English Novel Since 1945

Dust jacket for Greenfield's 1989 study of publishers' influences on authors' careers

dle which is 17 1/2 - 20 percent of. . . .

DLB: 17 1/2 to 20? Under this system the author is getting around 28 percent of the take, of the receipts?

GREENFIELD: Yes. If you take his royalty based on published price. Let's say we're talking about a twenty-five-dollar book as its official price when it hits the stores—yes, he's getting a 28 percent royalty based on that.

DLB: As opposed to 10 percent, 12 1/2 percent, 15 percent escalator. . . .

GREENFIELD: The usual formula, I believe, is for the successful, best-selling author in the States to get a flat 15 percent; not much more here, 17 1/2 percent perhaps. . . .

DLB: You have said that the plan had not been put into effect for any book yet because it requires an author who is powerful enough, who is a sure thing, to be able to be attractive to a publisher; and you have pointed out that if you have this sort of author the publisher is willing—even eager—to make an unrealistic advance so that for a book that might earn one million at best, the publisher will make an advance of two million which works out much better than 28 percent.

GREENFIELD: Sure. And of course there's the pathetic fallacy that it's based on the publisher's manufacturing profit. Shall we go into this?

If the publisher gets a big brand name, he knows he's going to sell 250,000 copies. He'll print 300,000; he'll have about 10 or 12 percent returned; but he'll net a quarter of a million sales. With a twenty-five-dollar book, after discounts to the chains and shops he's getting twelve or thirteen dollars per copy, and it costs him, say, six dollars to print and produce. So he's making about six or seven dollars a copy in the middle as his manufacturing profit, the difference between what it costs him to make it and what he's getting for it. Less overhead, of course. So on that reckoning if he sells a quarter of a million at six dollars a copy it's showing him one and a half million. He can give the author a million too much, and on his reckoning he's still making—at least on paper—half a million dollars profit. But, he has now cut his profit margin to a very considerable extent. So the books that *don't* sell a quarter of a million . . . if that book flopped and only sold a hundred thousand, then he's really behind the eight ball, isn't he? With all this money sloshing around they think it's logical—and if you say it quickly it is logical—but it's not leaving them any margin for error.

This is why so many publishing houses have changed hands. And you've also got this other business. . . . What usually happens when there's a slump, a new chief executive will be brought in, and he'll look at the list of his employees in a big house and fire 20 percent or more. So he's cut the overhead very substantially which reduces the loss. And they say, "My God this guy is good,

watch him!" And then he goes out—he needs to buy some brand names, so he rings up the agent and he says, "I'm offering big, big money for brand names. Tell me off the record, what does Martin Hotshot get from Hodder's, or whoever, Simon and Schuster?" And they say, "Oh, X," and he says, "I'll offer you twice that." And so he goes up and down the list, and of course as we know, in accounting practices, advances you've got out count as assets. They should count as debits because this is money you have promised to pay, but until you actually pay they count as assets. So at the end of a year or two when the top brass look at the books they say, "This is marvelous! This guy's cut the overhead and built up the assets, and we have all these wonderful new names. My wife goes to a cocktail party, and when she tells her friends we have Sidney Sheldon, Barbara Taylor Bradford, this one or that one in for drinks, her stock shoots up." Then this guy's head-hunted, and so he goes off to another crazy house for twice the salary to do the same thing.

DLB: Leaving behind the funny bookkeeping.

GREENFIELD: Exactly. And then, when it really works out, he's long gone. It's a pity it's happening that way. We are living in a mad, mad world. Talk about Paul Reynolds selling his grandmother; he'd get twice as much as before. So that I think is my prognosis of the future. I don't know whether it will work that way.

DLB: Anything you want to say by way of wrap-up?

GREENFIELD: Please God, realism will raise its tiny head at some point. The past is irrecoverable, I know, but I wish some of those traditions would come back. Books were—and a fairly good number of publishers still feel that books are—important: that they are valuable, that you treat them with loving care, that you keep the hucksters away from them. That's my hope and wish. I think it's doubtful it will ever be achieved again, but please God it will.

The Recovery of Literature: Criticism in the 1990s;
A Symposium

I. Postmodern Criticism:
A Statement

Walter Sullivan

Walter Sullivan, professor of English at Vanderbilt University, is known for his novels as well as several books of criticism, including *Death by Melancholy: Essays on Modern Southern Fiction* (1972). In 1988, as a part of the Southern Literary Studies series, edited by Louis D. Rubin, Jr., Professor Sullivan published *Allen Tate: A Recollection* (L.S.U.).

Deconstructionism was bad in theory and practice, detrimental to the work of writers of fiction and poetry partially because too many writers of fiction and poetry collaborated in the deconstructionist devaluation of the literary work of art. But a system of criticism based on the idea that the text is whatever the critic wants it to be couldn't endure for very long even in our debased society. Chaos is finite. As each critic adds a new deconstruction of a work of art, confusion increases, and ultimately the whole enterprise collapses on itself. But before the collapse came, the deconstructionists were able to destroy concepts of absolutes and ideals and thus discredit moral and aesthetic standards such as those formulated by Aristotle and Plato, Augustine and Aquinas, that had constituted the foundations of literary theory and criticism for thousands of years. Consequently, the demise of deconstructionism left an enormous intellectual and moral vacuum that was filled with political and social theories that are based on the lowest possible view of human nature: men and women as mere products of evolution, highly developed physical entities, bereft of a belief in God, or a knowledge of their own souls.

I have argued that the fatal flaw of the New Criticism was that it failed to provide for moral evaluations and consequently limited the scope of

Walter Sullivan (© Crichton Photography)

the aesthetic judgments its practitioners could make. Robert Penn Warren said, for example, that a poem was good insofar as it fulfilled the intentions of the author, but he declined to say that one successful poem might be better than another successful poem because of the moral significance of the subject. This is what Warren professed, but in practice, he and all the major New Critics made judgments in moral terms. The poems that they chose to write about were works of moral significance. This was true because they were moral human beings who had been taught Judeo-Christian ethics. To the end of his life Warren believed in moral absolutes.

148

In my judgment, the worst aspect of deconstructionism was that it made all moral considerations irrelevant. If the text said nothing, then the text was neither good nor bad, true nor false. At the end of the deconstructionist period—and it has ended; English faculties simply don't know it yet—there was left a moral vacuum that, the nature of vacuums being what it is, had to be filled. But the spiritually deprived generation now in charge of the critical establishment had nothing in themselves with which to fill it. Their only concepts of morality were political, cultural, and ultimately self-serving. In other words, the legacy of the deconstructionists was a value system, enforced with procrustean arrogance, that is false because it is relative to the core.

Years ago, Jacques Maritain said that the way to write a Christian novel is to be the best Christian you can possibly be and then write the best novel you can write. This advice seemed difficult even to so committed a Christian as François Mauriac. Even so, Maritain was onto something: morally dead writers produce morally dead literature. Morally dead critics compound the problem. The recovery of critical standards, like the recovery of literature in general, depends, at least in part, on the spiritual rejuvenation of us all.

II. The Decline in the Critical Discussion of New Literature:
George Garrett Interviews John W. Aldridge

Back from World War II, where he served as an infantryman in Europe, winning combat stars for Normandy, northern France, Rhineland, central Europe, and the Ardennes as well as the Bronze Star Medal, John W. Aldridge published his first influential critical book, *After the Lost Generation* (1951). Since then he has published six other critical studies, a novel, *The Party at Cranton* (1960), and a large number of book reviews and critical essays. He has taught at Vermont, Wyoming, Princeton, Sarah Lawrence, Queens, Hollins, among others; and he recently retired after more than twenty-five years of teaching at the University of Michigan. Forthcoming in 1992 are two critical books, *Talents and Technicians* (Scribners) and *Classics and Contemporaries* (Missouri).

GG: Right after World War II, when you began to publish influential criticism, the whole lit-

John W. Aldridge (photograph by Mary Grace Albert)

erary scene was very different—at least as far as criticism was concerned. It seems to me, at least in memory, that there was a lively, indeed *vital* exchange between the new, postwar generation of American writers and many of the critics. In memory it seems to me that we were *learning* from each other, all the time.

Lately, though, with the latest and newest directions in scholarship and criticism—the Marxists, still unreconstructed; the ideologues of all kinds; the feminists; the deadly Deconstructionists; and others—I have the feeling that most of the writers I know and know of are not paying a lot of attention to critics. They like and need good *reviews*, maybe more than ever. But they don't often learn much, if anything, from basic book reviews. What the hell happened to living, breathing, alive-and-kicking criticism? What happened to the *exchange* between critics and writers, a kind of dialogue with the *reader* (that lost and forgotten soul) in mind?

You have two new critical books coming out in the months ahead—*Talents and Technicians: Literary Chic and the New Assembly-line Fiction* (about the better-known younger American fiction writers) from Scribners in April and *Classics and Contemporaries* (a large selection of your essays on modern and contemporary writers) from the University of Missouri Press in May. Does it seem to you that, given the emphasis on current writing in both books, they will do anything to revive the kind of exchange I'm talking about?

JWA: I hope they will at least contribute. But let me go back a bit. My impression now is that the literary situation in this country right after World War II was very special, was unlike anything we have had since, and was probably, at least in its potential, most like the situation right after World War I. The young writers who began to appear in the late 1940s and early 1950s—and I think of Norman Mailer, Truman Capote, William Styron, Gore Vidal (yes, Vidal, who then showed promise of becoming a serious writer), and James Jones—seem actually to have thought of themselves as being part of a new literary renaissance at the same time that they supposed they were carrying forward the tradition of Hemingway, Fitzgerald, and Faulkner.

In fact, they assumed in their youthful arrogance that they were the contemporary replacements for those writers and were destined to create a body of work as important for our time as their work was to the 1920s and 1930s. This same expectation was shared by some critics, and I was one of them. I wrote about these young writers in my first book, significantly entitled *After the Lost Generation* [1951], as if they were indeed pretenders to the thrones of their distinguished predecessors.

I'm not sure that there was actually a dialogue or exchange going on between critics and writers at that time. But I do think that the postwar generation, because of their position in history and the still-living heritage of the 1920s generation, aroused the feeling in both critics and the general reading public that something of great significance was on the verge of happening, particularly in fiction, with the result that a good deal of attention was paid.

An illustration of this is the reception *After the Lost Generation* was accorded as the first critical book about the postwar writers. There were front-page reviews in both the Sunday *New York Times* and *New York Herald Tribune* book sections as well as reviews in the daily editions, an editorial in *Life*, essay-reviews in *Harper's*, the *Atlantic*, and *New Republic*, and an enormous number of notices in newspapers across the country. Readers were curious to know whether we were in fact about to experience a postwar literary renaissance like the one that followed the first war, and they were excited about the prospect. It is hard to imagine a critical book about current writers receiving that kind of attention today, although for selfish reasons I'd like to think it just might be possible.

But another big change is that until the New Criticism began to be academicized in the 1940s and even for some time after that, serious literary critics had in general a much closer relation to the world of contemporary creative writers than they do today. As you suggest, criticism has now all but abdicated its traditional role as a monitor and educator of taste and has nearly disappeared into linguistic and anthropological theory, the politics of race and gender, and the supposedly malignant manipulations of power. Literary works are read now in the universities as political texts, and those who do the reading are concerned, not with the quality of new writing, but with revising the canon and seeking out symptoms of political incorrectness.

In such a situation it is hard to believe that a practical critic like Malcolm Cowley once had a massive influence on the reputations of Hemingway and Faulkner, and that Edmund Wilson reviewing Hemingway's second book, *in our time* [1924], was influential on Hemingway's career in this country.

We also tend to forget that Robert Penn Warren, himself a New Critic, did important work in helping to elucidate Faulkner; that Wilson, in *Axel's Castle* [1931], effectively introduced American readers to European literary modernism; that Allen Tate, another New Critic, wrote powerfully about the creative work of his contemporaries, and so did R. P. Blackmur. Somewhat later, Granville Hicks did much to strengthen the reputation of one of our most neglected novelists, Wright Morris, while Leslie Fiedler probably did irreparable damage to James Jones's with his review of *From Here to Eternity* [1951].

Another closely related factor is the decline in authority of such a magazine as *Partisan Review*, at least as it once was back when it was the principal critical organ of literary modernism—that along with the disappearance of periodicals that once gave more than cursory attention to new creative work. I think of the *New York Herald Tribune Book Week*, which was once a serious competitor of the *New York Times Book Review*, and where for some years I at least was able to publish long reviews of around two thousand words on some new novel. The same was true of *Saturday Review*, which died in the early 1980s. I used to publish essays as long as four thousand words there, and in a piece that long you can manage to say something substantial about a book and even assemble some evidence to support your argument. Also in the early 1980s *Harper's* eliminated its book section altogether. But before that happened, I was able to publish there equally long essays on novels—specifically, Joseph Heller's *Good as Gold* [1979] and Styron's *Sophie's Choice* [1979].

Then there has been still another change and one that may have had a very great deal to do not only with the decline in critical discussion of new literature but with the decline of general public interest in new literature. My impression is that few novels any longer define and interpret our individual and/or national experience in a compelling way. In fact, our fiction has not done this since the early work of Mailer, Heller, and Vonnegut which functioned rather in the way that the fiction of their predecessors did. You will remember how instructive certain novels once were in introducing you to certain kinds of life you hadn't experienced—the almost magical effect on your young mind of *The Great Gatsby* [1925], *The Sun Also Rises* [1926], *A Farewell to Arms* [1929], *A Portrait of the Artist* [1916], *Ulysses* [1922], *Look Homeward, Angel* [1934], *All the King's Men* [1946]. These books, and there were others, served almost as guidebooks to life at the same time that they gave us the charged symbols of the significant preoccupations of the modern age. *Catch-22* [1961], *Slaughterhouse Five* [1969], and *The Armies of the Night* [1968] did much the same for the 1960s. But has there been any novel since that has illuminated the 1970s and 1980s in quite that way? I can't think of one, and the reason may be that, as I say in *Talents and Technicians*, the younger writers I discuss seem, for the most part, to be curiously divorced both from society and contemporary history and, therefore, to be operating in a kind of intellectual vacuum. The result is that the arena of so much of their fiction is reduced to the experience of the isolated self and the mostly trivial and commonplace housekeeping problems of daily life. They write stories about going to the supermarket, about buy-

ing items in shopping malls, or about people sitting around the kitchen table talking about their ex-spouses or how badly their parents have treated them. Unfortunately, these subjects tend not to be treated in a way that elevates them to universal significance. They may be of interest to the writers themselves but not to very many readers. Or they may be so familiar that, as T. S. Eliot put it, "they end their course in the desert of exact likeness to the reality perceived by the most commonplace mind." And I doubt that we much care to read the work of writers whose minds are commonplace.

GG: You are one of the very few critics who has had real, in-the-trenches experience as a book critic on television. Do you think that TV is compatible with books and reading? Can it work?

JWA: My experience as a book commentator on the MacNeil/Lehrer News Hour may or may not be instructive. It lasted about a year and came about when the program was extended to a full hour and someone decided that it might be interesting to devote a closing five- or six-minute segment to a review of some current book. I was one of four critics chosen to appear each month and was given complete freedom to choose the book or books to be discussed. The problem, especially for me, was that there was no script, no teleprompter. Everything was ad lib, and one had to try to say something sensible about a book in a very few minutes. A further problem was that Robin MacNeil, who conducted the sessions, clearly had not read the books, so he would begin the discussion by saying something like "Well, Jack, is this book a good *read*?" And you can imagine the kind of answer one had to fumble for. Or he would ask, "What is this book about?"

I concluded after a while—as apparently did MacNeil and Lehrer because the reviews ended after a year—that books can't be properly dealt with in a few minutes in a television news format. The reason is that if the book is a serious novel and, therefore, worth reviewing, a summary of the action, which is just about all one has time to give, tells us next to nothing about the quality of the work. You will see what I mean if you can imagine offering a description of the plot of *Ulysses*. A group of people can sit around a table and discuss a book or author for a half hour, and that will work on TV. A film can be discussed in terms of its characters and action, and footage from it can be shown, and that also, as many film review programs prove, will work on TV. But the medium is simply wrong for the responsible reviewing of books, not only because of the shortage of time but because books need to be *written about* at length and in some detail.

GG: For a good many years you have been a teacher as well as a writer. You have recently retired from the University of Michigan. Did teaching help or hurt your critical work? Do you miss teaching and the classroom now?

JWA: I am not by nature a public person. But in teaching I was forced to contrive the appearance of being one. I was an extremely shy, introverted only child, and well into young adulthood I was unable to speak at public gatherings without the embarrassment of having my voice shake. Teaching has, therefore, been stressful to me, and I have had to cope with it by becoming almost exclusively a lecturer and hiding behind my thoroughly prepared written text. I am told that I am a good lecturer. But if I am, it has cost me a great deal.

All this is to say that I've found teaching for the most part unpleasant, and ever since the day a year ago when I walked out of my campus office for the last time, I've not felt one twinge of desire to return to it. Of course there have been good moments. Once in a while one stirs the enthusiasm of serious students, and I've had very agreeable letters from some of them saying how much they took away from this or that lecture. But a big problem is that there is so little feedback, and one can go for years without knowing what, if anything, one's students do take away. It is rather like performing *Hamlet* two or three times a week before an audience that never applauds and after which there are no reviews.

Yet for a literary person it is the best way to make a living that there is. However, if one *is* a literary person, there is the problem that teaching is not one's natural medium. A writer or critic has a built-in expectation that if he has put together a first-rate lecture on Joyce or Mailer, it should elicit the same response it might get if it were published as an essay. And of course he would infinitely prefer to publish it as an essay because then it would have a chance of long life, while in the classroom it is likely to die with the end of the period. An outraged response to this might be: so you care more about having your work noticed and appreciated than you do about

educating your students. And my answer is that, yes, that is the way (most?) writers are.

GG: One thing the writers of fiction and poetry cling to is the hope (knowing it may be pure illusion) that they may be "discovered," maybe even championed, by a good critic. How much do you feel "discovery" is part of the critical responsibility? Who among the writers you have been reading lately, young or older writers, do you think deserve attention and "discovery"? Are there some inflated reputations you think may deserve a little taking-down to size? You have written persuasively about the downside of creative writing programs. Do you see any good things (or good *people*) coming out of them? You have personally known prominent American writers of several generations—Faulkner, for example, and Mailer— along with a host of very young and new writers. Do you sense any difference in the *kind* of person who writes? That is, is/was Faulkner different from Mailer and is Mailer a different type of man from the youngest generation of writers? I suppose I'm really asking if, now that writing is more accepted and "respectable," the writing life attracts a different kind of person than the rebels and walking wounded we knew of old?

JWA: I think that the discovery of new talent is and should be an important function of criticism. But for reasons we've already discussed, it is a function seldom performed these days. In my own case, I think that in a sense by giving their early work the first serious critical attention it received I "discovered" some of the writers I discussed in *After the Lost Generation*. Mailer later wrote in an introduction to a new edition of that book that I had given those writers their first sense of identity as a literary generation and that this is something every generation of writers needs to have. I also was one of the few critics to give serious attention to William Gaddis's *The Recognitions* when it was first published in 1955, and I'm told that my long and favorable review of his second novel, *JR* [1975], helped him to win a National Book Award. I think also that I helped to pioneer the at-the-time heretical view that Heller's *Something Happened* [1974] may actually be a more important achievement than *Catch-22*, and I've long been an admirer of Don DeLillo's work which has only fairly recently received serious recognition. Whether the young writers I discuss in *Talents and Technicians* will consider themselves to have been discovered or buried beneath a ton of rubble, I can't yet say.

In that book I give high marks to Lorrie Moore and T. Coraghessen Boyle; B's and B-pluses to Ann Beattie, Bobbie Ann Mason, Louise Erdrich, Mary Robison, and David Leavitt; low passes to Amy Hempel and Frederick Barthelme; and failing grades to Jay McInerney and Bret Easton Ellis. The reputations of Beattie, Mason, Erdrich, and Robison seem to me to have been inflated beyond the value of their work, while Moore and Boyle need to be taken far more seriously than they have been.

I think that Faulkner and Mailer—to take your two examples—are very different cases but alike in being writers obsessed with a powerful vision. And luckily they both had talent of sufficient size to accommodate it. They also were or are not only immensely gifted but extremely original; each was one of a kind and completely his own person.

It seems to me that the democratization of creative writing in the graduate writing programs has caused many small talents to be unduly and often cruelly encouraged, and it has led to a leveling of both talent and performance. These programs are founded on the specious proposition that serious creative writing is a trade that can be learned like carpentry, and that it involves learning how to put pieces of prose or poetry together so that they form ideally a seamless construction that is both efficient and attractive.

As apprentices to the trade of writing, the students master certain techniques, and a good many of them become indeed masters of technique in the sense that they learn how to write a graceful and, even now and then, a beautiful series of words. But then the problem becomes finding some kind of subject matter to be displayed by the excellent language, just as the carpenter requires pieces of wood to be put together. And this is where most writing students prove to be deficient. To paraphrase something Hemingway once said, they have the technique, all bright and shiny, and nothing to say. The result is the kind of productions I described earlier. They tend to write extremely well about materials so trivial and commonplace that the high quality of the technique is subverted by the poor quality of the material. They hold a mirror up to nature and reflect back a nature that is one we all perceive. Important writing should give us a recognizable reality but one never quite perceived in just that way be-

fore because it is illuminated by the writer's special insight.

In short, the writing programs on the whole seem to me to be turning out literary carpenters and construction engineers, but they cannot create talent. The result is that we now have literally hundreds of competent writers, of whom only a very few have something truly original to offer or the obsessiveness to keep them writing long enough to offer it. My impression of most of the students in these programs is that they are bright, conventional, not very literary, and might just as easily have entered law school or dentistry. It is, in the case of most of them, a real pity that they were not advised to do just that.

III. Something Serious, Something Important

The following are excerpts from a taped interview and conversation between George Core and Monroe K. Spears.

A reviewer needs time to say something serious, something important, if there is anything serious and important to say.

—Monroe K. Spears

This conversation took place late in 1991 in Sewanee, Tennessee, where both Spears and Core live. Monroe Spears has retired there after a career that included full-time faculty positions at Vanderbilt, Sewanee, and Rice University. He was editor of the *Sewanee Review* from 1952 to 1961. George Core is the present editor of the *Sewanee Review*. Spears is author of several important critical works—*The Poetry of W. H. Auden* (1963), *Hart Crane* (1965), *Dionysius and the City: Modernism in Twentieth Century American Poetry* (1972), and *American Ambitions* (1987). Forthcoming in 1992 from the University of Missouri Press is *Interworlds: Literary and Cultural Essays*. Spears is also the author of a book of poems—*The Levitator* (1975).

GC: Monroe, you have been involved in editing and publishing for over forty years. You came here exactly forty years ago to edit the *Sewanee Review*. And something I want to explore with you this morning is how book reviewing and criticism have changed over the past four decades.

MKS: Well, that is a very large subject, but a fascinating one. One thing that I think is basic to this kind of discussion—and, of course, I have in mind the academic as well as the general aspect of it—is the, so to speak, demographic, sociological aspect. In the 1950s the academic population was expanding, both faculty and students, and you had a group of very intelligent and somewhat older and more mature students coming in. And for this reason criticism seemed more important; that is, there was a necessity to teach these people how to read or improve their reading skills and also to deal with the modern literature which had not been fully digested or explained. And for that reason in the 1950s the job of criticism as seen in critical quarterlies seemed more vital, more essential than it does now simply because that job has pretty well been done now, and because, for many reasons, the academic population is contracting rather rapidly. There is not the same sense of urgency. And, of course, there is the obvious fact that criticism has now become much more specialized, that you have critical theorists who claim to have no particular obligation either to students or to potential students or to creative writers, but to be simply doing this job for its own sake. It is autotelic, in the fullest sense, I suppose you could say....

Then you have the creative writers who are now fully absorbed into the academy, but increasingly seem to be segregated from the English departments in separate programs or separate departments.

And then, of course, you have the literary scholars, far fewer of them than in the past, the historical scholars who keep on doing what they have always done....

But you have the phenomenon of English departments, to a surprising extent, being taken over by the faction of the theorists; and therefore possibly, in many institutions leaving the old-fashioned humane teaching of literature to the writing programs. Which is a curious development, indeed.

GC: When you first began, the scholars fought with the critics. Looking back on that, one might say that that battle turned out to be much more helpful to literature than what's going on at the present time, when the theorists seem to think they have parity with the creative writers.

Monroe K. Spears (photograph by Miriam Berkley)

On the other hand, you have the creative writers in a lot of places setting up their own programs to the extent that they are almost the tail-wagging dog of the English department. Which, as you say, is dominated by the theorists at this time.

MKS: Yes, that's a curious development. The latest issue of the *Virginia Quarterly Review* has a very interesting article by a woman named Janet McNew ["Whose Politics? Media Distortions of Academic Controversies," Winter 1992]. Have you happened to see that?

GC: No, I haven't read that.

MKS: She takes a position which simplifies it into a battle between the ancients and the moderns, as in Swift's *The Battle of the Books* [1794]. And she takes her stand firmly on the side of the moderns. It's an interesting piece. It is put more cogently than I've seen it put elsewhere that the conservatives, especially neo-conservative critics, people like Allan Bloom and E. D. Hirsch, are in fact radicals. They are the ones who are attempting to reverse a situation which was going along very nicely, according to her, until they began complaining about it. And she points out, quite rightly, that the media—the news magazines and newspapers and popular magazines of all kinds—just automatically take the side of the ancients. She goes on to argue that this is partly because before and especially after the First World War it was a part of the propaganda effort to emphasize the notion of Western Civilization as a coherent entity and something that should be the core of a liberal education. So her argument is, in brief, that there is a political bias behind the argument of the ancients.

And this seems to me interesting as a correction of what might be called knee-jerk conservatism. But it is ultimately quite false. The thing about the "ancients" that I find impossible to go along with is that while any sensible person has to see that there is no absolute criterion for distinguishing the good from the bad, the true from the false, or at least that it is madness to be absolutely sure that you have such a criterion, that is a very different thing from denying aggressively, and from the beginning, that it is even possible to have such a criterion and giving up the search for it. It seems to me that at least the more radical of the so-called theorists—like Derrida and his ilk—are essentially nihilists. They deny the possibility of any meaning, any coherence in intellectual life, denying not only the possibility of any standards of value, of any way of saying one thing is better than another, but the very notion of discrimination. It seems to me that to do this is to abandon the whole educational enterprise . . .

GC: It seems to me, Monroe, that literature has been lost, fallen between the cracks. What we were talking about is the old New Criticism and the related criticism by people you were publishing when you edited the *Sewanee Review*—the old Chicago neo-Aristotelians, the New York critics, and so on. In a way they succeeded too well, and now the theorists are trying to find a new tack for themselves. . . . The theorists say that what they are doing is as important as the literary enterprise, which no critics, to my mind, have ever said at any previous time. And then there are the writers all writing in a mechanical way they learned in these workshops . . .

[This leads Core and Spears to talk, judiciously, of the pros and cons of creative writing programs. Spears comments that the two of them

are talking "perhaps too exclusively" from an academic point of view, adding: "We can't help that, being in the academic environment ourselves." They turn the subject more specifically to book reviewing.]

MKS: There is always a tension, in publishing, between artistic motives and criteria and commercial motives and criteria. And publishing, after all, has always been a business, and making money has been a part of it. But it seems to me that now, far more than ever in the past, you have the pressure of "really big bucks"—millions and millions of dollars if a best-seller hits properly and is merchandised properly and then, perhaps, goes on to the movies. . . . This tends to have inevitably a distorting and sometimes a corrupting effect on the whole operation.

GC: What's happened (as we have talked about before) is that the publishing companies are being taken over by big holding companies. They have lost their independence. And then you have got the publishers, themselves, becoming "notables." They are being written about in the popular press, and they are vying for attention in the media among themselves and even with their own authors. The same thing is true even of agents—people we have laughed about in the past, like Swifty Lazar who himself may be better known than any writer in the country.

MKS: On the whole, book reviewing is less a department of criticism than it used to be. There are, of course, excellent book reviews being written and published, and there are many accomplished reviewers. I don't mean to make a miscellaneous attack. But because of the immense number of books being published and because of the competition in various ways for attention, there is tremendous pressure to keep the reviews short. And this, in itself, tends to stop any attempt at serious discussion. The review becomes primarily a news item . . . the *New York Times Book Review* is hardly ever willing to give a reviewer time enough to say anything sensible. There are some that do, fortunately. The quarterlies do publish long reviews. The *New York Review of Books*, although it runs very heavily to the political, does publish, occasionally, long, serious literary discussions. There are other places, too; but they tend to get crowded out . . .

GC: No matter how much manipulation by the media goes on, book reviews are absolutely essential in the promotion of a book.... The book review cannot be replaced by a blurb. No matter how many blurbs you get for a book from how many distinguished people, you still have to get the books reviewed.

MKS: But, of course, the sad fact about the commercial aspect of literature is that bad reviews do not have any noticeable effect on sales of a certain kind of fiction, at any rate. This sequel to *Gone With the Wind* [*Scarlett* (Warner)] has been number one on the *New York Times* bestseller list in spite of the fact that no critic, to my knowledge, has had the slightest kind word to say about it.

GC: But, of course, it has been reviewed.

[Moving to discuss changes in the practice of book reviewing, Spears recalls the days "when I was editing."]

MKS: You had first-rate people who were eager to do reviewing. I mean Randall Jarrell and James Dickey and Howard Nemerov and people like that. My impression is that nowadays that's not so much the case.

GC: The more established the person, the less likely he is to do any reviewing.

MKS: I am convinced, and I know you are, that book reviewing is an important function. Some people have argued there's no point in writing a negative review, that a bad book will sink of its own weight. But unfortunately I could cite quite a few examples to the contrary of bad books that might have been placed more accurately by reviews that pointed out what's the matter with them. And also it's an important way of ordering the intellectual world, to distinguish the good from the bad and to say what kind of standards one is employing and exactly what is the matter with it. Of course, even more important is pointing out why good books are good and what their outstanding qualities are and distinguishing the good from the bad in them, since nothing is either wholly good or wholly bad.

GC: We have to be grateful to somebody like Updike who keeps on reviewing ...

MKS: Yes!

GC: ... when most people of his age and stature have given it up. I don't think reviewing should just be left to young people who are starting out and trying to make their marks. I'd like to see critics, as you have done, continue reviewing books all their mature lives. To my mind book reviews can be one of the most engaging parts of criticism.

MKS: And, theorists to the contrary, a good review can sometimes be of use to the writer.

GC: I think we have both agreed that no matter how much the media does to manipulate authors in the literary marketplace, the book review is always central.

MKS: Of course, another way the media distort and corrupt is by making people celebrities, and then, simply because they are celebrities, their books are immediate best-sellers.

GC: I worry about literature, although I think that great literature will somehow always get written. But it does seem that the pressures on the writer are greater than ever now.... We're talking about a world, it seems to me, Monroe, in the academy and in the literary marketplace, that has too much in common with the world at large. Publishing used to be called a gentleman's profession. I don't know that there are many gentlemen left in it. Roger Straus may be one of the very few. And another one of our problems now is that we have got too damn many writers, people who call themselves writers, and too few readers. Everybody these days thinks he is a writer. And we may have fewer good writers than we have had in many a moon. Have you got any predictions about the future? Are we going straight to hell?

MKS: [laughs] No. I have always been suspicious of the old hell-in-a-handbasket syndrome. But I do think we are perhaps arriving at a situation where something is going to have to be done to curb the terrifying power of the media. And I don't know what. And I don't know who's going to do it....

Literary Research Archives VII:
The University of Virginia Libraries

Edmund Berkeley, Jr.
Director, Special Collection Department, Alderman Library

Literary collections at the University of Virginia might be dated from 1899, when the university received the gift of $10,180 from the estate of Alfred Henry Byrd, the income from which was to be used for the acquisition of Virginiana. But they are perhaps best dated from 1922, when the university—remarkably, because it has seldom spent money on such collections since—spent $800 to purchase the archives of John Henry Ingram, Edgar Allan Poe's English biographer.

This acquisition was a tentative step into the area of original research materials for the library. As Harry Clemons wrote in his history of the library, at that time "there had been no systematic organization of a rare book collection. Some rare items had been recognized among the gifts and isolated for special protection," including the few manuscripts. The library occupied and overwhelmed the Rotunda, the central building, which Jefferson had designed. The collections had outgrown the building chiefly because of the generous donations that followed the disastrous fire that destroyed the Rotunda and its annex in 1895 and which left only 17,194 volumes. "By June 1925 . . . the reported figure was 131,422, an increase of over sevenfold." Jefferson's handsome building had not been designed for a collection of this size, and planning for a new library building was begun in the mid 1920s with the university's president Edwin Anderson Alderman as a vigorous advocate. But the Great Depression slowed this effort.

Active efforts to build a rare-books collection began in 1929 when the southeastern wing of the Rotunda was set aside for what was designated the Virginia Collection, and certain books and the few manuscripts (2,177 in number) were moved into it. Frances Elizabeth Harshbarger was the first curator of the collection, and she was succeeded in 1934 by John Cook Wyllie, who had begun working in the library as a student assistant in late 1928. The rare-books and manuscripts collections grew during the 1930s, as did the efforts to secure a new library building.

A combination of a grant from the federal Works Progress Administration and a bond issue authorized by the state enabled construction of the new library, named for President Alderman, to begin in 1936, and it opened for use in April 1938. Notably for the literary collections, the new building included fine quarters for the Rare Books and Manuscripts Division and for the Tracy W. McGregor Library, which had been donated to the university in 1938 by McGregor's trustees. McGregor, who had spent much of his life in Detroit, had specified in his will that his library "be used to assist in the founding of a library of American history in a small institution of higher learning, having high ideals of education and reasonable means and likelihood of achieving those ideals." Because he had visited Charlottesville and was considering moving to the area, the trustees carefully considered the university as one possible home. Thomas R. Adams, in a talk on McGregor given in 1988 at a celebration of the fiftieth anniversary of the McGregor Library at the university, said, "Indeed John Cook Wyllie had had discussions with Mr. McGregor about having the books." And he further noted the influence of his father—Randolph Adams of the Clements Library, a friend and adviser of McGregor—who was sent by the trustees to visit the university in 1937. The trustees decided that the University of Virginia would be the home of the McGregor Library, and it arrived at a most opportune time. Harry Clemons, librarian when the gift was received, has written of it:

> The addition of the McGregor Library was a highly important factor in the research developments at the University of Virginia. This collection came to a small library at the moment when that library was attempting a new role. The significance of the collection was therefore much greater than it would have been in a library rich in such collections, or in a library not committed

The Alderman Library, University of Virginia (Special Collections, University of Virginia Library)

to an ambitious program. Moreover the conditions of the gift to a notable degree ensured its continued vitality. Altogether, this proved to be an outstanding example of constructive benefaction.

The trustees constructed as a memorial to McGregor the room in Alderman Library that bears his name. Its splendid dark paneling, bronze grillwork bookcases, handsome portrait, and fireplace make the room truly a fine memorial to McGregor.

The commitment of seventy-five hundred dollars per year by the McGregor trustees, with an additional twenty-five hundred dollars yearly from the university, enabled the McGregor Library to build its collections, both historical and literary, which numbered about 5,000 volumes concentrated in Americana, the New England Mathers, and English literature when they were received. The gift also included a reference collection of about 12,500 volumes.

"The earliest book in the collection is the first edition of Ptolemy's *Cosmographia*, printed in 1475," and it includes "the works of Strabo, Pomponius Mela, Solinus, Sacro Bosco, and Euclid" among many others. The "Dati metrical ver-

sion" (printed in Florence in 1493) of the Columbus letter "which first announced to Europe the results of Columbus' first voyage" is present. Other notable items include "one of the finest sets of Richard Hakluyt's *Principal Navigations* known, with splendid examples in both states of the famous Wright-Molyneaux map . . ." and "a fine set of the 'Great Voyages' of DeBry, which includes Hariot's *Virginia*," and many others.

McGregor had bought in the early 1930s William Gwinn Mather's personal library of over three hundred original editions and numerous secondary works that concentrate on Increase and Cotton as well as the minor Mathers. "Rich in materials concerning the early New England colonies, the collection throws into bold relief the essential differences between the early town life of the North and the plantation life of the South, and nicely complements the Americana."

The English literature section of the McGregor Library was the least strong among these riches, but included a good many notable items:

two Shakespeare folios and a Shakespeare quarto, a Kilmarnock Burns, an *Elegy Wrote in a Country Churchyard*, a complete first edition of all volumes of *Tristram Shandy*, many of the 19th century novels in original parts, a group of Conrad manuscripts; and, from a different point of view, such works as Adam Smith's *Wealth of Nations* and Hobbes' *Leviathan*. Many of the volumes, such as the *Great Expectations*, inscribed by the author, are of particular association interest.

McGregor had also collected letters or other writings by English literary figures, and, while most authors are represented by only a small amount of material, for a few such as Arthur Conan Doyle there is a sizable number of items. These manuscripts have been most useful both for research and in exhibits in recent years.

The year 1938 also brought to the library the extensive (approximately forty-five hundred volumes) library of Edward L. Stone, which contained many fine books "illustrative of the history of bookmaking." This important acquisition was "made possible by a grant from the Alumni Board of Trustees" of the university, a group that was often to support the library in succeeding years. Included in the collection of the Roanoke, Virginia, printer and collector were medieval manuscripts, incunabula, and materials illustrative of "the history and development of printing and of the graphic arts from the days of Gutenberg to the present. . . . The examples of fifteenth century printing number more than a hundred and include about thirty incunabula volumes. . . ." In recent years the collections of book and type designer Warren Chappell (long artist in residence at the university), of calligrapher and book designer Oscar Ogg, and of Ogham Press proprietor Willis W. Tompkins have come to the library to swell its holdings in the book arts.

Clemons notes that John Cook Wyllie undertook the herculean task, in the year after the Alderman Library was occupied, of searching the entire general collection to identify and transfer to the nascent rare-books collection those volumes that merited special handling and care. Among these were the books selected by Thomas Jefferson for the original library of the university; these had survived the 1895 fire in the Rotunda, and they remain a cornerstone of the rare-books collection today.

The year 1940 brought another endowment for the special collections with the gift of the Elizabeth Cocke Coles Fund by a bequest from Walter Derossett Coles; the income from this fund, like that of the Byrd Fund, has been used for Virginiana. These two funds continue today to provide very useful sums for the support of the acquisitions of Virginia imprints, books about Virginia, and manuscripts.

The university had acquired its first manuscripts collection in the early 1830s when the Lee family of Virginia placed a portion of its family papers in its custody. Through the nineteenth and early twentieth centuries other manuscripts, including letters by Jefferson, James Madison, James Monroe, and others, and certain university records were acquired and placed in the library. In 1930 Lester J. Cappon was appointed both as university archivist and to carry on a survey of manuscripts in the state. This effort was initiated by the mailing early that year of twenty thousand copies of a broadside which "earnestly called attention to the widespread destruction of Virginia's manuscript memorials of her past, and announced that the University of Virginia was now prepared to offer its aid in the preservation, the study, the interpretation, and the publication of the memorials of Virginia's social, industrial, political, and intellectual life." This appeal was effective, and constant travel by Cappon about the state in carrying on the survey made it possible for him to meet potential donors. The number of manuscripts began to grow, and had reached 500,000 items by the time the collections were moved down the slope from the Rotunda to the Alderman Library in 1938. Major gifts in the first year in Alderman brought the manuscripts totals to 1,155,000 items, and the numbers have gone up rapidly since, even during World War II, but especially in the decade after the end of the war, when Francis L. Berkeley, Jr., was curator of manuscripts. Again in the late 1970s and early 1980s, when the manuscripts department had the space and a full-time staff member able to travel for manuscripts acquisition, the collections flowed onto the shelves. Most of these collections were acquired in the early years either as gifts, bequests, or loans, but Clemons notes that certain benefactors such as Clifton Waller Barrett, William Andrews Clark, William Sobieski Hildreth, and Robert Coleman Taylor, among others, had either purchased manuscripts and presented them to the library, or had donated funds that enabled the library to purchase desired items. The development of the manuscripts collections chiefly through gifts has been the rule until recent years, when funds have more regularly permitted the purchase of manuscripts.

The Michael Sadlier-Robert K. Black Collection of Gothic Fiction was presented to the li-

Clifton Waller Barrett (left) and John Cook Wyllie at the dedication of the Barrett Library, 1960 (photograph by Ralph Thompson; Special Collections, University of Virginia Library)

brary in 1942 by Black, and he and Linton R. Massey later added materials to it, as has the library; the collection now numbers over one thousand titles.

> Sadlier amassed more than two hundred titles from the period 1770-1825, almost all in remarkable, unsophisticated condition. Black added other books so that the result provides an excellent survey of the genre. Present are the better-known forerunners of the "tales of terror," such as Walpole's *The Castle of Otranto* (1764) . . . , and classics such as Ann Radcliffe's *The Mysteries of Udolpho* (1794); even more impressive . . . is the complete "series of 'Northanger Novels. . . .' "

The postwar years were rich ones for the rare-book and manuscripts collections. Clifton Waller Barrett began his support of the library by donating Poe material and funds toward the acquisition of O. Henry items. Alexander Mackay-Smith generously presented part and sold the remainder of his fine music collection to the library in 1946. While music has not been an area of pri-

mary collecting, materials have been added, including papers of former music department faculty members such as Albert J. Swan, Randall Thompson, and Arthur Fickenscher. And the library holds perhaps fifteen thousand pieces of nineteenth- and twentieth-century sheet music, together with a small but useful collection of songsters, and much folk music collected by Arthur Kyle Davis, the WPA, and others.

On 26 February 1951 Linton Massey, president of the Bibliographical Society of the University of Virginia, presented a "special limited edition of *Notes on a Horse Thief* [1954], by William Faulkner," the first gift of what was to become one of its most notable collections. In succeeding years, Massey added materials to the Faulkner Collection, and in 1959 he deposited his splendid collection of Faulkner material in the library to be used in connection with the extensive archives lent by Faulkner in the landmark exhibition "Man Working," whose title was chosen by Faulkner. The 1968 catalogue of the collection, *"Man Working," 1916-1962 William Faulkner: A Catalogue of the William Faulkner Collection at the University of*

A corner of the Faulkner Room at the Alderman Library, with Faulkner's hacking jacket on the chair (Special Collections, University of Virginia Library)

Virginia, was compiled for Massey and demonstrates the vast riches of the collection: holograph or typescript drafts of *Soldiers' Pay* (1926), *Mosquitoes* (1927), *Flags in the Dust* (1974), *The Sound and the Fury* (1929), *Sanctuary* (1931), *Light in August* (1932), *Pylon* (1935), *Absalom, Absalom!* (1936), *The Wild Palms* (1939), *The Hamlet* (1940), and *The Mansion* (1959), and of more than fifty short stories, poetry, letters, drawings, and other material. After Massey's death in 1974, the library held another Faulkner exhibit to honor

Massey's contributions; the catalogue, *Man Collecting: Manuscripts and Printed Works of William Faulkner in the University of Virginia Library*, shows the growth of the Faulkner Collection in the fifteen years since the "Man Working" exhibit. Major acquisitions included title to the Faulkner archives, presented in 1970 by the William Faulkner Foundation to which Faulkner had bequeathed them at his death; the correspondence of Faulkner with Harold Ober, his literary agent; records of Faulkner's work in the People-to-People Program (see *DLB Yearbook: 1986*); a variety of letters and other materials concerning Faulkner's years at the university; Faulkner family materials from a variety of sources; and the university's newly acquired copy (one of six) of *The Marionettes* (1920).

Faulkner acquisitions have continued at the university, and important items such as the Faulkner files from Random House, screenplays from 20th Century-Fox and Metro-Goldwyn-Mayer, correspondence and other material from actress Ruth Ford, a carbon typescript of "Vision in Spring" from Mrs. Paul D. Summers, Jr., and large numbers of variant editions from the collection of Carl Petersen have been added. The most recent important item is an early unpublished draft of a portion of *Mosquitoes*, purchased in 1987.

English literature had always been important to the University of Virginia Library, and when in 1961 Tennyson scholar Edgar Finley Shannon, Jr., was appointed president of the university, friends and alumni purchased for the library the Templeton Crocker-Tennyson Collection ("containing virtually all of the poet laureate's first editions" plus letters and a few manuscripts of poems) in his honor. There it joined the Anthony Trollope Collection (a collection assembled by Michael Sadlier which includes many of Trollope's own copies of his writings) purchased by alumni in 1959. The library's collection of original and copied letters of Matthew Arnold is the basis for an edition being prepared by Professor Emeritus Cecil Y. Lang. Also available is the extensive collection of Richard Doddridge Blackmore letters begun by Professor Atcheson L. Hench and added to regularly by the library. Other notable British literature collections include the Victorius Evolution Collection, "possibly the largest [nearly five hundred volumes] gathering on the subject outside England," while gifts of Dickens's titles from William Tinker, Osa K. Lewis, and Lewis F. Kinsey have supplemented those in the McGregor Library; American editions of these works are often to be found in the Barrett Library. Recent interest in Alexander Pope has brought new volumes to the library that have been acquired through the generosity of several donors and through its own purchasing. Alumnus Arthur P. Bean, Jr., has made many gifts of material by Edith, Osbert, and Sacheverell Sitwell; the collection numbered over three hundred volumes in 1979 and has grown regularly since.

There are two major literary collections held by the library that lie outside American and British literature. One is that of Jorge Luis Borges which includes "more than a thousand individual items . . . in virtually all formats, spanning his career of sixty-five years. . . . This collection was begun in 1977, with the purchase of some 400 titles originally assembled by a long-time friend of the author, and it has grown through continued acquisitions on a title-by-title basis." Now included are every known first edition with later and variant editions, manuscripts, letters, and translations of Borges and his of Faulkner and Walt Whitman.

Douglas Huntly Gordon bequeathed to the University of Virginia at his death in 1986 his magnificent collection of 1,243 French books dating from the sixteenth to the nineteenth centuries, "arguably the most important collection of its kind in private hands" at the time of the bequest. "Over 600 [of Gordon's titles] were printed before 1600, many in bindings of the period. Almost all of the others are in elaborate morocco bindings by the finest French craftsmen of the eighteenth and nineteenth centuries."

Gordon, as a Harvard undergraduate, acquired his first book for the collection in 1923, a "first edition of the *Journal de Voyage de Michel de Montaigne*," and

> later . . . acquired all the major editions of Montaigne's *Essais* published in the author's lifetime and the works of virtually every important writer of the period: Ronsard, Du Bellay and their fellow members of the Pléiade group, Estienne Jodelle, Rémy Bellau, and Pontus de Tyard. Earlier Rhétoriqueur poets are included: Jean Molinet, Jean Marot, Jehan Meschinot, and Mellin de Saint Gelais, among hundreds more. . . . Jean Marot's son, Clément . . . is represented by several volumes . . . There are . . . contemporary poetical treatises such as Thomas Sébillet's *Art Poétique Francoys.* . . . Maurice Scève . . . is present here, as well as the *Oeuvres* (1556) of Louise Labé. . . . among Renaissance authors

> . . . are the works of Francois Rabelais . . . Marguerite de Navarra . . . the Estienne brothers, Robert and Henri. . . .

Unquestionably, the most important title in the collection is from a period later than the Renaissance. This is the magnificent thirty-six volume *Encyclopédie, ou Dictionnaire raisonné des Sciences, des Arts et des Métiers.* . . (1751-1780)—the Diderot Encyclopedia. There is a supplementary volume containing 300 proof papers with corrections, many in the hand of Denis Diderot. . . . There are other works by Diderot and a broad representation of literary culture of the Enlightenment from Montesquieu and Voltaire to l'Abbe Prévost . . . and Choderlos de Laclos. . . .

The nineteenth century is strongly represented by all the leading figures on that rich period of French literature and *fin de siècle* letters: Balzac, Victor Hugo, Alphonse Daudet, Prosper Mérimée, Maupassant, Alfred de Musset, George Sand, Théophile Gautier, Sainte Beuve, the Goncourts, Baudelaire, Anatole France, Edmond Rostand, Pierre Louys, Proust, and Pierre Loti.

The addition of the Gordon collection to the Alderman Library's holdings will provide an incomparable source of primary material. . . . Because Mr. Gordon's books are not available in editions held by . . . other American libraries, the University of Virginia can now be considered one of the most important American centers for research in French Renaissance and Enlightenment literature.

Gordon's bequest brought to the University of Virginia Library yet another imposing literary resource.

The historical collection and those of English literature, music, and others are indeed important ones, but the collections for which the University of Virginia Library is most noted today are those in American literature. The Faulkner Collection has been described, and those collections assembled by the late Clifton Waller Barrett and presented to the university in 1960 as the Clifton Waller Barrett Library of American Literature have made the library one of the preeminent centers for the study of American literature.

Beginning with his purchase in 1939 of a copy of Booth Tarkington's *Cherry* (1903), Barrett swept some 35,000 books and more than 112,000 manuscripts together with some portraits, numerous photographs, and occasional memorabilia into his American literature collection. Longtime dealer Franklin Gilliam said of Barrett in May 1991:

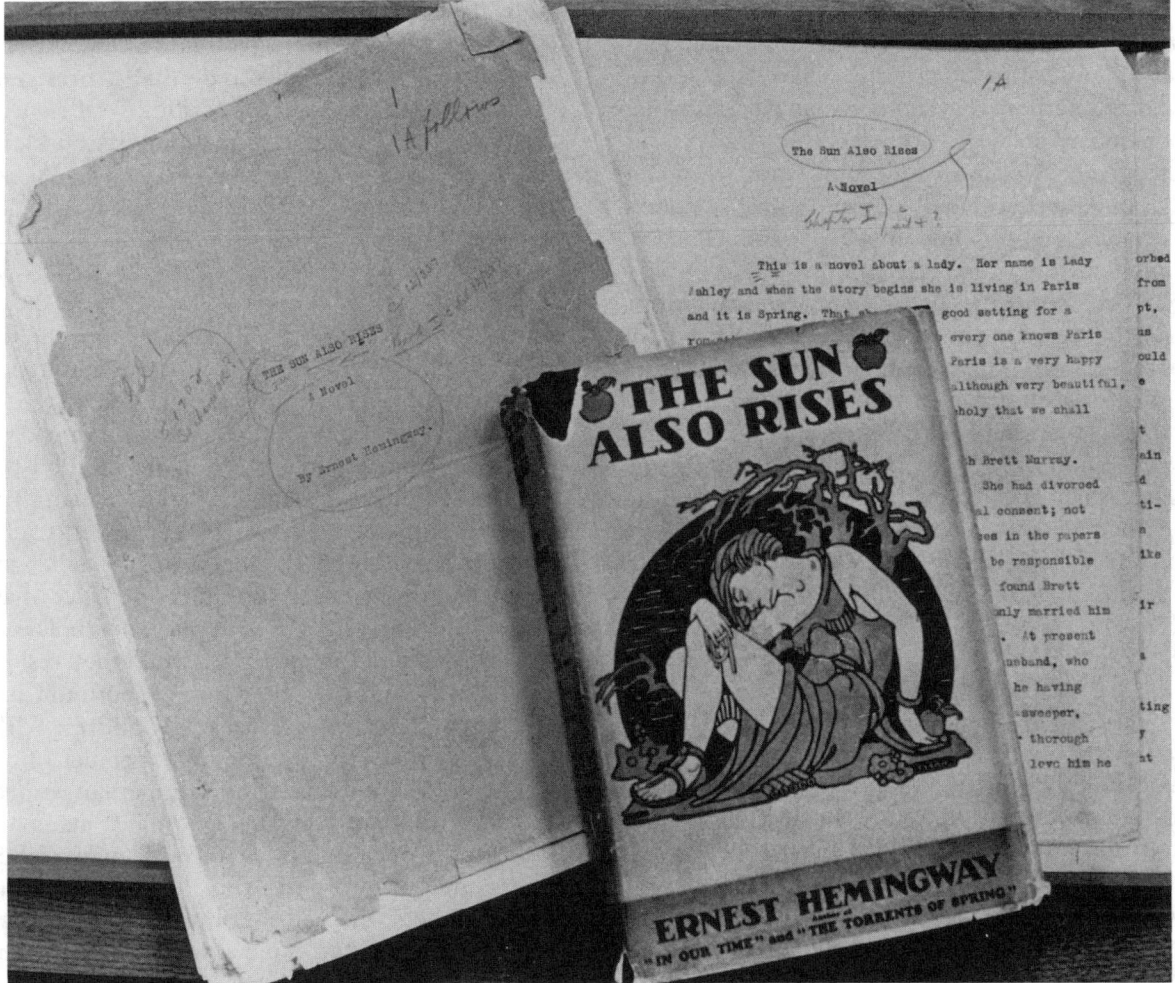

The setting copy for Ernest Hemingway's The Sun Also Rises *together with two unpublished chapters and a copy of the first edition of the novel, from the University of Virginia's American literature collections (photograph by Elizabeth Wilkerson; Special Collections, University of Virginia Library)*

He has a genuine fondness for American literature. I expect he has read a higher percentage of his books than any collector I know of. A large portion of his books have interesting inscriptions. He was quite interested in books authors gave their mothers. He enjoyed immensely pursing that side of it. So, for instance, he has a copy of *Walden* that Thoreau gave to his mother. . . . The phenomenal thing was the vision of his efforts. I know a little about what it takes to put a collection together and it is amazing what he has been able to do. It's a staggering achievement. . . . In the book collecting world his preeminence has been recognized for at least 35 years.

The plan followed by Barrett in acquiring materials has been best described by Herbert Cahoon in his remarks at the dedication of the Barrett Library in 1960:

The Clifton Waller Barrett Library takes as its province one hundred and seventy-five years of American literature, the years from 1775 to 1950. It contains, insofar as it has been possible to assemble them, all fiction, poetry, drama, and essays published by an American in book form up to and including the year 1875; for the years remaining it contains a very nearly complete collection of the works of every major American writer, as well as of those whose achievements were not of first rank but who, nevertheless, occupy a place in the literary history of the Republic. With the first editions are important later editions, many translations and periodical appearances, and a vast amount of biographical and critical material. Manuscripts and letters of quality have been brought together in such quantity that few similar collections can approach it in size and scholarly importance.

Recent surveys of the Barrett Library's holdings have revealed over eleven hundred individual author manuscripts collections. There are several hundred author collections of books for which no manuscripts were acquired. Mr. Barrett collected *all* American authors, men, women, African-American and other "ethnic" writers, prominent figures, and those who hoped to be prominent but remained obscure.

The Romantic period of American literature, the years from 1820 to 1870, may be the Barrett Library's strongest. Certainly some of its greatest treasures come from this period. The collections of authors such as Washington Irving, James Fenimore Cooper, William Cullen Bryant, Edgar Allan Poe, Henry Wadsworth Longfellow, and many others are extremely strong, and include such items as the manuscripts of *The Sketch Book* (1819-1820), *Salmagundi* (1807-1808), and others by Irving; Cooper's *Mercedes of Castile* (1841) and *The Two Admirals* (1845); and letters by Poe. Books by William Gilmore Simms, Thomas Buchanan Read, and Bayard Taylor "have virtually complete representation . . . ; for Read and Taylor the manuscripts outnumber those in any other collection and the file of letters from Simms is the largest to be found." The Longfellow collection Cahoon calls "exhaustive" because "Mr. Barrett had the good fortune and good judgment to acquire the Carroll A. Wilson collection of . . . Longfellow to combine with his own."

Barrett was especially proud that he was able to acquire the manuscript of Walt Whitman's *Leaves of Grass* (1855), a fascinating and "showy" manuscript written on pink, blue, and white papers of varying sizes. At the university's celebration of Barrett's seventieth birthday, Fredson Bowers spoke of his sight of this manuscript in September 1951 in Barrett's New York apartment where it was produced:

> perhaps with a slight puff of smoke and smell of brimstone from the next room. Mr. Barrett saw that I was rather shaken. . . . Machiavelli himself, he suggested: Suppose I sent this stuff down to Charlottesville and you look it over for me. I need a professional opinion. I don't know what's in this case—he lied with a straight face—and I'd appreciate any sorting out you could do. So I weakly said yes. . . .

Bowers's protests to Barrett that he was "a good Elizabethan type" who knew little of American literature did not sway him at all. The *Leaves of Grass* manuscript was promptly shipped to Charlottesville, where Bowers grew more and more fascinated with the textual puzzle that it presented. "I thought for a time of writing Waller what seemed to be the facts and shipping him back the red case. Then I said to myself, oh hell, I'll edit the damned thing myself. Famous last words. . . ." Barrett donated the manuscript to the library in 1954 while Bowers's edition of *Leaves of Grass* was in proof.

His method of drawing Bowers into the textual examination of this fascinating manuscript may have been unconventional, but Barrett's firm interest in scholarly use of his library was never far from his mind. He wrote in 1956 that "Since the library is made available for bona fide scholarly projects, many of the recent works relating to American literature including bibliographies, biographies and collections of letters have made use thereof." He encouraged scholars to use his books and manuscripts while they resided in New York and after they moved south to Charlottesville. Bowers added in his address, "I'm glad to say that I am not the only member of our faculty to fall from grace and Elizabethan respectability." And there were, and are, many, many others, some from this institution and many others across the country and from abroad, including large numbers who never detoured through Elizabethan texts but who came straight to the American.

There are numerous author collections from the period 1870-1910 that are very strong ones, such as that of Mark Twain, which includes hundreds of letters, important manuscripts, and "enough variants of [*Huckleberry Finn*, 1855] to satisfy any bibliographer." Bret Harte and Ambrose Bierce are here, and Cahoon called the Barrett Lafcadio Hearn collection the "finest Hearn collection ever assembled." Henry James was a particular favorite of Barrett's, and his collection is superb. The manuscript of *The Red Badge of Courage* (1895) is the centerpiece of the Stephen Crane collection and, indeed, is one of the great treasures of the Barrett Library. William Dean Howells stands with Eugene Field, Richard Harding Davis and his wife, and Jack London. And there are others, many others.

The author collections for American writers who flourished between 1910 and 1950 are often larger, particularly for manuscripts, than those for the earlier periods. The Robert Frost Collection includes "notebooks and poetical manuscripts, over forty letters mainly of the early peri-

TWILIGHT

Why am I first in thy so sad regard,
O twilight gazing from I know not
where?
I fear myself as one more than I guessed!
Am I instead of one so very fair?—
That thou art sorrowful and I oppressed?

High in the isolating air,
Over the inattentive moon,
Two birds sail on great wings,
And vanish soon.
(And they leave the north sky bare!)

The far-felt solitudes that harbor night,
Wake to the singing of the wood-bird's
fright.

By invocation, O wide silentness,
Thy spirit and my spirit pass in air!
They are unmemoried consciousness,
Nor great nor less!
And thou art here and I am everywhere!

I had two copies of Twilight printed and bound by a job printer in Lawrence Mass in 1894 probably out of pride in what Bliss Carmen and Maurice Thompson had said about the poem in it called My Butterfly. One copy I kept for myself and afterward destroyed. The other I gave away to a girl in St Lawrence University to show to her friends. It had no success and deserved none. But it unaccountably survived and has lately leaped into prominence as my first first. A few scattered lines in it are as much mine as any I was ever to write. I deliver it into your care my dear Bernheimer with the last request that you be not too fondly selfish with it, but consent to lend it once in a long long time to some important exhibition of my works as at the Jones Library in Amherst or the Baker at Dartmouth Boston February 1 1940   Robert Frost

The title poem in the only surviving copy of Robert Frost's first book and the inscription Frost wrote when he sold it to book collec-tor Earle J. Bernheimer (Barrett Library, University of Virginia Library)

od of his career, family papers, and about five hundred printed items: first editions, association copies, magazine appearances, books about, Christmas cards, and ephemera," much of this coming from the Roy Virgil Thorton collection of Frost. The files of Frost's biographer Laurence Thompson have been added. And the collection includes the only surviving copy of Frost's first book, *Twilight* (1894), of which two copies were printed. The library has published a facsimile edition of this unique book.

Barrett bought from Vachel Lindsay's widow what can only be called an archives, for it includes manuscripts, letters, papers, artwork, and other materials plus Lindsay's personal library. From descendants of Thomas Nelson Page was acquired a station wagon load of Page's papers. "Dreiser, Hemingway, Steinbeck and Faulkner may someday be considered the giants of American fiction in the first half of the twentieth century," Mr. Barrett wrote in 1956, and he continued, "These writers are represented [in the Barrett Library] in full measure. One of the latest acquisitions is the corrected manuscript of *The Grapes of Wrath* [1939]." This manuscript joined that of Hemingway's *Green Hills of Africa* (1935). In 1977 the typescript of *The Sun Also Rises* (1926), including the two unpublished chapters, was acquired by the library.

Sinclair Lewis, Marianne Moore, Ezra Pound (supplemented by the library's Harry Meacham-Pound Collection), Edna St. Vincent Millay, Thomas Wolfe, Eugene O'Neill, Katherine Anne Porter (the manuscript of *Ship of Fools*, 1962 was donated to the library), William Saroyan, and Sara Teasdale (supplemented a few years ago by a large collection acquired from a Virginia friend of her biographer, with support from the Associates of the Library), all are present.

Barrett's collecting of authors publishing after 1950 is described very well by Joan St. C. Crane, long the curator of American literature in the library:

> Mention must also be made of the contemporary and post-modern authors Mr. Barrett began collecting in the early 50s, knowing that from among them will emerge the major literary figures of the next century. The early works of most of these writers are all but unobtainable now.... Mr. Barrett had the perspicacity to buy their books at publication or before scarcity forced a dramatic escalation of prices.... Here lies a part of the wisdom of his method, which

also implies critical judgment of the direction American letters of distinction will take.... His choices bear witness to the soundness of his taste in modern literature and his eye for what will become the rarities of the future.

With Barrett's recent death, the University of Virginia and its library have lost their greatest benefactor, and the American literature collection its strong guiding force. He leaves behind the greatest assemblage of American literary materials ever brought together by an individual, and a strong tradition of encouraging the scholarly uses of these materials. This legacy poses a major challenge to the university and to the library and its faculty, both in the future collecting of material and in the encouragement of its use. Plans made by the university in honor of Barrett's ninetieth birthday—which include a professorship named for him, fellows who will be charged to use the materials in the Barrett Library, a Barrett symposium on American literature and a Barrett series in American literature to be published by the University Press of Virginia—will do much to meet this challenge.

The library's holdings include considerable American literary material that is technically not part of the Barrett Library. The Faulkner Collections have been described. From its earliest active days of collecting, the library has pursued Virginia literary groups and authors, those who have lived in Virginia, those who have been part of the university community, and those whose papers were discovered in Virginia, and has been quite successful in acquiring their papers and books. The list of these groups and writers now includes: Ann Beattie, William Stanley Braithwaite, James Branch Cabell, Erskine Caldwell, John Canaday, Virginius Dabney, John Dos Passos, Clifford Dowdey, Ellen Glasgow, Nancy Hale, Mary Johnston, Frances Parkinson Keyes, Michael Korda, Harry Meacham, Harry Edward Neal, Elizabeth Oakes-Smith, Agnes Rothery Pratt, Eudora Ramsey Richardson, Amelie Rives, Nancy Byrd Turner, the Virginia Folklore Society, and the WPA Folklore Project. These collections vary considerably in size and importance, but all contain useful source material.

The collection of John Dos Passos's papers is an extremely large one, and was begun in 1954 following the publication of *The Head and Heart of Thomas Jefferson* when Dos Passos donated the working materials for the book. The following year he presented manuscripts for *The Cho-*

sen Country (1951), *The Grand Design* (1949), and *The Prospect Before Us* (1950). Later, he served as writer in residence, and he continued his donations until his death. As Anne Freudenberg has written, Dos Passos frequently brought "stationwagon loads of manuscripts" in grocery bags which the two of them would review and mark as "'Rough Draft,' 'Second Draft,' 'Setting Copy,' and so on." Mrs. Dos Passos has lent a great deal of correspondence (including Dos Passos's correspondence with his agents, Brandt and Brandt), research notes, and other material to the library, and has generously made watercolors and other artwork available for exhibits. The collection today includes nearly all of the author's extant manuscripts as well as a modest number of books from his library, and Harold Weston's 1930 portrait. The collection has been augmented by gifts from friends of the Dos Passoses, and regularly by library purchases.

The library's literary collections have grown since 1922 chiefly by gift and bequest. It has been rare for the library to commit state funds for the purchase of manuscripts or rare books, and then only when the books or manuscripts were needed for university courses. Income from endowed funds has been available, especially for the acquisition of Virginiana. However, it was not until the founding of the Associates of the Library by Barrett in 1969 that general funds have been available. The associates established and have built an endowment fund for the special collections and have acted as a channel for contributions to these collections.

Most important for the development of the literary collections was the generous bequest from Robert B. and Virginia L. Tunstall that established in 1988 an unrestricted general acquisitions fund for the special collections department. The department uses part of the Tunstall income each year to acquire British literature. And finepress books, which also interested the Tunstalls (and for which there are no other funds), are now purchased. The department generally reserves the income from the Tunstall Fund for important acquisitions for which regular funds are unavailable.

Space has not permitted description of many of the library's other special collections, such as the Scott Collection of Sporting Books, the Taylor Collection of American Best Sellers, the libraries from "Elmwood" and from "Sabine Hall," the Franz Kafka Collection, the Izaak Walton Collection, the Hertz Collection of Classics,

the Streeter Railroad Collection, the Armed Services Editions Collection, the Great War Collection, the Barnard Shipp Collection of Voyages and Travels, and the Wilbur Cortez Abbot Collection of 17th Century English History and Literature. Space also does not permit any description of other literary collections at the university, those held by the archives of the Law School Library and by the Historical Collections and Services Section of the Health Sciences Library; both administer manuscripts, archives, and rare books in their academic areas.

Publications began in 1931 with the first of a twenty-year series, the *Annual Report of the Archivist University of Virginia Library*. The manuscripts department published its *News Notes* for many years. It was replaced with a biyearly publication, *Gatherings & Offerings*, in 1989, after the formation of the special collections department. Since the establishment of the associates, the group has sponsored ten issues of *Chapter & Verse*, the most recent appearing in May 1991. Numerous publications have appeared under the imprint of the McGregor Library, including *Dunmore's Proclamation of Emancipation* (1941), *Memoirs of a Monticello Slave* (1951), *Richard Oswald's Memorandum On the Folly of Invading Virginia . . .* (1953), and *A Brief Description of The Province of Carolina . . .* (1966); the most recent (1988) of these is *A Calendar of the Headquarters Papers of Brigadier-General John Forbes Relating to the Expedition Against Fort Duquesne in 1758*. In 1950 the library published *The Jefferson Papers of the University of Virginia*; this volume was reprinted in 1973 with a supplement. In the area of literature there have been such volumes as *The Tennyson Collections Presented to the University of Virginia in Honor of Edgar Finley Shannon, Jr.* (1961), *Robert Frost: A Descriptive Catalogue of Books and Manuscripts in the Clifton Waller Barrett Library University of Virginia* (1974), and *Carl Sandburg, Philip Green Wright, and the Asgard Press, 1900-1910: A Descriptive Catalogue of Early Books, Manuscripts, and Letters in the Clifton Waller Barrett Library* (1975). Exhibits have usually meant at least a keepsake, and often the publications, as those noted above for the Faulkner exhibits, have been quite substantial. A typical title from the substantial catalogues is *The American Writer in England: An Exhibition Arranged in Honor of the Sesquicentennial of the University of Virginia* (1969), while keepsakes may be represented by the last in the current series, *From Palm to Pine: Rudyard Kipling, 1865-1936* (1990).

The Bibliographical Society of the University of Virginia, founded in 1947, has been a distinguished supporter of bibliographical scholarship. It published the first volume of its distinguished annual *Studies in Bibliography* in 1948. The late Fredson Bowers edited every edition, including that for 1992. He will be succeeded as the Society's editor by David L. Vander Meulen, who has been the associate editor for several years. The Society has published many monographs, with the late John Cook Wyllie as its editor until his untimely death in 1968. Publications are now handled by the University Press of Virginia, and a list of those currently available appears in each issue of *Studies*. Some titles selected from the list of currently available publications give an idea of the Society's broad interests: Roger P. Bristol, *Supplement to Evans' American Bibliography* (1971); bibliographies by Stuart T. Wright and James L. West, III, including those for Randall Jarrell (1986), Reynolds Price (1986), and Peter Taylor (1988); G. Thomas Tanselle, *Textual Criticism and Scholarly Editing* (1990); David L. Vander Meulen, *Pope's Dunciad of 1728: A History and Facsimile* (1991); and Donald K. Fry, *Beowulf and The Fight at Finnsburgh: A Bibliography* (1969). Under the direction of its constitution, which states that the Society is "to foster an interest in books (including books in manuscript), maps, printing, and bibliography," the Society sponsors every other year a contest for student book collectors at the university. Led today by Irby Cauthen, president,

Kendon L. Stubbs, vice-president, and Ray W. Frantz, Jr., secretary-treasurer, the Society sustains the bibliographical tradition of the university.

Major problems face the rare-books and manuscripts collections. The stacks areas are entirely full, and were reported at 105 percent and 115 percent of capacity in a recent administrative report; this is possible only because materials are stored in the basement of the wing of Alderman, and in a student dormitory attic. Shelving has been erected in the department's Stettinius Exhibition Gallery, and consideration of whether to store new acquisitions in the Taylor Room or the south end of the McGregor Room is now under way.

Hope lies in the construction of a special collections library, a dream wafted about the university at least since the late 1960s. This building is expected to be one of the major goals for the university's next fund-raising campaign, scheduled to begin in 1993, in the 250th anniversary of Thomas Jefferson's birth. With a university president who worked in the departments as a student assistant while he was in graduate school, and who is a strong supporter of the programs of the special collections department, this dream may become a reality and provide a fitting home for the university's wonderful literary collections.

The Takarazuka Revue Company

Mary Scott Dye

An operatic version of F. Scott Fitzgerald's *The Great Gatsby* is the latest production of the Takarazuka Revue Company, a Japanese cultural institution that has enjoyed respect and prestige since its founding over seventy-five years ago in Takarazuka, Japan. This unique repertory company has built its international reputation by drawing upon the resources of Western literature and drama and adapting world classics to its operatic requirements. Though little known by Westerners, the company has become immensely popular in Japan by combining the most successful elements of traditional and modern opera with the drama of Eastern and Western plays.

One of the most notable aspects of the Takarazuka company is its cast. Comprised solely of unmarried women who are all graduates of the Takarazuka Music School, the company is divided into four troupes that alternately rehearse and perform in several different locations throughout the year. Each troupe has approximately seventy-five members. In addition to the Grand Theatre in Takarazuka City (about fifteen miles northwest of Osaka), the company operates a smaller theater in Tokyo. The company also regularly takes its revues on foreign tours. The adaptations of Western literature and drama are performed only in Japan.

The Takarazuka theater company was founded in 1914 by Ichizo Kobayashi, a well-educated entrepreneur who appreciated the arts as much as he excelled in business. His motivations for establishing the company were twofold: as president of the then-fledgling Hankyu Railways (now one of Japan's largest transportation networks), he hoped to increase traffic on the railroad line running between the large city of Osaka and the smaller town of Takarazuka. In addition, Kobayashi wanted to revitalize the classical Japanese Kabuki theater by incorporating modern dramatic elements. With both concerns in mind, he developed a recreation center in Takarazuka hoping to boost interest in his railroad and the theater. Live entertainment was added with the debut of the Takarazuka Choir's first play in spring 1914 at the Paradise Theater. The company presented popular folk and fairy tales in operetta form since the theater performances were originally intended for a juvenile audience.

The Takarazuka Music School (Takarazuka Ongaku Gakko) had been founded almost a year earlier on 15 July 1913 to train the "Takarasienne" for the stage. The first class consisted of sixteen students ranging in age from twelve to fifteen. Kobayashi became the school principal and established a high code of morality by selecting as school mottos: "Purity, Honesty, Beauty" and "One Highly Developed Art Form After Another." (Kobayashi served as principal—except for the decade from 1940 to 1950—until his death in 1957.)

The school required one year of study as a junior student and one year as a senior student. Discipline was strict to encourage proper artistic development. Junior students were expected to perform housecleaning chores at the school in addition to attending classes in music, dance, and acting. They were also taught to play musical instruments.

While in school, students were trained to perform either male (*otokoyaku*) or female (*musumeyaku*) roles upon graduation to the company, depending upon their interests, voice range, physical mannerisms, and size. Male roles were considered more prestigious although more intensive practice was required to perfect them. Once an actress established herself as an *otokoyaku* (a female playing a male), she rarely changed sex roles during her career.

As the music school's reputation grew, competition for admission increased. Today, applicants must be between the ages of fifteen and eighteen and must be graduates of junior or senior high school or be students in senior high school. Approximately forty girls per year (of up to one thousand applicants) are enrolled in the music school after completing a rigorous entrance examination that includes vocal and ballet tests and three interviews with school officials.

A scene from the Takarazuka Revue Company production of an adaptation of F. Scott Fitzgerald's The Great Gatsby

There are a total of forty-four staff members, thirty-eight of them teachers.

By 1921 the number of performers in the Takarazuka company (Takarazuka Kageki Dan) had increased, and the number of annual productions had doubled to eight, thus creating the need to divide into troupes. Upon entering a troupe performers are given stage names and nicknames by which they are known throughout their careers. The new graduates are still considered students, and a difficult regimen of training and practice continues. Each troupe has a star performer in male and female roles.

The first two troupes—named Moon and Flower—each prepared four shows a year. In 1924 the Takarazuka Grand Theatre was completed with a seating capacity of four hundred (it has since burned down and been reconstructed twice). A smaller Takarazuka theater, Bow Hall, is also regularly used. Eventually twelve productions per year were presented, so a third troupe (Snow) was added. The fourth and final troupe (Star) was created in 1933, one year before the opening of the Takarazuka Theatre in Toyko.

The music school and the theater became separate entities in 1939. As the company became better known and its performers matured, the types of plays changed to reflect the interests of an older audience. The typical Takarazuka audience had consisted primarily of women under the age of twenty-five. In accordance with Japanese tradition, the actresses who enter the school (and eventually the company) must retire from the company if they wish to marry. They are said to have "graduated" from the company. Some leave to pursue other acting careers, and many "Takarasienne" go on to professional careers in

television, in film, and on the stage. Others choose to make the Takarazuka company their career; some have remained active members for as long as forty years.

In the late 1930s Takarazuka began touring internationally. The company had expanded its repertoire to include lavish revues typical of the French, contemporary shows associated with Americans, and romances from either Western (Grand Romance) or Japanese historical (*ocho roman*) sources. There have been four mainland America tours between 1939 and 1989, all revues. A traditional dance known as *buyoshi* was also regularly performed. Takarazuka performances usually consist of the company's current musical (running about one and a half hours) followed by a revue or show (running about another hour). The musical is a fully plotted play, whereas the revues consist primarily of popular Japanese or Western show tunes. The high production values of a Takarazuka performance—including sets, staging, costumes, choreography, lyrics, orchestration, scenery, and lighting—have solidified the company's formidable reputation.

The first Takarazuka production based on a Western source—*Androcles and the Lion*—was presented during the company's third year. This production was followed by operettas about Joan of Arc, Christopher Columbus, and Cleopatra. Musicals featuring Hansel and Gretel, Cain and Abel, Jack and the Beanstalk, and even Santa Claus were also part of the early fare. By the late 1920s the French revue had become a favorite. In addition, adaptations of the operas Georges Bizet's *Carmen* (1875), Richard Strauss's *Elektra* (1909), and Giuseppe Verdi's *La traviata* (1853) were staged. As the company became more versatile,

A scene from the Takarazuka Revue Company production of an adaptation of Leo Tolstoy's War and Peace

Shakespeare was frequently presented, and many of his plays—including *Romeo and Juliet*, *Hamlet*, *Twelfth Night*, and *A Midsummer Night's Dream*—received multiple adaptations by the company. With the exception of Broadway musicals, adaptations from other sources feature original Japanese lyrics and music.

The company produced its first American musical in 1967 with a direct translation of *Oklahoma! West Side Story* followed a year later, and *Carousel* was presented next. Encouraged by the audience's reaction to this genre, Takarazuka produced *Brigadoon*, *The Apple Tree*, *South Pacific*, *Guys and Dolls*, and a second version of *Oklahoma!*, all in Japanese. Musicals from the London stage such as *Me and My Girl* were also warmly received.

Eventually Takarazuka was selecting Western material—primarily based on popular literature—for more than a quarter of its productions. American and European novels with romantic, idealized characters such as those found in *Don Quixote de la Mancha*, *The Scarlet Pimpernel*, *The Count of Monte Cristo*, and *Little Women* were all adapted by the company. Others included *Les Miserables*, *The Three Musketeers*, and *A Tale of Two Cities*. Modern American classics including Margaret Mitchell's *Gone With the Wind* and Ernest

Hemingway's *For Whom the Bell Tolls* have been well received, with *Gone With the Wind* enjoying five runs between 1977 and 1984.

The all-time favorite in the history of the company was its production of Ikeda Riyoko's *The Rose of Versailles*, which had five runs between 1974 and 1976 and a total audience of nearly one and a half million. *The Rose of Versailles* was well suited for the Takarazuka stage because its plot—set among the French aristocracy in the late eighteenth century—featured a female character who had been raised as a male. A strong Western idiom ran through the songs, solo and ensemble, as well as through the background music. The composer created a European pop feel (not rock or jazz, but closer to ballads and torch songs). The score was often centered in the minor mode and was highly chromatic, causing a slight Spanish flavor at times that may have seemed "off" to Western ears, given the plot, but it was also an effective mechanism for communicating the deceptions and intrigues of the court. The orchestration was fairly conventional (much like a Broadway musical) and communicated well, never distracting from the stage, even though harmonically the strings were thickly scored and the woodwinds were fairly independent and lively at times. The sets, while not cluttered with ornamentation, managed to capture effectively the opulence of Versailles, with clever use of large spaces and well-delineated areas.

The most recent production and current success is the Takarazuka company's adaptation of *The Great Gatsby*. The script was written and directed by Shuichiro Koike, with original lyrics and music by Kenji Yoshizaki and Masato Kai. Keaki Mori, the actress who portrayed Jay Gatsby, had previously portrayed Rhett Butler in the company's production of *Gone With the Wind*. Americans who saw *The Great Gatsby* considered it faithful to the content and spirit of the novel. Certain adjustments were required, however, to satisfy Japanese expectations. For example, Daisy Bu-

chanan (played by Yuki Ayu) was portrayed as a devoted mother in order to be acceptable to the Japanese audience. Although the company has increasingly drawn from the literature and drama of the West, revisions are necessary to ensure a melding of Oriental and Western cultures.

"Takarazuka is neither a reproduction of the Western opera nor of classical Japanese drama," said Haruhiko Saka, president of the company. "It is a completely new type of stage play which combines the two in harmonious fashion. . . . Guided by our motto of 'modesty, fairness and grace,' and supported by the Hankyu Corporation, we have continued to make history as the first revue company in Japan."

An Interview with James Ellroy

James Ellroy was interviewed by telephone on 27 January 1992 at his home, where he is revising *White Jazz*, the final volume in his L.A. Quartet. This interview was conducted by Richard Layman.

DLB: If my calculations are correct, as of the end of 1991 you've been a professional writer for ten years, during which you have produced ten published books and have gone from demanding four-figure to seven-figure advances. That's a pretty good ride.

ELLROY: Actually, I've been writing since January of 1979, so that's thirteen years. And the seven-figure advance is for three books. I pay a lot of taxes. I got married and divorced, and that's costly—but what the fuck. It's not bad.

DLB: How did it happen? How did you develop your career so surely?

ELLROY: I wrote the books that I wanted to. I addressed the craft with all the humility and

arrogance that I was capable of—that combination of thinking you're the greatest thing that ever walked and at the same time trying to be better, better, better, better, better. I think all good writers go through a period where they think their shit doesn't stink, and then they grow up a little bit. And, of course, I always wanted to be able to write more than one kind of book. I experimented—and I wrote larger and larger books. It was very satisfying to me to broaden the scope of my work.

DLB: You said you wanted to write more than one kind of book. What did you mean?

ELLROY: I've written books in the first person and in the third person. I've written crime novels set in contemporary times and crime novels set in historical periods. *White Jazz* (forthcoming, fall 1992), my most recent book, is quite stylistically advanced and difficult, so stylized that I had to tone it down a bit to thwart potential reader confusion.

James Ellroy (photograph by Michel Delsol)

DLB: But the point of style of *White Jazz* is concision—diarylike telegraphic language.

ELLROY: That's true. A lot of people couldn't follow the action, though, and I think I took it too far. The style is still there; it's still extremely concise and telegraphic, but not quite so difficult.

DLB: You said you wrote the books you wanted to write. What did you mean?

ELLROY: I didn't get hooked into a series character for the rest of my life.

DLB: Did you have a vision of what you wanted to achieve in your work from the beginning?

ELLROY: Yes. *Brown's Requiem* (1981), my first novel, was a first-person private-eye book. It's the most anecdotal and autobiographical

of my books and the most influenced by previous crime writers. My second book, *Clandestine* (1982), was set in 1951—because I wanted to write about the Red Scare era and wanted to base a plot partially on my mother's murder. Then I wrote a book called *L.A. Death Trip*, which was ultimately edited down into *Blood on the Moon* (1984)—and that initial draft was totally insane and undisciplined. It was turned down by seventeen publishers. In the original version of *Blood on the Moon* the killer and the detective blow up the Silverlake Reservoir and burn L.A. to the ground. I was younger then.

DLB: Do you think you would have been a writer if you had had a normal childhood?

ELLROY: I think it's almost impossible to answer questions like that. I can't see myself having done anything else under any different set of circumstances. The idea of doing anything else is so appalling to me.

DLB: It seems that your mother's death has been a driving force, if not a central focus, for several of your books, certainly *Clandestine* and *The Black Dahlia* (1987).

ELLROY: Yes, that's very true. It gave me a tremendous curiosity early on: I wanted to know *why*. It was an unsolved crime, and of course it left many unanswered questions in my mind. I wanted to understand the genealogies of violence, and I think my writing crime novels is a symbolic reworking of that event.

DLB: Do you understand it better now?

ELLROY: Yes. Of course, questions remain, and now I have adopted a more historical focus, because I want to be able to understand the crime of American history. That's what I'm doing now that the L.A. Quartet is completed— I'm re-creating America in the twentieth century through crime novels.

DLB: What do you mean by the crime of American history?

ELLROY: I want to put together historical genealogies and flesh them out with fictional details, so that I can re-create American history to my own specifications. Even if my reworkings are historically inaccurate, they will work on the level

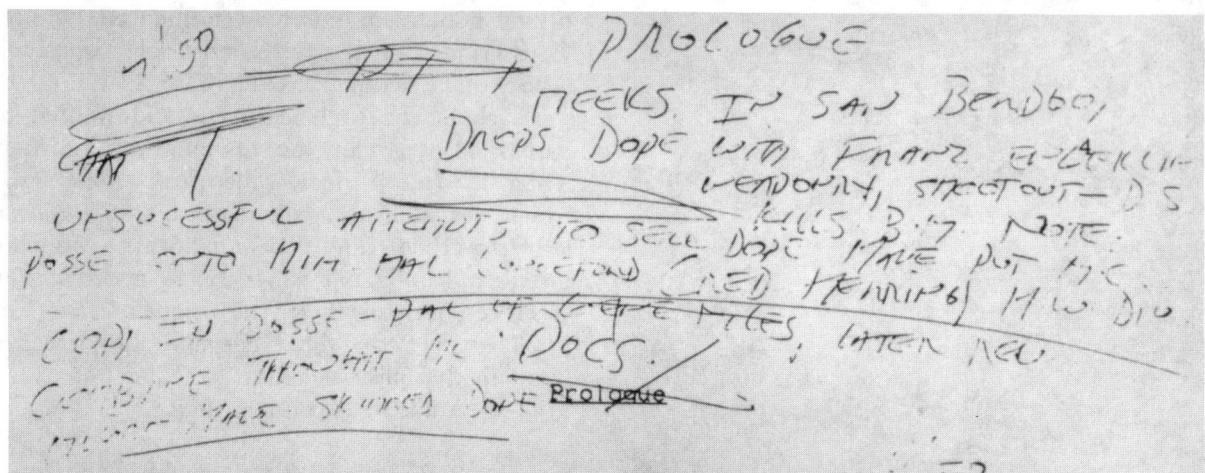

A set of confidential LAPD memos, dated ~~11/49~~.

William H. Parker, Deputy Chief and boss of the Patrol Bureau,

is gearing up for a mid-1950 run at Chief of Police - the City

Council is putting the job up for grabs in the wake of a series

of scandals and charges of ineptitude aimed at the current Chief

- William Worton. Parker assumes his number one rival will be

Deputy Chief Thad Green, LAPD's Chief of Detectives; he has

requested Intelligence Division, run by his pal Captain James

Hamilton, to glom him dirt dossiers on the Detective Division's

strong and weak points - the strengths and foibles of key men -

along with selected officers working Patrol and various

administrative assignments. Among the dossiers are:

1. Wendell "Bud" White - age 31, ~~Sergeant~~, working

the Central Station Detective squad. White is a feared

strongarm cop; is considered the toughest man in the LAPD;

excessive force complaints dot his record - the complaintants

arrested assault and battery perpetrators. As a child, White

witnessed his father beat his mother to death; his partner,

Officer Dick Stensland, is also volatile, drinks on duty and is

Pages from the typescript outline and the manuscript for Ellroy's L.A. Confidential *(Layman Collection; by permission of James Ellroy)*

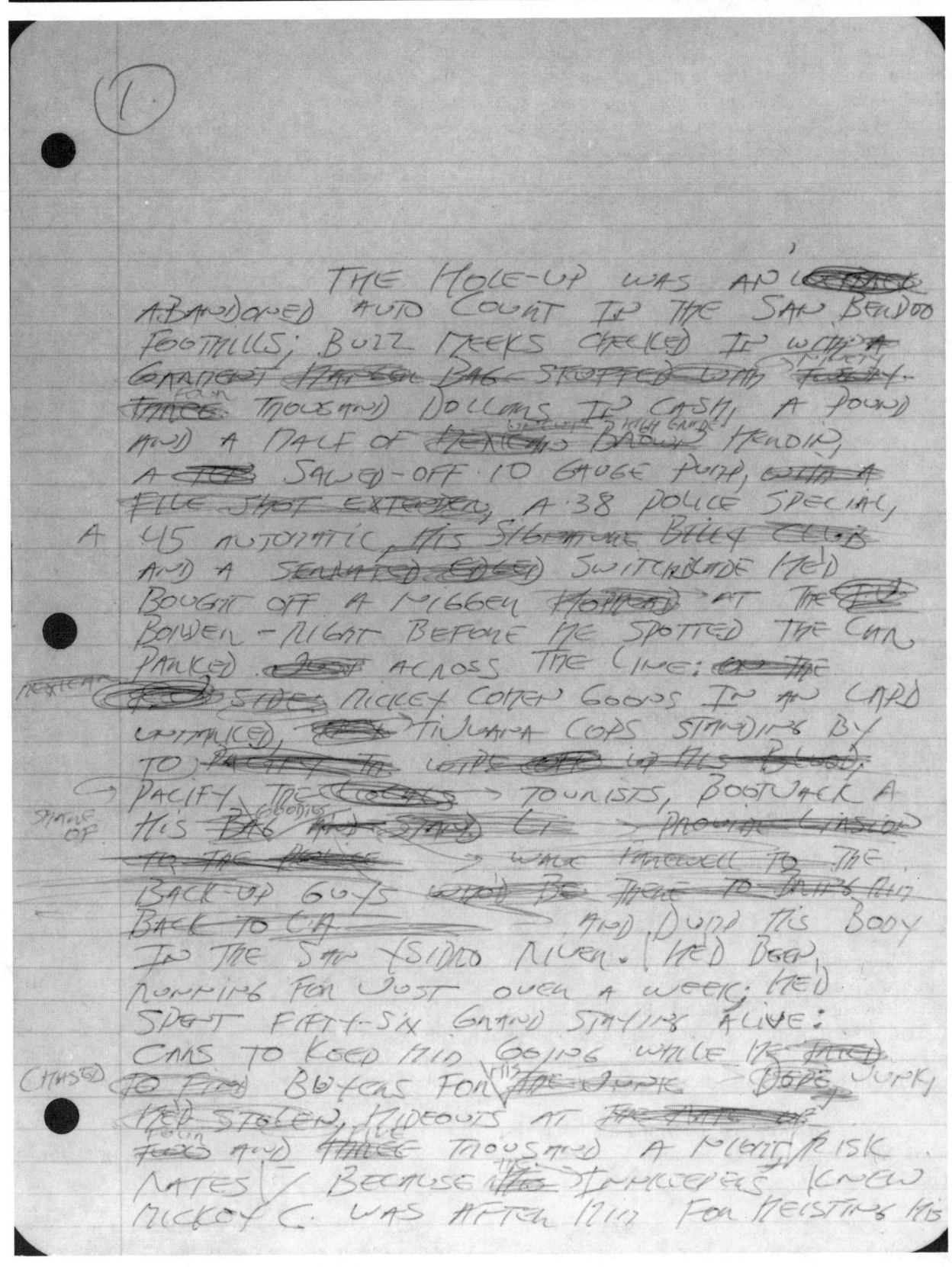

THE HOLE-UP WAS AN [strikethrough] ABANDONED AUTO COURT IN THE SAN BERDOO FOOTHILLS; BUZZ MEEKS CHECKED IN WITH A [strikethrough] BAG STUFFED WITH [strikethrough] THOUSAND DOLLARS IN CASH, A POUND AND A HALF OF [strikethrough] HEROIN, A [strikethrough] SAWED-OFF 10 GAUGE PUMP, [strikethrough] [strikethrough] A .38 POLICE SPECIAL, A .45 AUTOMATIC, [strikethrough] AND A [strikethrough] SWITCHBLADE HE'D BOUGHT OFF A NIGGER [strikethrough] AT THE [strikethrough] BORDER — RIGHT BEFORE HE SPOTTED THE CAR PARKED [strikethrough] ACROSS THE LINE; [strikethrough] MICKEY COHEN GOONS IN AN LAPD UNMARKED, [strikethrough] TIJUANA COPS STANDING BY TO [strikethrough] PACIFY THE [strikethrough] TOURISTS, BOOTJACK A [strikethrough] HIS [strikethrough] &[strikethrough] WAVE FAREWELL TO THE BACK-UP GUYS [strikethrough] AND DUMP HIS BODY IN THE SAN YSIDRO RIVER. HE'D BEEN RUNNING FOR JUST OVER A WEEK; HE'D SPENT FIFTY-SIX GRAND STAYING ALIVE: CARS TO KEEP HIM GOING WHILE HE [strikethrough] [strikethrough] BUYERS FOR HIS [strikethrough] DOPE JUNKY HE'D STOLEN, HIDEOUTS AT [strikethrough] [strikethrough] AND [strikethrough] THOUSAND A NIGHT, RISK RATES, BECAUSE THE INNKEEPERS KNEW MICKEY C. WAS AFTER HIM FOR HEISTING HIS of verisimilitude. The book I'm writing now— "American Tabloid"—is a fact-faction recounting of the underbelly of the Kennedy assassination. I'm fleshing out details on the assassination and related events right now—and I'm stepping into areas that other novelists haven't touched.

DLB: Why the Kennedy assassination?

ELLROY: Because in 1988 I read [Don DeLillo's] *Libra* . . .

DLB: Was *Libra* the beginning of your fascination with Kennedy's death?

ELLROY: Absolutely. I think it's a very great book—probably the book that's most influenced me in the past twenty years. The details in that book are so brilliantly worked out. DeLillo's telling of the story was so plausible and emotionally potent that I went out and read a lot of the Kennedy assassination quasi-fact theory books just on reflex. I noted that DeLillo utilized only the most interesting real-life characters, only the most potent historical events, only the most intelligent theories—and mingled them quite deftly. I refuse to play on his turf, and I suspect that his telling of the story is something approaching the literal truth. So I'm rising to the challenge of telling an overtold tale in a different fashion, with different characters and a different historical perspective—one that I think is historically and psychologically valid in its own right.

DLB: Do you have any comment on the Oliver Stone movie?

ELLROY: Yes—it's brilliantly snappy and well done and fatuous beyond words. He's got some stuff involving the conspirators that's wonderfully concise and droll and satirical. The Jim Garrison stuff is preposterous, and I think his overall thesis is crazy. Frankly, Stone made me root for the conspirators: they had panache.

DLB: Your approach to writing a book is remarkable. Would you go through the steps you take in developing an idea into a novel?

ELLROY: I start with basic ideas as to milieu, characterization, and plot and incident—call them initial notes. I then develop about forty dramatic incidents and start linking them, and before you know it the story begins fleshing itself

out. Logically, when you're dealing with narratives centered around homicide investigations as the books that I've written so far have been, there is a train of logic that needs to be followed, and I simply follow it as interestingly as possible. Concurrent with that I detail the personal lives of my characters: punchy and traumatic stuff. I then write very long and detailed outlines—with key motivational and investigatory information underlined. For example, the outline for *The Black Dahlia* was 142 pages; the outline for *The Big Nowhere* (1988), 155; the outline for *L.A. Confidential* (1990), 211; and the outline for *White Jazz*, 164. My agent, Nat Sobel—who's been my primary editor on the last four books—and I go over the outlines and fight a bit. He says, "No, don't do it this way," and I say, "No, you're crazy. I have to do it this way." He gives in and I give in, and the result—working with an editor this profoundly good—is that you've got the best story superstructure possible. Then I write the book, based on the outline with an improvisation factor of perhaps 15 percent worked in.

DLB: How did you come upon that method of composition?

ELLROY: It came to me instinctively—and I followed through haphazardly on my first several books. Then, because of the emotional import of writing *The Black Dahlia*—I had been obsessed with the actual case since I learned of it in 1959, six months after my mother's death, and was mildly daunted by the notion of writing the book—I wanted a particularly detailed outline to work from. I also wanted to develop a more complex plot than the ones that had driven my previous books. So, I wrote my first tremendously detailed outline, and it was such a spreading of the wings for me that I continued the process— upping the scope ante on *The Big Nowhere* and *L.A. Confidential*—certainly my most complexly plotted book. Basically, the outline process has become more and more essential to me.

DLB: What's the gestation period for a novel for you?

ELLROY: A few years. I've known that I was going to write the Kennedy book for about two and a half years now. Ideas for my next book work themselves out in my mind during the actual writing of the book that I'm on at the moment. It's a continuing narrative force always building inside me.

DLB: Do you bother to compare yourself to the competition?

ELLROY: Yes.

DLB: What's the basis of the comparison? I assume you don't compare yourself to the procedural detective novelists, although police procedure is central to your books; not to the so-called new hard-boiled writers, although your novels are clearly an extension of the hard-boiled tradition; not to horror writers, although there are certainly elements of horror and the grotesque in your work; not to the psychological thriller writers, such as Thomas Harris, although mental aberrations and dark obsessions mark your most memorable characters.

ELLROY: Comparisons get you nowhere. Masturbation gets you nowhere, but it's enjoyable. I practice both acts with approximately the same results: they feel good at the moment, then leave you yawning and perhaps ready to get back to writing fiction.

DLB: But a purpose of such comparisons is to identify the basis of your appeal so you can take advantage of it. You seem to have a firm sense of what readers like about your work.

ELLROY: What I work from emotionally is a powerful sense of awe at the potential for the crime novel form, and a concurrent sense that it has been largely untapped. What I work from is a desire to push the envelope, an arrogant desire to go too far mitigated now by a desire to learn to control my effects and address the craft with some humility. This sense of awe has steadily increased throughout the years. It's especially potent now that I'm published by Knopf—the publication of my first Knopf book is coming up. Being published by Knopf and being edited by the boss there is a fucking big thrill for me. I get a fucking boner from going into the Random House building and taking the elevator up to the twenty-first floor. It all feeds back into some emotional sense that crime fiction is a profoundly important populist voice, and that I can be a major voice within that collective voice. I feed on that. It helps me to focus. I have very few outside interests. This sense of awe that I work from continu-

ally prods me to look at the craft, look at the craft, look at the craft, analyze it and reach for that which is most intense and most horrifying inside me and around me.

DLB: In a time of politically correct thinking, hypersensitivity to anything that could possibly be construed as offensive by any party, your books stand out. Your characters are unabashed racists and sexists who delight in offending others. To what extent are your characters calculated to be offensive?

ELLROY: The extent is history. I write historical books. I attempt to show people involved in violent webs of intrigue who might realistically be expected to be involved in them: psychologically flawed people with bad character traits caught up in bad situations during historical times when political correctness didn't exist.

DLB: How do you respond to readers who are offended by such characters?

ELLROY: My response is twofold: either up your threshold for aberrant behavior or limit yourself to crime novels with traditionally sympathetic protagonists.

DLB: How do you respond to the people— some of them I think have been editors whom you respected—who have reacted against the grotesque elements in your books . . . the horrible violent perversions in a category beyond violence.

ELLROY: There are people—critics, editors, scholars—who think I've gone too far, and my response is: look at the horror of twentieth-century America and our continuing fascination with it. Address the issue chronologically, and you'll see that I was well ahead of the serial killer bandwagon that everybody and his brother and sister have jumped on subsequently. I wrote *Killer on the Road* (1986), also known as *Silent Terror*, back in 1984. It was a character study of the serial killer, and there have been six trillion serial killer books published since then—mostly bad and indifferent.

DLB: How have the movies treated you?

ELLROY: Kindly—lots of option money. I've had one book adapted into a film and options on most of them. It's money for nothing.

DLB: Money aside, do you have any feeling about whether you'd like to see a book made into a movie?

ELLROY: Money aside, I don't care.

DLB: How about stories? In the days of *New Black Mask* you wrote some pretty good stories.

ELLROY: They're funny, I think. I look back at them and see that they're funny and buffoonish, but I've never really found a voice as a short-story writer.

DLB: How much reworking and editing did Sonny Mehta request for *White Jazz*?

ELLROY: A good deal. I met Sonny at his pad two weeks ago to do the edit so we could get the book out in the early fall. He said that the only problem was that a couple of readers at Knopf found the style so difficult that they had a hard time following the story—something I'd heard from other people. Sonny showed me a bunch of query tags; I said, "Let me edit the book from scratch, add in words, retain the flavor of the style, but make it easier on readers," and he agreed. I think he was absolutely right, but this putting words back, taking words out—it's stupefying work.

DLB: How many interviews do you do a year?

ELLROY: At least a hundred.

DLB: Do you find them distracting?

ELLROY: Individually, no. What's distracting is going over to Europe and doing twelve or fourteen in a day. The challenge is to say something new and interesting.

DLB: That seems almost impossible with a hundred interviews, assuming that these hundred interviewers are asking you the same questions.

ELLROY: Very often they do, but, of course, you forget what people say.

DLB: The Kennedy book next. Do you know beyond that?

ELLROY: I want to write a book about the Wisconsin state police—two generations of cops, two generations of killers—a big, broad, state-police novel.

DLB: So, you're moving out of Los Angeles.

ELLROY: I'm moving out of L.A. I want to go to Wisconsin and bop around, see what I come up with and write a huge book out of it. Sooner or later I'd like to do a book about Huey Long, and a gangster novel—a book about the Jewish mobsters.

Center for Bibliographical Studies and Research at the University of California, Riverside

Charles L. Egleston

University of California, Riverside

In her 1990 announcement of the establishment of the Center for Bibliographical Studies and Research, Chancellor Rosemary S. J. Schraer of the University of California, Riverside, said, "the new center will enable the creation of extensive bibliographies worldwide and serve as an international focus of bibliographical scholarship." The director of the center is Henry L. Snyder, a historian specializing in eighteenth-century British political history. Two core projects, in existence at the university before the center was created, have been sponsored by it from its inception: the Eighteenth-Century Short Title Catalogue for North America (ESTC/NA, also directed by Snyder) and the Eaton Program in Science Fiction and Fantasy, whose director is George E. Slusser, a professor of comparative literature.

The ESTC/NA is a bibliography and union catalogue of materials printed in England and its dependencies, from 1701 through 1800, and draws together records created in three editorial centers: the British Library, the American Antiquarian Society, and ESTC/NA. In the first phase of the project, initiated in 1976, the British Library created the base file of the ESTC by recataloguing its own eighteenth-century English holdings in machine-readable form. Subsequently, it took responsibility for adding the holdings reported by British and European libraries to the base file. The American Antiquarian Society, through its North American Imprints Program (NAIP), revised in machine-readable form, and expanded, the relevant printed bibliographies for America (Charles Evans's *American Bibliography* [1903]) and Canada (Marie Tremaine's *A Bibliography of Canadian Imprints, 1751-1800* [1952]) and is responsible for cataloguing North American imprints from 1701 through 1800.

The North American editorial center for the ESTC, since 1990 a part of the Center for Bibliographical Studies and Research (CBSR), is responsible for entering records of eighteenth-century British imprints, or eighteenth-century items printed anywhere else in the world in the English language, held in North American libraries. As of April 1992 the ESTC data base held more than 355,000 separate bibliographic records. (A separate record is created for every edition or issue of a work.) Over one million individual copies, as reported by more than one thousand libraries worldwide have been matched to these records. More are added every day. ESTC is available on-line in North America through the Research Libraries Information Network (RLIN), a national computer network managed by the Research Libraries Group (RLG). Individuals can establish search accounts with RLIN through Internet or Telenet, two national communications networks available to many academic institutions. For scholars interested in other forms of access there is a microfiche edition of the ESTC (current to mid 1990) available from British Library Publications. As of December 1991 a CD-ROM version is in preparation.

ESTC is a union catalogue as well as a national bibliography. That is, it includes location information for individual copies. Like A. W. Pollard and G. R. Redgrave's *A Short-Title Catalogue of Books Printed in England, Scotland, & Ireland; and of English Books Printed Abroad: 1475-1640* (STC; 1926) which established the short-title catalogue tradition, it is an attempt to enumerate and describe the output of the English press for its time period. There are certain exclusions; the most notable are graphic items and periodicals issued more often than annually.

Unlike printed bibliographies and catalogues, ESTC is not limited to a few discrete access points. As in most data bases, it can be searched by personal and corporate author, by title, and by record identification number. In addition, searches can be made for key words in titles and notes, for place of imprint, for printers, publishers and booksellers, and for year of publication. The file is also indexed by contributing li-

179

Henry L. Snyder, director of the Center for Bibliographical Studies and Research, with Assistant Director Laura Stalker, demonstrating the ESTC data base at the 1987 Modern Language Association conference in San Francisco

brary and library call number. These searches can be combined with the logical operators "and," "or," and "not" to provide an immense variety of possibilities.

ESTC/NA bibliographers, like their counterparts at the British Library and North American Imprints Program, attempt to describe the composition of a copy which conforms to the intention of the publisher. Thus notes are added to say what is present or lacking (as defined by scholars) in each individual copy. The payoff for librarians and bibliographers of such in-depth cataloguing in a machine-readable format is immediate access to comparative data based on examination of copies held by the thousand or so contributing libraries. For the first time literary and historical scholars have access to the full range of eighteenth-century English printing and publishing, enabling the effective study of such things as popular literature, commercial and job printing, the provincial press, and literary forms not usually included in standard anthologies. Bibliographies organized by author, subject, or publisher can be produced in minutes, giving immediate hard

data to support hypotheses.

From the start the ESTC has been an Anglo-American project. A brief history of ESTC helps explain how CBSR came to be created. The ESTC project began with a 1976 conference in London of interested librarians and scholars to look at the possibility of creating a catalogue for the eighteenth century that was the equivalent of STC for its time period. The enormous number of eighteenth-century titles had precluded the manual file approach, but the advent of the computer seemed to make the idea feasible. The 1976 conference was followed by a British Library pilot project and by another conference at the Library of Congress the same year. Committees were set up on both sides of the Atlantic. Using some of the funds given to the British Library to separate itself from the British Museum, Donovan Richnell, then director general of the British Library, made the ESTC possible by committing the British Library to the recataloguing of its eighteenth-century British holdings. Robin C. Alston was named editor; a staff was engaged; and work began in 1977.

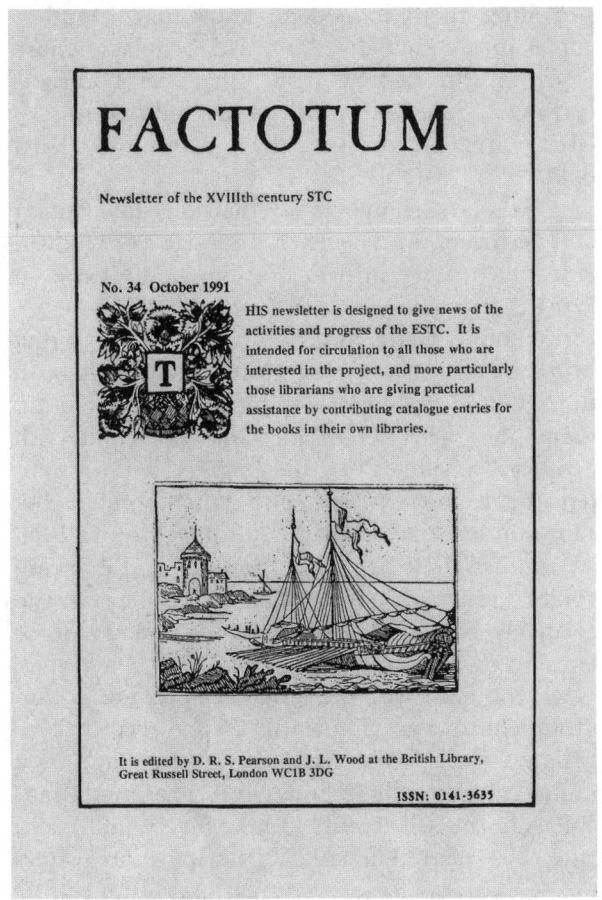

Front cover for the October 1991 issue of the ESTC newsletter, published by the British Library

Meanwhile the North American Committee for the ESTC was organizing the data-collecting efforts in the United States. Under the editorship of Thomas R. Adams of John Carter Brown Library, it was proposed first that Evans's and Tremaine's bibliographies and the *National Union Catalog: Pre-1956 Imprints* (NUC; 1968-1981) be read for relevant items held by North American libraries to add to the base file. A pilot project funded by the National Endowment for the Humanities (NEH) and conducted at the New York Public Library demonstrated that the records were too uneven to create a usable file. At that point responsibility for North American imprints in the ESTC was given to the American Antiquarian Society while ESTC/NA was made responsible for British imprints in North America. In mid 1978 Adams resigned from the North American committee because of other commitments. In September 1978 Henry L. Snyder of the University of Kansas became involved in the project when the steering committee unanimously elected him to replace Adams.

In January 1979 Snyder moved from Kansas to Louisiana State University, where he became dean of the College of Arts and Sciences. That year he obtained further funding from NEH and hired a team of cataloguers headed by Judith C. Singleton. Their first task was to match reports from North American libraries to a manual copy of the British Library's base file. For his part Snyder conducted a vigorous canvass of North American libraries with significant eighteenth-century holdings.

At first there was some resistance on the part of North American libraries to cooperating. Snyder traveled to many universities in the first six years of the project, both as director of ESTC/NA and as a dean at LSU, but wherever he went he would always visit the library to encourage reporting to the catalogue. Librarians and historians have been important to his success in getting libraries to report and maintaining funding for the project. Snyder says,

> "this project has worked because we have always had wonderful cooperation and support, and gradually that base has been expanded. There has always been wonderful support from the British Library. I remember one of the earliest places I went to was Harvard. One professor said, 'you will never get Harvard.' But I went to see Roger Stoddard, curator of rare books at Harvard. He introduced me to Ken Carpenter, who helped me get all of Harvard in. Harvard may be the best reported library in the country."

Snyder adds that it took this type of personal visit in many cases to build up the momentum for the project.

One other early problem that had to be overcome was the differences between names as used in the British Library and those used in the United States. The center has persuaded the British Library to redo the headings of the base file according to North American cataloguing standards and has taken the responsibility for adding the names to the on-line name-authority file maintained by the Library of Congress. The British Library, with distribution in the United States by CBSR, publishes *Factotum: Newsletter of the XVIIIth Century STC* for those who are interested in the activities and progress of the ESTC and its cataloguing centers. Particularly recommended is "Occasional Paper 5" (March 1987), an issue dedicated to searching strategies for ESTC on RLIN, by David Hunter.

ESTC/NA moved to the University of California, Riverside, in April 1986, where it is housed in the Tomás Rivera Library. The university has provided such a supportive environment that the project has not only thrived but has actually expanded. With special funding from NEH, ESTC/NA assumed responsibility for canvassing the Oxford and Cambridge college libraries and the Public Record Office for the data base. A canvass of selected Irish libraries, now being conducted, has been partially funded through ESTC/NA. In 1987 Snyder proposed to the International Committee for the ESTC that earlier periods of English printing, hitherto only covered by printed bibliographies, be added to the data base. The proposal was unanimously approved, and the English Short Title Catalogue (EngSTC) was born.

ESTC is the model for, and will comprise some 70 percent of, EngSTC, the largest bibliographic project ever attempted. It is a union catalogue, in machine-readable form, of all books, pamphlets, and single-sheet items produced in England or in English from the beginning of English printing (circa 1475) through 1800. For EngSTC, to the enormous number of ESTC records, center bibliographers (and some others, although most cataloguing will take place under center sponsorship), both in Riverside and at the Henry E. Huntington Library and Art Gallery, will add over forty thousand separate entries (and locations) from STC (circa 1475 through 1640) and from those items listed in Donald Wing's catalogue of books published from 1641 through 1700 (Wing). It is estimated that there will be five hundred thousand unique records with several million holdings when the EngSTC files are added to the ESTC data base for public access.

As an expanded ESTC, the EngSTC data base will obviate the scope limitations and lack of detail in existing bibliographies and catalogues of the handpress period, while preserving their achievements through citations to existing bibliographies. The enormous superiority of one computerized data base over the many print sources now used by librarians and scholars who must do research on the first 325 years of English imprints is obvious, both in terms of convenience and because of the various and numerous access points for searching. Moreover, the data base can be continuously updated and revised much more easily than the print counterparts. The EngSTC data base will enable librarians to catalogue accurately and uniformly their own collections while providing them immediate knowledge of other copies in the area and the world. Scholars, whose research will benefit from what the librarians learn, will be able to produce lists tailored to specific searches, and thus have immediate hard data.

Scholars should note that the description and verification practices of the EngSTC will provide much more information about the items in Wing than at present exists (and will add to the information in STC), to say nothing of the fact that Wing materials now will exist contextually with those two great foci of scholarship that surround them, the early Renaissance and the eighteenth century. In spite of this, the EngSTC will not render the hard-copy STC and Wing obsolete because individual scholars and libraries will be able to use these as ready reference and marking copies, easily carried about and not subject to the relatively high cost, and occasional system problems, of computer access.

Not only will the EngSTC provide bibliographic information, it will also direct the researcher to copies of the works in two ways. As a union catalogue its holdings information will enable scholars to identify copies for examination, and thus plan their research trips more effectively. Citations to several great microfilm sets of early English imprints give alternative access to the texts. The most important of these are University Microfilms's *Early English Books: Part I, 1475-1640*, *The Thomason Tracts*, and *Early English Books: Part II, 1641-1700* and Research Publications's *The Eighteenth Century*.

The new components are to be integrated with the on-line ESTC to create a complete set of full bibliographic records for all the entries that have been identified. With completion of the editorial phase, a complete EngSTC as it exists at that time will then be marketed, probably on compact disc. The file will continue to be available on-line through RLIN in North America. At that point a small staff will be maintained to make corrections and process any new entries or holdings in the EngSTC. Future maintenance of the EngSTC data base will be supported in part by royalties from sale of copies of the files.

The Center for Bibliographical Studies and Research is involved in many other projects. Because the ESTC has become a model for analogous national projects, the center is a major force in what is being called EuroSTC, an attempt to bring together the products of national cataloguing projects of materials published during the

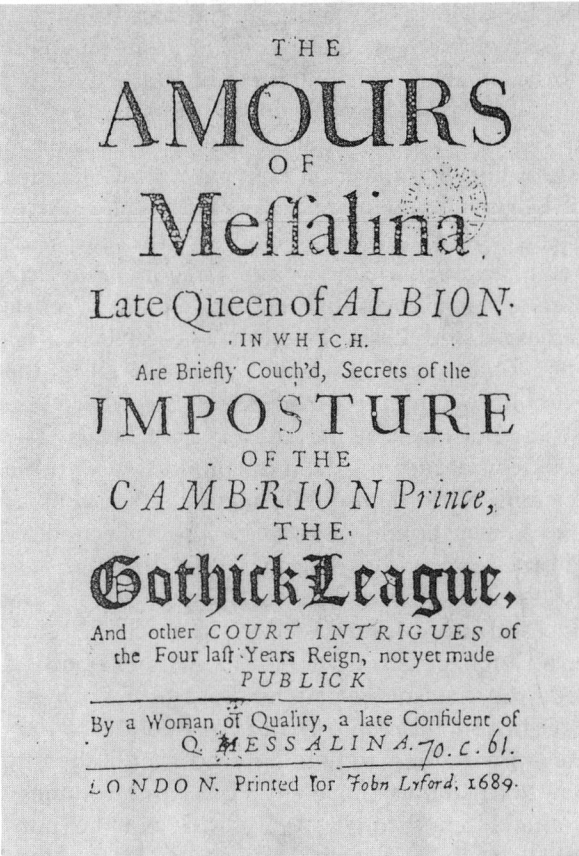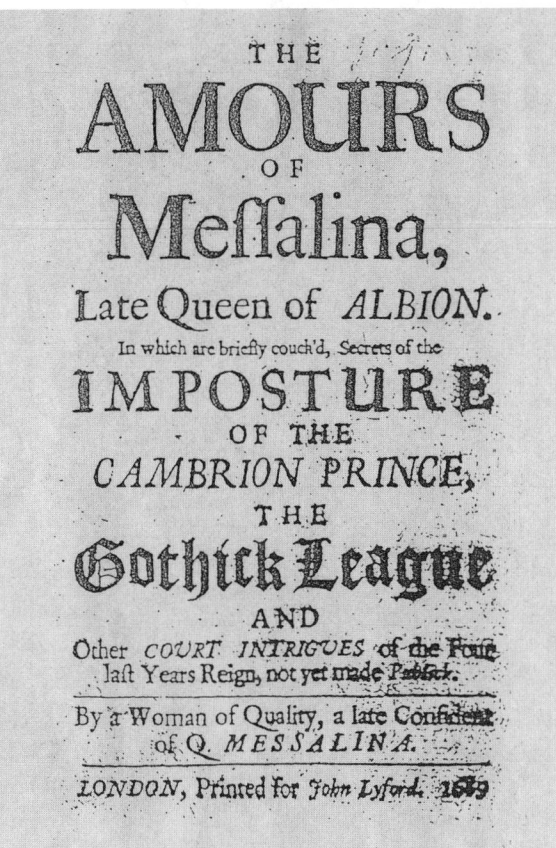

Title pages for two English editions of The Amours of Messalina, late Queen of Albion *(1689), an anonymous, scurrilous attack on Mary of Modena (1658-1718), queen of King James II, linking her romantically with Louis XIV, archenemy of England. During a ten-month period no fewer than fourteen editions—in English, French, Dutch, and Italian—were published in Europe. Differences in typography such as those exhibited by these title pages have revealed three separate 1689 English editions, and there may be one more English edition of that year. Before the EngSTC these editions had been undifferentiated in the standard bibliographies.*

handpress period in Europe. Negotiations are already under way with fifteen projects in twelve countries. Working in conjunction with RLIN, Snyder envisions a single computer-based file that will ultimately catalogue the entire European handpress. The center sees itself acting both as manager of the files in North America and as the agent to incorporate relevant holdings in the Western hemisphere. Through an extensive network of contacts in Europe the center is ideally placed to facilitate such proposals, in the future including interesting and varied internships abroad for North American students.

The other core project of the center is the Eaton Program in Science Fiction and Fantasy. The program is based on the university's J. Lloyd Eaton Collection of Science Fiction and Fantasy Literature, the largest catalogued collection of science fiction and fantasy in North America. The university has built on the foundation of the collec-

tion a major annual conference, a graduate degree program in comparative literature, a publication series, lectures, and a growing agenda of cooperation with like collections and programs, both within North America and internationally. The center's role is to further these programs.

The original Eaton collection was purchased by the university in 1969. Eaton, a physician in Oakland, California, was a fan of science fiction, horror, and fantasy who collected from the 1930s to 1953. His collection included obscure and rare examples of these genres from the 1880s to 1953. Eaton knew and corresponded with major science fiction writers Robert Heinlein, Ray Bradbury, Arthur C. Clarke, John Boucher, Robert Silverberg, Jack Vance, and also with Anthony Boucher (who compiled one of the first post-World War II anthologies of science fiction). Many of the first editions of works by these writers in his collection are signed. Eaton pub-

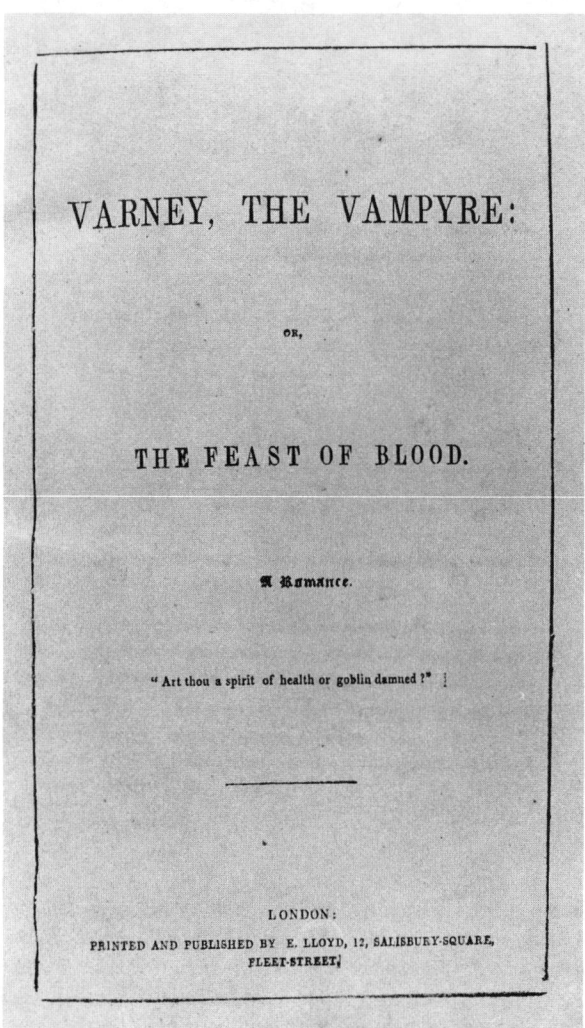

Title page for Varney, the Vampyre; or, the Feast of
Blood *(1847), from the collection formed by J. Lloyd Eaton,
and purchased by the University of California, Riverside,
in 1969*

lished *Rhodomagnetic Digest*, one of the first science-
fiction fanzines (reader newsletters). Among the
treasures of the original Eaton collection is one
of the few extant examples of the first edition of
Varney, the Vampyre; or, the Feast of Blood (London:
E. Lloyd, 1847). The core of the Eaton collection
was used by Arno Press to create the three sixty-
volume sets of science fiction, fantasy, and horror reprints that it published during the 1970s.

Cliff Wurfel, the university's head of special
collections, managed the Eaton collection until
1979, when George E. Slusser was hired as curator. The university began a program of acquisitions to cover the period from 1953 through
1973. Among key purchases was the Douglas
Menville Collection of over fifteen thousand
paperbacks, including Ballantine, DAW, and Ace

Doubles. Not all of this material had been pro-
cessed when G. K. Hall's three-volume catalogue
of the collection was published in 1983.

The first Eaton Conference was held in
1979. It featured science fiction writer Brian
Aldiss and literary critic Harry Levin of Harvard
University. Subsequent Eaton Conferences have
each featured a writer (including Theodore Stur-
geon, Samuel Delany, and Gregory Benford)
and a critic (including Harold Bloom, Fredric
Jameson, and Leslie Fiedler). The 1986 conference, on Philip K. Dick, was cosponsored by the
Sorbonne. The 1989 conference, on cyberpunk,
was cosponsored by the University of Leeds. The
1991 conference was held in conjunction with the
opening of the Maison D'Ailleurs in Yverdon les
Bains, Switzerland. Based on the collection of
Pierre Versins, the Maison D'Ailleurs holds the
largest collection of French language science fiction and utopian literature in the world. (French
is a language strength of the Eaton Collection
today. It has the largest holdings of French science fiction in North America.) Most of the conference proceedings to date have been published by
Southern Illinois University Press (nine volumes).
Volumes ten through twelve will soon be published by the University of Georgia Press. More
volumes are being prepared.

A comprehensive collection plan for the
Eaton Collection was established in 1983. Mysteries were excluded, and the focus of the collection
was expanded to include utopian fiction and imaginary voyages. In 1984 Tomás Rivera, then chancellor of the University of California, Riverside, organized a conference of graduate students and
faculty from all University of California campuses who were interested in the collection. His
untimely death that year halted work on any coop-
erative project.

Slusser was appointed a professor in comparative literature in 1989. Under his direction the
collection's holdings—to include materials in
French, Dutch, Spanish, Italian, Russian, Polish,
German, and other languages—are fully capable
of supporting the many activities of the program.
For example, there are some seventy thousand
monographs; thirty-five thousand to forty thousand fanzines (from the 1930s through the present); forty thousand North American superhero
comic books; over five thousand pulp magazines;
three hundred audio tapes; three hundred video
tapes of science fiction, fantasy, and horror
films; three hundred shooting scripts for such
films; fifteen hundred *Bandes dessinées* (illustrated

French narratives); the manuscripts of science-fiction writers, such as Gregory Benford, David Brin, and Dr. Robert L. Forward; a substantial run of Jules Verne first editions in French; a complete run of the French "Fleuve Noir" series (from 1953 to the present); and the Allan Adrian Collection of early utopian and imaginary travels from the seventeenth through the nineteenth centuries.

The California Newspaper Project is also headquartered at the center. The project takes its origin in the national United States Newspaper Program, sponsored by NEH in conjunction with the Library of Congress. The program is designed to record in the Online Computer Library Center (OCLC) the holdings of all U.S. newspapers in repositories and, where appropriate, in private collections throughout the United States. The goal is to create a machine-readable set of records for all surviving newspapers in OCLC as well as a union list of other U.S. newspapers published in the United States together with a record of holdings of originals and microproductions. The California Newspaper Project will create a complete set of records for California newspapers in OCLC as well as a union list of U.S. newspapers held in the state.

The University of California, Riverside, is committed to maintaining the programs of the Center for Bibliographical Studies and Research. Within the University of California system and internationally the center seeks to promote and coordinate courses and programs related to bibliography, the history of the book, and science fiction and fantasy. In October 1991 the center presented a proposal for a graduate school of library and information science at the University of California, Riverside. Such a school would fit well with the purposes of the center and the structure of the university, while fulfilling a regional need for trained librarians. Both nationally and internationally, the center and its professional staff are active in developing bibliographies, in establishing standards for bibliographic records, in aiding scholars directly, and in helping libraries bring their records under proper bibliographic control so as to better serve them.

The Vladimir Nabokov Archive in the Berg Collection of the New York Public Library: An Overview

James Goldwasser

The acquisition of the Vladimir Nabokov archive by the New York Public Library's Berg Collection of English and American Literature joins his papers with those of Virginia Woolf, W. H. Auden, and Sean O'Casey, as well as with the many other literary treasures that make the Berg Collection one of the great research archives in the United States. The addition of Nabokov to this collection is the culmination of an effort initiated by the late curator, Dr. Lola L. Szladits, after Nabokov's death in 1977 and brought to completion by a new regime at the NYPL through the agency of the New York rare book dealer Glenn Horowitz. The acquisition reflects Dr. Szladits's remarks on the Berg made in *DLB Yearbook: 1983*: "It is impossible to collect in one place all the written traces of a writing and reading man or woman. It is when all the pieces of a life and oeuvre are conflated, often from two or three continents, resting in private or public hands, relocated and recollected, often by two generations of scholar-writers, that biographical and critical studies of lasting importance emerge."

The Nabokov archive does not contain all of his written traces. In two forced emigrations (Russia to Germany and France; France to the United States) much material was abandoned or lost. In a series of donations beginning in 1958, Nabokov gave portions of his papers to the Library of Congress. The Berg archive, however, is hardly a collection of "leftovers." Organized and maintained by Nabokov himself during his last years in residence at the Montreux Palace Hotel, Switzerland, it documents his career in detail. Its scope, variety, and sheer bulk offer manifold opportunities for research into Nabokov's life and work as a novelist, poet, translator, scholar, teacher, and entomologist.

The papers occupy approximately one hundred linear feet of shelf space, with another forty feet holding books and magazines from Nabokov's Montreux library, each containing his contributions or mentioning him. From the earliest period there are poetry albums, scrapbooks, family correspondence, and memorabilia. Further, there is limited but important material relating to Nabokov's crucial transition from the Russian language to English. His years in America are represented by correspondence, manuscripts, notes, and annotated books. By far the most thoroughly preserved period is the post-*Lolita* years, when Nabokov had achieved international stature. The composition of new novels and editing of nonfiction works, the translation and revision of his earlier works, as well as the translation of many works into other languages are all well documented. Throughout the archive the presence of Véra Nabokov is evident as the author's adviser, agent, and amanuensis.

Nearly half of the archive consists of extensive correspondence both to and from Nabokov, his own letters being preserved in the form of carbon typescripts, holograph drafts, or photocopies. The letters provide a record of Nabokov's literary life, especially his relations with publishers and agents. Professional associates for whom substantial correspondence files are present include Jason Epstein, Allen Tate, James Laughlin, Stanley Kubrick, and the firms of McGraw-Hill, Putnam's, Doubleday, and the *New Yorker*. Particularly significant are the letters exchanged during Nabokov's futile first search for an American house willing to publish *Lolita* (1955). There is also meaningful personal and literary correspondence with such friends as Sylvia Berkman, Morris Bishop, Gleb Struve, and Bertrand and Lisbeth Thompson. A separate archival box contains Nabokov's complete correspondence with Edmund Wilson, including some three hundred pages of original Wilson letters. Smaller highlights are notable exchanges with Franz Hellens, Alfred Hitchcock, Alain Robbe-Grillet, and Peter Ustinov. These groups are supplemented by important Russian correspondence with close

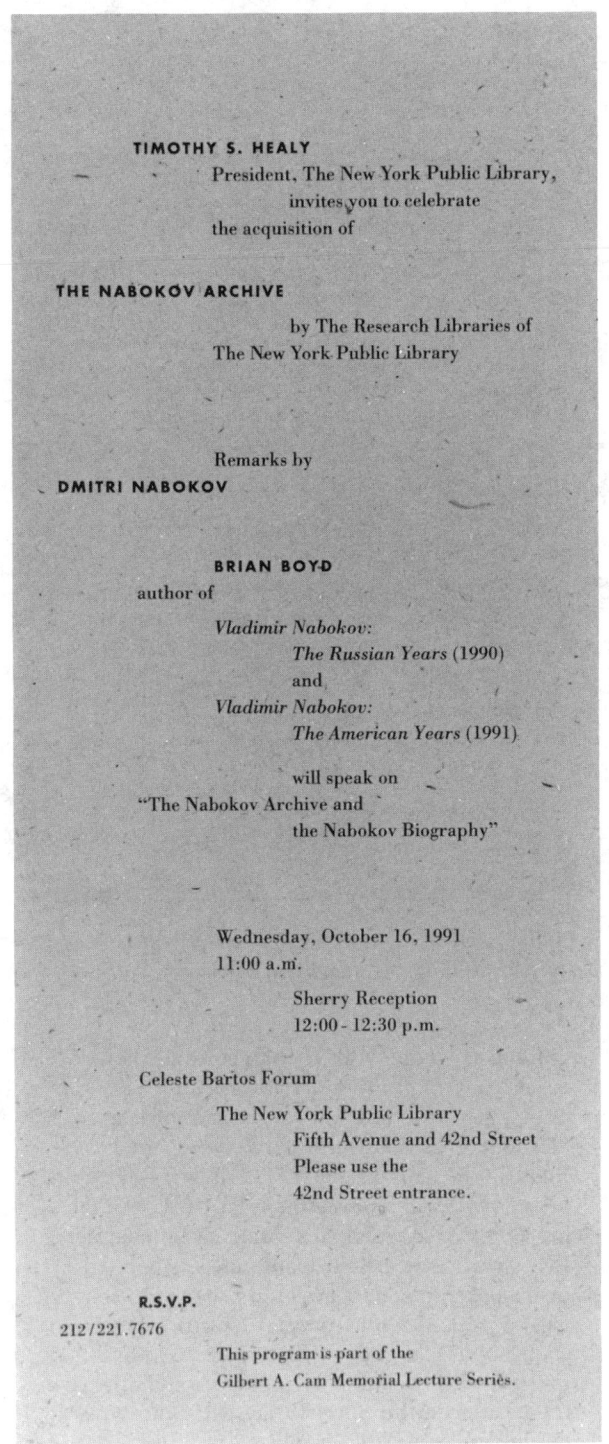

Invitation to the lectures and reception celebrating the acquisition of the Nabokov archive by the New York Public Library

friends and relatives: Elena Nabokov, Sergey Nabokov, Anna Feigin, Sonia Slonim, and others, revealing a great deal of the author's private life.

The most dramatic contents of the archive are the early notebooks and poetry albums. This material dates from as early as 1916 when Nabokov, as a teenager, wrote hundreds of lyrical poems, and runs up to 1931, when he was reaching the first flowering of his artistic ability under the pseudonym "V. Sirin." Particularly notable among these notebooks are those in which Nabokov has diagrammed the rhyme schemes of dozens of Russian poems using a visually striking method devised by Andrei Bely, which Nabokov learned from the poet Maximilian Voloshin. Other albums contain fair-copy transcriptions of Nabokov's own poems written out by his mother; still others include working drafts in Nabokov's hand, with his corrections, and clean typescripts. Of the hundreds of poems included in these notebooks, most remain either unpublished or untraced. All of this earliest material is in Russian, although one album contains a draft of "The Russian Song," (1923) one of his first attempts to write poetry in English.

A further series of notebooks dating from 1943 to 1977 is to be added to the archive at a later date. These diaries served the novelist as more than a record of appointments and travels. In them he recorded conversations, visual impressions, random observations, verse fragments, ideas for fiction, and remarks on works in progress. In an inventory he made of the archive, Nabokov's biographer Brian Boyd noted that "one of the 1951 diaries is something of a writer's workbook and was mined for ideas and curiosities for the next twenty years."

The archive is rich in autobiographical material: corrected typescripts of the memoir *Conclusive Evidence* (1951), dating from the serial publication of chapters in the *New Yorker*; a six-hundred-index-card manuscript of revisions for that work, published in 1967 as *Speak, Memory*, together with a completely revised four-hundred-page typescript. One of the more intriguing parts of the archive from the biographer's point of view is a massive accordion file for the 1973 volume *Strong Opinions*, keeping typescripts, annotated clippings, letters, and mimeographs of interviews, articles, and questionnaires. This material, much of which was not incorporated into *Strong Opinions*, includes complete, unedited interviews. But the most valuable of the biographical materials is a box containing index-card manuscript notes recalling twenty years of life in America for a projected second autobiography, tentatively titled "Speak On, Memory."

Index-card manuscripts were a hallmark of Nabokov's working method in his later years. He

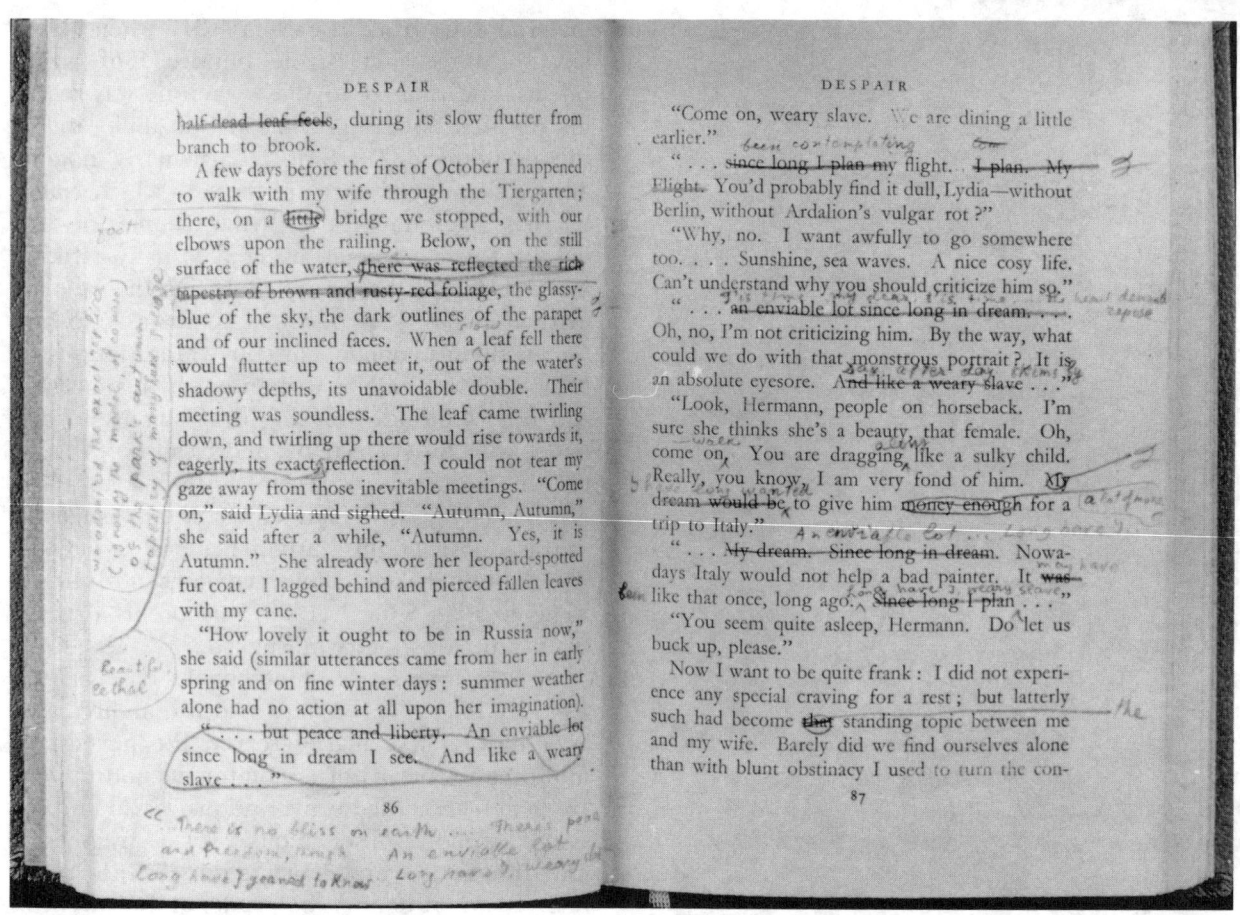

Nabokov's copy of his first English translation (1937) of Otchayanie *(1936), with revisions in his hand (Berg Collection of English and American Literature, New York Public Library, photograph by Peter Bittner). He published a new translation of this novel in 1966.*

once described to an interviewer the process of writing that is readily evident in the archive:

—the novel starts to breed by itself; the process solely in the mind, not on paper; and to be aware of the stage it has reached at any given moment, I do not have to be conscious of every exact phrase. I feel a kind of gentle development, an uncurling inside, and I know that the details are there already, that in fact I would see them plainly if I looked closer, if I stopped the machine and opened its inner compartment; but I prefer to wait until what is loosely called inspiration has completed the task for me. There comes a moment when I am informed from within that the entire structure is finished. All I have to do now is take it down in pencil or pen. Since this entire structure, dimly illumined in one's mind, can be compared to painting, and since you do not have to work gradually from left to right for its proper perception, I may direct my flashlight to any part or particle of the picture when setting it down in writing. I do not begin my novel at the be-

ginning. I do not reach chapter three before I reach chapter four, I do not go dutifully from one page to the next, in consecutive order; no, I pick out a bit here and a bit there, till I have filled all the gaps on paper. This is why I like writing my stories and novels on index cards, numbering them later when the whole set is complete. Every card is rewritten many times. About three cards make up one typewritten page, and when finally I feel that the conceived picture has been copied out by me as faithfully as physically possible—a few vacant lots always remain, alas— then I dictate the novel to my wife who types it out in triplicate (*Strong Opinions*, pp. 31-32).

First-draft index-card manuscripts of *Ada* (1969), *Transparent Things* (1972) and *Look at the Harlequins* (1974) illustrate that process vividly. Each card bears traces of heavy erasure and rewriting, but the completed texts, when compared to their respective typescripts, are remarkably whole. The "vacant lots" are few indeed, and once the autographed manuscript is completed in

Nabokov's legible hand, it is virtually ready for publication. While little has been preserved in the way of preparatory notes, it is likely that Nabokov habitually discarded such working materials. A suggestion to this effect is made by his holograph notation on the box containing the cards for his last novel, *Look at the Harlequins*: "To be destroyed unread if unfinished, VN 1973 (unnumbered cards only)."

As a creative procedure, this method was wholly different from Nabokov's approach to the translation of his own works. Nabokov worked comfortably in three languages. Like his contemporary Samuel Beckett, he was an accomplished author in his native tongue before reaching his artistic zenith and producing his best works in a second language. Both became emblems of an increasingly important issue in modern literature: the problem of language and translation. The Nabokov archive holds multiple opportunities for serious work on this problem.

The 1935 London edition of *Camera Obscura*, in addition to being the first of his books to appear in English (and one of the rarest in his canon), marked an important step in Nabokov's linguistic translation from Russian to English. A copy of the first edition in the Berg archive provides dramatic physical evidence of that shift. Wholly unsatisfied with the translation commissioned by the publisher from Winifred Roy, Nabokov set out in 1937 to revise the English version himself. The ultimate result was *Laughter in the Dark*, first published in the United States in 1938. The Berg copy of *Camera Obscura* has been thoroughly annotated by Nabokov on virtually every page, beginning with a list of alternate titles on the front endpaper ("Blindman's Buff," "The Dark Picture," "The Film," "The Coloured Ghost," and others) and amounting to a complete rewriting of the novel in its margins. The changes and annotations vary greatly, from the names of the characters down to the description and even illustration of details, ending with the transcription of a 1937 poem by Nabokov's contemporary Marina Tsvetaeva on the rear endpaper.

With the success of *Lolita*, Nabokov found a fresh demand from English readers for his earlier Russian works. Several translators collaborated with him in the effort: Michael Glenny (*Mary* [1970]), Michael Scammell (*The Defense* [1964], *The Gift* [1963]), and his son Dmitri (*King, Queen, Knave* [1968], *The Eye* [1965], *Glory* [1971], *Invitation to a Beheading* [1959], and *The Waltz Inven-*

tion [1966]). (Only *Despair* [1966], which he'd translated himself in 1937, did Nabokov revise entirely on his own: his extensively annotated copy of the 1937 edition now sits beside the *Camera Obscura* in the Berg Collection). Yet it would be unfair and inaccurate to describe these collaborative works with the simple epithet "translations." In transforming his early works out of their original Russian he preferred the term "*Englishing*." More than a process of literal translation, the rendering of an English text was, for Nabokov, a new imaginative work. As Dmitri Nabokov notes in a memo in the archive's file on the English version of *Glory*, "Many VN corrections represent authorial license to modify and update his own work, besides revising the translations as such. . . ."

In most every work the author/translator and the translator/collaborator can be seen cooperating in a special and most functional fashion. A first English version drafted by the translator is presented to Nabokov for his thoroughgoing revision—indeed, recomposition. Heavily corrected typescripts and galleys of *Mary*, *The Gift*, *The Waltz Invention*, *King, Queen, Knave*, *Glory*, as well as the various early stories that comprised the collections *Tyrants Destroyed* (1975), *A Russian Beauty* (1973) and *Details of a Sunset* (1976), all document this procedure. More than a simple record of the Nabokovian method of "Englishing," these translations represent the author's reformation of his earlier artistic self from the standpoint of his mature artistic vision.

The complex problem of translation is further addressed by the production of translations into other languages, especially French. Long under-noticed, Nabokov's fluency and creativity in French is revealed by the materials on the French editions of *Ada*, *The Eye*, *Pale Fire*, and *The Gift*, all of which were supervised by Nabokov himself. Here, the imaginative process of new creation gives way to the more literal approach of translation for its own sake. The translator's first rendering is scrutinized by Nabokov, who emends it carefully, always explaining in detail his alterations of words or sentences to emphasize the allusion, reference, or pun intended in the original. Although the translators of the French editions were given more liberty than their English-language counterparts, Nabokov retained the final word.

Finally, two works which Nabokov translated alone mark separate and distinctive achievements: his Russian version of *Lolita* (1967) and his annotated English translation of Aleksandr

Pushkin's *Eugene Onegin* (1964). The heavily revised holograph manuscript of the former is in twelve spiral-bound composition books, entirely filled with Nabokov's hand. Of the latter, abundant files of manuscript drafts, notes, copies, proofs, clippings, and correspondence trace the work's progress and production as well as the controversy it generated upon publication. Nabokov himself regarded these two translations as among his most important contributions to literature.

Other materials warranting mention are those covering Nabokov's academic and scientific work. These include files of lecture notes for his literature classes at Cornell and Wellesley and over two dozen teaching books with Nabokov's marginal annotations: works by Jane Austen, Anton Chekhov, Charles Dickens, Gustave Flaubert, Franz Kafka, Marcel Proust, Leo Tolstoy, and others. The annotations by Vladimir and

Véra Nabokov in a copy of Kafka's *Metamorphosis* amount to a virtual retranslation of that work into English. The portion of the archive labeled "Lepidoptera" includes a complete set of Nabokov's published papers in the field, some with his autograph corrections, as well as thousands of pages of manuscript and drawings of the wing patterns and genitalia of butterflies.

The Nabokov acquisition was marked with a ceremony in the New York Public Library's Celeste Bartos Forum on 16 October 1991, at which Brian Boyd and Dmitri Nabokov spoke. The texts of their remarks will appear in a forthcoming issue of the New York Public Library's annual bulletin *Biblion*. The archive will remain closed to researchers for two years until it has been completely catalogued. When it is opened, certain unpublished Russian material will be accessible on a restricted basis.

The British Library and the Regular Readers' Group

Brian Lake

Plans to move the British Library to a different site away from the British Museum have been under consideration for forty years. In 1972 the British Library was established as a separate institution, and following the failure to secure approval for building in Bloomsbury (the scheme would have meant the demolition of many historically listed houses) a railway goods yard next to St. Pancras Station was chosen as the place where all the collections, presently in nineteen different locations, would be "united under one roof." Both government and British Library readers have watched the slow completion of Britain's most expensive public building (£450 million) with trepidation: government because of the startling increase in costs, and readers because of concerns about the provision of services in the new building (half the size originally projected), the lack of commitment to complete the project, and the loss of familiar and much-loved facilities in Bloomsbury.

The year 1991 proved to be a particularly bad time for the library. The new building had been Margaret. Thatcher's monument—and Thatcher is no more. John Major and his arts minister, Tim Renton, want to be done with it. Only half the library is being built—it will be full of books when it opens, and there will be only 73 more reader seats than at present (1,176 instead of the 3,440 originally planned)—and the government is committed, at the moment, to selling off the rest of the site. On top of all this, there are serious problems with the new building. The first books were supposed to be moved to St. Pancras in June 1991. Now contractual delays and numerous faults with the mobile shelving system have delayed the start of the move indefinitely.

At the same time, government funding for acquisitions has been cut back severely, leaving many departments without book-buying budgets at all, and both readers and library staff are in dispute with library management. While the library assistants have been on strike because of regrad-

A 1928 photograph of the main reading room at the British Museum, redesignated the British Library in 1972

ing which would put junior assistants in the same pay bracket as cleaners, July 1991 saw the publication of a damning memorandum to the arts minister entitled *Is the British Library Falling Down?* The Regular Readers' Group, unable to enter into a formal consultation process with management, felt forced into publicizing serious concerns, while at the same time suggesting the practical benefits of retaining use of the Round Reading Room and North Library, and the associated storage facilities at Bloomsbury, in light of the limited provision of both reader and storage space at St. Pancras. Better to have books ten minutes away from St. Pancras in purpose-built shelving, rather than in Yorkshire, as the British Library proposes. Because of cutbacks, the number of computer terminals for use by readers at St. Pancras has been reduced to 150. There are also "inherent" (the library's word) problems with 180 moving shelving miles. First of all, there were "whipping, vibration, and jolting," and, after twenty different identified design faults, came the revelation that the paint work on the shelves is below specification.

Despite the readers' arguments, British Library chairman Commander Saunders Watson, chief executive Brian Lang, and the minister for the arts have stuck to their guns and offer no compromises. A second report, *Bloomsbury AND St. Pancras. A Future for the British Library*, was published in November 1991 and addressed to the prime minister, John Major. This report expanded on the concerns, while advocating practical solutions to apparently insoluble problems. The grand opening of the first phase scheduled for 1993 is unlikely to take place as building work will not be finished, and the shelving defects will take at least two years to rectify. The first move of books will not happen until 1994 at the earliest.

Readers regard British Library management as blinkered in its approach, apparently unwilling to review the situation in the light of changed circumstances. Chairman Saunders Watson wrote to the Regular Readers' Group early in 1992 that it was the unanimous view of the British Library Board that "the Library should take the fullest possible advantage of the greatly improved storage conditions and automated services which will become available when the new building is completed." Such generalizations have failed to satisfy the skeptics. A letter from a Canadian professor of English to the Regular Readers' Group summed up the feelings of the majority:

> I love the Round Reading Room. It seems to me a positively miraculous environment for study, making reference material (especially the catalogue) accessible and one's neighbours inconspicuous. Nevertheless I have never hitherto argued for its retention, on the grounds that after the move Readers ought as far as humanly possible to be on the same site as the books. If this is not to be the case, then the whole argument for aban-

doning the Panizzi reading room falls to the ground, and if you are campaigning for its retention I should like to join you.

In short, if St. Pancras was going to be as originally planned, Bloomsbury would become a happy memory. St. Pancras is, however, only half a library, and the old reading rooms must not be abandoned. There may be a benefit in the delay if the government can be persuaded of the advantages which would accrue from combining the old and the new: not an ideal solution but a practical one.

An Interview with David Rabe

See also the Rabe entry in *DLB 7: Twentieth-Century American Dramatists*.

David Rabe was born on 10 March 1940 in Dubuque, Iowa. While studying for his M.A. in theater at Villanova University in 1964, Rabe was drafted into the army. He served from January 1965 to January 1967 and spent the last eleven months of his tour of duty in Vietnam. He took his degree in 1968. In 1971 two of his plays, *The Basic Training of Paulo Hummel* and *Sticks and Bones*, opened in New York City. Rabe has been highly acclaimed for his work in the theater and has also written screenplays for many films, including *Streamers* (1983) and *Casualties of War* (1989). Rabe was interviewed at his home by telephone on 25 June 1991. The interview was conducted by Ronald S. Baughman.

DLB: Would you give me a brief history of your military training and experience?

RABE: I was drafted in '65. I went in through Fort Jackson, had my basic in Fort Gordon, went next to Fort Belvoir in Virginia, and then Fort Mead in Maryland. From Mead I shipped out to Vietnam. At that time we went by

ship, which was sort of unusual in the Vietnam experience, but in the beginning, in that first massive buildup—which is what I was part of—troops went by boat. I was stationed at Long Binh, which was a short distance—maybe twenty-something miles—outside Saigon. Long Binh at that time was almost nonexistent. It was a very rough place, not dangerous—well, it was fairly dangerous—but I mean it was primitive. I understand from people who were there five years later that it had everything but Burger King. It became a huge, huge base camp. That's where we established the hospitals, and the nearest primary one was the 91st EVAC. That's where I was stationed the whole time.

DLB: And you worked in a field-hospital support group?

RABE: In a support group yes; not in the actual hospital but around it. When there were massive casualties, which happened once or twice when I was there, I got more involved in the actual hospital. But for the most part, I spent my time in the beginning doing construction, primarily building and digging and a lot of guard duty and driving. And then we put up tents, lived in tents, and built hootches. A lot of the time went

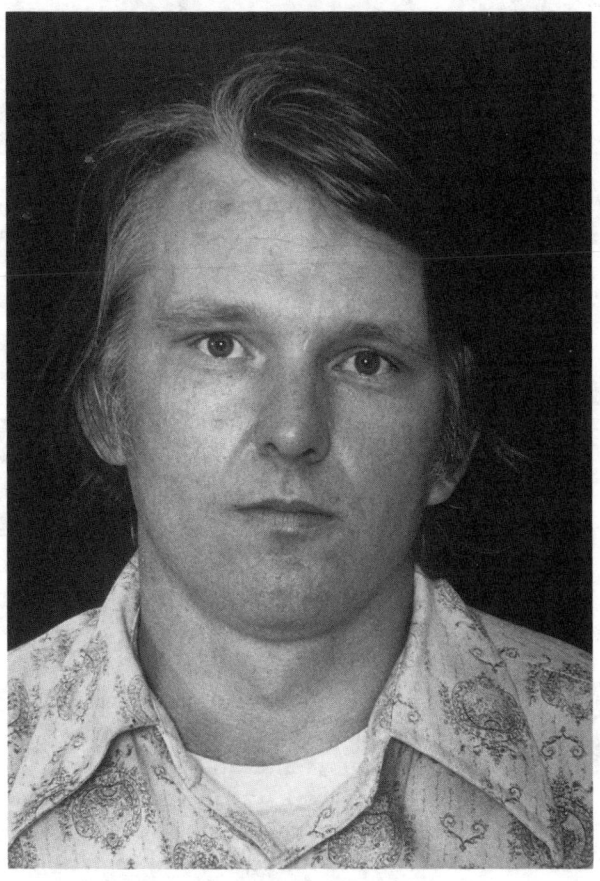

*David Rabe, circa 1975 (photograph copyright
Frederic Ohringer)*

into that kind of work. It took a long time to get
it all set up. Unless there was a massive casualty,
we weren't really involved in hospital work.

DLB: When there was a massive casualty
rate, what did you do then?

RABE: There was spillover, and extra people were needed to carry people around. Sometimes our areas were taken over as hospital beds
for the less seriously wounded. But it was, again,
just basically kind of logistical stuff.

DLB: You were discharged as a specialist
fourth class in January of 1967, is that right?

RABE: Right.

DLB: Did you come back by boat?

RABE: No, I flew back, into San Francisco—
or Oakland—wait, where did we fly into? I think
we flew into San Francisco.

DLB: Was it one of those surreal flights in
the sense that twenty-four hours before you were
in Vietnam and then the next day back in the
U.S.?

RABE: Yes, that part of it was very bizarre.
It's so surreal you don't even know it's surreal. It
feels very good, and then you land and that feels
good. It's as if you don't know that it's surreal—
at least, I didn't—until I got further along. But it
is. It's bizarre, but it's what you've been thinking
about, and it feels good. At least, that was my experience. But literally it was twenty-four hours and
you're home—or it might have been thirty-some
hours—and you're out of the army, as in my
case, not just out of Vietnam, but out of the
army. The surreal impact in my case didn't happen for about a week. You're still there emotionally in Vietnam for a long time, even though
you're not. And I don't know, I'm sure a boat is
far more transitional in a way; it would give you
far more time to adjust to coming back. There
was no particular trauma to the event itself, but
there was in the aftermath.

DLB: Where did you go after you arrived in
the U.S.?

RABE: I went home to Dubuque, and I
stayed there for, oh I don't know, a few months,
knocking around. At the time I thought I kind
of wanted to go back to Vietnam as a journalist. I
wrote letters to different people. But I didn't really want to go back, do you know what I mean?
I wanted to, but I didn't really. I didn't follow
through. I wrote some letters, and I didn't get
any positive response, so I gave up. I kind of
thought I wanted to, or ought to want to or something, but I gave it up quickly. I had gone from college straight into graduate school, and after I
was in graduate school at Villanova for a year, I
quit. I knocked around about a year, and that's
when I got drafted. I had been interested in writing while in graduate school, and people in graduate school somehow had kept track of me and my
whereabouts, and they were aware that I was
back from the war. They contacted me at home,
and one of my professors called and wanted to
know whether I wanted to come back to finish
on an assistantship. I said no at first, and then
some more time went by, and he called again. I
ended up going there. Then after I was there for
a while, I received a Rockefeller play-writing
grant. This was probably close to a year after I

was out of the army. I don't remember exactly, but it was roughly six months before I went back to Philadelphia. And then another six months before this grant came my way.

DLB: You mentioned in the introduction to *The Basic Training of Pavlo Hummel* that you had been trying to write novels, and had the grant been for novel writing, you might have turned to prose fiction rather than to drama.

RABE: Yes, that's true. At the time I couldn't conceive of how to capture the experience of the war on stage. And so I was struggling to try to write about the war but hadn't gotten very far. I'd been more or less stymied in the novel form. So when this grant came I thought, well, I'll write these plays.

DLB: Let's discuss your Vietnam trilogy. Did you encounter any Sergeant Brisbees while you were in Vietnam?

RABE: Well, yes and no. I can't say I had that conversation, but I encountered people one way or another—whether it was just seeing them in some cases—who were in some version of that extremity. I wouldn't say that they were exactly like Brisbee, but they were some version of him. As I was saying before, I couldn't imagine how to capture the experience of Vietnam on stage because at the time I was thinking about the stage in realistic terms. When I actually started writing for the theater, I discovered that there were different forms of metaphoric levels that I could create. That discovery enabled me to get at the experience in a metaphoric way and accounts for a Sergeant Brisbee in a sense. In the theatrical life, you are not only able—but I feel that I am obligated—to create these sort of larger, not strictly literal, figures. And so a Brisbee comes into being. He's literally accurate in terms of what could happen and what the wounds could be, but in terms of his vision or point of view he is a larger-than-life embodiment, almost of the unconscious of someone like that. So, as I say, it was that discovery that enabled me to write for the stage and feel that I was touching—or beginning, at least—to encompass some of the experience by not being realistic. And that is how a Brisbee came about.

DLB: You realized very early in your writing that realism may not have anything to do with the-atricality, and that you were more interested in the art of the theater than in rendering something realistically.

RABE: The very term *realistic* lays a certain claim on the truth and reality, which is spurious because it's simply a convention. The realistic play does not encompass as much reality as Shakespeare, that's for sure. It's not really accurate. Realism involves a set of conventions that came into being at a certain point and were revolutionary, I guess, when they appeared but are aberrant to the real thrust of theater. By not being realistic I am not abandoning reality or the truth or whatever those things are, but I adopt a more theatrical set of conventions to get at my material. And that's what I started to see, and once I did see that then I was able to address the experience of the war, which had been largely intuitive in me. I had experienced the war through a kind of osmosis. I saw numerous things, but as we've discussed, I was not in a combat unit and never really was in that daily grind. There were occasional threats and alerts and attacks on a nearby ammo dump. The place I was in when Tet came was jeopardized. I wasn't there, but when Tet hit a lot of that area was attacked. So my experience wasn't direct experience. The direct experience was one thing, and then there was a lot of absorbing and hearing and talking to guys and incorporating experience. So the theatrical form in the long run was the best for me, I think.

DLB: As opposed to the novel?

RABE: Yes. I think, now. I didn't feel that at the time, but I think it was.

DLB: Just being close to or within that environment is combat zone enough, isn't it?

RABE: Well, I guess that's my story. That's what happened to me because I absorbed it somehow, and I was close enough. When I came home, when I was home for a while, I was alienated, or whatever the proper word is, from the States and from anybody who hadn't been over there. Millions of guys could go through it and not be able to write about it. Being where I was, I ended up writing what I did, which was based on my experiences. I feel fairly confident that I would have been—I was disordered enough by the experience I had, just being around the chaos of it. I doubt that I could have handled the

BILL

I mean, do you just turn off. Be a robot. ~~and you just do as you're told like all the others~~ all marching in a row—all in a line, all dressed alike, thinking alike—goddamn hundred, million machines. ~~~~

SANDRA

Bill, I really feel like I ought to go; ~~MMMMMMMMMMMMMMMMM~~

BILL

I'm not ready.

SANDRA

Just walk me down to a cab.

MICKEY

Sandra, relax; you don't want to go.

SANDRA

You don't understand, Mickey. Really.

~~PAVLO~~

~~I'll walk you down to a cab.~~

SANDRA

Would you?

PAVLO

Sure. What's your coat.

SANDRA

(AS PAVLO EXITS)

The blue one. You see, mickey, it's my landlord—I haven't been able to ~~MMMM~~ rest properly for weeks—he's homosexual, do you see— openly admits it, and not that I think he should hide it—but it must be getting out of hand for the poor thing. He's headed for a real crash real soon, ~~~~ because he sent me this terribly hysterical letterbegging me ~~~~ me to move out immediately because he can't stand to have me ~~~~ above him anymore—he hates women so bad, ~~~~ And it was just a really gross awful letter. ~~MM~~ H just sits down there sometimes listening to whatever sound I might make above him—~~just that thin floor between us~~ and he thinks about me— sees me move, ~~~~ and when I have company, ~~MM MMMMM~~ a boy, or Bills over~~MMMMMMM—~~, I guess he's down there raving. ~~~~ I feel so badly for him—it must be awful for him, but it's worse for me.

(PAVLO HAS RETURNED DURING THIS, LISTENED, HELPED
HER ON WITH HER COAT.)

BILL

You're gonna be a general son and make us all prouad.

Page from the revised typescript for The Basic Training of Pavlo Hummel *(Boston University, Mugar Memorial Library, by permission of David Rabe)* full thing. I'm not sure. You never know because you deaden some part of yourself.

DLB: Pavlo at one point is called a liar, and then Mickey calls him a "mythmaker"; in many ways, Pavlo is a mythmaker, isn't he?

RABE: Yes, lacking any personality, or sense of identity, he's forever trying to devise one, and so he makes up an identity; he sees the possibility of an identity in a story that he makes up about himself. And it's almost as if he is so lacking in an authentic self that he tries to create a self by controlling or modifying and shifting the impression he's making. He's entrenched, or he's infatuated with certain myths about what will make him successful, or make him a man, or make him a soldier, or give him an identity. He's both a mythmaker and a myth believer.

DLB: He believes the myth of the macho soldier figure, and he wants to get discharged out of the hospital so he can go to a combat unit?

RABE: Right. It is as if he is in need of an authentic experience for himself, sort of a validation of himself, and so he feels that combat is how he'll get it. The agenda of his lack of personality, or lack of identity, propels him in the face of his experience toward this ultimate destination, which is where he ends up. And in those circumstances he thinks that being in a certain kind of unit and having a certain reputation will grant him that selfhood. There were guys like that, and there were guys who thought it was all bullshit. But there's a certain thing that he does capture, I think, that most people in the army are prone to, drawn to, which is the myth of the army.

DLB: Do you see Pavlo as an archetypal figure of the middle-class boy who grew up on all the John Wayne-Iwo Jima stories?

RABE: Well, he's that, but he's not quite because he's a little more impoverished emotionally, I think, than most middle-class guys. But, yes, in a way he shares that. Or he's a more extreme case. His father is gone. His blindness is neurotic; he has a blindness to what is happening in front of him. What he's accomplishing is very strong. But it's the same dynamic that you are describing, or that Ron Kovic has described in *Born on the Fourth of July* [1976]. It is similar to that im-

pulse, only a lot of guys in those circumstances attribute that phenomenon just to being young and inexperienced or having had these movies thrown at them since they were little; whereas with Pavlo I feel there is the addition of a real psychic wound, which makes him more universal. It's not merely his youth and inexperience. He's got a real gap in his psychological makeup.

DLB: The psychic wound of his nonfamily?

RABE: Yes, of what he's trying to create, what he's trying to attain. Maybe that's why he's trying to make the army into his family and the soldiers into his brothers, which is what we all do. I did it when I was in, and it's sort of what the army is built on. That's how it functions. We all have those buttons and those various needs, and they get tapped by the army. That's how they make the army work.

DLB: Do you see a progression from Pavlo to David in *Sticks and Bones*? Are they part of a character continuum?

RABE: You know, a friend of mine said something to me once that I think is spooky; it was as if this guy had ESP. I never did understand it. But he hadn't read *Sticks and Bones*. *Pavlo* had just opened in New York. It was already written, but not many people knew of it—it was just a manuscript. I didn't know this guy very well at the time. But we were in a bar talking one night, and he was going on about this section toward the end of act 1 of *Pavlo* where Pavlo says: "If I could be bone, Ardell; if I could be bone. In my deepest part or center, if I could be bone." He's talking about the desire to be hard and impenetrable and invulnerable, using "bone" as the key image. This friend said, "You know, you're going to write a play," or, "Your next play's going to be *Bones Comes Home*." I said, "What?" And he was just sort of ranting on, based on whatever had happened to him that made him say this to begin with. So except for that conversation, I wouldn't have thought that there is a continuity. In a sense there is a way in which David is a kind of ghost of Pavlo, or is Pavlo's dream of being bone and coming home, because David is also impenetrable. The curious thing about the play and David is that everybody wants to sympathize with him, but he's really rough. I remember when the play was first performed; it was a liberal audience, and they wanted to sympathize with this guy who was coming home and who was against the war. But he was so unpleasant and so obsessive and fanatical in his single-mindedness. He was hard to root for or to align with. And it made the audiences very frustrated, which is why the play is difficult to make work, but that's the way it *should* work. And the audience should be thrown back to an identification with Ozzie and then left with that because that's who the audience is, no matter what their politics.

DLB: You forced the American public to re-examine their "sentimental myth," their sense of sympathy, by asserting that the issues were deeper and stronger than that.

RABE: Yes. The sentimental to me was very infuriating when I came back. The sympathies were well meant, but the experience was harder, tougher. It just was not an accurate picture. Sentimentality couldn't get near the true kinds of emotions. Plus, I was in a frame of mind as I wrote the play that was much like David's. I wanted to distress people to the extent that I felt the event was distressing, not enlist their sympathy. So it was the most difficult play for me to write.

DLB: I remember the first time I taught *Sticks and Bones*, it stunned my class and me. I had initially approached it as if this was a play through which we could feel superior to Ozzie, Harriett, and Ricky, but it doesn't work that way.

RABE: No, it doesn't, or it shouldn't. It won't. No, I've seen productions that have tried to do it that way exclusively, and it just doesn't get to the end. Good productions of it are very funny, but the laughter is coming from a savage place. You're not just laughing at it, and by the end of it it's just deranged and disturbing. And you are forced into, you're compelled into, an alliance with the family in spite of yourself. The truth is that—if you eliminate the politics and look at the dramatic action—Ozzie is just trying to stay sane basically, and what David is offering him is madness. There may be a deep, and who knows, an absolute truth in that madness if Ozzie went in with him, but it's a pretty harrowing request. He goes about as close as most people would dare to go to accepting madness. Ozzie backs out. And certainly from an actor's point of view he's the great part.

DLB: Which actor do you think played the part of Ozzie best?

RABE: I've never seen it played fully. I saw a couple of guys get close. One guy played it on the college level who was wonderful. Tom Aldridge was very good in the TV version and was good on stage, but he was never really the right person. He ended up doing it, and he worked wonderfully and hard, but I always wanted a more physically substantial person. I feel that he should be a large man and more of an obvious kind of American symbol, a more powerful figure, an American ideal, a male father figure. I don't know; I don't know who. Whoever plays Ozzie should attempt to go as far as he can. The family faces the issue that basically David is telling them they'll be very happy when he fills the house up with corpses. Actually, Ozzie is almost on the verge of accepting that view in a strange way until Ricky intervenes. So that when he comes out—I don't know, it's almost irreducible—he is settling for a form of sanity that's based on immense falsehoods, which is sort of how sanity works. I mean, sanity's foundation is immense falsehoods, and that's what he's doing. Tom Aldridge certainly did that as well as the other people I've seen; it's just that I've always had in my mind someone like George C. Scott, that kind of figure, in that era, when he was that age—that kind of very huge force of a man.

DLB: Are you working consciously to explore the falsehoods on which we have based our sanity?

RABE: I didn't set out to do that. I was thinking simply about wrestling with the experience of the war. No, I was really in the midst of it, I think. I was really in that wrestling match, and I was trying to figure those things out, a kind of life-and-death struggle. And I didn't resolve it and that's why it ends the way it does.

DLB: The third part of your trilogy is *Streamers*, a play that you have identified as being written with few changes.

RABE: I don't really look at it as trilogy. I include *The Orphan* in the Vietnam plays, and I see it as four plays the way I wrote them. I've never quite decided which is the fourth play, whether it's the order in which they were written or whether I would scramble them if they were ever

(handwritten:) WHAT:
CARLYLE
YOU AND ROGER ARE SITTIN' ON
RICHIE, RIGHT?   2-13

                            BILLY
He's not queer if that's what you're sayin'. A little
effeminate but that's all, no more; if that's what you're
sayin'.

                      (handwritten: MYSELF) CARLYLE
I'd like to get some a him if he a good punk is what I'm sayin'. That's
what I'm sayin'. We can make us some arrangements--I got ~~MHMM~~ wheels,
we can go into town sometime, there's these people got~~M~~ this whore house,'
they take care a ~~you~~, and then cause we so friendly, you just let me
have some a your punk every now and then, I bet. ~~Whata you lookin' at~~.

                            BILLY
He don't do that stuff.

                            CARLYLE
What stuff.

                            BILLY
Listen, man; I don't feel too good, you don't mind.

                            CARLYLE
What stuff?

                            BILLY
What you're thinkin'.

                            CARLYLE
What ... am I thinkin'?

                            BILLY
You ... know ...

                            CARLYLE
Yes, I do. It in my head, that how come I know. But how
do you know? I can see your heart, Billy, boy, but you
cannot see mine. I am unknown. YOU ... are known.

                            BILLY
                      (Slowly)
You just ... talk fast and keep movin', don't you? Don't ever
stay still.

                            CARLYLE
Words to say my feelin', Billy, boy.

                      (RICHIE enters)

There he is. There he be.

                            RICHIE
He's one of them who hasn't come down far out of the trees,
yet, Billy; believe me.

Page from the revised typescript for Streamers *(Boston University, Mugar Memorial Library, by permission of David Rabe)* put together. It's curious, you can look at them as a sequence of plays and find their development. If you look at them in a literal or sequential way, you would go from *Pavlo* to *Streamers* to *Sticks and Bones*, but that arrangement doesn't make any sense emotionally. And if you look at them in their thematic progression, so to speak, or the way their view of the war gets larger, you would go from *Pavlo* to *Sticks and Bones* to *Streamers* to *Orphan*. The true progression though is probably the sequence in which they are written, which is the emotional life. And on the basis of the emotional life, *Streamers* in a strange way is the most forgiving of all the plays and, thus, should be fourth. I don't allow *The Orphan* to be excluded in any conversation. And, in fact, recently I saw a production of it at Barnard College at New York, and it was really quite stunning. The reception, which was fascinating, was a reception from kids—those who were in the audience, those who were performing, plus the reviewers were all college students—twenty years after the fact. They were very taken with it; the reception and the critical approach was quite gratifying to me. It made me realize that the play—which I've always loved—had a life. And it does. If people twenty years later can do it and make sense out of it and be thrilled by it—which they were—it's there. I still have kind of a pet peeve about the play's reception, but—not really—that's not true. I was going to say I had a pet peeve about the play's critical reception, but it's not true. The production in New York was bad, and the script wasn't finished. It was a confusing experience for the audience. The critics couldn't see what wasn't there. The play has since been worked on quite a bit at various times and various productions. So it's a different play than the one that was done in New York. To address what you were saying before, though, *Streamers* may be the most controlled, I guess. In its craft *Streamers* is perhaps the most controlled of the plays.

DLB: You have stated that *Streamers* came to you almost whole in a way that some of the other plays didn't.

RABE: Yes, that's true. *Streamers* and *Hurly Burly* probably were the most complete. They came in a certain way that didn't allow for a lot of fiddling around.

DLB: Is that a particularly gratifying feeling for a writer?

RABE: Yes. The way *Streamers* came was so peculiar. It came in a series of chunks that were separated over a seven-year period. And yet each chunk was more or less complete. There wasn't much room for alteration. It was very weird. Part of *Streamers* was the first thing I wrote when I came home and started writing again. I wrote something like a thirty-page one-act play in—I don't know—five hours, in some sort of rush. Then nearly four years later I rewrote that one-act play and turned it into a fifty-page play, again in this same kind of rush, in maybe a day or two. Then about three years later I did it again, and it was the play. The writing covered over seven years, and yet if you took the actual writing hours, you'd probably not have more than three days. And it was basically the play with only minor changes in rehearsal.

DLB: Had you been thinking about these various chunks?

RABE: The first part I just wrote, and then it was, in fact, done as a one-act play at Villanova. After that I went through long periods without thinking about it; then suddenly I'd find myself thinking about it and make certain additions to expand it. I always knew that it wasn't finished. Early in my career, when I had not had a play done in New York, a guy wanted the option on the fifty-page version for a production in New York. I wouldn't do it because—I remember the decision was very difficult to make—I just knew it wasn't finished in some way that I didn't understand. So I turned that production down. Then it was nearly another, I'd say, year and a half or two before *Pavlo*. The final phase of rewriting came another couple of years after that. So it's very weird. I mean, that had never happened before.

DLB: For a then-unknown playwright that had to be a difficult decision.

RABE: Yes. It was going to be an Off-Broadway production, but it was New York. And, yes, it was very difficult to turn down. It wasn't difficult in one sense because I knew I couldn't do the play the way it was. Yet, part of me was very upset because there was no way to know whether I'd get another chance at New York.

DLB: You've said that *Goose and TomTom* was a breakthrough play for you, primarily because of your realization of how the characters' language creates its own reality, rather than imitating or describing a reality. Do you still feel that way?

RABE: It's a feeling that informed that play, or it was discovered in that play, and then it informed *Hurly Burly* and a lot of the subsequent work. It's a liberating notion—and another step away from the realistic or well-made play—which has enabled me to grasp a lot of other theatrical writing. Shakespeare's characters are not speaking about some reality that exists around them, that preexisted and that now they're describing. Their reality is being devised as they speak. It's a subtle idea, and it can sound as if I'm saying little when I say it. This approach, however, has helped me break further away from the realistic notion that what people say expresses some idea that they have or some event that's already happened to them, and that it's proportionate to what the other person says; instead, everybody's spinning these spider webs of language.

DLB: So that the reality is contained on the stage and becomes timeless in that regard, is that right?

RABE: Yes. And it can be done in what would appear to be a realistic play in terms of how characters speak; in other words, *Hurly Burly* is a play like that, and yet to me it is not a play in which there is ever any exposition, in which you could say this character is telling the truth and that character is lying. Each character is in his or her own world, and none knows exactly what the plot of the play is; they're all preceding with their own agenda. They think they are telling the truth, but they're not. You can't say that so-and-so is right and so-and-so is wrong. People do make such judgments; and you can create this technique within what appears to be a realistic framework, but then it's no longer realistic in the traditional sense.

DLB: You've said that you came to Shakespeare late in your life, that you really hadn't taken Shakespeare inside you.

RABE: There was a part of me that was very rational and literal minded, and I had a difficult time knowing what the hell he was talking about. It was only when I realized that he's talking about exactly what he says, that he started to

make sense. That is what he's talking about, and not about something else. When he refers to the soul he means a soul. He's not talking about somebody's unconscious or their neurosis. The heavens are the heavens, and the planets are just that—the planets; he's actually very literal in a sense. It's just that his world is not what we think of as the world, as the literal world. His world as he writes about it is all up front; thus, the mysteries. I was always trying to equate the language to something else, and, consequently, he seemed overwritten, or I couldn't follow it. It was as if I was trying to translate him, which I think a lot of people do. Both scholars and directors are always trying to find a modern equivalent to translate him by. But I personally don't think that's how it works. He's operating in some sort of language of the soul or of the psyche or archetypes or the spirit or something that is alien to us in a way unless we just open up to him.

DLB: Earlier you had mentioned your comedy. Your humor is funny; yet it has an edge that's quite disconcerting.

RABE: There's no question that part of what the work does is comic when it's at its best; that's probably true of every play of mine. I don't know how it came to be. It just seems to me that the feeling about life that the plays try to embody is a comprehensive feeling. There is a strange mix in life. The laughter usually comes out of a giddy quality, almost a disorientation sometimes. I don't know how to interpret it myself.

DLB: In *Lear*, when the blinded Gloucester wants to die by jumping off a cliff at Dover, his son, Edgar, says, "Yes, here's a huge cliff," and Gloucester jumps, thinking he is committing suicide. Yet, because it's only a short fall, he is not dead. It's funny yet dreadful. Does this scene characterize your comedy as well?

RABE: To an extent. When I read *Lear* after having had my eyes opened to Shakespeare, I saw how that kind of playfulness abounds— both the theatrical playfulness and the cosmic playfulness. The level he's operating at was a revelation for me. The next step is to go into the bleakest and most harrowing kind of direct emotion. Of course, Shakespeare also has written wonderfully pure comedies. Although I personally feel that there is a great darkness in a lot of his

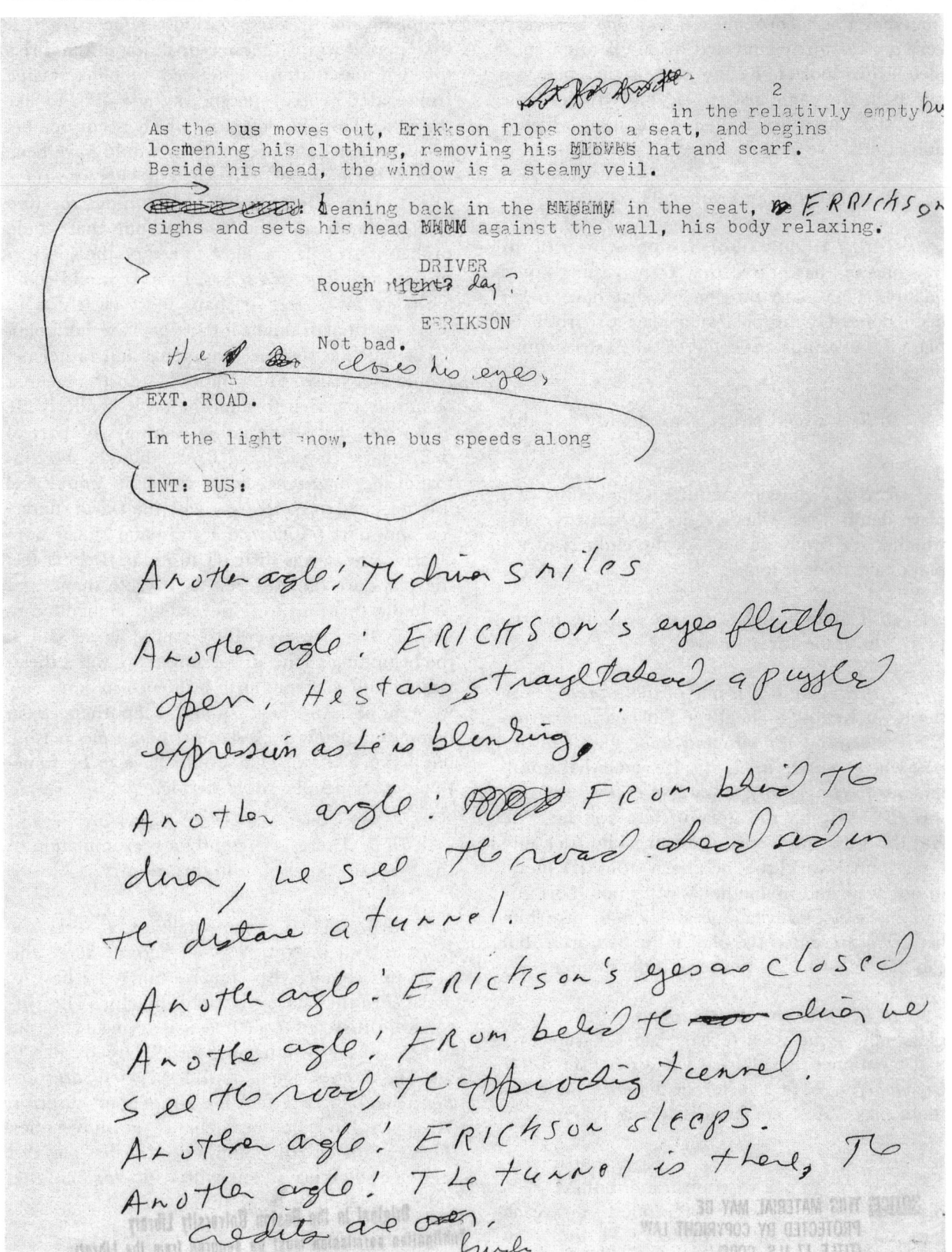

Page from the revised typescript for **Casualties of War** *(Boston University, Mugar Memorial Library, by permission of David Rabe)*

comedies that people miss. *Much Ado* is a very, very dark comedy, and that quality is often completely overlooked. By the end of that play, no one is in the same reality. He has written some plays that are pure comedies, though, which I don't think I've ever done.

DLB: Do you think you will?

RABE: I don't know. I suppose in a funny way one of these three that I am writing could qualify. There are three plays that have never been done. Of my published plays or produced plays, I don't think any could be called strict comedies.

DLB: I would struggle to identify any that way.

RABE: I guess by definition the ending of a play determines whether it's a comedy, not whether it's funny or not. So, the endings of my plays have done it to me.

DLB: This spring you were working on the play "Those the River Keeps."

RABE: That one is one of the three. "Those the River Keeps" is about the Phil character from *Hurly Burly* and his wife and some guy from his past who shows up in his life. It's somewhat simultaneous to *Hurly Burly*, to parts of *Hurly Burly* anyway. Basically it's the story of him and his wife and this guy who is sort of inviting him back into the criminal world that he's been from. It's literal in one way, and in another way it's not. This guy and his sort of invitation/seduction to take him back. We presented the play at the McCarter, but I'm not sure what its future is at the moment.

DLB: How do you feel about your Vietnam plays now some twenty years later? Earlier you had mentioned that Barnard had performed *The Orphan*. You have a different audience now for those plays. Your audience is twenty years old in some cases.

RABE: Well, it's curious, and I think each play would have a different reception—they each face different kinds of problems, I think, in terms of seeming pertinent, to the degree that they would be judged capable of escaping their Vietnam categorization. *The Orphan* was very interesting. These kids just accepted the play and its at-

tempt to link up these various elements of that time period with Greek myth, although the director told me that there tended to be a feeling from older people—people my age—not to like the play. The kids loved it, which is curious because someone my age or older would have been part of the initial experience. The kids who came to it without any preconceived attitudes received it as a play. *Pavlo* would be the one that would probably struggle the most to escape the specifics of the war. *Sticks and Bones*, I think, would stand a chance to be seen perhaps more clearly in its more essential dramatic lines, which are not political as much as they are emotional and rather demonic in a sense. The politics of and the feelings about the war that formed the plays—and my life as I wrote them—are going to always be part of these plays. In *Sticks and Bones*, though, the dramatic line might be clearer; people would feel less obligated to sympathize with the David character and might follow the dramatic story more clearly. *Streamers* is difficult to judge. I don't feel the plays are dated. I felt as I wrote them, and feel now, that they were never quite embedded finally in their time period because, as we said at the beginning of this discussion, there was a theatricality and a metaphoric influence in how they were done. And that should keep them from being completely locked into their time period, but I don't know. That would have to be something other people would decide.

DLB: There is currently a reexamination of the Vietnam experience in this country.

RABE: There's some talk of a *Sticks and Bones* revival in New York at Second Stage this year, this coming year, but it's not set. I have to make sure they have the right director. The person who directed *The Orphan* is trying to get an Off-Broadway production, too. I'd really like to see *The Orphan* again, and I may let *Sticks and Bones* happen, if I feel it's got a good director. My plays have the best chance at universities. They're not exactly community theater plays or summer stock plays. Their life is in regional theaters and in universities.

DLB: David, there's something called Vietnam chic now. It had become quite chic to talk and write about Vietnam. How do you feel about that?

RABE: Well, I don't know. It's not—you know, I think when some of that happens it's offensive, but it's just part of the process of—you know, it's hard to answer such a question without having a specific piece of work that I'm commenting on or thinking about. In general, it struck me as odd—at first kind of offensive, and then odd, and then sort of typical of how things are dealt with. It's a superficial way of dealing with important events—to turn them into fashion.

DLB: Are you thinking of the play *Miss Saigon*, for example?

RABE: I didn't go to *Miss Saigon*. But I think that's sacrilegious, frankly. I was invited to an event, and I wouldn't go. I was also invited to write about it, and I wouldn't do that either, because I knew from the get-go I would attack it—no matter what it was, I was going to attack it. But it's sort of inevitable. It's the pattern of what happens to major events such as the Vietnam War. I remember when—I think I was still living at home and probably hadn't even gone to college or been in the army yet when *Hogan's Heroes* came on TV; I was offended. I thought that making jokes about Nazis was a way of defusing, or reducing, the whole experience. It was a way of preparing for the next phase of the Nazis' madness so it could come back again.

DLB: Is Vietnam an aberration in American military history? Was it a unique war?

RABE: That's a very complicated question because I think that it certainly was politically traditional. Vietnam was a manifestation of political ideas that go back to the beginning of the country, to westward expansion. To me Vietnam was a manifestation of the same political thrust that covered the Indians. In terms of how it was fought, it certainly was not unique. Strategically it was almost identical to Korea in the kind of restraints that were put on the troops. The war took place in a long, narrow country that sticks out in the water and at the halfway point is divided. American soldiers could do certain things, but could not do other things. We couldn't invade, take the ground, and hold it and move on. The goals were political. Vietnam was basically fought in the same way as Korea, strategically. How Vietnam is different is in the fact that the politics and the bare bones of the event were perceived fully for the first time by Americans and

were protested; the raw nature of the war was revealed. There was a political response that differed. Since then the basic political thrust has been reestablished, and the powers that be understood the mistakes they made in terms of public relations. They'll never do that again. And although I'm happy in some ways that there is no draft, I think an all-voluntary army is a very dangerous entity in this regard.

DLB: Tim O'Brien has a passage in his novel *Going After Cacciato* [1978] in which the character Doc Peret discusses this very idea with a Captain Rhallon of the Iranian Savak. Doc says, in effect, that all one needs to do is just change the name of the war and you still have the feel of it, the smell, the experience of it. In that sense Vietnam is not aberrant, but this war did have some unique qualities to it, too, didn't it?

RABE: Yes, the uniqueness was the people in the war at the time, the specifics of the weaponry. Korea was unique, you know what I mean? The difference was the way in which it went on. Anybody who participated—all of those participants—created the uniqueness of it. Then there was the incredible length of the Vietnam War. The length of the war created the possibility that people who were eight when the war started could have ended up in it. Or they were twelve when the war began, then went to college, protested against the war, and then later were fighting over there. There was a strange amalgam and mixture of people and feelings. I doubt that the sense of absurdity was higher in Vietnam than in the combat situations in Korea, except that during Korea no one at home was attacking you or saying you were foolish, which is a huge difference. And the year's rotation was a big difference. I don't know my Korean War history that well, but I don't think that was the case there. That year put a strange stress on people. Vietnam was horribly unique, and it wasn't. It was this mixture of differing elements that made it unique, and the influx or the intrusion of television translated it in a way. But just the sheer length of the war, the basic flow of battle, I think— although one involved frozen terrain while the other was a jungle—was radically different from Korea. But then World War II had both frozen terrain and jungles.

DLB: You bring up an interesting point— the Vietnam soldier's year rotation had a way of making the individual even more isolated. A soldier served according to the calendar rather than the demands of particular battles.

RABE: I believe it made us know in our souls that nothing was at stake for the country, so that we knew that somewhere—whether we ever thought it the whole time we were there, whether it ever consciously crossed our minds—we knew somewhere in our bones that there was nothing really at stake, certainly not survival, or they couldn't do that. If important concerns were at stake you would have to stay till you won. I think in a strange way that was the poison. It worked; people were glad to have it. The government thought it was going to trick people, placate them, into going along with the war. But on some level it poisoned everybody. Everybody was on a different schedule. People were arriving, other people were leaving, you know, people were experienced and inexperienced.

DLB: Do you go to any of the movies about Vietnam?

RABE: I've seen a lot of them, but I haven't seen all of them.

DLB: How do they strike you?

RABE: I don't know. They each had their own virtues and vices. I didn't care much for the kind of story line of *Platoon*, but I thought that Oliver Stone caught the feel of Vietnam better than anybody else. The story line to me supported the heroic myth a little too much, but the actual feel of the place and the combat and the chaos of things, I think, Stone caught better than anybody else. I didn't see *Born on the Fourth of July*. I thought *Casualties of War* was fucked up, about halfway fucked up, halfway good. I thought *Full Metal Jacket* was fascinating, but not the last part. Did you see it?

DLB: Yes, I did.

RABE: I thought that they would have just shot that girl in two seconds at the end. You know that strange scene where they all kind of hesitate? That was garbage.

DLB: The basic training section of the movie I thought was probably its strongest element.

RABE: Yes. Have you ever read the book it's based on?

DLB: Yes, I have.

RABE: Well, the book is powerful. Kubrick is one of the great filmmakers around, I think, but I've never been able to figure out why he didn't go with how the book ended, which was far more harrowing than the movie ending. So, none of the movies have been to me a fully satisfying experience. But having dealt with Hollywood myself, I know how difficult it is to get anything that even vaguely resembles reality.

DLB: Is Hollywood a subject about which you have strong responses?

RABE: It's one of these things—biting the hand that feeds me at the moment. I have more opportunity to write for Hollywood than I do for the theater. The theater is disappearing from the planet. And I do write these movies, and they pay the bills. But it's problematic. You know, it's very, very difficult to get anything done that really has integrity, or that attempts to have integrity, that wants to really reflect life or reality. They're all into genres, and it's difficult.

DLB: When you see a film such as *Full Metal Jacket*, do you respond as a playwright, as a filmmaker, as a Vietnam vet, or all three of those?

RABE: Well, I think with something like that movie, it was all three elements. The first response I think to me is one in which I am responding as myself. I don't pick it apart as it goes or study the way it was made. As with *Full Metal Jacket*, I went along with the movie. I had read the book before I saw the movie. So I was kind of flabbergasted when the ending came along. I have technical thoughts at moments when the movie sort of asks me to in a way. But I try to let the movie take me with it. Primarily my response to something that pertains to Vietnam is as someone who has thought about it a lot and still has deep feelings about it. Which is why when I was involved in *Casualties of War*, and it turned into something that I thought was not what we—the director, the producer, and I—had agreed upon, and something that didn't reflect the script that I had turned in, I was very disturbed. If that had happened with another movie I had written that wasn't about Vietnam, it would not have disturbed me anywhere near as much. But I'll never write another one about Vietnam, and I wish I hadn't written that one. But I thought we had a chance. I went into the project thinking that it would go a certain way, but it didn't. I'm not ashamed of the whole thing, but I feel that it is not what it could have been, and a large part—several parts of it are embarrassing.

DLB: It's a very effective movie in many regards. The language itself is so much more accomplished than other war movies I've seen about Vietnam. What disturbed you most of all about it?

RABE: There were several scenes in the early part which were put into a different order than they were intended to be in, which in a strange way screwed up our ability to follow Erickson, the Michael J. Fox character, as he went into this experience. Then there were several scenes added and several other scenes cut from the script. Several short scenes were added for the purpose of making the Michael J. Fox character understand the moral ramifications of his situation almost immediately. What I had tried to write was something in which those ramifications would be fairly clear to the audience, but it would also be clear to the audience that anybody in those circumstances would have had reason to misunderstand them. I had a scene where, after the first battle, they stopped at a whorehouse that was a farmhouse. That way the audience would have known that *some* farms were whorehouses. And so there was a reason for him not to quite know what to do for a long period of time and to try to talk Meserve and the other people out of what they were doing, to wonder if she was a VC or if she was a whore? And even if she was one or both, did that mean that what they were doing was right? A scene was added in which Erickson stands with the mother and sister of the girl and says, "I'm sorry." They probably would have killed him. He wouldn't have done that anyway. The last thing a soldier would do is let himself be separated from his people. The addition of this scene made it clear that he knew what was right and what was wrong at that moment. And if he knew it at that point, then a lot of the next part of the script lost tension and drive. But mainly what it did is separate him from the other soldiers, made him a good guy and them bad, and that was not what I had intended. The scenes that were cut would have

helped tighten his relationship with them so he would have had more loyalty, or more trouble breaking away from them, even though he would have come to know the situation as it was, and even though they would—when they realized that he was not with them—be willing to consider killing him. But that was supposed to evolve slowly, rather than how it was done—right from the get-go. Then there were certain lines that I wrote in the last scene with the girl about it all being a dream and passages which I wrote under duress. In fact, there was a dream, when Erickson had a nightmare in which these soldiers attempted a retaliation on him and his family; he woke up on the subway screaming, which would have given the girl some reason to know that he'd had a dream, something to talk about. I never liked the lines; I never wanted the lines. They said to me, "If you don't do it, we'll write them, and you'll do it better than us, so why don't you do it?" I fought desperately once the movie was edited to get those lines out so that nothing would happen between him and her at the end except that they would say hello and goodbye in Vietnamese. The only exchange of language would have been "Cai, Co" "Cai, Ung," and they would have looked at each other, and that would have been that. There were a couple of other things, too. I had problems with their trying to blow Erickson up with a grenade. That was perhaps okay, but that he then faced them down and beat the guy with a shovel undermined the dramatic tension of the trial scene because two things happened: once they clearly tried to murder him, the ambiguity of the trial scene was lost; and once he hit the guy with the shovel, he was top dog; he had won. So in a sense, the movie was over; the dramatic reversal had happened. That shouldn't have happened until she says hello to him. So I had quarrels with moral and thematic ideas and also structural elements.

DLB: Yet, it's quite a moving, effective film.

RABE: I guess it is. Some people find it very much so. There are people who try to convince me of that. But it could have been a great movie; it could have had a moral richness, an ambiguity and richness comparable to what *Paths of Glory* has where things are not clear-cut—or it's clear-cut, but it doesn't win out in a clear-cut way.

DLB: I hope someday the director and producer will listen to the playwright. That would be helpful.

RABE: Yes, it would, wouldn't it? At least when we're right. We're always right.

The First Edition Library/Collectors' Reprints Inc.

Mary Scott Dye

Every book collector knows that immaculate copies of important first editions are rare and, consequently, expensive. First editions of significant books that are readily available *and* affordable are unheard of. How, then, are Henry and Mary Reath and Kemp Battle, owners of Collectors' Reprints, Inc.—a small but thriving Manhattan-based specialist publisher—able to offer "1940 Hemingways at the 1940 price?" They aren't. But they are producing the next best thing: first edition facsimiles, with dust jackets, of America's most acclaimed novels.

"The original editions of America's great literary classics have long been out of circulation, available, at great expense, only through the rare book trade," state the company owners, who began making the classics accessible to readers of more modest means when they organized the First Edition Library series in 1987. With annual sales of $1.25 million last year generated by more than twenty-six thousand customers, the response has been anything but modest. The Reaths and Battle acknowledge a tremendous debt to helpful publishers, rare book librarians, antiquarian book dealers, and private collectors who have assisted in their quest for knowledge about the rare book business and who have supplied volumes that would otherwise have been too costly for them to reproduce in facsimile.

Each First Edition Library reprint is identical to its original counterpart with two exceptions: the printing process (offset rather than letterpress) and consumer cost (an average of thirty dollars a book rather than three hundred dollars or, in many cases, three thousand dollars or more). That they are printed on acid-free paper instead of the now-disintegrating stock commonly used in the early to mid twentieth century en-

Front cover for the First Edition Library facsimile of Twain's 1885 novel, one of two nineteenth-century works reproduced in the series

sures the books' longevity. No detail has been overlooked by the Reaths and Battle when a book is being planned and produced: dust jackets, sewn bindings, paper weight and finish, endpapers, illustrations, typefaces (including some for which materials no longer exist), cover colors and designs, and typographical errors or "issue points" are all meticulously duplicated. Print runs aver-

Some of the facsimiles produced by Collectors' Reprints for the First Edition Library

age around five thousand per volume.

Henry Reath, a former Doubleday executive, brought both editorial and marketing experience to Collectors' Reprint when he and his wife, Mary, a former English teacher, founded the company in 1987. Kemp Battle contributed his skills as an investment banker and Doubleday subsidiary rights manager. The three function as equal partners, but all agree it was Henry Reath, a self-described minor book collector, who discovered the large, untapped market for quality facsimiles of first editions. "He was talking with a friend who was a rare book dealer," said Mary Reath, "and he thought it was remarkable that modern twentieth-century firsts were printed on paper that was disintegrating and that their prices were increasing so dramatically. I think right then and there Henry was curious. . . . We thought about this being America's century as far as literature and about the way graphic art and the development of dustjackets came together at the same time. It was a project that would have risks, but be worth trying."

Along with Ernest Hemingway's *The Sun Also Rises* (1926), *A Farewell to Arms* (1929), *For Whom the Bell Tolls* (1940), and *The Old Man and the Sea* (1952), all offered by the First Edition Library, readers have been able to choose from a total of twenty-six books thus far (an average of nine per year) by authors that include F. Scott Fitz-

gerald (*The Great Gatsby* [1925]—the first book published in the series, *This Side of Paradise* [1920], and *Tender Is the Night* [1934]), William Faulkner (*As I Lay Dying* [1930], The Sound and the Fury [1929], and *Light in August* [1932]), John Steinbeck (*Tortilla Flat* [1935], Of Mice and Men [1932], and *The Grapes of Wrath* [1939]), and Edith Wharton (*Ethan Frome* [1911]). Forthcoming books include James Baldwin's *Go Tell It on the Mountain* (1953), Theodore Dreiser's *Sister Carrie* (1900), Sinclair Lewis's *Babbitt* (1922), Marjorie Kinnan Rawlings's *The Yearling* (1938), and the company's first collection of short stories, Hemingway's *Men Without Women* (1927). Walt Whitman's *Leaves of Grass* (1855) will be the first volume in a new poetry series planned for 1992 and the only volume produced on a letterpress to date.

Collectors' Reprints has also explored nineteenth-century classics by producing facsimiles of Mark Twain's 1885 novel *Huckleberry Finn* (one of its biggest sellers), and recently *Tom Sawyer* (1876). "We're testing the waters," said Mary Reath about nineteenth-century literature. "From my point of view I like working on different types of things, and from a production point of view, as far as we feel we can accomplish something that's pretty faithful [to the original], we're open to it. If you go much beyond the nineteenth century the production was so totally different that it would be out of the question for us to make those books."

Locating pristine copies of first editions, and especially first edition dust jackets, from which to produce the film for the facsimiles has often been a difficult task for the company. "In order to make a book we must first acquire a copy of the title," said Mary Reath. "We don't always buy a dustjacket because they're usually in pretty bad shape. We have a good working relationship with the Beinecke—the Rare Book Library at Yale—and they have a marvelous collection of dustjackets that are in quite good condition, though they still require a lot of repair once the photograph has been taken. There are many first editions that only cost five or six hundred dollars in dustjackets, and we've bought a lot of those. It's when a book starts to cost four thousand dollars that it doesn't make sense for us to purchase that particular title." (The Reaths and Battle were fortunate to have access to Fitzgerald's copy of *The Great Gatsby*—complete with a pristine jacket—from his scrapbook in the Fitzgerald archives at Firestone Library. A mint-condition copy of the same book recently sold for ten thousand dollars.)

In most cases reprint rights have been readily granted by publishers or trustees of authors' estates with Collectors' Reprints paying royalties. "We have been able to acquire all the rights that we wanted," said Mary Reath. "I can't think of a title that we have wanted to do that we haven't been able to do. The only one that comes to mind is *Catcher in the Rye*, and that's because the first edition had a photograph of Salinger on the back and he won't allow it to be reproduced. The publishers have been great, though; they really have looked on it as an important adjunct to the manufacturing and distribution of their titles."

The reactions of librarians and scholars to the appearance and content of First Edition Library volumes have always been a matter of utmost importance to the Reaths and Battle. Great care has been exerted to prevent their facsimiles from being circulated by unscrupulous parties as true first printings. Each First Edition Library volume is clearly identified as such by a small FEL logo on the back inside flap of the dust jacket and a printed disclaimer on the copyright page. The year of publication and the words *printed on acid-free paper* are also included on the copyright page.

Collectors' Reprints operates as a mail order business that offers individual volumes for sale at $34.95 each or $29.95 for regular subscribers. Each volume comes with a descriptive card providing information about the author and the history of the book.

Bertram Rota and His Bookshop

Anthony B. Rota
Bertram Rota Ltd. Booksellers

Cyril Bertram Rota was born in London in June 1903. Cyril to his family and friends of early years, he was later known almost exclusively by his middle name, given to him after his maternal grandfather, the scholar-bookseller Bertram Dobell (1842-1914), discoverer of Thomas Traherne and publisher of James Thomson ("City of Dreadful Night") and champion of various bookselling causes (such as the retention of the so-called sixpenny shelves outside Charing Cross Road bookshops).

Because of the shortage of men on the labor market toward the end of World War I, Bertram's mother yielded to the pleas of her brothers, Percy and Arthur Dobell, to let her son leave school and go straight to work for them in the antiquarian bookselling business they had inherited from their father. Percy told his sister Eva: "I will teach the boy all I know." My father used to say, without any bitterness, that all he was actually taught in his four years with his uncles was how to tie a neat parcel—something, he continued, that stood him in good stead for the rest of his life. That was what he was taught: what he learned for himself was a different matter, and by 1923 he was ready to put it into practice on his own account. Not wishing to cause any conflict within the family, he looked for a field of bookselling which would not be in competition with his uncles. His natural predilection for the moderns (he was later to lecture on them at London's Working Men's College) made the newly developing field of first editions of modern English literature a natural and happy choice. It was a field that he made virtually synonymous with his own name, and it is fair to say that he, together with Percy Muir and A. T. Miller (of Frank Hollings), effectively codified the best practices.

The business began in a suite of upstairs rooms in Charing Cross Road. The starting capital was exactly one hundred pounds, a sum borrowed from his mother, who had painstakingly scraped it together over the years by saving from the housekeeping money which formed virtually

Bertram Rota in 1957

all the wages of her husband, a "corrector of the press" (that is, newspaper proofreader). Bertram supplemented this meager seed corn with what he could earn in the evenings by playing the drums in a dance band. At weekends he played the timpani in an amateur symphony orchestra. With no staff to help him, he would shut the shop at lunchtime and eat a sandwich while traveling to view auction sales.

The young firm's first catalogue was published in 1923. The celebrated collector A. E. Newton made it his practice to be the first customer of new entrants to the trade, and the first purchase he made from my father was a copy of Samuel Butler's utopian novel *Erewhon* (1872). Visiting California in 1963, Bertram found the selfsame copy, now with Eddie Newton's bookplate, on the shelves of the Los Angeles dealer

Max Hunley, and, of course, he snapped it up. It is among my most cherished books today.

In 1927 the firm moved to a narrow shop in Davies Street in the West End of London. It was here that T. E. Lawrence was a visitor. The next move, in 1934, was to larger premises near at hand in Old Burlington Street, where Bertram was joined by Percy Lauder, a boy recruited straight from Bertram's old school, Hornsey County. Lauder stayed until called for war service around 1940. By that time the business had moved again, this time to Bodley House in Vigo Street, actually a set of chambers in Albany, whence John Lane had published *The Yellow Book* and many of the celebrated works of the 1890s, which were Bertram Rota's stock-in-trade. The building suffered a direct hit from a bomb in the course of the Blitz, but most of the stock was salvaged. (The next catalogue, No. 66, was entitled *Brands from the Burning*.) The business continued from temporary quarters next door. It was then that Bertram volunteered for a commission in the Royal Air Force, where he served with distinction in the fields of photographic interpretation and target intelligence. A loyal team of women and part-timers (including the bibliographer Eric Osborne, himself serving as a special constable, and the poet Kenneth Hopkins) kept the business ticking over, with direction from Bertram in off-duty hours.

After the war he was joined by a then youthful Anthony Newnham, later to trade on his own, but who, under Bertram's tuition, trained his natural instinctive flair for a good book to an awesome level. In 1952 I joined the firm myself: we had then reached Catalogue No. 90. I worked with my father in Vigo Street for fourteen happy years, during which time my close colleague George Lawson was recruited, as was our stalwart shop manager, Peter Scott, to whom we owe our interest in books of the Great War—see Catalogue No. 245, for example. Ronald Taylor came to us, by way of Blackwell's and the Folio Society, to take care of books published before 1870. With these additions we were now pushing out the walls of Bodley House and in 1965 decided to move again—literally across the road to the palatially decorated ground floor of a modern building in Savile Row. The journey was so short that we carried all the books over by hand—and even sold one while it was in transit.

Alas Bertram did not live to enjoy his comfortable new quarters for long: a heart attack carried him off on 3 December 1966 when he was only sixty-three. He had established the firm's reputation throughout the English-speaking world. The forewords of bibliographies were peppered with acknowledgments of his help. He had built (or largely contributed to) some of the best modern collections in private hands (notably the George Lazarus collection of D. H. Lawrence). He was a regular consultant and adviser to such institutions as the Berg Collection at the New York Public Library and the newly burgeoning Harry Ransom Humanities Research Center at the University of Texas. His advice to collectors remains valid today: "Don't just follow fashion: collect what *you* admire. Buy the best copy you can reasonably expect to find. The books you don't buy that are the ones you regret." Many of the more important libraries and archives that the firm has handled came up in my father's lifetime. They include H. G. Wells's manuscripts, now at the University of Illinois (in 1953); the Eddie Marsh archive, now in the Berg Collection, New York Public Library (Marsh, editor of *Georgian Poetry*, was patron to the best young poets and painters of the 1920s); the correspondence files of the literary agent J. B. Pinker; the library of the economic historians J. L. and Barbara Hammond; and much else. Subsequently we handled such archives as those of Hilaire Belloc (together with his library), now at Boston College; Lawrence Durrell, now at Southern Illinois University; John Lane, now at the Harry Ransom Humanities Research Center, University of Texas; the poet and publisher John Rodker, also at the Harry Ransom Humanities Research Center; the file copies of John Murray's publications, now at the University of North Carolina at Chapel Hill; Edward Thomas's manuscript journals; Evelyn Waugh's letters to Lady Diana Cooper, at the British Library; and major manuscripts by D. H. Lawrence, Somerset Maugham, and Edith and Osbert Sitwell.

In the years since my father's death much has happened, but I do not think any changes the firm has made have been at variance with the ethos that he established. We have had the fortune to continue to recruit and retain good people, a prime example being John Byrne, who works with me on manuscripts and archives and who is responsible for looking after our interests in private press books. We purchased the stock, reference libraries, and good will of two other firms, Frank Hollings and G. F. Sims. We moved from rented property to premises that we own in Covent Garden. We have issued more than a hun-

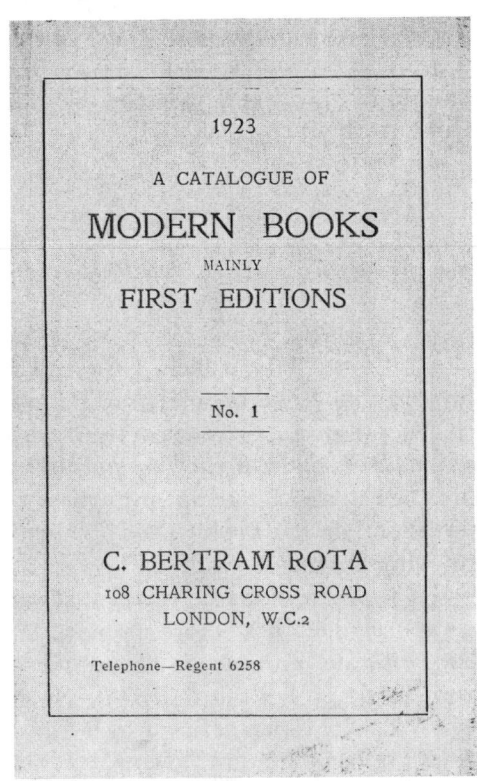

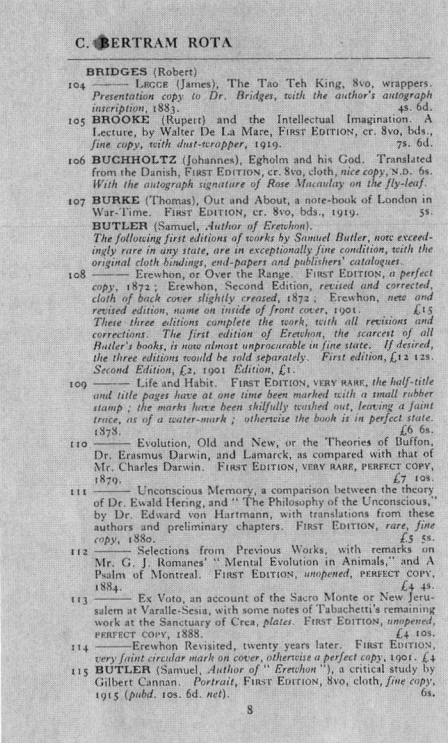

Front cover and page from Bertram Rota's first catalogue (Special Collections, Thomas Cooper Library, University of South Carolina). His first sale was item number 108, bought by book collector A. E. Newton.

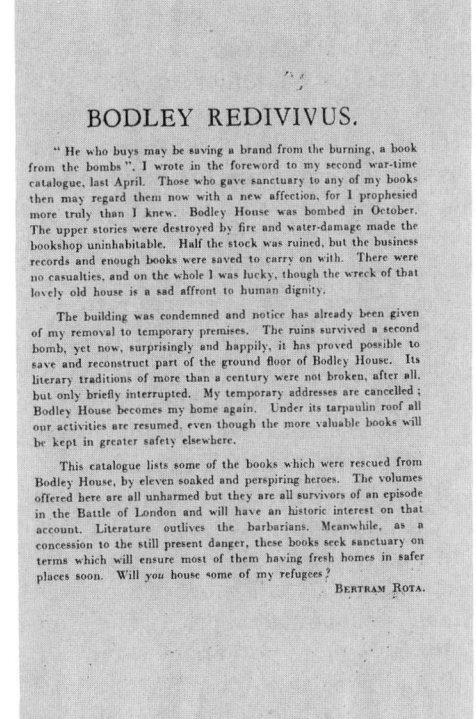

Cover and introduction from Rota's catalogue of the books he recovered from his bookshop after it was bombed by the Germans during World War II (Special Collections, Thomas Cooper Library, University of South Carolina)

dred further catalogues, some specialized (for example, No. 180, Rossetti family books; No. 244, books by the Powys family; No. 192, The Printer and the Artist), but the main thrust remains the same: first editions of English literature from about 1890 to the present day. It has to be said that many—indeed a majority—of the books we buy are sold in the shop or by special quotation before they can be listed in one of our printed catalogues, but I believe it remains true that those catalogues, taken together, provide a reliable index to the market in first editions and to changes in bibliographical taste and technique.

How have taste and technique evolved? In a nutshell the range of authors actively collected has narrowed, collections are formed in greater depth, and fine condition and the presence of the dust jacket have become the criteria for purchase decisions. Fashion plays a larger part than at any time since the boom days of high prices for John Galsworthy's *The Forsyte Saga* (never a truly rare book). One month everyone wants J. R. R. Tolkien, the next D. M. Thomas, and the month after that Salman Rushdie. Meanwhile the works of good, solid writers such as Arnold Bennett, George Moore, and, save for the rarities, Rudyard Kipling, lie neglected on the shelves.

The depth of present-day collecting makes a happier picture. Where collectors used to be content with having the first edition of a book as published in the author's own country (the practice known as "following the flag"), and could only rarely be persuaded to have the first edition produced on the other side of the Atlantic *even if it could be proved to have appeared earlier*, the virtues of having both English *and* American first editions is now widely accepted. The same is true of revised editions, foreign translations, and serializations too—which means that author collections formed today are far more interesting and have far more research potential, both from the textual standpoint and from the bibliographical.

It was always the best policy to pay a premium for a really fine copy, but the emphasis on fine condition has never been greater than it is today. Indeed copies that fall short of fine state are hard to sell at almost any price. The dust-jacket, once merely seen as an ephemeral protection to guard (and later also to advertise) a book during its transit from bindery to customer, then to be discarded, has now come into its own. Today it is rightly seen as an integral part of the book, with much to tell us about the author, the book's publishing history—and for that matter,

the history of publishing. If I deplore the switch to what one of my colleagues calls "flavor of the month" bookselling, I welcome the other changes almost without reservation.

ON BEING 100

The introduction to Catalogue 100, which was issued in Spring 1955

So this is how it feels. Nearly fifty years before my time I find myself in one sense a centenarian. Assuming the privilege of the old I permit myself to look back to the day in 1923 when, just turning twenty, I put up my sign at the foot of the flight of stairs which led to my first bookroom in Charing Cross Road.

Catalogue No. 1, in the format which I have always retained, lies before me now. It is modest, but I look at it with the eye of a father for his first-born. Beside it lies this Catalogue No. 100. Looking over the long series which came between them I reflect that, with Dowson, I have been faithful in my fashion. The moderns, to whose mast I nailed my flag, have sailed steadily on, even if the seas were sometimes choppy; and I offer still the works of those who are newly launched as well as of those who have triumphantly arrived.

Who, I wonder, bought the first edition of T. S. Eliot's "The Waste Land" from Catalogue 4 in 1924 for 7s. 6d.—and would he care to sell it back to me now? "Prufrock" was up to £3 3s. in Catalogue 13 in 1929 but costs nearly ten times as much to-day. The published price of 7s. 6d. seems reasonable enough for a dust-wrappered copy of the first edition of Mary Webb's "Precious Bane" in 1927, the day before Prime Minister Stanley Baldwin's broadcast praise of it brought me twenty orders the next morning. Presentation copies of Baron Corvo's "Stories Toto Told Me" at £2 2s. in 1925 and of Joyce's "Portrait of the Artist as a Young Man" at £9 9s. in 1928 have well justified the faith of the buyers. James, Chesterton, Lawrence, Huxley, Maugham, Pound and Graham Greene were going for comparative songs in those days.

It is true that there have been falls from the dizzy pinnacles of the late nineteen-twenties, but in looking back one sees the steady appreciation of worthy work—a comforting reflection for collectors of judgement. The lesson is as clear to-day, when we may be confident that these times are producing creative work as deserving of pre-

Bertram Rota (right) and Anthony B. Rota in the Rota bookshop in Bodley House, on Vigo Street, circa 1957

servation and as likely to bring reward in growing value as well as in the pleasure of possession.

Nine catalogues were issued before my Charing Cross Road book-rooms were forsaken in 1927 for a small bookshop in Davies Street. Twenty-three more came from that address by 1934 and another seventeen were published from a larger shop in Old Burlington Street by 1937, before our removal to our permanent home in John Lane's lovely old "Bodley Head." Since 1937 Nos. 50 to 100 have come from Bodley House. My single-handed efforts of 1923 are now shared by seven helpers, including my son, whose birth coincided with Catalogue 22. We survived the war, with all the men away in the forces, and we arose phoenix-like from the ashes to which a bomb reduced us in 1940.

Though incorporated as a company in 1942, for convenience, the business did not change the personal character which has been my constant aim and pleasure and which has so richly rewarded me in a chain of world-wide friendships. Not a day fails to refresh my gratitude to the collectors, librarians and fellow-

booksellers who have been such faithful friends for so long.

Turning over my hundred catalogues again I note especially No. 25, the inscribed library of John Gawsworth (enlivened with sketch-portraits and potted biographies); No. 29, an irreplaceable collection of signed proof engravings by Stephen Gooden; No. 36, a representative library of 100 first editions for £100; No. 55, which offered "A Thousand Bargains" (and fluttered some dovecotes); No. 59, a chronological catalogue of Twentieth Century Novels; No. 64, in which I prophesied more truly than I then knew the impending bomb disaster of 1940, and No. 66, which offered the brands rescued from that burning.

After the war No. 75 assembled nearly nine hundred first editions of poetry and No. 80, "The Art of the Printed Book," became our most ambitious effort, listing eight hundred and fifty private press books. Since 1949 another score of catalogues has led us through six more years to the round figure now achieved.

This hundredth list is representative of our general stock and includes a collection of first editions of fiction of the nineteen-thirties in remarkably fine state. Our catalogues, however, only hint at the many important books, manuscripts, collections and archives which we acquire and sell privately and of which I am glad to give news to buyers about whose special interests I am advised.

Now, with my little centenary reminiscence over, I renounce the unlived second half-century of years which I began by assuming, and I am off to assemble books for Catalogue 101.

Bertram Rota

By WAY OF INTRODUCTION

The introduction to Catalogue 200, which was issued in Winter 1975/1976

This is the two hundredth in our regular series of catalogues devoted in the main to first editions, private press books and modern literary autographs. In it we list two hundred items which are currently in our stock and which are representative of the material in which we specialise. In addition to nineteenth and twentieth century literature, there are some rare books of earlier periods as well as drawings and engravings of literary interest.

It has been said that regular swimmers should not waste too much time taking the temperature of the water. Nevertheless publication of this catalogue does seem an appropriate moment for what Sir Francis Meynell called a "prospectus and retrospectus"—a looking forward and a looking back.

Our first catalogue was published in 1923 from an upstairs room in Charing Cross Road. Since then we have published catalogues at an average rate of about four a year (rather fewer during the war years), remaining, like Dowson, faithful in our fashion to the modern first editions in which we specialise. They still form the cornerstone of our business, although perhaps we now place greater emphasis on modern fine printing than was once our habit. Moreover our acquisition of Frank Hollings' bookshop in 1969 marked our commitment to strengthening our stock of earlier books. Happily Hollings' former proprietor, Mr. A. T. Miller, still makes his services available to us as a consultant and indeed he is regularly to be found at Savile Row.

In a foreword to our one hundredth catalogue, issued in the Spring of 1955, my father,

Bertram Rota, picked out those of his catalogues which lived particularly in his memory. As I look back over the second century I recall particularly some of the association copies in Catalogue 111: Norman Douglas' *Siren Land* inscribed to Hugh Walpole, Gilbert's *Songs of a Savoyard* inscribed to George Grossmith and *Du Côté de Chez Swann* inscribed by Proust to Prince Manuel Bibesco. Then in Catalogue 116 I was proud to offer the original engraved wood blocks by David Jones for *Gulliver's Travels* and *The Book of Jonah*. There was Catalogue 122 with manuscripts and drawings by Beerbohm; and an autograph catalogue, number 142, including one hundred and sixty-one letters from Beardsley to Raffalovich and fifty-two letters from Baron Corvo to the literary agent, J. B. Pinker. Catalogue 143 was one of a number to echo something we first tried in 1947: a catalogue devoted to modern poetry with a foreword by a contemporary poet. Sir John Betjeman and Edward Lucie-Smith have both been good enough to contribute introductions to recent catalogues in this series. I have always taken great personal pleasure and satisfaction in these more specialised catalogues, which seem to me to be of more lasting worth than any general compilation.

Number 150, issued in 1967, was something of a celebratory catalogue. Among the good things it contained were the manuscript of Iris Murdoch's first novel, *Under the Net*; some original wood blocks of Thomas Bewick; Eliot's *Poems*, 1920, inscribed to Virginia Woolf, and a collection of fifty-one cockerel devices engraved by a wide range of artists for use in the books of the Golden Cockerel Press. But the item in 150 which brought the largest number of orders was a set of Leonard Smithers' rare book catalogues.

Catalogue 158 offered—and reproduced—a pencil drawing by Charlotte Brontë. Catalogue 166 listed Mme. Daudet's copy of *Lettres de Mon Moulin*; *Ulysses* inscribed by Joyce to Augustus John; and corrected proofs of Ezra Pound's first *Cantos*. Catalogue 180, the first catalogue of our fiftieth year, was devoted to books from the libraries of Christina, Dante Gabriel and William Michael Rossetti. More recently Catalogue 186, *One Hundred Rare Books*, began with Sir Edward Marsh's commonplace book containing one hundred poems written in the hands of their authors, almost every famous name in English poetry in the first half of the twentieth century being represented. That item was hard to follow but the catalogue also included John Berryman's manuscript account of Dylan Thomas' death and a copy of *Hadrian VII* inscribed by Baron Corvo to his brother.

The only catalogue for which we have ever made a charge—two pounds—was number 192, *The Printer and the Artist*. This described more than 1,300 private press and illustrated books from the United Kingdom, Europe and America. *The Book Collector* called it a "notable opportunity" to compare the Anglo-American press movement with similar work in Europe. *Das Börsenblatt* said it would retain "a lasting significance" and—rather to our surprise—*The Financial Times* declared that it made "compulsive reading"! Be that as it may, number 192 was the only catalogue to vary from the present format.

Over the years a number of our customers have complimented us on the physical appearance of our catalogues. It is a fundamental part of our philosophy that those who live by the printed word should do their best to see that it is *well* printed and happily there have always been members of the firm who have interested themselves in this aspect of our work. Since Catalogue 125 (1961) they have benefited from the freely given advice of Mr. John Ryder, who has been responsible for the more successful of our cover designs. To him and to our long-suffering printers we remain most grateful.

As Mr. Simon Nowell-Smith has pointed out (in *The Book Collector* Volume 16, No. 1, Spring 1967), our catalogues fall short of providing a perfect "microcosm of book price history in the modern field." This is chiefly because many of the more obvious "highspots" go directly to customers who have expressly asked for them and so do not pass through the printed catalogues at all. Even so the catalogues mirror changes in taste and fashion over half a century—and they certainly show the steady upward march of prices. As a firm we have always set our face against recommending books as investments *per se*, but, given that there are other reasons for buying books in the first place, it must be a source of satisfaction to their owners to see their realisable value increase.

Despite the present economic instabilities, rare book prices—at least in the field of modern literature—still do not look excessive. Indeed many first editions of worth-while books by contemporary authors look positively cheap by the side of the current published prices of new books. It has been argued that the days of the hand-produced book are numbered (we discussed this proposition in the foreword to *The*

Printer and the Artist), and if the supply is to be cut off, then the price of the better products of the private presses can move in only one direction.

But the largest single influence on demand and supply in my generation of bookselling has undoubtedly been the growth in the pattern of buying by university libraries. Whether or not, as some authorities suggest, this institutional purchasing is now past its zenith, the fact remains that many hundreds of thousands of rare books which used to circulate from one private collection to another via the bookshops have now been removed from the market for all time. I see the results of this in the diminishing frequency with which such staple items of my company's stock of first editions as, let us say, *Salomé*, *Tess of the D'Urbervilles* and the pre-war novels of Elizabeth Bowen and Ivy Compton-Burnett come on to the market. The moral is clear and scarcely needs to be pointed.

Now, to paraphrase a remark of my father's from Catalogue 100, I am off to assemble books for Catalogue 201.

Anthony Rota

INTRODUCTION

Anthony Rota's introduction to Catalogue 244, which was issued in 1987 and presents the Powys Family collection of Lloyd Emerson Siberell

There are several notable examples in English literature of families producing in one generation two or more siblings who have both or all achieved distinction as writers. The most celebrated instance of this happy phenomenon probably remains the Brontë sisters; the most recent, Margaret Drabble and her sister, Antonia (A.S.) Byatt. The twentieth century case which perhaps comes most readily to mind is that of the Sitwell family, with Edith, Osbert and Sacheverell writing between them a vast body of work, but the record for the number of brothers and sisters achieving publication is almost certainly held by the Powyses.

John Cowper Powys (1872-1963), with his highly individual philosophy, attempted in his novels to explain the meaning of life in terms of ancient myths and elemental forces. Llewelyn Powys (1884-1939) is known as much for his essays and stories as for his novels, *Dorset Essays*, *Apples Be Ripe* and *Love and Death* being good examples of his work in each of those three forms. Theodore

Francis Powys (1875-1953) wrote allegorical stories of good and evil and may best be remembered as the author of *Mr Weston's Good Wine*. A. R. Powys (1881-1936), an architect and secretary of the Society for the Protection of Ancient Buildings, wrote books on *The English Parish Church* and *The Repair of Ancient Buildings*. Littleton Powys (1874-1955) became headmaster of Sherborne Preparatory School and published two volumes of autobiography. (His second wife was the novelist Elizabeth Myers.) Philippa Powys (1886-1963) wrote poetry and a novel. Marian Powys (1882-1970) published an authoritative book on lace-making.

John Cowper, Llewelyn and T. F. Powys all present an interesting bibliography, but this is particularly true of John Cowper, whose long sojourn in the United States caused a number of his books to be published first, and sometimes only, in America. Certainly between them the writing members of the Powys family set an intriguing challenge to collectors.

One of the first to rise to that challenge was the Ohio bibliophile Lloyd Emerson Siberell. His *Bibliography of the First Editions of John Cowper Powys*, Cincinnati, 1934, was a pioneering work, and along with Dante Thomas's *Bibliography of the Writings of John Cowper Powys*, Mamaroneck, New York, 1975, and Derek Langridge's *John Cowper Powys: A Record of Achievement*, London, 1966, is cited in this catalogue. Mr. Siberell strove ceaselessly to promote the cause of the Powys Brothers and was instrumental in procuring American publication of Llewelyn's *A Baker's Dozen*, for which he provided the introduction. His own Powys collection was assiduously formed and was comprehensive in its scope. We contributed many books to it from the 1930s until the 1970s and are proud to have been able to purchase it in its entirety in 1986. This catalogue lists the printed books that it contained. A supplement offering contributions to periodicals and various ephemeral pieces is available on request. For the record, it should be stated that some manuscript material from the collection, including the holograph manuscript of *Wolf Solent*, has already been sold by private treaty.

Virtually every book in the collection carries Mr. Siberell's "Auburn Crest" bookplate, normally tipped-in rather than pasted down. The presence of the bookplate is not mentioned in the individual descriptions. Many of the books are inscribed to Mr. Siberell. The inscriptions from John Cowper Powys are so characteristic of the author that we have tended to quote them in full for the interest of our customers.

We hope that reading the catalogue—and perhaps ordering from it—will give you as much pleasure as we had in preparing it, and as Lloyd Siberell had in assembling the books.

New Literary Periodicals: A Report for 1991

Richard R. Centing
Ohio State University

The following report on new literary periodicals, the fifth in a series of annual reports scheduled to appear in the *Dictionary of Literary Biography Yearbook*, documents scholarly journals, annuals, newsletters, and reviews launched in 1991, along with some 1990 titles that had not come to our attention by press time last year. Any 1991 titles that we missed will be covered in the 1992 *Yearbook*. These descriptions are not meant to be evaluative, although we do stress the importance of a few titles. By highlighting outstanding facets of each serial, our intention is to bring them to the attention of librarians and scholars for purposes of collection development and scholarly submission, and to alert indexing services of the need for the inclusion of new titles in their core lists. Please contact the author with any comments on the report for 1991 or suggestions for inclusion in the 1992 report.

Quondam et Futurus: A Journal of Arthurian Interpretations (Memphis State University, English Department, Memphis, Tennessee 38152) is a quarterly combination of two previous titles, *Quondam et Futurus* (1980-1990) and *Arthurian Interpretations* (1986-1990). The reformatted journal is an official publication of the North American Branch of the International Arthurian Society; the journal is devoted to study of the Arthurian romances. The first issue of the new journal (spring 1991) includes six scholarly articles on such subjects as the source of the Grail stories, *Sir Gawain and the Green Knight*, Sir Thomas Malory, and Alfred, Lord Tennyson's *Idylls of the King*. Four book reviews and a column of news and events conclude the issue. It is guided by an international editorial board and edited by Henry Hall Peyton III.

The semiannual *Hagiography Society Newsletter* (c/o the editor, Sherry L. Reames, University of Wisconsin, Department of English, 600 North Park Street, Madison, Wisconsin 53706) promotes communication among scholars whose research involves the study of early Christian or medieval saints' legends. The first issue, February 1991, includes a twenty-eight-page directory of

"Researchers in Medieval Hagiography." The directory includes the scholars' names, addresses, lists of publications, and information on their current projects, for example, "Motif-Index of early Irish saints." The Hagiography Society sponsors sessions at the annual International Congress on Medieval Studies in Kalamazoo, Michigan.

The debut of the annual *Journal of Anglo-Italian Studies* (University of Malta, Institute of Anglo-Italian Studies, Malta) was in 1991. The attractively printed 160-page issue handles typefaces for Italian and English articles with great skill. It includes well-reproduced illustrations and meticulously edited footnotes and references that are complex yet highly readable. The contents include a tribute to the scholar Mario Praz, who died in 1982, and articles on the relationship of Percy Bysshe Shelley's *The Triumph of Life* to Petrarch and Dante; Charles Dickens's and William Wordsworth's knowledge of Italy; the Grand Tour in the seventeenth century; and Italian writing on the Wars of the Roses. The credentials of the contributors could be amplified, as the journal usually only provides the names of the institutions where they are affiliated, that is, Peter Brand (University of Edinburgh).

My last survey of journals devoted to James Joyce (1882-1941) was in the *DLB Yearbook* periodicals report for 1990. An addition to the Joyce industry is *Odyssey* (James Joyce Society of London, The Polytechnic of North London, Faculty of Humanities, Prince of Wales Road, London, England NW5 3LB). First issued in autumn 1990, the irregular, eight-page newsletter reports on Joycean conferences, reviews new books, and publishes the papers of members. "James Joyce and Nationalism," by the newsletter's editor, Caroline Hyland, is a summary of a paper given to the James Joyce Society of London on 8 February 1990.

Scholarship on T. S. Eliot (1888-1965) has received periodical attention in the *T. S. Eliot Newsletter* (1974), the *T. S. Eliot Review* (1975-1977), and the continuing *Yeats Eliot Review* (1978-). The *T. S. Eliot Annual* (Macmillan Press, Ltd., Hound-

Front cover for the first issue of the annual edited by Edward Chaney and Peter Vassallo

mills, Basingstoke, Hampshire, England RG21 2XS) is a substantial, hardbound annual that was first published in 1990. Edited by a long-time Eliot scholar, Shyamal Bagchee, University of Alberta, Canada, the contents include eight scholarly articles and six signed book reviews. The books reviewed were published from 1981 to 1984, and no explanation is given for their lateness. Persons who influenced Eliot, such as Arnold Bennett, Oscar Wilde, and Tristan Tzara, are studied, as well as the topics of rhetoric and classicism. One section, called "Occasional Monograph," runs forty-two pages and is devoted to the relationship of "The Love Song of J. Alfred Prufrock" to modern literary criticism. The author is Stanley Sultan, professor of English at Clark University, Boston. Another section, "Review Essay," runs thirteen pages and surveys the relationship of Eliot to the philosophy of F. H. Bradley.

Jack London (1876-1916) has had numerous serials devoted to him over the years. The

best recent publication has been the *Jack London Newsletter*, which began in 1967 and ceased in 1991. Still issued on an occasional basis is *What's New About London, Jack?*, which began in 1971. The Jack London Society, which was founded December 1990, now issues its own informal newsletter, *The Call: The Official Newsletter of the Jack London Society* (The University of Texas at San Antonio, Division of English, San Antonio, Texas 78249). Published semiannually in six pages, it contains notices on new books, dissertations, seminars, and a short article on "Approaches to Teaching Jack London." *The Call* also announces that a new annual, *Jack London Journal*, is planned for 1992.

The *Rawlings Journal* (The Rawlings Society, University of Florida, Department of English, Gainesville, Florida 32611) was first issued in 1988 as an annual devoted to the writings of Marjorie Kinnan Rawlings (1896-1953), author of *The Yearling* (1938). Although born in Washington, D.C., Rawlings settled in Florida, the locale of most of her work. The *Rawlings Journal* quickly evolved into the present *Journal of Florida Literature* (Illinois State University, Department of English, Normal, Illinois 61761). It is now edited by Rodger L. Tarr, a professor at Illinois State University, who has expanded the journal to include discussion of any writer who uses Florida as a subject. Despite the expansion, the new annual, called volume two and dated 1989-1990, contains nothing but articles on Rawlings, such as "Gender and Mothering in The Yearling" and "Marjorie Kinnan Rawlings's Theory of Composition."

During April 1991 the F. Scott Fitzgerald Society issued its first *Newsletter* (c/o Ruth Prigozy, Hofstra University, English Department, Hempstead, New York 11550), which is promised to be published "several times during the year." The Society, which was founded 28 December 1990, has discussed the possibility of a future scholarly journal devoted to Fitzgerald, a function clearly not filled by this informal *Newsletter*. The newsletter includes a summary article on the important work of the Hemingway Society and outlines the plans of the Fitzgerald group. It also prints two letters from Budd Schulberg relating to his acceptance of an appointment to the Society Board and his remarks on Fitzgerald's reputation at his death. There are five informative obituaries of persons associated with Fitzgerald, a checklist of new primary and secondary materials, and other short notes. The coeditors are Jackson R. Bryer, Alan Margolies, and Ruth Prigozy.

American poet and novelist Charles Bukowski (1920-   ) now has a single-author publication devoted to him called *Sure: The Charles Bukowski Newsletter* (c/o the editor, Edward L. Smith, P.O. Box 1183, Ojai, California 93024). It is published three times a year, with the first issue dated May 1991. *Sure* seeks to track Bukowski's recent writings and share opinions about his life and work. News about recent books is included, as well as cassettes, CDs, postcards, and T-shirts. One article, "The Classical Buk," surveys Bukowski's interest in classical music. Letters to Bukowski and details about films based on his work are also published. The newsletter is illustrated with photographs and drawings of Bukowski, and some illustrations are by Bukowski, who lends his support to the venture.

The first issue of the semiannual *American Drama* (University of Cincinnati, Department of English, ML 69, Cincinnati, Ohio 45221) was published in fall 1991. It begins with an "Address" given on the occasion of the establishment of the Helen Weinberger Center for the Study of Drama and Playwriting, 4 April 1990, at the University of Cincinnati. The first essay demonstrates that Tennessee Williams was influenced by Margaret Widdemer's *The Rose-Garden Husband* (1915), a novel mentioned briefly in *The Glass Menagerie*. It relates to the guilt felt by Williams concerning his mentally unstable sister, Rose. A ground-breaking essay discusses "David Mamet's Homosocial Order" where women are excluded or marginalized. A section called "Playwright's Forum" is devoted to an interview with Arthur Miller that took place at "Miller's Roxbury, Connecticut home on August 2, 1990." The interview was conducted by Steven R. Centola (Millersville University, Pennsylvania). Another essay compares Miller to Sam Shepard, and Miller is also one of the subjects of a group book review of three books written by Miller, Elia Kazan, and Clifford Odets. The editorial board includes luminaries such as Ruby Cohn and Donald Wilmeth. The editor is Norma Jenckes, Department of English, University of Cincinnati.

Drama Criticism (Gale Research Inc., 835 Penobscot Building, Detroit, Michigan 48226) is an annual reference tool providing biographical, critical, and bibliographical information on "the most frequently studied playwrights of all time periods and nationalities." Volume one (1991) covers James Baldwin, William Wells Brown, Karel

Front cover for the newsletter edited by Edward L. Smith

Capek, Mary Chase, Alexandre Dumas (fils), Charles Fuller, Nikolay Gogol, Lillian Hellman, Christopher Marlowe, Arthur Miller, Yukio Mishima, Richard Brinsley Sheridan, Sophocles, and Thornton Wilder. Each entry includes biographical and critical introductions to the playwright's life and achievement, excerpts from the playwright's commentary on his work, excerpts from critical commentary on the playwright, excerpts from production reviews, and a list of references at the end entitled "Further Reading." A portrait of the playwright is included at the beginning of each entry (Sophocles is represented by a photograph of a statue). Illustrations of productions are also included, for example, a contemporary depiction of the original "Screen Scene" of *The School for Scandal* (1777). The level of presentation seems to be geared toward undergraduates and theatergoers. The editor of the 576-page volume is Lawrence J. Trudeau.

The oversized *Euromaske: The European Theatre Quarterly* (Delo/Revije, Titova 35, VIII, YU 61000, Ljubljana, Yugoslavia) is an English-language theater periodical that first appeared in fall 1990. Lavishly illustrated and covering all aspects of current activity in European theater, *Euromaske* reviews new productions, interviews technical specialists, profiles companies, reviews books and serials, and provides an intensive examination of national cultural policy. The third issue, spring 1991, interviews the Hungarian-born German director George Tabori. The "Outside Europe" column surveys theatrical developments in Siberia. Many notable practitioners contribute to this avant-garde bellwether, such as Clive Barker, editor of the *New Theatre Quarterly*, writing on the national theaters of Britain. Video recording of dance is discussed, reports are given on international conferences, and the holdings of research institutes are described. The editors are Dušan Jovanović and Dragan Klaić.

Beverley Byers-Pevitts, dean, College of Humanities and Fine Arts, University of Northern Iowa, is the editor of the semiannual *Theatre Topics* (Johns Hopkins University Press, Journals Publishing Division, 701 West 40th Street, Suite 275, Baltimore, Maryland 21211). This peer-reviewed journal focuses on performance studies, dramaturgy, and theater pedagogy. Published in cooperation with the Association for Theatre in Higher Education, each issue includes anywhere from seven to nine articles and article responses. The subjects range from Harold Pinter to Peter Sellars, from Alaskan Eskimo theater to vocal training. It is well illustrated with reproductions of stage designs, photographs of productions, or documentation of such specifics as Alaskan tamborine-style drummers. The September 1991 *Theatre Topics* profiles JoAnne Akalaitis, whom the late Joseph Papp named as his successor as director of the New York Shakespeare Festival. Andrea J. Nouryeh (St. Lawrence University) calls Akalaitis an "important" director with an "eclectic style." The first issue (March 1991) includes a feminist analysis of children's theater and calls for "responsible social relations and context" in drama presented to children.

Laura Furman, the editor of the quarterly *American Short Fiction* (The University of Texas Press, Journals Department, P.O. Box 7819, Austin, Texas 78713), announces the intention of this journal to publish original stories "of all genres and all lengths, up to and including the novella." Its first issue is dated spring 1991. Some of her writers are published here for the first time, although many are established names such as Joyce Carol Oates, Hortense Calisher, Ursula K. LeGuin, and Tama Janowitz. There are no book reviews or essays about short fiction. *American Short Fiction* is published in cooperation with the Texas Center for Writers and with the *Sound of Writing* (a short-story magazine of the air broadcast on National Public Radio).

Mary Rohrberger, professor in and head of the Department of English, University of Northern Iowa, is editing the semiannual *Short Story* (Texas Southmost College, 83 Fort Brown, Brownsville, Texas 78520), which first appeared in spring 1990. It publishes original stories, essays on the genre, and reviews of new books in the field. The contributors are mostly American, as are the subjects of the essays and reviews, such as Willa Cather, Eudora Welty, and Richard Kostelanetz. There are some theoretical pieces such as "Defining the Short Story and Certain Limitations of Reader-Oriented Theory."

The "Eclectic Literary Forum," called *ELF* (ELF Associates, Inc., P.O. Box 392, Tonawanda, New York 14150), is a quarterly review featuring stories, poetry, essays, and miscellaneous tidbits about the cultural scene. The first issue, spring 1991, encompasses such diverse subjects as Seneca Indian legends and the teaching of freshman writing through baseball metaphors. One poet from Springfield, Ohio, is a retired professor of German, Kurt Fickert. His poem "A Sepia Snapshot" is a nostalgic look at a childhood photograph with precise references to "Flexible Flyer sleds" and a "Kodak Brownie" camera. The best-known poet is Judson Jerome, poetry columnist of *Writer's Market*. The editor, C. K. Erbes, refers to his contributors as "word painters." The cover illustration depicts an elf white-water rafting.

"High Octane Poetry" is the promise of *Gas* (New College of California, 50 Fell Street, San Francisco, California 94102), a 132-page quarterly review devoted solely to poetry and poetic prose. The first issue, winter 1990, features eight poems by Charles Bukowski (whose newsletter *Sure* is examined in this survey). Other contributors include Robert Creeley, Alice Notley, and Dana Gioia. The poetry is nontraditional, using various free-verse forms, concrete approaches, beat rhythms, and L=A=N=G=U=A=G=E-school techniques, with references to icons of modern culture such as Henry Miller, Gary Snyder, James Baldwin, and "Jimmy" (James) Schuyler. There are advertisements for presses such as Black Sparrow and Smithereens. Tom Clark is the editor, and he contributes a cartoon satire from a work entitled *The Thousand Year Empire*.

Gatherings: The En'Owkin Journal of First North American Peoples (Theytus Books, En'Owkin Centre, 257 Brunswick Street, Penticton, B.C., Canada V2A 5P9) is an annual literary publication of the En'Owkin International School of Writing. It was first issued in fall 1990 and is edited by David Gregoire (an Okanagan Indian). The contributors (men and women, young and old, Canadian and American) have included poetry and stories that evoke Native themes. The first essay, "Concepts of Anger, Identity and Power and the Vision in the Writings and Voices of First Nations Women," by Kerrie Charnley, mourns the silencing of Native language by European immigrants. Another essay on "The Disempowerment of First North American Native Peoples and Empowerment Through Their Writing," by Jeannette Armstrong, recounts five centuries of aggression by "foreign peoples" (white men) that destroyed Native civilization; it is the duty of Native writers through "discourse and dialogue" to create a new vision for Native North Americans. The second annual, fall 1991, continues to utilize literary forms for the expression of insights into the condition of Native peoples.

A bimonthly that began January/February 1991, *In the Company of Poets* (P.O. Box 10786, Oakland, California 94610) is a place of publication for poets and a market adviser offering practical tips to the novice. The editor, Jacalyn Robinson, refers to her magazine as *ITCOP* and enthuses about the "magic of the written word." One featured poet, Eddie Holan, says he is "currently seeking a publisher." Every issue has a column called "Write Ideas" by a popular poet, Selma Glasser, who has appeared on television talk shows. The contributors represent a multicultural spectrum that includes an Ethiopian, an African-Cherokee, and an Ojibwa Indian from Canada. There are short descriptions of other literary magazines and news about grants. The magazine also publishes short stories and visual art, although the bulk of the content is poetry.

Literati Internazionale (Literati Internazionale, 213 W. Institute Place, Suite 207, Chicago, Illinois 60610) is a semiannual featuring multicultural literary and visual arts. The "Premiere Issue" was published early in 1991. It is published in collaboration with the English department of Southern Illinois University, Edwardsville, and includes fiction, poetry, artwork, and essays. An essay by Henry Miller about a black painter, "The Amazing and Invariable Beauford DeLaney," is reprinted from the origi-

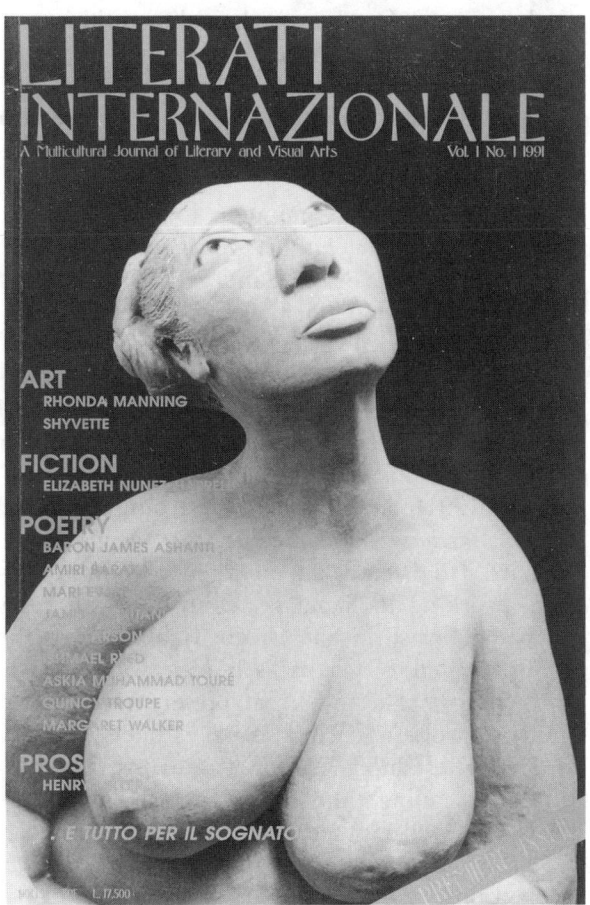

Front cover for the first issue of the journal edited by L. McGraw-Beauchamp and A. C. McGraw-Beauchamp

nal *Outcast* chapbook of 1945. The poetry editor is Eugene B. Redmond, and there are more than thirty poems in the first issue. Some of the artwork reproductions are in full color, giving *Literati* the dimension of a fine-arts journal. The editors are L. McGraw-Beauchamp and A. C. McGraw-Beauchamp.

Pulphouse: A Weekly Magazine (Pulphouse Publishing, Box 1227, Eugene, Oregon 97440) is the latest product of Pulphouse Publishing, a firm that specializes in science fiction, horror, and fantasy. One line features short-story paperbacks, such as *Journey to the Goat Star* by Brian W. Aldiss (1989). Novels are published by a division called Axolotl Press. Their new magazine was launched with an "Issue Zero" on 1 March 1991, with the "Premier Issue" dated 1 June 1991. The attractive weekly includes fiction by accomplished writers such as Andre Norton, Kristine Kathryn Rusch, and Edward Bryant. There is some poetry included, as well as cartoons, book reviews, and novel excerpts. An important development in the sixth issue, 25 October 1991, is the addition of a column called "Ask Uncle Harlan" by the outspoken Harlan Ellison. The column's format has Ellison writing responses to letters to the editor about pulp fiction. The editor and publisher is Dean Wesley Smith.

Exhibiting a commitment to excellent writing, the *Santa Fe Literary Review* (Haven Hill Press, P.O. Box 8018, Santa Fe, New Mexico 87504) is an independent literary quarterly concentrating on poetry, fiction, essays, and artwork. The editor, Colleen Rae, teaches writing to adults in Santa Fe and is a graduate of the University of Chicago's creative-writing master's program. Her short story "God's Will" is in volume one, number 1 (1991), and an excerpt from her novel *Dream Warriors* is included in the second issue. Richard Goldstein, "an emergency room physician" working in Santa Fe, contributes an essay on being Jewish in San Diego, California, in the 1950s. Steven E. Counsel's line drawings, black-and-white graphics of great power, have graced the first two issues. He also writes poetry for the review. The editor calls for a return to a "literature of meaning" and cites Ernest Hemingway's "A Clean, Well-Lighted Place" as a touchstone.

An independent little magazine, *World Letter* (Jon Cone, 2726 E. Court Street, Iowa City, Iowa 52245) is an irregular compilation of poetry and fiction, first appearing in 1991. Henry Miller fan Irving Stettner, who edits his own little magazine, *Stroker*, contributes "Paris, Mon Amour," identified as an excerpt from a novel-in-progress, *Beggars in Paradise*. "O Paris, let me sing about you . . ." is a typical example of Stettner's style. Another underground figure, Morty Sklar, founder of The Spirit That Moves Us Press, offers a poem, "Forgetting My Life." Its plain style evokes memories of "1960 electro-shock therapy." A representative of the L= A= N= G =U =A =G =E poets Charles Bernstein, ends his poem "Searchless Warrant" with four words: "trampolines of the spleen." *World Letter* also includes some new translations of various psalms and fiction fragments of Chandler Brossard.

The newsstand-glossy *XX!st Century* (Rizzoli International Publications, Inc., 300 Park Avenue South, New York, New York 10010) is a little bit *Esquire* and a little bit *Bomb*, an assemblage of interviews, photographs, essays, and reviews attempting coverage of the contemporary world with an emphasis on the arts. The first issue is dated winter 1991/1992, and its stated frequency is three times a year. The editor is Gini Alhadeff. Literary topics receive serious attention, with the inaugural issue featuring an essay by the currently lauded novelist Harold Brodkey, "The Animal Life of Ideas," discussing the process of writing. The Pulitzer Prize-winning poet James Schuyler, who died 12 April 1991, is represented by a sampler of poems followed by excerpts from his *Diary*. Schuyler is also interviewed by Raymond Foye. This interview was conducted two weeks before Schuyler died and describes Schuyler's lifestyle at the Chelsea Hotel, New York City. "The New Negroe," an excerpt from Darryl Pinckney's forthcoming first novel, *High Cotton*, is included, as well as a preview of Peter Sellars's first film, *The Cabinet of Dr. Ramirez* (a remake of *The Cabinet of Dr. Caligari*).

Connotations: A Journal for Critical Debate (Waxmann Publishing Company, P.O. Box 1318, New York, New York 10028) is published three times a year by Waxmann Verlag in Münster, Germany. Its first issue is dated March 1991. The editors are Inge Leimberg, Lothar Cěrny, Michael Steppat, and Matthias Bauer, and their editorial address is at the Westfälische Wilhelms-Universität in Münster. The language of publication is English, and it claims to focus on the "semantic and stylistic energy" of literature from the Middle English period to the present. The contributors are from Simon Fraser University, Vanderbilt University, Duke University, the University of Wisconsin, and Cambridge. Only one article is from the editorial base in Münster. The subjects covered range from *Doctor Faustus*, *Twelfth Night*, and *Marcus Tullius Cicero*, to a comparison of the fiction theories of Henry James, H. G. Wells, and Ford Maddox Ford.

Constructive Criticism: A Journal of Construct Psychology and the Arts (Center for the Study of Construct Psychology and the Arts) is a quarterly that began in March 1991. The term *construct psychology* is taken from the teachings of George Kelly (1905-1967), a professor of psychology at Ohio State University, who developed his ideas in his book *Psychology of Personal Constructs* (1955). The editor of *Constructive Criticism*, Cintra Whitehead, has a Ph.D. in English and psychology from the University of Toledo. It is her belief, following Kelly, that personality theory is the branch of psychology most relevant to psychological literary criticism. Hence, her self-generated journal contains five articles, all of which are written by Whitehead. Most of the references are to literary topics, and two of the longest essays are the reason we have included this journal in our sur-

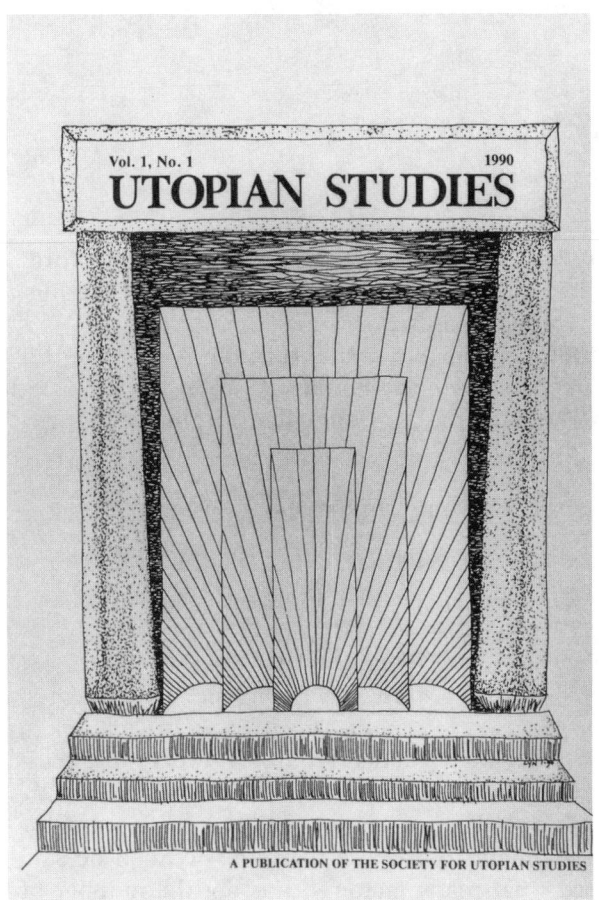

Vol. 1, No. 1   1990

UTOPIAN STUDIES

A PUBLICATION OF THE SOCIETY FOR UTOPIAN STUDIES

Front cover for the first issue of the journal edited by Lyman Tower Sargent

vey: a sixty-nine-page article, "Construing Hamlet," that surveys the psychoanalytic approach to Shakespeare's masterpiece and even "suggests innovative constructs for directors and actors to use in performance"; and a fifteen-page article on Sophocles' *Oedipus Rex* that touches on Sigmund Freud's interest in *Oedipus Rex* as the key to *Hamlet*. The journal concludes with an original short story by Whitehead, "La Dame de Charité," that applies construct psychology to a Christmas setting. The editor has issued a call for papers with construct interpretations of novels, poetry, essays, films, television, and other arts.

Although distributed free of charge by a trade publisher, *The English Poetry Full-Text Database Newsletter* (Chadwyck-Healey Ltd., Cambridge Place, Cambridge, England CB2 1NR) has research applications. This occasional reporting service informs the scholarly community about the progress of Chadwyck-Healey's project to con-

vert the works of all English poets from 600 to 1900 into an electronic data base available on a CD-ROM. The project will take at least three years to complete, and the newsletter discusses such things as their editorial principles and software requirements. The first issue is dated December 1991.

The Society for Utopian Studies, an interdisciplinary, international association founded in 1975, sponsors the semiannual *Utopian Studies* (University of Missouri—St. Louis, Department of Political Science, St. Louis, Missouri 63121). The editor, Lyman Tower Sargent, is a professor of political science at the University of Missouri—St. Louis. Her editorial defines utopias as "social dreams (sometimes nightmares) that range from fantasy to blueprint." The first contribution is a valuable "Bibliography of Utopian Fiction by United States Women 1836-1988" by Carol Farley Kessler, associate professor of English, American studies, and women's studies at Penn State Delaware County Campus. The bibliography includes detailed annotations; for example, Eleanor DeForest's *Armageddon: A Tale of the Antichrist* (1938) depicts "an anti-Semitic and anti-feminist dystopia set in California and Palestine." The articles discuss Aldous Huxley, Toni Morrison, the problem of modernity, and late-nineteenth-century utopian texts. There are around thirty book reviews, including reviews in English of foreign works. The first issue of *Utopian Studies* (1990) is dedicated to Eugenio Battisti (1924-1989), a utopian scholar who organized conferences in Italy in 1983, 1986, and 1989.

The *Yearbook of Interdisciplinary Studies in the Fine Arts* (Edwin Mellen Press, P.O. Box 450, Lewiston, New York 14092) is a large annual devoted to comparative studies of literature, music, drama, and the visual arts. It is edited by two professors from Ohio University (Athens), William E. Grim and Michael B. Harper. The title page cites it as a 1989 publication, copyright 1990, and it was distributed in 1991. The scholarly articles include numerous literary topics, such as one on Benjamin Britten's 1954 opera rendition of Henry James's *The Turn of the Screw*, and another comparing Henry David Thoreau's view of the Maine wilderness to the panoramic landscapes of the painter Frederic Church (1826-1900). Other subjects cover a broad spectrum, including Paul Celan, Edouard Manet, and Bertolt Brecht. There are five very short book reviews.

Fredson Thayer Bowers

(25 April 1905 - 11 April 1991)

CHRONOLOGY:

1905: Birth, New Haven, Connecticut, 25 April

1925: Brown University, Ph.B.

1934: Harvard University, Ph.D.

1936-1938: Instructor in English, Princeton University

1938-1946: Assistant Professor of English, University of Virginia

1942: Marriage to Nancy Hale

1942-1946: Commander, USNR, Naval Communications, Washington, D.C.

1946-1948: Associate Professor of English, University of Virginia

1948-1957: Professor of English, University of Virginia

1948-1991: Founding Editor, *Studies in Bibliography*

1954: Rosenbach Lecturer in Bibliography

1957-1968: Alumni Professor of English, University of Virginia

1958: Sandars Reader in Bibliography, Cambridge University

1959: James Lyell Reader in Bibliography, Oxford University

1961-1968: Chairman, Department of English, University of Virginia

1964: Bicentennial Medal, Brown University

1968-1975: Linden Kent Memorial Professor of English, University of Virginia

1968: Corresponding Fellow, British Academy

1968: Gold Medal of the Bibliographical Society, London

1968-1969: Dean of the Faculty, University of Virginia

1969: President, South Atlantic Modern Language Association

1970: Doctor of Letters, Brown University

1970: Doctor of Letters, Clark University

1971-1972: Research, Scholar, Villa Serbelloni Research Center, Bellagio, Italy

1971: Thomas Jefferson Award, University of Virginia

1972: Fellow of the American Academy of Arts and Sciences

1972: Visiting Fellow, All Souls College, Oxford

1973: Doctor of Humane Letters, University of Chicago

1974: Visting Fellow, All Souls College, Oxford

1975-1991: Linden Kent Professor Emeritus, University of Virginia

1986: Julian Boyd Award of the Association for Documentary Editing

1991: Death, Charlottesville, Virginia, 11 April

Fredson Bowers, Master Teacher

Irby B. Cauthen, Jr.
University of Virginia

For his students, Fredson Bowers was a master teacher; for some, and I was one, he was *the* best one. Part of his mastery was his respect for his students. On more than one occasion he said that what really mattered was not the number of cards bearing his name in the library's card catalogue but his students. That respect for them was coupled with his rigor and justice.

According to the students' stories about his life in graduate school, Bowers worked hard to keep himself financially solvent; he played the saxophone in dance bands, ate more chicken than he liked because it was given as part of his pay, and then would go to his room—or the library— to prepare for the next day and the rest of his life as a teacher. He seems never to have stinted in his demands upon himself and came to expect the same kind of dedication from his students. A holiday was not for him a time of rest: one of the most complicated assignments that I remember from his bibliography class was to be completed over the Thanksgiving weekend. And his students knew that it had to be done. What he expected of them, he demanded of himself in class. He was jealous of every minute of class time, pausing only briefly to light another cigarette or to remove from that long holder the little bit that was left from the previous cigarette.

Bowers's rigor extended to his explication of a text: never was a puzzling line left unexplained, and the explanation was always clear

Nancy Hale Bowers and Fredson Bowers, Woodburn, Charlottesville, Virginia

and definitive. To read *Hamlet* under his guidance was like seeing an old friend in new guises. From the too solid/sullied/sallied flesh to Hamlet's recognition scene in act 5, the play opened up through his guidance. And he—even if some critics do not—knew what Milton meant, even in the most obscure passages. He along with a few could safely have conversed with Milton and, I believe, with Milton's God.

Bowers was not only awesome in his detailed explanations of literature, but he saw the larger issues. As one of his students said, he knew when to switch from a movement through particularities to the larger general intellectual history that would provide the imaginative concept for the passage. He saw matters clearly and could define how literature fit within the vast universe of art and life.

His rigor was extended to our answers to his questions. One student once said, "Well, it is a reason although it may be wrong." His reply, quickly, gently, but firmly phrased, was that it was better to have no reason than a wrong one.

That rigor was part of his justice. If one could decipher his hand, which had been skilled in cryptography and in itself looked like a code, one would recognize the justice and perception of Bowers's comments upon one's essay. He read

what his students wrote as carefully as if he were to publish it; he saw what each was trying to say and where each had failed or succeeded. The comments were always measured, not necessarily flattering. He was like Chaucer's knight,

He nevere yet no vileynye [rudeness] ne sayde
In all his lyf unto no maner wight.

He always, it seems, had his students first in mind. We knew something of his own research, but while his methods influenced him, his findings did not necessarily intrude on his teaching. At least once he did bring that research into the class, and one student remembers the occasion well. Fred announced to the class that was reading in the Metaphysical poets that the material he was to speak of had never been published and was restricted to use in that class. The listening student said that he had never heard anything of that kind before; no undergraduate teacher had ever said anything at that level of professionalism. "I suddenly realized that I had entered another level of literary study: I had been told that I was a member of the profession. It was an exciting moment, a coming of age."

Bowers's teaching was not confined to the classroom. He delighted in bringing some recordings from his extensive record collection (he reviewed most of them for a Richmond newspaper) to the Grounds about an evening a month and played them for us in a spacious and acoustically perfect room. He always had something to say, briefly, of course, and perceptively, before playing them. He opened up new worlds for those of us who were, against his knowledge, almost musically illiterate. This was another side of him that we did not see in class, and yet it was an extension of his innate ability to teach.

I remember he said once that many of George Lyman Kittredge's students wanted to teach just as Kittredge did—and that was impossible. Both Kittredge and Fred Bowers developed their own characteristic manner, and no one could successfully emulate them. Many of Fred's students wanted to teach like him, but that, too, was impossible. His knowledge, his insistent yet judicious demands upon his students, and his respectful judging of them were his alone. We who sat with him in the classroom knew we could not equal him. But he gladly taught us (and a great deal, too), and we gladly learned much from him.

Fredson Bowers
and *Studies in Bibliography*

George Walton Williams
Duke University

In his commendatory foreword to volume twenty of *Studies in Bibliography*, Sir Frank Francis, then director and principal librarian of the British Museum, immediate past president of the Bibliographical Society, noted that persistence is not unfamiliar among bibliographical editors—"A. W. Pollard set the pace with his forty years' editorship of *The Library*." With no intention to compete or outdo, Fredson Bowers in 1991 completed an editorship of forty-three years, forty-four volumes. That editorship has not been single-handed—L. A. Beaurline and David L. Vander Meulen serving as assistant and associate editors from, respectively, 1964 to 1974 and 1988 to date—but it has clearly been single-minded in its dedication to excellence. Sir Frank continued: "The prestige [that the Bibliographical Society of the University of Virginia] now enjoys and the great success it has had are substan-

tially the image of its Editor"; and very properly he asserted that the "rigidly uncompromising standards" that Bowers applied to *Studies* are "in part at least the fruits of his association" with the members of the Bibliographical Society (of London). Bowers would certainly have acknowledged that debt, though he must have taken quiet satisfaction in Sir Frank's simile that "*Studies* sprang into being full-grown and fully armed, like Minerva from the head of Jupiter, whose thunderbolts she wielded from time to time."

Volume one "came forth," as a *TLS* reviewer put it, "to astonish all the bibliographers of Europe." It was entitled *Papers of the Bibliographical Society of the University of Virginia*—a title that became the subtitle in volume two, replaced by *Studies in Bibliography*; and it is interesting to note, looking back on it, how deeply "Virginian" it was even as its style and standards astonished the bibliographers of Europe. (The first two articles dealt with concerns of Thomas Jefferson.) Of seventeen contributors, ten were associated with Mr. Jefferson's university: three were faculty members, five were graduate students, two were alumni; one author taught at a private school in the state. The remaining seven represented American scholarship more generally: bibliographer-librarians: Giles Dawson and J. G. McManaway at the Folger, Rudolph Hirsh at the Library of the University of Pennsylvania, Curt F. Buhler at the Pierpont Morgan; bibliographer-faculty members: G. J. Eberle at Loyola (New Orleans) and Allan H. Stevenson at Illinois Institute of Technology; one graduate student from another university, Guy A. Battle at Duke. These categories in the profession—librarians, faculty members, graduate students—have always formed the core of contributors, but to them have been added bibliographers from publishing houses, from printing houses, from bookstores. Over the years the number of contributors with academic affiliations has increased, but among the authors in the most recent five volumes there still remains a good representation of librarians, publishers, and operators of bookstores. Nonprofessional book lovers are also present.

Geographical distribution has changed markedly. The first foreign scholar to appear in the pages of *Studies* was Sir Walter Greg, whose seminal study, "The Rationale of Copy Text," appeared in volume three. Sir Walter was joined in the same volume by Ernst Kyriss of Stuttgart, and they were followed in volume four by H. Teerink of the Netherlands, and G. I. Duthie of

*Oil portrait of Fredson Bowers by T. Turner
(Bruccoli Collection)*

Scotland. In volume thirteen half of the contributors of the major articles were from overseas. Most foreign contributors have been English—Philip Gaskell, Cyprian Blagden, John Russell Brown, Alice Walker, Harold Jenkins, Kenneth Povey; others have been Scots—R. H. Carnie; Dutch—Johann Gerritsen; Canadian—R. H. Woof; and the list goes on, with scholars from Australia and New Zealand.

The *TLS* article mentioned above includes a "bibliographical analysis" of the first twenty volumes of the series. To that may be added the fact that *Studies* was published by the society from 1948/49 through 1963; the typical colophon for these early years reads "designed, composed, and printed by the William Byrd Press" (a Virginia printing house named for a famous Virginian). Volume four, an exception, was "produced at the University of Virginia Press" as were also volumes nine through sixteen. Volume seventeen bore the imprint "Published for [the society] by the University Press of Viginia." That imprint is still current. The first twenty-one volumes carried an acknowledgement of the funding provided by anonymous donors, by the Research Council of the Richmond Area University Center, and by the University of Virginia Research

Committee. Since 1968 there has been no mention of such generosity; presumably the funding is now an aspect of the general operation of the press.

Of the hundreds of articles and notes in the volumes of the series, I count some twelve major articles and eleven notes written by the editor himself. Always attentive to the niceties of protocol and with seemly modesty, Bowers placed his own brief (published) contribution to volume one in final position in the volume. Only in volume twenty-six does one of his own studies occupy first position in a volume, a place which he regularly reserved for persons or topics of particular distinction. The article, "Marlowe's *Doctor Faustus*: The 1602 Additions," he evidently believed to be of major import, more significant than any other in that volume. That study, however, reveals another quality in Bowers's contributions to the series. It is one of three articles—the other two appeared in volume twenty-five—dealing with Christopher Marlowe; the group of three reflects Bowers's other scholarly work: his edition of Marlowe's plays appeared from Cambridge in 1973. Similarly, his interest in editions of American authors is reflected in notes in volumes seventeen and twenty-two: the first stating "Some Principles for Scholarly Editions of Nineteenth-Century American Authors," the second examining Crane's *The Red Badge of Courage*. His continuing work on the Beaumont and Fletcher canon is reflected in articles in volumes twenty-seven and forty-one, with studies of *Beggars' Bush* and *Henry VIII* testifying to his activities in that series as well, specifically volume three and volume seven. Many papers, of course, demonstrate an interest in Shakespeare's texts, especially *Hamlet* and *All's Well*. But there are general and theoretical papers also such as that in volume forty-one "Greg's Rationale of Copy Text Revisited."

One aspect of Fredson Bowers's editorial activity cannot be underestimated—the attention given to graduate students at Virginia and, indeed, at other institutions. As has been noted, of the original contributors to volume one, just over one-third were graduate students, five being his own. Because Bowers recognized the need for young scholars to be presented to the profession and tested against its standards, he encouraged students to publish; and yet I do not recall that as a graduate student I ever "submitted" anything to *Studies*. But Bowers knew what his students were doing and what was being done under other mentors in the department. I remember, for example—before I even knew what it was to publish—finding a comment beside a footnote on a paper of mine: "Has this been noted before? I think you could publish this"; and in high excitement off went a note to *The Explicator*. On another paper: "I think we could print this in *Studies*." Bowers sought out from students material that was suitable for *Studies*, and he saw to it that what he printed was made even more suitable than it had been. Reading galley proofs on my second "submission" to *Studies*, I was surprised to find set up in type in the center of my article paragraphs I had never seen before. When I asked him what had happened, Bowers acknowledged that they were his: he had had a few thoughts on the topic of my paper and had just slipped them into my argument. "That's what a good editor does," he explained. And so his thoughts became part of my article and were published as if mine. Some months after publication of these "joint" thoughts, W. W. Greg commented on them in an article of his; he particularly praised me for certain insights; they were Bowers's insights, of course. By this silent editorial accretion, a graduate student was helped on his way, an article was strengthened, and a volume of *Studies* was made a better book. Though such supplements were, I am sure, rare and probably were not offered to the work of mature scholars, this one represented the concern for both the student and the scholarly level of the volume.

More significant, surely, for the health of the entire enterprise was Bowers's readiness to publish material that directly or indirectly attacked him or his dearly held theories. John Russell Brown's article on the nonutility of old spelling in texts edited for modern readers and D. F. MacKenzie's acute, well-informed, and challenging "Printers of the Mind" are instances of this sort of fairness. For the first of these, a rejoinder by Arthur Brown appeared in the same volume; the pair constituted an open debate. For the second no immediate answer was at hand; its influence, tempering too easy or too enthusiastic assurance, has been salutary in textual editing. It was a valuable corrective, and Bowers recognized it as such, his standards being originality and rigor of argument, not political correctness. This attitude has been one of the principal causes maintaining the high standard of *Studies in Bibliography* throughout more than two score of years.

Fredson Bowers as a Critic of Renaissance Dramatic Literature

George L. Geckle
University of South Carolina

Fredson Bowers will probably always be best known as the greatest American bibliographer and textual critic. For those of us who were fortunate enough to study with him, he will always remain one of the best teacher-scholars. And for those of us who are students, teachers, and scholars of Renaissance dramatic literature, he will continue to be both our mentor and one of our most discerning literary critics. Perhaps it is more than coincidence that his first and last major scholarly publications, *Elizabethan Revenge Tragedy 1587-1642* (1940) and *Hamlet as Minister and Scourge and Other Studies in Shakespeare and Milton* (1990), separated by fifty years, bracket his career as securely and appropriately as solid gold bookends.

Elizabethan Revenge Tragedy, first published by Princeton University Press, is still in print. As Bowers tells us in a postscript to the first Princeton paperback edition (1965), the book is a condensation of his Harvard dissertation of 1934 (and is appropriately dedicated to his mentor, George Lyman Kittredge). Rather too modestly, Bowers also tells us that "graduate students still seem to find it of use" and that because it has remained in print and "effectively inhibited the production of other surveys on the same subject," one may find "some reason to continue to keep it in print." Well, the reason for its astonishing longevity is the fact that it is still the standard critical work in the field. The first chapter, "The Background of Revenge," is, for instance, a learned compendium of both the folk and legal history of revenge in England. It contains information on the *talion* ("the strict law of like for like"), the wergeld (the value set upon a man's life), the feud, the indictment (which "introduced almost in its entirety the system of state justice which operates today"), malice forethought or prepensed (with the interesting ramification illustrated by *Hamlet*'s Claudius, who "is guilty of first-degree murder, and not of manslaughter, when Gertrude dies of the poison he has intended for Hamlet"), much on Elizabethan social and religious mores, and the following conclusion about the Elizabethan audience's probable attitude toward stage-revengers:

> . . . the audience at the theaters seems to have made the customary compromise between a formal set of religious and moral ethics and an informal set of native convictions. Under these circumstances—and the evidence of the tragedies bears out the theory—the revenger of the drama started with the sympathy of the audience if his cause were good and if he acted according to the typically English notions of straightforward fair play.

After a chapter on the Senecan, Italian, and French backgrounds of revenge tragedies, Bowers devotes his third chapter to Kyd's *The Spanish Tragedy* and to the so-called *Ur-Hamlet*. His interest in the structure of English Renaissance tragedy—of paramount importance in his last book—is here made evident in his definition of the crucial Kydian type of revenge play:

> This revenge constitutes the main action of the play in the sense that the audience is chiefly interested in the events which lead to the necessary revenge for murder, and then in the revenger's actions in accordance with his vow. The revenge must be the cause of the catastrophe, and its start must not be delayed beyond the crisis.

Moreover, here in this same chapter is characteristic Bowers—a rigorously logical mind applied to the solution of problems in the analysis of the structure of *The Spanish Tragedy*, including Kyd's reasons for the delay of revenge, the madness of his revenger Hieronimo, and the "change marked by the [*Vindicta mihi*] soliloquy [in III.xiii] from open to dissembling action . . . forced upon Hieronimo." Bowers concludes: "Once Hieronimo adopted the Italianate Machiavellian tactics, he immediately lost the absolute admiration of his audience."

It is in his ensuing discussion of Kyd's *Ur-Hamlet* that we can find a discussion of the seminal problem that would eventually lead Bowers to his famous and influential subsequent essay "Hamlet as Minister and Scourge" (1955): that is, the problem of the relationship between the revenger, the sympathies of the Elizabethan audience, and the concept of God's justice:

> One can imagine an Elizabethan sympathizer pointing out that Hamlet was justified [in killing by mistake the Polonius character instead of the Claudius character] since he could not ap-

peal to legal justice. But the inevitable and unanswerable reply would come that Hamlet must therefore await God's justice. If he anticipates divine vengeance, he must pay the penalty: given his sympathetic characterization he is a hero, but he must die. But God sometimes uses human instruments as the agents for the heavenly vengeance. If Hamlet is such an agent, does he not operate under God's favor? . . . Heaven may be using Hamlet—and even Hieronimo—as its agent, but that does not remove guilt. . . .

We are here close to the deductive reasoning that led fifteen years later to the minister and scourge rationale. And in his sixth chapter Bowers makes another observation that would lead years later to another well-known essay. Returning to a discussion of Kyd's Hieronimo, Bowers argues that

> . . . it may be stated with justice that the audience sentimentally sympathized with the Kydian hero revenger and hoped for his success, but only on condition that he did not survive. Thus his death was accepted as expiation for the violent motives which had forced him to override the rules of God and, without awaiting the slow justice of divine retribution, to carve out a bloody revenge for himself. . . . Who but an incurable sentimentalist could conceive of Hamlet's receiving the crown after the death of Claudius, marrying, and living happily ever after? The grand sacrifice—death in victory—was the revenger's only possible lot.

Here, of course, we have the source for "Death in Victory: Shakespeare's Tragic Reconciliations" (1967).

The latter chapters of *Elizabethan Revenge Tragedy* contain a survey and structural analysis of such major revenge plays as Marlowe's *The Jew of Malta*, Shakespeare's *Titus Andronicus*, Marston's *Antonio's Revenge*, *The Revenger's Tragedy* (by Tourneur or Middleton), Chapman's *The Revenge of Bussy D'Ambois*, Tourneur's *The Atheist's Tragedy*, Middleton's *Women Beware Women*, Beaumont and Fletcher's *The Maid's Tragedy*, Webster's *The White Devil* and *The Duchess of Malfi*, Middleton and Rowley's *The Changeling*, Ford's *'Tis Pity She's a Whore* and *The Broken Heart*, and Shirley's *The Cardinal*, as well as a host of less important plays in the genre. It is a remarkably full and thorough survey, drawing on a deep and broad scholarship (as the notes attest), of one of the two most important types of English Renaissance tragedy (the other being *De casibus* tragedy). And in his powerful concluding chapter, which summarizes the main sources and stages of revenge tragedy, Bowers makes a strong case for the preeminence of the genre:

> The great tragic theme of the sixteenth- and seventeenth-century teaching is this theme of God's revenge for sin. Writers of tragedies, both dramatic and non-dramatic tragedies, were necessarily preoccupied with this fundamental teaching. And all Elizabethan tragedy must appear as fundamentally a tragedy of revenge if the extent of the idea of revenge be but grasped.

Elizabethan Revenge Tragedy 1587-1642 has done as much as any single work of dramatic criticism in this century to establish the "great tragic theme" of those earlier centuries.

Because it was only published in January 1990, it is not possible to determine what the long-term influence of *Hamlet as Minister and Scourge and Other Studies in Shakespeare and Milton* (University Press of Virginia) will be. The thirteen essays in the book were all originally published either in scholarly journals or festschrifts between 1955 and 1982, but at least one of them, "Hamlet as Minister and Scourge" (*PMLA*, 70 [1955]), has already had a significant influence on subsequent *Hamlet* studies, as is evidenced, for example, in the work of David Bevington, whose highly successful editions of *The Complete Works of Shakespeare* and *The Bantam Shakespeare* have spread the ideas of Bowers. Because they are now gathered in one place, it is probably safe to say that this "collection of separate but thematically linked essays," which "share a common background from the active teaching of a relatively few plays in the Kittredge manner of close analysis," will do much to solidify Bowers as a powerful force in the criticism of Renaissance drama.

Aside from the evidence of Kittredge's influence in the rigorously logical and analytical close textual analysis of a large number of Shakespeare's comedies, histories, and tragedies, as well as Milton's *Samson Agonistes*, the two most evident links between all of the essays is the emphasis upon dramatic structure and upon a Christian ethos. "Aristotle's *Poetics* led to plot as the most important factor with which to start; thus Shakespeare's dramatic structure as a revelatory means of analysis came to the fore." However, both Shakespeare's "special interest in character" and the considerable differences between his civilization and that of the Greeks led to consideration of "the profound changes that may be observed between the Sophoclean and the Shakes-

Fredson Bowers and graduate student in 1955 with the second Hinman Collator, Alderman Library, University of Virginia

pearean tragic ethos." Whereas Greek tragedy represented "the characters' futile struggles against Fate to no ultimate purpose save stubborn human resistance to the vagaries of indifferent or hostile gods and the darkly sensed force of Fate," Shakespeare's "Christian world picture" represented "an ethic based on free will and its accompanying personal responsibility for action" and contained the crucial "concept of reconciliation as a critical Shakespearean tragic doctrine." The "analysis of dramatic structure," therefore, affords the means to understand the way Shakespeare not only "conceived his plays" but also "controlled the reactions of his audience to the understanding of character and action according to his intentions." In essence, then, the main thrust in Bowers's literary criticism is to make clear the meaning of the text in question. This is the approach of the older historical criticism at its best, a methodology and scholarship not currently fashionable but certainly an approach that has a venerable history and one that will, one may venture to argue, outlast most of the postmodern academic "isms."

The opening essay, "Death in Victory: Shakespeare's Tragic Reconciliations" (1967), is a tour de force that had its gestation, as mentioned above, in *Elizabethan Revenge Tragedy*. With logic and clarity Bowers argues forcibly that "Hamlet's tragic error" occurs not in III.ii or III.iii (as many have asserted) but in III.iv, and that the error, "the impulsive killing of Polonius in mistake for the King" becomes "Hamlet's alienation from Heaven by his inability to wait upon a non-criminal revenge that God would in due course have arranged for His minister." Moreover, it follows logically from the evidence set forth in Bowers's earlier book that Hamlet's "crack in . . . patience, or fortitude, and his instant springing into action at the cry behind the arras, . . . led him in his momentary weakness to commit a crime that on the Elizabethan stage must inevitably be repaid by death." The analysis of *Hamlet* is interwoven with a discussion of retributive vs. corrective justice, the Old Law vs. the New Law, the concept of catharsis, the *Oedipus* plays, and *Samson Agonistes*. Bowers concludes that although both Hamlet and Samson are justly punished by death the audience knows "that a higher equity stemming from mercy will bring them to their rest" and that this knowledge "reconciles the audience to the tragic penalty that justice must exact."

The importance of both *Hamlet* and *Samson Agonistes* to Bowers as both teacher and scholar is well known, and his last book bears testimony to their crucial position in his critical thinking. *Hamlet*, of course, is the work that dominates the criticism. Of the thirteen essays in *Hamlet as Minister and Scourge*, six have *Hamlet* in the title, and four of the others (the first four in the book) include considerable discussion of the play. "Hamlet as Minister and Scourge," the fifth essay in the book, is, of course, given particular attention. As the dust jacket notes: "The title essay was cited in the seventy-fifth anniversary issue of *PMLA* as one of the nine articles published there in the past seventy-five years 'which have really affected the course of scholarship and criticism.' " One of the most tightly reasoned essays, "Hamlet as Minister and Scourge" can also be traced back to Bowers's *Elizabethan Revenge Tragedy* (in his discussion of the *Ur-Hamlet*). The argument of the essay originates from Hamlet's lines in III.iv— "But heaven hath pleas'd it so / To punish me with this [the mistakenly murdered Polonius], and this with me, / That I must be their scourge and minister"—and develops from the distinctions between scourge (an instrument of vengeance) and minister (an agent of good) and con-

cludes with arguments for Hamlet's ultimate reconciliation with Heaven (albeit at the expense of his life) in V.ii.

The concept of reconciliation also figures prominently in "Milton's *Samson Agonistes*: Justice and Reconciliation" (1978), the last essay in the book. Although it might at first glance seem odd that Bowers included an essay on a closet drama in his collection, upon reflection the logic of the decision becomes clear. First of all the play poses, like *Hamlet*, problems, and Bowers liked to solve problems. For example, his instructions to his students in his Milton seminar at the University of Virginia were to be original and to solve a problem in the major assignment, a 6000- to 7000-word term paper. In his closely reasoned and logically organized lectures on *Samson Agonistes*, he focused upon two problems that he considered crucial and that had not been adequately addressed by previous critics. With aplomb and authority, he took issue particularly with Dr. Johnson, who had argued that Milton's work had no middle, that is, climax, because there was no cause-and-effect order to the three visitations of Manoa, Dalila, and Harapha. Secondly, Johnson, overlooking the words "persuaded inwardly" in Milton's Argument, had argued that Samson did not act out of necessity when he went to the feast at the end of the play. Drawing upon his impressive knowledge of Aristotle, Greek tragedy, Shakespearean tragedy, and Christian theology, Bowers over a period of several weeks inexorably demolished his formidable critical opponent. It was an impressive display that exuded both mastery of his material and true critical authority. The essence of those lectures is found in the printed essay, which is argued with rigorous logic.

As Bowers says in his essay: "Two related problems face any critic of *Samson Agonistes*. The first is the precise nature of the misunderstanding that Samson and the other characters have of God's purpose for him after his blinding, a purpose not finally manifested until the catastrophe. The second is the exact means, as dramatically represented, by which the misunderstanding is eliminated and a reconciliation is brought about." *Samson Agonistes*, argues Bowers, is "a redemptive tragedy not on the Greek but on the Shakespearean model, in which the hero after his tragic error wins through to a death in victory that justifies such a trust as Horatio's that flights of angels will sing Hamlet to his rest." Given these premises, supported by a thorough knowledge of

Milton's canon, Bowers develops a tight argument, based upon distinctions between Old Testament (or retributive) and New Testament (or redemptive) justice, to solve the first problem, that is, God's purpose for Samson after the blinding. The solution is to understand the nature of redemptive justice:

> The purpose of punishment under the system of equity—mercy added to justice—that governs redemptive justice is to lead man to an understanding of the will of God when his own will has crossed divine purpose and alienated him from the supporting signs of grace. That man, so taught, can return to God's favor is the healing message of *Samson Agonistes* and its justification of the ways of God to man.

Samson does submit himself to the will of God once more, but "must pay the law by dying in order to win the victory." Bowers solves the second problem, the means by which "misunderstanding is eliminated and a reconciliation is brought about," through an elaborate analysis of the structure of *Samson Agonistes* which draws upon analogy with "the three stages of repentance as worked out in Book I of Spenser's *Faerie Queene* in accord with the conventional teachings of the church." It is a tour de force and far too intricate to be summarized here, but one must surely agree that Bowers proves that at his end "Samson fulfills his original mission" and that "in the new action at the temple Samson is a God-guided man once more."

Bowers's love of problem solving can be seen throughout his last book, and almost always the focus is upon plot and ethical issues. The major exception is "Hamlet's 'Sullied' or 'Solid' Flesh: A Bibliographical Case-History" (1956), but this exception, in fact, proves the main point also, for in arguing on bibliographical evidence that the *sallied* (flesh) found in the First and Second Quartos is to be preferred over the Folio's *solid*, Bowers not only solves a "celebrated Shakespearean crux" but does so for literary reasons. That is, what is the meaning of Shakespeare's text? As Bowers says, *sallied* can be preferred "on the belief that Hamlet's feeling his flesh to be soiled by his mother's incestuous marriage is not a far-fetched idea." The issue is, of course, an ethical one, but ethical issues cannot, in Bowers's view, be separated from dramatic structure, because, as he says in his preface, that is the way Shakespeare "controlled the reactions of his audience to the understanding of character and action." For example, Bowers argues in the second essay (but actually the last published), "Climax and Protagonist in Shakespeare's Dramatic Structure" (1982): "Shakespeare's tragedies are pyramidal in structure." It follows logically that: "In a pyramidal plot structure [the] climax occurs in the third act, the fourth and fifth then being devoted to the falling action as the play descends to its catastrophic resolution." The emphasis upon structure leads to analysis and discovery of the climax in such plays as *Hamlet, Antony and Cleopatra, Macbeth, Much Ado about Nothing, Twelfth Night, The Tempest, Measure for Measure, As You Like It, The Merchant of Venice,* and *Henry IV*, part 1, with passing reference at the end of the essay to *King Lear*. In fact, two of the most powerful essays in *Hamlet as Minister and Scourge* are devoted to these last two plays, that is, "The Structure of *King Lear*" (1980) and "Theme and Structure in *King Henry IV, Part 1*." The *Lear* essay is a masterful analysis in which Bowers proves that even though the play is a "fifth-act tragedy" with the climax of the story occurring in I.i, the second storm scene, which changes Lear's character for the better, is nevertheless the turning point of the play's action. In the *Henry IV*, part 1, essay, a combination of two papers published in 1966 and 1970, Bowers demonstrates that Prince Hal is "a supremely rational Renaissance man," not to be viewed, as so many modern critics view him, as a cold-hearted, hypocritical Machiavel.

In the last-mentioned essays, as in all of the rest, Bowers's twofold interest is in structure and ethics. It was always so, for at the very end of *Elizabethan Revenge Tragedy* he had remarked: "The closing of the theaters was really a blessing in disguise. In the breathing space afforded by the Commonwealth's inhibition, the tragic drama found a relief from its dependence on empty ingenuity and worn-out tragic conventions which had lost all touch with the problems of human life and ethics, and all interest in the human soul." It is clear from *Hamlet as Minister and Scourge and Other Studies in Shakespeare and Milton* that Fredson Bowers never lost "touch with the problems of human life and ethics" nor lost "interest in the human soul." Both books stand as fitting monuments to an outstanding scholar, critic, and gentleman.

Fredson Bowers and the Cambridge Beaumont and Fletcher

Robert Kean Turner
University of Wisconsin—Milwaukee

Mr. Bowers's editorial work—from Shakespeare and Marlowe through Dryden and Fielding to Whitman, Hawthorne, Crane, and William James—and the power of his copious theoretical writing on analytical bibliography and textual criticism inaugurated a new era of scholarship. Having written the authoritative book in its field—*Principles of Bibliographical Description* (1949; itself a product of and rule book for a descriptive bibliography of Restoration drama that is, according to report, finished but unchecked)—a lesser man might have felt justified in devoting himself to music reviewing, sophisticated stamp collecting, and the finer points of Irish wolfhounds, contract bridge, and single malt whiskey. Endowed with vast energy and a sharp and restless intellect, however, Bowers found powerful satisfaction in a firm and selfless commitment to the life of the mind.

His Harvard dissertation, which appeared in 1940 as *Elizabethan Revenge Tragedy 1587-1642*, was for its time an accomplished work of classification and description; its exposition of the Kydian revenge formula remains a staple of criticism. As early as 1936, however, in connection with an interest in Jonson, he was reading Dekker and moving from literary criticism (which, of course, he never abandoned) toward textual studies. In *Library* (1936-1937) appeared "Bibliographical Problems in Dekker's *Magnificent Entertainment*," an explanation of anomalies in reprinting on the supposition that standing type was carried from one printing house to another. The article may show that work had begun on the Dekker edition, but it is important for another reason. In the same volume W. W. Greg's magisterial and much more comprehensible rebuttal was published; printed sheets, not type, had done the traveling. Later Mr. Bowers was to say that Greg's demonstration of his bibliographical ineptitude led him to serious study of the subject; once embarrassingly caught, he was never going to be wrong again in that way if he could help it. His first published work as an editor, however, was nei-

ther a revenge play nor a bibliographical foray but a manuscript play attributed to Thomas Randolph, *The Fary Knight*. It appeared in 1942, the year in which Mr. Bowers volunteered for military service. Scholarship shelved almost entirely, he served until 1946 as a naval officer.

In the late 1940s he made important discoveries showing how evidence from early printed books could be brought to bear on textual problems. During that period too he proposed to the Syndicate of the Cambridge University Press that he prepare a critical, old-spelling edition of Dekker's plays, its method to reflect the theories R. B. McKerrow had formulated for the Oxford Shakespeare as modified by the more advanced and influential ideas of Greg. The assignment of responsibilities was to affect profoundly the rest of his scholarly career. However much they may have recognized that the edition was needed, the syndics were perhaps reluctant to entrust it entirely to a relatively unknown American; or it may have been that, as Bowers put it, "other projects in being did not permit [him] to suggest a larger undertaking than the presentation of the text and appropriate material." Responsibility for the edition was therefore divided in a fashion that was to seem unfortunate to many critics. Although Bowers was to prepare the texts and provide textual apparatus, John Crow, an English scholar who had published little but who was reputed to (and perhaps did) know everything, was to provide their explanation and presumably a literary evaluation of each as well as discussions of canon, sources, stage history, and the like. In other editorial collaborations, one editor typically will handle text and commentary for one part of a canon and another will handle text and commentary for the rest. It has been asserted that the division of labor adopted for *Dekker* was hopelessly flawed: from this perspective it is imperative that he who makes the text also explains it. Actually, the *Dekker* arrangement is not impossible; indeed, a textual specialist and a literary critic may discover it stimulating if they work so closely together as to derive mutual inspiration. In the instance of *Dekker*, however, such a collaboration never happened. Handsomely printed, *Dekker* volume one appeared in 1953 comprising five plays and Dekker's addition to *Sir Thomas More*, all equipped with textual introductions, footnotes showing substantive departures from the copytexts, lists of press-variants found in the copytexts, lists of emended accidentals, and notes explaining not the meaning of the texts but why the editor had emended or why not. What struck nearly every reviewer as anomalous was that the scholar responsible for putting down the words he believed Dekker wrote seldom or never said what he thought Dekker meant by them. To an early review of this sort, Bowers responded in the *Library* that literary apparatus by another hand would be published in a later volume; as to the voluminous textual apparatus, he wrote, "I hold it incumbent on a critical old-spelling editor to provide for the reader the entire body of evidence from which he derived his text. . . . I hold it an axiom that an editor is bound to present faithfully the evidence for his treatment of the text." In the opinion of some, however, the *Dekker* apparatus went far beyond such evidence; regarding the apparatus of another edition modeled on *Dekker*, a critic who is also a textual scholar commented that its effect "is to draw attention away from matters of critical, linguistic, and literary significance towards superficial, accidental, and trivial matters." Nevertheless, the edition was so clearly superior to any other then available except the Herford and Simpson *Jonson* that it was generally welcomed despite reservations. R. C. Bald wrote in *Modern Philology*:

> It is now almost fifteen years since the late R. B. McKerrow's *Prolegomena to the Oxford Shakespeare* appeared. In the intervening years there has been a good deal of discussion on the principles and techniques of editing, in which Professor Bowers has taken an active part, but until now there has been no attempt to apply the results of this discussion to a body of texts. Bowers' edition . . . of Dekker is thus the first concrete example of the "New Editing"; it is likely to serve as a model for future editors of old authors.

It did, even when other editors disagreed with Bowers in principle and in practice. Volume two was published in 1955, three in 1958, and four in 1961. The promised literary introductions, notes, and commentary were finally forthcoming in four volumes published in 1980, the work of the eminently capable Cyrus Hoy.

Despite considerable scholarly opinion to the contrary, Bowers decided while *Dekker* was in progress that the strictly textual techniques of editing it represented should be extended to the work of other Renaissance playwrights (and, as it developed, to American writing as well). Since he knew that many Renaissance scholars would have preferred it otherwise but never directly answered them, one can only speculate as to why.

There was precedent, of course; the first and second Cambridge editions of Shakespeare (1863-1866 and 1891-1893) and the first Cambridge's popular offspring, the Globe edition (1864), had no literary apparatus except for a glossary in the Globe. Glover and Waller's ten-volume *Beaumont and Fletcher* (1905-1912) was furnished with collations only; a projected two volumes of literary notes were left to other hands that never grasped them. Furthermore, what could happen if one tried to do everything was apparent from the history of the Herford and Simpson *Jonson*. Volume one of that series was published in 1925 and volume two, the last, in 1952; after Herford's death in 1931, Percy Simpson had virtually to devote his life to *Jonson*. Moreover, Bowers to some extent shared with others the idea that textual criticism is very significantly a logical exercise based on the physical evidence found in the early versions of the texts, work more objective and hence more dependable than literary interpretation, especially of the sort that contaminated textual reasoning. As he wrote in *On Editing Shakespeare*,

> Bibliography may be said to attack textual problems from the mechanical point of view, using evidence which must deliberately avoid being colored by literary considerations. Non-bibliographical textual criticism works with meanings and literary values. If these last are divorced from all connection with the evidence of the mechanical process that imprinted meaningful symbols on a sheet of paper, no check-rein of fact or probability can restrain the farthest reaches of idle speculation.

One may trace his opinion to several brilliant triumphs achieved through acute observation and reasoning; he demonstrated, for instance, that the variants in only certain forms of *The Magnificent Entertainment* were authoritative because they resulted from Dekker's proofreading and that in the second edition of *The Honest Whore* variants were authoritative or not depending on whether they were found in standing or in reset type. *Q.E.D.* was an expression he loved. It should also be said that his intellectual powers could sometimes lead him into the wilderness because his premises were wrong; his mistaken general ideas about Elizabethan proofreading and about running titles as providers of information about the speed of typesetting are cases in point. He really was a bibliographer of the mind. But probably the chief reason for his decision to produce other austerely textual editions was his conviction that scholars generally were capable of furnishing their own glosses and interpretations whereas producing the text upon which these exercises were based required a special training, talent, and dedication. Convinced he was right, he declined to compromise, adverse opinion notwithstanding.

Some of the tasks required in preparing a critical edition—the collation of all extant copies of the copy-text to discover press-variants and the historical collation of editions to discover emendations—require little more than industry and a clear head; the inventive parts of the job, the determination of the history of the text, which can be especially challenging when more than one substantive version survives, and the delicate choices sometimes involved in emendation demand stringent intellectual and critical discipline. Nevertheless, all the work can usually be handled by a trained subordinate working under supervision. Such editions of Elizabethan plays had been around for some time, Bullen's turn-of-the-century variorum Beaumont and Fletcher being an especially relevant instance, and Bowers himself had edited *Merry Wives* for the Pelican Shakespeare under the direction of Alfred Harbage. Long before *Dekker* was completed it evidently occurred to Bowers that with his guidance his students could handle a large corpus. As early as 1950, when Cyrus Hoy began as a doctoral dissertation his expert study of the authorship of the Beaumont and Fletcher canon and soon afterwards when other Bowers students attempted editions of a couple of the more textually difficult plays, groundwork for the Beaumont and Fletcher edition was laid. Just after Christmas 1960, with some seasonal jubilation Bowers announced to several of his former students the agreement-in-principle with the Cambridge University Press. The edition would run to ten volumes. He would contribute at least one text to each volume and as general editor set policy and oversee the work of the subordinate editors, originally L. A. Beaurline, Irby B. Cauthen, Jr., Cyrus Hoy, Robert K. Turner, and George Walton Williams. The object was to establish the texts of the fifty-two works in the Beaumont and Fletcher canon. As he put it in "Old Spelling Editions of Dramatic Texts,"

> to establish the text, the editor . . . must attempt to recover what the author actually wrote—in his final intentions—as closely as bibliographical tech-

niques, linguistic analysis, and critical intelligence can guide him. In complex cases he must separate the authority of the substantives (the author's final words) from the authority of the accidentals (the texture of spelling, punctuation, capitalization that clothe these substantives); and by any necessary eclectic selection contrive that form of the text that in all its details most closely corresponds to what would have been the authorial intentions in print; in other words, present the words of an author in their most authoritative recoverable form.

The extensive basic training his contributing editors required for this enterprise Bowers undertook with the greatest possible generosity, patience, and good will. "The Text of This Edition," the essay which was to appear in volume one, set the ground rules, but their interpretation required some encyclicals, which were typically addressed to "Dear Colleagues and Partners." Queries and appeals for help were carefully and fully answered; ignorance and wrongheadedness were courteously set right, although it was always clear that the editors were finally responsible for their own judgments. No detail was too trivial for scrupulous attention and often detailed response. One of the founding editors recalls that "the easy way was not his way"; he was a demanding taskmaster. And yet while he expended great care and pains on this launching, Bowers, among other activities, was getting the Hawthorne edition established, editing *The Marble Faun* for it, running the Department of English at the University of Virginia, and supervising *Studies in Bibliography*.

Beaumont and Fletcher volume one was published in 1966. It was a remarkable production, the printer's copy for the texts being mounted Xeroxes of the copy-texts, heavily altered in manuscript to emend both accidentals and substantives as well as to achieve accord with the edition's style. On top of the editor's markings were those of Bowers, whose hand was so dreadful that sometimes he could not read it himself. (This technique was continued through volume five, after which CUP rebelled and demanded typed copy throughout.) The volume received about the same kind of reviews that had greeted *Dekker*. Kenneth Muir in *Shakespeare Studies* stated:

> There does not seem to be any intention of providing such notes [as Cyrus Hoy would supply for *Dekker*] for the Beaumont and Fletcher volumes. It need hardly be said that such notes would

The Life | in the | Studio | [fleuron] | NANCY HALE |

[device: Bunker Hill monument with L B in oval] | Boston

Little, Brown and Company   Toronto

[1-7]^{16}, pp. [i-ix] x-xi [xii-xiii] xiv, [1-3] 4-209 [210]

     (pp. 13, 31, 46, 53, 63, 75, 85, 96-99, 115, 125, 141,

     156, 172, 197 unnumbered)   *paper notice every numbers*

p. i: blank; p. ii: 'BOOKS by NANCY HALE' (15 titles);

p. iii: hf.tit. 'The Life in the Studio'; p. iv: blank; p. v:

title; p. vi: 'COPYRIGHT ©xxxxx 1957, 1962, 1963, 1965, 1967,

1968, 1969 BY NANCY HALE | xxxxxx[all rights reserved notice] |

LIBRARY OF CONGRESS CATALOG CARD NO. 69-16965 | FIRST EDITION |

[credits to New Yorker, Ladies Home Journal, Virginia Quarterly

Review] | Published simultaneously in Canada | by Little,

Brown & Company (Canada) Limited | PRINTED IN THE UNITED

STATES OF AMERICA'; p. vii: 'To John C. Coleman'; p. viii:

blank; p. ix: 'Foreword'; p. xii: blank; p. xiii: 'Contents';

~~p. 1: 'ONE | Family Ties | [fleuron]; p. 2: blank; xxxxx~~

pp. 3-209 text, beginning '[row of fleurons] | What Haunts Thee

in Ford Shapes' with 2-line heading capital; p. 210: blank.

Fredson Bowers's proposed model entry for the Pittsburgh Series in Bibliography

-2-

p. 1: sec.tit. 'ONE | Family Ties | [fleuron]'; p. 2: blank;

pp. 3-95, text of pt. 1 beginning '[row of fleurons] | What

Haunts Thee in Fond Shapes' with 2-line heading cap; p. 96:

blank; p. 97: sec.tit. 'TWO | The Loosening | [fleuron]';

p. 98: blank; pp. 99-209, text of pt. 2 (same typography);

p. 210: blank.

One

FAMILY TIES

Two

THE LOOSENING

~~Typography~~ Such and such, such and such point, 30 lines

per page; running-heads versos part titles, rectos story titles.

Leaf   x   mm., wove ~~xxx~~ off-white paper, all/edges trimmed.

Endpapers heavier wove stock, one leaf pasted to cover, other

free.

-3-

<u>Binding</u>: 3/4 dark-brown buckram, front cover blindstamped

with device; back cover blank.   Spine light-brown buckram

lettered in dark brown: 'HALE | [fleuron] | <u>The</u> | <u>Life</u> | <u>in the</u> |

<u>Studio</u> | [fleuron] | <u>Little,</u> | <u>Brown</u>'.

<u>Dustjacket</u>: [front: dark brown background, drawing of mother

[*coated* | *White stock,*]

to right, white-rimmed oval photograph of father to lower left.

Lettering: [white] <u>Nancy Hale</u> | [light brown] <u>The Life</u>|<u>in the</u>|

<u>Studio</u> | [white, lower right] <u>An Affectionate Recollection</u> |

<u>of Some Singular Parents</u>'; front flap: blurb concluded on back

flap; notation, '<u>Jacket Design by Martha Lehtola</u> '. Spine:

light-brown background, lettering in dark brown, '<u>Hale</u> | [oval

photo of father] | <u>The</u> | <u>Life</u> | <u>in</u> | <u>the</u> | <u>Studio</u> | [drawing

of mother in hexagonal frame] | [white] <u>Little</u>, <u>Brown</u>'. Back:

photo of author by University of Virginia Dept. of Graphics.

Lower right, code number 338699.

greatly increase the value of the edition. One wonders, indeed, whether it is really possible to establish a reliable text without being able to explain every line of it; and it seems a pity that the knowledge so acquired should not be shared with the reader. In *Cupid's Revenge*, for example, there are five or six words for which the reviewer would have liked assistance, and there must be other Elizabethan scholars almost as ignorant.

Philip Edwards, who was to produce an excellent edition of Massinger on a different plan of collaboration, remarked: "The great value of the new edition of the plays . . . is not only that this fine material is made available, but that a standard text is being established. The disadvantages [include] the exiguity of elucidation and explanation as against a lavishness of textual and bibliographical matter." And Clifford Leech noted: "There is no doubt that here at last we shall have an edition we can use. . . . If, in one respect or another, we may feel it could have been done differently, that is because there are areas for debate in the whole matter of editing seventeenth-century dramatic texts. What is indubitable is that the task is being performed with splendid care." Volume two followed in 1970 without the participation of I. B. Cauthen, Jr., who had been called away by administrative work; volume three in 1976; volume four in 1979 (with Hans Walter Gabler, one of Bowers's most talented postdoctoral students, replacing L. A. Beaurline, called away by his *Jonson*); volume five in 1982; volume six in 1985; and volume seven in 1989. Bowers's own contributions through volume seven included editions of *The Masque of the Inner Temple and Gray's Inn, Cupid's Revenge, Beggars' Bush, The Woman's Prize, The Wild-Goose Chase, The Loyal Subject, Henry VIII,* and *The Two Noble Kinsmen.* His edition of *Barnavelt* will appear in volume eight, now in press. As his life drew with increasing discomfort to an end, he began to work more and more on the edition; he hoped to see it finished, and the mechanical nature of some of the work seemed to provide relief for physical distress. For volume nine, also in press, he completed editions of *The Sea Voyage, The Maid in the Mill,* and *The Elder Brother* and for volume ten *The Fair Maid of the Inn.* Volume ten, to which Hoy, Williams, and Turner will also contribute, is now in preparation. All experienced scholars, all in their sixties, the three survivors nevertheless are strangely at sea. One put it this way:

This is August 1991. I am now working on the apparatus for my last play. As I fidget over the pages of tedious notes and infinitesimal details, I realize that they will not pass under Fred's scrutiny. I ask myself: "What difference will it make? What effect will his absence have on the quality of the editing of this last play?" I sense, indeed, a vacuum of power and direction. The enterprise has no engine to take it over the last hill, no driver to keep it in the right way. But, of course, it has thirty years of momentum and thirty years of imaginative guidance and defining of the right way. Vol. 10 will make it over the hill just as Fred wanted it to and expected it would. Still, in personal terms, there will not be hassles over the lining of Fletcher's verse (fortunately, this play has few serious problems), there will not be the differences over how to link short lines or what to do with them at the head of long speeches. There will not be those near-illegible squiggles on my neat pages proposing tentatively—as it were—that the comma should not be changed to a colon and explaining that the copy-text really made sense without emendation. There will not be the presence of an intellect freshly considering the play as a whole, not solely line by line. What will be lacking is the quality of tempering: adjusting to a universal standard the apparent inconsistencies of the single play, correcting misjudgments and restraining individual flights of editorial fancy, assisting with wise restraint in the handling of vexing cruces. I sense already—and the typescript is far from complete—a vacuum. It is no longer possible to say: "How will Fred react to this?" Instead, I find myself saying: "I know how Fred would react to this. I don't need to send it to Charlottesville. I just need to use, without asking, the control and discipline which after thirty years have been ingrained, have been internalized as part of the edition." That's it; he is still the teacher.

The Editorial Style of Fredson Bowers

Ignas K. Skrupskelis
University of South Carolina

My impression of Fredson Bowers centers on the image of a man who in a few hours in Harvard's Houghton Library could examine hundreds of pages of manuscripts and produce reams of virtually illegible notes describing paper, watermarks, folds, inks, foliation. No doubt this reflects great native capacity, but, more importantly, it reflects mastery of method. Some philosophers claim that the goal of philosophy is to produce a language of maximum clarity to displace the vagaries and ambiguities of common speech. Bowers perfected a language of maximum clarity for describing books and manuscripts. As an amateur in bibliography, I did not realize how imprecise was my commonsense use of terms such as *edition, printing, manuscript*. I did not understand what a discarded verso was or a false start or why it was important to distinguish between a holograph and a typescript. Bowers's notation was both precise and economical. A mass of information about a text could be recorded using very little space. And Bowers himself was a master of his method.

It is a method which places great demands upon a scholar because he must work in terms of a complete documentary record. To compile this record requires much time and great patience and, as William James might have put it, a capacity for not being bored. The scholar must abandon his intuitions, his preferences wherever possible and work in terms of the factual data, in an effort to remain faithful to the author and his final intentions. The task of reducing this documentary record to some order, establishing the history of transmission, deciding the degree of authority to be assigned to the different documents, is intellectually quite challenging because thousands of small and seemingly disconnected details must be placed in a very complex web of relations. Bowers always could find order where an amateur could find only a mass of stray and disconnected facts.

Bowers was very much a theoretician who enjoyed seeing his theory at work and gloried in its capacity to overcome great difficulties. Perhaps in William James the most challenging text from an editorial point of view was James's psychical research paper "Report on Mrs. Piper's Hodgson-Control." I thought the paper hardly worth reprinting because it was long and consisted mainly of trivia supplied by insipid ghosts. In any case, science had not moved in the direction James had hoped, so that now the piece had no theoretical interest. Bowers was excited by the challenge to his editorial theory. Could he arrange the surviving documents in such an order that it would exhibit James's final intentions? There was a manuscript, and, more importantly, there were two printed texts differing in wording and punctuation, and both could be considered authoritative as far as final intentions were concerned. Bowers devised

a theory that one version was set from a copy of the unrevised proof of the other. The theory solved some problems but "complicated certain questions of textual authority." In the end, in some cases, the "doctrine of final intentions" had to be set aside and readings adopted because in the editor's view they represented the "superior revision." James's posthumously published *Some Problems of Philosophy* also posed great textual difficulties because there were two typescripts which James had revised independently of each other. The first editor had pretty much followed his own tastes and in addition had improved the text on his own authority. It is to *Some Problems* that Bowers pointed in defense of his own more objective editorial practices.

The notion of objectivity is central to Bowers's editorial theory. The final text should not reflect what the editor liked or thought interesting but what the author himself wanted to write. But Bowers was quite flexible in the application of his theory. Different authors require different treatments, and even different books cannot be edited in the same way. The editorial theory was a guide to the understanding of the individuality of a particular author or work. It was never a simple matter of adopting as copy-text the first printing of the first edition. It was a much more subtle process of adjusting editorial practices to the work habits of an author. Did an author revise extensively in proof? Did he make corrections in his copies? Was he careful in matters of punctuation and capitalization? Editorial decisions had to respect an author's practices.

It is easy to caricature Bowers as a man immersed in pedantry for the sake of pedantry. It is easy to view him as Smedley Force, someone who curled up in bed to read "elegant and urbane footnotes" and assigned graduate students the task of deciding whether the missing closing quotation mark on one page was the same as the extra quotation mark twenty pages later. I cannot say what Bowers was like in his early years, and I have heard rumors of an authoritarian taskmaster. Perhaps the Bowers I knew during the last twenty years of his life when we worked together on the William James edition was much mellowed. I found him quite willing to support and encourage those in whom he had confidence. Not much given to words of praise, he still managed to convey warmth and appreciativeness. And he was anything but a pedant. On the contrary, he was always ready to solve a problem with a guess, with a conjecture, if in his view the problem was not worth much time. When on one occasion I spent a fruitless day hunting an insignificant fact because I was certain that I would get the answer in just a few more minutes, Bowers scolded me for wasting valuable time. The extent of the effort had to be proportioned to the value of the information being sought.

Bowers usually responded to accusations of pedantry with an instrumental defense: textual criticism which leads to purified and authoritative texts is a necessary condition of any interpretative scholarship. Bowers and his followers could always produce amusing examples of how typographical errors have misled interpreters, how apparently difficult texts were mere products of careless printing. Some philosophers claimed that critical and definitive editions of philosophical texts were not important because the corrections which resulted from the process almost never made a difference to philosophical interpreters. James, for example, still remained a pragmatist in his conception of truth, no matter what his final intentions regarding punctuation and wording were. Bowers responded by pointing out the numerous places in which significant corruptions have been removed from the text and by arguing that editorial work was important even when it did not result in significant changes. Readers need to be confident that the troublesome comma, the unexpected capital letter, the inaccurate quotation came from the author himself and were a part of the "texture of meaning," to use a very suggestive Bowersism. In possession of a properly edited text, an interpreter could proceed with confidence. Theoretically this defense rests on a refusal to separate style from content, the rejection of the belief that ideas can be abstracted out of the texture of meaning in which they were expressed. Bowers, I think, properly saw that James himself was very much on his side:

> James was a conscious and dedicated stylist, less perhaps for aesthetic reasons than for purposes of clarity, precision, and readability, on which he set high store. I cannot conceive that he ever distinguished style from content—the two were so synonymous in his thinking that to separate them would foster an artificial dichotomy. Indeed, his criticism of murky thinking in philosophers and psychologists was that it was produced by murky writing, especially in the Germans.

James, who labored at great length even on the accidentals and who was interested in the book-

production process, would have agreed that the distinction between style and content is an artificial one, an expression of an intellectualistic way of thinking.

In answering the critics who claimed that the techniques of textual criticism while useful in literature had no application to philosophical texts, Bowers could not have known that he was stepping into a controversy concerning the nature of philosophy. He thought that concerning textual criticism philosophers represented a "midposition," between literary scholars, most of whom recognize the need for modern editing, and historians who deliberately reject such methods. I think in this he was mistaken. On the whole, philosophers are simply indifferent, content to use in their research the same paperbacks which they acquired in graduate school. It is virtually impossible to find in a philosophy journal a review of a critical edition which pays significant attention to the editorial work. Many philosophers consider the task of philosophy to be the assertion or denial of propositions, timeless entities expressible in one language as easily as in another. From this point of view, for example, James's pragmatism, is not the inextricable product of a certain personality and a certain culture, it is the assertion of certain falsehoods (or truths) about the relations between truth and practice and meaning; propositions which are independent of the mode in which they are expressed. Of course, these propositions can only be expressed in a certain style. But the good interpreter will set aside the accidentals of expression and extract from a text its core propositions. These propositions can then be examined to discover whether they are true or false. The philosophical critics of Bowers, in effect, insist that philosophers with certain limited interests form the only audience which editors of philosophical texts should take into account. In fact, most philosophers write for many audiences. Some read James in search of philosophical truths, others because they find his work inspiring, still others enjoy his style, and others find social, intellectual, and linguistic records of James's time. A critical edition is intended to serve the needs of various readers, and an editor should not work with just one audience in mind.

For Bowers, I think, textual criticism was not simply a device for producing better texts but also a means of controlling and stimulating the critical imagination. His method requires that the critic attain great intimacy with his author, understanding not just the finished product but the process of production as well. In some cases, it might be a trivial consideration that an author first inserted and then deleted a comma. But in others, it might be quite illuminating. And it is impossible to know with certainty whether a particular comma is of the first kind or of the second. It will be trivial as long as no conflicts of interpretation arise. It will be trivial as long as no theories are developed which need just that fact. Facts by themselves, as James believed, neither have nor lack value. It all depends on the interest which the investigator takes in them. In "Editing a Philosopher," Bowers asks concerning the imprecision which some commentators find in James: "Was this lack of precision due to James's inability to express himself precisely or to the fact that the ideas themselves were not always clearly defined in his mind?" These are surely important questions for James's interpreters to answer. Bowers rightly points out that they cannot be answered without the sort of data which textual criticism provides.

Bowers himself, in my view, did what he did not because he thought it was useful but because it was part of his enjoyment of literature. The Bowers I knew enjoyed what he was doing. He enjoyed challenges to his theories, he liked books, he liked being intimate with authors. And he liked doing things with style, whether driving his Mercedes 250 SL from Charlottesville to Folly Cove in one day or producing urbane footnotes.

Fredson Bowers as Music Critic

David L. Vander Meulen
University of Virginia

When Fredson Bowers developed an interest, whether it was in Irish wolfhounds, Restoration drama, foreign cars, or microwave cooking, he pursued it to the point of expertise. But his various preoccupations tended to be evident only to the audience that was immediately involved; seldom were there any public cross-references between activities, despite the commonality of their guiding principles. Now and then hints would appear; contributors to *Studies in Bibliography*, for instance, learned that the colorful stamps on envelopes from the editor had to be returned for the sake of what seemed to be some serious collecting interest in Charlottesville. Likewise in the Bowers home, Woodburn, itself: visitors entering the

grand living room graced with portraits by Lilian Westcott Hale, the mother of his wife, Nancy Hale, would ordinarily have no sense of the textual work being carried on in his study down a short hall to the left nor of what lay behind the folding doors on either side of the dining room entry to the right. Occasionally, however, the doors might be open, revealing twenty-eight speakers built into the wall, with rows of sound recordings above and below them.

These records were the trophies of work in four decades, from May 1939 to November 1966, when he wrote almost twelve hundred columns reviewing about five thousand records for the Sunday editions of the *Richmond Times-Dispatch*. John Denniston, who has compiled a list of these (on deposit in the Special Collections Department of the University of Virginia's Alderman Library), and to whom I am deeply indebted for access to the list and for his observations on it, calculates that the articles contain approximately 21,307 column inches of type—about a third of a mile. The byline of what became the most important series of record reviews in the state never included anything more than the author's name, though from February 1963 the column added his photograph. The title varied, as if in search of the perfect pun: initially "Music on Records," it gained or lost a definite article, the opening word, and the plural of the final one. In 1944 the preposition changed, and for a time the column became "Music Off the Records." The "on"-again "off"-again dialectic reached a stasis in 1950, when the title assumed its final form, "Music Off Records" (except for three issues in the final year, when the original 1939 title resurfaced).

The column appeared nearly every week over those twenty-eight years, except for three significant gaps: June 1942 through February 1946; September 1952 into June 1953 (when Bowers was in England on a Fulbright Fellowship); and April through July 1959 (when he was in Oxford as the Lyell Reader in Bibliography). The arrangements in the intervals of the 1950s suggest how institutionalized the column and its author had become. Both times it continued, first over the initials "H.F.E." and then as "By F. E. Kirby (For Fredson Bowers)." The hiatus in the 1940s corresponds with Bowers's service as a commander in the U.S. Naval Reserve; wartime duty may explain the dearth of reviews, though he had warned his readers on 7 June 1942 that "Owing to the cut in record releases [because of a shortage of materials and a union recording ban, as

Page from a manuscript draft for Bowers's 1961 lecture "The Ideal Record Collector," given at the Virginia Museum of Fine Art (5691-F, Manuscripts Division, Special Collections Department, University of Virginia Library) he pointed out on 26 December 1943], this column will appear in the future only once or twice a month as records become available for review."

The subject of the column was always classical recordings. During the early 1940s a weekly feature entitled "On the Popular Side," by Norman Towe, considered especially the music of swing bands; it was printed immediately adjacent to the Bowers one, but it always began at least a couple of inches lower on the page. In the early days "Music on Records" was also accompanied by advertisements. In a practice that many current newspapers find inappropriate, the 21 July 1940 column, for instance, is followed by two ads that mention records reviewed inches above, and by a third that offers to provide "the New Records reviewed on this page by Fredson Bowers." In historical perspective, similarly placed ads in 1943 offering to pay cash (six cents a pound) for used records seem to offer commentary on the vanity of human wishes.

Despite the general unfamiliarity in literary and bibliographical circles with this part of his canon, personal acquaintances were well aware of the strong musical involvement, if for no other reason than that they were often the recipients of records as Christmas or birthday gifts. This secondary use of the records had its own good results: according to Bowers's daughter Joan Stout,

> My love for music was inculcated into me because my father sent me many of the records he had reviewed. The collection grew—and being heavy (they were in those days mostly 78s) it became a challenge for me to truck them all forward and back to boarding school in the late 40s—but I listened to every one!

Bowers and his wife were regulars at the University's Tuesday Evening Concerts, a visiting artists series that he also would dangle as a lure to prospective faculty members. When traveling he would waste no opportunity to attend live performances. A letter in 1979 summarizes the afterhours activity of a week in London: Stoppard's *Night and Day*, three ballet evenings, and *The Return of Ulysses*, by Montiverdi—"firstclass singing" by the Kent Opera Company. Special visitors to Woodburn were treated to public performances of the best of his collection, one comprehensive enough to draw on for any taste. One couple tells of how, upon returning from a New York trip to see Strauss's opera *Elektra*, Bowers virtually re-created their experience by playing at full amplification a twenty-minute excerpt from an-

other Strauss opera, *Ariadne auf Naxos*. For a demonstration of the system's effectiveness, a Princeton alumnus was favored with a recital by the Princeton organist Carl Weinrich. (In the course of the performance, Nancy Hale, whose interest in the details of musical history was as small as her capacities for irony and deflation were great, observed that "I always enjoy listening to Segovia.")

The reviews continued until, said Bowers, "I ran out of adjectives." How they developed in the first place is less clear. He began what apparently is the inaugural essay, on 19 November 1939, in full stride, with no introductory explanation: "The most important symphonic recording of the month is . . ." His general musical interest is slightly more definable. As an undergraduate at Brown University from 1921 through 1925 he was involved in "Musical Clubs" all but his first year and took music classes his third year. As a senior—at age nineteen—he was part of the Varsity Quartet and leader of the Glee Club. His eldest son, Fredson, Jr., recounts other expressions of musical interest:

> When I was a boy, I discovered an old guitar down in the cellar in considerable disrepair and with half its strings missing. I asked my father about it, and he told me that when he was a student at Brown University his tuition was covered by scholarship but he had to earn money for expenses. He became the leader of a small jazz band in which he played saxophone and Hawaiian guitar. Knowing my father's later love for classical music, it is difficult to imagine him playing a hot sax in local night clubs in the Providence area.

The chief aspects of most of the reviews are present already in the very first one. The length is typical—about twenty column inches (though during World War II it dropped as low as seven). The procedure proves conventional: to start, without introduction, with the most important new release and then to look at a handful more (here, three) as space allows. The features considered are also standard: the work itself, the performance, and the recorded reproduction. Because the column is first of all about records, the second and third features customarily receive the most attention, though in this opening review he includes more discussion than usual of the musical work:

[Brahms's First Symphony] is one of the world's best-loved symphonies, and rightly, for the progression from the deep tragedy of the first movement through the pathos of the andante to the superhuman triumph of the finale is so tremendous that a conductor must eschew all cheap effects and think altogether in terms of the larger phrases and the long line of the music.

The conductor does what is required, the orchestra responds appropriately, and the recording is a success:

Weingartner allows the music to speak for itself as it is so fully capable of doing. He never drags the tempo, but his crispness of beat does not hurry his players and cause them to scant their phrasing. . . . The London Symphony is not one of the world's very greatest orchestras, but it is entirely satisfactory here, and the recording is exceptional. . . . With the possible exception of the Telefunken set recorded in Germany by Jochum and the Berlin Philharmonic, this recording is the best made and one which displaces not only the earlier Columbia version but also the Victor sets recorded by Stokowski and by Walter.

The rhetorical stance here also proves characteristic. Bowers assumes an interested audience and thus can dispense with an introduction. The ability to make multiple comparisons confirms the knowledge and credibility of the reviewer, while actually making them provides the practical advice that is largely the reason for the column's existence. This representative willingness to serve the reader shows up again toward the end of the column. About a Bach sonata, Bowers points out that it "is the best of the three that he wrote for these instruments, and beautifully played here, but to an extent it is best appreciated by a full-fledged lover of Bach. For the ordinary listener there are more important Bach recordings."

This concern for the audience also shows in other ways. By providing information that is up-to-date, that smacks of privileged trade gossip, and that discusses changes in public policy as they affect records, Bowers creates readers more informed than they are likely to be by any other means—and also strengthens his own authority as a guide. On 7 December 1941, he passes on the news that "Columbia has just announced that it will issue no new records in January since December will be filled entirely with manufacturing Christmas orders and catching up with back orders." On 20 July of that year he had discussed rumors about a price increase and a tax on records; his delineation of the questions was forceful, and his recommendations firm:

So far as I have been able to learn, these are the facts. . . . Hence if readers wish to escape the tax, they had better stock up early since there is no telling when the tax will be levied.

There . . . is such a record shortage at the moment that a price increase may come in the future. . . . People using steel needles had definitely better stock up since shortages are developing and half tone needles, for example, are almost unobtainable.

Or he might sound the alert about faulty pressings:

I wish to warn readers, however, that they should play each record side before purchase. My review copy was very badly pressed, only Sides 2 and 10 being free from some fault. . . . [25 April 1943].

Finally, most of the columns of the 1940s concluded with an invitation to send enquiries about the care or selection of records—some columns add "needles"—which "Mr. Bowers will gladly answer." The tag for the 7 July 1940 column put the offer more strongly: "Mr. Bowers will be glad to advised [sic] at great length by letter on records reviewed in his column or on the selection of past recordings."

The air of authority was nonetheless accompanied by a recognition of possible fallibility and acknowledgement that his opinions were merely that—his opinions. On 1 February 1942 he revised some earlier verdicts:

Three recent statements I have made need some correction now that I have been able to play the records on a better machine. The recording of the Toscanini Rhine Journey album is much better than I indicated. . . . The recording of the Spalding-Primrose album of Mozart's Sinfonia Concertante is less good than I indicated. . . . Finally, further listening has convinced me that Heifetz's playing of the Brahms First Violin Sonata is even more unsatisfactory than I indicated.

A column at the end of that year (13 December) was typical in its awareness of his subjective judgment and taste:

Here is the annual list of what in my purely private opinion have been the most distinguished albums of the past year. No individual can make up a list of the ten best albums of 1942 that will represent universal opinion.

He promptly substantiated that observation himself: "Moreover, when I tried to make a list of 10, I found I could not sacrifice a single one out of the 12." He made the identical point the following year, observing that any individual's opinion appeared "against his background of prejudices and preconceived likes and dislikes of music, musicians, and recording techniques" (5 December). The same diffidence occurs in specific comments about individual composers. He acknowledges that Samuel Barber, for instance,

is extremely well thought of, but for myself I have always thought his music rhetorical rather than truly expressive, and usually thin in content for the form chosen. But this is only a personal opinion, and I can well imagine others finding this well-written sonata ingratiating [31 December 1950].

Bowers's most extensive discussion of music comes not in these reviews but in an unpublished talk on "The Ideal Record Collector" at the Virginia Museum of Fine Arts in Richmond on 5 March 1961. (The manuscript and typescript are now in Alderman Library and are quoted by permission.) In it he argues that to enjoy music (a goal that he sees as desirable) one must understand its language.

Music is just as much a language as the sounds that form words constitute a language. Musical notes played according to a choice of instruments and in preconceived combinations communicate an emotion, even something of an idea—certainly some form of transferred experience—as much as words can, and oftentimes better than words can, just as a painting is better at the essence of physical description than words.

Language is communication *between people*: "The real basis of understanding musical language is the simple ability to hear what the composer is saying. This sounds elementary, but it is not." The disc he would give if he could to every beginning record collection in order to learn the language of music is Beethoven's "Archduke" trio. "This music may not assault the heavens," he says, "but it strikes home instantly to the heart. It can be listened to with sympathy and appreciation in almost every mood. It is, in short, perfection." It is significantly "human," then, especially because it communicates both beauty and emotion. He speaks of music giving him shivers up his spine, of feeling his back muscles "squinch up" with pleasure. That principle explains why Bowers is cool to Gustav Holst's *Planets*, which he considers "music more of the head than the heart" (23 July 1944) but also why he likes Ernst Bloch's *Three Jewish Poems* ("a lyric beauty . . . a softness"; 9 April 1961), Marian Anderson's singing ("the rare combination of magnificent voice and heartfelt feeling"; 18 April 1943), and the work of William Walton. This composer, he says, "is definitely separated from the too great number of modern composers who are technically proficient, but have really nothing to say. He is brilliant, intense, complex in mood, and warm in feeling" (15 February 1942). Gustav Mahler's Symphony No. 9 "is the greatest symphony of the twentieth century," in part because of the transmission of serene faith and reconciliation made from composer to listener.

On the other hand, Bowers also warns against following one's instinctive reaction of dislike to a new work. Not all composers will have the accessibility of Bowers's favorite, Mozart. "Be venturesome," he admonishes, as he predicts a revival of Richard Strauss and prophesies—five years before the opera's premier at the Metropolitan Opera House—that "Some day you may even hear *Die Frau ohne Schatten* at the Met, a wonderfully original and imaginative work of large proportions." Patience is also important. Copland's *Appalachian Spring* requires "a few hearings . . . for a proper understanding and appreciation of the virtues of this music"; the "starkness and angularity" of Copland's style are actually the "just container of deeply felt emotion kept in restraint and free from sentimentality" (26 May 1946). It took him longer to adjust to Alban Berg's opera *Wozzeck*, but it too occurred. On 27 January 1952 Bowers wrote that "it is probably not for the ordinary music listener but for those with more specialized tastes." It still seemed "strong meat" on 19 December 1965, "But study now possible on records will convince all but the completely conventional musical sympathy that here is a modern masterpiece."

Regardless of one's critical principles, one needs to determine a tone to employ in applying them. That of Bowers in these reviews is often hyperbolic in praise ("It is really a stunner" or "the boys choir sing like angels") and seldom caustic in criticism. Severity is often only implicit; on 14 January 1945 Bowers presents a list of albums which "seem to me to have been worth the recording," rather than castigating the ones that have not been. In considering a problematic setting of the Second Idyll of Theocritus on 6 October 1957, he emphasizes what could be done rather than what has been: "How better to handle such a problem is, I think, exemplified on. . . ." Nonetheless the temperature of the remarks sometimes rises. Inexplicably a famous name pops up in an unrelated discussion: "Fortunately this work was recorded by Monteux rather than Stokowski . . ." (15 May 1949); a few years earlier the reference had been more direct, though not more favorable: "Stokowski with his exaggerations and musical posturings succeeds in turning in the dullest performance I have ever heard of this masterpiece" (1 February 1942).

As John Denniston has pointed out, Bowers was also less than enthusiastic about "the young American composer-conductor Leonard Bernstein," to whom Columbia Records gave "a considerable publicity boost in a series of records devoted to him and his works": "So far as I am concerned, it is movie-house music eloquently played but fundamentally empty. . . . The records then move to the cheaper CL series (where they should have started)" (18 November 1956). Bernstein's stock had not risen by the time of the next review, on 25 August 1957: "One can doubtless ignore ML-5182, with Leonard Bernstein conducting the New York Philharmonic in the Stravinsky Firebird Suite and Tchaikovsky Romeo and Juliet Fantasy. Both have appeared in versions by conductors of much superior attainments to Bernstein's small talent." Nor did the passage of a few more years help. On 21 October 1962 Bowers wrote: "Bernstein may be suffering from phonographic over-exposure. His new record of the Berlioz . . . is curiously obtuse to the Berlioz idiom. Bernstein can whip up a vigorous Orgy of the Brigands finale, but in the March of the Pilgrims and in Serenade he is insensitive to Berlioz' subtle orchestral effects and thus the pleasure of the hearer is considerably lessened in the relentlessly flamboyant treatment and the coarseness of the texture." To say as he did on 4 August 1963, that "This record shows both Bernstein's typical strengths and weaknesses" therefore signaled a major advance. But praise for Bernstein was never to be unequivocal. On 3 November of that year he noted, "As usual with Bernstein, his interpretation is rich and romantic, full of energy, and with due account taken of the inner voices of the orchestra. This being so, it is a pity that. . . ."

In all his record reviewing, Bowers remained acutely aware of the material elements of the transmission of sound. With such long coverage, his columns provide a chronicle of developments in the recording industry. Some were social; Bowers often alludes to James Petrillo, the president of the American Federation of Musicians who beginning in 1942 led a strike against record companies and significantly curtailed their production. But most were technological, and Bowers tracked developments in this area as modern computer buffs do in theirs. Unlike some of those modern counterparts, however, he was able to communicate his insights to a popular audience. During the record shortage of 1944 he wrote four articles on the fate of records after the war; his special interest was the effect of frequency modulation for broadcasting, and he explained how it works and how one might test the quality of a radio-phonograph. In 1948 he devoted two columns to the competing long-play systems of 33 1/3 and 45 rpm, and the following year he considered the prospects for tape recording. In 1958 the record industry revolutionized itself again, this time by introducing stereophonic recordings. Again he was enthusiastic, and he of course reviewed the demonstration records that awed with their depiction of a train moving from one end of the living room to another; "good directionalism" became a touchstone in future reviews.

Although Bowers's work on the record reviews and on bibliographical and textual study had no visible connection, they shared many common principles. The empiric approach is fundamental to both; for the records that meant playing one of them one hundred times to test the wear (30 December 1945), or timing the silence as RCA-Victor's new long-playing records changed (10 April 1949). Equally basic is the recognition that musical works, like literary ones, are conveyed by physical means, and that the material conveyance can profoundly affect the aesthetic object. Many of the distinctions can be identified only by comparison with other recordings; collation of different copies becomes as important for records as for books. For such study one needs to know the circumstances of each form of the work; it therefore becomes important to determine whether Beethoven's *Jena* or First Symphony was written first. What is perhaps most surprising is the role that authorial intention plays in the record criticism. The Richmond talk specifies how the composer and the listener must communicate; even artists such as Jascha Heifetz are criticized for "dominat[ing] the work in a manner never *intended* [italics added] by the composer" (22 March 1942).

The chief point of Bowers's Richmond talk was an apparent oxymoron: one must discipline the mind in order to participate fully in the fun of music. He was serious about the fun: "Have a good time. Have a good time," that paper ended. That rigor is perhaps what made him loathe the playing of background music during dinner parties; music was such important fun that it needed one's full attention. It was also what characterized the last known time that he listened to music with visitors. Again, his oldest son describes the scene:

> About a month before he died, our daughter Carolyn and her husband Mark visited Dad in Charlottesville, and they expressed a desire to hear his built-in stereo system. He obliged by locating a favorite record, swinging wide the large doors covering the speakers which were located on either side of the entrance to the dining room, and cranking up the volume to its apparently customary earsplitting level. Carolyn tells us that they stood there for 15 minutes with him, not wanting to break his concentration while Dad gazed through the massive living room windows towards the Blue Ridge Mountains and occasionally commented on some technical aspect of the music.

Engagement and enjoyment. The discipline and concentration that propelled the regimen of weekly record reviews for nearly thirty years provided their reward many times over.

Working with Fredson Bowers
Matthew J. Bruccoli
University of South Carolina

From 1961 to 1991 I worked with Fredson Bowers on *The Centenary Edition of the Works of Nathaniel Hawthorne, The Works of Stephen Crane*, Vladimir Nabokov's lectures, and *The Cambridge Edition of F. Scott Fitzgerald*; he helped plan the Pittsburgh Series in Bibliography, and he advised me during my term as director of the Center for Editions of American Authors.

It was not a case of elective affinity. We met in 1954 when I was a graduate student at the University of Virginia, and it took a long time for us to overcome our wariness of each other. After he

directed my dissertation on Fitzgerald. I accepted his invitation—it was stronger than that—to work with him on the Hawthorne Edition because it was a splendid career opportunity; but I did so prepared to be his flunky. I was gratified, and remain grateful, that from the start I was a partner. He expected me to argue with him, and he was pleased when—infrequently—I carried my points. He was generous about sharing credit. There was never a problem about rank: we worked together and did not play silly authority games because we both knew that he was The Great Man. Fred didn't even object when I repunctuated him.

Later, when I was officially in charge of some of our projects, we worked the same way. Usually Fred drafted an editorial policy statement, and I made the work plan; then we divided up the jobs. An example of our working arrangement is provided by the sample entry that Fred drafted for the Pittsburgh Series in 1970. It was accompanied by three single-spaced pages of advice and questions. I then modified this material into the standard Pittbib entry format.

Failed scholars derive comfort from alleging that successful scholars have their work done by their students. Since Fred was the most productive literary scholar of his time—as well as the best—he was the subject of envious chitchat. Bowers's name went on his own work. He did not have teams of ghosts. Who the hell could have done his work for him? Even when he farmed out routine collations, he checked the results by doing his own back-up collations. When Fred was asked how he got so much work done, he would usually reply that "A change is as good as a holiday." On a given day he would work on two or three projects. He had trained himself to switch from job to job while keeping all of the details in his head.

Those who know Bowers's thinking only from his dense prose may be relieved to know that he discussed editorial problems in a kind of shortmouth. There were three main practical rules:

1—"Good for man or beast": This meant that a text and the apparatus accompanying it had to be usable by different categories of readers. He was always concerned about the usability of an edition.

2—"If you knows a better 'ole . . . ": This one puzzled hearers unfamiliar with the Bruce Bairnsfather Great War cartoon. It usually signified that an editor had to work with available evi-

-7- TITN

has ~~not~~ gone unchallenged by posterity. Self-censorship is sometimes
a prominent reason for a change in authorial expression, but closely
related to this is the influence of outside opinion that has succeeded
in convincing an author, however reluctantly, that if his book is to
succeed to his hopes it must undergo some major alteration. An
author's reliance on such outside opinion as to a book's reception
instead of his ~~ix~~ own creative force that produced the version under
criticism has not always been found--as remarked--to be in his
ultimate best interest. Most authors are right in the end when they
trust to their instincts and their ^original^ creative plan. We may take this
as applying with particular ~~fore~~ weight to Fitzgerald's acceptance
of what the critics believed to be a ^serious^ flaw. The depth of his
acceptance of the flashback as 'a serious fault' cannot be estimated--
how much he convinced himself in his desire for a reversal of the
book's initial reception remains unkowable. What is of textual importance to an editor is the distinction between the internal forces
that generated Fitzgerald's recognition of the ~~advisability of~~
desirability of removing the lengthy incident of the governess at
Innsbruch and the external forces that (post-creation) led him to
want to ensure the future success of the novel by convincing himself
that ~~r~~the critics' view of the flashback was correct.

        In fact, it is the present editor's opinion that the critics
were wrong. Fitzgerald's reason for agreement--that the true beginning was tucked away in the middle óf the book--is an ambiguous one,
for not every true beginning must actually come at the start of a
narrative, as Greek tragedy shows us. In short, ~~xh~~ conventional
chronological structure is not always the best. As exemplified in
The Last Tycoon, in his best work Fitzgerald had a strong sense that
the past is always an integral part of the present, and the present
of the past. This sense is strongly pointed by the use of the

Fredson Bowers's editorial plan for F. Scott Fitzgerald's Tender Is the Night *in the* Cambridge Edition of the Works of F.
Scott Fitzgerald

-8- TITN

flashback in <u>Tender</u>. It is of importance, of course, that its beginning in medias res on the beach and ~~its~~ the subsequent party, with the reader led ~~led~~ by Rosemary's dazzled reactions, produces a brilliant start that, with its accompanying mystery, draws the reader instantly into ~~the xxxxxx~~ these people's affairs. But it is more important that the insight and coloration of this immensely successful opening has an important role in causing a reader to understand and to estimate at their true value the anterior events that are later to be introduced in Switzerland. In turn, these initial episodes ~~in retrospect~~-- lead to a retrospective understanding of the hinted but never explicit mysteries and nuances of the opening, so that once the flashback has concluded in Switzerland and we are brought back to the present it is with a greater understanding, a jelling one might say, of the central situation of the book in Diver's dilemma and the failure to/solve it. One other consideration is appropriate. When a narrative has been structured in a particular way, the balance of the treatment rests accordingly. The ~~narrative~~ account of the earlier events in Switzerland and of the ironic consequences up to the opening on the beach is written with the technique of a catching-up of the narrative. Merely to rearrange the sequence of events to a chronological order does violence to the balance of opening and then in a sense a reprise in the original book. There can be little question that if Fitzgerald had reordered the events at some stage in the composition, even so late as the book's galley proofs, the early events would have been differently narrated ~~with~~ since there could be no reliance on the reader's understanding of them ~~because~~ resulting of his view of the Divers in their introduction on the Riviera. <u>Tender</u> is not so mechanically conceived and executed as to yield to post creation restructuring in such an important matter that has dictated the treatment both of start and of middle. In the sense of

-9- TITN

'might-have-been' we can envisage a novel that Fitzgerald himself
   composed, *or*
had |revised, to read in chrolonological order, but it would be a

fundamentally different novel from what results in the Cowley edition
                    bodily   *without the necessary reworking.*
when the middle is ∧transferred to the beginnkng/ This is no doubt

special/pleading, but the concept is true. Scribner exhibited the

right attitude when the firm issued in paperback the originally

conceived (and in fact the only published) version as a substitute

for Cowley's extrapolation of Fitzgerald's ʀᴍᴋʀx letter to Perkins

and his note in his private copy. This is one instance where an
                 despite his after-the-event wishes.
author's own version must be respected/ To choose the Cowley

ordering as the base-text for a critical edition would be an act of
                  inner
violence to the ∧conherence of authorial ᴄʀᴇᴀᴛɪᴏɴ. conception and

execution. The pressure that Fitzgerald felt to popularize his novel

was illegitimate. His capitulation to what he conceived of as public
     ni   *should*
opion, no matter how rationalized, ᴍᴜsᴛ not be permitted to tear
   ∧
a_part the living fabric of the novel as he wrote it.

   Once this central question of structure is settled, the rest of

the editing of Tender Is the Night falls into place. The first-edition

base-text has flaws in factual detail that must be corrected beyond

what has yet been done. The stylistic revisions and the two cuts in

Fitzgerald's marked copy must be inserted to produce his final

preserved intentions. It is of some importance to reduce the amount
                                   characterostic of
of housestyling by a return, especially, to Fitzgerald's ∧lighter
                                       n
punctuation whenever it is not ʀᴇxɪɢᴇɴᴛ negligent or too awkwardly
                        but acceptable
idiosyncratic. His older-fashioned ∧system of compounding can be

restored. Much of this ɪɴᴛ conventionalizing of the texture can be
                                        forms in the
established as housestyling by comparison of the ∧galley proofs with

the alterations of the book, although fewer can be detected as part
                                                  revisory
of the earlier transmission. Fitzgerald's own autograph punctuation
                                                ∧

dence; but sometimes it meant that we would do it Fred's way unless I could convince him that there was a better hole.

3—"A little bit pregnant": This indicated that one bad editorial decision resulted in proliferating textual problems.

Another Bowers expression was "fairest flower of English amateurism"—applied to certain scholars who did not meet his standards of professionalism.

Although we were separated by hundreds of miles, we maintained close touch and arranged to meet when our trips intersected. He introduced me to single-malt scotch, but I drew the line at snuff. We usually talked before undertaking big projects that were not collaborations. I am convinced that he asked my advice to give me pleasure. The best advice I provided was to dissuade him from undertaking an edition of Bret Harte; I pointed him at Stephen Crane instead. But I stupidly failed to encourage his desire to acquire a Porsche when he was eighty: he wanted me to talk him into it.

Our last collaboration was the Cambridge F. Scott Fitzgerald edition, and our last phone talk concerned the *Gatsby* galleys. Fred was ill and tired and unhappy (his Nancy died in 1988) when we started work on Fitzgerald; but he wrote a superb rationale of base-text to accommodate Fitzgerald's habit of revising and rewriting through every stage of composition. After reading *Tender Is the Night* for the first time he wrote a brilliant memo on the structure of the novel.

The last time I saw Fred was when I came to Charlottesville to supervise the videotaping of two of his lectures ("Hamlet as Minister and Scourge" and "Death in Victory: Shakespeare's Tragic Reconciliations"). He was very tired, and I wanted to give him a nap break between lectures; but he insisted on doing them back-to-back because he was uncertain about his strength later in the day. He taped the second lecture without blowing a line.

Fredson Bowers was a good master, and I was a fortunate apprentice.

Checklist

Si monumentum requiris, circumspice

Fredson Bowers often remarked that "the only monument I want is in the Library of Congress catalogue." This checklist is restricted to

the books he wrote and the editions in which he had a major responsibility. His hundreds of scholarly articles are not listed.

The Dog Owner's Handbook (Boston: Houghton Mifflin, 1936);

Elizabethan Revenge Tragedy 1587-1942 (Princeton: Princeton University Press, 1940);

A Fary Knight or Oberon the Second; A Manuscript Play Attributed to Thomas Randolph (Chapel Hill: University of North Carolina Press, 1944), Editor;

Principles of Bibliographical Description (Princeton: Princeton University Press, 1949);

The Dramatic Works of Thomas Dekker (Cambridge: Cambridge University Press, 1953-1961), Editor;

On Editing Shakespeare and the Elizabethan Dramatists, Rosenbach Fellowship in Bibliography Publications (Philadelphia: University of Pennsylvania Library, 1955);

Whitman's Manuscripts: Leaves of Grass (1860), A Parallel Text (Chicago: University of Chicago Press, 1955), Editor;

Textual and Literary Criticism (The Sandars Lectures in Bibliography 1957-58) (Cambridge: Cambridge University Press, 1959);

The Centenary Edition of the Works of Nathaniel Hawthorne (Columbus: Ohio State University Press, 1962-1975), General Editor;

William Shakespeare: The Merry Wives of Windsor (Baltimore: Penguin, 1963), Editor;

Bibliography and Textual Criticism (The Lyell Lectures, 1959) (Oxford at the Clarendon Press, 1964);

Hamlet: An Outline Guide to the Play (New York: Barnes & Noble, 1965);

The Dramatic Works in the Beaumont and Fletcher Canon (Cambridge: Cambridge University Press, 1966-   ), General Editor;

John Dryden: Four Tragedies (Chicago: Chicago University Press, 1967), Editor;

John Dryden: Four Comedies (Chicago: Chicago University Press, 1967), Editor;

The Works of Stephen Crane (Charlottesville: University Press of Virginia, 1969-1975), Editor;

The Complete Works of Christopher Marlowe (Cambridge: Cambridge University Press, 1973), Editor;

Stephen Crane The Red Badge of Courage: A Facsimile Edition of the Manuscript (Washington, D.C.: Bruccoli Clark/NCR Microcard Editions, 1973), Editor;

Tom Jones; The History of a Foundling, by Henry Fielding (Middletown, Connecticut: Wesleyan University Press; Oxford: Oxford University Press, 1974), Editor;

Essays in Bibliography, Text, and Editing (Charlottesville: University Press of Virginia for the Bibliographical Society of the University of Virginia, 1975);

The Works of William James (Cambridge: Cambridge University Press, 1975-), Textual Editor;

Vladimir Nabokov, *Lectures on Literature* (New York: Harcourt Brace Jovanovich/Bruccoli Clark, 1980), Editor;

Vladimir Nabokov, *Lectures on Russian Literature* (New York: Harcourt Brace Jovanovich/Bruccoli Clark, 1981), Editor;

Vladimir Nabokov, *Lectures on Don Quixote* (New York: Harcourt Brace Jovanovich/Bruccoli Clark, 1983), Editor;

Leon Kroll: A Spoken Memoir, with Nancy Hale Bowers (Charlottesville: University Press of Virginia, 1983), Editor;

Hamlet as Minister and Scourge and Other Studies in Shakespeare and Milton (Charlottesville: University Press of Virginia, 1989);

Death in Victory: Shakespeare's Tragic Reconciliations, Eminent Scholar/Teachers Videotape (Detroit: Omnigraphics, 1990);

Hamlet as Minister and Scourge, Eminent Scholar/Teachers Videotape (Detroit: Omnigraphics, 1990);

The Great Gatsby (Cambridge: Cambridge University Press, 1991), Textual Consultant.

Theodor Seuss Geisel
(Dr. Seuss, Theo. LeSieg)
(2 March 1904 - 24 September 1991)

See also the Geisel entry in *DLB 61: American Writers for Children Since 1960: Poets, Illustrators, and Nonfiction Authors.*

BOOKS: *And to Think That I Saw It on Mulberry Street*, as Dr. Seuss (New York: Vanguard Press, 1937; London: Country Life, 1939);

The 500 Hats of Bartholomew Cubbins, as Dr. Seuss (New York: Vanguard Press, 1938; London: Oxford University Press, 1940);

The Seven Lady Godivas, as Dr. Seuss (New York: Random House, 1939);

The King's Stilts, as Dr. Seuss (New York: Random House, 1939; London: Hamish Hamilton, 1942);

Horton Hatches the Egg, as Dr. Seuss (New York: Random House, 1940; London: Hamish Hamilton, 1942);

McElligot's Pool, as Dr. Seuss (New York: Random House, 1947; London: Collins, 1975);

Thidwick, The Big-Hearted Moose, as Dr. Seuss (New York: Random House, 1948; London: Collins, 1968);

Bartholomew and the Oobleck, as Dr. Seuss (New York: Random House, 1949);

If I Ran the Zoo, as Dr. Seuss (New York: Random House, 1950);

Scrambled Eggs Super!, as Dr. Seuss (New York: Random House, 1953);

The Sneetches, and Other Stories, as Dr. Seuss (New York: Random House, 1953);

Horton Hears a Who!, as Dr. Seuss (New York: Random House, 1954);

On Beyond Zebra, as Dr. Seuss (New York: Random House, 1955);

Signs of Civilization!, as Dr. Seuss (La Jolla, Cal.: La Jolla Town Council, 1956);

If I Ran the Circus, as Dr. Seuss (New York: Random House, 1956; London: Collins, 1969);

The Cat in the Hat, as Dr. Seuss (New York: Random House, 1957; London: Hutchinson, 1958);

How the Grinch Stole Christmas, as Dr. Seuss (New York: Random House, 1957);

The Cat in the Hat Comes Back!, as Dr. Seuss (New York: Beginner Books, 1958; London: Collins, 1961);

Yertle the Turtle, and Other Stories, as Dr. Seuss (New York: Random House, 1958; London: Collins, 1963);

Happy Birthday to You!, as Dr. Seuss (New York: Random House, 1959);

One Fish Two Fish Red Fish Blue Fish, as Dr. Seuss (New York: Random House, 1960; London: Collins, 1962);

Green Eggs and Ham, as Dr. Seuss (New York: Beginner Books, 1960; London: Collins, 1962);

Ten Apples Up on Top!, as Theo. LeSieg, illustrated by Roy McKie (New York: Beginner Books, 1961; London: Collins, 1963);

Dr. Seuss' Sleep Book, as Dr. Seuss (New York: Random House, 1962; London: Collins, 1964);

Hop on Pop, as Dr. Seuss (New York: Beginner Books, 1963; London: Collins, 1964);

Dr. Seuss' ABC, as Dr. Seuss (New York: Beginner Books, 1963; London: Collins, 1964);

The Cat in the Hat Dictionary, by the Cat Himself, as Dr. Seuss, with Philip D. Eastman (New York: Beginner Books, 1964);

I Wish That I Had Duck Feet, as Theo. LeSieg, illustrated by B. Tokey (New York: Beginner Books, 1965; London: Collins, 1967);

Fox in Socks, as Dr. Seuss (New York: Beginner Books, 1965; London: Collins, 1966);

I Had Trouble in Getting to Solla Sollew, as Dr. Seuss (New York: Random House, 1965; London: Collins, 1967);

Come Over to My House, as Theo. LeSieg, illustrated by Richard Erdoes (New York: Beginner Books, 1966; London: Collins, 1967);

Dr. Seuss' Lost World Revisited: A Forward Looking Backward Glance, as Dr. Seuss (New York: Award Books, 1967);

The Cat in the Hat Songbook, as Dr. Seuss (New York: Random House, 1967);

The Foot Book, as Dr. Seuss (New York: Random House, 1968; London: Collins, 1969);

The Eye Book, as Theo. LeSieg (New York: Random House, 1968; London: Collins, 1969);

I Can Lick 30 Tigers Today, and Other Stories, as Dr. Seuss (New York: Random House, 1969; London: Collins, 1970);

My Book About Me, By Me, Myself. I Wrote It! I Drew It!, as Dr. Seuss, illustrated by McKie (New York: Random House, 1969);

Mr. Brown Can Moo! Can You?, as Dr. Seuss (New York: Random House, 1970; London: Collins, 1971);

I Can Draw It Myself, as Dr. Seuss (New York: Random House, 1970);

I Can Write—By Me, Myself, as Theo. LeSieg (New York: Random House, 1971);

The Lorax, as Dr. Seuss (New York: Random House, 1971; London: Collins, 1972);

In a People House, as Theo. LeSieg, illustrated by McKie (New York: Random House, 1972; London: Collins, 1973);

Marvin K. Mooney, Will You Please Go Now?, as Dr. Seuss (New York: Random House, 1972; London: Collins, 1973);

The Many Mice of Mr. Brice, as Theo. LeSieg, illustrated by McKie (New York: Random House, 1973; London: Collins, 1974);

Did I Ever Tell You How Lucky You Are?, as Dr. Seuss (New York: Random House, 1973; London: Collins, 1974);

The Shape of Me and Other Stuff, as Dr. Seuss (New York: Random House, 1973; London: Collins, 1974);

Wacky Wednesday, as Theo. LeSieg, illustrated by George Booth (New York: Beginner Books, 1974; London: Collins, 1975);

There's a Wocket in My Pocket!, as Dr. Seuss (New York: Random House, 1974; London: Collins, 1975);

Great Day for Up!, as Dr. Seuss, illustrated by Quentin Blake (New York: Random House, 1974; London: Collins, 1975);

Because a Little Bug Went Ka-Choo!, by Geisel and Michael Frith, as Rosetta Stone (New York: Beginner Books, 1975);

Would You Rather Be a Bullfrog?, as Theo. LeSieg, illustrated by McKie (New York: Random House, 1975);

Oh, The Thinks You Can Think!, as Dr. Seuss (New York: Random House, 1975; London: Collins, 1976);

The Cat's Quizzer, as Dr. Seuss (New York: Random House, 1976; London: Collins, 1977);

Hooper Humperdink ...? Not Him!, as Theo. LeSieg (New York: Random House, 1976; London: Collins, 1977);

Please Try to Remember the First of Octember!, as Theo. LeSieg, illustrated by Arthur Cummings (New York: Beginner Books, 1977);

I Can Read With My Eyes Shut, as Dr. Seuss (New York: Random House, 1978);

Oh Say Can You Say?, as Dr. Seuss (New York: Beginner Books, 1979);

Maybe You Should Fly a Jet! Maybe You Should Be a Vet, as Theo. LeSieg, illustrated by Michael J. Smullin (New York: Beginner Books, 1980);

The Tooth Book, as Theo. LeSieg, illustrated by Roy McKie (New York: Beginner Books, 1981);

Hunches in Bunches, as Dr. Seuss (New York: Random House, 1982);

The Butter Battle Book, as Dr. Seuss (New York: Random House, 1984; London: Collins, 1984);

You're Only Old Once, as Dr. Seuss (New York: Random House, 1986; London: Fontana, 1986);

The Tough Coughs as He Ploughs the Dough: Early Writings and Cartoons by Dr. Seuss, edited by Richard Marschall (New York: Morrow, 1986);

I Am Not Going to Get Up Today, as Dr. Seuss (New York: Random House, 1987; London: Collins, 1988);

Oh, The Places You'll Go!, as Dr. Seuss (New York: Random House, 1990; London: Collins, 1990).

BOOKS ILLUSTRATED: *Boners* (New York: Viking, 1931);
More Boners (New York: Viking, 1931).

MOTION PICTURES: *Your Job in Germany*, screenplay by Geisel, U.S. Army, 1946; released as *Hitler Lives*, Warner Bros., 1946;

Design for Death, screenplay by Geisel and Helen Palmer Geisel, RKO Pictures, 1947;

Gerald McBoing-Boing, screenplay by Geisel, Columbia, 1951;

The 5,000 Fingers of Dr. T, screenplay by Geisel and Allen Scott, Columbia, 1953.

TELEVISION: *How the Grinch Stole Christmas*, CBS, 18 December 1966;

Horton Hears a Who, CBS, 19 March 1970;

The Cat in the Hat, CBS, 10 March 1971;

Dr. Seuss on the Loose, CBS, 15 October 1973;

Hoober-Bloob Highway, CBS, 19 February 1975;

Theodore Seuss Geisel (portrait by Everett Raymond Kinster, commissioned by the trustees of Dartmouth College)

Halloween is Grinch Night, ABC, 28 October 1977;
Pontoffel Pock, Where Are You?, ABC, 2 March 1980;
The Grinch Grinches the Cat in the Hat, ABC, 20 May 1982.

A TRIBUTE

from JUDY BLUME

I met Dr. Seuss once, in 1978, when we were speakers, together with Maurice Sendak, at the first Children's Book and Author Breakfast at the American Booksellers Association convention in Atlanta. It was the highlight of my professional life. I told him that when I was a student teaching in 1960, I always read one of his books to my class when I was being evaluated. He made me look good.

I told him when I began to write, a few years later, I wanted to write rhyming picture books, exactly like his, but I wasn't very good at it so I had to try novels, instead.

I told him how much fun it was to share his books with my own children, and how they learned to read using *Hop on Pop* and *The Cat in the Hat*.

I told him, as I clutched my note cards in a sweaty hand, that I was terrified of addressing the large audience that awaited us. He pulled a single piece of paper from his breast pocket and with trembling hands showed me his speech, which was very brief and in rhyme. "I'm too insecure to speak in public without rhymes," he explained.

I loved him for that and for all his books and for all the pleasure he has brought, and will continue to bring, to kids around the world.

If I could, I'd tell him that I have a grandchild now—my first—who, at three months, already has his own copy of *Green Eggs and Ham*!

A TRIBUTE —————————————————

from ROBERT CORMIER

Dr. Seuss was a wonderful companion to everyone in our family—young and old—at one time or another. (I was thrilled that we shared the same publisher for a while, although we never met.) Meanwhile, the delights of *Hop On Pop* still echo in my ears, particularly as I recall a tedious seven-hour drive through New England's back roads when my wife, Connie, read the book incessantly to a restless three-year-old while everyone else in the car—ranging in ages from nine to the forties—cringed at yet another "We see the bee. . . ." But the words were music to that child and, now in tender retrospect, to these aged ears as well. Speaking of age, *You're Only Old Once* also proved a delight as a lighthearted affectionate gift to me from Connie, proving that Dr. Seuss is indeed a writer not only for the ages—but for all ages.

A TRIBUTE —————————————————

from ROBERT COOVER

It was that year, 1968. Mid-February. Pacifist rage was sweeping the nation, and especially among the young, being dragged away to die in a stupid war virtually no one believed in. The University of Iowa, where I was teaching, was, like so many universities, on the boil. Resistance was mounting, passive protest was giving way to more aggressive action, vigilante police teams had been created and thrown into battle, heads had been bloodied, students hospitalized and arrested and charged with conspiracy. And worse seemed likely to come. Certainly, the stakes were rising, all one's energies were about to be consumed, arrest of sympathetic faculty looked inevitable, tedious entanglements with the law and with the administration—we decided to break away to Mexico for a couple of quiet weeks before the storm.

Drove down with three small kids and my wife's guitar, our rationale being an intensive master course with her Argentinian teacher, then in Mexico City. We took a room in an old mouse-infested hotel in the city center with brass spittoons in the lobby and I minded the children while Pilar practiced. And it was while reading a Dr. Seuss book to them that my eye fell on the little Cat-in-the-Hat symbol on the front cover: "I CAN READ IT ALL BY MYSELF." It looked

like a campaign button. And it occurred to me that this goofily anarchical and highly creative generation now on campus had all been brought up on these Dr. Seuss stories, their childhood years being his heyday, that their favorite songwriter Bob Dylan was a kind of grown-up (but not too grown-up) Dr. Seuss, that tripping was not unlike a visit from the mischievous Cat, and that their ambivalent enthusiasm for Eugene McCarthy, a winsomely goofy character in his own right (just then surprising Lyndon Johnson in the New Hampshire primaries), was a deflected desire to nominate their Cat in the Hat as the next president of the United States of America. I rented a room up on the roof of the hotel where the maids hung out the laundry and, as time allowed, wrote "The Cat in the Hat for President."

When we got back to Iowa City, in and around the teaching and the disruptive activities of that spring, I revised the story and rushed it to my editor Hal Scharlatt at Random House in the hopes that Random House author Dr. Seuss (only now known to me as Ted Geisel) might be willing to illustrate it and get it out before the elections. Silence descended. We eventually learned that Geisel (or his agent: did he ever read it?) viewed it with fear and loathing, and had told the Random House nabobs that he would leave Random House and take his multimillion-dollar business with him, not merely if they published it, but if they allowed that story to be published *anywhere* (I was a Random House author, wasn't I? if they could not control me, he would have to find a more fearless publisher), with the result that the story had been slipped into a locked drawer and the word to my editor was that it did not exist. Hal got a copy to Ted Solotaroff, then the editor of *New American Review*, and it eventually ran in their autumn issue, just in time for elections. But not without more resistance from Dr. Seuss and his agents. Several cover designs were rejected, the story title was stripped from the front cover, there were ominous threats of suits that would effectively close down that magazine forever. I wrote to Geisel and got back a not unfriendly reply from his agent (Dr. Seuss was on a honeymoon), and the story at last appeared, albeit with restrictions and well concealed from most of the reading public.

It took twelve more years before the story was at last allowed to appear in book form, and then missing its title, using instead its original subtitle: *A Political Fable*. Probably this was just publisher timidity; Ted Geisel himself no longer seemed to care. He had sent me a courteous note some years before, but now did not reply when I wrote to him. It was a new era. The war was over and already forgotten. The creatively anarchical generation of the 1960s had given way to the dour boring hustlers of the yuppie generation, brought up, not on Dr. Seuss (few could even read), but on TV commercials. Similar sort of jingles (you can sing it by yourself), but different message. Politics, though, was still the same.

Graham Greene
(2 October 1904 - 3 April 1991)

Richard Hauer Costa
Texas A & M University

See also the Greene entries in DLB 13: British Dramatists Since World War II: Part One; DLB 15: British Novelists, 1930-1959: Part One; DLB Yearbook: 1985; DLB 77: British Mystery Writers, 1920-1939; DLB 100: Modern British Essayists: Second Series; *and* CDBLB 7: Writers After World War II, 1945-1960.

BOOKS: *Babbling April* (Oxford: Blackwood, 1925);

The Man Within (London: Heinemann, 1929; Garden City, N.Y.: Doubleday, Doran, 1929);

The Name of Action (London: Heinemann, 1930; Garden City, N.Y.: Doubleday, Doran, 1931);

Rumour at Nightfall (London: Heinemann, 1931; Garden City, N.Y.: Doubleday, Doran, 1932);

Stamboul Train (London: Heinemann, 1932); republished as *Orient Express* (Garden City, N.Y.: Doubleday, Doran, 1933);

It's a Battlefield (London: Heinemann, 1934; Garden City, N.Y.: Doubleday, Doran, 1934; revised edition, New York: Viking, 1962);

England Made Me (London & Toronto: Heinemann, 1935; Garden City, N.Y.: Doubleday, Doran, 1935) republished as *The Shipwrecked* (New York: Viking, 1953);

The Bear Fell Free (London: Grayson & Grayson, 1935; Folcroft, Pa.: Folcroft, 1977);

The Basement Room, and Other Stories (London: Cresset, 1935);

Journey Without Maps (London & Toronto: Heinemann, 1936; Garden City, N.Y.: Doubleday, Doran, 1936);

A Gun for Sale: An Entertainment (London & Toronto: Heinemann, 1936); republished as *This Gun for Hire* (Garden City, N.Y.: Doubleday, Doran, 1936);

Brighton Rock (New York: Viking, 1938; London & Toronto: Heinemann, 1938);

The Lawless Roads (London & Toronto: Longmans, Green, 1939); republished as *Another Mexico* (New York: Viking, 1939);

The Confidential Agent (London & Toronto: Heinemann, 1939; New York: Viking, 1939);

Twenty-Four Short Stories, by Greene, James Laver, and Sylvia Townsend Warner (London: Cresset, 1939);

The Power and the Glory (London & Toronto: Heinemann, 1940); published simultaneously as *The Labyrinthine Ways* (New York: Viking, 1940); republished as *The Power and the Glory* (New York: Viking, 1946);

British Dramatists (London: Collins, 1942);

The Ministry of Fear: An Entertainment (London & Toronto: Heinemann, 1943; New York: Viking, 1943);

The Little Train (Norwich: Jarrold, 1946; New York: Lothrop, Lee & Shepard, 1958);

Nineteen Stories (London & Toronto: Heinemann, 1947; New York: Viking, 1949);

The Heart of the Matter (Melbourne, London & Toronto: Heinemann, 1948; New York: Viking, 1948);

Graham Greene

Why Do I Write? by Greene, Elizabeth Bowen, and V. S. Pritchett (London: Marshall, 1948; Folcroft, Pa.: Folcroft, 1969);

The Third Man and The Fallen Idol (Melbourne, London & Toronto: Heinemann, 1950); abridged as *The Third Man* (New York: Viking, 1950);

The Little Fire Engine (Norwich: Jarrold, 1950); republished as *The Little Red Fire Engine* (New York: Lothrop, Lee & Shepard, 1953);

The Lost Childhood, and Other Essays (London: Eyre & Spottiswoode, 1951; New York: Viking, 1952);

The End of the Affair (Melbourne, London & Toronto: Heinemann, 1951; New York: Viking, 1951);

The Little Horse Bus (Norwich: Jarrold / London: Parrish, 1952; New York: Lothrop, Lee & Shepard, 1954);

The Living Room: A Play in Two Acts (Melbourne, London & Toronto: Heinemann, 1953; New York: Viking, 1954);

The Little Steamroller: A Story of Adventure, Mystery and Detection (London: Parrish, 1953; New York: Lothrop, Lee & Shepard, 1955);

Essais Catholiques, translated (into French) by Marcelle Sibon (Paris: Edition du Seuil, 1953);

Twenty-One Stories (London, Melbourne & Toronto: Heinemann, 1954; New York: Viking, 1962);

Loser Takes All (Melbourne, London & Toronto: Heinemann, 1955; New York: Viking, 1957);

The Quiet American (Melbourne, London & Toronto: Heinemann, 1955; New York: Viking, 1956);

The Potting Shed: A Play in Three Acts (New York: Viking, 1957; London, Melbourne & Toronto: Heinemann, 1958);

Our Man in Havana: An Entertainment (London, Melbourne & Toronto: Heinemann, 1958; New York: Viking, 1958);

The Complaisant Lover: A Comedy (London, Melbourne & Toronto: Heinemann, 1959; New York: Viking, 1961);

A Burnt-Out Case (London, Melbourne & Toronto: Heinemann, 1961; New York: Viking, 1961);

In Search of A Character: Two African Journals (London: Bodley Head, 1961; New York: Viking, 1961);

A Sense of Reality (London: Bodley Head, 1963; New York: Viking, 1963);

Carving a Statue: A Play (London: Bodley Head, 1964);

The Comedians (London: Bodley Head, 1966; New York: Viking, 1966);

Victorian Detective Fiction: A Catalogue of the Collection Made by Dorothy Glover & Graham Greene, by Greene and Dorothy Glover, edited by Eric Osborne (London, Sydney & Toronto: Bodley Head, 1966);

May We Borrow Your Husband? And Other Comedies of the Sexual Life (London, Sydney & Toronto: Bodley Head, 1967; New York: Viking, 1967);

Modern Film Scripts: The Third Man, by Greene and Carol Reed (London: Lorrimer, 1968; New York: Simon & Schuster, 1969);

Collected Essays (London, Sydney & Toronto: Bodley Head, 1969, New York: Viking, 1969);

Travels With My Aunt: A Novel (London, Sydney & Toronto: Bodley Head, 1969; New York: Viking, 1970);

A Sort of Life (London, Sydney & Toronto: Bodley Head, 1971; New York: Simon & Schuster, 1971);

Collected Stories (London: Bodley Head/Heinemann, 1972; New York: Viking, 1973);

The Pleasure-Dome: The Collected Film Criticism 1935-40, edited by John Russell Taylor (London: Secker & Warburg, 1972) republished as *Graham Greene on Film: Collected Film Criticism, 1935-1940* (New York: Simon & Schuster, 1972);

The Honorary Consul (London, Sydney & Toronto: Bodley Head, 1973; New York: Simon & Schuster, 1973);

Lord Rochester's Monkey: Being the Life of John Wilmot, Second Earl of Rochester (London, Sydney & Toronto: Bodley Head, 1974; New York: Viking, 1974);

The Return of A. J. Raffles: An Edwardian Comedy in Three Acts Based Somewhat Loosely on E. W. Hornung's Characters in "The Amateur Cracksman" (London, Sydney & Toronto: Bodley Head, 1975; New York: Simon & Schuster, 1976);

The Human Factor (London, Sydney & Toronto: Bodley Head, 1978; New York: Simon & Schuster, 1978);

Doctor Fischer of Geneva, or the Bomb Party (London: Bodley Head, 1980; New York: Simon & Schuster, 1980);

Ways of Escape (London: Bodley Head, 1981; New York: Simon & Schuster, 1981);

Monsignor Quixote (Toronto: Lester & Orpen Dennys, 1982; London: Bodley Head, 1982; New York: Simon & Schuster, 1982);

J'Accuse: The Dark Side of Nice (London: Bodley Head, 1982);

Getting to Know the General: The Story of an Involvement (London: Bodley Head, 1984; New York: Simon & Schuster, 1984);

The Tenth Man (London: Bodley Head, 1985; New York: Simon & Schuster, 1985);

The Captain and the Enemy (London: Bodley Head, 1988; New York: Viking, 1988);

Yours, Etc.: Letters to the Press, 1945-1989, edited by Christopher Hawtree (New York: Viking Penguin, 1990);

The Last Word and Other Stories (London: Reinhardt, 1990; New York: Viking, 1991).

Editions and Collections: *Three Plays* (London: Mercur, 1961);

Graham Greene: The Collected Edition, with introductions by Greene (London: Bodley Head/ Heinemann, 1970-   );

The Portable Graham Greene, edited by Philip Stratford (New York: Viking, 1973; Harmondsworth, U.K.: Penguin, 1977);

Shades of Greene: The Televised Stories of Graham Greene (London: Bodley Head/Heinemann, 1975; New York: Penguin, 1977);

Why the Epigraph? (London: Nonesuch, 1989);

Reflections (London: Reinhardt, 1990; New York: Viking, 1991).

PLAY PRODUCTIONS: *The Living Room*, London, Wyndham's Theatre, 16 April 1953;

The Potting Shed, New York, Bijou Theatre, 29 January 1957; London, Globe Theatre, 5 February 1958;

The Complaisant Lover: A Comedy, London, Globe Theatre, 18 June 1959; New York, Ethel Barrymore Theatre, 1 November 1961;

Carving a Statue, London, Haymarket Theatre, 17 September 1964; New York, Gramercy Arts Theatre, 30 April 1968;

The Return of A. J. Raffles, London, Aldwych Theatre, 4 December 1975;

Yes and No and *For Whom the Bell Chimes*, Leicester, Haymarket Studio, 20 March 1980.

MOTION PICTURES: *Twenty-one Days*, screenplay by Greene and Basil Dean, Columbia, 1937; released as *21 Days Together*, Columbia, 1940;

The Future's in the Air, commentary by Greene, Strand Film Unit, 1937;

The New Britain, commentary by Greene, Strand Film Unit, 1940;

Brighton Rock, screenplay by Greene and Terence Rattingan, Pathé, 1946; rereleased as *Young Scarface*, Mayer-Kingsley, 1952;

The Fallen Idol, screenplay by Greene, British Lion, 1948; rereleased, Selznick International, 1949;

The Third Man, screenplay by Greene, British Lion, 1949; rereleased, Selznick International, 1950;

The Stranger's Hand, screenplay by Greene and John Stafford, British Lion, 1954; rereleased, Distributors Corporation of America, 1955;

Loser Takes All, screenplay by Greene, British Lion, 1956; rereleased, Distributors Corporation of America, 1957;

Saint Joan, screenplay, adapted from Bernard Shaw's play, by Greene, United Artists, 1957;

Our Man in Havana, screenplay by Greene, Columbia, 1960;

The Comedians, screenplay by Greene, M-G-M, 1967.

OTHER: *The Old School: Essays by Divers Hands*, edited by Greene (London: Cape, 1934);

H. h. Munro, *The Best of Saki*, introduction by Greene (London: Lane, 1950; New York: Viking, 1961);

The Spy's Bedside Book: An Anthology, edited by Greene and Hugh Greene (London: Hart-Davis, 1957; New York: Carroll & Graf, 1985);

Ford Madox Ford, *The Bodley Head Ford Madox Ford*, volumes 1-4 edited by Greene (London: Bodley Head, 1962-1963);

An Impossible Woman: The Memoirs of Dottoressa Moor of Capri, edited by Greene (London, Sydney & Toronto: Bodley Head, 1975; New York: Viking, 1976);

Victorian Villainies, edited by Greene and Hugh Greene (Harmondsworth, U.K. & New York: Viking, 1984).

SELECTED PERIODICAL PUBLICATIONS—UNCOLLECTED:

FICTION

"The Lieutenant Died Last," *Collier's*, 105 (29 June 1940): 9-10;

"Men at Work," *New Yorker*, 17 (25 October 1941): 63-66;

"Proof Positive," *Harper's*, 195 (October 1947): 312-314;

"A Drive in the Country," *Harper's*, 195 (November 1947): 450-457;

"The Hint of an Exploration," *Commonweal*, 49 (11 February 1949): 438-442;

"The Third Man," *American Magazine*, 147 (March 1949): 142-160;

"Church Militant," *Commonweal*, 63 (6 January 1956): 350-352;

"Dear Dr. Falkenheim," *Vogue*, 141 (1 January 1963): 100-101;

"Dream of a Strange Land," *Saturday Evening Post*, (19 January 1963): 44-47;

"Beauty," *Esquire*, 59 (April 1963): 60, 142;

"Root of All Evil," *Saturday Evening Post*, 237 (7 March 1964): 56-58;

"Invisible Japanese Gentleman," *Saturday Evening Post*, 238 (20 November 1965): 60-61;

"Blessing," *Harper's*, 232 (March 1966): 91-94;

"Story," *Vogue*, 149 (1 January 1967): 94-95.

NONFICTION

"Middle-brow Film" *Fortnightly*, 145 (March 1936): 302-307;

"Ideas in the Cinema," *Spectator*, 159 (19 November 1937): 894-895;

"Self-Portrait," *Spectator*, 167 (18 July 1941): 66, 68;

"H. Sylvester," *Commonweal*, 33 (25 October 1949): 11-13;

"The Catholic Church's New Dogma: Assumption of Mary," *Life*, 29 (30 October 1950): 50-52;

"Malaya, the Forgotten War," *Life*, 31 (30 July 1951): 51-54;

"The Pope Who Remains a Priest," *Life*, 31 (24 September 1951): 146-148;

"The Return of Charlie Chaplin: An Open Letter," *New Statesman and Nation*, 45 (27 September 1952): 344;

"Indo-China," *New Republic*, 130 (5 April 1954): 13-15;

"Last Act in Indo-China," *New Republic*, 132 (9 May 1955): 9-11; (16 May 1955): 10-12;

"The Catholic Temper in Poland," *Atlantic Monthly*, 197 (March 1956): 39-41;

"In Search of a Character," *Harper's*, 224 (January 1962): 66-74;

"Return to Cuba," *New Republic*, 149 (2 November 1963): 16-18;

"Nightmare Republic," *New Republic*, 149 (16 November 1963): 18-20;

"Reflections on the Character of Kim Philby," *Esquire*, 70 (September 1968): 110-111.

Literary history is replete with the names of writers who reversed A. E. Housman's "Athlete Dying Young," whose names far outlived their performance. Edward (Ted) Driffield, Somerset Maugham's fictional "last Victorian" in *Cakes and Ale* (1930), was like that. When Graham Greene died in his eighty-seventh year on 3 April 1991, not even his detractors dared placed him in the Driffield position. His fifth collection of short fiction, *The Last Word and Other Stories* (1990), appeared in the United States and Britain only a few weeks before his death. In fact, novelist Frank Tuohy, whom Greene much admired, several years ago called the octogenarian the only living British writer "to have had a complete literary career, moving from strength to strength."

When a writer dies who has been a household name for over a half-century and whose productivity never allowed his name to be missing from the major review outlets on either side of the Atlantic, the rush to judgment is both prompt and daunting. If one of the measures of a writer is the caliber of the commentary, Graham Greene truly "matters." But Greene has always been praised with faint damning.

Greene's most popular novel—yet the one most soundly damned in certain high places—is *The Heart of the Matter* (1948), a fictional study of damnation itself. The book was scorned on doctrinal lines, charged with being neither true to life nor art, and seen by a onetime worshiper as providing a retreat from the world for readers who themselves wallowed in versions of self-pity, a version of which dooms the novel's protagonist.

Evelyn Waugh (like Greene, a convert in his twenties from the Church of England to the Roman Catholic church) entered into a public row with his then-casual friend over the fate of Maj. Henry Scobie, a British colonial policeman in West Africa, who in the novel commits suicide out of pity for his wife and his mistress. Because Scobie was a fallen Catholic his suicide could be construed as a plea for divine forgiveness. Waugh, as a practicing Catholic, objected. "To me," wrote Waugh, "the idea of willing my own damnation for the love of God is either a very loose poetical expression or a mad blasphemy, for the God who accepted that sacrifice could be neither just nor lovable."

Greene, flattered, responded: "I did not regard Scobie as a saint, and his offering his damnation up was intended to show how muddled a mind full of goodwill could become." Thirty-two years later, in *Ways of Escape* (1981), Greene came down hard on his profitable millstone of a book, wearied as he had become by Catholic rebukes on Scobie's fate. "I was not so stupid as to believe that [salvation or damnation] could ever be an issue in a novel. Besides, I have small belief in the doctrine of eternal punishment (it was Scobie's belief not mine). Suicide was Scobie's inevitable end . . . a subject for a cruel comedy rather than a tragedy."

Kingsley Amis has often exploited this flipside of solemnity, and Greene has often been the target of this comic writer's respectful aim. In *Lucky Jim* (1953), Amis fires off a sniper's round, although behind the camouflage of anonymity. In the midst of a self-destructive liaison with a fake-suicide compulsive named Margaret Peel, Jim Dixon remembers "a character in a modern novel who was always feeling pity moving in him like a sickness, or some such jargon. The parallel was very apt: he felt ill." Two novels later, in *I Like It Here* (1958), Amis stations a nonwriting writer named Garnet Bowen in a ship's lounge, where he sees a book whose jacket proclaims it "the new Graham Greene." Bowen ekes out a living teaching English literature to "foreign persons," who ask him questions not about Evelyn Waugh, Somerset Maugham, James Joyce, or Graham Greene but about "Ifflen-Voth," "Zumzit-Mum," "Shem-Shoice," and "Grim Grin".

Bowen says he has nothing against "Grim Grin" personally or aesthetically but "wishes he would die soon so that his lectures on him would not keep having things added to them every eighteen months or so. Perhaps it would be better in the long run to set his teeth and make the switch to E. M. Forster (who hadn't written a new novel in 30 years). The New Graham Greene, like most of the old Graham Greenes, was about abroad. Extraordinary how the region kept coming up."

For Graham Greene, "abroad" was terra incognita where, far from seeking material for novels, he sought to regain a lost sense of insecurity, an antidote, only occasionally achieved, for chronic boredom. "I hadn't the courage for suicide," he confesses in *Ways of Escape*, so he brought his troubled spirit to troubled places. At the height of his powers, he imposed an aura of peril throughout the 1950s: three months of travel in Malaya during the Emergency in 1951; four winters in Vietnam reporting the French wars for the Sunday (London) *Times* and *Le Figaro* from 1951 to 1955; in Kenya reporting the Mau Mau outbreak for the *Times* in 1953; and the furthest escape of all, to a leprosarium in the final days of the Belgian Congo in 1958.

The Greene who trekked these outposts in what we now call the Third World saw the same poverty, shabbiness, and human misery as his exact contemporary George Orwell—sights that forever turned the two upper-class Englishmen against officialdom and empire. Orwell's vision extended to "other" worlds. Greene scoffed at utopian blueprints. His journeys "represented a distrust of any future based on what we are."

Greene fiercely took issue with those who questioned the journalistic accuracy of his fiction. "I have sometimes wondered whether they go round the world blinkered. This *is* Indochina. . . . this *is* Mexico, this *is* Sierra Leone. . . . I have been a newspaper correspondent as well as a novelist. I assure you that the dead child lay in the ditch in just that attitude. In the canal of Phat Diem the bodies stuck out of the water."

In his world, in which evil dominates, Greene takes a good-bad man and puts him in a situation where his potentials for evil and good inevitably collide, where what is at stake transcends integrity. If the character is really good while seeming bad, nothing will serve him better than his vulnerability. Greene paves hell with heavenly intimations until, finally, innocence—that is, freedom from a controlling guile or cunning—takes over everything, even corruption, and a state that Greene calls grace is reached. In Greene's major novels the protagonist's fall is always fortunate because it strips him of everything, including his disguises: bad Catholic (Scobie), bad writer (Bendrix in *The End of the Affair*, 1951), drunken diplomat (Brown in *The Comedians*, 1966), flawed clergyman (the whiskey priest in *The Power and the Glory*, 1940), inept idealist (Pyle in *The Quiet American*, 1955). Always in the wings, urging the character on, is a figure he will have to discern on his own, a figure called, for want of a better name, God.

God, in fact, hardly enters Greene's fiction until *A Gun for Sale* (1936), when the killer Raven, trapped by a betrayal, reaches out for a God he does not believe in. Later, action is allegorized in God's image, as in *The Power and the Glory*. The journal entries of Sarah Miles in *The End of the Affair* show her infidelity with Bendrix pitted against God's will in such a way as to make God an actual character. Consistently, in the key works, Greene uses God as a kind of reference. What happens over and over again in Greene is like something that occurs perhaps once in Ernest Hemingway's work—near the end of *The Sun Also Rises* (1926). When Brett Ashley informs Jake Barnes that deciding not to be a bitch is "sort of what we have instead of God," Jake replies, "Some people have God . . . quite a lot." It is usually that way in Greene's religious novels, God either honored in the breach or dishonored in the observance.

Graham Greene was born 2 October 1904 at Berkhamsted, Hertfordshire, England, to Charles Henry Greene, headmaster of Berkhamsted School, and Marion R. Greene. He was one of six children. The parents were cousins, both born with the family name Greene, and Robert Louis Stevenson was a first cousin of Marion Greene's.

Although *The Lost Childhood* (1951) is the title of a memoir Greene wrote in his forties, there is no writer in whom less of childhood has been lost. The penance childhood pays to disillusion is a common theme in his earliest stories. Many of these stories are analogues of the painful life he appears to have led "on a border" between two "countries," that of his family and that of his father's school. It is difficult to know how

much of Greene's proclaimed hatred of school is intellectual and how much, in the words of Douglas Jerrold, is "merely emotion recollected in hostility to life in general." Peter Quennell, Greene's contemporary at Berkhamsted, recalls him as a potential Pierrot, a wearer of a "rather woebegone mask" concealing "a great capacity for cynical humor. . . . [Reading his books] I sometimes feel that I am confronting the spirited schoolboy in a more accomplished and more portentous guise." More recent commentators—John Bayley and David Pryce-Jones, for example—do not credit as the beginning of a continuum the teenage Graham's melodramatic assaults on boredom. "Playing a moody Russian roulette with his father's revolver, as Greene claimed to have done, was a response to be understood as any teenager's refusal of what must lie ahead. The world, it seemed, had to be like that," a disenchanted Pryce-Jones observes.

Berkhamsted School, nevertheless, was the place where evil became an article of faith, "a land of stone stairs and cracked bells ringing early [where] one was aware of fear and hate. . . . One met for the first time characters, adult and adolescent, who bore about them the genuine quality of evil. . . . And so faith came to one—shapelessly, without dogma, a presence about a croquet lawn, something associated with violence, cruelty, evil across the way. One began to believe in heaven because one believed in hell, but for a long time it was only hell one could picture with a certain intimacy." This sense of hell as more credible than heaven is another way of saying that corruption acquired innocence. It would be a theme the writer would never tire of playing on.

It is not surprising, then, that in a writer for whom adolescence lay like a dread palimpsest over everything, stories whose protagonists are boys should interweave innocence and corruption. In "The Basement Room" the author's childhood is symbolized dually by the worlds of the nursery, where young Philip Lane spends most of his time, and the basement living room of the butler Baines, Philip's idol, and his bitchy wife. When his parents go on holiday, Philip penetrates the green baize door of childhood into Baines's quarters, where he lives every word of the butler's made-up stories. However, in the dramatically limited perception of the boy, fantasy gives way to a series of too-intimate-too-soon brushes with the world of adults. Philip is startled, during one of his flights beyond the baize door, to find Baines kissing a girl, Emmy, whom he has introduced as his niece. Philip is, finally, the witness to a struggle between the Baineses which ends with the wife falling down the staircase to her death. "The whole house had been turned over to the grown-up world," Philip feels. He will shut it all out. Let them keep to their world; he will keep to his. He runs away only to be found by a policeman. In his innocence about involvements with the secrets of adults, he blurts out, "It was all Emmy's fault!" He had adored Baines: "Baines had involved him in secrets, fears he didn't understand. That was what happened when you loved—you got involved; and Philip extricated himself from life, from love, from Baines."

By reversing every assumed value, a later story, "The Destructors," flips innocence into an unaccustomed controlling position over corruption. Time and place—the World War II blitzkrieg of London—are ripe for it, and Greene makes the most of his opportunity. Philip Lane has grown to early teens as Trevor, son of a patrician family reduced by the war to neighborhood caste. Trevor joins the Wormsley Common Gang who know him only as "T." He takes over the gang by audacity, making it clear there is to be no more kids' stuff—petty thievery or cadging rides from unwary conductors. Instead, they will systemically demolish the common's last standing buildings, a house and loo belonging to an elderly man who has offered them chocolates, a gesture they view as a bribe. They dub Thomas, the householder, "Old Misery." They work, Greene writes, "with the seriousness of creators—and destruction after all is a form of creation." They will dismantle Old Misery's house, with its two-hundred-year-old corkscrew staircase, from the inside, and bring down to their level a building that, to Trevor, is invisibly held up "by opposite forces."

Opposite forces generate, as they do all of Greene's longer works, this shorter one which leads off a list of Greene's own favorites ("I believe I have never written anything better"). T. and his gang dispossess the old man, but they are not thieves; they burn his seventy bank notes one by one. T. admits to wanting "to see Old Misery's face when we're through," but he denies hating him. "There'd be no fun if I hated him." For Trevor, hate and love—opposing forces—are "soft . . . hooey. There's only things."

They maneuver Thomas into his own loo, then lock the door behind him. While they put fin-

ishing touches on the demolition, Thomas, half-suspecting, ponders the Bank Holiday and an unfavorable horoscope ("They speak in parables and double meanings"). The gang makes him "comfortable" by passing in a blanket and throwing buttered penny buns and sausage rolls over his wall. Early next morning a driver starts the lorry that he has parked by Thomas's house. The lorry, having been tied to a strut of the house, completes Trevor's fiendish achievement. The driver, even in the face of Old Misery's misery, breaks into convulsive laughter—opposing forces at work to the end: "Nothing personal, but you got to admit that it's funny." "The Destructors," like "The Basement Room," is about youth at bay. In the first, goodness loses out to forces it cannot understand; in the second, to forces it understands too well. Innocence and depravity—opposing forces—have joined hands.

Greene, a lifelong sufferer from a despairing romanticism that is associated with boredom, wonders "how all those who do not write, compose or paint can manage to escape the madness, the melancholia, the panic fear which is inherent in the human condition." One wonders how close *his* situation, up to the age of thirty, brought him to despair, so conventional was it. He read modern history at Balliol College, Oxford. While there, as a perverse prank, he joined the Communist party as a dues-paying member—the amount he paid has been estimated at twenty-eight cents—for a period variously reported as from four to six weeks. That caprice would haunt Greene thirty years later.

Between coming down from Oxford with a second-class degree in 1925 and joining the *Times* the following year, Greene published a collection of poetry, *Babbling April*, which he subsequently disavowed, and joined the Roman Catholic church, an action which helped determine the course (and cause) of his life. His authorized biographer, Norman Sherry, conveys in exhaustive detail Greene's state of mind during his plodding instruction and, finally, baptism ("a humiliating ordeal" were Greene's words for them over a half-century later) but leaves no doubt that it was less the force of his convictions than the woman he loved which sustained him. "I had made the first move with a view to my future marriage, but now the land had given way under my feet and I was afraid of where the tide would take me," Greene wrote forty-five years later in *A Sort of Life* (1971).

A year after his conversion, Greene married Vivien Dayrell-Browning. The couple had a son and a daughter but separated in the 1960s. He maintained a warm relationship with his daughter, Caroline Bourget, and his final hospitalization for the leukemia which proved fatal was in Switzerland, the daughter's adopted country. His son, Francis, lives in Devon, England.

In the decade following his conversion and marriage Greene worked mostly as an editor on the *Times*, a job he relinquished only after the publication of his first novel, *The Man Within* (1929), and the guarantee from Heinemann and Doubleday of a six-hundred-pound advance. The book was a modest success, selling eight thousand copies.

Greene became a popular success with the publication of his fourth novel, *Stamboul Train* (1932; published in the United States as *Orient Express*, 1933). He employs the train speeding from Ostend to Istanbul as the setting for his first thriller of international espionage. Pryce-Jones regards this novel as a distinct advance on the three apprentice works, in which Greene's attempts to reveal his characters' inner lives were like "clumsy asides in a play." In *Stamboul Train* "the lull of the journey is an illusion: one and all are being borne to a destiny as much as to a destination, and they will be harried all along the line. . . . [T]he very fact of travelling deviates or at least deflects them from their purposes. That is in the nature of life." And betrayal prior to a fall is in the nature of Greene.

Stamboul Train was followed by two novels, *It's a Battlefield* (1934), a work deriving from Greene's hero Joseph Conrad's *Secret Agent* (1907) [the protagonist is even named Conrad Drover], about the repercussions in the lives of various Londoners of the conviction of a Communist for the murder of a policeman, and *England Made Me* (1935); published in the United States as *The Shipwrecked*, 1953), about the empty lives of a Swedish millionaire named Krogh and those around him. Both novels were ignored by the public on both sides of the Atlantic. By 1935, bored and experiencing marital problems, Greene, with a £350 advance, hiked through the jungles of Liberia. The result was *Journey Without Maps* (1936), the first evidence that Greene would win recognition as a travel writer, too.

A clue to where Greene was heading—his commitment to dealing with his own crisis of faith even though it could not yet make itself known to him with the clarity of a controlling

philosophy—is that he was drawing a distinction between drama and melodrama. The distinction prompted him, for a time, to partition his fiction into novels and "entertainments." His reputation rising with every book, these labels caused little stir either in him or in his growing audience.

Brighton Rock (1938) was a milestone in Greene's career, a work whose rubric its creator shifted from novel to entertainment to novel. A. A. DeVitis puts Greene's reasons well: "What had been before *Brighton Rock* a deeply felt religious outlook became with this novel the frame of reference within which the action developed. . . . [Now] it was Greene's Roman Catholicism that gave coherence and meaning to the narrative." The Catholic-writer label Greene seemed always to have deplored was first affixed with *Brighton Rock* and cemented forever with *The Power and the Glory* and *The Heart of the Matter*. "At a stroke," he wrote in *Ways of Escape*, "I found myself regarded as a Catholic author in England, Europe and America—the last title to which I ever aspired."

Brighton Rock deals overtly with the questions which, years later, prompted Evelyn Waugh to refer to Greene as the "most distinguished" of his contemporaries, "a writer equipped to take as his subject the gravest questions that face the destiny of a man and to write about them convincingly": sin, damnation, salvation. From its opening sentence ("Hale knew, before he had been in Brighton three hours, that they meant to murder him."), the novel presents all the ingredients of a thriller—rival mobs and vendettas, betrayals and chases to the death, a grisly (and fake) suicide pact involving one of the gang leaders, Pinkie, and Rose, his 16-year-old victim—both slum-born Catholics—who is left pregnant with the child of the dead killer.

The religious theme comes to the fore in a confessional scene after Pinkie's death. It clarifies, for the first time in his fiction, ideas which will come to dialectical fullness in subsequent books. Rose expresses to a priest her conviction that Pinkie is damned and says she wants to be damned too. The priest speaks of the "appalling . . . strangeness of the mercy of God." When Rose mentions that Pinkie was a Catholic, the priest answers, summing up not only the theme of this novel but a major theme in all of Greene's religion-oriented works: "*Corruptio optimi est pessimi.* . . . I mean—a Catholic is more capable of evil than anyone. I think perhaps because we be-

Greene in 1939 (Bassano Studios). During 1939, Greene published three books in addition to working on The Power and the Glory *(1940).*

lieve in him—we are more in touch with the devil than other people."

Brighton Rock is the quintessential example of that series of fast-paced works in which politics and religion, rightly understood, merge and which Greene once labeled entertainments: *The Confidential Agent* (1939), *The Ministry of Fear* (1943), and *The Third Man* (1950). In the epigraph to *The Honorary Consul* (1973), a strong novel published in his sixty-ninth year, Greene quotes Thomas Hardy: "All things merge in one another—good into evil, generosity into justice, religion into politics. . . . " This sense of the blending of politics and religion helps explain why, according to Frank D. McConnell, "Greene often seems most 'religious' when he is writing about spies and policemen . . . and most 'political' when he is writing about priests and saints."

For Harold Bloom, however, only *Brighton Rock* overcomes the "theological tendentiousness" of the later and more famous *The Power and the Glory* and *The Heart of the Matter*. "[I]t is all one thing, Greene's shot out of hell, as it were. Pinkie persuades us to believe that [*sic*] the nameless whis-

key priest . . . and . . . the colonial policeman . . . cannot."

George Stade faults Greene for "mythification, especially when what's being mythified is the raw material of an entertainment. A pox on Graham Greene! Who needs his wretched allegories?" Stade's question, clearly intended to be rhetorical, merits a response. The respondent may be one who read Greene with the fascination of romance-hungry youth but for whom going back to Greene in mid-life "is like trying on clothes which are too small, an effort between clumsiness and embarrassment." David Pryce-Jones, writing for the London *Times Literary Supplement* a week after Greene's death, goes on to find in Greene's vast readership an audience that "welcomed the retreat from reality . . . wanted to feel sorry for themselves. . . . Greene showed them how this could be done."

These, however, are minority reports. R. W. B. Lewis has written for the majority. He finds in *Brighton Rock*, *The Power and the Glory*, and *The Heart of the Matter* a trilogy which released "the special energy and 'vision' that would characterize Greene as a writer of stature . . . [seeking] all the truth of things [lying] hidden in the darkness: whether of slum-ridden Brighton, of a squalid [Mexican] prison cell, or of a West African night of wonder and despair."

Graham Greene went to Mexico in the late winter of 1937-1938. He had been commissioned by a London publishing house to study the plight of the Mexican Catholic church, which had for over a decade been engaged in a running feud with the revolutionary government. Nothing was further from his thoughts in Mexico than the writing of a novel, he recalls in his preface to the Viking critical edition of *The Power and the Glory*. He was in Villahermosa when by accident he came on traces of his principal character. A villager told him of the last priest in the state. The priest had baptized the villager's son, giving him a girl's name, for he was so drunk he could hardly stand for the ceremony, let alone remember a name. Afterward he had disappeared into the same mountains on the borders of Chiapas through which Greene, astride a mule, rode that winter on his way to Las Casas, where the churches were still standing but with priests *prohibido*. It was not a happy journey. The West was edging its way to World War II, the Italian pope was dying, and Greene was suffering from dysentery and the knowledge that he might be as much persona non grata in England as British diplomats were in Mexico. A libel action had been brought against him by Shirley Temple for remarks he had made in a film review. The case was settled for thirty-five hundred pounds, including two thousand pounds for Temple, but at the time Greene feared he might be arrested on his return. So it was that he extended his stay to eight weeks and accumulated material for his best novel.

The incidents on which the plot of *The Power and the Glory* are based can be found in his second travel book, *The Lawless Roads* (1939; published in the United States as *Another Mexico*), a straightforward plea for the religious practices of Catholicism. Since the provinces of Tabasco and Chiapas were remote and communication nonexistent, the physical conditions of the journey must have seemed a repetition of those he recalled in 1936 from his first—to Liberia.

The Power and the Glory enables Greene to deploy his opposite forces in an Aristotelian fashion. Complication in the Mexican interior leads inevitably to tragic resolution. Religion and materialism are embodied by a priest and a police lieutenant. As soon as the two protagonists, never named except by their vocations, are matched, Greene's most powerful novel takes on the air of a parable. The action is right out of the entertainments—a chase—but much extended. Triangulated by three legs (three meetings), the action moves from the first, in a village where the priest has sought refuge and celebrated mass, to a second, in a prison where the priest is confined on a charge of drunkenness, to the final, the arrest leading to his execution.

The priest is tracked by a mestizo—a half-caste—who forces him to return to the village to attend to a dying gangster, a grown-up Pinkie, a Catholic who might be saved by confession and whom the police have used as an involuntary decoy in their ambush. The priest's case is not so extreme as Pinkie's, for the former has the plea of suffering from his earnest moral intentions whenever he is sober enough to concentrate. By paying with his life, he attains salvation, which apparently was denied Pinkie. Greene's question, as a Catholic writer, is whether the priest is a saint. Pryce-Jones is cogent on this point which he answers in the affirmative. The priest becomes a saint "because of the stress towards repentance set up by his sins, much as Rose is something of a saint because of her shouldering of the burdens of Pinkie's sins. . . . Certainly the priest never fails to mortify himself whenever his con-

science is brought into play: perhaps his self-knowledge should be seen as humility instead of realism. He admits to the lieutenant that he had stayed in the province partly to have the satisfaction of being the last priest when the others had run away, and partly out of pride, and he is angrily answered by the lieutenant that he will be a martyr. 'Oh no. Martyrs are not like me. They don't think all the time—if I had drunk more brandy, I shouldn't be so afraid,' the priest replies."

The Power and the Glory is Greene's plea for the priest's heroic, or, in religious terms, saintly, status despite constant self-humiliation, a status that allows him to die for his faith despite his impulse for self-preservation. Given the fortification of belief, *felix culpa* (doctrinally translated as the "fortunate fall") takes on imperatives no less deterministic than the hamartia ("tragic flaw" or "error") of classical tragedy. In Greene's works, the humiliated, like the humble, can inherit the earth. He has said that of all his novels the one that most satisfied him is *The Power and the Glory*.

If one has to be a Christian to be convinced of the apotheosis of the whiskey priest, one has to disbelieve, in order to praise the later work, that the tenets of any organized religion should be invoked as aesthetic considerations. Otherwise, it is difficult to believe that Scobie's motives in *The Heart of the Matter* adequately explain his actions. Perhaps for George Orwell, who deplored colonialism, it was second nature to wonder why Greene did not simply play out Scobie's dilemmas in a London suburb instead of in West Africa. "All [Scobie] is interested in is his own progress toward damnation. The improbability of this shows up against the colonial setting, but it is an improbability that is present in *Brighton Rock* as well, and that is bound to result from foisting theological preoccupations upon simple people anywhere."

The aesthetic question, then, is inseparable from the religious. For the nondoctrinaire reader who finds nothing honorific about being damned, novels like *The Heart of the Matter* and *Brighton Rock* may seem too special. Orwell puts the problem well when he concludes that, in Greene, hell becomes "a sort of high-class night club, entry to which is reserved for Catholics only, since the others. . . . are too ignorant to be held guilty. . . ." If one forgets that Greene was a Catholic novelist—and he always insisted that he was a writer who just happened to be a Catholic—it is inescapable that self-humiliation lies at the

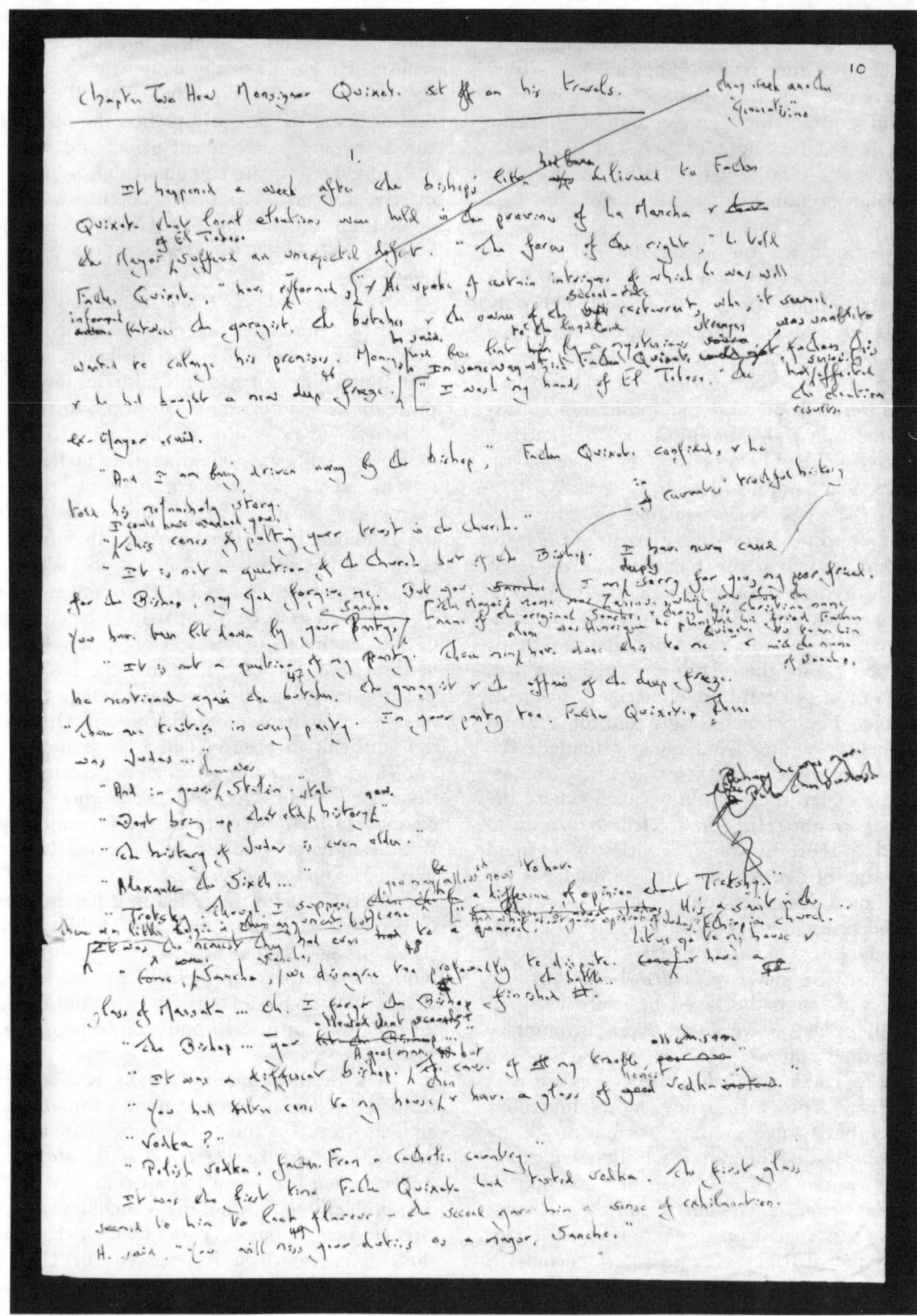

Pages ten and eleven from the manuscript for Greene's last novel, Monsignor Quixote *(Graham Greene Papers, Department of Special Collections, Georgetown University Library, by permission of the Estate of Graham Greene)*

11.

"I plan to take a holiday. I have not stepped outside El Toboso for five years. If only I had a car..."

Father Quixote thought of Rocinante. His mind wandered. In the vein of the night watchman. I have no desire to go there,

"Mexico is too far, Deville it is too cold. East Germany — she have seen too many Germans in Spain.

Suppose Father Quixote thought, I am expelled to Rome. Rocinante could never not greater distance. The Bishop had even spoken of the mission field. Rocinante was near the end of her days. He couldn't leave her to die by some roadside in Africa to be cannibalized for the sake of a gear-box or a door-handle.

"San Marino is the nearest state where the Party rules. Another glass, Father."

Without thinking Father Quixote extended his hand.

"What will you do, father, away from El Toboso?"

"I shall obey orders. I will go where I am sent."

"To preach to the converted?"

"That is an easy answer, Sancho. I doubt if anyone is ever fully converted."

"Not the Pope?"

"Perhaps, poor man, not even the Pope. Who knows what he thinks at night, is his faith when he says his prayer?

"And yourself?"

"Oh, I am as ignorant as anyone in the parish. I have read one book, that is all, when I studied, but one forgets..."

"All the same you believe, all that nonsense, God, the Trinity, the Immaculate Conception..."

"I want to believe. I want others to believe."

"Why?"

"I want them to be happy."

"Let them drink a little vodka than. That's better than a make-believe."

"It wears off. It's wearing off now."

"So does belief."

Father Quixote looked up with surprise. He had been gazing with a certain wistfulness at the last drops in his glass.

"Your belief?"

"And your belief."

"Why do you think that?"

"It's life, father. It is dirty work. Belief dies away like the desire for a woman. I doubt if you are an exception to the general rule."

"Do you think it would be bad for me to have another glass?"

"Vodka has never done anyone any harm."

"I was astonished the other day at how much the Mayor of Mopoto drank."

"Where is Mopoto?"

"In British infidelity."

heart of the matter. As Edmund Wilson was obliged to point out about Harold Frederic's *Damnation of Theron Ware* (1896), a novel he cherished, "I doubt whether a great novel can be written around a central character who, having been made sufficiently attractive for the reader to share his emotions, is at the end so abjectly humiliated." For some, surely, Wilson's regrets are also assignable to all but *The Power and the Glory* among Greene's religious novels.

In *The End of the Affair*, the religious theme is inseparable from the plot. Greene clothes adultery in holy writ. The plot is easily summarized. Maurice Bendrix hopes to write a novel about a civil servant and takes Sarah, the wife of a ministry official, out to lunch. It is wartime, and London is under the blitzkrieg. They have an affair which ends abruptly, leaving Bendrix unhappy and jealous. After a lapse of two years—by now the war is over—Bendrix meets Henry, the deceived husband, and the chance encounter leads to the explanation of Sarah's conduct. The story is told in both past and present tenses. Bendrix is the narrator, but a forty-page interlude consisting of Sarah's diary, to which Bendrix is illicitly made privy after he has jealously set a private investigator on Sarah's trail, becomes a dramatic device which enables Greene to give Sarah's account of the affair.

The End of the Affair is a modern religious novel that cannot be for everyone. It relies on the reader's believing that something even proclaimed atheists might do in an emergency—Sarah prays that the lover she assumes killed in an air raid be spared and to that end enters into a contract with God—can change the bargainer's life forever. Specifically Greene requires acceptance of at least four fictionally unearned developments—miracles—the most implausible of which is the gratuitous insertion of evidence that, when very young, Sarah had been secretly baptized as a Catholic by her mother.

Ten years after *Affair*, Greene returned to a shabby setting that calls to mind his first African novel. In *A Burnt-Out Case* (1961), he also moved beyond mounting a case for any particular dogma. He beaches his Faustian seeker, appropriately named Querry, in a Congo leprosarium where, like other Greene heroes, he experiences a rebirth of concern for human suffering and becomes martyred by it. Querry is a Catholic architect of world renown who has sought refuge in the leprosarium, where his spiritual impasse equates to the lepers' physical condition. He has come to the end of his tether, a stage further even than Scobie or Bendrix: "I haven't enough feeling left for human beings to do anything for them out of pity." In the Congo, however, his rehabilitation becomes possible because he sees the worst of suffering. His rebirth apparent in his efforts to design a new hospital, Querry dies meaninglessly, a victim of the mistaken assumptions and stupidities of others.

Although political considerations do not override his novels, Greene did not escape unscathed the McCarthyite anticommunism of America in the 1950s. Early in 1952, through the American consul in Saigon, Greene applied for a visa to enter the United States. That he was admitted briefly amid difficulties and then denied the visa Greene blamed on the U.S. attorney general. "That it could seriously be thought that Graham Greene would carry the contagion and infect us is a fair measure of the intelligence and the precision of the authors of the McCarran Act," editorialized *Commonweal*. "McCarran and McCarthy might sacrilegiously have met Mr. Greene on his arrival, with bell and book and candle to drive from his spirit the last few traces of germs." As is usually the case, the rebuff became grist for the writer's mill. Eviction generated journalistic invective: a spirited defense of the concept of "Disloyalty" and an open letter, "Dear Mr. Chaplin," castigating Senator Joseph McCarthy and his Hollywood supporters and urging British writers and actors to refuse to sell stories or appear in films sponsored by any organization that included "these friends of the witch-hunter."

In *The Quiet American*, his "Vietnam novel," Greene dramatizes the necessity of disloyalty in the face of a destructive idealism. Although his most polemical novel came more than three years after the denial of his visa, some American reviewers saw a connection, and nearly all criticized the book for its anti-American fervor. The novel counterpoises Fowler, an English journalist, and Pyle, the American of the title. Fowler, middle-aged, sophisticated, and safe, is a self-proclaimed atheist who nevertheless frequently addresses himself to God. Pyle is thirty-two, Harvard-reared, innocent, and full of intellectual idealism, enthusiasm, and danger. Greene brings into vivid relief the old problem—the fearful price of innocence—and shows, as Bernard Shaw does in his major plays, that behind innocence lurk unconscious arrogance and a self-righteous streak of moral blindness.

The Comedians was apparently Greene's signal that he would no longer write about no-longer-young, not-quite-happy men with tedious and/or dangerous jobs in seedy locales. A. A. DeVitis finds this Haitian novel to be "the gloomiest as well as the most challenging" of Greene's works and Brown an antiheroic practitioner of an innocent nihilism which, witness to farce and macabre humor though it is, cannot mask despair. "Brown makes no real commitment to anything, not to love, not to religion, not to God, not to innocence. It is only right that at the novel's end he becomes a partner in an undertaking business . . . ; symbolically and literally he serves the dead."

If Querry of *A Burnt-Out Case* fingered his lack of faith like a sore he wanted to get rid of, Greene may well have fingered his guilt-obsessed Scobies and uncommitted Browns like sores *he* wanted to get rid of. After *A Burnt-Out Case* and the bleak outlook of *The Comedians*, it is the moments of rich if bitter humor that scintillate in most of Greene's last books. In *Our Man in Havana* (1958) and *Travels With My Aunt* (1969), he gives expression fully to his gift for comedy. The former combines exciting satire on the exploits of the British secret service abroad with wry commentary on Fulgencio Batista's decadent Cuba with its stupid bureaucracy. The latter is a jeu d'esprit about a dotty old lady with a delightfully wicked past. Aunt Augusta takes it upon herself to initiate her inhibited middle-aged nephew into grotesqueries beyond his conception. Their trip becomes a montage of places where Greene had set his previous books.

The central point of much of Greene's writing is suicide—in Catholic doctrine the most deadly sin. In his play *The Living Room* (1953) his interpretation of it is not a doctrinal one. The audience is left feeling that the heroine's (Rose Pemberton's) soul is saved, if anyone's is, and the message of the play is not Catholic propaganda but of far wider appeal. It is a plea to believe in a God whom Father Browne, the girl's confessor, admits may not exist, but belief can only do good not ill, and without it we cannot help ourselves. Although Rose's suicide will probably be the only answer visible to most people, Father Browne's unshakable faith, his calm acceptance of her death, implies that there is another, but that the struggle for it must be unceasing.

Another play, *The Potting Shed* (1957), makes combined use of the Lazarus theme and the framework of the detective story. James Callifer has come to his father's deathbed hoping to learn what in his life makes him incapable of experiencing any deeply felt emotion. In the second act it is learned that James had been a suicide at fourteen but had returned to life after the boy's Uncle William had promised God his only valuable possession—his faith—to spare the boy he loved. This miracle is crucial and strongly reminiscent of the miracles in *The End of the Affair*. After God answers Sarah Miles's prayer, sparing Bendrix, she proceeds to greater and greater awareness of his existence. Unlike Sarah, William Callifer goes on in his existence without faith until he is given proof of the miracle.

The Complaisant Lover: A Comedy (1959) stands in relation to the earlier pair of plays as *Our Man in Havana* relates to the novels and the preceding entertainments. This play is a brisk, witty, oftentimes farcical treatment of the triangle situation Greene had used in several of his novels as well as in *The Living Room*. But, where the emphasis in the novels and the first play falls on the emotional and spiritual complications of characters involved in basically tragic situations, in *The Complaisant Lover* it falls on the comic involvements of a domestic tragedy.

"There is a point . . . in the careers of important and prolific novelists," writes Thomas F. Staley in *Commonweal*, "when each new book becomes a piece in the larger picture of their total work, and the entire picture becomes far more important than the latest piece." Staley is writing about *Monsignor Quixote* (1982), which is perhaps Greene's best novel written after his seventy-fifth year, but the words could be applied to all his writings after *The Honorary Consul*. The latter relates the story of the politically motivated kidnapping of Charlie Fortnum, a minor British functionary in South America. The novel's major characters exemplify the kinds of personal sacrifices one must make in order to live in good conscience in a world where there is too much tyranny and injustice. A minor machismo novelist endures privation; a priest joins the radical underground movement; a physician gives up a lucrative Buenos Aires practice. All three hope their sacrifices will in some way help the poor.

Of *Monsignor Quixote*, Staley concludes that Greene's concern, dramatized first in his early masterpiece *The Power and the Glory*, remains steadfast: the transforming power of illusion and the transforming power of love.

As he approached his eightieth year, the rarely interviewed Greene made no effort to deny that writing, which he always viewed as a means to fend off boredom, no longer sustained him. He told John Vinocur that he was entering accounts of his dreams into a journal—"more than 800 pages, indexed by letter, like the phone book so that I can find a dream about the sea or a hotel or Khrushchev or Haiti." Norman Sherry recently reported that, just before his death, Greene awarded him publishing rights to the dreams. He wished also to set the record straight on a variety of sore matters. It had been made out that he didn't like the United States, which he last visited in the 1960s, and that he once said he would prefer living in the Soviet Union to California. "The comment was meant to be ironic. I would end my days much quicker in Russia than in California, because the Russians take writing seriously, so I would soon find myself in a gulag, which is in a way a compliment to a writer. Whereas one might drag out one's years in California in some backwater."

Graham Greene the writer lived most of his eighty-six years under a torment of faith, of which his politics were the merest suggestion. He is the supreme exemplar in twentieth-century fiction of the guilt-obsessed writer who has worked through corruption-of-innocence so thoroughly that he has brought it out on its other side as innocence-of-corruption.

Interviews:

Martin Shuttleworth and Simon Raven, "The Art of Fiction III: Graham Greene," *Paris Review*, 1 (Autumn 1953): 24-41;

"New Honor and a New Novel: Interview," *Life*, 60 (4 February 1966): 43-44;

G. D. Phillips, "Graham Greene: On the Screen: Interview," *Catholic World*, 209 (August 1969): 218-221;

Michael Mewshaw, "Greene in Antibes," *London Magazine*, 17 (June-July 1977): 35-45;

Marie-Francoise Allain, *The Other Man—Conversations with Graham Greene* (London: Bodley Head, 1983);

John Vinocur, "Graham Greene: Waiting for the Words," "Weekend," *International Herald Tribune*, 8 March 1985, 7;

John Mortimer, "I'm an Angry Old Man, You See," *Spectator* (14 June 1986): 9-12.

Bibliographies:

William Birmingham, "Graham Greene Criticism: A Bibliographical Study," *Thought*, 27 (Spring 1952): 72-100;

Francis Wyndham, *Graham Greene, Bibliographical Series of Supplements to British Book News on Writers and Their Work*, no. 67 (London: Longmans, Green, 1955);

Maurice Beebe, "Criticism of Graham Greene: A Selected Checklist with an Index to Studies of Separate Works," *Modern Fiction Studies*, 3 (Autumn 1957): 281-288;

Phyllis Hargreaves, "Graham Greene: A Selected Bibliography," *Modern Fiction Studies*, 3 (Autumn 1957): 269-280;

Jerry Don Vann, *Graham Greene: Checklist of Criticism* (Lexington: University of Kentucky Press, 1970);

Robert H. Miller, *Graham Greene: A Descriptive Catalog* (Lexington: University of Kentucky Press, 1979);

R. A. Wobbe, *Graham Greene: A Bibliography and Guide to Research* (New York & London: Garland, 1979);

A. F. Cassis, *Graham Greene: An Annotated Bibliography of Criticism* (Metuchen, N.J.: Scarecrow Press, 1981).

Biography:

Norman Sherry, *The Life of Graham Greene, 1904-1939* (New York: Viking, 1989).

References:

Judith Adamson, *Graham Greene and Cinema* (Norman, Okla.: Pilgrim Books, 1984);

Jacob H. Adler, "Graham Greene's Plays: Technique versus Value," in *Graham Greene: Some Critical Considerations*, edited by Robert O. Evans (Lexington: University of Kentucky Press, 1963);

Walter Allen, *Tradition and Dream: The English and American Novel from the Twenties to Our Time* (London: Phoenix House, 1964);

Kenneth Allott and Miriam Farris Allott, *The Art of Graham Greene* (New York: Russell & Russell, 1963);

John Atkins, *Graham Greene: A Biographical and Critical Study* (New York: Roy Publishers, 1958; revised edition, London: Calder & Boyars, 1966);

Atkins, "Two Views of Life: William Golding and Graham Greene," *Studies in the Literary Imagination*, 13, no. 1 (1980): 81-96;

W. H. Auden, "The Heresy of Our Time," *Renascence*, 1 (Spring 1949): 23-24;

Saul Bellow, "The Writer as Moralist," *Atlantic Monthly*, 211 (March 1963): 58-62;

Gwenn R. Boardman, *Graham Greene: The Aesthetics of Exploration* (Gainesville: University of Florida Press, 1971);

Arthur Calder-Marshall, "Graham Greene," in *Living Writers: Being Critical Studies Broadcast in the B.B.C. Third Programme*, edited by Gilbert Phelps (London: Sylvan, 1947), pp. 39-47;

Calder-Marshall, "The Works of Graham Greene," *Horizon*, 1 (May 1940): 367-375;

A. F. Cassis, "The Dream as Literary Device in Graham Greene's Novels," *Literature and Psychology*, 24 (Spring 1974): 99-108.

Francis X. Connolly, "Inside Modern Man: The Spiritual Adventures of Graham Greene," *Renascence*, 1 (Spring 1949): 16-24;

Donald P. Costello, "Graham Greene and the Catholic Press," *Renascence*, 12 (Autumn 1959): 3-28;

Beekman W. Cottrell, "Second Time Charm: The Theatre of Graham Greene," *Modern Fiction Studies*, special Greene issue, 3 (Autumn 1957): 249-255;

Maria Couto, *Graham Greene: On the Frontier: Politics and Religion in the Novels* (New York: St. Martin's Press, 1988);

Richard Creese, "Abstracting and Recording Narration in *The Good Soldier* and *The End of the Affair*," *Journal of Narrative Technique*, 16 (Winter 1986): 1-14;

David Daiches, "The Possibilities of Heroism," *American Scholar*, 25 (Winter 1956): 94-106;

A. A. DeVitis, *Graham Greene*, new and revised (Boston: Twayne, 1986);

Denis Donoghue, "Secret Sharer," *New York Review of Books* (19 February 1981): 14-18;

William D. Ellis, Jr., "The Grand Theme of Graham Greene," *Southwest Review*, 41 (Summer 1956): pp. 239-250;

Quentin Falk, *Travels in Greeneland: The Cinema of Graham Greene* (London & New York: Quartet Books, 1984);

Georg M. A. Gaston, *The Pursuit of Salvation: A Critical Guide to the Novels of Graham Greene* (Troy, N.Y.: Whitsun, 1984);

Richard Gilman, "Up from Hell with Graham Greene," *New Republic*, 154 (29 January 1966): 25-28;

Alan Grob, "*The Power and the Glory*: Graham Greene's Argument from Design," *Criticism*, 2 (Winter 1969): 1-30;

Henry A. Grubbs, "Albert Camus and Graham Greene," *Modern Language Quarterly*, 10 (March 1949): 33-42;

David Leon Higdon, "Saint Catherine, Von Hugel 28714 and Graham Greene's *The End of the Affair*," *English Studies*, 62 (January 1981): 46-52;

Paul Hogarth (illustrator), *Graham Greene Country Visited by Paul Hogarth*, Foreword and Commentary by Graham Greene (London: Pavilion Books, 1986);

Richard Hoggart, "The Force of Caricature: Aspects of the Art of Graham Greene, with Particular Reference to *The Power and the Glory*," *Essays in Criticism*, 3 (October 1953): 447-462;

Samuel Hynes, ed., *Graham Greene: A Collection of Critical Essays* (Englewood Cliffs, N.J.: Prentice Hall, 1973);

Douglas Jerrold, "Graham Greene, Pleasure-Hater," *Harper's*, 205 (August 1952): 50-52;

Richard Kelly, *Graham Greene* (New York: Ungar, 1984);

Frank Kermode, "Mr. Greene's Eggs and Crosses," *Encounter*, 16 (April 1961), 69-75; reprinted in his *Puzzles and Epiphanies* (New York: Chidmark, 1963), pp. 176-187;

J. P. Kulshrestha, *Graham Greene: The Novelist* (New Delhi: Macmillan of India, 1977);

Francis L. Kunkel, *The Labyrinthine Ways of Graham Greene* (New York: Sheed & Ward, 1959);

F. N. Lees, "Graham Greene: A Comment," *Scrunity*, 19 (October 1952): 31-42;

Laurence Lerner, "Graham Greene," *Critical Quarterly*, 5 (1963): 217-231;

R. W. B. Lewis, "The Trilogy," in his *The Picaresque Saint: Representative Figures in Contemporary Fiction* (New York: Lippincott, 1959), pp. 239-264;

Lewis and Peter J. Conn, eds., *The Power and the Glory: Text and Criticism* (New York: Viking, 1970);

David Lodge, *Graham Greene* (New York: Columbia University Press, 1966);

François Mauriac, "Graham Greene," in his *Men I Hold Great* (New York: Philosophical Library, 1951), pp. 124-128;

Mary McCarthy, "Graham Greene and the Intelligentsia," *Partisan Review*, 11 (Spring 1944): 228-230;

Frank D. McConnell, "Perspectives: Graham Greene," *Wilson Quarterly*, 5 (Winter 1981): 168-186;

James L. McDonald, "Graham Greene: A Reconsideration," *Arizona Quarterly*, 27 (Winter 1971): 197-210;

Greene in his apartment in Antibes, France (photograph by Graham Wood/Daily Mail)

Marie-Beatrice Mesnet, *Graham Greene and the Heart of the Matter* (Westport, Conn.: Greenwood, 1972);

Jeffrey Meyers, ed., *Graham Greene: A Revaluation* (New York: St. Martin's Press, 1990);

Conor Cruise O'Brien, "A Funny Sort of God," *New York Review of Books*, 18 (18 October 1973): 56-58;

Sean O'Faolain, "Graham Greene: I Suffer; Therefore, I Am," in his *The Vanishing Hero: Studies in Novelists of the Twenties* (London: Eyre and Spottiswoode, 1956): 73-97;

George Orwell, "The Sanctified Sinner," in *The Collected Essays, Journalism and Letters of George Orwell*, edited by Sonia Orwell and Ian Angus (New York: Harcourt, Brace & World, 1968);

Gene D. Phillips, S.J., *Graham Greene: The Films of His Fiction* (New York: Teachers College Press, Columbia University, 1974);

Orville Prescott, "Comrade of the Coterie," in his *In My Opinion* (Indianapolis: Bobbs-Merrill, 1952), pp. 92-109;

V. S. Pritchett, "The World of Graham Greene," *New Statesman* (4 January 1958);

David Pryce-Jones, *Graham Greene* (New York: Barnes & Noble, 1967);

Peter Quennell, *The Sign of the Fish* (London: Collins, 1960);

Michael Routh, "Greene's Parody of Farce and Comedy in *The Comedians*," *Renascence*, 26 (Spring 1974): 139-151;

Anne T. Salvatore, *Greene and Kierkegaard: The Discourse of Belief* (Tuscaloosa: University of Alabama Press, 1988);

Marc Silverstein, "After the Fall: The World of Graham Greene's Thrillers," *Novel*, 22 (Fall 1988): 24-44;

Roger Sharrock, *Saints, Sinners and Comedians: The Novels of Graham Greene* (Notre Dame, Ind.: University of Notre Dame Press, 1984);

Philip Stratford, *Faith and Fiction: Creative Process in Greene and Mauriac* (Notre Dame, Ind.: University of Notre Dame Press, 1964);

Stratford, Introduction to *The Portable Graham Greene* (New York: Viking, 1973);

Brian Thomas, *An Uncertain Fate: The Idiom of Romance in the Later Novels of Graham Greene* (Athens: University of Georgia Press, 1980);

John Updike, "The Passion of Graham Greene," *New York Review of Books*, 37 (16 August 1990): 16-17;

Richard J. Voorhees, "The World of Graham Greene," *South Atlantic Quarterly*, 50 (July 1951): 389-398;

Ronald Walker, *The Infernal Paradise: Mexico and the Modern English Novel* (Berkeley & Los Angeles: University of California Press, 1978);

Evelyn Waugh, "Last Steps in Africa," *Spectator*, 208 (27 October 1961): 594-595;

Peter Wolfe, *Graham Greene: The Entertainer* (Carbondale, Ill.: Southern Illinois University Press, 1972);

George Woodcock, "Mexico and the English Novelist," *Western Review*, 21 (Autumn 1956): 21-32;

Morton Dauwen Zabel, "Graham Greene: The Best and the Worst," in his *Craft and Character in Modern Fiction* (New York: Viking, 1957), pp. 76-96.

Papers:

The Humanities Research Center, University of Texas at Austin, has manuscripts and typescripts of most of Greene's books, plus working drafts and final manuscripts of various short stories and articles, as well as much of the correspondence. There are Greene holdings at the Lilly Library, Indiana University; the Pennsylvania State University Library; the Library of Congress; and the British Library.

A TRIBUTE

from MARGARET DRABBLE

I never met him, but have read and reread his works over the years, greatly admiring the moral honesty, the bleakness, the despairing compassion, the restlessness, and the deep seriousness of his vision of life and death. Novels such as *The End of the Affair* and *The Heart of the Matter* affected me profoundly—as, in later years, did works such as *A Burnt-Out Case*. I can say that as a young person I learned a good deal about the world from him.

Many years ago he generously wrote me a fan letter about my novel, *The Millstone*. I was so impressed I feared it was a hoax. I hope I still have it, but haven't seen it for years. Then, about four years ago, I was inspired by a radio version of his play *The Potting Shed* to write him a letter thanking him for all he had meant to me over the years. He wrote back, reminding me of the letter he had once written me, saying that he himself had always been uncertain about the value of *The Potting Shed*, and apologizing for using a typewriter instead of writing by hand. He was the most courteous of men.

A TRIBUTE

from JOHN LE CARRÉ

As a young writer, I looked up at Greene as a role model, and nothing in my writing life has made me happier than the supremely generous support he gave to my early work. As a diplomat in Bonn, I blushed for him when he stood on the Eastern side of the Berlin Wall and made some unhappy comment about preferring it there to here. I thought his anti-Americanism too much. I thought him daft about the possible marriage of Communism and Christianity, and dafter still in his defence of Kim Philby. When I attacked him on Philby in print, I incurred his wrath and for a while was appointed a fully paid-up Graham Greene Unperson, guilty of all the sins of modern man, of which the chief, I fear, was ingratitude for his encouragement—though typically, between loosing off his salvoes at me, he sent me kindly messages through intermediaries.

I only met him a couple of times, once in Vienna and once in Paris. We drank a lot and he treated me with overwhelming courtesy. Occasionally I wrote to him—once, I remember, to commiserate about a shabby review of one of his novels by Kingsley Amis, and once from Phnom Penh to tell him that while in Saigon I had re-read *The Quiet American* and found it even more wonderful than before. He replied at once, asking me to visit the Phnom Penh museum and find out whether it still displayed the bowler hat with ostrich feathers with which, he said, Cambodian kings had once been crowned. To my sadness I had to report to him that the museum had been flattened by a *plastique*, or was it a rocket? The last time I wrote to him was a couple of years back. I don't remember exactly what prompted me, but it was probably yet another hatchet job by yet another small talent looking to play the giant killer. In my letter I said that, lest either one of us should go under a bus, I wanted to tell him how much his work had meant to me, and how he had been an inspiration to me throughout my writing life. I thanked him again for his support, and, however inadequately, for the magic of his writing. By then, of course, Greene was already becoming a little too old for his reputation. The British literary bureaucracy really had nothing left to do but try to shake him off his pedestal. It was wasting its breath. Greene will be alive and kicking in English letters long after his detractors have departed their insular stage. For he had what they can only dream of: wit and grace and character and story, and a transcendant, universal compassion that places him for all time in the ranks of world literature.

© David Cornwell 1991

TWO TRIBUTES

from NORMAN SHERRY

I knew him to be 70, with a reputation as the greatest writer in English, the most elusive personality of his generation, a legend in his own time—mysterious, aloof, unpredictable—and a tenacious guardian of his privacy.

Yet when I first met Graham Greene in 1974, it was a "young" author who popped his head round the door of the morning room of the Savile Club asking, each word well masticated, whether I was Professor Sherry. We shook hands, and his smile of blue blindness (which I mistook for a direct and innocent gaze), suggested he was ready for anything and anyone—even his future biographer. He was without a trace of self-importance. Rashly, I assured myself, he was not "an old fox" (his description) or even old.

With access to private letters, his willingness to assist by letter or interview, I thought his life could be written in half a dozen years. Biographers are sublime optimists, else they would not write full-length biographies in contrast to which a trip to darkest Africa is a bagatelle.

In writing Greene's life, I tried to probe his uniqueness—it did not, under scrutiny, disappear like ice under heat. And suddenly 12 years had elapsed before I completed Volume One—a thousand and a half pages of typescript. My obsessive years of research had produced an excess, and I felt fear and wonder as to how it would be put together. It had grown hydra-headed and as I struck off one head two shot up in its place. I remember making a note in my diary: "be sure to pare down the surrounding detail and centre on crucial points only." When the battle of the book was over, I had ripped 500 pages from my text.

Well, it didn't need to be so difficult. I could have used a simpler biographical method. Couldn't Greene's life be viewed as a journey from innocence to experience, from comparative rags to certain riches? Wasn't his story the case of a man sensitive to contemporary movements? And his journeys to the trouble spots of the world, even exploring where no white man had been before, wasn't this a throwback to Livingstone and Stanley, Burton and Speke? A Victorian schoolboy's dream fulfilled—though he was motivated by the daring of despair. He was seeking adventurous disaster in lost, forgotten places with the persistence of a determined suicide (which in part he was). If death came, his diaries prove, he would welcome it. Yet paradoxically he was always shooting the rapids, it was in a sound canoe. But to come to such views prior to research would mean that truth wasn't being served. I'd have come ready-armed with a template, seeing only what I wished to see.

So I researched on a grand scale collecting material by the ton. I spread my net wide and the method was heartbreaking, not helped by Greene's nature—for if he was not aloof, or unpredictable, he *was* elusive. In interviews he was preternaturally alert, "Set a watch, O Lord, before my mouth and a door round my lips" his motto.

Once I asked him to expand his comments on his boyhood attempts at suicide. It was likely that here lay the seeds of the complicated nature of Greene. He refused. That refusal led me in search of Old Boys at his school, many scattered around the world, to ask about Greene's early days, events 60 years old. When I had completed the research dealing with Greene's breakdown and written it up, three years had run headlong into the past. But there were no limits to what I would do to understand Greene, even (tongue in cheek) at one time approaching a witch, a graphologist and a fortune-teller. But if the master craftsman's soul had the mark of God upon it or was set in storm, he'd not allow me to be sole guardian of his secrets or to mine the dark side of his nature. Indeed conscience would make cowards of us both.

Greene had a ready answer for his biographer: "They [his friends] have a right to deal with my private life without involving theirs." Here was a cop-out, which initially thwarted any flanking movement. But a life, like a decaying tooth, will out, tracks will be found, discoveries made.

Perhaps, finally, Greene will unburden himself, for though a biographer might reveal a flaw in the old man's majesty, he is, inevitably, his subject's last disciple. Maybe others, knowing Greene, will come forward. Please, friend or enemy, get in touch, the second volume is just 60,000 words on. But do it quickly, I have only months left before I go to that leper colony in West Africa, and . . . but that is another story.

© Norman Sherry, reprinted from the Independent, *8 December 1990*

He knew he was played out and he was fearless. Most of us facing death would feel like a cornered rat. Not Greene. This last year he has been fighting for his life and knew this to be his last great battle. Tired, exhausted, frail, his body wasted, his mind, functioning like a perfectly oiled machine, was crystal clear: not a comma out of verbal place.

In 1978 I had just returned from the rain forests of Tabasco and the high mountains of Chiapas in southwest Mexico where I had found the model for his Judas figure—he who prowls sinister in *The Power and the Glory*. On return I met Graham in a tiny unassuming room in the Ritz. Upon learning that I had found *his* man 40 years afterwards in a tiny Mexican village up in the mountains he was ecstatic. I had done a sketch of Judas whom I found in a little white mountain church and as I entered the courtyard there were Mexican men within with white shirttails hanging, heads bowed and great sombreros in their hands. A rough sign asserted that "The pay for a Christian is poor but the rewards endless" and sitting alone was a dirty figure with hardened excrement on his hands.

Greene seeing this sketch in red ink spoke to me about his original coming to that village in the mountains, of how on riding a mule in those terribly precipitous hills he had finished up with ticks in his backside and had used heated beeswax to extract them. From that point we talked of the writing life and the hold it had on him. He who had often spoken of how writing allowed one to keep one's sanity said unexpectedly, "I'll die with a pen in my hand."

And that is what he did. My letters in recent months have been going back and forth at furious rate. I've known him for 17 years, and struggled with his biography for 15 and plied him, I thought, with every possible question—some answers were furtive, others cunning, others informative but not going to the heart of his matter.

So now, near the end of his life, I had tough questions still crying to be answered and Greene, fulfilling his prophesy made that Wednesday afternoon in the Ritz, tousled and tugged away at my unending questions. He ignored Mr. D while that great miscreant readied himself to fall on the greatest living writer of our generation.

He did not mind dying. He had no fear, which is a mystery to those of us who are lapsed Catholics. He looked forward to crossing his last frontier. His biographer in contrast looks upon death as a metaphysical scandal, an extraterrestrial Saddam Hussein whose great hands close down on life everywhere, hands which never cease their obscene game. He is gone. But, believers and nonbelievers, those who have loved his novels over 60 years, let me call you like the faithful to look up in the sky. If there be a star, it will be he.

© Norman Sherry, reprinted from the Guardian, *4 April 1991*

Fletcher Markle

(27 March 1921 - 22 May 1991)

See also the Markle entry in *DLB 68: Canadian Writers, 1920-1959*, First Series.

PUBLISHED WORKS: *Sometime Every Summertime*, in *Radio's Best Plays*, edited by Joseph Liss (New York: Greenberg, 1947), pp. 349-365;

Brainstorm Between Opening and Closing Announcements, in *All the Bright Company: Radio Drama Produced by Andrew Allan*, edited by Howard Fink and John Jackson (Kingston: Quarry / Toronto: CBC Enterprises, 1987), pp. 23-38.

MOTION PICTURES: *V-1: The Story of the Robot Bomb*, screenplay by Markle, British Ministry of Information, 1944;

Jigsaw, screenplay by Markle and Vincent McConnor, United Artists, 1949.

TELEVISION: *Telescope*, by Markle and others, CBC, 1963-1969;

Festival, by Markle and others, CBC, 1963-1969;

That's Hollywood, by Markle and others, ABC, 1977-1978.

RADIO: *Imagine Please*, CKWX Vancouver, 1940-1941;

"Action of the Tiger," "Another Year," "Christopher the Cricket," "Postscript to a First Love," "Presenting Mr. Charles," "This Land Is Ours," "With Heart We Sing"; adaptations of: J. Jefferson Farjeon's "The Appointed Date," W. L. George's "The Artistic Truth about Señor Pérez," Monica Marsden's "Front Page Splash," Peter J. Harkins's "This Was a Man," and Rachel Reynolds's "When Charlot Comes Home," for *Theatre Time*, CBC, 1941;

"Brainstorm Between Opening and Closing Announcements," "For the Love of Mike," "The Gilbys of Millbrook," "He and She," "Journey to Eternity," "One to Get Ready," "Simple as ABC," "There Was a Young Man" (4 parts), "They Come and Go and That's the Way It Is," and "Unfinished Blues," for *Baker's Dozen*, CBC, 1942;

Fletcher Markle (courtesy of Dorothy Markle)

"29:40", "Home Is Where You Hang Your Heart," "Great God Gadget," "A Day in the Life," "Tears, Idle Tears," "The Warrior Looks Homeward," "Who Do You Think You Are?," "Wonderful Charlie," "He and She" (enlarged version); adaptations of: Eugene O'Neill's *Ah, Wilderness!*, Prosper Mérimée's *Carmen*, Hamilton Basso's *The Great Lady*, Marcel Pagnol's *Topaze*, and Christopher Morley's *The Trojan Horse*, for *Stage*, CBC, 1944-1958;

"To Be Announced," "Sometime Every Summertime," "Blood," "Thunder and a Woman in Green," "For Future Reference," "Here's Harry," "Illusion," "Marcia," "Three's Company," "Midnight Town is Full of Boys," "The Trouble with You," and "Darling," for *Radio Folio*, CBC, 1945.

Fletcher Markle's radio dramatizations provided an introduction to literature for people of my generation. When I was in high school I learned about many works and authors through *Studio One* (1947) and the *Ford Theatre* (1948). The first production on *Studio One* was *Under the Volcano*.

As writer, actor, director, and producer Fletcher Markle enlarged the scope of radio and of his listeners. Although he went on to successes in telly and movies, his work in radio—before he was twenty-seven—properly earned him the accolade "boy wonder." His radio play *Sometime Every Summertime*, first produced in 1945, was a superb matching of talent and medium.

Much later Fletcher and I became friends when we met at a lunch and talked about the books I had discovered through him. I am grateful for that friendship—and grateful for all that he taught me.

—*M. J. B.*

Véra Nabokov
(5 January 1902 - 7 April 1991)

from DMITRI NABOKOV

For Mother's Funeral

11 April 1991

On the eve of a risky hip operation two years ago, my brave and considerate mother asked that I bring her favorite blue dress, because she might be receiving someone. I had the eerie feeling she wanted that dress for a very different reason. She survived on *that* occasion. Now, for her last earthly encounter, she was clad in that very dress.

It was Mother's wish that her ashes be united with those of Father's in the urn at the Clarens cemetery. In a curiously Nabokovian twist of things, there was some difficulty in locating that urn. My instinct was to call Mother and ask her what to do about it. But there was no Mother to ask.

I miss most, perhaps, her nightly kiss on my accident-burned little finger, her nightly warning to drive or jog carefully even if I was traveling three hundred meters, and her desire for a phone call to reassure her that I was safe at bed-time, whether I was in Montreux or on some distant continent.

I shall miss her love and tenderness for the natural kingdom and the artistic one, and wish she could comment on my style even as I speak now. I shall remember, when I told her a pelican had made its way up to the 26th floor of a Florida tower, how she said "that's a big effort for a pelican," or her comment that the heart of a rhinoceros must be pounding in panic as it ran beneath the presumably harmless aircraft that was filming it. I shall remember, too, with what joy she read the great poets—even Dante and Leopardi who wrote in a language she had not been trained in—and the evenings we spent reading to each other Pushkin or Lermontov, or Nabokov. I shall treasure the love she instilled in me for the great painters. I shall sorely miss the encyclopedic precision and splendid taste with which she assisted me on countless occasions.

Véra Nabokov was always reserved and modest about her important literary contributions. But even in her eighties she helped with the preparation of many editions of her husband's works, wrote an introduction for a Russian edition of his poems, assisted in the compilation of a collection of his letters, dedicated immense effort to the Russian translation of *Pale Fire*, and checked my first novel with a motherly but most objective eye. It is perhaps appropriate

Vladimir and Véra Nabokov (Bruccoli Collection)

that some original research of hers, in connection with Pushkin's "Queen of Spades," has just been published by Ardis in America, in a final, Nabokovian, issue of the *Russian Literature TriQuarterly*.

The saddest events seem to occur on the most beautiful days of the year. And it was almost as if Mother had held on tenaciously until the day I was to return from America and surrendered when my arrival was delayed. But when, after the dreaded phone call, I rushed back to spend Mother's last day with her, I was sure that, even though she was no longer strong enough to speak, she knew I was holding her hand and stroking her hair, and that, as her faithful companion Madame Landi put it, she expired gently, like a candle that has burned down. And while her material incarnation has now been completely reduced to ashes, I am kept buoyant by an optimism that Father, Mother, and I have long shared: although we did not participate in any for-

mal religious denomination, we have always known that things do not all end here, that pity and beauty are not wasted, and that one day we shall be rejoined.

It is sad to lose a loved one, but good to be loved. *My* love and thanks go to all those who have shown their affection by coming here today, or by writing, or by calling. A few of you have said some words. Several faithful Nabokovians have sent small statements from far away. You have already heard some of them. There are two more, which I shall now transmit to you.

Professor Stephen Jan Parker, founder of the Nabokov Society and publisher of *The Nabokovian*, writes:

On such occasions American custom asks for personal testimony—the recollection of special moments. But my memory is crowded with myriad such moments, each of them special, precious, personal. In Judaic belief it is held that personal immortality resides on this earth—in the lives of the people whom we have touched. My life, in this regard, has been profoundly marked by the grace of Véra Evseevna Nabokov—by the example of her selflessness, her concern for others, her maternal strength and wisdom, her rigorous honesty, her intellectual strength, her powers of loyalty and commitment. And those fabulous eyes—those blue, bright, radiant eyes that encompassed and sparkled and challenged—and made one glad to be in her presence, and to be alive.

Brian Boyd, who gleaned much from Mother while preparing his superb biography of Vladimir Nabokov, says:

> He dedicated his books to her; she dedicated her life to him. His genius, her loyalty, their love made a story that readers the world over will not soon forget.

Vladimir Nabokov himself, in *Speak Memory*, wrote:

> The years are passing, my dear, and presently nobody will know what you and I know. Our child is growing; the roses of Paestum, of misty Paestum, are gone; mechanically minded idiots are tinkering and tampering with the forces of nature that mild mathematicians, to their own secret surprise, appear to have foreshadowed; so perhaps it is time we examined ancient snapshots, cave drawings of trains and planes, strata of toys in the lumbered closet.

He also wrote, in a poem I have recently translated:

> Good God, in this eerie, alien world,
> letters of life, and whole lines,
> have been transposed by the typesetters. Let's fold
> our wings, my lofty angel.

Reprinted from The Nabokovian, *26 (Spring 1991).*

A TRIBUTE

from BRIAN BOYD

In the fifty-two years she was married to Vladimir Nabokov and the fourteen years she outlived him, Véra Nabokov served him at various times as agent, archivist, bibliographer, business manager, chauffeuse, cook, editor, lawyer, muse, research assistant, secretary, sharebroker, teaching assistant, translator, and typist. People who never knew her have often supposed that someone who could do so much for another person must have left little of herself. Far from it. Véra Nabokov was never meekly submissive—after learning to shoot a pistol in Germany in the early 1920s, she regularly carried one around in her purse—but always proud, determined, unbending. She showed no qualms about disagreeing with anyone, even, as tape recordings of them together show, with the husband to whom she was so devoted.

I have also served Nabokov in many capacities: as archivist, bibliographer, biographer, and critic. Véra Nabokov anticipated me in all of these. She had, for example, written an excellent synopsis of *The Gift* to interest English-language publishers in translating the book. Since the early 1920s, she had maintained scrapbooks of Nabokov's verse and prose and of reviews of his work, without which some of these fugitive pieces might have taken decades more to be discovered. She compiled a bibliography of her husband's works for the French periodical *L'Arc* in 1962, and supplemented that with much more as Dieter Zimmer, Andrew Field, Stephen Parker, and Michael Juliar began to compile their bibliographies of Nabokov.

Although she also worked in a sense as Nabokov's first biographer, keeping records of their numerous addresses in America, maintaining a diary that tracked the triumph of *Lolita*, assembling chronologies of his life for publishers and others, biography was not something she looked on with favor. Nabokov himself ends his memorial tribute to his friend Vladislav Khodasevich: "But let us turn to the poetry." For him, the work was all that mattered, all that should survive. Véra's passion for privacy—inherited from her parents, rather than learned from her husband—greatly outstripped even Nabokov's. She wanted her husband to reap all the glory she thought he deserved, but despite all she had done for his oeuvre, she wanted none of it for herself. "You would be closer to the truth, Mr. Boyd," she told me at one stage, "if you kept me right out of the biography." Once she laughed at the idea that people supposed *she* must be like her husband. "In what ways were you different, then?" I asked, hoping to elicit capsule descriptions of their characters and the distinctions between them. But instead she simply revealed herself by her reticence and her admiration: "Oh, everybody was different from *him*." The only times she would tell me about herself were when I did not have pen in hand—and would have to rush away and commit to paper all I could remember of, say, the fascinating adventures her family underwent in escaping from Bolshevized Russia in 1918-1920.

To me she showed an odd combination of formal reserve and almost maternal solicitude. Partly because of an age difference of fifty years, partly because of her wariness about biography, partly because her deafness made easy conversation impossible, we remained on surname-only terms for years, although for about fifteen months of that period I saw her every day. At the same time she worried about whether I was eating enough (she sent coffee and sandwiches down the corridor to the archive where I was working) or whether I had enough clothes (she passed on to me some of her husband's jackets and shoes, not my style or size but treasured anyway). She had read and liked several hundred pages of my critical work on Nabokov, but only when she read the first chapter of the biography did she write back on a first-name basis.

That particular instance of her reserve may have been because she was anxious that the world should realize that Nabokov was a good person as well as a good writer, and she could relax only when she felt I was not determined to impugn Nabokov's character. She herself was stern in her judgment of others, especially for any hint of cruelty (in particular toward children or animals), and rather unforgiving. As she told me once, she was inclined to see the negative side of things and people first, where her husband was much more predisposed to the positive. (I have suggested in both volumes of the biography that this may have influenced the development of Nabokov's art, from the direct radiance of the early work to a testing of that vision in the inversions of worlds like *Invitation to a Beheading* or *Lolita*.) But she too had a passion for the remembered past, a desire to see the present through the prisms of imagination, and a hope (in her case, more that than Nabokov's quiet conviction) that the future might offer something beyond

life where the treasures of the past and the present might linger on. Like her husband she also had a delight in detail (a trifle lost in translation, a vivid little dog in a Carpaccio painting, a luminous finger in La Tour, a bird's eye or tail flicking outside the window). Unlike Nabokov, she had a keen interest in politics, and she seemed half-shocked, half-delighted that he had never once voted.

Because of her poor health in her teens and early twenties, Véra saw little of high school and nothing of university. At times she was aware of her lack of formal education—she felt she had no head for abstract thinking—but more than made up for it with her love of culture and her passionate reading. One of her *dames de compagnie*, a woman of Swiss peasant stock, told me: "She doesn't know how to live. All she does every summer"—when the Nabokovs would rent a chalet in the Alps—"is sit and read."

Nabokov thought his wife had a formidable command of Russian. Her command of English could also be stunning. Though on occasion she might not quite retrieve a word she knew very well and reach for a bookish substitute no native English speaker would ever pick ("greensward" for "lawn" is one case I recall), she spoke with flair and color, and looked over the grammar, the imagery, the accuracy, and the logic of written English with an intensity that must have saved even Nabokov a few faux pas. Certainly she spotted flaws in my English and softened the blows by saying: " '*Ya pridiravus*' (I am quibbling)." She had learned Italian in her sixties in order to check the translation of her husband's verse into the language of Leopardi, and it was a stirring sight to see her in her eighties, when she could barely hold a pen, still correcting volume after volume of translations of her husband's books into French, German, or Russian, the proofs of new editions of his fact or fiction, or the interminable typescript of a new biography. She may not have been *my* muse—but she was without doubt my most exigent editor.

Isaac Bashevis Singer

(14 July 1904 - 24 July 1991)

Lawrence S. Friedman
Indiana University at Purdue University, Fort Wayne

See also the Singer entries in *DLB 6: American Novelists Since World War II*; *DLB 28: Twentieth-Century American-Jewish Fiction Writers*; and *DLB 52: American Writers for Children Since 1960: Fiction.*

BOOKS IN ENGLISH: *The Family Moskat*, translated by A. H. Gross (New York: Knopf, 1950; London: Secker & Warburg, 1966);

Satan in Goray, translated by Jacob Sloan (New York: Noonday, 1955; London: Owen, 1958);

Gimpel the Fool and Other Stories, translated by Saul Bellow and others (New York: Noonday, 1957; London: Owen, 1958);

The Magician of Lublin, translated by Elaine Gottlieb and Joseph Singer (New York: Noonday, 1960; London: Secker & Warburg, 1961);

The Spinoza of Market Street, translated by Martha Glicklich, Cecil Hemley, and others (New York: Farrar, Straus & Cudahy, 1961; London: Secker & Warburg, 1962);

The Slave, translated by Isaac Bashevis Singer and Hemley (New York: Farrar, Straus & Cudahy, 1962; London: Secker & Warburg, 1963);

Short Friday and Other Stories, translated by Joseph Singer and others (New York: Farrar, Straus & Giroux, 1964; London: Secker & Warburg, 1967);

In My Father's Court, translated by Channah Kleinerman-Goldstein, Gottlieb, and Joseph Singer (New York: Farrar, Straus & Giroux, 1966; London: Secker & Warburg, 1967);

Zlateh the Goat and Other Stories, translated by Elizabeth Shub and Isaac Bashevis Singer, illustrated by Maurice Sendak (New York: Harper & Row, 1966; Harmondsworth, U.K.: Longman, Young, 1970);

Selected Short Stories of Isaac Bashevis Singer, edited by Irving Howe (New York: Modern Library, 1966);

Mazel and Shlimazel; or, The Milk of A Lioness, translated by Shub and Isaac Bashevis Singer, illustrated by Margot Zemach (New York: Far-

Isaac Bashevis Singer (photograph copyright Jerry Bauer)

rar, Straus & Giroux, 1967; London: Cape, 1979);

The Manor, translated by Joseph Singer and Gottlieb (New York: Farrar, Straus & Giroux, 1967; London: Secker & Warburg, 1968);

The Fearsome Inn, translated by Shub and Isaac Bashevis Singer, illustrated by Nonny Hogrogian (New York: Scribners, 1967; London: Collins, 1970);

When Shlemiel Went to Warsaw and Other Stories, translated by Isaac Bashevis Singer and Shub, illustrated by Zemach (New York: Farrar, Straus & Giroux, 1968;

Harmondsworth, U.K.: Longman, Young, 1974);

The Séance and Other Stories, translated by Roger H. Klein, Hemley, and others (New York: Farrar, Straus & Giroux, 1968; London: Cape, 1970);

A Day of Pleasure: Stories of a Boy Growing Up in Warsaw, translated by Kleinerman-Goldstein and others, illustrated with contemporary photographs by Roman Vishniac (New York: Farrar, Straus & Giroux, 1969; London: MacRae, 1980);

The Estate, translated by Joseph Singer, Gottlieb, and Shub (New York: Farrar, Straus & Giroux, 1969; London: Cape, 1970);

Joseph and Koza; or, The Sacrifice to the Vistula, translated by Isaac Bashevis Singer and Shub, illustrated by Symeon Shimin (New York: Farrar, Straus & Giroux, 1970);

Elijah the Slave, translated by Isaac Bashevis Singer and Elizabeth Shub, illustrated by Antonio Frasconi (New York: Farrar, Straus & Giroux, 1970);

A Friend of Kafka and Other Stories, translated by Isaac Bashevis Singer, Elizabeth Shub, and others (New York: Farrar, Straus & Giroux, 1970; London: Cape, 1972);

An Isaac Bashevis Singer Reader (New York: Farrar, Straus & Giroux, 1971);

Alone in the Wild Forest, translated by Isaac Bashevis Singer and Shub, illustrated by Zemach (New York: Farrar, Straus & Giroux, 1971);

The Topsy-Turvy Emperor of China, translated by Isaac Bashevis Singer and Shub, illustrated by William Pène du Bois (New York & London: Harper & Row, 1971);

Enemies, A Love Story, translated by Aliza Shevrin and Shub (New York: Farrar, Straus & Giroux, 1972; London: Cape, 1972);

The Wicked City, translated by Isaac Bashevis Singer and Shub, illustrated by Leonard Everett Fisher (New York: Farrar, Straus & Giroux, 1972);

A Crown of Feathers and Other Stories, translated by Isaac Bashevis Singer, Lauru Colwin, and others (New York: Farrar, Straus & Giroux, 1973; London: Cape, 1974);

The Hasidim, with Ira Moskowitz (New York: Crown, 1973);

The Fools of Chelm and Their History, translated by Isaac Bashevis Singer and Shub, illustrated by Uri Shulevitz (New York: Farrar, Straus & Giroux, 1973);

Why Noah Chose the Dove, translated by Shub, illustrated by Eric Carle (New York: Farrar, Straus & Giroux, 1974);

Passions and Other Stories, translated by Isaac Bashevis Singer and others (New York: Farrar, Straus & Giroux, 1975; London: Cape, 1976);

A Tale of Three Wishes, illustrated by Irene Lieblich (New York: Farrar, Straus & Giroux, 1975);

A Little Boy in Search of God; or Mysticism in a Personal Light, with Moskowitz, translated by Joseph Singer (Garden City, N.Y.: Doubleday, 1976);

Naftali the Storyteller and His Horse, Sus, and Other Stories, translated by Joseph Singer, Isaac Bashevis Singer, and others, illustrated by Zemach (New York: Farrar, Straus & Giroux, 1976; Oxford: Oxford University Press, 1977);

A Young Man in Search of Love, translated by Joseph Singer (Garden City, N.Y.: Doubleday, 1978);

Shosha, translated by Joseph Singer and Isaac Bashevis Singer (New York: Farrar, Straus & Giroux, 1978; London: Cape, 1979);

Old Love, translated by Joseph Singer, Isaac Bashevis Singer, and others (New York: Farrar, Straus & Giroux, 1979; London: Cape, 1980);

Nobel Lecture (New York: Farrar, Straus & Giroux, 1979; London: Cape, 1979);

Reaches of Heaven: A Story of Baal Shem Tov (New York: Farrar, Straus & Giroux, 1980);

The Power of Light: Eight Stories for Hanukkah, illustrated by Lieblich (New York: Farrar, Straus & Giroux, 1980);

Lost in America (Garden City, N.Y.: Doubleday, 1981);

The Collected Stories (New York: Farrar, Straus & Giroux, 1982; London: Cape, 1982);

The Golem, illustrated by Uri Shulevitz (New York: Farrar, Straus & Giroux, 1982; London: Deutsch, 1983);

Yentl the Yeshiva Boy, translated by Marion Magid and Elizabeth Pollet (New York: Farrar, Straus & Giroux, 1983);

The Penitent (New York: Farrar, Straus & Giroux, 1983; London: Cape, 1984);

Love & Exile: A Memoir (Garden City, N.Y.: Doubleday, 1984; London: Cape, 1985);

Stories for Children (New York: Farrar, Straus & Giroux, 1984);

The Image and Other Stories (New York: Farrar, Straus & Giroux, 1985; London: Cape, 1986);

Gifts (Philadelphia: Jewish Publication Society, 1985);

The Death of Methuselah and Other Stories (New York: Farrar, Straus & Giroux, 1987; London: Cape, 1988);

The King of the Fields (New York: Farrar, Straus & Giroux, 1988; London: Cape, 1988);

Scum (New York: Farrar, Straus & Giroux, 1991; London: Cape, 1991).

With Isaac Bashevis Singer's death on 24 July 1991 in Surfside, Florida, the Yiddish language lost its most eloquent voice, and the vanished world of Jewish Poland lost its most evocative memorialist. Author of more than thirty books—all in Yiddish, the language of his Warsaw childhood—he achieved international fame with the translation of his works, first into English, eventually into many other languages as well. The widespread appeal of his writing, evidenced by his many literary awards, including the 1978 Nobel Prize, came despite his lifelong devotion to a dying language and a shattered culture. A self-styled curator of a sociology engulfed by the Holocaust, Singer was also a consummate artist whose historicity was rarely an end in itself. The Nobel Prize citation praised his "impassioned narratives, which, with roots in a Polish-Jewish cultural tradition, bring universal human conditions to life."

Isaac Bashevis Singer was born on 14 July 1904 to Bathsheba Zylberman Singer in Leoncin, Poland, a provincial town northeast of Warsaw. Pinhos-Mendel, Singer's father, was a Hasidic rabbi whose ecstatic pietism was tempered by the no less pious rationalism of his wife, herself the descendant of a rabbinical line from Bilgoray, an obscure village in eastern Poland. When Singer was four, his family moved to Warsaw where his father established a rabbinical court on Krochmalna Street. Teeming with Jewish life—and low-life—Krochmalna Street would be the nexus of Singer's many literary evocations of Warsaw settings. *In My Father's Court* (1966), Singer's memoir of his first eighteen years, recalls an upbringing of material poverty offset by spiritual wealth. Imbued with his father's belief that the world outside their shabby quarters was *tref* (unclean), the ten-year-old Singer first confronted an opposing worldview when he visited the artist's studio of his elder brother, Israel Joshua. The powerful contrast between his brother's secular rationalism and his father's pious religiosity created the moral dialectic upon which much of Singer's fiction is based.

In 1917 Singer accompanied his mother to Bilgoray, where, far from the worldliness of Warsaw, he would spend four crucially formative years. So remote was Bilgoray that it had remained virtually unchanged for hundreds of years. There, recalled Singer, in a "world of old Jewishness I found a spiritual treasure trove.... Time seemed to flow backwards. I lived Jewish history." Yet it was also in Bilgoray that Singer first read August Strindberg, Ivan Turgenev, Leo Tolstoy, Guy de Maupassant, and Anton Chekhov in Yiddish translations provided by post-World War I American aid to Polish villages. The writer who most shook his Jewish orthodoxy, however, was Benedict de Spinoza, whose philosophy "created a turmoil" in Singer's brain. Several of Singer's fictional heroes are similarly disturbed, torn between traditional belief and Spinozistic skepticism.

In 1921 Singer enrolled at the Tachkemoni Rabbinical Seminary in Warsaw at the behest of his parents. Soon bored with his studies, however, he gave them up to work as a translator and proofreader for *Literarische Bletter*, a Yiddish literary magazine which published his first stories. Undoubtedly Singer's transformation from rabbinical student into secular writer was greatly influenced by the example of his older brother. Still, the decision to live by writing may also have reflected an erosion of religious faith as well as the heady intellectual ambience of Warsaw, then the center of the Yiddish literary world. After a brief flirtation with Hebrew, Singer elected to write exclusively in Yiddish, the language of the Jewish masses. In 1932 he became an editor of *Globus*, a Yiddish literary journal which serialized his first novel, *Satan in Goray*, in 1934. A demon-ridden tale of messianic fanaticism set in seventeenth-century Poland, *Satan in Goray* "could never have been written," admitted Singer, "without having lived in Bilgoray." With its exotic setting and equally exotic characters wed to a modern critical sensibility, *Satan in Goray* anticipates a good deal of Singer's subsequent fiction.

By the mid 1930s a combination of public and personal events made life in Warsaw increasingly uncongenial for Singer. Added to the growing menace of Nazism and the worsening conditions for Polish Jewry was the breakup of Singer's family. His father had died in 1929; his mother

First page of the 25 February 1955 issue of the New York Yiddish-language newspaper Forverts, *featuring the first installment of "mayn tatns bezdn-shtub" (My Father's Rabbinical Court). Singer's memoir of his father was translated into English and published in 1966 as* In My Father's Court *(courtesy of YIVO Institute for Jewish Research).*

and younger brother remained in Galicia; his married sister was in England; and Israel Joshua, his revered older brother, had emigrated to the United States. Moreover, Runya, the mother of the only child Singer would ever sire, and a fervent Communist, was preparing to depart with their son, Israel, born in 1929, for the U.S.S.R. So in 1935 Singer followed his older brother to New York where Israel Joshua had permanently settled. There he began writing for the *Jewish Daily Forward*, a Yiddish newspaper to which he contributed regularly for the rest of his life. It was in the *Forward* that the great majority of his stories and novels first appeared prior to their translation and publication in book form.

At first Singer was depressed about the future of Yiddish in America: "for five or six or maybe seven years I couldn't write a word," he later recalled. But his association with the *Forward*, his widening circle of Jewish friends and acquaintances, and especially his 1940 marriage to Alma Haimann, a German émigré, lightened his outlook. In 1943, the year he became a U.S. citizen, his creative impasse was broken with five new short stories which were published along with a new Yiddish edition of *Satan in Goray*. Among the stories is one of Singer's masterpieces, "The Destruction of Kreshev," a terrifying account of demonic possession on the order of *Satan in Goray*. In the story, the eerily prescient Holocaust imagery of the novel is again present, this time intensified by its evocation of actual events. Similar end-of-the-world scenarios fusing God's wrath and Jewish devastation recur in several of Singer's most powerful later works.

The Family Moskat (1950), the first novel Singer wrote in the United States, was a radical departure from the surrealistic *Satan in Goray*. A sweeping panorama of East European family life, *The Family Moskat* is a Jewish version of Thomas Mann's *Buddenbrooks* (1901), a novel which Singer had translated into Yiddish shortly before leaving Warsaw. It is equally a homage to Israel Joshua, whose most famous novels were also long family chronicles. Singer began *The Family Moskat* in 1945, the year after Israel Joshua's untimely death, dedicating the novel "to my late brother, I. J. Singer, author of *The Brothers Ashkanazi*. To me he was not only the older brother, but a spiritual father and master as well." Similarly indebted to Israel Joshua and again serving to perpetuate his memory was another chronicle of Jewish family life, so huge that it ran in the *Forward* for two years (1953-1955), and its eventual publication in English translation required two volumes: *The Manor* (1967) and *The Estate* (1969). Taken together these novels extend Singer's historical panorama backwards, opening in 1863 and closing in the early years of the twentieth century when *The Family Moskat*, which concludes with Hitler's 1939 invasion of Poland, begins.

Although an English translation of *The Family Moskat* had been published to enthusiastic reviews in 1950, it was Saul Bellow's masterful translation of "Gimpel the Fool" in the May 1953 *Partisan Review* that brought Singer to the attention of a wider audience. One of Singer's greatest and lastingly popular stories, "Gimpel the Fool" features the sort of simple but pious man already established in Yiddish literature by Sholem Aleichem. The idea that simple piety is the Jews' best defense against worldly corruption is equally the point of "The Old Man" and "The Little Shoemakers," two more of Singer's finest tales in *Gimpel the Fool and Other Stories* (1957). This first of his many volumes of short fiction is often singled out as evidence that Singer was at his best as a short-story writer.

To the virtue of piety Singer added another of his recurrent themes—the value of repentance—in two novels of spiritual redemption: *The Magician of Lublin* (1960) and *The Slave* (1962). Their heroes succumb to worldly temptation symbolized by liaisons with Gentile women, but ultimately regain their spiritual equilibrium through willed acts of expiation. Like nearly all of Singer's fiction, these two novels make it clear that spiritual fulfillment may be achieved solely within the matrix of traditional Jewish belief. Yet Singer himself maintained that religion required neither dogma nor revelation. Although he never lost his belief in God, he personally scorned the very orthodoxy that his fiction valorizes. Nevertheless he habitually distrusted secular philosophies and social panaceas; and his fiction is often based upon the collision between old and new orthodoxies. The three short-story collections of the 1960s—*The Spinoza of Market Street* (1961), *Short Friday and Other Stories* (1964), and *The Séance and Other Stories* (1968)—echo the moral concerns of the novels. Typical of their subject matter are two harrowing tales in *Short Friday*: "Blood" and "Zeidlus the Pope." In the former, blood lust leads a woman from animal slaughter to adultery to Christian conversion. Her loss of humanity, symbolized by her eventual transformation into a werewolf, is the logical culmination of her initial renunciation of the spirit for the flesh. In "Zeidlus the Pope" the title character, flushed with intellectual pride, abandons the rigors of Judaism for the imagined rewards of Christianity and ends up blind and destitute in the grip of Satan, who drags him off to hell. These tales of damnation are leavened by ones such as "Short Friday," which ends with the death of a simple, pious, and loving couple who ascend together to Paradise.

Short Friday and Other Stories is also noteworthy for Singer's first use of American settings. Thus two masterful stories, "Alone" and "A Wedding in Brownsville," retain Singer's familiar characters (Polish Jews) and style (an amalgam of the real and the supernatural) but are located in Miami Beach and New York respectively. And while Judaism is understandably even more diluted in postwar America than it was in prewar Poland, the heroes of both stories are saved by acts of faith. American settings grow increasingly common in the story collections of the 1970s, as does Singer's reliance on first-person (often autobiographical) narration. Jewish refugees from eastern Europe, many of them concentration camp survivors, frequent the stories in *A Friend of Kafka and Other Stories* (1970), one-third of which deal with immigrants to the United States "The Cafeteria," located in Singer's own Upper West Side New York neighborhood and told in the first person, is typical in its setting, characterization, and narration. Although its apparent subject is Esther, a concentration camp survivor, "The Cafeteria" reveals as much about its author's life in the 1960s as it does about hers. Half of the stories in the 1973 collection, *A Crown of Feathers*, deal with life in America in an increasingly personal manner. In "A Day in Coney Island," for example, a recognizably autobiographical account of Singer's adventures in Brooklyn shortly after his arrival in the United States is given only the thinnest of fictional patinas.

In the 1975 collection, *Passions*, some of the stories recount the adventures of a middle-aged Jewish writer, transparently Singer himself. And *Old Love* (1979), the last short-story collection of the 1970s, again mirrors the life of its aging author. It is also in this volume that Singer reiterated and expanded a favorite theme: the value of love, notably in its redemptive capacity. But now it is, as Singer confessed in his author's note, the "love of the old and the middle-aged that is recurring more and more in my works of fiction." Of course Singer's view that "the young are just beginners and that the art of loving matures with age and experience" reflected not only the mainly autobiographical subject matter of *Passions* and *Old Love* but the ripe years of their author/protagonist.

As Singer came to rely more and more heavily on bits of his life to sustain his stories and novels of the 1970s, the line between fiction and autobiography became blurred. Indeed, many ostensibly fictional episodes mirror ones portrayed in Singer's several volumes of memoirs. The first and richest of these volumes, *In My Father's Court*, Singer called a "literary experiment," an attempt "to combine two styles—that of memoirs and that of belles-lettres." Its deliberate blurring of literary genres not only mirrored the technique of much of his fiction but had an identical purpose: to portray "a life and environment that no longer exist and are unique." Subsequent volumes of memoirs recall Singer's early childhood, adolescence, and sexual initiation (*A Little Boy in Search of God*, 1976); his further liaisons with women and his initial literary successes (*A Young Man in Search of Love*, 1978); and his lonely and depressed early years in New York (*Lost in America*, 1981). More than *In My Father's Court*, the three later volumes reflect real-life episodes that reappear thinly veiled as fiction in which Singer figures either as his own protagonist or as the faithful confidant and recorder of other people's stories.

Shosha (1978), which memorializes the prewar Jewish community of Warsaw on the eve of its destruction, is Singer's most self-reflexive novel. His only novel written entirely in the first person, *Shosha* merely fictionalizes the autobiographical contents of *A Young Man in Search of Love*, published in the same year. Aaron Greidinger, the writer-hero of *Shosha* and Singer's alter ego, memorizes every sight and sound before fleeing Warsaw, so that his work, like Singer's, will have the power to reanimate the vanished past. But the most powerful Singer novel of the 1970s is *Enemies, A Love Story* (1972), which succeeds despite—or perhaps because of—its muting of autobiography. The first of Singer's novels to be set in the United States, *Enemies* was also the first to focus on the Holocaust survivors who would largely people his subsequent fiction. Among the protagonists of Singer's novels, only Herman Broder of *Enemies* spends World War II entirely in Poland; and no other Singer novel is so relentlessly determined by the Holocaust and its aftermath. Broder is a post-Holocaust version of Asa Heshel Bannet, the hero of *The Family Moskat*, and like him (and Singer) is a former rabbinical student. Two faces of the quintessential Singer protagonist, Broder and Bannet are alienated from God and helpless without him. They trade traditional Judaism for mindless hedonism in the cynical belief that lust is the common denominator of human behavior. Both men routinely betray women, father unwanted children, alternate between spasms of frenetic but aimless activity and periods of near paralysis, and simply disappear at the end of their respective novels. And both sporadically yearn for the redemption which they know can be achieved only by returning to the traditional Judaism which simultaneously attracts and repels them. In their loss of faith that triggers existential angst, in their essential loneliness and homelessness, in their ultimately unresolved or incomplete identities, Broder and Bannet most powerfully typify the modern Jewish intellectual of Singer's fiction.

Although Broder and Bannet victimize themselves, as Jews they are equally the victims of a history epitomized most terribly by the Holocaust. The tragic knowledge that the Jewish community of Poland was snuffed out by Hitler is never far from the surface of Singer's fiction. The shadow of the Holocaust looms even over *Satan in Goray* and *The Slave* (1962), novels set in the remote past. Historically, Singer's Polish fiction terminates in 1939 with the Nazi bombardment of War-

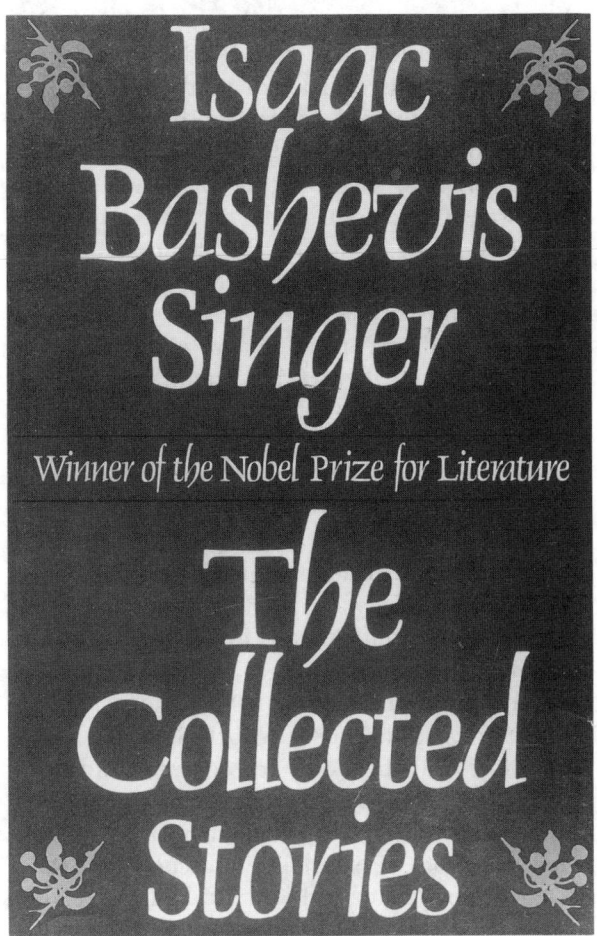

Dust jacket for Singer's 1982 selection of his stories

saw that closes *The Family Moskat*. And the subsequent decimation of the Jewish community is reflected in the typical dramatis personae—holocaust survivors—of his American settings. Branded permanently by the Holocaust, these "lucky" few are likely to regard themselves as the living dead. Thus even Dr. Solomon Margolin, the respected and affluent hero of "A Wedding in Brownsville," is a burned-out case: "Hitler's carnage and the extinction of his family had rooted out his last hope for better days, had destroyed all his faith in humanity." Such chronic despair afflicts many of Singer's Holocaust survivors, some of whom—like Masha, who kills herself in *Enemies*—can see little reason for living.

The hopelessness engendered by suffering and loss often evokes in Singer's Holocaust survivors the same contempt for an unclean world that his father incessantly professed in Warsaw. They read the Holocaust as the awful culmination of the many persecutions that constitute Jewish history. Its lesson powerfully seconds Rabbi

Pinhos-Mendel Singer's certainty that the invariably hostile world beyond his balcony (i.e., beyond the precinct of Jewishness) must be shunned as well as feared. Intimations of extinction die slowly if at all for Holocaust survivors, aging refugees who encounter in the Manhattan of Singer's fiction a world in which the dress and customs, the Yiddish language, and the religious beliefs of Jews seem barely to exist. Enveloped by a dominant secular culture—which seems to consist as often of American Jews as of Gentiles—refugees typically and pitifully cling to the vestigial remnants of a shattered past. As they witness the headlong secularization of American Jews, the fear arises in Singer's Holocaust survivors that the annihilation of the Jewish people so nearly accomplished by Hitler will be completed in the United States. It is no wonder that the refugees are prone to forget what Singer in his Nobel Prize address identified as the characteristic Jewish outlook incarnated in the Yiddish language: "gratitude for every day of life, every crumb of success, each encounter of love ... It does not demand and command but it muddles through, sneaks by, smuggles itself amidst the powers of destruction, knowing somewhere that God's plan for creation is still at the very beginning."

Singer's own attitude toward the God who is rarely absent from his fiction was ambivalent. While disclaiming religious dogma and revelation, he was unwavering in his belief in God's existence: "The belief in God is as necessary as sex. Whatever you call him—nature or higher power—doesn't matter. The power that takes care of you, and the farthest star, all this is God." Yet Singer's fiction depicts a world in which a silent God perpetrates or at least permits actions inexplicable to victims who must "do all the guesswork" about why they suffer. And the evidence of history powerfully suggests that God has betrayed his chosen people: "The Almighty keeps promising things, and He doesn't keep his word. What hasn't He promised us Jews!" In the end, Singer's Jews, like Singer himself, can only fall back on the commonplace that God works in mysterious ways. If they are to maintain their faith in God despite what appears to be divine indifference if not callousness, they must take the long view of history: "It took him 2,000 years to get us to Israel."

Although God may reward believers—such as the pious couple of "Short Friday" who die and ascend to heaven together—and punish transgressors—such as the title character in "Zeidlus the Pope" whose apostasy earns him hell—the world he presides over in Singer's fiction is characteristically evil. Symptomatic and symbolic of worldly evil is betrayal, nearly the quintessential human act for Singer: "I would say a great part of human history is a history of self-betrayal and betrayal of others." Given that history, some of his protagonists opt out of it. Men who have their own share of betrayals to live down turn their backs on the world in conscious acts of penance. So disenchanted grows Yasha Mazur, the hero of *The Magician of Lublin* (1960), that he ends up having himself bricked into a doorless hut whose one tiny window provides his only outside contact. He renames himself Jacob the Penitent, reverts to traditional Jewish dress, and dedicates himself to holy scripture. But it is Joseph Shapiro, the title character of *The Penitent* (1983), who rails most endlessly against worldliness. A Holocaust survivor who has won material success at the expense of moral failure, Shapiro grows terminally disillusioned with secular life in postwar New York. *The Penitent* is cast in the form of his extended diatribe against the spiritual malaise of the modern world. Unlike Mazur, whose penitence took the form of self-imprisonment as the only guarantee against worldly temptation, Shapiro elects to return to the sanctified Jewish past by emigrating to Israel and leading a traditional Jewish life. Yet Israel too is infected by the incubus of worldliness against which Shapiro can protect himself only by keeping to the ultraorthodox Meah Shearim district of Jerusalem. Singer's bitterest indictment of modernity, *The Penitent* is also a restatement of a central theme of his fiction: that only by living a life consistent with traditional values can a Jew retain his essential identity in a fallen world.

Joseph Shapiro's spiritual rebirth incarnates the value system at the heart of an invariably moral fiction. For Singer, the human soul is a battlefield where forces of good and evil eternally war. A typical character is born into a traditional Jewish home, is seduced by worldly aspirations, and is either saved or damned according to whether he abandons or persists in waywardness. While the Holocaust forever cancels the possibility of actually returning home, the penitent can, like Shapiro, do so symbolically. Shapiro explains that *Der Baal Tschuve* (the Yiddish title of *The Penitent*) "means one who returns—I came back home." In deliberately reenacting the age-old story of the prodigal son, such penitents regain those moral values expressed by "Jewishness." Thus the sexuality, criminality, and demonology

which fill Singer's pages and unnerve his orthodox Jewish critics are portrayed as deviations from the normative ideals of piety and humility. Irving Howe judged Singer to have remained faithful to the values traditionally celebrated by Yiddish writers: "The virtue of powerlessness, the power of helplessness, the company of the dispossessed, the sanctity of the insulted and the injured—these finally, are the great themes of Yiddish literature."

The full sweep of Singer's treatment of these and other themes is best appreciated via *The Collected Stories* (1982), his personal selection of forty-seven of the more than one hundred stories he had previously published in eight separate volumes. Perhaps reflecting his theory that only in the short story can a writer attain perfection, this volume contains much of his best work. *The Collected Stories* was hailed by critics as the single volume most emblematic of the literary values for which Singer had won the Nobel Prize. Not that any additional proof of his merit was required. For, unlike many Nobel laureates whose best work was belatedly recognized and long past, Singer had maintained a remarkably high level of output and achievement over half a century. The Nobel Prize neither rescued him from obscurity nor dramatically multiplied his readership. Already a world-famous writer whose work was widely available in translation, Singer viewed the award as a tribute to Yiddish and to its speakers rather than a means of personal aggrandizement. In honoring him, therefore, the Swedish Academy honored a people and a way of life immortalized by his fiction.

In 1966, already world famous for his novels and stories, Singer published his first children's book, *Zlateh the Goat and Other Stories*. Consisting partly of folktales recollected from his Polish childhood and partly of the by-product of his rich fantasy life, this volume and its several successors evolved naturally from the aesthetic of his adult fiction. The demons and devils that haunt *Satan in Goray*, even the lovers of *The Slave*, find their counterparts in the children's stories. Indeed Singer often maintained, not entirely facetiously, that in an era "when literature is losing its address and the telling of stories is becoming a forgotten art, children are the best readers." *A Day of Pleasure: Stories of a Boy Growing Up in Warsaw* (1969), an autobiographical account of Singer's first fourteen years taken largely from *In My Father's Court*, won him his first National Book Award (a second came for *A Crown of Feathers and*

Other Stories). Accepting the award for *A Day of Pleasure*, Singer enumerated "only ten" of the "five hundred reasons why I write for children," in the exact words he would repeat on 10 December 1978 at the banquet in Stockholm's City Hall following the Nobel award ceremony. The list recapitulates his lifelong advocacy of story telling as the primary raison d'être of fiction. Because children have no use for literary critics, psychology, or sociology; because they read not to alleviate their guilt or to decipher impossibly obscure texts; because they still believe in God, the family, and the supernatural; and perhaps most of all because they "love interesting stories," Singer argued that children were his best readers.

The success of his children's books reflects the scope of Singer's popular as well as critical acclaim. Several of his works were adapted for stage and screen, with varying degrees of success. With Eve Friedman, Singer turned his story "Teibele and Her Demon" into a 1979 play which closed after two dozen Broadway performances. "A Play for the Devil," written for the stage, was performed Off Broadway in 1984. "Yentl the Yeshiva Boy," a short story blown up into a 1983 wide-screen musical vehicle for Barbra Streisand as Yentl, got lukewarm reviews and a disparaging notice from Singer himself. Perhaps the most artistic cinematic adaptation of a Singer work is Paul Mazursky's 1989 version of *Enemies, A Love Story*, which won nearly unanimous critical, if not popular, acclaim.

Two weeks after his death, Singer was affectionately remembered by Israel Shenker, a writer and former reporter for the *New York Times*. Shenker recalled their first interview in 1968 at the Jewish dairy restaurant where Singer, a longtime vegetarian, took many of his meals. About the author who would go on to write thirty books and innumerable short stories and to win the Nobel Prize, Shenker was struck by his "peculiar relationship to God: man to Man, personal and frank, sometimes unforgiving." Although God too often failed to keep his word—especially to the Jews—Singer remained grateful for his gift of the "many fantasies" that made writing a joy rather than a chore. Singer's "mind teemed with eternal questions and with plain-spoken answers," remembered Shenker. "In talk and in writing he was forthright and intense, not a tentative rose water soul given to pallid thought and half-hearted expression." To Shenker, Singer "appeared inoffensive and vulnerable"—like the typical Jew of his fiction. The "odds-on-favorite" in

the event of "a contest for the palest, least colorful man on New York's Upper West Side," Singer was as dynamic intellectually as he was unprepossessing physically. "Part prophet, part scold, writer of genius, ironist, pessimist and cynic," Singer "conveyed . . . the burden of experience shaped by trials, transformed by imagination, weighted by reflection, leavened by humor."

What Singer achieved transcends even the imposing task—to memorialize a vanished people in a vanishing language—that he assigned to his work. He was more than "the recorder of a lost world, the preserver of a vanished sociology," maintained the author Cynthia Ozick in her 1982 *New York Times* review of *The Collected Stories of Isaac Bashevis Singer*. His faithful reproductions of the Jewish past "are only seeds for his febrile conflagrations." No mere curator, Singer was rather "an artist and transcendent inventor," Ozick concluded. Ultimately, Singer's achievement was the very one that he claimed for the serious writer. In his Nobel Prize acceptance speech he argued that in the writer—whose pessimism like his own "is not decadence but a mighty passion for the redemption of man"—is vested the hope of rescuing civilization. While the writer must never forget his primary obligation to entertain, he must seek eternal truths as well. Only the persistence of hope, continued Singer, sustained Jews like himself whose people have endured endless persecution. And new hopes always arose to convince him that humanity may yet be redeemed; and that the writer, indistinguishable from the prophet in the Jewish tradition, may point the way to "new horizons and new perspectives—philosophical, religious, aesthetical, and even social."

Bibliography:

Jackson R. Bryer and Paul E. Rockwell, "Isaac Bashevis Singer in English: A Bibliography," in *Critical Views of Isaac Bashevis Singer*, edited by Irving Malin (New York: New York University Press, 1968), pp. 220-265.

References:

Edward Alexander, *Isaac Bashevis Singer* (Boston: Twayne, 1980);

Marcia Allentuck, ed., *The Achievement of Isaac Bashevis Singer* (Carbondale: Southern Illinois University Press, 1969);

Irving H. Buchen, *Isaac Bashevis Singer and the Eternal Past* (New York: New York University

Dust jacket for Singer's 1991 novel, the last to be translated and published before his death

Press / London: University of London Press, 1968);

Lawrence S. Friedman, *Understanding Isaac Bashevis Singer* (Columbia: University of South Carolina Press, 1988);

Paul Kresh, *Isaac Bashevis Singer: The Magician of West 86th Street* (New York: Dial, 1979);

Irving Malin, *Isaac Bashevis Singer* (New York: Ungar, 1972);

Malin, ed., *Critical Views of Isaac Bashevis Singer* (New York: New York University Press, 1969);

David Neal Miller, *Fear of Fiction: Narrative Strategies in the Works of Isaac Bashevis Singer* (Albany: State University of New York Press, 1985);

Sanford Pinsker, "The Fictive Worlds of I. B. Singer," *Critique*, 11 (1969): 26-39;

Israel Schenker, "The Man Who Talked Back to God," *New York Times Book Review*, 11 August 1991;

Ben Siegel, *Isaac Bashevis Singer* (Minneapolis: University of Minnesota Press, 1969);

Clive Sinclair, *The Brothers Singer* (London: Allison & Busby, 1983);

Isaac Bashevis Singer and Richard Burgin, *Conversations with Isaac Bashevis Singer* (Garden City, N.Y.: Doubleday, 1985);

Singer and Irving Howe, "Yiddish Tradition vs. Jewish Tradition: A Dialogue," *Midstream*, 19 (1973): 33-38.

A TRIBUTE

from IRVIN FAUST

Isaac Bashevis Singer has, of course, left his literary and cultural imprint on us all, but he is especially valid and necessary to those writers based in New York City. His essence remains strong on the Upper West Side, on Broadway, Amsterdam Avenue, on Sherman and Verdi Squares. I, for one, will always be grateful that he lived and worked here (I say that, too, for my father, who was an avid reader of the *Forward*). Much of my own work deals with the clash of cultures in this terrific, impossible town, so, as I think about it, I am part of a literary chain that gained permanency, if not birth, from Singer. The rush to America's gateway continues; the clashing, the internal and external conflicts are as tough as ever; as fine as Abe Cahan and Henry Roth were in capturing them, I. B. Singer remains the great one, the writer who consistently spun art from lives we thought were humdrum.

A TRIBUTE

from DANIEL FUCHS

One gorgeous story after the other, set in the old country; in Sea Gate at the tip of Brooklyn, where the ocean liners go by; on Manhattan's Upper Broadway, in the restaurants and apartment buildings; in the Miami golden *medina*—that is what I. B. Singer did all his lifetime, without pause, a wellspring, a Yiddish Charles Dickens. He made a rich tumbling world of his own. At times he was smug and a little wearying in his perfection, but always there was the scent of holiness over his people, to redeem him and exalt them—the mystics and scholars, the merchants, go-betweens and matchmakers; the wonderful luxurious middle-aged widows and sweethearts, the forever insatiable middle-aged gentlemen. Someday, five years from now or ten, they will be all put on the stage, the stories brought together, artfully composed (probably by the BBC), and it will be a wonder.

A TRIBUTE

from SANFORD PINSKER

For Isaac Bashevis Singer, the assorted -isms that professors value—Freudianism, symbolism, cubism, surrealism, and countless others—were very much beside the literary point. What a story needs, he kept insisting, is an "address," a place where a reader could imagine sending a letter. After all, nobody can address anything to characters who do not live in a specific place (a country, a city, a street, an apartment number) and who do not resemble human beings. And nobody will be interested in a story if it looks like somebody else's story, or worse, as if it had been written by a committee of famous writers, English professors, and literary critics. No, Singer insisted again and again, a story must begin with an author who really believes that he or she is the only one who could tell this story.

At the same time, however, when Singer visited my classes at Franklin and Marshall College, he did not want to give students the impression that writing was easy. As he pointed out, even with a good story in your head, a beginning writer needs a friend. Not a parent, not a boy- or girlfriend, not even a kindly, encouraging teacher. No, a young writer needs to make friends with his or her wastebasket, to fill it up with pages until it is overflowing; and then to empty it and fill it up again.

This Singer is, of course, familiar to those lucky enough to have heard him lecture and field questions from the audience. It is also the Singer that has been the subject of several television documentaries. He was a charmer of the first water, the sort of person who could pull memorable quips out of his pocket like breath mints. Indeed, not since Mark Twain has an American writer been such a darling of journalists, academic critics, and perhaps most of all, common readers.

However, the best illustration of how strongly Singer felt about keeping stories at an arm's distance from external interferences may be an anecdote that, so far as I know, never became part of his public shtick: It seems that Singer was once invited to read a story to a group of Yiddishists in

Brooklyn. They begged him to come, even though they were too poor to be able to pay him. But, their spokesman argued, at least he would be among *landsmen*, people who understand Yiddish, and not like what happens when he visits fancy-shmancy colleges and people make fun of his accent. As Singer put it to me, "What could I do? These are old people (as if he were not!), so I went. The cab ride to Brooklyn cost me thirty-five dollars. And when I finally arrived, who was there?—maybe twelve people altogether. So, I read them a new story.

"No sooner am I finished than the first person gets up and says the following: 'This is not a good story. This is not a Zionist story. I spit on your story.' And he proceeded to spit on the floor in anger, and then to sit down. At that point the next person gets up and says: 'This is not a good story. This is not an Orthodox story. This is a dirty story, so I also spit on your story.' And like the first man, he spit on the floor in anger and sat down. Others objected that the story was not a 'socialist' story or a 'nice' story or even a properly 'Yiddish' story; but about one thing they agreed: it was definitely not a *good* story. In fact, one man spit on the story twice— once because it was not a Zionist story and once because it was not an Orthodox story. So, from twelve people I collected thirteen spits!"

This seemed an excellent opportunity for me to remind Singer that he is hardly the first artist who could number himself among the misunderstood; but only a fool would interrupt an I. B. Singer anecdote. Besides, I was anxious to find out what he said to his antagonists. I didn't have to wait long. "So, I told them," he began, "it cost me thirty-five dollars to the taxi to get here and it will cost me another thirty-five dollars to get home. Already a clear loss of seventy dollars! Now I am giving thirty dollars to your treasurer, so it will be a hundred dollars. And why am I giving him so much money. I will tell you. So that he can buy writing paper and pencils for each of you. You should go home immediately and write stories. Then when you have your next meeting you will have exactly the stories you want. And better than this, you won't have to call me anymore!"

On afternoons when I grow weary of the demands some readers make for stories about "representative" (that is, happy, well-adjusted, politically correct) Jews or blacks or feminists or Hispanics or gays or whatever, I remember Singer's words, and find myself pulling one of his books from the shelf. It doesn't take long before you are transported to a world where the faces one meets are simultaneously strange and familiar. Great stories have always packed precisely that power, and whatever else he might have been, Isaac Bashevis Singer was one of the world's great storytellers.

A TRIBUTE

from NORMAN MAILER

Isaac Bashevis Singer saved me from writing a novel I would otherwise have embarked upon, and probably to dubious outcome. I was preparing a novel on the East European Jews of the nineteenth-century ghetto when I came across Singer's work, and realized that a good, young, enterprising writer must not go near what a great writer has already accomplished. Needless to say, I then read everything by him over the next few years.

A TRIBUTE

from ROBERT GIROUX

These remarks were delivered during a tribute to Isaac Bashevis Singer held at the Poetry Center of the 92nd Street Young Men's and Young Women's Hebrew Association on Monday, 4 November 1991.

Isaac Bashevis Singer called himself, with irony, a nineteenth-century writer, and, in a sense, he was. But has any other century produced greater fiction or better novelists? Isaac's work was neither old-fashioned, and if you think it was, you haven't read his story "Two" in the collection *Old Love*, nor was it new-fashioned. It was outside fashion altogether. His popularity transcended fashion because he wrote about recognizable human beings, a lesson rejected by all too many writers today. The writer he most resembles, in my opinion, is Charles Dickens: in his prolific output, in his vitality and humor, in the variety of his characterizations, and in the ingenuity and humanity of his stories.

In 1979 Simon Weber, the editor of the *Daily Forward*, told me that Isaac had not once, since 1939, missed his biweekly appearance in the paper, a span of forty years. Not only did the *Forward* serialize his longer works, like *The Family Moskat* and *The Manor*, but twice every week they

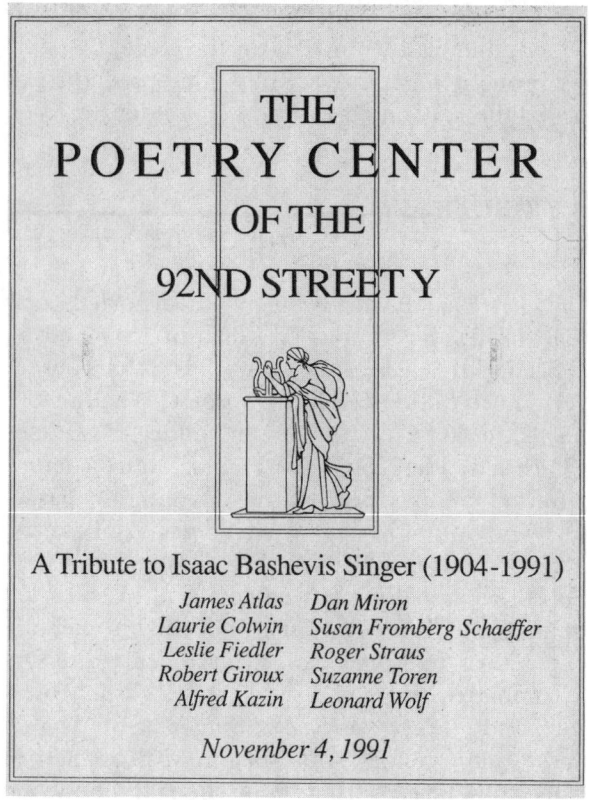

THE
POETRY CENTER
OF THE
92ND STREET Y

A Tribute to Isaac Bashevis Singer (1904-1991)

James Atlas	*Dan Miron*
Laurie Colwin	*Susan Fromberg Schaeffer*
Leslie Fiedler	*Roger Straus*
Robert Giroux	*Suzanne Toren*
Alfred Kazin	*Leonard Wolf*

November 4, 1991

Program cover for a tribute held in Singer's memory in New York City (courtesy of the Poetry Center of the 92nd Street Y and YIVO Institute for Jewish Research)

printed everything he wrote in Yiddish. This included the nine novels that have appeared in English, the two novels yet to be translated, hundreds of stories, the best of which have appeared in his ten collections in English, from "Gimpel the Fool" to "The Death of Methuselah." He also wrote numerous books for children, as well as sketches, memoirs, and short pieces of a speculative and humorous nature under various pseudonyms. His death is an enormous loss to literature.

Once I visited Isaac and Alma in their attractive Belnord apartment on Eighty-sixth Street, where he showed me his Yiddish typewriter. I asked if he had ever started to publish a novel in Yiddish before he had actually reached the last page, as Dickens is said to have done. "Yes," he said, "and once I changed the plot when someone wrote in pleading for me to spare a poor sick character who was about to die. So I gave a few more years. But I always knew before I began writing how the novel would end."

I first met Isaac around 1959, when the Noonday Press merged with our firm. Cecil Hemry, the Noonday editor, and a talented novelist himself, had already published translations of *Satan in Goray* and *The Magician of Lublin* and he edited for us that wonderful novel *The Slave*. When Cecil left to become the editor of the Ohio University Press, I succeeded as Isaac's editor. My first book with him was *The Spinoza of Market Street* and I edited all the FSG books thereafter, excepting the children's books, up to the most recent novel, *Scum*, translated by Rosaline Dukalsky Schwartz. It was not only interesting to work with Isaac, it was also fun. When I first took him to lunch, we went to the Players Club on Gramercy Park, and I discovered he was a vegetarian and an abstemious eater. We had reached a first-name basis, his books were selling reasonably well, though they were not yet best-sellers (this is long before the Nobel Prize, the movie sales, and so on), and Isaac said, "You know, Robert, I never in all my life thought I would be rich."

In 1978 at the Nobel Prize ceremony, when the king presented him with the leather-bound Nobel diploma, he said he opened it expecting to find a check for $185,000. Instead, he found a card with a message "Call at the Cashier's Office in the morning after 9 A.M." When he told me this, he added, "Robert, I was there at 9:01." On the plane going over, I mentioned that the Nobel Prize was beyond doubt the most prestigious literary prize in the world. "Robert," he said, "if the award didn't pay $185,000, nobody would pay the slightest attention." On the evening of the award itself, his son, Israel Shamir, who was in the room next to mine at the hotel, put on the white tie and tails required for the banquet and handed me a camera. "If I don't bring back a photo," he said, "no one in my kibbutz will believe I'm wearing this outfit."

Isaac attended a gathering at the Jewish Community Center in Stockholm, at the request of several thousand people who had been expelled from Poland nine years earlier. He was the first Jewish writer to meet with them and the occasion was emotional and moving. People wept at the sight of their countryman, but as soon as he began to speak in Yiddish, he had them all laughing. He wanted to demonstrate the richness of Yiddish and one example is the various words for a poor man. He said English had only a few synonyms like pauper and beggar but Yiddish had sixty-six such words. And they roared as he started to cite them. The secretary of the Swedish Academy told us that Isaac was the most popular recipient of the Nobel Prize in all his many years of secretaryship.

One last story. Not so many years ago, the superintendent of West Point called and asked if Mr. Singer would speak to the cadets. Someone had endowed a series of lectures on the topic of freedom with a fee of $10,000 for a one-hour talk, preceded by a full-dress parade of the entire cadet corps honoring the lecturer. When I told Isaac, assuming he would accept at once, he said, "Robert, I can't go there. I don't know any generals." And he also said, "the subject of freedom is too abstract, what can I say?" After a great deal of persuasion, he finally agreed to talk about the freedom of the writer. And the superintendent told us that he was more popular than any other lecturer because he made the cadets laugh. During the dress parade, as the troops marched by with their white-trousered legs moving in perfect unison, Isaac whispered in a low voice, "It looks to me as if a few of these men are women." It's a story Charles Dickens could never have written.

The story "Two," that I mentioned at the beginning of my lecture, is a story that Charles Dickens could never have written—about outcasts living together, one of whom passes as a woman. When the truth comes out in the village, they are both destroyed. And this is Isaac's conclusion, "They were buried behind a fence late at night without anyone to follow their hearses or to say kaddish. But one morning the cemetery watchman saw a board on their grave with an inscription from the second book of Samuel. 'Lovely and pleasant in their lives and in their deaths they were not divided.' " As a social thinker Isaac may have been conservative, but as a writer he was a genius.

A TRIBUTE

from ROGER STRAUS

These remarks were delivered during a tribute to Isaac Bashevis Singer held at the Poetry Center of the 92nd Street Young Men's and Young Women's Hebrew Association on Monday, 4 November 1991.

We are here tonight to pay homage to Isaac Bashevis Singer and to celebrate his life and work. As his publisher and friend for over thirty years, I had the unique privilege of knowing Isaac and publishing no less than nineteen novels, fourteen books for children, and nine collections of short stories. Isaac Singer was every publisher's dream. We not only acted as his publisher, but we also handled foreign rights and film rights for most of his work. If we had been out of touch—as we often were—for a few days or a few weeks, Isaac's first question on the telephone, or in the restaurant, to me would be, "How is our business, Roger?" I would then report to him. I should say, parenthetically, that the restaurant part of our life together was pretty bad. I always accused Isaac of taking me to every greasy spoon in New York. He had, of course, some particular ones—not only the dairy restaurants but some of the others; the last one I think we spent a lot of time at was the American Restaurant. I had another distinguished author called Gaylord Houser, who introduced me to the wheat burger, but Isaac introduced me to the vegetable burger. I'm not sure which was worse, but we ate a lot of pseudoburgers together in one way or another.

I would report to Isaac on how our business was, and the kind of reports that I would give him were that he had a new publisher in Spain, or he was on the best-seller list in Italy—where, by the way, he is now; I had a fax this morning from Italy saying *Scum* was just published in Italy; it started off as number ten on the best-seller list in that country, and that would have given him great pleasure to know what was going on there. Also, if we were negotiating film rights, we had some ups and downs on that. He wasn't very happy with most of the films that were made of his work. Of course, there was the famous situation with Barbra Streisand that I'm too refined to go into now, but Isaac was quite outspoken on what he liked and what he didn't like, and what he hoped was going to happen and what did or didn't happen.

He loved the flow of information from abroad as well as the local successes that came to him, including honorary degrees. He would count them up and he would say to me, "I'm going to Badbreath, Arkansas, to get an honorary degree," or "I'm going to Harvard to get an honorary degree. It's my seventeenth, I think, Roger." And he liked that kind of thing a lot, it sort of turned him on, and it was really sort of amusing to see how that happened. I remember also a citation from the mayor that he got, it was this huge thing that the mayor schlepped up to him; I think that he was rather surprised with that one.

Our high point as his publishers, of course, was in 1978 when Isaac won the Nobel Prize for lit-

erature. It was a great trip; he had an absolutely marvelous time. I can see him now in his white tie and tails walking down the aisle with one arm—I won't say around—but with the princess of Sweden with one arm in his, and as he passed my wife he said, "Dorothea, look, I'm walking with this princess," and it was really quite an interesting sight. Actually, up until then, he had not received the worldwide acclaim that we at Farrar, Straus and Giroux felt was his due. But with that award everything changed. There was literally no country in the world that did not wish to publish a translation of his work, and these translations, I might add, were always from the American edition, edited and published by us and carefully supervised by Isaac. Even to this day in Sweden, which is really quite interesting, because Nobel Prizes come and go as they say, but Isaac Singer, book after book, had best-sellers in Sweden. *Scum* is a best-seller taken by book clubs and so forth and so on, and if you walk into a better Swedish bookstore, you will see at least a half a dozen of Isaac's books—children's books, adult books, and so forth and so on—displayed there. He was then and is now a highly acclaimed writer that the Swedes are just in love with—were then and are now.

As you know, the reason that the control was from the American edition was that Isaac wrote in Yiddish, and the vast majority of his stories, novels, and the like first appeared in the *Jewish Daily Forward*. This work was then reworked, in most instances by Isaac, and then released to his publishers. I'm happy to be able to announce for the first time here, that there will be two more books by Isaac that we shall release in the next two or three years. The first will be *The Certificate*, which is currently being translated by Leonard Wolf, who is here tonight and who will be talking to you later. This will be followed by another book of Isaac's that he often talked about entitled *Shadows on the Hudson*. All of these works will be carefully supervised, not only by us but by his widow, Alma, who is here this evening and who is his literary executor. And finally, we shall be publishing in due course the complete stories of Isaac Singer, and there are still one or two yet to be translated. You will be hearing tonight from our distinguished panel of guests about Isaac's work.

I shall end this introduction merely by saying that I shall miss that voice on the telephone saying, "Roger, how is our business?" For the business of publishing Isaac was a great joy.

A TRIBUTE —————————————————

from SAUL BELLOW (as read by Roger Straus)

These remarks were delivered during a tribute to
Isaac Bashevis Singer held at the Poetry Center
of the 92nd Street Young Men's and Young
Women's Hebrew Association on Monday, 4 November 1991.

My friend Saul Bellow, who, unfortunately,
I do not publish—and let his present publisher
beware—cannot be with us tonight, but he has
asked me to read a message that he prepared for
this evening.

In the early fifties when I was completing
Augie March, I was approached by an acquaintance, Eliezer Greenberg, and invited to translate
Singer's "Gimpel the Fool." Singer's name was familiar to me, because my father—who followed
his serials in the *Forward*, pronounced "Forvitz"—
was an early fan, and urged me to read him. Somehow I had never found the time.

Together with Irving Howe, Greenberg was
preparing an anthology of Yiddish fiction and he
asked me to do the Singer story. I said I couldn't
possibly, and listed the usual neurotic complaints.
Patient Eliezer heard me out, most sympathetic,
and said it could be done without strain. The
work would not only be easy, but even restora-
tive, he promised. The late Greenberg was a man
of great charm, and in those days a kind word
would bring tears to my eyes. "Listen," he said,

"you will sit at the typewriter, I will read the
story, you will do it line by line, nothing to it."

He was right. The circumstances couldn't
have been more pleasant: the season was spring,
the air was soft, the birds were twittering. And so
amid twittering and clattering and banter, we produced an American version of "Gimpel." *Partisan
Review* published it, and paid me a fee of ten
bucks.

When I met Singer years later, I asked him
why he had never asked me to translate any
other stories. "Quite simply," he said, "they'll say
it's you and not me." He was absolutely true to
himself. Polonius would have loved him for that.
He was not Mr. Nice Guy. He rejected Americani-
zation absolutely. No smooth finish for Bashevis.
No cosmetics. I knew very well what *that* was
about and I liked him all the more for it. In him
I recognized the kinks of my father's—and my
own unreconstructable, hereditary disposition.

I tried to do right by him in my own fashion. When he won the Nobel Prize I sent him a
congratulatory note in Yiddish. He answered me
with matching politeness, but he also conveyed—
in one of the few references he ever made
to "Gimpel," oblique, of course—that one story
didn't make a career. He didn't need me. Nor anyone else. His gifts were great and he was right to
emphasize his independence.

Well, God bless him, I say, or I'm inclined
to say, knowing he'd accept no blessing recommended by me or any mortal. It would *have* to
come from God, direct.

Alden Whitman

(27 October 1913 - 4 September 1990)

Alden Whitman was a member of the planning board of the *Dictionary of Literary Biography* series and served on the first advisory board.

BOOKS: *Labor parties, 1827-1834: Initial Steps in Independent Political Action During the Formative Years of Workers' Organization in the U.S.* (New York: International [circa 1943]);
Portrait, Adlai E. Stevenson: Politician, Diplomat, Friend (New York: Harper & Row, 1965);
Triumph Out of Tragedy (New York: New York Times, 1968);
The Obituary Book (New York: Stein & Day, 1971);
Come to Judgment (New York: Viking, 1980);
Independent Documentarians and Public Television: A Task Force Report to the National News Council (New York: the Council, 1980).

OTHER: Adlai Ewing Stevenson, *AS: A Stevenson Sampler 1945-1965*, selected by Whitman (New York: Harper & Row [circa 1965]);
American Reformers: An H. W. Wilson Biographical Dictionary, edited by Whitman (New York: Wilson, 1985).

A TRIBUTE _____

from MAHONRI SHARP YOUNG

Alden Whitman (photograph, New Haven Register)

Alden Whitman invented the Great American Obituary, and it died with him. "Brief lives," he liked to call them, and not so brief at that; Lindbergh's ran to several pages, and Alden got two bylines that day, rare for the *New York Times*. Lindbergh made the front page as of right, but Alden got the front page for people who had never been there before. That's the hard way; but there are many roads to Parnassus.

He was highly regarded in the trade; apparently in journalism, as in music, you can tell. He was born in Nova Scotia, his father's family having left Long Island after the Revolution. He spent eight years on the *Herald Tribune* and twenty-five on the *Times*. He liked to take the late shift. Nobody else wanted it, and they needed an experienced man to handle whatever came in after the newspaper was made up. If war broke out, he telephoned. Otherwise he rewrote the wires and rear-

ranged the paper. He liked that. Much of the best writing these days is in newspapers, and Alden wrote a lot of it. About two-thirds through his copy there were often two or three sentences that told you where Alden and his subject stood. They were not necessarily the same.

He interviewed his subjects and wrote the story before they died, which is much more life-like than typing against the clock with the file from the morgue in front of you. He got extraordinary cooperation. As Harry Truman said, "I know why you're here and I want to help you all I can." Every man in his eighties is familiar with the main event.

Alden never dropped a name in his life, though he knew an impossible range of people. He also knew *everything*, and maybe more. "Don't look it up, ask Whitman." But memory and desire don't make a writer. (He knew T. S. Eliot at Harvard when he was an undergraduate, about the time he got his teeth knocked out by a nightstick.) He listened, and his copy was clean. I have never known a man or woman who disliked him. All kinds of people would do all kinds of things for him. He was a personal friend of Lindbergh, and traveled with him in the Philippines. They made a rare pair.

In his gracious and witty "Viewpoint" on Alden in the *Wall Street Journal*, Michael Gartner, an old newspaperman himself, says that "if Alden Whitman had been writing the obituary of Alden Whitman, Whitman would have talked to Whitman, too, about Whitman's membership in the Communist Party for 13 years, about his refusal to name other members, his conviction and reversal and second conviction for contempt of Congress." And about the disposition of the case, thrown out by the Supreme Court: record clear.

At one of our regular Tuesday lunches in Bridgehampton, he said that he would never regret his association with the Communist Party. He could be astonishingly frank, on his own terms. I am sure that he never said anything that he did not mean to say, but, most courteous of men, he did not always answer direct questions. The only people I ever heard him speak harshly about were those who gave names.

In his last couple of years, Alden was in poor shape, but thanks to his wife, Joan, he rarely missed a Tuesday lunch. Like many Americans *de vieille souche*, he was in love with France; for the grand occasions of life, he had a long cape. He died a few minutes outside the French border. As he had requested, his ashes were scattered over Paris. At one of our last lunches, when we were not sure whether Alden was listening, we were trying to remember the name of that racetrack outside Paris.

"Chantilly."

Reprinted from The Century Association Yearbook 1991.

Literary Awards and Honors Announced in 1991

ACADEMY OF AMERICAN POETS AWARDS

FELLOWSHIP
J. D. McClatchy.

LAMONT POETRY SELECTION
Susan Wood, *Campo Santo* (Louisiana State University Press).

HAROLD MORTON LANDON TRANSLATION AWARD
Robert Fagles, *The Iliad* (Viking).

PETER I. B. LAVAN YOUNGER POET AWARD
Nicholas Christopher, J. Allen Rosser, Peter Schmitt.

WALT WHITMAN AWARD
Greg Glazner, *From the Iron Chair* (Louisiana State University Press).

AMERICAN ACADEMY AND INSTITUTE OF ARTS AND LETTERS AWARDS

ACADEMY-INSTITUTE AWARDS IN LITERATURE
Edgar Bowers, Christopher Davis, Jaimy Gordon, Rachel Ingalls, J. D. McClatchy, Harry Matthews, Albert F. Moritz, James Schevill.

AWARD OF MERIT FOR THE NOVEL
Walter Abish.

MICHAEL BRAUDE AWARD FOR LIGHT VERSE
Gavin Ewart.

WITTER BYNNER PRIZE FOR POETRY
Thylias Moss.

E. M. FORSTER AWARD IN LITERATURE
Alan Hollingshurst.

GOLD MEDAL FOR POETRY
Richard Wilbur.

SUE KAUFMAN PRIZE FOR FIRST FICTION
Charles Palliser, *The Quincunx* (Ballantine).

ROME FELLOWSHIP IN LITERATURE
Mary Caponegro.

RICHARD AND HILDA ROSENTHAL FOUNDATION AWARD FOR LITERATURE
Joanna Scott, *Arrogance* (Simon & Schuster).

JEAN STEIN AWARD FOR FICTION
Cormac McCarthy.

HAROLD D. VURSELL MEMORIAL AWARD IN LITERATURE
Ursula K. Le Guin.

MORTON DAUWEN ZABEL AWARD IN POETRY
Gordon Rogoff.

BANCROFT PRIZES

Lizabeth Cohen, *Making a New Deal: Industrial Workers in Chicago, 1919-1939* (Cambridge University Press).

Laurel Thatcher Ulrich, *A Midwife's Tale: The Life of Martha Ballard Based On Her Diary, 1785-1812* (Knopf).

BAY AREA BOOK REVIEWERS ASSOCIATION AWARDS

CHILDREN'S LITERATURE
Ellen Kindt McKenzie, *Stargone John* (Henry Holt).

FICTION
Ella Lefland, *The Knight, Death, and the Devil* (William Morrow).

NONFICTION
Linda Niemann, *Boomer—Railroad Memoirs* (University of California Press).

POETRY
Thomas Centolella, *Terra Firma* (Copper Canyon Press).

IRMA SIMONTON BLACK AWARD

Barbara Abercrombie, *Charlie Anderson*, illustrated by Mark Gradkin (Margaret K. McElderry).

JAMES TAIT BLACK MEMORIAL PRIZE

BIOGRAPHY
Claire Tomalin, *The Invisible Woman: The Story of Nelly Ternan and Charles Dickens* (Viking).

FICTION
William Boyd, *Brazzaville Beach* (Sinclair-Stevenson).

BOLLINGEN PRIZE

Laura (Riding) Jackson.
Donald Justice.

THE BOOKER PRIZE

Ben Okri, *The Famished Road* (Cape).

BOOTS ROMANTIC NOVEL OF THE YEAR

Susan Kay, *Phantom* (Delacorte).

BOSTON GLOBE—HORN BOOK AWARD

FICTION
Avi, *The True Confessions of Charlotte Doyle* (Orchard/Richard Jackson).

RANDOLPH CALDECOTT MEDAL

David Macaulay, *Black and White*.

COMMON WEALTH AWARD OF DISTINGUISHED SERVICE TO LITERATURE

Adrienne Rich.

COMMONWEALTH WRITERS PRIZES

BEST BOOK
David Malouf, *The Great World* (Chatto & Windus).

BEST FIRST BOOK
Pauline Melville, *Shape-Shifter* (Women's Press/Picador).

JOHN DOS PASSOS PRIZE FOR LITERATURE

Larry Woiwode.

DRUE HEINZ LITERATURE PRIZE

Elizabeth Graver, *Have You Seen Me?* (University of Pittsburgh Press).

FELLOWSHIP OF SOUTHERN WRITERS AWARDS

CLEANTH BROOKS AWARD
Eudora Welty.

SPECIAL AWARD
Andrew Lytle.

GOLDEN KITE AWARDS

FICTION
Avi, *The True Confessions of Charlotte Doyle* (Orchard/Richard Jackson).

NONFICTION
Jim Murphy, *The Boys' War* (Clarion).

PICTURE-ILLUSTRATION
Crescent Dragonwagon, *Home Place*, illustrated by Jerry Pinkney (Macmillan).

GUGGENHEIM FELLOWSHIPS FOR LITERATURE AND LITERARY AND CULTURAL STUDIES

Madison Smartt Bell, Thomas Boyle, John Brewer, David Carroll, Vincent J. Cheng, Carolyn Chute, Constance S. Congdon, Fred Curchack, Jean Bethke Elshtain, Tom Englehardt, Helene P. Foley, Regenia Gagnier, Francine Du Plessix Gray, Edward L. Greenstein, Kenneth Gross, N. Katherine Hayles, Cheryl Temple Herr, Linda Hogan, John T. Irwin, Rachel Jacoff, Mark Jarman, Herbert Leibowitz, Olga Matich, Lorrie Moore, Vasudha Narayanan, Felicity A. Nussbaum, Katherine F. Pantzer, Mary Louise Poovey, Jeremy D. Popkin, Francine Prose, Velcheru Narayanu Rau, Claude Rawson, Jeffrey T. Schnapp, Laurie Sheck, Jane Shore, Debora Kuller Shuger, Diana Trilling, David Underdown, Joseph S. Viscomi, Calvert Watkins, Samuel Weber, Liliane Weissberg, Dana Wier, Alan Williamson, Brenda Wineapple.

O. B. HARDISON, JR., POETRY MEDAL

Brenda Galvin.

O. HENRY AWARD

Brian Wooley, "A Family Nightmare" (*Dallas Life*).

INGERSOLL PRIZES

FICTION
Mario Vargas Llosa.

HISTORY
John Lukacs.

IRISH TIMES—AER LINGUS INTERNATIONAL FICTION PRIZE

Louis Begley, *Wartime Lies* (Knopf).

JERUSALEM PRIZE

Zbigniew Herbert.

JANET HEIDINGER KAFKA PRIZE

Karen Tei Yamashita, *Through the Arc of the Rain Forest* (Coffee House Press).

Valerie Martin, *Mary Reilly* (Doubleday).

ROBERT F. KENNEDY AWARDS

Myles Horton.
Chico Mendes.

LANNAN LITERARY AWARDS

FICTION
Sandra Cisneros, Alexander Theroux, John Edgar Wideman.

NONFICTION
Christopher Hitchens.

POETRY
William Bronk, Chrystos, Herbert Morris, Pattiann Rogers.

LIBRARY ASSOCIATION MEDALS

CARNEGIE MEDAL
Gilliam Cross, *Wolf* (Oxford).

KATE GREENAWAY MEDAL
Dyan Sheldon, *The Whales' Song*, illustrated by Gary Blythe (Hutchinson Children's Books).

RUTH LILLY POETRY PRIZE

David Wagoner.

RUTH LILLY POETRY FELLOWSHIP

Gregory A. Sellers.

LOS ANGELES TIMES BOOK AWARDS

BIOGRAPHY
T. H. Watkins, *Righteous Pilgrim: The Life and Times of Harold Ickes, 1874-1952* (Henry Holt).

CURRENT INTEREST
E. J. Dionne, *Why Americans Hate Politics* (Simon & Schuster).

FICTION
Allan Gurganus, *White People: Stories and Novellas* (Knopf).

HISTORY
Nicholas Lemann, *The Promised Land: The Great Black Migration and How It Changed America* (Knopf).

ROBERT KIRSCH AWARD
Ken Kesey.

POETRY
Philip Levine, *What Work Is* (David McKay).

ART SEIDENBAUM AWARD
David Wong Louie, *Pangs of Love* (Knopf).

MACARTHUR FELLOWS

Paul Berman, Taylor Branch, Mary Jo Buhle, Alice Fulton, Guillermo Gomez-Pena, Jerzy Grotowski, W. Lewis Hyde, Harlan Lane, Patricia Locke, Marcel Ophuls, Arnold Rampersad, Gunther Schuller, Julie Taymor, Eleanor Wilner.

JOSEPHINE MILES AWARD

Gerald Haslam, *That Constant Coyote* (University of Nevada Press).

HARRIET MONROE POETRY AWARD

Allen Ginsberg.

NATIONAL ARTS CLUB MEDAL OF HONOR FOR LITERATURE

Philip Roth.

NATIONAL BOOK AWARDS

FICTION
Norman Rush, *Mating* (Knopf).

MEDAL FOR DISTINGUISHED CONTRIBUTION TO AMERICAN LETTERS
Eudora Welty.

NONFICTION
Orlando Patterson, *Freedom* (Basic/HarperCollins).

POETRY
Philip Levine, *What Work Is* (David McKay).

NATIONAL BOOK CRITICS CIRCLE AWARD

BIOGRAPHY
Robert Caro, *The Means of Ascent: The Years of Lyndon Johnson* (Knopf).

CRITICISM
Arthur C. Danto, *Encounters and Reflections: Art in the Historical Present* (Farrar, Straus & Giroux).

FICTION
John Updike, *Rabbit at Rest* (Knopf).

GENERAL NONFICTION
Shelby Steele, *The Content of Their Character: A New Vision of Race in America* (St. Martin's Press).

POETRY
Amy Gerstler, *Bitter Angel* (North Point Press).

REVIEWING
Molly Giles.

NATIONAL JEWISH BOOK AWARDS

IRA AND JOSHUA ABER AWARD
Shalom Sabar, *Ketubbah: Jewish Marriage Contracts of Hebrew Union College Skirball Museum and Klau Library* (Jewish Publication Society).

GERRARD AND ELLA BERMAN AWARD FOR JEWISH HISTORY

Elisheva Carlebach, *The Pursuit of Heresy: Rabbi Moses Haqiz and the Sabbatian Controversies* (Columbia University Press).

SANDRA BRAND AND ARIK WEINTRAUB AWARD FOR AUTOBIOGRAPHY AND MEMOIR

Irving Louis Horowitz, *Daydreams and Nightmares: Reflections of a Harlem Childhood* (University Press of Mississippi).

WILLIAM AND JANICE EPSTEIN AWARD FOR FICTION

Chaim Potok, *The Gift of Asher Lev* (Knopf).

JEWISH CONTEMPORARY LIFE

Daniel J. Elazar and Harold M. Waller, *Maintaining Consensus: The Canadian Jewish Polity in the Postwar World* (Jerusalem Center for Public Affairs/University Press of America).

JEWISH THOUGHT

Neil Gillman, *Sacred Fragments Recovering Theology for the Modern Jew* (Jewish Publication Society).

LEON JOLSON AWARD FOR HOLOCAUST WRITING

Leni Yahil, *The Holocaust: The Fate of European Jewry, 1932-1945*, translated by Ina Friedman and Haya Galai (Oxford University Press).

MORRIS J. AND BETTY KAPLUN AWARD FOR WRITING ON ISRAEL

Sergio I. Minerbi, *The Vatican and Zionism: Conflict in the Holy Land 1895-1925*, translated by Arnold Schwarz (Oxford).

SARAH H. AND JULIUS KUSHNER AWARD FOR SCHOLARSHIP

Gavin Langmuir, *History, Religion & Antisemitism* (University of California Press).

MARCIA AND LOUIS POSNER AWARD FOR CHILDREN'S PICTURE BOOK

Roni Schotter, *Hanukkah!*, illustrated by Marilyn Hafner (Little, Brown).

ANITA AND MARTIN SHAPOLSKY AWARD FOR CHILDREN'S LITERATURE

Nava Semel, *Becoming Gershona*, translated by Seymour Simckes (Viking Penguin).

JOHN T. NEWBERY MEDAL

Jerry Spinelli, *Maniac Magee* (Little, Brown).

SCOTT O'DELL AWARD FOR HISTORICAL FICTION

Pieter Van Reuen, *A Time of Troubles* (Scribners).

PEN LITERARY AWARDS

FAULKNER AWARD FOR FICTION

John Edgar Wideman, *Philadelphia Fire* (Henry Holt).

PEN/MARTHA ALBRAND AWARD FOR NONFICTION

Gerand Marzorati, *A Painter of Darkness: Leon Golub and Our Times* (Viking).

PEN/BOOK-OF-THE-MONTH CLUB TRANSLATION PRIZE

Fyodor Dostoyevski, *The Brothers Karamazov*, translated by Richard Pevear and Larissa Volokhonsky (North Point Press).

ERNEST HEMINGWAY FOUNDATION AWARD

Bernard Cooper, *Maps to Anywhere* (University of Georgia Press).

PEN/JERARD FUND AWARD

Lydia Yuri Minatoya, *Talking to High Monks in the Snow: An Asian Odyssey* (forthcoming).

PEN/NORMA KLEIN AWARD

Cynthia Grant.

PEN MEDAL FOR TRANSLATION

William Weaver.

PEN/REVSON FOUNDATION FELLOWSHIP

Lucia Maria Perillo.

PEN/SPIELVOGEL-DIAMONSTEIN AWARD

Martha C. Nussbaum, *Loves's Knowledge: Essays on Philosophy and Literature* (Oxford University Press).

RENATO POGGIOLI TRANSLATION AWARD
Liana Millu, *Smoke Over Birkenau*, translated by Lynne Sharon Schwartz (Jewish Publication Society, forthcoming).

ΦBK BOOK PRIZES

RALPH WALDO EMERSON AWARD
Carl N. Degler, *In Search of Human Nature: The Decline and Revival of Darwinism in American Social Thought* (Oxford University Press).

CHRISTIAN GAUSS AWARD
Richard Altick, *The Presence of the Present: Topics of the Day in the Victorian Novel* (Ohio State University Press).

EDGAR ALLAN POE AWARDS

BEST FIRST MYSTERY NOVEL
Patricia Daniels Cornwell, *Post Mortem* (Scribners).

BEST MYSTERY NOVEL
Julie Smith, *New Orleans Mourning* (St. Martin's Press).

BEST ORIGINAL PAPERBACK
David Hendler, *The Man Who Would be F. Scott Fitzgerald* (Bantam).

BEST PLAY
Rupert Holmes, *Accomplice*.

BEST SHORT STORY
Lynne Barrett, "Elvis Lives."

BEST YOUNG ADULT NOVEL
Chap Reaven, *Mote* (Delacorte).

BIOGRAPHICAL/CRITICAL STUDY
John Conquest, *Trouble Is Their Business: Private Eyes in Fiction, Film, and Television 1927-1988* (Garland).

ROBERT L. FISH MEMORIAL AWARD
Jerry F. Sharky, "Willie's Story."

GRANDMASTER
Tony Hillerman.

THE POETS' PRIZE

John Haines, *New Poems: 1980-88* (Story Line Press).

Mark Jarman, *The Black Riviera* (Wesleyan University Press).

PRIX GONCOURT

Pierre Combescot, *Les Filles du Calvaire*.

PULITZER PRIZES

BIOGRAPHY
Steven Naifeh and Greg W. Smith, *Jackson Pollack: An American Genius* (Crown).

HISTORY
Laurel Thatcher Ulrich, *A Midwife's Tale: The Life of Martha Ballard Based on Her Diary, 1785-1812* (Knopf).

LITERATURE
John Updike, *Rabbit at Rest* (Knopf).

NONFICTION
Edward O. Wilson and Bert Holldobler, *The Ants* (Belknap Press of Harvard University Press).

POETRY
Mona Van Duyn, *Near Changes* (Knopf).

REA AWARD FOR THE SHORT STORY

Paul Bowles.

TURNER TOMORROW AWARD

Daniel Quinn, *Ishmael*.

WHITBREAD AWARDS

BIOGRAPHY
Ann Thwaite, *A. A. Milne: His Life* (Faber & Faber).

CHILDREN'S NOVEL
> Peter Dickinson, *AK* (Gollancz).

FIRST NOVEL
> Hanf Kureishi, *The Budda of Suburbia* (Faber & Faber).

NOVEL AND BOOK OF THE YEAR
> Nicholas Mosley, *Hopeful Monsters* (Secker & Warburg).

POETRY
> Paul Duncan, *Daddy, Daddy* (Blackstaff Press).

JOHN WHITING AWARD

Terry Johnson, *Imagine Drowning*.

WHITING WRITERS' AWARDS

Stanley Crouch, Rebecca Goldstein, Allegra Goodman, John Holman, Cynthia Kodohata, Scott McPherson, Thylias Moss, Rick Rofihe, Anton Shammas, Franz Wright.

Checklist: Contributions to Literary History and Biography

This checklist is a selection of new books on various aspects of literary and cultural history, including biographies, memoirs, and correspondence of literary people and their associates.

Peter Ackroyd, *Dickens*. New York: HarperCollins, 1991.

Carol Angier, *Jean Rhys: Life and Work*. Boston: Little, Brown, 1991.

Brian Boyd, *Vladimir Nabokov: The American Years*. Princeton, N.J.: Princeton University Press, 1991.

Nicholas Boyle, *Goethe: The Poet and the Age, Volume One: The Poetry of Desire, 1749-1790*. New York: Oxford University Press, 1991.

Mikhail Bulgakov, *Manuscripts Don't Burn: Mikhail Bulgakov: A Life in Letters and Diaries*. Edited by J. A. E. Curtis. London: Bloomsbury, 1991.

John Cheever, *The Journals of John Cheever*. Edited by Robert Gottlieb. New York: Knopf, 1991.

Günter Eich, *Pigeons and Moles: Selected Writings of Günter Eich*. Translated with an introduction by Michael Hamburger. Columbia, S.C.: Camden House, 1991.

Didier Eribon, *Michel Foucault*. Translated by Betsy Wing. Cambridge, Mass.: Harvard University Press, 1991.

The Facts-On-File Bibliography of American Fiction: 1919-1988. Edited by Matthew J. Bruccoli and Judith S. Baughman. New York: Facts-On-File, 1991.

Michael Ffinch, *John Henry Newman: A Biography*. San Francisco: Harper, 1991.

F. Scott Fitzgerald, *The Short Stories of F. Scott Fitzgerald*. Edited by Matthew J. Bruccoli. New York: Scribners, 1991.

Zelda Fitzgerald, *The Collected Writings of Zelda Fitzgerald*. Edited by Matthew J. Bruccoli. New York: Scribners, 1991.

Germany and Europe; The Politics of Culture. Columbia, S.C.: Camden House, 1991.

David Gilmour, *The Last Leopard: A Life of Giuseppe di Lampedusa*. New York: Pantheon, 1991.

George Gissing, *The Collected Letters of George Gissing, 1881-1885*. Edited by Paul F. Matthiesen, Arthur C. Young and Pierre Coustillas. Athens: Ohio University Press, 1991.

Graham Greene, *Reflections*. Selected and introduced by Judith Adamson. New York: Reinhardt/Viking, 1991.

N. John Hall, *Trollope: A Biography*. New York: Oxford University Press, 1991.

Gertrude Himmelfarb, *Poverty and Compassion: The Moral Imagination of the Late Victorians*. New York: Knopf, 1991.

The Ideological Crisis of Expressionism: The Literary and Artistic German War Colony in Belgium, 1914-1918. Columbia, S.C.: Camden House, 1991.

Paul Johnson, *The Birth of the Modern: World Society, 1815-1830*. New York: HarperCollins, 1991.

Peter Stephan Jungk, *A Life Torn by History: Franz Werfel, 1890-1945*. London: Weidenfeld and Nicolson, 1991.

David Lehman, *Signs of the Times; Deconstruction and the Fall of Paul de Man*. New York: Poseidon, 1991.

R. W. B. Lewis, *The Jameses: A Family Narrative*. New York: Farrar, Straus and Giroux, 1991.

Robert Bernard Martin, *Gerard Manley Hopkins: A Very Private Life*. New York: Putnam's, 1991.

Diane Wood Middlebrook, *Anne Sexton: A Biography*. New York: Houghton Mifflin, 1991.

Edwin Haviland Miller, *Salem Is My Dwelling Place: A Life of Nathaniel Hawthorne*. Iowa City: University of Iowa Press, 1991.

Lesley Milne, *Mikhail Bulgakov: A Critical Biography*. Cambridge: Cambridge University Press, 1991.

Penelope Niven, *Carl Sandburg: A Biography*. New York: Scribners, 1991.

V. S. Pritchett, *The Complete Essays*. London: Chatto & Windus, 1991.

Ellenda Proffer, *Vladimir Nabokov: A Pictorial Biography*. Ann Arbor, Mich.: Ardis, 1991.

Jean Paul Sartre, *Ecrits de Jeunesse*. Edited by Michel Contat and Michel Rybalka. Paris: Gallimard, 1991.

Paddy Scannell and David Cardiff, *A Social History of British Broadcasting, Volume One: 1922-1939: Serving the Nation*. Oxford: Blackwell, 1991.

Arthur M. Schlesinger, Jr., *The Disuniting of America: Reflections on a Multicultural Society*. Knoxville, Tenn.: Whittle, 1991.

Michael Sheldon, *Orwell: The Authorized Biography*. New York: HarperCollins, 1991.

Song of Love: The Letters of Rupert Brooke and Noel Oliver. London: Bloomsbury, 1991.

Emily Toth, *Kate Chopin*. London: Century, 1991.

John Updike, *Odd Jobs: Essays and Criticism*. New York: Knopf, 1991.

Kurt Vonnegut, *Fates Worse Than Death: An Autobiographical Collage of the 1980s*. New York: Putnam's, 1991.

Whitman In His Own Time: A Biographical Chronicle of His Life, Drawn from Recollections, Memoirs, and Interviews by Friends and Associates. Edited by Joel Myerson. Detroit: Omnigraphics, 1991.

John Worthen, *D. H. Lawrence: The Early Years, 1885-1912*. New York: Cambridge University Press, 1991.

CATALOGUES

"The Bible in the Lilly Library." Prepared and described by Joel Silver. Bloomington: Lilly Library, University of Indiana, 1991.

"Mark Twain: Selections from the Collection of Nick Karanovich." Prepared and described by Nick Karanovich, William Cagle, and Joel Silver. Bloomington: Lilly Library, Indiana University, 1991.

Necrology

Irwin Allen—2 November 1991
Carl Allensworth—22 October 1991
William Ball—30 August 1991
George Granville Barker—27 October 1991
Allen Barnett—14 August 1991
Patricia Robbins Beatty—9 July 1991
Anthony Bliss—10 August 1991
Gavin Gail Borden—19 December 1991
Julie Bovasso—14 September 1991
Fredson Thayer Bowers—11 April 1991
Myron Brinig—13 May 1991
Luther Slade Brown—29 June 1991
Aaron Burns—16 July 1991
Niven Busch—25 August 1991
Socrates K. Butsikares—8 August 1991
Lydia Cabrera—19 September 1991
Frank Capra—3 September 1990
George N. Cavalero—6 December 1991
Kathleen Coburn—23 September 1991
John Crosby—7 September 1991
Donald Day—22 July 1991
Meindert DeJong—16 July 1991
George T. Delacorte, Jr.—4 May 1991
John Dillon—5 November 1991
Jack Donahue—27 July 1991
James J. Fahey—23 September 1991
Roberta Feuerlicht—4 October 1991
Roy Fuller—28 September 1991
Ernest Kellogg Gann—19 December 1991
Mary Virginia Gaver—31 December 1991
Addison Gayle, Jr.—4 October 1991
Theodor Seuss Geisel—24 September 1991
Natalia Ginzburg—7 October 1991
Marcus Aurelius Goodrich—20 October 1991
Graham Greene—3 April 1991
Milton Greenstein—29 July 1991
Herve Guibert—27 December 1991
Daniel Haberman—8 August 1991
Tibor Halasi-Kun—19 October 1991
Elaine Halperin—21 July 1991
Caroline Thomas Harnsberger—29 June 1991
Alan A. Harper—19 October 1991
Howard Haycraft—12 November 1991
Peter Heyworth—1 October 1991
Wolfgang Hildesheimer—21 August 1991
Claude Hill—10 December 1991

David Armine Howarth—2 July 1991
Benjamin Hunningher—21 November 1991
George P. Hunt—6 July 1991
Yusuf Idris—1 August 1991
Alvin Illig—2 August 1991
Laura Riding Jackson—2 September 1991
Herb Jaffe—7 December 1991
Judson Jerome—5 August 1991
Helene Mullins Johnson—26 October 1991
Edward Joseph—24 September 1991
Arthur Klar—15 October 1991
John Kobal—28 October 1991
Jerzy Kosinski—3 May 1991
Paul Henry Lang—21 September 1991
Jan Josef Lipski—10 September 1991
Artur Lundkvist—11 December 1991
Joseph Russell Lynes—14 September 1991
Fletcher Markle—22 May 1991
Robert Maxwell—5 November 1991
Robert Motherwell—16 July 1991
Véra Nabokov—7 April 1991
Howard Nemerov—5 July 1991
Leonard C. Odell—4 October 1991
Russell O'Neil—18 December 1991
Joseph Papp—31 October 1991
Italo Pietra—4 September 1991
Irwin H. Pizer—8 July 1991
Catherine M. Prelinger—31 August 1991
Martha Pulliam—11 July 1991
James Revson—11 July 1991
Louise Dickinson Rich—9 April 1991
Keith Carlton Robertson—23 September 1991
Earl Robinson—20 July 1991
James Schuyler—12 April 1991
Mort Shuman—3 November 1991
Benjamin Siegel—31 July 1991
Isaac Bashevis Singer—24 July 1991
Virginia Sorensen—24 December 1991
Grace Zaring Stone—29 September 1991
Lou Stoumen—20 September 1991
Eleanor Regis Sullivan—12 July 1991
Horace Sutton—26 October 1991
Jack Tannen—10 December 1991
Thomas Tryon—4 September 1990
Nikiforos Vrettakos—4 August 1991
Sebastian Walker—16 June 1991

Edward Neighbor Waters—27 July 1991

Hans Weigel—12 August 1991

John O. Whedon—22 November 1991

Alden Whitman—4 September 1990

Sir Angus Wilson—31 May 1991

Asher Wolk—16 November 1991

Hsin-Nung Yao—18 December 1991

Frank Yerby—29 November 1991

Philip Young—4 October 1991

Hallie Burnett Zeisel—3 September 1991

Contributors

Cumulative Index

Dictionary of Literary Biography, Volumes 1-115
Dictionary of Literary Biography Yearbook, 1980-1991
Dictionary of Literary Biography Documentary Series, Volumes 1-9

Cumulative Index

DLB before number: *Dictionary of Literary Biography*, Volumes 1-115
Y before number: *Dictionary of Literary Biography Yearbook*, 1980-1991
DS before number: *Dictionary of Literary Biography Documentary Series*, Volumes 1-9

A

D

E

F

G

H

I

K

L

M

N

O

P

Y

Z

ISBN 0-8103-7601-6

90000

(Continued from front endsheets)

80: *Restoration and Eighteenth-Century Dramatists,* First Series, edited by Paula R. Backscheider (1989)

81: *Austrian Fiction Writers, 1875-1913,* edited by James Hardin and Donald G. Daviau (1989)

82: *Chicano Writers,* First Series, edited by Francisco A. Lomelí and Carl R. Shirley (1989)

83: *French Novelists Since 1960,* edited by Catharine Savage Brosman (1989)

84: *Restoration and Eighteenth-Century Dramatists,* Second Series, edited by Paula ⁿ Backscheider (1989)

85: *Austrian Fiction Writers After 1914,* edited by James Hardin and Donald G. Daviau (1989)

86: *American Short-Story Writers, 1910-1945,* First Series, edited by Bobby Ellen Kimbel (1989)

87: *British Mystery and Thriller Writers Since 1940,* First Series, edited by Bernard Benstock and Thomas F. Staley (1989)

88: *Canadian Writers, 1920-1959,* Second Series, edited by W. H. New (1989)

89: *Restoration and Eighteenth-Century Dramatists,* Third Series, edited by Paula R. Backscheider (1989)

90: *German Writers in the Age of Goethe, 1789-1832,* edited by James Hardin and Christoph E. Schweitzer (1989)

91: *American Magazine Journalists, 1900-1960,* First Series, edited by Sam G. Riley (1990)

92: *Canadian Writers, 1890-1920,* edited by W. H. New (1990)

93: *British Romantic Poets, 1789-1832,* First Series, edited by John R. Greenfield (1990)

94: *German Writers in the Age of Goethe: Sturm und Drang to Classicism,* edited by James Hardin and Christoph E. Schweitzer (1990)

95: *Eighteenth-Century British Poets,* First Series, edited by John Sitter (1990)

96: *British Romantic Poets, 1789-1832,* Second Series, edited by John R. Greenfield (1990)

97: *German Writers from the Enlightenment to Sturm und Drang, 1720-1764,* edited by James Hardin and Christoph E. Schweitzer (1990)

98: *Modern British Essayists,* First Series, edited by Robert Beum (1990)

99: *Canadian Writers Before 1890,* edited by W. H. New (1990)

100: *Modern British Essayists,* Second Series, edited by Robert Beum (1990)

101: *British Prose Writers, 1660-1800,* First Series, edited by Donald T. Siebert (1991)

102: *American Short-Story Writers, 1910-1945,* Second Series, edited by Bobby Ellen Kimbel (1991)

103: *American Literary Biographers,* First Series, edited by Steven Serafin (1991)

104: *British Prose Writers, 1660-1800,* Second Series, edited by Donald T. Siebert (1991)

105: *American Poets Since World War II,* Second Series, edited by R. S. Gwynn (1991)

106: *British Literary Publishing Houses, 1820-1880,* edited by Patricia J. Anderson and Jonathan Rose (1991)

107: *British Romantic Prose Writers, 1789-1832,* First Series, edited by John R. Greenfield (1991)

108: *Twentieth-Century Spanish Poets,* First Series, edited by Michael L. Perna (1991)

109: *Eighteenth-Century British Poets,* Second Series, edited by John Sitter (1991)

110: *British Romantic Prose Writers, 1789-1832,* Second Series, edited by John R. Greenfield (1991)

111: *American Literary Biographers,* Second Series, edited by Steven Serafin (1991)

112: *British Literary Publishing Houses, 1881-1965,* edited by Jonathan Rose and Patricia J. Anderson (1991)

113: *Modern Latin-American Fiction Writers,* First Series, edited by William Luis (1992)

114: *Twentieth-Century Italian Poets,* First Series, edited by Giovanna Wedel De Stasio, Glauco Cambon, and Antonio Illiano (1992)

115: *Medieval Philosophers,* edited by Jeremiah Hackett (1992)

Documentary Series

1: *Sherwood Anderson, Willa Cather, John Dos Passos, Theodore Dreiser, F. Scott Fitzgerald, Ernest Heming-*